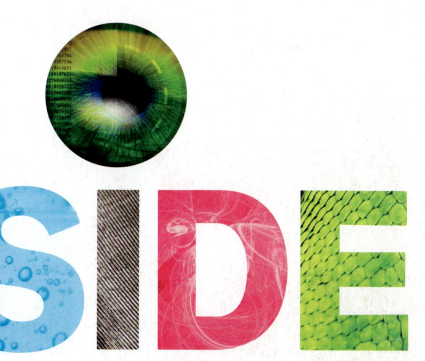

INSIDE

LANGUAGE, LITERACY, AND CONTENT

PROGRAM AUTHORS

David W. Moore

Deborah J. Short

Alfred W. Tatum

Josefina Villamil Tinajero

 NATIONAL GEOGRAPHIC    Hampton-Brown

Acknowledgments

Grateful acknowledgment is given to the authors, artists, photographers, museums, publishers, and agents for permission to reprint copyrighted material. Every effort has been made to secure the appropriate permission. If any omissions have been made or if corrections are required, please contact the Publisher.

Almanac Music, Inc., c/o The Richmond Organization: LAST NIGHT I HAD THE STRANGEST DREAM Words and Music by Ed McCurdy. TRO - © Copyright 1950 (Renewed), 1951 (Renewed), 1955 (Renewed) Folkways Music Publishers, Inc., New York, NY. Used by Permission.

Acknowledgments continue on page 678.

Neither the Publisher nor the authors shall be liable for any damage that may be caused or sustained or result from conducting any of the activities in this publication without specifically following instructions, undertaking the activities without proper supervision, or failing to comply with the cautions contained herein.

The National Geographic Society
John M. Fahey, Jr., President & Chief Executive Officer
Gilbert M. Grosvenor, Chairman of the Board

National Geographic School Publishing
Hampton–Brown
www.NGSP.com

Printed in the United States of America
RR Donnelley, Willard, OH

ISBN: 978-0-7362-7981-9

12 13 14 15 16 17 18 19
10 9 8 7 6 5 4 3

Contents at a Glance

Unit	Focus on Genre	Focus on Vocabulary	Language & Grammar Function	Grammar	Reading Strategy	Writing
1	Narrative Writing: Fiction, Nonfiction	Word Parts: Compound Words, Suffixes	Ask and Answer Questions Give Information Express Ideas and Opinions	Complete Sentences Nouns Action Verbs	Plan Your Reading: Preview, Predict, Set a Purpose	Paragraph Personal Narrative
2	Elements of Fiction: Plot, Character, Setting	Relate Words: Synonyms, Antonyms, Cognates	Define and Explain Retell a Story Engage in Conversation	Subject Pronouns Verb Forms: *Be* and *Have* Indefinite Pronouns	Monitor Your Reading	Summary Paragraph Modern Fairy Tale
3	Organization of Ideas: Chronological Order, Problem and Solution	Word Parts: Prefixes, Suffixes	Ask for and Give Information Describe Summarize	Present and Past Tense Verb Forms: *Be*	Ask Questions	Problem-Solution Paragraph Problem-and-Solution Essay
4	Organization of Ideas: Comparison and Contrast	Context Clues: Definition, Example, and Restatement; Jargon and Specialized Language; Denotation and Connotation	Make Comparisons Define and Explain Clarify and Verify	Subject and Predicate Nouns Prepositions Subject and Object Pronouns	Make Connections	Research Report
5	Nonfiction Text Features	Context Clues: Multiple-Meaning Words, Jargon	Describe Make Comparisons Elaborate	Adjectives and Adverbs	Visualize	Poem in Free Verse Business Letter Friendly Letter
6	Author's Purpose and Word Choice	Figurative Language: Simile, Metaphor and Personification; Idioms; Shades of Meaning	Express Opinions Engage in Discussion Justify	Complete Sentences Compound Sentences Complex Sentences	Make Inferences	Character Sketch Literary Response
7	Organization of Ideas: Logical Order, Cause and Effect	Word Origins: Borrowed Words, Roots, Mythology	Tell an Original Story Summarize Give and Follow Directions	Possessive Adjectives Participles Participial Phrases	Determine Importance	Cause-and-Effect Paragraph Cause-and-Effect Essay
8	Persuasive Writing: Argument and Support	Context Clues: Technical Vocabulary, Jargon, Specialized Language	Persuade Negotiate Use Appropriate Language	Present, Past, and Future Tense Present Perfect and Past Perfect Tense	Synthesize	Persuasive Essay

Reviewers

We gratefully acknowledge the many contributions of the following dedicated educators in creating a program that is not only pedagogically sound, but also appealing to and motivating for middle school students.

Literature Consultant

Dr. René Saldaña teaches English and education at Texas Tech University and is the author of *The Jumping Tree* (2001) and *Finding Our Way: Stories* (Random House/ Wendy Lamb Books, 2003). More recently, several of his stories have appeared in anthologies such as *Face Relations, Guys Write for GUYS READ, Every Man for Himself,* and *Make Me Over,* and in magazines such as *Boy's Life* and *READ.*

Texas English Language Proficiency Standards (ELPS) Consultant

John Seidlitz is an independent educational consultant and is the author of Sheltered instruction Plus: A Guide for Texas Teachers of English Learners. He is the creator of "Tips for instructing ELLS" part of the ELL student Success Initiative of the Texas Educational Agency. As co-developer with Bill Perryman of the Perspective-Based Learning™, he works with teachers across the country implementing strategies that promote academic language development for all students and the use of perspective in the classroom. He currently serves as member of the SIOP ® National faculty. He served teachers at ESC Region 20 in San Antonio and South Texas as an educational specialist. He is a former social studies and ESL teacher and also served as a secondary ESL program coordinator.

Teacher Reviewers

Idalia Apodaca
English Language Development Teacher
Shaw Middle School
Spokane, WA

Pat E. Baggett-Hopkins
Area Reading Coach
Chicago Public Schools
Chicago, IL

Judy Chin
ESOL Teacher
Arvida Middle School
Miami, FL

Sonia Flores
Teacher Supporter
Los Angeles Unified School District
Los Angeles, CA

Brenda Garcia
ESL Teacher
Crockett Middle School
Irving, TX

Rebecca S. Gigliotti-Barton
ESL Teacher
Marble Falls Independent School District
Marble Falls, TX

Kristine Hoffman
Teacher on Special Assignment
Newport-Mesa Unified School District
Costa Mesa, CA

Dr. Margaret R. Keefe
ELL Contact and Secondary Advocate
Martin County School District
Stuart, FL

Julianne Kosareff
Curriculum Specialist
Paramount Unified School District
Paramount, CA

Lore Levene
Coordinator of Language Arts
Community Consolidated School District 59
Arlington Heights, IL

Laura Elfrez Lopez
Intermediate Bilingual Teacher
Aldine Independent School District
Houston, TX

Natalie M. Mangini
Teacher/ELD Coordinator
Serrano Intermediate School
Lake Forest, CA

Laurie Manikowski
Teacher/Trainer
Lee Mathson Middle School
San Jose, CA

Patsy Mills
Supervisor, Bilingual-ESL
Houston Independent School District
Houston, TX

Juliane M. Prager-Nored
High Point Expert
Los Angeles Unified School District
Los Angeles, CA

Patricia Previdi
ESOL Teacher
Patapsco Middle School
Ellicott City, MD

Dr. Louisa Rogers
Middle School Team Leader
Broward County Public Schools
Fort Lauderdale, FL

Rebecca Varner
ESL Teacher
Copley-Fairlawn Middle School
Copley, OH

Hailey F. Wade
ESL Teacher/Instructional Specialist
Lake Highlands Junior High
Richardson, TX

Cassandra Yorke
ESOL Coordinator
Palm Beach School District
West Palm Beach, FL

Program Authors

David W. Moore, Ph.D.
Professor of Education
Arizona State University

Dr. David Moore taught high school social studies and reading in Arizona public schools before entering college teaching. He currently teaches secondary school teacher preparation courses in adolescent literacy. He co-chaired the International Reading Association's Commission on Adolescent Literacy and is actively involved with several professional associations. His twenty-five year publication record balances research reports, professional articles, book chapters, and books. Noteworthy publications include the International Reading Association position statement on adolescent literacy and the *Handbook of Reading Research* chapter on secondary school reading. Recent books include *Developing Readers and Writers in the Content Areas (5th ed.)*, *Teaching Adolescents Who Struggle with Reading (2nd ed.)*, and *Principled Practices for Adolescent Literacy*.

Deborah J. Short, Ph.D.
Senior Research Associate
Center for Applied Linguistics

Dr. Deborah Short is a co-developer of the research-validated SIOP Model for sheltered instruction. She has directed quasi-experimental and experimental studies on English language learners funded by the Carnegie Corporation of New York, the Rockefeller Foundation, and the U.S. Dept. of Education. She recently chaired an expert panel on adolescent ELL literacy and coauthored a policy report: *Double the Work: Challenges and Solutions to Acquiring Language and Academic Literacy for Adolescent English Language Learners*. She has also conducted extensive research on secondary level newcomer programs. Her research articles have appeared in the *TESOL Quarterly*, the *Journal of Educational Research*, *Educational Leadership*, *Education and Urban Society*, *TESOL Journal*, *Social Education*, and *Journal of Research in Education*.

Alfred W. Tatum, Ph.D.
Associate Professor and
Director of UIC Reading Clinic
University of Illinois at Chicago

Dr. Alfred Tatum began his career as an eighth-grade teacher, later becoming a reading specialist and discovering the power of texts to reshape the life outcomes of struggling readers. His current research focuses on the literacy development of African American adolescent males, and he provides teacher professional development to urban middle and high schools. He serves on the National Advisory Reading Committee of the National Assessment of Educational Progress (NAEP) and is active in a number of literacy organizations. In addition to his book *Teaching Reading to Black Adolescent Males: Closing the Achievement Gap*, he has published in journals such as *Reading Research Quarterly*, *The Reading Teacher*, *Journal of Adolescent & Adult Literacy*, *Educational Leadership*, *Journal of College Reading and Learning*, and *Principal Leadership*.

Josefina Villamil Tinajero, Ph.D.
Associate Dean, Professor,
College of Education
University of Texas at El Paso

Dr. Josefina Villamil Tinajero specializes in staff development and school-university partnership programs, and consulted with school districts in the U.S. to design ESL, bilingual, literacy, and biliteracy programs. She has served on state and national advisory committees for standards development, including English as a New Language Advisory Panel of the National Board of Professional Teaching Standards. She is currently Professor of Education and Associate Dean at the University of Texas at El Paso, and was President of the National Association for Bilingual Education, 1997–2000.

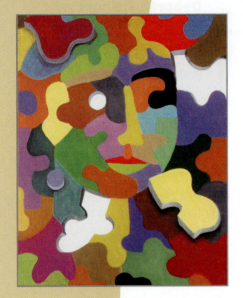

Decision Point

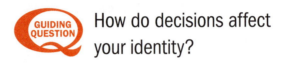

GUIDING QUESTION How do decisions affect your identity?

Pages 1W–65W

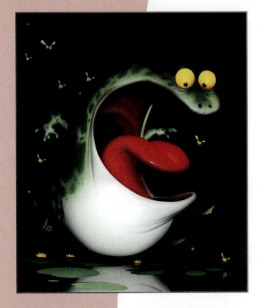

Stand or Fall

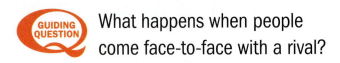

GUIDING QUESTION What happens when people come face-to-face with a rival?

ELPS Focus: 1.A.2 use prior experiences to understand meanings in English; 4.C.3 comprehend English vocabulary used routinely in written classroom materials

ELPS Focus: 1.A.2 use prior experiences to understand meanings in English

UNIT SKILLS

Writing
Summary Paragraph
▶ **Modern Fairy Tale**

Pages 66W–107W

Unit **3**

Making a Difference

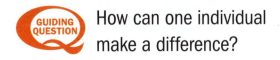 **GUIDING QUESTION** How can one individual make a difference?

Pages 108W–147W

x

At Home in the World

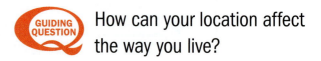 **GUIDING QUESTION** How can your location affect the way you live?

UNIT SKILLS

WRITING

INSIDE
LANGUAGE, LITERACY, AND CONTENT

Pages 148W–225W

Unit 5

Our Precious World

 GUIDING QUESTION What makes the environment so valuable?

> **ELPS Focus:** 1.A.1 use prior knowledge to understand meanings in English; 4.C.3 comprehend English vocabulary used routinely in written classroom materials; 4.F.1 use visual and contextual support to read grade-appropriate content area text; 4.F.2 use visual and contextual support to enhance and confirm understanding

> **ELPS Focus:** 1.A.1 use prior knowledge to understand meanings in English; 4.F.3 use visual and contextual support to develop vocabulary needed to comprehend increasingly challenging language; 4.F.8 use support from peers and teachers t develop vocabulary needed to comprehend increasingly challenging language

UNIT SKILLS

Vocabulary Study

Literary Analysis

Listening & Speaking

Writing ✏

Poem in Free Verse
Business Letter
Friendly Letter

Pages 226W–261W

Unit 6

CONFLICT AND RESOLUTION

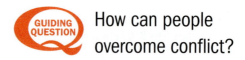

GUIDING QUESTION How can people overcome conflict?

UNIT SKILLS

Pages 262W–303W

Unit 7

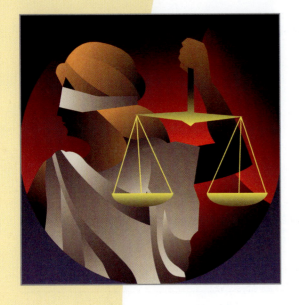

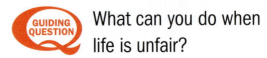
Fair Is Fair

GUIDING QUESTION What can you do when life is unfair?

UNIT SKILLS

Writing ✎
▶ Cause-and-Effect Paragraph

▶ Cause-and-Effect Essay

Pages 304W–345W

Unit 8

Food for Thought

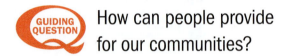

How can people provide for our communities?

ELPS Focus: 4.F.10 use support from peers and teachers to develop back-ground knowledge needed to comprehend increasingly challenging language

ELPS Focus: 1.C acquire basic and grade-level vocabulary

UNIT SKILLS

Pages 346W–385W

xx

Genres at a Glance

▼ Grasshopper on a flower in South Africa

▲ Close-up of a green sea turtle

Puzzled, 2006, Elizabeth Rosen.
Acrylic on canvas, courtesy of Morgan Gaynin, Inc., New York.

Critical Viewing: How are the decisions you make like the pieces of a puzzle?

Focus: 1.B.1 monitor oral language production and self-correct; 2.C.1 learn new language structures heard during classroom instruction and interactions; 2.C.2 learn new expressions heard classroom instruction and interactions; 2.E.3 use linguistic support to enhance and confirm understanding of complex and elaborated spoken language; 2.F.1 listen to and derive meaning variety of media to build and reinforce concept attainment; 2.F.2 listen to and derive meaning from a variety of media to build and reinforce language attainment; 2.I.1 demonstrate listening hension of complex spoken English by following directions; 2.I.3 demonstrate listening comprehension of complex spoken English by responding to questions and requests; 3.B.1 expand ternalize initial vocabulary by learning and using high-frequency words necessary for identifying and describing people, places, and objects; 3.B.3 expand and internalize initial vocabulary by g and using routine language needed for classroom communication; 3.C.3 speak using a variety of sentence types with increasing accuracy and ease; 3.F.2 give information ranging from concrete ary to abstract and content-based vocabulary; 3.G.1 express opinions on a variety of social and grade-appropriate academic topics; 3.G.2 express ideas on a variety of social and grade-appropriate ic topics; 4.F.4 use visual and contextual support to develop grasp of language structures needed to comprehend increasingly challenging language; 4.F.9 use support from peers and teachers to n grasp of language structures needed to comprehend increasingly challenging language; 5.D.1 edit writing for standard grammar and usage, including subject-verb agreement

Decision Point

GUIDING QUESTION

How do decisions affect your identity?

Read More!

Content Library

Making Healthy Choices
by Carolyn Newton

Leveled Library

Stuck in Neutral
by Terry Trueman

Facing the Lion
by Joseph Lemasolai Lekuton and Herman Viola

Surviving Hitler
by Andrea Warren

Internet
InsideNG.com

- Find out more about choosing a name.
- Explore Kenya.
- View the many types of homes people live in.

Focus on Genre

Narrative Writing in Fiction and Nonfiction

Narrative writing tells a story. It can be fiction or nonfiction.

How It Works

When the story is made up, the narrative is **fiction**.

> I was in a rush that night, so I took my favorite shortcut. Then I heard footsteps behind me. I called out, "Who's there?"

The words spoken by the characters are called dialogue.

When the story is about real people and events, it is **narrative nonfiction**.

> As a young writer, Ted Geisel decided to change his name to Dr. Seuss. When he died in 1991, he had written more than 50 books.

The details about people, places, and events are facts.

Whether fiction or nonfiction, a narrative is always told through someone's eyes. This is its **point of view**, the position from which events are told.

In **first-person point of view**, the narrator, or person telling the story, tells only what he or she knows.

> I was in a rush that night, so I took my favorite shortcut. Then I heard footsteps behind me.

These words signal first-person point of view:

I	me
my	mine
we	us

In **third-person point of view**, the narrator tells what others do, but is not part of the events.

> As a young writer, Ted Geisel decided to change his name to Dr. Seuss. When he died in 1991, he had written more than 50 books.

These words signal third-person point of view:

he	she
his	her
they	their

When you read a narrative, pay attention to the signal words to help you **identify** the narrator's point of view.

Academic Vocabulary
- **identify** (ī-**den**-tu-fī) *verb*
  When you **identify** something, you name it or tell what it is.

Practice Together

Read these narratives aloud. As you read, listen for clues that signal first-person or third-person point of view.

How the World Was Named

Long, long ago, a wise ruler decided that everything in her land needed a name. So she went outside and called the tall, green things *trees* and the huge, brown shapes *mountains*. Then she invited others to share their ideas, too. "What fun!" said her husband, as he looked up at everything.

Saturday's Game

I can't stop thinking about last Saturday at the soccer stadium. My team ran onto the field. Suddenly, the ball was at my feet. I remembered that Coach had taught us to make quick decisions. I passed the ball to my teammate Marco, who was near the goal. He kicked the ball and scored our first goal! I made a good decision.

Try It!

Read the following narrative aloud. Is it told in first-person or third-person point of view? How do you know?

Baseball and Bravery

Among America's heroes is the baseball player Jackie Robinson. In 1947, he decided to join the Brooklyn Dodgers. It was a brave choice because Robinson was the first African American to play Major League Baseball. Some white fans yelled at him. Although he got angry, he did not yell back. Instead, he played baseball and became a popular player. Through his actions, he led the way for other African Americans to enter the Major Leagues.

▲ Jackie Robinson was elected to the Baseball Hall of Fame in 1962.

There are different kinds of first- and third-person points of view. If the narrator has a **subjective** point of view, he or she knows one or more characters' thoughts and feelings. If the narrator knows all the characters' thoughts and feelings, he or she has an **omniscient** point of view. If the narrator knows the thoughts and feelings of only one character, he or she has a **limited omniscient** point of view.

In some cases, the narrator doesn't know any of the characters' thoughts and feelings. This is called an **objective** point of view.

Focus on Vocabulary

ELPS: 1.A.1 use prior knowledge to understand meanings in English

Use Word Parts

A **suffix** is a word part added to the end of a base word. The suffix changes the part of speech and the meaning of the word.

Many suffixes come from other languages. The suffix *-ful* comes from Anglo-Saxon. It means "full of." Add it to the noun *fear* and you change the noun into an adjective. The new word *fearful* means "full of fear."

EXAMPLE

fear + ful = fearful

How the Strategy Works

When you read, you may come to a word you don't know. **Analyze** the meanings of the word parts to understand the whole word.

EXAMPLE   You cannot go to the store **shoeless**.

1. Look closely at the word to see if you already know any of the parts.
2. If the word has a suffix, cover it up.   **shoe**less
3. Think about the meaning of the base word.
4. Uncover the suffix and determine its meaning.
5. Put the meanings of the word parts together to define the whole word. Be sure the meaning makes sense in the passage.

Follow the Strategy in Action to figure out the meaning of *wonderful*.

> **W**ho are you really? What makes you who you are? Is it your body? Is it your brain?
>
> New discoveries have given us more knowledge about how our <u>wonderful</u> brains work. Even as babies, we already seem ready to learn. What we learn and when we learn it shapes how we continue to learn.

Strategy in Action

❝ I see the suffix *-ful* in this word. I'll cover it. I already know the base word *wonder*. I know *-ful* means 'full of.' So *wonder* + *ful* means 'full of wonder.'❞

☑ **REMEMBER** You can use the meanings of word parts to figure out the meanings of unknown words.

Academic Vocabulary
- **analyze** (a-nu-līz) *verb*
  When you **analyze**, you separate something into parts and examine, or study, it.

Practice Together

Read this passage aloud. Look at each underlined word. Find the word parts. Put their meanings together to figure out the meaning of each underlined word.

Suffix	Meaning
-ful	"full of"
-able, *-ible*	"can be" or "can do"
-ion, *-tion*	"act of"
-less	"without"

YOUR BRAIN
The Mind-Body Connection

You know that you use your brain to make decisions. You also know that your brain is part of your body. The connection between the brain and the rest of the body is one that scientists study carefully.

Your brain is a powerful organ. Your brain helps you make decisions about what to do with your body. For example, suppose you choose to stay up late. Then you skip breakfast.

The next morning your mind may not be as sharp as usual. You might feel dizzy and act careless.

Rest, food, exercise, stress, and even the air around you affect your brain. The understanding that taking care of your body takes care of your brain can be remarkable. Those choices may affect how well you make other decisions.

Try It!

Read this passage aloud. What is the meaning of each underlined word? How do you know?

The Decision

I have an important decision to make. Should I stay on the volleyball team or join the speech and debate team? I don't know what to do. I feel helpless and can't make a decision. I love playing volleyball and don't want to give it up. It's one of the most enjoyable sports to play. I want to join the speech and debate team to improve my speaking skills. I think the experience will be useful for me. The only problem is that they both have weekly practice at the same time. I can't do both at the same time. Which selection should I make? Do I try something new, or should I stick with what I do best?

American Names

by Tony Johnston

Divercity, 2005, Elizabeth Rosen. Acrylic on chipboard, collection of the artist.

Build Background

What's in a Name?

Digital Library **InsideNG.com**
🧭 View the video.

▲ Our names tell people who we are.

Connect

Anticipation Guide Think about your name and what it means to you. Then tell whether you agree or disagree with these statements.

Anticipation Guide

	Agree	Disagree
1. Your name is an important part of who you are.	_____	_____
2. All names have a special meaning.	_____	_____
3. People judge others based on their names.	_____	_____

Language & Grammar

ELPS: 2.C.1 learn new language structures heard during classroom instruction and interactions; 2.E.3 use linguistic support to enhance and confirm understanding of complex and elaborated spoken language; 2.I.1 demonstrate listening comprehension of complex spoken English by following directions; 2.I.3 demonstrate listening comprehension of complex spoken English by responding to questions and requests; 3.C.3 speak using a variety of sentence types with increasing accuracy and ease

1 TRY OUT LANGUAGE
2 LEARN GRAMMAR
3 APPLY ON YOUR OWN

Ask and Answer Questions

CD

Look at the photos and listen to the interview. Then ask your partner a question about himself or herself. Answer your partner's question with a statement or an exclamation.

PICTURE PROMPT and INTERVIEW

Who Are You?

Madu

Sheila: Madu, where are you from?

Madu: I am from Egypt.

Sheila: What does your name mean?

Madu: My name means "of the people."

Sheila: What do you like to do?

Madu: I ride my bike! I love my bike. It gives me freedom.

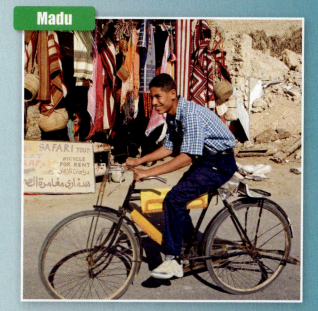

Sheila: Eva, what is something special about you?

Eva: I love music. I can play four instruments. Guitar is my favorite.

Sheila: How do you spend your free time?

Eva: I practice my music. I also babysit a lot.

Sheila: What are your goals for the future?

Eva: I want to be a music teacher. I want to teach children to play music.

Eva

Use Complete Sentences

A complete sentence has two parts: the **subject** and the **predicate**. The **subject** tells whom or what the sentence is about. The **predicate** often tells what the subject does.

Subject	Predicate
My mother	named me.

To find the parts in most sentences, ask yourself:

1. Whom or what is the sentence about? Your answer is the **subject**.
2. What does the subject do? Your answer is the **predicate**.

Sentence	Whom or What?	What Does the Subject Do?
My father named me.	My father	named me
My name comes from Swahili.	My name	comes from Swahili

In a command, the subject is understood. You do not usually say the subject when you give the command.

Four Types of Sentences

1. A **statement** tells something.
   My name is special.
2. A **question** asks something.
   What is your name?
3. An **exclamation** expresses a strong feeling.
   That is a cool name!
4. A **command** tells someone what to do.
   Tell me your name.

Practice Together

Match each subject to a predicate. Say the new sentence.

1. My brother
2. His name
3. His teachers
4. His friends
5. My father

a. shares his name with my father.
b. calls my brother by his real name.
c. comes from an African word.
d. use his nickname.
e. use his real name.

Try It!

Match each subject to a predicate. Use your own information. Say the new sentence.

6. My name
7. My friend
8. My _____
9. My teachers
10. My friends

a. use my full name.
b. prefers my nickname.
c. use nicknames.
d. comes from _____.
e. named me.

▲ Their names unite them.

Interview a Friend

ASK AND ANSWER QUESTIONS

Many things make each person special. Find out more about a friend by asking questions.

Work with a partner to write six questions, one for each question word. Think about what you want to learn.

Question Word	Asks About	Example Question
Who?	a person	Who is your best friend?
What?	a thing	What are your hobbies?
Where?	a place	Where were you born?
When?	a time	When is your birthday?
Why?	a reason	Why is your name special?
How?	an explanation	How do you go to school?

Take turns asking and answering the questions with your partner. Then share what you found out about your partner with the whole group. After listening to the information shared, tell what you learned.

HOW TO ASK AND ANSWER QUESTIONS

1. When you want information, you ask questions. Start your questions with *Who, What, Where, When, Why,* or *How.*

2. Give information in your answer to show that you understood the question. Use complete sentences.

> Where does your name come from?

> My name comes from an African Swahili word. It means *king.*

USE COMPLETE SENTENCES

Use complete sentences when you answer your partner's questions. Make sure each sentence has a **subject** and a **predicate** .

Question: Why is your name special?

Answer: **My dad** **shares my name** .

Prepare to Read

ELPS: 1.A.2 use prior experiences to understand meanings in English; 3.A practice producing sounds of newly acquired vocabulary in a manner that is comprehensible; 4.D use prereading supports to enhance comprehension of written text

Learn Key Vocabulary

Rate and Study the Words Rate how well you know each word. Then:

1. Pronounce the word. Say it aloud several times. Spell it.
2. Study the example.
3. Tell more about the word.
4. Practice it. Make the word your own.

Rating Scale

1 = I have never seen this word before.

2 = I am not sure of the word's meaning.

3 = I know this word and can teach the word's meaning to someone else.

Key Words

culture (kul-chur) *noun*
▶ page 20

A **culture** is a set of beliefs and customs that a group of people share. Dancing is a custom found in many **cultures**.

disfavor (dis-fā-vor) *noun*
▶ page 16

When you show **disfavor**, you show that you don't like something. A thumbs down is one way to show **disfavor** about something.
Base Word: **favor**

doubt (dowt) *noun*
▶ page 18

When you feel **doubt**, you are not sure. The girl had **doubts** about the food.

erase (e-rās) *verb*
▶ page 15

When you **erase** something, you make it go away. We can **erase** mistakes when we write.
Synonyms: **delete, remove**
Antonym: **add**

excessive (ik-ses-iv)
adjective ▶ page 15

When something is **excessive**, it is too much. That is an **excessive** number of pancakes for one person.

pact (pakt) *noun*
▶ page 22

A **pact** is a promise between people. Friends might make a **pact** to always help each other.

scrape (skrāp) *verb*
▶ page 18

When you **scrape** something, you damage it. Did you **scrape** your knee when you fell?

shame (shām) *noun*
▶ page 18

When you feel **shame**, you feel badly about something you did. She felt **shame** about the mistake she made.
Antonym: **pride**

Practice the Words Complete a Vocabulary Example Chart. Connect your prior experiences with each Key Word.

Word	Definition	Example from My Life
doubt	a feeling of not being sure	I have doubts about how I did on my math test.

Vocabulary Example Chart

Reading Strategy: Plan Your Reading

Good readers make a plan before they read. When you read a story, look it over first. Think about what might happen in the story.

Reading Strategy
Plan Your Reading

HOW TO PREVIEW AND PREDICT

1. Look at the title, turn the pages of the story, and look at the pictures. Read the first few paragraphs. What do you think this story is about?
2. As you read, use details to decide, or predict, what will happen next in the story.

Strategy in Action

Here's how one student previewed and made predictions.

Look Into the Text

American Names

My name's Arturo, "Turo" for short. For my father, and my grandfather, and *his* father, back and back. Arturos— like stacks of strong adobe bricks, forever, my grandmother says.

Really, my name *was* Arturo. Here's why: Three years ago our family came up from Mexico to L.A.

Prediction Chart

Detail	My Prediction
The title has the word *names* in it.	I think this story is going to be about names.
The first paragraph talks about names, too.	

Practice Together

Reread the passage above. Follow the steps in the How-To box to make your own prediction. Make a Prediction Chart like the one above. As you read "American Names," write the details you find and your predictions on your chart.

Focus on Genre

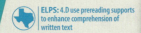

ELPS: 4.D use prereading supports to enhance comprehension of written text

Realistic Fiction

Realistic fiction is about people, relationships, and problems like those in real life. Often the main character is the narrator and tells the story from his or her point of view. Look for **first–person pronouns** that are clues to the first–person point of view.

> Luckily, I had some English when I got here. "It is good to have Eeenglish in your pocket," my parents pressed us always . . .

Your Job as a Reader

Reading Strategy: Plan Your Reading

As you read, keep making predictions. Look at the details and pay attention to what the narrator says to help you predict what might happen next. Write the details and your predictions on your Prediction Chart.

American Names

by Tony Johnston

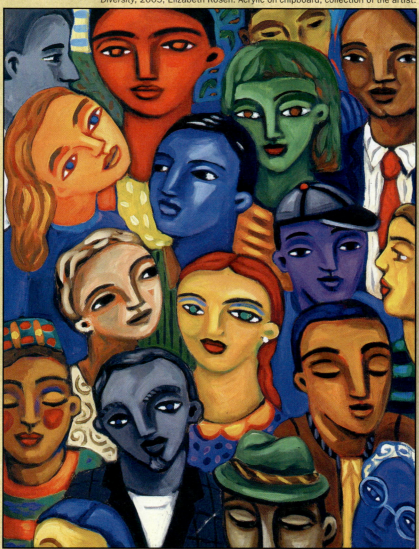

Diversity, 2005, Elizabeth Rosen. Acrylic on chipboard, collection of the artist.

▲ **Critical Viewing: Effect** Study the faces in the image. What ideas do you think the image expresses about people?

Online Coach

My name's Arturo, "Turo" for short. For my father, and my grandfather, and *his* father, **back and back**. Arturos— like stacks of strong adobe bricks, forever, my grandmother says.

Really, my name *was* Arturo. Here's why: Three years ago our family came up from Mexico to L.A. From stories they'd heard, my parents were worried for our safety in "that **hard-as-a-fist** Los Angeles." But Papi needed better work.

Rosa, my little sister, wailed, "'Nighted States, no! Too dark!" My brother, Luis, and I pretty much **clammed up**. I guess **numbed** by the thought of leaving our home, and a little scared, too, about the tough **barrio**.

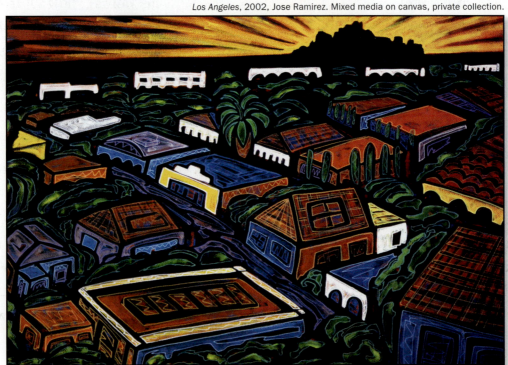

Los Angeles, 2002, Jose Ramirez. Mixed media on canvas, private collection.

▲ **Critical Viewing: Design** What impression is created by the artist's choice of details and colors in this painting of Los Angeles?

In Other Words
back and back the same name passed down from father to son
hard-as-a-fist big tough city
clammed up stayed quiet
numbed still upset
barrio neighborhood

Like some random, windblown weeds, we landed in L.A., home to movie stars and crazies and crazy movie stars.

Luckily, I had some English when I got here. "It is good to have Eeenglish in your pocket," my parents pressed us always, "*por las cochinas dudas.*" For the dirty doubts, that is. Just in case. So, for the dirty doubts, we've all got a little English.

In school, I get Miss Pringle. Miss Pringle's okay, I guess. She's always kind of floating where she goes, and talking in a bright and airy way. My friend Raúl says she's got **excessive** sparkle." Raúl loves weird words.

ANYWAY, first day of school, Miss Pringle, all chipper and bearing a rubbery-dolphin smile, says, "Class, this is Arthur Rodriguez." Probably to make things easier on herself. Without asking. **Ya estuvo**. Like a used-up word on the chalkboard, Arturo's **erased**.

Who cares? Not me. With such a name as Arthur, I'll fit in at this school real well. Like a pair of chewed-up Nikes. Not stiff and stumblingly new. American names are cool. Frank. Mike. Jake. They sound sharp as nails shot from guns.

I'm not the only one who's **been gringo-ized**. There's Jaime and Alicia and Raúl. Presto change-o! With one breath of teacher-magic, they're James and Alice and Ralph. (Our friend Lloyd, alias Rat Nose, is already a gringo, so his name's untouchable.)

When we're together, we joke about our new names.

"So, '*mano*," Raúl says with **bravura** (another one of his words), "how's it feel to be Arthur, like a Round Table guy?"

"*Muy* cool." I slip into full *pocho*, an English-Spanish mix.

"Hey, Alice," I say.

"Yeah?"

"Seen Alicia?"

She scans the hall. Digs in her backpack. "No, man. She's *gone*."

We all laugh. But I notice Alicia's eyes, like two dark and hurting bruises. I fluff it off, easy as dandruff flakes in a TV ad.

My parents hate that I'm Arthur. I mean, totally H-A-T-E. I can tell because when

> I'll fit in at this school real well.

In Other Words
Ya estuvo. That was it. (in Spanish)
been gringo-ized become American
'*mano* brother (short for *hermano* in Spanish)
bravura courage (in Spanish)
Muy Very (in Spanish)

Literary Background
According to legend, or a traditional tale, King Arthur ruled England around 500 C.E. It is believed that he formed the **Round Table**, a group of brave knights, to protect England.

El Lonche, 1993, Simon Silva. Oil on canvas, private collection.

I break this news, my mother starts cooking excessively. Her way of organizing the world. My father goes carefully quiet.

Most parents I know would spit out choice curses if their children chose names that hurt their ears. Maybe even smack them. Not mine. Mami and Papi are like two soft doves. They **work on a policy of gentleness**. They've never touched us in anger. Never **talked severely**. So their silent **disfavor** hits harder than the sting of slaps. Tough tortillas. I'm going gringo.

Key Vocabulary
disfavor *n.*, dislike, disapproval

In Other Words
work on a policy of gentleness try to be nice always
talked severely yelled at us

Before You Move On

1. **Confirm Prediction** Was your prediction correct? How does Arturo react to his new American name?
2. **Compare** Did Arturo's parents have the same reaction? Explain.
3. **Personal Connection** If you were Arturo, would you have corrected Miss Pringle? Why or why not?

Predict
Will Arturo and his friends miss their real names?

The one who hates my name most is my *abuelita*. Grandmother always dresses in cricket-black, in *luto* for my grandfather, who died. She's eighty-something. So old, her skin looks like it's woven from brown cobwebs. She's got two braids wound so high on her head, they must have been growing during her whole life. Unlike my parents, Abuelita's no dove. Like a little fighting rooster, she's got *bravura* to spare.

Even though she's **feisty**, God guides her life. She closes most conversation with an after-breath of "*Dios mediante*," God willing.

Since Grandfather died, she lives with us. She came all the way from Aguascalientes, Mexico, on a Norteño bus, with only her prayer book, a photograph of Grandfather, and her *molcajete*.

A *molcajete's* a three-legged grinding stone, carved of lava spit from some old volcano. It's hollowed and pitted, like a cupped hand scarred with acne. Abuelita uses it to grind chilies. For salsa and stuff. Takes longer than forever. Jeez! She could do it with one *zzzzzip* of the blender switch! If that lava-lump was mine, I'd chuck it out.

"Theeesss name Arter—eeet burns in my earsss like poissson." Since my **Spanish's a little crippled from pouring the English on**, Abuelita hisses her English to be sure I can't escape her point. *Muele, muele, muele.* She grinds her disfavor into me at every chance. The heat of peppers fills her voice as she **pulverizes** chilies extra vigorously, for some tasty Mexican dish. If my new name were a chili pepper, she'd pulverize that, too.

At every chance she turns "Arturo" on her tongue, like a pearl.

What does *she* know, this thin-as-an-eyelash old woman from Hot Waters, Mexico? Man, this is L.A. To get by, you need American names.

Apart from problems of names, here there are problems of gangs. Like those saber-toothed tigers in pits of tar, kids get sucked into them. For protection from invaders from other areas. Or to have a place to go, or something to do. Even some old guys, fathers with kids, are gang members.

My father's the kind of person who removes his hat in a restaurant and blesses his plate of tacos. Not prime gang material. I hope I'm not, either. Though the pull at school is pretty strong, I keep looking for something else to do.

My friends live on my block. All the time they come over to hang out in Abuelita's kitchen. They're there now, **dragged by their noses**. By the pure power of chili dust. And the tang of cilantro.

When they enter, she pinches their

If my new name were a chili pepper, she'd pulverize that, too.

cheeks and claims they are "***muchachos muy lindos***" and calls them by their true names: Jaime, Alicia, Raúl.

"*Hola*, Lloyd." She aims a dripping spoon straight for Rat Nose. "You love *menudo*? You taste."

Abuelita speaks with such excessive *bravura*, each name <mark>scrapes</mark> my mind like the *scritch-scritching* claws of a feisty rooster.

"Jeez!" I say to myself, cringing with <mark>shame</mark>. But my friends seem totally unfazed. Even pleased. Raúl's got a heart tattoo (not real, just inked on). It's so big, it blues his muscle. Grinning, he pumps his tattoo for Abuelita. *¡Caray!* Don't they remember? We peeled off those old names, like onion skins. Still, a worm of <mark>doubt</mark> squirms in my mind.

My friends slump themselves over the arms of chairs like overcooked noodles and chat easily with my grandmother. Alice's eyes—at the sound of her real name, they **flame up**, bright with excessive sparkle. *Por* please!

Key Vocabulary

<mark>scrape</mark> *v.*, damage, injure
<mark>shame</mark> *n.*, a bad feeling
<mark>doubt</mark> *n.*, an uncertain feeling

In Other Words

dragged by their noses because they smelled good food
muchachos muy lindos very nice kids (in Spanish)
flame up show excitement

Before You Move On

1. **Confirm Prediction** Was your prediction correct? How do the friends react when Abuelita uses their real names?

2. **Character's Point of View** Why does Arturo "cringe with **shame**"?

3. **Compare and Contrast** How are Arturo and Abuelita similar and different?

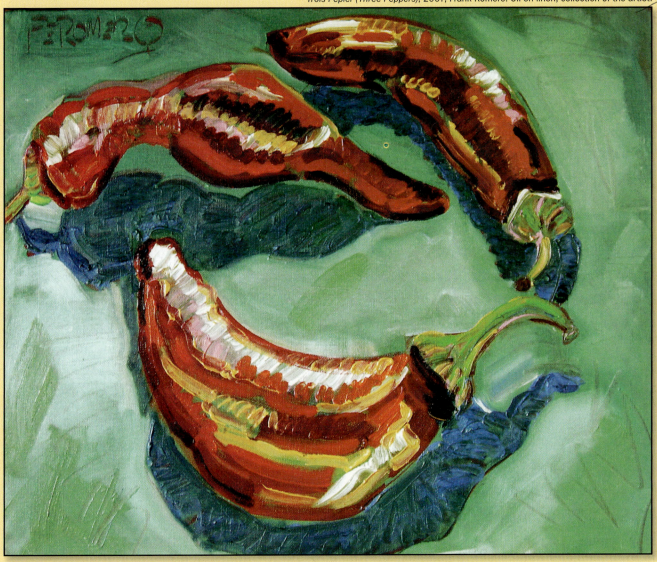

Trois Pepier (Three Peppers), 2007, Frank Romero. Oil on linen, collection of the artist.

▲ **Critical Viewing: Design** How does the artist's use of shadows and colors create energy?

Arturo discovers something important about his culture. What will he do next?

One night I'm struggling with geography homework. Trying to map out where Marco Polo went. *Hijos*, did that guy get around! His route **looks like some bad knitter's tangled yarn**. Like my sister Rosa's when she's trying to learn.

Through the blinds, my room's banded with moon. Everything's quiet. Even the crickets are sleeping. Then I hear something. Mumbling. Coming from Abuelita's room. Our rooms are back to back. Like when you check your size against somebody else.

My room's painted white. But Abue's, it's totally Mexican pink, the color she believes the Mexican flag should be. Her walls dance with *calacas*, skeletons, of all sizes and materials—clay, wood, wire, papier-mâché. Abue **thumbs her nose at** Death.

Abuelita's talking to Grandfather, muttering to the ghost of his photograph, I bet.

"Arturo," she says, holding that word in her mouth gently, like a highly breakable egg. She speaks Spanish only.

"He's a good boy, our Turo. Just a little bit mixed up. One day, *Dios mediante*, he will recognize how good is your name. One day he will know what it means— Arturo. He is me. He is you. And all before. And all to come."

I hear a long, moist sigh then. Like the breath of a tired teakettle. I hear tears glaze her voice. I feel a blaze of embarrassment to be listening in on this private conversation.

My heart feels squeezed out. Abuelita has known all along what I should have known. It's okay to be Arturo. **What a *menso*-head I am.** *Un idiota de primera.* To give up my name. It's to give up my family. To let myself—all of us—be erased to chalkboard dust.

In this moment my history holds me. Like a warm *sarape*. I feel tears come. In this moment I want to hug Abuelita.

I look out my window. At the half-moon. Like a perfectly broken button.

It's late. But I call my friends anyhow. "*Por* please," I joke, "come over."

Key Vocabulary

culture *n.*, the beliefs and values of a group

In Other Words

looks like some bad knitter's tangled yarn is everywhere; is not direct

thumbs her nose at is not scared of

What a *menso*-head I am. I am so stupid.

sarape blanket (in Spanish)

"*¿Ahora?*"

"Now. *Ahoritita.*"

And they come—Ralph and Alice and James and Rat Nose—all expectant and wondering what in *diablos* is going on. Before any of them can **wedge a word in, I blurt**,

"We're taking back our names. **We don't, we're *borrados*.** Blotted out."

"You mean 'Rat Nose' is dead?" Ralph moans. "Such an *excelente* and rodential name?"

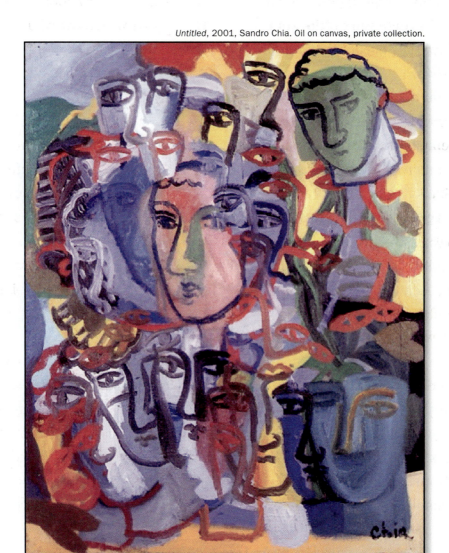

Untitled, 2001, Sandro Chia. Oil on canvas, private collection.

▲ **Critical Viewing: Theme** How does this painting relate to the theme of identity?

In Other Words
¿Ahora? Now? (in Spanish)
Ahoritita Right now. (in Spanish)
wedge a word in, I blurt say anything, I say quickly
We don't, we're *borrados*. If we don't, we're erased.

"Rat Nose lives. We'll call ourselves whatever we want, but those teachers can't make us into someone new. Those teachers, they must be *formal*."

They're pretty cool with that. Especially Alice. Little stars bloom in her eyes. Ralph's **already itching** for morning, he says, so he can **apprise** Miss Pringle. I itch to apprise my family, now snoring deeper than zombies. Especially Abuelita.

We make a pact. Right there in her chili-laden kitchen. On the most Mexican thing around—one by one we place our hands on Abuelita's *molcajete*, ugly as a pockmarked thug.

In solemn ceremony we retrieve our names. Ourselves. Into the bold night air we say with utmost bravura:

¡Raúl!

¡Alicia!

¡Jaime!

¡Lloyd!

¡Arturo!

When we apprise her of our stand on names, Miss Pringle's pretty surprised. But she limps along with it. (A result of "the incident" is that other kids go for their own "name-reclaimment.")

Not long after, they're selling T-shirts and plants and stuff at school. To raise funds for a computer. I buy a little cactus, **prickly** to touch and with one red bloom.

After school, I give it to Abuelita: "Ta-*ta!*" she laughs when I **spring** it from behind my back, and she hugs me with the gift between us, but somehow we don't get poked.

"*¡Ay, Arturo, **mi pequeño** cactus!*" Abuelita exclaims. Like I'm prickly sometimes, but **have a chance of flowers.**

Santa Fe Roadside Prickly Pear, 2007, Claudette Moe. Acrylic on canvas, collection of the artist.

Key Vocabulary

pact *n.*, a promise or agreement between people

In Other Words

already itching so excited
apprise tell
In solemn ceremony we retrieve our names. Very seriously, we take back our Spanish names.
prickly sharp
spring quickly take
mi pequeño my little (in Spanish)
have a chance of flowers mostly good

Abuelita's prickly but full of goodness. As far from gangbangers as Papi is. I wish I could be like her, getting people's names back for them—or something important like that. So far I'm just hanging out. Being like some weird L.A. weather report: prickly—with a chance of flowers. ❖

About the Author

Tony Johnston (1942–) grew up in California and spent fifteen years living in Mexico. She likes books that "come from the heart." When she was in sixth grade, her teacher had students keep journals of words they came across and loved or hated. "Ever since, I've been keeping lists of the wonderful words I bump into. Whenever I can, I toss them out like flowers, hoping that others will catch them and love them and hold onto them—and use them."

Before You Move On

1. **Confirm Prediction** Was your prediction correct? How did family and **culture** affect Arturo's decision?
2. **Character and Plot** How did Arturo change from the beginning to the end of the story? What events caused the change?

Saying Yes

by Diana Chang

"Are you Chinese?"
"Yes."

"American?"
"Yes."

5 "Really Chinese?"
"No...not quite."

"Really American?"
"Well, actually, you
see..."

10 But I would rather say
yes

Not neither-nor,
not maybe,
but both, and not only

15 The homes I've had,
the ways I am

I'd rather say it
twice,
yes

Before You Move On

1. **Paraphrase** Explain in your own words what the poet means by "both, and not only."

2. **Compare** How is the message in the poem similar to Arturo's experience in "American Names"?

Connect Reading and Writing

Vocabulary
culture
disfavor
doubt
erase
excessive
pact
scraped
shame

CRITICAL THINKING

1. **SUM IT UP** Make a Character Chart that shows how Arturo changes. Use the chart to summarize the story.

Character Chart

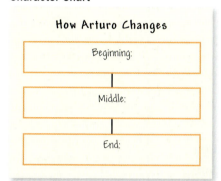

2. **Interpret** Arturo says he is **erased** when Miss Pringle changes his name. What does he mean? How might he feel **shame**?

3. **Analyze** Look at the Anticipation Guide you filled out before you read the story. Do you want to change any of your answers now? Why or why not?

4. **Draw Conclusions** What does Arturo realize about his **culture**? How is this similar to or different from the message in "Saying Yes"? With a partner, share reasons that support your conclusions.

READING FLUENCY

Intonation Read the passage on page 634 to a partner. Assess your fluency.

1. I read
   a. great   **b.** OK   **c.** not very well

2. What I did best was _____ .

READING STRATEGY

Plan Your Reading
Share with a partner the predictions you made as you read the selection. What clues did you find to support them?

VOCABULARY REVIEW

Oral Review Read the paragraph aloud. Add the vocabulary words.

If you move to another country, you experience a new _____ . You may enjoy some customs and show _____ toward others. You may have _____ about whether you fit in, or feel _____ that others may see you as different. Well, don't _____ who you are. Change is never easy. Sure, a few changes are good, but _____ changes make it seem as if your feelings were being _____ against stone. Make a _____ with family members to share the best of both countries.

Written Review Imagine you are a friend of Arturo's. Write an explanation of the **pact** you made. Use at least five vocabulary words.

WRITE ABOUT THE GUIDING QUESTION

Explore Identity
How does **culture** affect a person's identity? Reread the selections to find examples that support your ideas. Then write your opinion.

Connect Across the Curriculum

 **ELPS:** 2.C.4 learn academic vocabulary heard during classroom instruction and interactions

Literary Analysis

Analyze Text Structure: Plot

> **Academic Vocabulary**
> • **identify** (ī-**den**-tu-fī) *verb*
>   When you **identify** something, you name it or tell what it is.

What Makes a Story? A story's plot can be divided into parts:

- The **conflict** is the problem to be solved.
- **Complications** are events that make the conflict worse.
- The **climax** is the turning point of the story.
- The complications that lead to the climax are called the **rising action**.
- The events that happen after the climax are called the **falling action**.
- The **resolution** is the way the conflict ends.

Learn About Story Maps When you read a story, **identify** events that determine the plot. You can use a Story Map to record these events and **identify** the plot.

Story Map

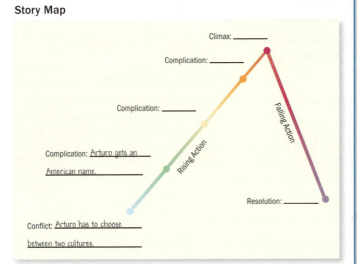

Practice Together

Start the Story Map Read the following passage with your class. What **complications** , or events, do you notice? How do they affect the conflict?

> ANYWAY, first day of school , Miss Pringle . . . says, "Class, this is Arthur Rodriguez." Probably to make things easier on herself. Without asking. *Ya estuvo.* Like a used-up word on the chalkboard, Arturo's erased.

Try It!

Complete the Story Map Copy the Story Map. Complete it with events in the story. Use the map to discuss this question with a partner: What lesson does Arturo learn?

Vocabulary Study

Use Compound Words

Academic Vocabulary

- **compound** (kahm-**pownd**) *adjective*
  Something that is **compound** is made up of two
  or more parts.

Sometimes two words combine to create a **compound** word. Often, the
meaning of a **compound** word is closely related to its two base words:

<u>birth</u> + <u>day</u> = <u>birthday</u>

> *Birth* means
> when I was born. *Day*
> is time. Birthday
> must mean the day
> I was born.

Study Compound Words Work with a partner. Find the base words for each
of these **compound** words from "American Names."

1. grandmother (p. 14)
2. windblown (p. 15)
3. backpack (p. 15)
4. something (p. 17)

Discuss the meanings of the two base words in the **compound** word. Then
decide the meaning of the new word. Reread the sentence in the selection.
Do you understand it differently now?

Write Sentences Write sentences that use each of these **compound**
words. Trade sentences with your partner.

Research/Writing

Report About Names of Places

SOCIAL SCIENCE

Academic Vocabulary

- **research** (rē-surch) *verb*
  When you **research** something, you collect
  information about it.

Arturo moves to Los Angeles, which is Spanish for *the angels*. What name
do you want to **research**?

1. **Focus Your Topic** With a partner, brainstorm
   names of places, people, or things to **research**.
   Use a Topic Triangle to help you focus your topic:
   - Write the general topic in the top band.
   - Think about one aspect of the general topic.
     Write this in the middle.
   - Narrow this topic even more in the bottom band.

2. **Research** **and Write** Use the Internet to research
   and take notes about your topic.

3. Synthesize, or combine, your information in a
   short, written report. Then switch reports with a
   partner. Check that your partner's report has a
   focused topic.

Topic Triangle

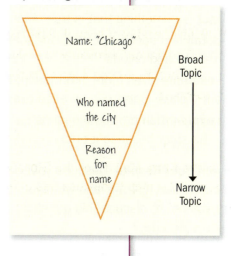

Name: "Chicago"

Broad Topic

Who named the city

Reason for name

Narrow Topic

Research/Speaking

Collect Data

SOCIAL
SCIENCE

ELPS: 2.C.4 learn academic vocabulary heard during classroom instruction and interactions

> **Academic Vocabulary**
> • **culture** (kul-chur) *noun*
>   **Culture** includes the beliefs, attitudes, and behaviors shared by a group of people.

❶ **Research and Collect Data** Arturo likes the special foods his grandmother cooks. Many groups have foods that are special to their **culture** . Choose a food from a specific **culture** to research, such as Mexican food.

Use the Internet to research and learn more about your topic.

Internet InsideNG.com

✦ Access a search engine. Use search words like *traditional foods* and the culture you're interested in.

Ask: What are traditional foods from this **culture** ? For example, these are some traditional Mexican dishes: enchiladas, quesadillas, menudo, salsa, and guacamole.

❷ **Narrow the Topic** Focus your topic by asking a specific research question. Ask: Which three dishes are the most popular? For example, these are the most popular Mexican dishes: salsa, guacamole, and quesadillas.

❸ **Support Your Research** Use two or three authoritative sources to support your topic. Authoritative sources contain trustworthy, reliable, and factual information. These are some examples of authoritative sources: an encyclopedia, an important research report, an interview with a trusted expert, and a dictionary.

❹ **Gather and Share Information** Synthesize information such as facts, details, examples, and explanations to describe three dishes to the class.
* A **fact** is something that is true. Fact: Salsa is a sauce.
* A **detail** is a specific point about something. Detail: Salsa contains tomatoes and onions.
* An **example** gives more information. Example: Salsa can be used in many dishes. Salsa can be used over rice, meat, or in tacos.
* An **explanation** provides reasons for something. Explanation: Salsa can be spicy because it often includes chili peppers.

❺ **Present Your Results** Describe your dishes to the class. Tell why you chose that **culture** and what you learned about it. Use the data you gathered to discuss this question: How is food important to a person's **culture** ?

Ask and Answer Questions

Role-Play Work with a partner. Role-play an interview with a character from the story to learn about his or her ideas about culture. Ask questions that begin with *who, what, where, when, why,* and *how.* Trade roles. Answer your partner's questions with complete sentences.

> Why do you like the name Arturo?

> I share it with my father and grandfather and his father.

ELPS: 1.B.2 monitor written language and self-correct

Write About Your Name

Study the Models An effective sentence is clear, interesting, and complete. A complete sentence has a subject and a predicate. When you use complete sentences, your writing is clear.

NOT OK

Arturo and his friends get new names from their teacher. Their teacher didn't ask them first. Miss Pringle them new names. At first, like their gringo-ized names. Arturo's parents hate his new name. His grandmother it even more. One night, learns why.

> The reader thinks: **"What did Miss Pringle do?"** The sentence isn't clear because it is not complete.

OK

Arturo and his friends get new names from their teacher. Their teacher didn't ask them first. Miss Pringle assigned them new names. At first, they like their gringo-ized names. Arturo's parents hate his new name. His grandmother hates it even more. One night, Arturo learns why.

> This writer uses complete sentences with a subject and predicate.

Add Sentences Think of two sentences to add to the OK model above. Be sure to use complete sentences.

🖊 **WRITE ON YOUR OWN** Write about the importance of your name. Is it important to always use your formal name? What if someone calls you something else? When is it OK to use a nickname—for example, Ed instead of Edward? Review your writing and correct any sentences that are not complete.

▲ Friends often have nicknames for each other.

REMEMBER

A complete sentence has both a subject and a predicate.

A Lion Hunt

by Joseph Lemasolai Lekuton with Herman Viola

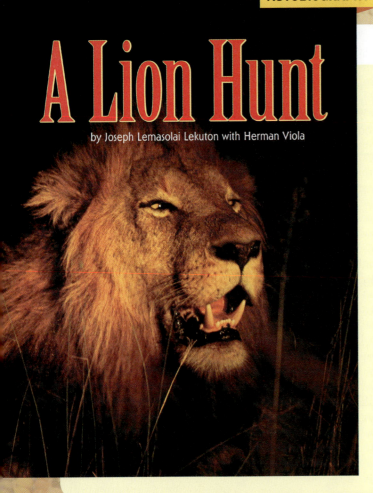

SELECTION 2 OVERVIEW

▶ **Build Background**

▶ **Language & Grammar**
Give Information
Use Nouns in Sentences

▶ **Prepare to Read**
Learn Key Vocabulary
Learn a Reading Strategy
Plan Your Reading

▶ **Read and Write**
Focus on Genre
Autobiography
Apply the Reading Strategy
Plan Your Reading
Critical Thinking
Reading Fluency
Read with Expression
Vocabulary Review
Write About the Guiding Question

▶ **Connect Across the Curriculum**
Literary Analysis
Analyze Text Structure: Point of View
Vocabulary Study
Use Suffixes
Listening/Speaking
Tell a Story
Discuss Different Viewpoints
Language and Grammar
Give Information
Writing and Grammar
Write About Bravery

Build Background

Connect

Group Discussion Dangerous events force us to make quick decisions. Is it always brave to face danger? Discuss this question with your group. Give examples of when being brave might be a good choice and when it might not be a good choice.

Learn About Bravery

Whether as a writer or a warrior, Joseph Lemasolai Lekuton knows what it means to be brave. He had to prove his bravery to become a Maasai warrior.

Digital Library
InsideNG.com
View the video.

▲ Joseph Lemasolai Lekuton

Give Information

CD

Listen to the chant and chime in.
Listen to the CD for more information.
What does it tell you about lions?

 ELPS: 1.B.1 monitor oral language production and self-correct; 2.F.1 listen to and derive meaning from a variety of media to build and reinforce concept attainment; 2.F.2 listen to and derive meaning from a variety of media to build and reinforce language attainment; 3.B.1 expand and internalize initial vocabulary by learning and using high-frequency words necessary for identifying and describing people, places, and objects; 3.F.2 give information ranging from concrete vocabulary to abstract and content-based vocabulary; 4.F.4 use visual and contextual support to develop grasp of language structures needed to comprehend increasingly challenging language; 4.F.9 use support from peers and teachers to develop grasp of language structures needed to comprehend increasingly challenging language

CHANT

The Lion

The lion is a great big cat.

It's as simple as that—

A lion is a great big cat,

With great big claws,

And great big teeth,

And a great big taste

For any kind of meat.

If you see a lion

Just tip your hat

And scat!

Use Nouns in Sentences

A **noun** names a person, place, thing, or idea.

thing   person   place   idea

A **lion** watches a **boy** in the **field**. **Danger** is near.

	More Nouns
Person	boy, brother, friend, hunter
Place	field, school, village
Thing	cloud, rock, shoe, stick
Idea	bravery, danger, silence

A **singular noun** names one person, place, thing, or idea.
A **plural noun** names more than one person, place, thing, or idea.

* To make most nouns plural, just add **-s**.
   hunter + -s = hunters   Two **hunters** track the lion.

* If the noun ends in **s**, **z**, **sh**, **ch**, or **x**, add **-es**.
   dish + -es = dishes   They take **dishes** to the camp.

* If the noun ends in **y**, look at the letter before the **y**.
   If it is a consonant, change the **y** to **i**. Then add **-es**.
   story + -es = stories   At the camp, they hear many **stories** about lions.

* If the letter before the **y** is a vowel, just add **-s**.
   boy + -s = boys   Many **boys** hunt the lion.

* Some nouns have special plural forms.
   man—**men**   **Men** cheer the hunters.
   foot—**feet**   The hunters' **feet** are sore.

Practice Together

Tell if the noun in the box names a person, place, thing, or idea. Say the plural form of the noun. Then say the sentence and add the plural noun.

1. | bush | At least two lions are in the _____.
2. | brother | The _____ walk slowly away.
3. | foot | Their _____ move silently.
4. | field | The _____ are suddenly empty.

Try It!

Tell if the noun in the box names a person, place, thing, or idea. Write the plural form of the noun on a card. Then say the sentence to a partner and add the plural noun.

5. | snake | Even the _____ move quickly away.
6. | fox | _____ hide fast.
7. | boy | The _____ yell for help.
8. | family | Their _____ are worried about them.

▲ Danger is near.

Tell About Your Favorite Animal

GIVE INFORMATION

Find a picture of your favorite animal. Use an encyclopedia book or an online encyclopedia to find information about the animal. Tell a partner about your animal.

HOW TO GIVE INFORMATION

1. Think about the information you want to include. What do you want to say?
2. Use details and specific nouns to give precise information.

Lakes are good homes for bullfrogs.

To get started, draw pictures of your favorite animal. Show where it lives. Show what it eats. Show where it sleeps and how it behaves around people.

USE SPECIFIC NOUNS

When you tell about your animal, use many details that give information. Use nouns that give your partner a clear, precise picture of the people, animals, places, things, or ideas that you tell about. Which words on the scale below are the most precise?

NOT SPECIFIC ➤ **SPECIFIC**

person	scientist	▶ frog scientist	▶ herpetologist
animal	amphibian	▶ frog	▶ North American bullfrog
place	North America	▶ United States	▶ eastern United States
thing	lots of things	▶ frog food	▶ snakes, worms, and insects
idea	time	▶ lifespan	▶ 7 to 9 years

Not precise: The animal lives in water.
Someone wrote about bullfrogs' food.
Bullfrogs are native to North America.

Precise: The North American bullfrog lives in ponds.
A herpetologist wrote that North American bullfrogs eat snakes, worms, and insects.
North American bullfrogs are native to the eastern United States.

▲ Bullfrogs live in ponds.

Prepare to Read

ELPS: 3.A practice producing sounds of newly acquired vocabulary in a manner that is comprehensible; 4.D use prereading supports to enhance comprehension of written text; 5.A learn relationships between sounds and letters to represent sounds when writing in English

Learn Key Vocabulary

Rate and Study the Words Rate how well you know each word. Then:

1. Pronounce the word. Say it aloud several times. Spell it. Write it.
2. Study the example.
3. Tell more about the word.
4. Practice it. Make the word your own.

Key Words

bravery (brā-vu-rē) *noun*
▶ page 38

Bravery means courage, or not being afraid. Firefighters show **bravery** when they put out fires.
Base Word: **brave**

brotherhood (**bruth**-ur-hood) *noun* ▶ page 42

A **brotherhood** is a close group of people. A sports team can be a **brotherhood**.

decision (dē-si-zhun) *noun*
▶ page 42

A **decision** is a choice. You make a **decision** when you choose clothes to wear each day.
Base Word: **decide**

defend (dē-fend) *verb*
▶ page 38

When you **defend** something, you protect it. A mother animal **defends** her young.
Synonyms: **protect, guard**
Antonym: **attack**

pride (prīd) *noun*
▶ page 38

When you feel **pride**, you feel good about something you or someone else does. The boy felt **pride** when he graduated from high school.

society (so-sī-i-tē) *noun*
▶ page 47

A **society** is a group of people who share beliefs and goals. In American **society**, we value public discussions of key issues.

symbol (sim-bul) *noun*
▶ page 38

A **symbol** is an object that stands for something else. In the U.S., the Bald Eagle is a **symbol** of power.

warrior (wor-ē-yur) *noun*
▶ page 38

A **warrior** is someone who protects his people. Some **warriors** hunt animals for food.
Synonyms: **hunter, fighter**

Practice the Words With a partner, make an Expanded Meaning Map for each Key Word.

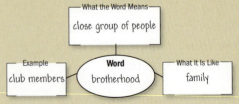

Expanded Meaning Map

Reading Strategy: Plan Your Reading

Good readers **preview** a selection to see what it is about. Then they decide why they will read the selection. This means they **set a purpose** for reading.

Reading Strategy
Plan Your Reading

How to Preview and Set a Purpose

1. Look at the title. What do you think the selection is about?
2. Read the first sentence. Now what do you think?
3. Ask yourself: *What do I want to find out?* Your answer is your purpose for reading.

Strategy in Action

Here's how one student previewed and set a purpose.

Look Into the Text

title

A Lion Hunt

first sentence

I'M GOING TO TELL YOU the lion story. Where I live in northern Kenya, the lion is a symbol of bravery and pride. Lions have a special presence. If you kill a lion, you are respected by everyone. Other warriors even make up songs about how brave you are. So it is every warrior's dream to kill a lion at one point or another.

PREVIEW

The title and first sentence are about lions.

SET A PURPOSE

I'll read on to find out . . .

Practice Together

Now it's your turn to look into the text. Reread the passage above. Follow the steps in the How-To box to do your own preview. Then set a purpose for reading "A Lion Hunt."

ELPS: 4.D use prereading supports to enhance comprehension of written text

Autobiography

An autobiography is narrative nonfiction in which the writer tells the story of his or her life or of an important experience in it. The author of an autobiography is the narrator. He or she tells the story from **first-person point of view**.

The narrator often uses the words *I*, *me*, *we*, and *us*. Look for words that show the **first-person point of view**.

> It took us all day to get there, but at sunset we were walking through the gap in the acacia-branch fence. . . . At night we could see fires in the distance.

Your Job as a Reader

Reading Strategy: Plan Your Reading

You've previewed the selection. What purpose did you set for reading it? Read on to find out what you want to know.

A Lion Hunt

by Joseph Lemasolai Lekuton with Herman Viola

Online Coach

Find out what the narrator thinks about lions.

I'M GOING TO TELL YOU the lion story. Where I live in northern Kenya, the lion is a **symbol** of **bravery** and **pride**. Lions have a special presence. If you kill a lion, you are respected by everyone. Other **warriors** even make up songs about how brave you are. So it is every warrior's dream to kill a lion **at one point or another**. Growing up, I'd had a lot of interaction with wild animals—elephants, rhinos, cape buffalo, hyenas. But at the time of this story—when I was about 14—I'd never **come face-to-face with** a lion, ever. I'd heard stories from all the young warriors who told me, "Wow, you know yesterday we chased this lion—" bragging about it. And I always said, "**Big deal**." What's the big deal about a lion? It's just another animal. If I can **defend** myself against elephants or rhinos, I thought, why not a lion?

I was just back from school for vacation. It was December, and there was enough rain. It was green and beautiful everywhere. The cows were giving plenty of milk. In order to get them away from **ticks**, the cattle had been taken down to the lowlands. There's good grass there, though it's drier than in the high country, with some rocks here and there. There are no ticks, so you don't have to worry about the health of the cattle, but the area is known for its fierce lions. They roam freely there, as if they own the land.

Key Vocabulary
symbol *n.*, something that represents something else
bravery *n.*, having no fear
pride *n.*, self-respect
warrior *n.*, a hunter
defend *v.*, to protect from attack

▲ Giraffes, impalas, zebras, and gazelles near Lake Nakuru. Lake Nakuru National Park, Kenya

I spent two days in the village with my mom, then my brother Ngoliong came home to have his hair braided and asked me to go to the cattle camp along with an elder who was on his way there. I'd say the cattle camp was 18 to 24 miles away, depending on the route, through some rocky areas and a lot of shrubs. My spear was broken, so I left it at home. I carried a small stick and a small club. I wore my *nanga*, which is a red cloth, tied around my waist.

Cultural Background

Here is Lekuton as a Maasai warrior, wearing some of his finest traditional beads.

It took us all day to get there, but at sunset we were walking through the gap in the **acacia-branch fence** that surrounded our camp. There were several cattle camps scattered over a five-mile **radius**. At night we could see fires in the distance, so we knew that we were not alone. As soon as we got there my brother Lmatarion told us that two lions had been terrorizing the camps. But lions are smart. Like thieves, they go somewhere, they look, they take, but they don't go back to the same place again.

Well, that was our unlucky day. That evening when the cows got back from **grazing**, we had a lot of milk to drink, so we were well fed. We sat together around the fire and sang songs—songs about our girlfriends, bravery songs. We **swapped** stories, and I told stories about school. The others were always curious to understand

▲ Maasai men and boys watching their cattle.

Cultural Background
The **Maasai** are a famous warrior tribe in Kenya whose lives center on herding cattle. The Maasai move frequently in search of water and good grazing lands. The success of the Maasai is measured by the number of cattle they have.

school. There were four families in the camp, but most of the older warriors were back at the village seeing their girlfriends and getting their hair braided. So there were only three experienced warriors who could fight a lion, plus the one elder who had come down with me. The rest of us were younger.

We went to bed around 11:30 or 12. We all slept out under the stars in the cattle camp—no bed, just a **cowhide** spread on bare soil. And at night it gets cold in those desert areas. For a cover I used the nanga that I had worn during the day. The piece of cloth barely covered my body, and I kept trying to make it longer and pull it close around me, but it wouldn't stretch. I curled myself underneath it trying to stay warm.

Everything was silent. The sky was clear. There **was no sign of** clouds. The fire was just out. The stars were like millions of diamonds in the sky. One by one everybody fell asleep. Although I was tired, I was the last to sleep. I was so excited about taking the cows out the following morning.

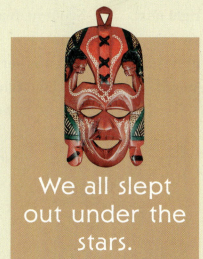

We all slept out under the stars.

During the middle of the night, I woke to this huge sound—like rain, but not really like rain. I looked up. The starlight was gone, clouds were everywhere, and there was a drizzle falling. But that wasn't the sound. The sound was all of the cows starting to pee. All of them, in every direction. And that is the sign of a lion. A hyena doesn't make them do that. An elephant doesn't make them do that. A person doesn't. Only the lion. We knew right away that a lion was about to attack us.

The other warriors started making a lot of noise, and I got up with them, but I couldn't find my shoes. I'd taken them off before I went to sleep, and now it was **pitch black**. Some warriors, when they know there's danger, sleep with their shoes in their hands and their spears right next to them. But I couldn't find my shoes, and I didn't even have a spear. Then the lion made just one noise: *bhwuuuu!* One huge roar. We started running toward the noise. Right then we heard a cow making a **rasping**, **guttural** sound, and we knew that the lion had her by the throat.

In Other Words

cowhide cow skin
was no sign of were no
pitch black completely dark
rasping, guttural coughing, choking

Before You Move On

1. **Author's Point of View** What is the narrator's opinion about lions?
2. **Summarize** What events occurred the first night at the cattle camp?
3. **Inference** Were the warriors prepared to fight the lion? Why or why not?

COWS WERE EVERYWHERE. They ran into one another and into us, too. We could hear noises from all directions—people shouting, cows running—but we couldn't see a thing. My brother heard the lion right next to him and threw his spear. He missed the lion—and lucky for the rest of us, he missed us, too. Eventually, we began to get used to the darkness, but it was still difficult to tell a lion from a cow. My brother was the first to arrive where the cow had been killed.

The way we figured it was this: Two lions had attacked the camp. Lions are very intelligent. They had **split up**. One had stayed at the southern end of the camp where we were sleeping, while the other had gone to the northern end. The wind was blowing from south to north. The cows smelled the lion at the southern end and **stampeded** to the north—toward the other waiting lion.

When I asked my brother, "Hey, what's going on?" he said, "The lion killed Ngoneya."

Ngoneya was my mother's favorite cow and Ngoneya's family was the best one in the herd. My mother depended on her to produce more milk than any other cow. She loved Ngoneya, really. At night she would get up to pet her.

I was very angry. I said, "I wish to see this lion right now. He's going to **see a man he's never seen before**."

Just as we were talking, a second death cry came from the other end of the camp. Again we ran, but as we got closer, I told everyone to stop. "He's going to kill all the cows!" I told my brother. And I think this is where school thinking comes in. I told him, "Look. If we keep on chasing this lion, he's going to kill more and more. So why don't we let him eat what he has now, and tomorrow morning we will go hunting for him." My brother said, "Yes, that's a good idea," and it was agreed. For the first time I felt like I was part of the **brotherhood** of warriors. I had just made a **decision** I was proud of.

Key Vocabulary
brotherhood *n.*, a close group of people
decision *n.*, a choice someone makes

In Other Words
The way we figured it was this We decided this is what happened
split up hunted separately
stampeded went together quickly
see a man he's never seen before be afraid of me

It was muddy, it was dark, we were in **the middle of nowhere**, and right then we had cows that were miles away. They had stampeded in every direction, and we could not protect them. So we came back to camp and made a big fire. I looked for my shoes and I found them. By that time I was bruised all over from the cows banging into me, and my legs were bloody from the scratches I got from the acacia thorns. I hurt all over.

We started talking about how we were going to hunt the lion the next day. I could tell my brother was worried and wanted to get me out of danger. He said, "Listen, you're fast, you can run. Run and tell the people at the other camps to come and help. We only have three real warriors here; the rest of you are younger."

"**No way**," I said. "Are you **kidding** me? I'm a warrior. I'm just as brave as you, and I'm not going anywhere." At this point, I hadn't actually seen the lion, and I absolutely refused to leave.

▲ Nighttime on the Savannah, or grasslands of Kenya, offers little protection from lions.

In Other Words
the middle of nowhere a place far from everything else
No way No
kidding joking with

My brother said, "I'm going to ask you one more time, please go. Go get help. Go to the other camp and tell the warriors that we've found the two lions that have been terrorizing everyone, and we need to kill them today."

And I said, "No, I'm not going."

So he said, "Fine," and sent the youngest boy, who was only about eight.

When daylight came, I took the little boy's spear and walked out from the camp with the others. Barely 200 yards away were the two lions. One had its head right in the cow, eating from the inside. And one was just lying around: She was full. As we approached them, we sang a lion song: "We're going to get the lion, it's going to be a great day for all of us, all the warriors will be happy, we'll save all our cows."

As we got closer, the older man who was with us kept telling us to be careful. We should wait for help, he said. "This is dangerous. You have no idea what lions can do." But no one would listen to him.

The other guys were saying, "We can do

We came face-to-face with the lions.

it. Be brave, everyone." We were encouraging each other, **hyping ourselves up**.

My brother was so angry, so upset about our mother's favorite cow that he was crying. "You killed Ngoneya," he was saying. "You are going to **pay for it**."

Everyone was **in a trance**. I felt that something inside me was about to burst, that my heart was about to come out. I was ready. Then we came face-to-face with the lions. The female lion walked away, but the male stayed. We formed a little semicircle around the male, with our long spears raised. We didn't move. The lion had stopped eating and was now looking at us. It felt like he was looking right at me. He was big, really big. His tail was thumping the ground.

He gave one loud roar to warn us. Everything shook. The ground where I was standing started to tremble. I could see right into his throat, that's how close we were. His mouth was huge and full of gore from the cow. I could count his teeth. His face and mane were red with blood. Blood was everywhere.

In Other Words
hyping ourselves up making each
  other excited
pay for it be punished
in a trance focused

The lion slowly got up so he could show us his full **presence**. He roared again. The second roar almost broke my eardrums. The lion was now pacing up and down, walking in small circles. He was looking at our feet and then at our eyes. They say a lion can figure out who will be the first person to spear it.

I edged closer to my brother, being careful not to give any sign of lifting or throwing my spear, and I said, "Where's that other camp?"

My brother said to me, "Oh, you're going now?" He gave me a look—a look that seemed to say, You watch out because someone might think you are afraid.

But I said, "Just tell me where to go." He told me. I gave him my spear. "It will help you," I said, and then I **took off** in the direction of the other cattle camp. No warrior looked back to see where I was going. They were all concentrating on the lion.

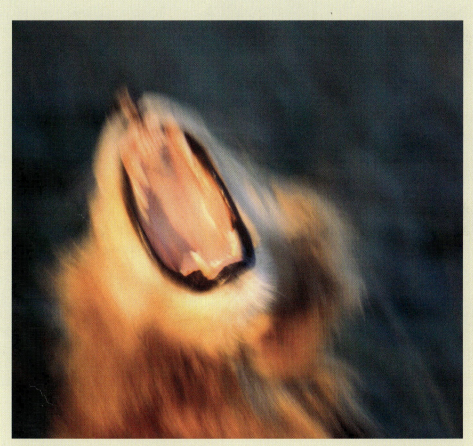

▲ A male lion roars, ready to attack.

Before You Move On

1. **Summarize** How did the warriors plan to get the lions?
2. **Paraphrase** Tell in your own words what the narrator's brother wanted him to do.
3. **Confirm Prediction and Judge** What did the narrator do when he saw the lion? Do you think he did the right thing? Explain.

Find out what others think of the narrator's decision to run away.

AS I RAN TOWARD THE NEXT CAMP I saw that the little boy had done his job well. Warriors were coming, lots of them, chanting songs, asking our warriors to wait for them. The lion **stood his ground** until he saw so many men coming down, warriors in red clothes. It must have seemed to him that the whole hillside was red in color. The

▲ The Maasai wear a lot of red clothing. The color red represents power and is sacred. The Maasai also use a red dye to draw on their skin. They make the dye by mixing clay with water or animal fat.

In Other Words
stood his ground was ready to fight

lion then started to look for a way out.

The warriors reasoned that the lion had eaten too much to run fast and that the muddy ground would slow him up. They thought they could run after him and kill him. They were wrong. As soon as they took their positions, the lion surged forward and took off running. The warriors were left behind. There was nothing they could do except pray that they would meet this lion again.

From that time on, I knew **the word in the village was** that I had run away from the lion. There was no way I could prevent it.

"You know the young Lekuton warrior?"

"Yeah."

"He was afraid of the lion."

My brother tried to support me, but in our **society**, once word like that gets out, that's it. So I knew that I'd have to prove myself, to prove that I'm not a coward. So from then on, every time I came home for vacation, I went to the cattle camp on my own. I'd get my spear, I'd get my shoes. Even if it was 30 miles from the village, I'd go on my own, through **thick and thin**, through the forest and deserts. When I got there I'd take the cattle out on my own. Always I hoped something would attack our cattle so I could protect them. ❖

About the Author

Joseph Lemasolai Lekuton wrote about his life experiences in the book *Facing the Lion: Growing up Maasai on the African Savanna*. In 2006, National Geographic named the author an Emerging Explorer for his many accomplishments. Today, Lekuton lives in Kenya and serves as a member of parliament in the Kenya National Assembly.

Key Vocabulary
society *n.*, group of people who share a common purpose

In Other Words
the word in the village was people were saying
thick and thin easy and difficult areas

Before You Move On

1. **Summarize** What did people in the village think of the narrator after the lion hunt? How did the narrator react?
2. **Theme** How does this selection relate to the unit theme?

From Kenya to America and Back Again

◄ The family of Joseph Lemasolai Lekuton, who was born in northern Kenya, is part of a sub-group of the Maasai, called the Ariaal.

Joseph Lemasolai Lekuton was fourteen at the time the events in this narrative took place. He wanted to prove to his tribe that he was a brave warrior. As he grew up, Lekuton did prove himself in many ways.

Lekuton's soccer skills earned him a scholarship to an excellent high school in Kenya. Lekuton did so well in high school that he earned a full scholarship to an American college.

After graduating from college, Lekuton became a social studies teacher in Virginia. He strived to teach his students the benefits of both tribal life and a western education. He linked Kenyan and American cultures by organizing school trips to Kenya. "Cultures can learn so much from each other," he said. "We may be divided by bodies of water and masses of mountains but as human beings we all identify with the same fundamental things."

Lekuton continued to help Kenya. His work helped provide educational opportunities and clean water to villages there. For his service to the country, Lekuton became the youngest recipient of Kenya's Order of the Grand Warrior in June of 2001.

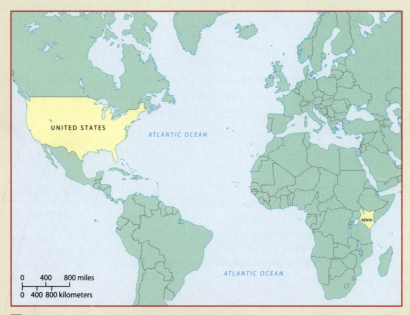

UNITED STATES

ATLANTIC OCEAN

ATLANTIC OCEAN

KENYA

0   400   800 miles
0   400 800 kilometers

▲ **Interpret the Map** How far away is the United States from Kenya?

Connect Reading and Writing

Vocabulary

bravery

brotherhood

decisions

defend

pride

societies

symbol

warriors

CRITICAL THINKING

1. **SUM IT UP** Create a Sequence Chain to record the order of events in this selection. Write one event in each oval. Use the chain to summarize the autobiography.

Sequence Chain

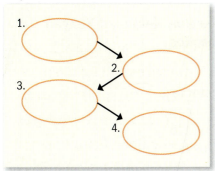

2. **Compare** In "American Names" and "A Lion Hunt," both narrators make **decisions** that affect their identities. Explain how the decisions are alike and what the decisions are a **symbol** of.

3. **Evaluate** When the narrator sees the lion, he makes a **decision**. How might this action show fear or **bravery** in his **society**?

4. **Explain** Recall the group discussion you had about **bravery**. How have your ideas changed after reading the selection?

READING FLUENCY

Expression Read the passage on page 635 to a partner. Assess your fluency.

1. I read
   a. great   **b.** OK   **c.** not very well

2. What I did best was _____ .

READING STRATEGY

Plan Your Reading
Tell a partner how previewing and setting a purpose helped you understand what you read.

VOCABULARY REVIEW

Oral Review Read the paragraph aloud. Add the vocabulary words.

> Some _____ depend on _____ for survival. They hunt for food. They _____ people from attack. Together, they feel great _____ in their common _____ . Sometimes they hunt lions. Then they must show great _____ because lions are dangerous. They have to make quick _____ because lions are fast. Lions are also a _____ of strength.

Written Review Imagine that Lekuton made a different **decision**. Write a new ending for the selection. Use four vocabulary words.

WRITE ABOUT THE GUIDING QUESTION

Explore the Decision Point

Was Lekuton's **decision** an act of **bravery** or **pride**? How did it affect his identity? Find details from the selection that support your ideas.

Connect Across the Curriculum

Literary Analysis

Analyze Text Structure: Point of View

> **Academic Vocabulary**
> - **connection** (ku-**nek**-shun) *noun*
>   The **connection** between two things is something they have in common.

How Is the Story Told? Sometimes a story is told by a narrator in the story. Other times, the narrator is someone outside of the story. The **connection** between what is told and who tells the story is the point of view.

First-Person or Third-Person In the first-person point of view, a narrator tells his or her own personal story using words like *I, me, my, we, us,* and *our.* In third-person point of view, the narrator tells about events that happened to someone else. So instead of using words like *I* and *me,* the narrator uses words like *he, she,* and *they.*

Subjective or Objective In a subjective point of view, the narrator knows one or more characters' thoughts and feelings. In an objective point of view, the narrator doesn't know any characters' thoughts or feelings.

Omniscient or Limited Omniscient A narrator with an omniscient point of view knows the thoughts and feelings of all the characters. A narrator who knows the thoughts and feelings of only one character has a limited omniscient point of view.

Practice Together

Find Signal Words Reread the beginning of "A Lion Hunt." The following passage shows how it would change if it were told from third-person point of view. Read the passage with your class. Find the words that signal third-person point of view.

> Leukton likes to tell the lion story. Where he lives in northern Kenya, the lion is a symbol of bravery and pride. Lions have special presence. If a person kills a lion, then that person is respected by everyone.

Try It!

Write a Paragraph On a separate sheet of paper, continue to rewrite the first few paragraphs of the selection using third-person point of view. Share your rewritten paragraphs with a partner. Evaluate which point of view tells a more powerful story.

Vocabulary Study

Use Suffixes

Suffix	Meaning
-ful	full of
-ness	quality or state of
-ous	full of
-ly	in the manner of

Academic Vocabulary
- **analyze** (**a**-nu-līz) *verb*
  When you **analyze**, you separate something into parts and examine, or study, it.

A **suffix** is a word part at the end of a base word. The suffix changes the meaning of the base word.

```
  base word      suffix

    fit      +   -ness   =   fitness
```

Fit is an Anglo-Saxon root that means "the right shape." *Fitness* must mean "the state of being in shape."

Use Base Words Work with a partner. Cover up the suffix on each of these words from "A Lion Hunt." Find the base word. Then **analyze** the meaning of the base word. Uncover the suffix and determine its meaning. Put the meanings of the word parts together to define the whole word.

1. darkness
2. dangerous
3. painful
4. careful
5. slowly
6. freely

Write a sentence using each word. Trade sentences with a partner. Discuss how each suffix affects the meaning of the base word.

Listening/Speaking

DRAMA

Tell a Story

Academic Vocabulary
- **specific** (spi-**sif**-ik) *adjective*
  When something is **specific**, it is definite or particular.

Imagine listening to Lekuton tell "the lion story." He would probably tell some parts slowly and speak quietly. He would probably change the sound of his voice and make facial expressions to show fear, pride, or anger.

Tell a small group a story about an important, **specific** event in your life.

1. Use a different rate and volume to tell different parts of your story. Slow down and speak quietly to build suspense or show certain emotions, such as sadness. Speed up and speak more loudly to show excitement.

2. Use the sound of your voice to keep the listeners interested. For example, change your voice to show someone else's dialogue.

3. Use gestures and facial expressions that match your story.

After you tell your story, ask your audience which parts they liked the best and why. Was it what your story was about or how you told it?

ELPS: 2.C.4 learn academic vocabulary heard during classroom instruction and interactions; 2.G.1 understand the general meaning of spoken language regarding familiar to unfamiliar topics

Listening/Speaking

SOCIAL SCIENCE

Discuss Different Viewpoints

Academic Vocabulary
- **decision** (dē-si-zhun) *noun*
  A **decision** is a choice or a resolution.

Lekuton made a **decision** that affected how others viewed him. He decided to run for help during the lion hunt even though he might appear to be a coward. What if everyone in his village gathered after the lion hunt to discuss what happened? What do you think they would say about him? Imagine that you are part of the discussion in the village, and have the discussion with a group.

1 Choose a Viewpoint Tell your viewpoint to the group. Was what Lekuton did brave? Or did he act cowardly?

2 Share Your Ideas Share your reasons for your viewpoint. For example, "I think Lekuton was brave because he went to get help." Use examples from the story to support your reasons.

▲ Different viewpoints make discussions interesting.

3 Listen and Respond to Other Viewpoints Listen carefully and respectfully to others in the group to hear their viewpoints. Build on others' ideas. For example, "When you said that Lekuton gave his spear to his brother, that reminded me that Lekuton wanted to help. So, I do not think he was a coward."

4 Notice Any Bias Some people in the discussion might have a bias. A bias is a particular or personal reason for thinking one way. Someone who has a bias usually makes his or her decisions or judgments based on emotions, not facts. For example, Lekuton's mother might say he was brave without hearing the facts. As his mother, she may have a hard time thinking anything negative about her son.

If someone in the discussion has a bias, it is better to ask a question about his or her thinking than say something like, "You are wrong!" For example, you might ask Lekuton's mother "Why do you think he was brave?"

5 Tell What You Discovered Summarize your discussion for the class to show you that you understood the general meaning. Did you change your point of view, or did it stay the same after your discussion? Tell what you discovered about the different viewpoints and reasons for each person's viewpoints.

Language and Grammar

Give Information

Group Share With a group, give information about the place you are from or the place where you live now. Think about what you want to say. Use specific nouns to give detailed, precise information.

> My city has a large natural habitat zoo. Its African exhibit has five miles of walkways.

Writing and Grammar

Write About Bravery

Study the Models To make your writing interesting, use nouns that say exactly what you mean.

JUST OK

> I read a <u>thing</u> about lions. A <u>boy</u> went on a hunt to a <u>place</u> with some <u>people</u>. The <u>boy</u> wanted to prove <u>something</u>. Then the lion killed some <u>cows</u>. The <u>boy</u> ran away. He was sorry and tried to prove his <u>bravery</u> later.

These nouns are not specific. The reader thinks: "What 'thing' did the writer read? Where was the hunt?"

BETTER

> I read a <u>story</u> about lions. A <u>teenager</u> went on a hunt in <u>Kenya</u> with <u>his brother and an elder</u> from his <u>village</u>. The <u>teenager</u> wanted to prove his <u>bravery</u>. Then the lion killed <u>his mother's favorite cows</u>. The <u>teenager</u> ran away. He was sorry and tried to prove his <u>bravery</u> later.

The writer used specific nouns. The reader will have a better picture.

Add Sentences Think of two sentences to add to the BETTER model above. Be sure to use specific nouns.

✎ WRITE ON YOUR OWN Write a short personal narrative about a time when you were brave. Explain the consequences of your bravery. Use specific, precise nouns. Use a singular noun for "one" and a plural noun for "more than one."

REMEMBER

- To make most nouns plural, add -**s**.
- If the noun ends in **s**, **z**, **sh**, **ch**, or **x**, add -**es**.
- If the noun ends in **y** after a consonant, change the **y** to **i**. Then add -**es**.
- Some nouns have special forms.

▲ A warrior proves his bravery.

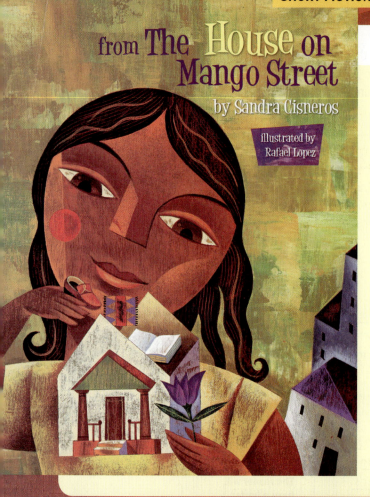

from The House on
Mango Street
by Sandra Cisneros

illustrated by
Rafael Lopez

Build Background

Explore Homes and Houses

What does home mean to you? Discover what it means to others.

Connect

Quickwrite "Good things come to those who wait" is a common expression. But that may not always be true. Often, people must make decisions to follow their dreams. What is your biggest dream in life? What steps will you take to make it happen?

Digital Library

InsideNG.com
◉ View the images.

▲ People identify strongly with their homes.

Language & Grammar

1 TRY OUT LANGUAGE
2 LEARN GRAMMAR
3 APPLY ON YOUR OWN

Express Ideas and Opinions

CD

ELPS: 2.C.2 learn new expressions heard during classroom instruction and interactions; 2.E.3 use linguistic support to enhance and confirm understanding of complex and elaborated spoken language; 2.F.1 listen to and derive meaning from a variety of media to build and reinforce concept attainment; 2.F.2 listen to and derive meaning from a variety of media to build and reinforce language attainment; 3.B.3 expand and internalize initial vocabulary by learning and using routine language needed for classroom communication; 3.G.1 express opinions on a variety of social and grade-appropriate academic topics; 3.G.2 express ideas on a variety of social and grade-appropriate academic topics; 5.D.1 edit writing for standard grammar and usage, including subject-verb agreement

Study the painting and the quotation.
Listen to the ideas and opinions of others.

Amy: A girl stands at a window. I think she's waiting for someone to visit her.

Andrew: I disagree. I see water and a boat. I think she wants to leave home and sail across the water.

Laura: In my opinion, she's daydreaming about what she will be when she is older.

Amy: Maybe you are right. The quotation makes me think she's dreaming about her future.

Andrew: In my opinion, the quotation is too simple. It takes more than a dream to reach your goals.

What do you see in the painting? What is your opinion?

PICTURE PROMPT

Young Girl at the Window, 1925, Salvador Dali. Oil on board.

"The future belongs to those who believe in the beauty of their dreams."

—Eleanor Roosevelt

1 TRY OUT LANGUAGE
2 LEARN GRAMMAR
3 APPLY ON YOUR OWN

Use Action Verbs

- **Verbs** tell what a person *does*, *has*, or *is*. An action verb tells what a person does.

  EXAMPLE   Marie **writes** about her goal.

- A complete predicate in a sentence often tells what the subject does. The **verb** is the most important word in the predicate.

Sentence	Complete Predicate	Verb
Marie **writes** about her goal.	**writes** about her goal	**writes**
She **dreams** about traveling around the world.	**dreams** about traveling around the world	**dreams**

- The **verb** has to agree with, or match, the subject. Add **-s** to the verb if the subject tells about one place, one thing, or one other person.

  EXAMPLES   Marie **tells** her sister.
                       The girls **tell** their mother.

Practice Together

Say each sentence with the correct verb.

1. Marie (read/reads) books about different countries.
2. She (plan/plans) many adventures.
3. Marie's sister (help/helps) her plan.
4. The sisters (eat/eats) at different kinds of restaurants.
5. The girls (learn/learns) about many cultures.

Try It!

Read each sentence. Write the correct verb on a card. Then say the sentence with the correct verb.

6. The girls (discover/discovers) new ideas.
7. Their mother (help/helps) them make plans.
8. Marie (want/wants) to go far away.
9. Her sister (agree/agrees) with her.
10. Their friends (send/sends) them information, too.

▲ A reader discovers new ideas.

Tell a Partner

EXPRESS IDEAS AND OPINIONS

Everyone has ideas and opinions. How do you think this photo shows a dream or a goal? What's your opinion about it?

Gather your ideas and opinions in a chart.

My Ideas	My Opinions
That building is very tall.	In my opinion, the girl looks small next to the building.
It must be in a big city.	I think she might be moving there.

Then use your chart to tell a partner what you think. Trade roles. After listening to each other, tell what you learned.

HOW TO EXPRESS IDEAS AND OPINIONS

1. To express an idea, tell what you see.
2. To express an opinion, tell what you think or feel. Give reasons for your opinion.

> I think the girl wants to work in that building.

USE VERBS

Think about the **verbs** you will use when you express your ideas and opinions. The verbs you use need to agree with the subjects of your sentences.

Remember to add **-s** to the verb if the subject is singular.

Singular subject: The girl **stares** at the skyscraper. I think she has a goal.

Plural subject: Many people **work** in the building. I think it's in a big city.

Prepare to Read

 ELPS: 2.A.1 distinguish sounds of English with increasing ease; 3.A practice producing sounds of newly acquired vocabulary in a manner that is comprehensible; 4.D use prereading supports to enhance comprehension of written text; 4.F.1 use visual and contextual support to read grade-appropriate content area text

Learn Key Vocabulary

Rate and Study the Words Rate how well you know each word. Then:

1. Pronounce the word. Say it aloud several times. Spell it.
2. Study the example.
3. Tell more about the word.
4. Practice it. Make the word your own.

Key Words

appreciate (u-**prē**-shē-āt)
verb ▶ page 66

When you **appreciate** something, you understand its importance. You **appreciate** an umbrella when it rains.

despite (di-**spīt**) *preposition*
▶ page 66

Despite means even though or without regard to. The man felt cold, **despite** his warm jacket.

disgusted (di-**skus**-tid)
adjective ▶ page 67

To be **disgusted** means that you dislike something. Some people are **disgusted** by frogs.

expectation
(eks-pek-**tā**-shun) *noun* ▶ page 62

An **expectation** is something you look forward to or have ideas about. We had great **expectations** about our project.
Base Word: **expect**

landlord (**land**-lawrd) *noun*
▶ page 62

A **landlord** is a person who owns land or buildings. My **landlord** always makes sure the building is clean.

rent (**rent**) *noun*
▶ page 62

When you pay **rent**, you pay money to the owner of a property to live there. The mother paid **rent** for the family's apartment every month.

strength (**strength**) *noun*
▶ page 66

Strength is the quality of being powerful. The **strength** of the storm destroyed many homes.

temporary (tem-pa-**rair**-ē)
adjective ▶ page 64

When something is **temporary**, it lasts only a short time. They had **temporary** housing and would soon move.

Practice the Words Make a Study Card for each Key Word. Then compare your cards with a partner.

> **expectation**
>
> **What it means:** something you look forward to or have ideas about
>
> **Example:** My expectation about the party was right—it was fun!
>
> **Not an example:** I had no idea how the book would end. I had no expectations.

Study Card

Reading Strategy: Plan Your Reading

Before you read a story, look it over. Decide what it is about. Then think about what you might learn.

HOW TO PREVIEW AND PREDICT

1. Before you read, look quickly at the title and pictures. Ask yourself: *What is this story about?*

2. Read the first few paragraphs. Look for clues that give information about the characters.

3. As you read, make predictions about what the characters will do.

Strategy in Action

Here's how one student previewed and made predictions.

Look Into the Text

Hmm, she lives on the third floor.

"My preview tells me she lives in an apartment."

You live *there*?

There. I had to look to where she pointed—the third floor, the paint peeling, wooden bars Papa had nailed on the windows so we wouldn't fall out. You live *there*? The way she said it made me feel like nothing. *There.*

Practice Together

Now it's your turn to look into the text. Reread the passage above and make your own prediction. Follow the steps in the How-To box. As you read, continue to make predictions about what the characters will do. Then keep reading to confirm whether your predictions are correct.

ELPS: 4.D use prereading supports to enhance comprehension of written text; 4.F.1 use visual and contextual support to read grade-appropriate content area text

Short Fiction

Short fiction tells a brief story about imaginary people, places, things, or events. The **words, actions, and feelings of the characters** , or people in the story, guide the events that take place.

> You live *there*? The way she said it made me feel like nothing. *There*. I lived *there*. I nodded.
>
> I knew then I had to have a house. A real house.

Your Job as a Reader

Reading Strategy: Plan Your Reading

As you read, make predictions. Use what characters think, say, and do as clues.

> **WHAT THE CHARACTER SAYS**
>
> I knew then I had to have a house.
>
> **PREDICTION**
>
> The character will look for a house.

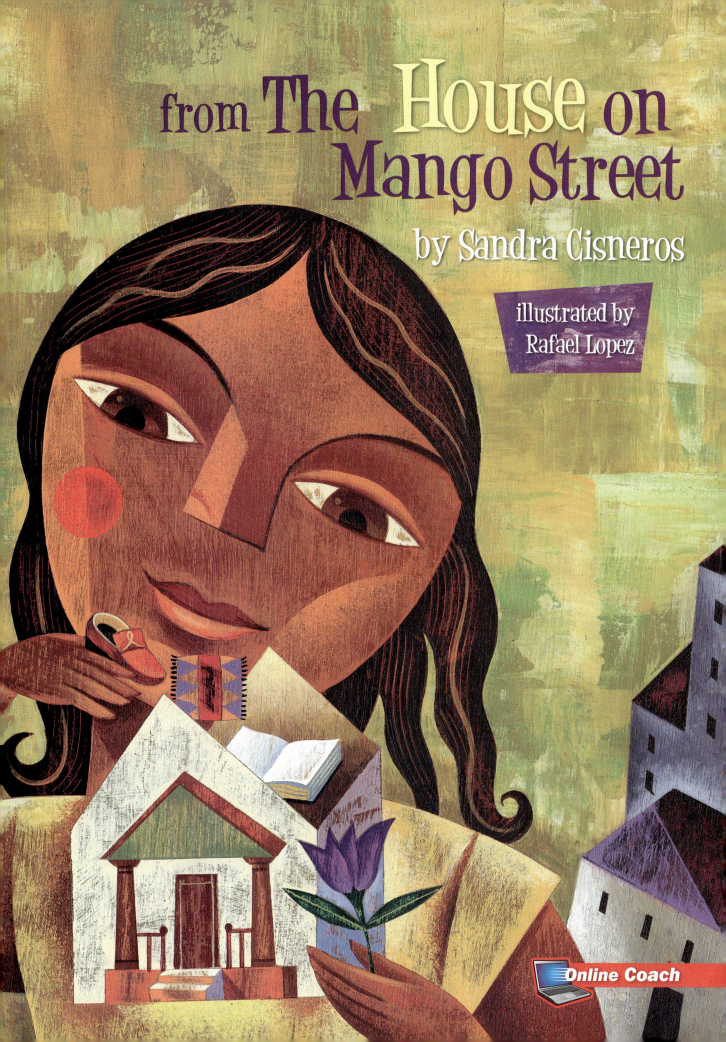

Set a Purpose

Find out if the family's new house matches the girl's expectations.

The House on
Mango Street

We didn't always live on Mango Street. Before that we lived on Loomis on the third floor, and before that we lived on Keeler. Before Keeler it was Paulina, and before that I can't remember. But what I remember most is moving a lot. Each time it seemed there'd be one more of us. By the time we got to Mango Street we were six— Mama, Papa, Carlos, Kiki, my sister Nenny and me.

The house on Mango Street is ours, and we don't have to pay **rent** to anybody, or share the yard with the people downstairs, or be careful not to make too much noise, and there isn't a **landlord** banging on the ceiling with a broom. But even so, it's not the house we'd thought we'd get.

We had to leave the **flat** on Loomis quick. The water pipes broke and the landlord wouldn't fix them because the house was too old. We had to leave fast. We were using the washroom next door and carrying water over in empty milk gallons. That's why Mama and Papa looked for a house, and that's why we moved into the house on Mango Street, far away, on the other side of town.

They always told us that one day we would move into a house, a real house that would be ours for always so we wouldn't

Key Vocabulary

expectation *n.*, something that a person looks forward to

rent *n.*, money paid to live on an owner's property

landlord *n.*, a person who owns land or buildings

In Other Words

flat apartment

have to move each year. And our house would have running water and pipes that worked. And inside it would have real stairs, not **hallway stairs**, but stairs inside like the houses on TV. And we'd have a basement and at least three washrooms so when we took a bath we wouldn't have to tell everybody. Our house would be white with trees around it, a great big yard and grass growing without a fence. This was the house Papa talked about

In Other Words
hallway stairs stairs shared by everyone in the building

Language Background
Apartments and flats refer to the same type of housing, or style of buildings where people live. The term *apartment* is more commonly used in North America.

when he **held a lottery ticket** and this was the house Mama **dreamed up** in the stories she told us before we went to bed.

But the house on Mango Street is not the way they told it at all. It's small and red with **tight** steps in front and windows so small you'd think they were holding their breath. Bricks are crumbling in places, and the front door is **so swollen** you have to push hard to get in. There is no front yard, only four little elms the city planted by the curb. Out back is a small garage for the car we don't own yet and a small yard that looks smaller between the two buildings on either side. There are stairs in our house, but they're ordinary hallway stairs, and the house has only one washroom. Everybody has to share a bedroom—Mama and Papa, Carlos and Kiki, me and Nenny.

Once when we were living on Loomis, a nun from my school passed by and saw

You live there ?

me playing out front. The laundromat downstairs had been boarded up because it had been robbed two days before and the owner had painted on the wood YES WE'RE OPEN so as not to lose **business**.

Where do you live? she asked.

There, I said pointing up to the third floor.

You live *there*?

There. I had to look to where she pointed—the third floor, the paint peeling, wooden bars Papa had nailed on the windows so we wouldn't fall out. You live *there*? The way she said it made me feel like nothing. *There.* I lived *there*. I nodded.

I knew then I had to have a house. A real house. One I could point to. But this isn't it. The house on Mango Street isn't it. For the time being, Mama says. **Temporary**, says Papa. But I know how **those things go**.

Key Vocabulary
temporary *adj.*, for a short time

In Other Words
held a lottery ticket dreamed of winning money
dreamed up thought about
tight small, narrow
so swollen too big for the frame so
business customers
those things go plans can change

Before You Move On

1. **Narrator's Point of View** How do the girl's **expectations** of a real house compare to the house on Mango Street?
2. **Compare and Contrast** How is life on Mango Street like and unlike life on Loomis?
3. **Inference** Why does the girl "feel like nothing"? Explain.

▲ **Critical Viewing: Effect** How do you think the girl feels? How do the colors, shapes, and angles help create this mood?

Four Skinny Trees

They are the only ones who understand me. I am the only one who understands them. Four skinny trees with skinny necks and pointy elbows like mine. Four who do not belong here but are here. Four **raggedy excuses** planted by the city. From our room we can hear them, but Nenny just sleeps and doesn't **appreciate** these things.

Their **strength** is secret. They send ferocious roots beneath the ground. They grow up and they grow down and **grab the earth between their hairy toes and bite the sky with violent teeth** and never quit their anger. This is how they keep.

Let one forget his reason for being, they'd all droop like tulips in a glass, each with their arms around the other. Keep, keep, keep, trees say when I sleep. They teach.

When I am too sad and too skinny to keep keeping, when I am a tiny thing against so many bricks, then it is I look at trees. When there is nothing left to look at on this street. Four who grew **despite** concrete. Four who reach and do not forget to reach. Four whose only reason is to be and be.

Key Vocabulary

appreciate *v.*, to understand the value of something
strength *n.*, the quality of being powerful
despite *prep.*, even though

In Other Words

raggedy excuses worn and weak trees
grab the earth between their hairy toes and bite the sky with violent teeth use their roots and branches to hold on

A **Smart** Cookie

I could've **been somebody**, you know? my mother says and sighs. She has lived in this city her whole life. She can speak two languages. She can sing an opera. She knows how to fix a TV. But she doesn't know which subway train to take to get downtown. I hold her hand very tight while we wait for the right train to arrive.

She used to draw when she had time. Now she draws with a needle and thread, little knotted rosebuds, tulips made of silk thread. Someday she would like to go to the ballet. Someday she would like to see a play. She borrows opera records from the public library and sings with **velvety lungs** powerful as morning glories.

> I could've been somebody, you know?

Today while cooking oatmeal she is Madame Butterfly until she sighs and points the wooden spoon at me. I could've been somebody, you know? Esperanza, you go to school. Study hard. That Madame Butterfly was a fool. She stirs the oatmeal. Look at my *comadres*. She means Izaura whose husband left and Yolanda whose husband is dead. Got to take care all your own, she says shaking her head.

Then out of nowhere: Shame is a bad thing, you know? It keeps you down. You want to know why I quit school? Because I didn't have nice clothes. No clothes, but I had brains.

Yup, she says **disgusted**, stirring again. I was a smart cookie then.

Key Vocabulary
disgusted *adj.*, feeling ashamed

In Other Words
been somebody become someone important
velvety lungs a beautiful voice
comadres godmothers (in Spanish)

Before You Move On

1. **Interpret** Describe the trees. How are the trees a symbol of the narrator's life?
2. **Opinion** What do you think about the mother's decision to quit school? Why? Discuss with a partner.

A **House** of My Own

Not a flat. Not an apartment in back. Not a man's house. Not a daddy's. A house all my own. With my porch and my pillow, my pretty purple **petunias**. My books and my stories. My two shoes waiting beside the bed. Nobody to **shake a stick at**. Nobody's garbage to pick up after.

Only a house quiet as snow, a space for myself to go, **clean as paper before the poem**.

⯅ **Critical Viewing: Setting** What details do you see in this image? How do they relate to the text?

In Other Words
petunias flowers
shake a stick at get mad at
clean as paper before the poem
    a place that no one has lived
    in before

▲ **Critical Viewing: Plot** Describe this image. How does it relate to the girl's experience in the text?

Mango Says
Goodbye Sometimes

I like to tell stories. I tell them inside my head. I tell them after the mailman says, Here's your mail. Here's your mail he said.

I make a story for my life, for each step my brown shoe takes. I say, "And so she trudged up the wooden stairs, her sad brown shoes taking her to the house she never liked."

I like to tell stories. I am going to tell you a story about a girl who didn't want to belong.

We didn't always live on Mango Street. Before that we lived on Loomis on the third floor, and before that we lived on Keeler. Before Keeler it was Paulina, but what I remember most is Mango Street, sad red house, the house I belong but do not belong to.

I **put it down on paper** and then the **ghost does not ache** so much. I write it down and Mango says goodbye sometimes. **She does not hold me with both arms.** She sets me free.

In Other Words
put it down on paper write
ghost does not ache memories do not hurt me
She does not hold me with both arms. My past does not stop me.

One day I will pack my bags of books and paper. One day I will say goodbye to Mango. I am too strong for her to keep me here forever. One day I will go away.

Friends and neighbors will say, What happened to that Esperanza?

Where did she go with all those books and paper? Why did she **march** so far away?

They will not know I have gone away to come back. For the ones I left behind. For the ones who **cannot out**. ❖

About the Author

Sandra Cisneros

Throughout her childhood, **Sandra Cisneros** (1954–) and her family moved many times. She read books to make a home in her imagination. There was a book called *The Little House* that she checked out of the library over and over again. The house in the story was her dream house. Soon Cisneros started writing her own stories. In 1984, she published *The House on Mango Street*. Now she lives in a house of her own in San Antonio, Texas.

In Other Words
march go
cannot out are not able to leave

Before You Move On

1. **Character's Motive** Why does the girl write about the house on Mango Street?
2. **Check Prediction** The text doesn't give the answer, but it gives more evidence. What do you think now: Will the girl "say goodbye to Mango"? Why or why not?

Connect Reading and Writing

Vocabulary

appreciate

despite

disgust

expectations

landlord

rent

strengths

temporary

CRITICAL THINKING

1. SUM IT UP Complete a Character Description Chart about Esperanza to show what her thoughts and actions show about her. Include her **expectations** and her **strengths**.

Character Description Chart

What the Character Thinks	What the Character Does	What this Shows About the Character

2. Draw Conclusions Mama's life does not match her **expectations**. What does Esperanza learn from Mama's experiences?

3. Compare Esperanza doesn't want to have to pay **rent** to a **landlord** anymore. How is her dream house different from the other places she has lived?

4. Make Judgments Think about all three selections. **Despite** mistakes, Arturo, Lekuton, and Esperanza all make important decisions. Whose decision do you think was the hardest? Explain.

READING FLUENCY

Phrasing Read the passage on page 636 to a partner. Assess your fluency.

1. I read

   a. great   **b.** OK   **c.** not very well

2. What I did best was _____ .

READING STRATEGY

Plan Your Reading
What clues did you use to make your predictions about the characters? Were your predictions right? Tell a partner.

VOCABULARY REVIEW

Oral Review Read the paragraph aloud. Add the vocabulary words.

People have different _____ about their homes. Some people pay _____ to a _____ . Some people want to own a home. Every kind of home has different _____ . Most people _____ their homes even if they are _____ . Sometimes people must put up with a home, _____ the _____ they might feel about it.

Written Review Draw a house for Esperanza. Write captions to explain why she would **appreciate** this home. Use at least four vocabulary words.

WRITE ABOUT THE GUIDING QUESTION

Explore Personal Decisions

Esperanza's **expectations** and disappointments lead her to make a decision about her future. Reread the selection. Then explain what she did and why.

Connect Across the Curriculum

 ELPS: 2.C.4 learn academic vocabulary heard during classroom instruction and interactions; 1.E.3 internalize new academic language in speaking activities; 5.B.2 write using content-based grade-level vocabulary

Literary Analysis

Analyze Theme

> **Academic Vocabulary**
> • **analyze** (a-nu-līz) *verb*
>   When you **analyze**, you separate something into parts and examine, or study, it.

What Is the Story's Message? The title "The House on Mango Street" tells you a topic. The topic is what the story is about. For example, in this story, the main character wants a house of her own. A story also has a **theme**, or message, about the topic. Authors usually don't tell the readers the theme. The readers have to figure it out.

To identify the theme of the story, pay attention to the **thoughts, words, and actions of the characters** . These clues will help you **analyze** the theme.

> We didn't always live on Mango Street. Before that we lived on Loomis on the third floor, and before that we lived on Keeler. Before Keeler it was Paulina, and before that I can't remember. But what I remember most is moving a lot. Each time it seemed there'd be one more of us.

Practice Together

Make a Theme Chart What message do you think the author wants to tell? First, identify important **clues** about the characters in the story. Use a Theme Chart to keep track of the clues. Then use what you learn about the characters to **analyze** the theme of a story.

Theme Chart

Important Event	What the Character Thinks, Says, and Does	What the Character Learns and How She Changes
Family moves to Mango Street		

Create your own Theme Chart. Work with the class to add more clues from the story.

Try It!

Tell About the Theme Add another detail, or clue, from the story. Then review all the clues. What do you think is the theme of the story? Use the clues to write a sentence about the message of the story.

Vocabulary Study

Use Word Parts

Suffix	Meaning
-ion	condition or action
-ful	full of

Academic Vocabulary
- **connection** (ku-**nek**-shun) *noun*
  The **connection** between two things is something they have in common.

If you see a word with a **suffix** or a **compound word** that you do not know, analyze the base word. To figure out the meaning of a word with a suffix, cover the part of the word that is not the base word. Here you see that *protect* is the base word.

protection = **protect** + **ion**

In a compound word, the **connection** of two base words makes a new word.

bird + **house** = **birdhouse**

Find Base Words Work with a partner. Find the base words in these words from the selection. Cover up the part that is not a base word. Find the **connection** between the base word and the meaning of the whole word.

1. downstairs (p. 62)
2. washroom (p. 62)
3. expectation (p. 62)
4. hallway (p. 63)
5. everybody (p. 63)
6. powerful (p. 67)

Write a Description Use at least three of these words to write about your own home. Share your description with a partner.

Research/Writing

MATH

Find Area

Academic Vocabulary
- **identify** (ī-**den**-tu-fī) *verb*
  When you **identify** something, you name it or tell what it is.

How can you **identify** the actual size of a place? Measure its area. Area is length multiplied by width.

width = 8 inches

length = 11 inches

Area: 88 square inches

① **Practice** Practice **identifying** area by measuring a sheet of paper.

② **Measure** Measure the length of the paper with a ruler. Write down the number. Then, measure and note the width.

③ **Multiply** Multiply the two sides to **identify** the area. For example, 11 inches x 8 inches = 88 square inches.

④ **Discuss Your Findings** Compare your results with a partner to see if you both **identified** the same area.

ELPS: 2.C.4 learn academic vocabulary heard during classroom instruction and interactions; 3.E share information in cooperative learning interactions; 3.G.2 express ideas on a variety of social and grade-appropriate academic topics

Media/Speaking

Design a Home

MEDIA & TECHNOLOGY

Academic Vocabulary
- **specific** (spi-**sif**-ik) *adjective*
  When something is **specific**, it is definite or particular.

Esperanza had **specific** opinions about what makes a house a home. What **specific** things do you think make a house a home?

1 **Discuss Homes** With a small group, discuss the question: What makes a house a home? As you state your opinion, make sure you support it with **specific** details. For example:
- An unsupported opinion: Furniture is good in a house.
- A supported opinion: I think a house is a home when it has a room with comfortable chairs and couches where family can gather.

As you tell your opinion about what you want in a home, use visuals as support as well. If you can easily sketch what you want, you probably have a good **specific** idea. If you can't easily sketch it, like the unsupported opinion above, your idea is probably not **specific** enough.

After your discussion, list at least five things that your group chose as important features of a home.

2 **Collect Ideas** Collect and cut out pictures of various homes and decorated rooms. Choose pictures that show the **specific** things your group wants in a home.
- Use the Internet to find pictures and take virtual tours of homes.

  Internet InsideNG.com
  Access a search engine. Use search words related to your **specific** topic.

3 **Organize Your Design Team** Set a deadline for the completion of your design. Have each member of your team choose a task:
- Draw the outside of your home.
- Use graph paper to draw the floor plan of each room.
- Write a description of the special features that make the house a home.

4 **Share Your Design** Present your drawings to the class. Give each team member a set amount of time to present. Have one person in the group describe the five features that are special about your home. Listen to each presentation. Then discuss the **specific** advantages of each team's design.

ELPS: 3.G.1 express opinions on a variety of social and grade-appropriate academic topics; 3.G.2 express ideas on a variety of social and grade-appropriate academic topics

Express Ideas and Opinions

Pair Share With a partner, share your ideas and opinions about what you want to do when you are older. Give reasons for your opinions. Be sure the verbs you use agree with the subjects of your sentences.

> I want to be a chef. I think it's exciting to create new dishes.

Write with Colorful Action Words

Study the Models When you write, you want to catch your reader's interest. One way to do that is to use colorful action verbs. Many verbs tell what someone or something does—*eats, nibbles, munches, gobbles, gulps, devours*. These action verbs can be boring, like *eats*, or they can give a colorful, vivid picture, like *gobbles* or *devours*.

JUST OK

> Esperanza <u>looks</u> at the house on Mango Street. Four trees <u>grow</u> in the front near the street. Bricks on the house <u>break</u> slowly. The front door doesn't want to open.

The reader thinks: **"This writing is plain."**

BETTER

> Esperanza <u>frowns</u> at the house on Mango Street. Four trees <u>grab</u> the earth in the front near the street. Bricks on the house <u>crumble</u> slowly. The front door <u>clings</u> to the house. It doesn't want to open.

The reader thinks: **"This is better. The verb 'frowns' helps me know that Esperanza doesn't like what she sees."**

Add Sentences Think of two more sentences to add to the BETTER model above. Try to use colorful verbs from the chart.

Instead of . . .	Try a colorful verb like . . .
go	crawl, hobble, walk, hurry, race
look at	glance at, notice, observe, gaze, watch
laugh	grin, giggle, chuckle, cackle, howl
talk	chat, chatter, discuss, speak
write	jot down, scribble, record, compose

WRITE ON YOUR OWN Write about something you learned from Esperanza. Use colorful action verbs in your sentences. Use some action verbs from the chart or try a thesaurus. It can help you find more precise and colorful verbs.

REMEMBER
- Add **-s** to the action verb only when the subject is singular.

  One tree grow**s** in the backyard.

Compare Across Texts

Compare Universal Themes

"American Names" and "The House on Mango Street" tell about people trying to relate to the world around them. What is the **connection** between their themes?

How It Works

Collect and Organize Ideas You can use a chart to help you compare ideas across these two texts. What questions might help you compare?

Comparison Chart

Question	"American Names"	"The House on Mango Street"
1. What situation bothers each narrator?	Arturo is trying to fit in at school. His teacher calls him "Arthur."	Esperanza has moved many times. She would like a place of her own in which to feel at home.
2. What decisions do the narrators make?		

Practice Together

Study and Summarize Ideas Compare the answers for question 1, then summarize. Think about ways the texts are alike.

> The speakers of "American Names" and "The House on Mango Street" do not feel comfortable. Arturo feels trapped between his Hispanic culture and his new American one. Esperanza feels trapped in small houses in a crowded city.

Try It!

Copy this chart to collect answers for question 2. Summarize them. You can use this frame to help you express your comparison.

The narrators of "American Names" and "The House on Mango Street" want to feel _____.
Arturo agrees to the new name at first, then realizes _____. Esperanza cannot _____,
but she can use her mind. To feel more free, she _____. Both narrators deal with their
situations by _____.

Academic Vocabulary
- **connection** (ku-**nek**-shun) *noun*
  The connection between two
  things is something they have
  in common.

Decision Point

GUIDING QUESTION How do decisions affect your identity?

Reflect on Your Reading

Think back on your reading of the unit selections. Discuss what you did to understand what you read.

Focus on Genre **Narrative Writing**

In this unit, you learned about fiction and nonfiction. Choose a selection from the unit and explain to a partner what makes it fiction or nonfiction. Find examples of its point of view.

Reading Strategy **Plan Your Reading**

As you read the selections, you learned how to preview and predict to help you understand the narratives. Discuss with a partner how you might use this strategy with other kinds of texts.

Explore the

Throughout this unit, you have been thinking about decisions and identity. Choose one of these ways to explore the Guiding Question:

- **Discuss** With a group, discuss the Guiding Question. Give examples from real life of decisions that affect who you are. Compare them to decisions in the selections.

- **Describe** Each selection describes a place that affects the main character's identity. Describe a place that is important to you. Give details to help listeners see it in their minds.

- **Write** Write a persuasive essay about a common type of decision. Explain why people should or shouldn't make this decision. Be sure to clearly establish your position, consider and respond to other views, and anticipate and answer reader concerns and counter-arguments. Support your position with logically organized evidence, including facts and opinions.

Book Talk

Which Unit Library book did you choose? Explain to a partner what it taught you about decision making.

UNIT LIBRARY

Content Library

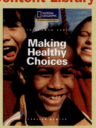

Leveled Library

▲ **Critical Viewing:** Study the details of this image. What do you think will happen next?

Stand or Fall

 GUIDING QUESTION

What happens when people come face-to-face with a rival?

 ELPS Focus: 1.B.1 monitor oral language production and self-correct; 1.E.2 internalize new basic language in writing activities; 2.E.1 use visual support to enhance and confirm understanding of complex and elaborated spoken language; 2.G.5 understand the main points of spoken language regarding familiar to unfamiliar language; 2.I.2 demonstrate listening comprehension of complex spoken English by retelling or summarizing spoken messages; 3.B.2 expand and internalize initial vocabulary by retelling simple stories and basic information; 3.B.3 expand and internalize initial vocabulary by learning and using routine language needed for classroom communication; 3.C.1 speak using a variety of grammatical structures with increasing accuracy and ease; 3.H.3 explain with increasing specificity and detail

Read More!

Content Library

Amazing Animals
by Kate Boehm Nyquist

Leveled Library

Romiette and Julio
by Sharon M. Draper

Speak
by Laurie Halse Anderson

The Forbidden Schoolhouse
by Suzanne Jurmain

Internet
InsideNG.com

- Discover how different animals survive.
- Find out about other traditional tales.
- View images of dragons.

Focus on Genre

 ELPS: 1.A.2 use prior knowledge to understand meanings in English; 4.C.3 comprehend English vocabulary used routinely in written classroom materials

Elements of Fiction

▶ **Plot**
▶ **Character**
▶ **Setting**

Every story has at least three parts, or <mark>elements</mark>—plot, characters, and setting. These <mark>elements</mark> of fiction work together to build a story.

Plot: How It Works

The **plot** is what happens in the story. It is what the characters experience.

- Plots are based on a **conflict**, or problem, that the main character faces.
- The plot develops during the **rising action** as complications occur and the characters try to solve the problem.
- The turning point in the plot is called the **climax**.
- **Falling action** leads from the climax to the **resolution**, the stage where the problem is solved at the end of the story.

Read "A Walk in the City" aloud to see the stages of the plot.

Content-Area Words

This lesson contains several words that are routinely used in written language arts classroom materials.
plot
character
setting

A Walk in the City

One afternoon a girl named Red walked into the city to take soup to her sick grandmother. She suddenly heard a barking sound behind her. Red turned around and saw a dog staring at her. <u>She was scared of dogs</u> so she started to walk faster. The dog followed her. "How am I going to get rid of this dog? What should I do?" Red wondered.

The dog kept following Red. Then he started to whine. Suddenly, she remembered the soup in her hands. She set down the soup, and the dog ate it up. <u>After he finished, he came up to her. She stood still, not moving. Then he licked her foot and wagged his tail.</u>

She realized he had been hungry and might be lost. She read his tag. The address was right next to her grandmother's apartment! So Red continued to her grandmother's, with the dog following her.

setting
character

conflict

rising action

climax

resolution

Academic Vocabulary

- **element** (el-u-munt) *noun*
  An **element** is one part of a whole.

Plot: Practice Together

Read "A Walk in the City" again. As you read, listen for events of the plot and tell where they go on this Plot Diagram.

Character: How It Works

Characters are the people or animals that take part in the plot.

- Each character's traits, actions, words, and decisions affect what happens in the plot.
- Writers tell readers about their characters by:
    - saying directly what the character is like
    - showing the characters' thoughts, words, and actions
    - telling what other characters think of him or her.
- These writing techniques are called **characterization**.

See these techniques in action as the writer characterizes Kit Fox below.

Plot Diagram

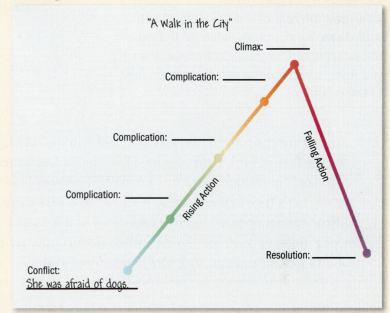

"A Walk in the City"

Climax: _____
Complication: _____
Complication: _____
Rising Action
Complication: _____
Falling Action
Resolution: _____
Conflict:
She was afraid of dogs.

A Foxy Challenge

The sun was setting as Kit Fox left her desert den. Hunting had not been good the night before, and she was hungry. She needed to find food, so she trotted off across the dry land hunting for food. Soon, Kit Fox saw Roadrunner with a fresh meal in his beak. Roadrunner looked up nervously. Foxes and birds are usually enemies in the desert.

"Ah, I see that you have a yummy mouse for your evening meal," Kit Fox said. She eyed the bird's catch hungrily. "That must have been easy for you to catch. I've heard that you are very speedy."

Telling about the character directly

Character's words and actions

Academic Vocabulary

- **characterization** (kair-ik-tu-**ris**-ā-shun) *noun*
  The way writers show their characters is called **characterization**.

Character: Practice Together

Now read the rest of the story aloud with your class. As you read, listen for the ways the writer characterizes Roadrunner. After you read, complete the activities listed next to the passage.

Character Description Chart

Character	What the Character Is Like	How I Know
Kit Fox	hungry	writer tells about the character directly
Kit Fox	friendly	her words and actions

Roadrunner dropped his meal and held it in his claws. "Oh, yes, I am the fastest bird in this desert. I have never lost a race!"

"Never?" questioned Kit Fox. "I don't believe you. I am very fast myself. Let's race to that cactus. We'll see who gets there first."

Roadrunner counted to three and raced to the cactus. Kit Fox never caught up with him. In fact, when Roadrunner returned, Kit Fox was gone. Gone, too, was Roadrunner's meal.

1. **Make a Character Description Chart for both Kit Fox and Roadrunner. Include new information about Kit Fox you learn from the end of the story.**
2. **How would the plot change if Roadrunner were more clever than Kit Fox?**

Setting: How It Works

Setting is the time and place where a story happens.

- Setting includes the customs and the way people think at that time and place. During the course of the story, the setting may change.
- The time and place affect how the characters think and act.
- Setting also affects the plot. For example, a story set in a hot desert would probably not include characters being caught in a hurricane.

See how one writer uses the **element** of setting.

A Foxy Challenge

The sun was setting as Kit Fox left her desert den. Hunting had not been good the night before, and she was hungry. She needed to find food, so she trotted off across the dry land hunting for food. Soon, Kit Fox saw Roadrunner with a fresh meal in his beak. Roadrunner looked up nervously. Foxes and birds are usually enemies in the desert.

The time and place

Customs of the time and place

Setting: Practice Together

Now read a different version of this story aloud with your class. As you read, listen for details about the setting. After you read, complete the activities next to the passage.

It was almost midnight when Kit Fox left her den in the alley behind the trash bin. Hunting had not been good the night before because of the storm and flooding, and she was hungry. She needed to find food, so she crept along the alley hunting for food. Soon, Kit Fox saw Roadrunner with a rain-soaked meal in his beak. Roadrunner looked up nervously. It was dangerous for a bird to be out this late, especially around strangers.

1. Describe the time and place and what the characters think.
2. Compare the different settings in these two versions of "A Foxy Challenge."
3. With a partner, predict how the plot of the second version would be different from the first plot as a result of the different setting.

Try It!

Read the following passage aloud and answer the questions about the <mark>elements</mark> of fiction. Tell how you know.

A Music Caper

"Who stole my new CD?" shouted Rudy from his room. He was getting ready for school.

One by one, Rudy approached his family members. He knocked on his sister's door. "Cara, give me back my CD," he said. She opened the door. "I don't have it Rudy," she replied. Rudy looked around. His CD was not there.

Then he went to his brother's room. "Andrew, where is my new CD?" "I don't have it, Rudy," he replied.

"Mom, Dad, have you seen my new CD?" Rudy said as he searched the kitchen. He looked everywhere but still couldn't find it. "I don't have it, Rudy," his mom said. "Rudy, you've asked each one of us, and you've searched every room. We don't have it," his dad said.

Rudy was not convinced. If his new CD was missing, someone must have taken it. He sat at the breakfast table sulking.

Later as Rudy sat on the bus to school, he reached into his backpack to get his science book. As he searched for the book, he felt a square shape. Rudy had found his new CD. It had been in his backpack all along!

That day after school, Rudy apologized to his family. Then they all sat down together to listen to his new CD.

1. What is the setting?
2. Who are the characters and what are they like?
3. What is the conflict?
4. How does the main character resolve the conflict?
5. How would the plot be different if the characters were fish and the setting was the ocean?

Focus on Vocabulary

 **ELPS:** 1.A.2 use prior experiences to understand meanings in English

Relate Words

Synonyms are words with similar meanings that describe the same concept. No two synonyms mean exactly the same thing. They have specific definitions and different shades of meaning. For example, one word might have a much stronger meaning than its synonym does.

> **EXAMPLE**   Amber had to play hard to **beat** her opponent,
> but she was finally able to **vanquish** the other player.

Knowing the specific meaning of a synonym and how it relates to other words can help you better understand what you read. A Synonym Scale like the one below can help you sort out the shades of meaning of words that describe the same concept.

Synonym Scale

beat   triumph   vanquish

How the Strategy Works

The more words you know about a concept, the better you will be able to express your own thoughts and understand exactly what someone says.

1. Every time you read, take the opportunity to learn new words.
2. Put words into groups, or categories, to see how they relate to one another. This will help you understand their specific definitions.
3. Use a Synonym Scale to rank synonyms from weakest to strongest.

Use the strategy to figure out how the underlined words relate to each other.

> Our school tennis team won the city finals this year. My sister Jana is the team captain. People say Jana is the best player on the team. Everyone was <u>excited</u> about our victory. Jana was <u>thrilled</u> because she won every one of her games.

Strategy in Action

" *Excited* and *thrilled* both mean a shade of 'happy,' but I think a player would be happier to win than fans would be, so *thrilled* must be stronger than *excited*."

☑ **REMEMBER** Using shades of meanings and knowing how synonyms relate to one another can help you understand a word's specific meaning.

Academic Vocabulary
- **relate** (ri-lāt) *verb*
  When you **relate** things, you show how they are connected.

Practice Together

Read this passage aloud. Then, work with your class to make a Synonym Scale for the underlined words.

The Sound of Drums

Someone gave my upstairs neighbor a drum set for his birthday. He has been practicing on those drums ever since, and the sounds coming through the ceiling are driving me crazy!

At first, he spent hours <u>tapping</u> a simple beat with one drum stick. It was quiet, so I didn't mind too much.

Then he moved on to learning how to play the bass drum. He seems to enjoy <u>thumping</u> loudly on the bass. The sound coming through the ceiling is giving me a headache.

I have started <u>pounding</u> on the ceiling to get him to quiet down. It isn't working. He keeps practicing.

I am afraid that next I'll hear him <u>clashing</u> the cymbals. That will wake up the whole building!

Then all the neighbors will be <u>knocking</u> on his door complaining about the noise!

Try It!

Read the following passage and notice the underlined synonyms. Which year had the best tasting barbeque? How do you know?

It's All in the Family

Every August, brothers Joe and George compete to see who makes the best barbeque. They have had this cooking rivalry for years, and the family loves it. Relatives from around the country come to picnic and enjoy the brothers' food. Everyone votes to decide which barbeque is the best that year.

Two years ago, Joe's entry won the contest. People called it "<u>tasty</u>." Last year George won. Everyone declared that his special sauce made with cranberries was <u>scrumptious</u>. This year was different. Both men had experimented with strange ingredients. Neither brother's barbeque was even <u>appetizing</u>! The family voted against them both and decided they should work together from then on.

On the Menu

by Susan E. Goodman

Build Background

Watch Animals in Nature

How does an animal survive in nature? Animals have different ways of protecting themselves. They may hide, run, or try to blend in with their environment.

Connect

Play a Game Make cards with pictures of animals on them. Show a card to a partner. Does this animal hunt other animals? Is this animal hunted by other animals? Put each card in a *Hunter* or *Hunted* pile. Do some cards belong in both piles?

Digital Library

InsideNG.com
◉ View the video.

▲ This grasshopper blends into the grass so that other animals won't see it.

Language & Grammar

ELPS: 1.E.2 internalize new basic language in writing activities; 2.E.1 use visual support to enhance and confirm understanding of complex and elaborated spoken language; 3.B.3 expand and internalize initial vocabulary by learning and using routine language needed for classroom communication; 3.C.1 speak using a variety of grammatical structures with increasing accuracy and ease; 3.H.3 explain with increasing specificity and detail

1 TRY OUT LANGUAGE
2 LEARN GRAMMAR
3 APPLY ON YOUR OWN

Define and Explain CD

Study the photo. Read the labels, which contain commonly used classroom language. Listen to the information.

PICTURE PROMPT

How Does an Octopus Disappear?

Octopuses have well-developed brains. They are smart animals.

head

eye

Octopuses have very good eyesight. They have a large eye on either side of their heads.

An octopus has eight arms called tentacles. They are attached to the octopus's head. Each tentacle has two rows of suckers on it.

tentacle

ink

An octopus squirts ink to protect itself. The ink forms a cloud. It looks like smoke. The octopus "disappears" in the ink.

Use Pronouns as Subjects

A **pronoun** refers to a noun. A **subject pronoun** is a pronoun that is the subject of a sentence.

Subject Pronoun	Example Sentence
• Use **I** to talk about yourself. • Use **we** to talk about another person and yourself.	• **I** study ocean animals. • <u>Lisa and I</u> read books about the ocean. **We** study the photos.
• Use **you** to talk to another person. • Use **you** also to talk to more than one person.	• **You** are a good photographer. • Class, **you** are all good photographers.
• Use **he** to talk about one man or boy. • Use **she** to talk about one woman or girl. • Use **it** to talk about one thing, place, or idea. • Use **they** to talk about more than one person, place, thing, or idea.	• The <u>diver</u> photographs an octopus. **He** uses an underwater camera. • <u>Lisa</u> studies octopus behavior. **She** is amazed by their ability to hide. • The <u>octopus</u> squirts ink. **It** escapes quickly. • <u>Octopuses</u> have eight arms. **They** also have good eyesight.

Practice Together

Say each sentence with the correct subject pronoun.

1. Mark and I study a photo of an octopus. (We/They) are curious.
2. The poison of some octopuses is dangerous. (He/It) can hurt people.
3. The scientist takes a picture of an octopus underwater. (She/They) swims away slowly.
4. Octopuses are not good swimmers. (He/They) use their arms to crawl on the ocean bottom.

Try It!

Write the correct subject pronoun on a card. Then say the sentence and add the pronoun.

5. Octopuses are very smart animals. (We/They) can change how they look.
6. Sometimes an octopus cannot trick its enemy. Then (they/it) uses ink to disappear.
7. A diver examines an octopus. (He/They) wears special gloves.
8. My sister and I want to learn more about octopuses. (We/You) do research on the Internet.

▲ A scientist examines the suckers on an octopus.

Tell About an Animal's Behavior

DEFINE AND EXPLAIN

Animals act in all kinds of ways that can surprise us. Which animal do you want to find out more about?

Work with a partner to research an animal. Find out how the animal behaves and what makes it special. Use books, the Internet, or other sources to find information about the animal you choose.

Download a photo or draw a picture of the animal. Label its body parts. Include interesting facts about the animal's behavior with your labels.

With your partner, show your picture to a group of classmates. Tell your classmates how your animal behaves. Explain the interesting facts you discovered.

▲ A good explanation includes details.

HOW TO DEFINE AND EXPLAIN

1. Explain the meaning of the word or topic.
2. Give details or examples.
3. Use visuals for explanations.

> Two rows of suckers are on each arm of the octopus. They are used for tasting things.

USE PRONOUNS AS SUBJECTS

Think about the pronouns you will use in your explanation.

First use a **noun** to tell about your animal. Then use a **subject pronoun** to refer to it. Remember, a subject pronoun can refer to a subject noun.

Subject noun: The **octopus** changes color to trick enemies.

Subject pronoun: **It** can blend into the background.

ELPS: 3.A practice producing sounds of newly acquired vocabulary in a manner that is comprehensible; 4.D use prereading supports to enhance comprehension of text; 4.F.1 use visual and contextual support to read grade-appropriate content area text

Learn Key Vocabulary

Rate and Study the Words Rate how well you know each word. Then:

1. Pronounce the word. Say it aloud several times. Spell it.
2. Study the example.
3. Tell more about the word.
4. Practice it. Make the word your own.

Key Words

adaptation (a-dap-**tā**-shun) *noun* ▶ page 101

An **adaptation** is a feature or behavior that helps animals survive. This cat's arched back is an **adaptation** that protects it.

advantage (ad-**van**-tij) *noun* ▶ page 97

When you have an **advantage**, you have a better chance to succeed than others. If you are stronger or faster, this is an **advantage**.

camouflage (**kam**-a-flazh) *noun* ▶ page 96

Camouflage is a color or pattern that helps people or animals hide. Lions use **camouflage** to help them hide when they hunt.

disguise (dis-**gīz**) *noun* ▶ page 94

When you wear a **disguise**, you try to look different from what you normally look like. A **disguise** can help people or animals hide.

predator (**pre**-du-tur) *noun* ▶ page 94

A **predator** is an animal that eats other animals for food. Lions and tigers are **predators**.
Antonym: **prey**

prey (**prā**) *noun* ▶ page 102

Prey is an animal that other animals eat. A mouse is **prey** for a snake.
Antonym: **predator**

survive (sur-**vīv**) *verb* ▶ page 96

When you **survive**, you stay alive. In cold weather, you need warm clothes to **survive**.

threat (thret) *noun* ▶ page 96

A **threat** is a danger. Clouds show the **threat** of a storm.
Synonym: danger

Practice the Words Make an Example Web for each Key Word. Work with a partner to think of examples.

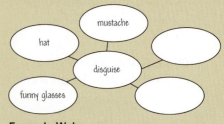

Example Web

Reading Strategy: Monitor Your Reading

What do you do when you read something that you don't understand?
Try to **reread** the text or **read on** to make it clear, or clarify ideas.

Reading Strategy
Monitor Your Reading

HOW TO CLARIFY IDEAS

1. As you read, stop when you don't understand something.

2. If the text is unclear, read it again. Start at the beginning of the paragraph.

3. If you still don't understand, keep reading. Look for information that helps you figure things out.

Strategy in Action

Here's how one student clarified ideas.

Look Into the Text

> Some animals hide by looking like the places where they live. To see how this works, let's look at the leafy sea dragon. You may never have heard of this sea creature, but it is a master of disguise.
>
> The sea dragon is covered with skin that looks like leaves, which helps the dragon look like a piece of seaweed. A hungry meat-eater would stay away from anything that looks like seaweed.
>
> Leaf-like skin is just one part of the sea dragon's disguise.

I don't understand what "master of disguise" means.

" To figure it out, I reread the paragraph. "

I'm still not sure what "master of disguise" means.

" When I read on, I learn that it means the sea dragon looks like something else. "

Practice Together

Reread the passage. Stop when you read something you do not understand.
Write it on a sticky note. Follow the steps in the How-To box to clarify ideas.

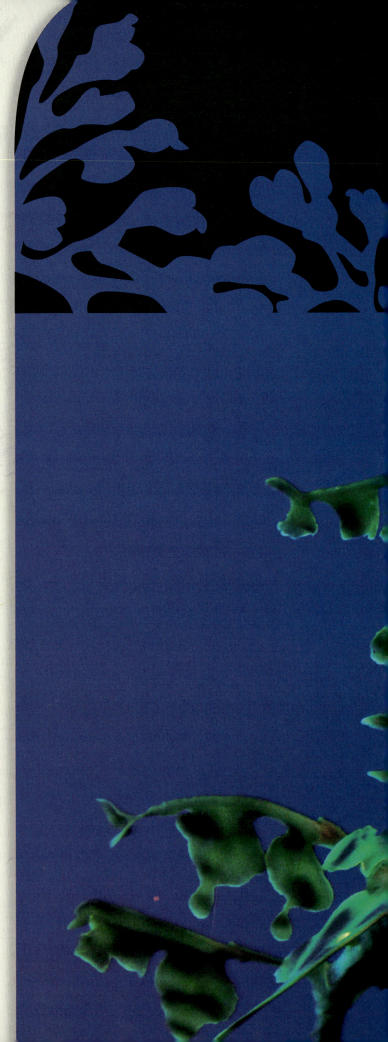

ELPS: 4.F.1 use visual and contextual support to read grade-appropriate content area text

Science Article

A science article is nonfiction writing that tells about ideas and information in the natural world. It gives facts about animals, environments, discoveries, or other science topics. It does not include opinions or commonplace assertions.

Science articles are usually organized with **headings** and **labels** that explain the ideas.

Master of Disguise

Over time, animals n  developed many ways to stay away from predators. A predator is an animal that hunts and eats other animals. Hiding is one of the best ways to stay alive.

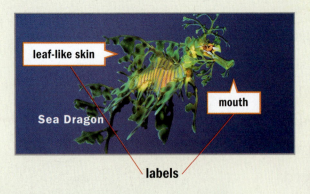

leaf-like skin

mouth

Sea Dragon

labels

Your Job as a Reader

Reading Strategy: Monitor Your Reading

As you read, make sure you understand the text. If there is something in the text that is confusing, **reread** or **read on** to figure it out.

On the Menu

by Susan E. Goodman

Is that seaweed? Look again. The sea dragon's disguise helps the sea dragon stay off another fish's menu. Hiding is one of many animal tricks for staying alive.

Online Coach

Staying Alive

Staying alive can be a big challenge for some animals, especially when other animals want to eat them. Read on to discover the **self-defense tricks** that animals use to stay alive.

Master of Disguise

Over time, animals have developed many ways to stay away from **predators**. A predator is an animal that hunts and eats other animals. Hiding is one of the best ways to stay alive.

Some animals hide by looking like the places where they live. To see how this works, let's look at the leafy sea dragon. You may never have heard of this sea creature, but it is **a master of disguise**.

The sea dragon is covered with skin that looks like leaves, which helps the dragon look like a piece of seaweed. A hungry **meat-eater** would stay away from anything that looks like seaweed.

Leaf-like skin is just one part of the sea dragon's disguise. Its fins make another part. They are small. They slowly push the dragon

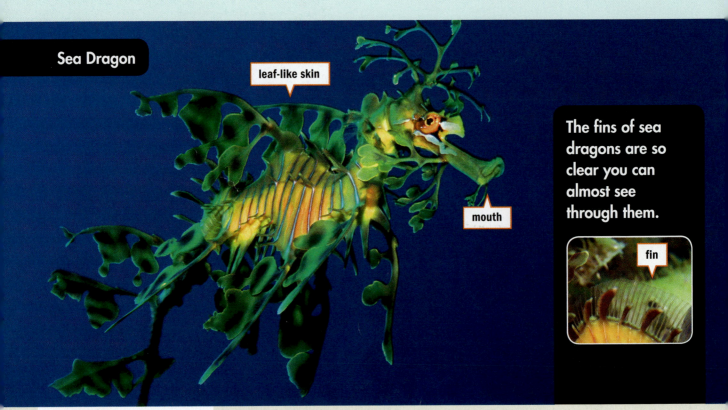

Sea Dragon

leaf-like skin

mouth

The fins of sea dragons are so clear you can almost see through them.

fin

Key Vocabulary

predator n., an animal that eats other animals

disguise n., a different look that keeps someone or something from being recognized

In Other Words

self-defense tricks ways to protect oneself

a master of very good at

meat-eater animal that eats other animals

through the water. So the dragon looks like it's floating—just like seaweed.

The sea dragon's mouth completes its disguise. The mouth looks like just another seaweed stem. There are even small "leaves" at the end! Yet it's actually a tube that works like a straw. That mouth is great for **slurping up** the dragon's favorite food—sea lice. Yum!

Show-Offs

The leafy sea dragon hides to stay safe, while other animals stay safe by showing their colors. They want other animals to see them.

Scientists call these bright colors warning colors because the colors tell predators to stay away.

You have probably seen animals that have warning colors. Think, for instance, of all those insects that buzz by you on warm days. When one flies by, you likely **swat it away**. But what happens when a yellow bug flies in your face? Do you swat it? Or do you jump away?

You guessed it. Yellow is a warning color. It tells you that the pesky pest might be a bumblebee or a yellow wasp, and you don't want to bug those insects.

Some grasshoppers show off their own bright colors. A few are even red and blue. Those colors don't just look **spiffy**, they also tell predators to stay away.

Of course, hungry predators sometimes ignore the warning. They still go after the grasshopper. If that happens, the grasshopper has **a backup defense**. It makes lots of foam, and the foam tastes so bad that the predator won't do it again.

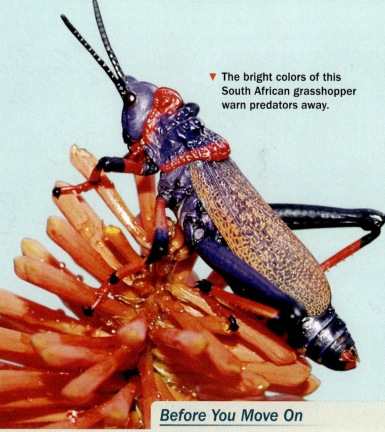

▼ The bright colors of this South African grasshopper warn predators away.

In Other Words
slurping up eating
swat it away hit it with something
   to make it go away
spiffy nice, pretty
a backup defense another way
   to protect itself

Before You Move On

1. **Details** What parts of the sea dragon give it a good **disguise**?
2. **Cause and Effect** Why do some animals hide and others show off their colors?

Blending In

Many animals use colors to match the place they live in. This is called camouflage. Some even change colors with the seasons.

The snowshoe hare has rusty brown fur in summer so it **blends in with** the colors of fields. In fall, the hare loses its brown fur and grows thick white fur. The new fur matches the snow in winter and keeps the hare warm.

On the Ball

Color doesn't offer enough protection for some other animals, so they have different defenses that help them survive in the wild.

The armadillo needs all the defenses it can get. It is only about two feet long and weighs 15 pounds. It has small teeth, so it cannot even bite to protect itself.

Instead the armadillo has **an armored** shell. The armor is made out of **bony plates**. Armor protects this animal from bumps and

Rolling, Rolling, Rolling. . .

1 At the first sign of a threat, an armadillo tries to run away. If that doesn't work, the armadillo stops.

2 Then, the armadillo begins to tuck itself into a ball. It folds its head and legs inside its shell.

Key Vocabulary
camouflage *n.*, colors that help animals hide
survive *v.*, to continue to live
threat *n.*, danger

In Other Words
blends in with matches
an armored a protective
bony plates a hard covering

bruises. Another **advantage** of the armor is that it makes it much harder for a predator to eat an armadillo.

An armadillo does not just rely on its armor, though. It has a couple of other tricks. When an armadillo spots a predator, it first tries to run away. A scared armadillo **darts for** the safety of its burrow. A burrow is an underground home.

But that's just the beginning. If an armored armadillo cannot get away, it hides in its shell. First it tucks in its legs and ears. Then it rolls its shell together. It turns itself into a living ball. It's an animal **roll-up**.

Most hungry hunters don't know how to eat an armadillo roll-up. They can **prod and poke** and toss the roll-up around, but they cannot find a tasty bite to eat.

3 Finally, the armadillo tucks its tail next to its head. Now the shell covers the animal's whole body.

4 After rolling itself into a ball, the armadillo is safe. Predators cannot find a tasty morsel to eat.

Key Vocabulary
advantage *n.*, something that helps

In Other Words
darts for runs to
roll-up that looks like a ball
prod and poke push and hit it

Before You Move On

1. **Describe** Use the photos and details from the text to tell what an armadillo looks like.
2. **Cause and Effect** What does the armadillo do to protect itself against a **threat**?

Lying Lizard

Like the armadillo, the frilled lizard tries to run away when it **spots** a predator. It darts up a tree, or it hops on its back legs and dashes across the forest. But that doesn't always work.

Sometimes the lizard can't just run away.

When that happens, it tries to **bluff its way out of becoming a tasty treat**. It pretends to be bigger than it really is, and it also acts **tough**.

The lizard opens its mouth as wide as it can. The skin around its neck pops

Before

The frilled lizard looks harmless most of the time.

In Other Words

spots sees
bluff its way out of becoming a tasty treat look like something it isn't so that it won't get eaten
tough mean

Science Background

Frilled lizards live in northern Australia's hot, dry forests. They are appropriately named after their neck frill that opens when they want to scare off a predator. Their color allows them to hide because they match the land and the trees they live on.

out like an umbrella. The lizard hisses and whips its long tail around. This makes the lizard look bigger and scarier than usual.

These moves often work, and they scare some predators away. Other hungry hunters may not be scared exactly, but they go looking for other snacks. Few animals want to **mess with this crazy critter**.

Either way, the lizard wins. It lives to eat its own supper of delicious insects and spiders.

After

To scare a predator away, the lizard spreads its skin.

In Other Words
mess with this crazy critter bother this strange animal

Before You Move On

1. **Explain** How does the lizard protect itself against a <mark>predator</mark>?
2. **Compare** How are a lizard's defenses like those of other animals?

School Safety

Many fish live in groups, or schools. That's because **there is safety in numbers**.

At the first sign of trouble, schooling fish swim as close together as they can get. Then the school makes lots of twists and turns. All that movement makes it hard for predators to make a meal out of just one fish.

Many other animals also stay safe by moving in groups. Predators cannot see individuals in a large group.

In Other Words

there is safety in numbers it is safer to swim with other fish than to swim alone

By swimming in schools, fish make themselves harder to catch.

Common Defenses

These are only a few of the ways that animals escape predators. They have other defenses, too.

Just look around. Cats arch their backs to look big and scary. Green grasshoppers blend into grass. Claws and teeth help animals fight.

These **adaptations**, or useful traits, are quite different. Yet they share one purpose. They all keep an animal from **landing on the menu**.

Key Vocabulary
adaptation *n.*, a feature or a behavior that lets an animal stay alive

In Other Words
landing on the menu getting eaten by another animal

Before You Move On

1. **Paraphrase** Tell in your own words how moving in groups helps some animals **survive**.
2. **Problem and Solution** Name an animal from the article and tell how it defends itself against a **predator**.

Looking for Prey

Camouflage helps animals hide from hungry predators. Did you know that it also helps predators hide from their **prey**? Why would predators need to hide? Sometimes they need help finding—and catching—dinner.

Some predators are awfully slow, and they can't run as fast as their prey. Camouflage lets them **sneak up at their own pace**.

Other predators are quick but sneaky. Clever coloring helps them hide from view. They lie in wait, hoping a meal will wander by. Surprise! The predator snaps up its prey.

A Bump on a Log

One predator that uses camouflage is the crocodile. Have you ever noticed the shape of a crocodile's head or the appearance of its skin? These features **help the beast nab** its next meal.

A crocodile can stay underwater for hours. It lies perfectly still in a river or lake with only its eyes and nostrils showing above the surface. It looks around and watches for food.

The crocodile's skin is rough and bumpy. In **murky** water, it looks a lot like a floating log—except that this log can bite. When an animal comes near, the crocodile leaps forward and **snatches** its prey.

A crocodile hides as it waits for its prey.

Key Vocabulary
prey *n.*, an animal that is eaten by another animal

In Other Words
sneak up at their own pace quietly approach when they are ready
help the beast nab help the animal catch
murky dark
snatches takes, grabs

A death adder moves its tail from side-to-side to attract prey.

Trick or Treat

Death adders are sneaky snakes. Like crocodiles, they use tricks to **scare up** their food.

A death adder's coloring makes it hard to see. The snake is mostly brown. When it lies on brown ground, it blends right in. Death adders **just love hanging out** under leaves and grass—which makes them even harder to see.

But there's one thing a death adder leaves in plain view: its tail. Why does it do this? That's simple. The tip of its tail looks like a worm. When a small animal approaches for a snack—wham! The adder strikes. It's trick-or-treat, animal style. ❖

In Other Words
scare up find, catch
just love hanging out enjoy hiding

Before You Move On

1. **Explain** How does the crocodile use camouflage?
2. **Paraphrase** Use your own words to tell how a death adder finds food.

Find the Adaptations

Animals have many adaptations that help protect them from predators. Some animals have colors that match the places they live. Some have shapes that make them hard to see. Figure out and explain these nature puzzles.

What to Do

❶ Look closely at each photo.

❷ Find the animal and describe its color and shape.

❸ Explain how its color and shape help it survive.

Snowshoe Hare   Thorn Bug Insects   Lizard

Snake   Spider   Tree Frog

▲ Some animals use camouflage so well that you can look right at them and not see them.

Before You Move On

1. **Text Feature** Why are numbered steps often part of text that gives direction?

2. **Instructions** Is there any missing or extra information in the instructions?

Connect Reading and Writing

Vocabulary
adaptations
advantage
camouflage
disguise
predators
prey
survive
threat

CRITICAL THINKING

1. SUM IT UP Decide what kind of **adaptation** each animal from the selection makes. Does it look different or does it act different? List the animal in the correct category on a Classification Chart. Then write a sentence about what you learned.

Classification Chart

Looks Different	Acts Different

What I Learned: _____

2. Describe Tell how **prey** protect themselves from **predators**.

3. Interpret The headings give clues about how animals **survive**. Choose two headings. Tell how each heading describes that animal's survival skills.

4. Explain What kinds of **threats** do animals in the selection face? What other animals do you know that face these **threats**?

READING FLUENCY

Phrasing Read the passage on page 637 to a partner. Assess your fluency.

1. I read
   a. great   **b.** OK   **c.** not very well

2. What I did best in my reading was _____.

READING STRATEGY

Clarify Ideas
Show a partner one part of the text that confused you. Tell your partner how you clarified ideas.

VOCABULARY REVIEW

Oral Review Read the paragraph aloud. Add the vocabulary words.

Every animal wants to _____, or stay alive. Some animals hunt other animals. They are _____. The animals they hunt are called _____. Animals use different _____ to stay safe. Sea dragons are protected by their _____. Armadillos roll into a ball if there is a _____. Animals also use adaptations to catch prey. Crocodiles use _____ to look like a log. This gives them an _____ over their prey.

Written Review Make picture cards for the animals from the selection. Write captions on the backs of the cards describing the animal and how it **survives**. Use four vocabulary words.

WRITE ABOUT THE GUIDING QUESTION

Explore What It Takes To Survive a Rival
Which **adaptation** from the selection do you think is the most amazing? Reread the selection to find examples that support your opinion.

Connect Across the Curriculum

ELPS: 4.K demonstrate and expand comprehension by employing analytical skills

Literary Analysis

Analyze Text Structure: Cause and Effect

> **Academic Vocabulary**
> • **structure** (struk-chur) *noun*
>   A **structure** is how parts are arranged or organized.

What Is Text Structure? Text **structure** is the way the writer organizes his or her ideas. A writer chooses the type of **structure** that shows the information in a clear way.

What Is a Cause-and-Effect Text Structure? A cause-and-effect text **structure** shows what happens and why. A cause is why something happens. An effect is what happens because of the cause. Often there are several causes and effects in one selection.

Practice Together

Analyze Cause and Effect The writer of "On the Menu" chose to use a cause-and-effect text structure to show information about animal adaptations. By analyzing the causes and effects, you can learn what animals do and why. For example, what happens when insects show off their bright colors or make a lot of foam? Work with your class to put the answer in a chart like this one.

Cause-and-Effect Chart

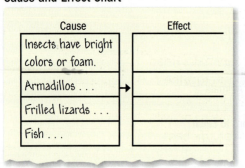

Cause	Effect
Insects have bright colors or foam.	
Armadillos . . .	
Frilled lizards . . .	
Fish . . .	

Try It!

Complete the Cause-and-Effect Chart Reread "On the Menu" to find the causes and effects of adaptation for other animals. Add them to the chart. Use the chart to answer this question: What do animals do to survive? Share your answers with a partner.

Relate Words: Synonyms

Academic Vocabulary
- **relate** (ri-lāt) *verb*
  When you **relate** things, you show how they are connected.

Synonyms are words that mean about the same thing, but have different shades of meaning. You can see how words **relate** to one another in a thesaurus, a book that lists synonyms.

Revise Sentences Rewrite these sentences by replacing the underlined words with more specific synonyms. Use a thesaurus to find the synonyms.

1. The armadillo's hard shell makes it an <u>unpleasant</u> meal for predators.
2. To escape predators, the frilled lizard <u>moves</u> across the forest floor.
3. Some animals are so <u>little</u> that large predators can't find them.
4. Elephants and other <u>strong</u> animals have very few predators.

Research Animal Vision

Academic Vocabulary
- **specific** (spi-**sif**-ik) *adjective*
  When something is **specific**, it is definite or particular.

HEALTH & SCIENCE

ELPS: 1.D speak using learning strategies; 2.G.1 understand the general meaning of spoken language regarding familiar to unfamiliar topics; 3.D.1 speak using content area vocabulary in context to internalize new English words

Eyesight is important to animals. Yet some animals see poorly and still survive.

1 **List Animals** In a group, brainstorm a list of about twenty animals. Read the list aloud and pick **specific** animals that you will research together. Make a chart of at least five animals. Make predictions about each animal's eyesight. Listen to each other's ideas. List the animals you will research in order, from the animal that the group thinks sees the best to the animal the group thinks sees the worst.

2 **Conduct Research** Follow your research plan by using search strategies to collect facts about each animal in print sources and online. See if your predictions are correct. Take steps to evaluate the different sites to make sure the information is reliable.

3 **Discuss Your Findings** Once you research each animal, summarize your findings by revising your chart. Share your findings with the class, taking turns reading aloud the research from your chart. Discuss which predictions were correct and which ones were not. If you have trouble with words, use hand gestures or familiar words to describe what you mean. Listen to the other groups' presentations and ask questions.

ELPS: 3.D.1 speak using content area vocabulary in context to internalize new English words; 4.I.2 expand reading skills; 5.B.2 write using content-based grade-level vocabulary

Research/Speaking

Explore Animal Adaptations

GEOGRAPHY

Academic Vocabulary
- **summarize** (sum-u-rīz) *verb*
  When you **summarize** something, you cover the main points briefly.

The animals in "On the Menu" have adapted to survive where they live. How have other animals adapted to their habitats?

1 Choose a Topic Work with a partner and research a specific habitat like the desert. Find out which animals live in this habitat and how they have adapted to it. Then choose one of those animals to research. As a group, plan goals and deadlines for completing your research.

2 Summarize Your Information Write down the information you find about your animal's adaptations. A good way to understand and remember important information is to **summarize** it. When you **summarize**, you state the main idea and only the most important details, usually in a sentence or two. With your partner, write a summary that tells how your animal survives in its habitat. Follow these steps:

- Read your information. What is it mostly about? This is the main idea.
- Note important details. Decide which to include and which to leave out.
- Write a short summary of the information. Be sure to use the words *adaptation* and *habitat*.

Original Information:

> The <u>snowshoe hare</u> has rusty brown fur in summer so it <u>blends in with the colors of fields</u>. In fall, the hare loses its brown fur and grows <u>thick white fur</u>. The new fur <u>matches the snow in winter</u> and keeps the hare warm.

Summary:

> The snowshoe hare survives by blending in with its environment. In the summer, its brown fur blends in with the fields. In the winter, its white fur matches the snow.

This is a good summary because it's short and covers the main idea and only the important details.

3 Share Your Summary Present your summary to your class to tell what you and your partner discovered. Set time limits for each speaker.

Language and Grammar

Define and Explain

Pair Share With a partner, choose one animal from the story. Work together to talk about and explain the special features of this animal. Use correct subject pronouns. Monitor your understanding of what your partner says.

> The armadillo has an armored shell. The armor is made of bony plates.

> The bony plates protect the armadillo. They also keep predators from eating the armadillo.

Writing and Grammar

Write About an Animal

Study the Models The first time you name your animal, use a noun. After that, use a subject pronoun to talk about the same thing. Don't keep repeating the same noun. This will keep your reader's interest because you will have smooth sentences.

JUST OK

> The leafy sea dragon is a true master of disguise. The leafy sea dragon has skin that looks like leaves. The leafy sea dragon has clear fins. The fins are so clear you can almost see through them! The fins propel the sea dragon slowly through the water. Another part of the sea dragon's disguise is its mouth. The mouth looks like a seaweed stem. The mouth even has small leaves at the end!

The reader thinks: "All the sentences sound the same!" That's because the writer repeats the same noun.

BETTER

> The leafy sea dragon is a true master of disguise. It has skin that looks like leaves and clear fins. The fins are so clear you can almost see through them! They propel the sea dragon slowly through the water. Another part of the sea dragon's disguise is its mouth. It looks like a seaweed stem and even has small leaves at the end!

This mix of nouns and pronouns brings variety to the sentences.

Add Sentences Think of two more sentences to add to the BETTER model above. Be sure to use correct subject pronouns.

✏️ **WRITE ON YOUR OWN** Write about a different animal in the selection. How does it protect itself? How does it trick predators? Use the animal's name in the first sentence. Then use the correct subject pronoun after that.

REMEMBER

Use the correct subject pronoun.

Singular (One)	Plural (More than One)
I	we
you	you
he, she, it	they

The Three Chicharrones

by Patricia Santos Marcantonio
illustrated by Bill Mayer

SELECTION 2 OVERVIEW

▶ **Build Background**

▶ **Language & Grammar**
Retell a Story
Use Forms of the Verbs *Be* and *Have*

▶ **Prepare to Read**
Learn Key Vocabulary
Learn a Reading Strategy
Monitor Your Reading

▶ **Read and Write**
Focus on Genre
Modern Fairy Tale
Apply the Reading Strategy
Monitor Your Reading
Critical Thinking
Reading Fluency
Read with Intonation
Vocabulary Review
Write About the Guiding Question

▶ **Connect Across the Curriculum**
Literary Analysis
Analyze Characters and Plot
Vocabulary Study
Relate Words: Cognates
Media/Speaking
Make a Comic Book
Viewing/Speaking
Plan a Community
Language and Grammar
Retell a Story
Writing and Grammar
Write About a Folk Tale

Build Background

Explore Creative Storytelling

What makes an old story new? Author Patricia Santos Marcantonio uses fresh ideas to retell an old favorite.

Connect

What If? How would the story of "The Three Little Pigs" be different if it happened in your town today? How would the story be different if it was on TV, in a movie, or in a graphic novel? Work with a partner to think of ideas. Share them with the class.

Digital Library
InsideNG.com
⊘ View the images.

▲ A scene from "The Three Little Pigs"

Language & Grammar

ELPS: 2.E.1 use visual support to enhance and confirm understanding of complex and elaborated spoken language; 2.I.2 demonstrate listening comprehension of complex spoken English by retelling or summarizing spoken messages; 3.B.2 expand and internalize initial vocabulary by retelling simple stories and basic information

1 TRY OUT LANGUAGE
2 LEARN GRAMMAR
3 APPLY ON YOUR OWN

Retell a Story CD

Listen to a Vietnamese folk tale about a rooster.
Then listen to this retelling of the folk tale.

FOLK TALE

The Rooster and the Jewel

There is a rooster who is all alone.
He is very hungry and weak.

He wanders around the countryside,
looking everywhere for food. He can't
find anything to eat.

Then the rooster finds a shiny
stone on the ground. He stares
at it for a long time.

Finally, he says, "People would fight
over this jewel. It would be valuable
to them. But to me, the jewel is
worthless because I cannot eat it.
Shiny stones will not keep me alive."
And the starving rooster continues
to look for food.

1 TRY OUT LANGUAGE
2 LEARN GRAMMAR
3 APPLY ON YOUR OWN

Use Forms of the Verbs *Be* and *Have*

The verbs *be* and *have* have special forms to tell about the present.

Present of *Be*

Forms of *Be*	Negative
I **am**	I'm **not**
you **are**	you **aren't**
he, she, or it **is**	he, she, or it **isn't**
we **are**	we **aren't**
they **are**	they **aren't**

Present of *Have*

Forms of *Have*	Negative
I **have**	I **don't have**
you **have**	you **don't have**
he, she, or it **has**	he, she, or it **doesn't have**
we **have**	we **don't have**
they **have**	they **don't have**

Use the correct form of the verb.

EXAMPLES **Forms of *be***

Present: The rabbit **is** more like a human in tales.

Negative: He **isn't** exactly like an animal.

EXAMPLES **Forms of *have***

Present: The rabbit **has** human traits in tales.

Negative: He **doesn't have** many animal traits.

Practice Together

Say each sentence. Then say it again and make the sentence negative.

1. I (am/are) interested in folk tales.
2. Most countries (have/has) folk tales.
3. Often, a folk tale (have/has) a lesson.
4. A hero (is/are) clever.

Try It!

Say each sentence. Write the negative form of the verb on a card. Then say the negative sentence.

5. The animals in folk tales (have/has) human traits.
6. The villains (is/are) evil.
7. Sometimes a folk tale (have/has) magic objects.
8. Usually, the stories (is/are) short.

▲ A coyote and a rabbit are characters in a Mayan folk tale.

Tell the Group a Folk Tale

RETELL A STORY

People enjoy listening to others tell stories. You may have heard stories or folk tales from your own family. Like folk tales, television dramas show people solving problems. At home or at the library, go online and find a re-broadcast of a television drama. Listen for the words that the characters use as they solve the problem. Then prepare to retell the story.

Refer to the pictures on pages 111 and 112 for visual help. Make a story map like the one below to remember what happens. List the important details you want to include.

Story Map

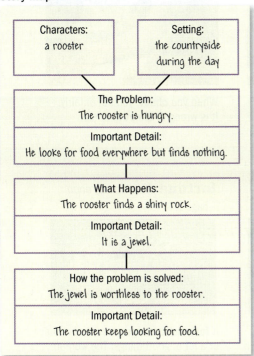

Now retell your story to a group of classmates.

> A rooster is all alone and very hungry. He looks everywhere for food.

HOW TO RETELL A STORY

1. Introduce the characters and setting.

2. Use details to tell about the problem.

3. Use more details to tell how the problem is solved.

USE CORRECT FORMS OF *BE* AND *HAVE*

When you retell your story, be sure to use the correct form of *be* and *have*.

In the Present: The rooster **is** hungry. He **has** no food.

In the Negative: He **isn't** happy. He **doesn't have** any food to eat.

ELPS: 2.B recognize elements of the English sound system in newly acquired vocabulary; 3.A practice producing sounds of newly acquired vocabulary in a manner that is comprehensible; 4.F.3 use visual and contextual support to develop vocabulary needed to comprehend increasingly challenging language; 4.F.8 use support from peers and teachers to develop vocabulary needed to comprehend increasingly challenging language

Learn Key Vocabulary

Rate and Study the Words Rate how well you know each word. Then:

1. Pronounce the word. Say it aloud several times. Spell it.
2. Study the example.
3. Tell more about the word.
4. Practice it. Make the word your own.

Key Words

advice (ad-vīs) *noun*
▶ page 118

To give **advice** means to share wise words. Parents give **advice** to their children.

business (biz-nis) *noun*
▶ page 127

A **business** is where you do work for money. Some people's place of **business** is in an office.

cheat (chēt) *verb*
▶ page 124

When you **cheat**, you act unfairly. It is wrong to **cheat** on a test.

deal (dēl) *noun*
▶ page 120

A **deal** is an agreement. If you agree to mow your neighbor's lawn for money, you have made a **deal** with your neighbor.

deserve (di-zurv) *verb*
▶ page 124

When you **deserve** something it means you have worked hard to earn it. If you study hard for a test, you **deserve** a good grade.

fortune (for-chun) *noun*
▶ page 118

A **fortune** is a large amount of money or a lot of good things. The woman worked hard to earn her **fortune**.

frustration (frus-trā-shun) *noun* ▶ page 126

If you feel **frustration**, you feel angry that you can't do something. If you do not understand your homework, you may feel **frustration**.
Related Word: **frustrated**

property (prop-er-tē) *noun*
▶ page 120

Property is what someone owns, like a house or land. People can sell their **property** to someone else.

Practice the Words Make a Category Chart. List each Key Word under Noun or Verb. Work with a partner to think of sentences for each word.

Noun	Verb
advice	cheat

Category Chart

Reading Strategy: Monitor Your Reading

As you read, you may see words that you don't know. Ask yourself, "What could this mean?"

Reading Strategy
Monitor Your Reading

HOW TO CLARIFY VOCABULARY

1. As you read, stop when you come to a word you don't know. Look for other words that give you clues to the meaning.

2. Use the clues to figure out what the unfamiliar word might mean.

3. Use the meaning you guessed in the sentence. Does the sentence make sense?

Strategy in Action

Here's how one student clarified the meaning of the words *bade farewell*.

Look Into the Text

And so the brothers hugged and bade farewell to each other and their father. They got into their cars and drove off in three different directions.

Pereza hadn't gone very far when he saw a small piece of land for sale at 120 *pesos*. On the land was a bale-mountain of straw. He said to himself, "A house of *paja* does seem foolish, but I can build it in no time and then take a nap."

I'm not sure what "bade farewell" means.

"The clue words make me think the brothers are leaving so they are probably saying goodbye."

Practice Together

Reread the passage. Follow the steps in the How-To box to figure out the meaning of the word *directions*.

Focus on Genre

ELPS: 4.F.3 use visual and contextual support to develop vocabulary needed to comprehend increasingly challenging language

Modern Fairy Tale

A fairy tale is a short, made-up story that has been told over the years. A modern fairy tale puts a new twist on an old story.

The **plot**, or events, of a fairy tale often tell about good and evil. The **setting** of most fairy tales is either a castle, the country, or a forest. The **characters** are usually simple and have one **character trait**, such as silly or mean.

Modern Version of "The Three Little Pigs"

> "Can't we stay here a little longer, Papá?" drawled Pereza, yawning, for he was lazy.

Your Job as a Reader

Reading Strategy: Monitor Your Reading

As you read, stop at unfamiliar words. Then look for other words in the text that are clues to the meaning of the unknown word.

The Three Chicharrones

by Patricia Santos Marcantonio
illustrated by Bill Mayer

Papá Chicharrón smiled at his three sons. Each had curly black hair, small dark eyes, tiny ears, and round, round stomachs, just like their father.

"Pereza, Gordo, and Astuto, it's time for you to **go into the world** and make your **fortunes**."

He handed them each little bags. "You'll receive the same **number of *pesos*** I received from my *papá* when I was your age."

They opened their bags and found two hundred coins.

"Can't we stay here a little longer, *Papá*?" **drawled Pereza**, yawning, for he was lazy.

"This is impossible. How can we make our way in the world like this?" **whined** Gordo, who always looked for the quickest way to everything.

"I'll do my best, *Papá*," said Astuto, who always worked hard.

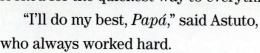

Watch for the wolf at the door.

"With two hundred *pesos* and a lot of work, I did well for myself." Their father spread his arms out, **indicating** his large house. "Now, get packed, *hijos*."

The next morning, the Chicharrones were ready to **set out**.

"Don't be greedy like a *cerdo*." Their father grunted his **advice**. "And this is the most important thing to remember: Watch for the wolf at the door. He will try to take all you have, but you won't know it until you have nothing left."

"What?" replied Pereza, who had only half listened, while Gordo recounted his money.

"*Gracias* for the useful words, *Papá*," Astuto said.

And so the brothers hugged and **bade farewell** to each other and their father. They got into their cars and drove off in three different directions.

Key Vocabulary

fortune *n.*, a large amount of money

advice *n.*, wise words

In Other Words

go into the world live by yourselves
number of *pesos* amount of money
drawled Pereza said Pereza slowly
whined complained
indicating pointing to

hijos children (in Spanish)
set out go on their journeys
cerdo pig (in Spanish)
Gracias Thank you (in Spanish)
bade farewell said goodbye

Pereza hadn't gone very far when he saw a small piece of land for sale at 120 *pesos*. On the land was a bale-mountain of straw. He said to himself, "A house of **paja** does seem foolish, but I can build it in no time and then take a nap."

He bought the land and built his house, which he called the **Casa de Paja**, and indeed, the work did not take long. Pereza slept for the rest of the day, too lazy to spend his other *pesos*.

Meanwhile, Gordo had traveled a little

In Other Words

paja straw (in Spanish)
Casa de Paja House of Straw (in Spanish)

Language and Literary Background

Sometimes a writer gives a name to the characters to show what they are like. *Chicharrones* is Spanish for "pork rinds." The names of the three Chicharrones–Pereza, Gordo, and Astuto–are the Spanish words for laziness, fat, and astute (or smart).

farther down the road when he saw a parcel of land for sale at 150 *pesos*, which came with a gigantic pile of **piñon**-tree sticks.

"Sticks are a good start," he told himself. "With the rest of the money, I can gamble and make more money so I can have a big fine house. I can't wait too long to get rich."

Gordo closed the **deal** on the land and built his house of *piñon* sticks. As soon as he finished what he called **Palacio Piñon**, he got in his car and headed off to build the rest of his fortune at cards.

Astuto drove the farthest, stopping only when he spotted the exact land he wanted. The **property** had a nice view of the valley and included a tower

of adobe bricks. The land cost 220 *pesos*, so he sold his car to make up the difference.

Taking his time, Astuto built his house of adobe. He didn't mind the sweat and **toil** because he knew he would end up with a strong home. When he was finally done, Astuto searched for a job.

Meanwhile, at the *Casa de Paja*, Pereza had just finished taking another nap.

"Maybe **mañana** I'll start looking for work. But it's too nice of a day for that. I think I'll go fishing instead. I can sleep a little as I wait **for a bite**."

Just then came a *rap-tap-tap* on the door. Pereza peered out his window. "Let me introduce myself. I'm Dinero Martínez. And I'm going to make you rich."

> ## Just then came a rap-tap-tap on the door.

Key Vocabulary

deal *n.*, agreement to purchase or do something
property *n.*, someone's house and land

In Other Words

piñon pine nut (in Spanish)
Palacio Piñon Pine Nut Palace (in Spanish)
toil hard work
mañana tomorrow (in Spanish)
for a bite to catch a fish

Before You Move On

1. **Paraphrase** Use your own words to retell the father's **advice** to his sons as they left home.
2. **Compare and Contrast** What did each brother do after he left home? How were their actions similar and different?

Dinero Martínez was tall and skinny, with big ears and eyes that looked **not merely hungry to make a deal, but famished**. He wore a hairy gray suit and carried a big black briefcase. Parked out front was his *jalapeño*-green sports car.

Pereza opened the front door a little. "Do I have to do any work to get rich?"

"Not at all, young **señor**. I'll give you top *peso* for your house and land—top *peso* I say, and you don't have to **lift a fingernail** except to sign." Dinero was smooth as his

In Other Words

not merely hungry to make a deal, but famished
  untrustworthy and evil
señor sir (in Spanish)
lift a fingernail do any work

Language and Literary Background
The name Dinero is the Spanish word for money. The author chose this name for the evil character to show his greed.

shiny car and offered double what Pereza had paid in the first place.

"**Bueno**." Pereza yawned.

The ink wasn't even dry on the papers when Dinero's eyes turned hard as rusty coins. "Chicharrón, you must leave. There's soon going to be a huff and a **soplo**, and down goes your silly *casa*. Just look over there."

A bulldozer rumbled along.

Pereza was hardly out of his straw house before the machine chugged and churned and *Casa de Paja* was flat.

"Foolish Chicharrón, you would have gotten five times more for this land if you weren't so lazy. But I caught you napping." Dinero laughed and laughed as he tacked up a sign: FUTURE **SITE** OF A NEW HOTEL.

In Other Words
"Bueno." "Good." (in Spanish)
The ink wasn't even dry on the papers when Right after signing
soplo puff (in Spanish)
site location

"No matter," Pereza said with a shrug. "I have money. But all this dealing has made me tired." He drove away, looking for a good place to take a nap.

A few days later, Gordo was busy planning a party for his gambling friends when he heard a knock.

Dinero Martínez was at the door.

"I'm going to make you rich," Dinero said.

Gordo's eyes became wide.

Dinero **did more of his smooth-talking**, and soon Gordo **was signing on the dotted line**. All the while, Gordo told himself that he would take the money and place larger bets to get rich even faster.

After Gordo sold the land, Dinero **bellowed**, "Bring on the bulldozer!"

Along came the machine, and down went the *Piñon Palacio* in a huff and a *soplo*.

I'm going to make you rich.

"Chicharrón, you could have gotten a lot more *pesos*. Now it's too late, so get off my land," Dinero ordered Gordo, who started packing his car.

"Gordo!" he heard someone call.

Up the road, Pereza was walking with a suitcase in hand.

"What happened to your car?" Gordo asked.

"Someone stole all my money when I fell asleep by the side of the road, and I had to sell my car to buy food," Pereza said, rubbing his feet.

"Ah, I see that you've met Dinero Martínez."

"He just showed up at my door," Gordo replied.

"Never mind, Brother. Get in my car. We'll go to the racetrack and win big, then we'll buy even more land."

The brothers turned for a last look and saw a sign go up where Gordo's house had once stood: COMING SOON: NEW CASINO.

In Other Words

did more of his smooth-talking told more lies
was signing on the dotted line agreed to sell his house
bellowed cried out loudly

Before You Move On

1. **Confirm Predictions/Plot** Was your prediction correct? What happens to Pereza after he makes the **deal** with Dinero?

2. **Analyze** Who is more foolish, Pereza or Gordo? Give reasons from the text.

But Dinero Martínez wasn't through with the Chicharrones. A few days later, he showed up at the house of Astuto.

"***Buenas tardes***, young *señor*. I am ready to make you a great offer on your land and house." Dinero straightened his tie.

Astuto listened because he was polite. He also smiled because he knew what his land was worth.

"Thank you, Señor Martínez, but I am not interested in selling," Astuto said.

Dinero **upped** his offer.

Astuto felt **deep down in his pudgy stomach** that this Martínez in the hairy gray suit was trying to **cheat** him.

"Again, no thanks," the brother said.

Dinero's eyes became **red slits of anger**. "You are making a mistake, Chicharrón."

"That may be," Astuto replied, "but you are the one leaving **empty-handed**."

Dinero got in his sports car and zoomed away.

From the other direction came Pereza and Gordo, walking with their suitcases. They had lost all their money betting and had had to sell Gordo's car for food.

"***¡Hermanos!***" Astuto called out happily.

At supper, Gordo and Pereza told their brother how they had failed to listen to their father's advice and had lost their homes to a wolf who showed up at the door.

"I **deserved** what I got," Pereza said. "I was too lazy to keep my land or money."

"*Ay, yi, yi.*" Gordo slapped his head. "I wanted to take the fast road to a good life. I gambled and lost."

Then and there, Pereza promised to work hard and Gordo vowed never to make another wager.

"No, my brothers, you haven't lost everything. We have each other," Astuto said.

Key Vocabulary
cheat *v.*, to act unfairly
deserve *v.*, to get what you have earned

In Other Words
Buenas tardes Good afternoon (in Spanish)
upped increased
deep down in his pudgy stomach very sure
red slits of anger very small because he was angry
empty-handed with nothing
"***¡Hermanos!***" "Brothers!" (in Spanish)

"We will live together."

"But what about Dinero Martínez?" Gordo said.

"He doesn't look like the type to give up so easy," Pereza added.

Astuto grinned. "We are the Chicharrones, and we can handle him if we work together."

Gordo, Pereza, and Astuto laughed and settled down for a nice evening before the fire, snacking on pork rinds and salsa.

The next day, Dinero warned the brothers that Astuto's land was located in a **flood plain** and would be filled with water when it stormed.

Astuto wouldn't sell.

The next day, Dinero told the brothers that a freeway was going to be built right through their land. He would **take it off their hands** for more than the freeway department would ever pay.

"No, *gracias*," Astuto replied.

Dinero returned and advised the brothers that the house was in the path of several tornadoes known to hit at springtime, so they would be better off selling than being swirled away.

The brothers wouldn't budge.

"CHICHARRONES!" Dinero bellowed with <mark>frustration</mark>, because this was the first time in his **sleazy** career that he could not close a deal. "Someday my bulldozer *will* come with a huff and a *soplo*, and well, you know the rest…"

"How do we get rid of this pest?" Gordo asked that night at supper.

"I have a plan," Astuto said.

"Of course you do," Pereza replied. "That's why we love you."

The following morning, Gordo and Pereza were out working in the garden. They talked loud to each other because they knew Dinero was listening around the corner.

"I'm really looking forward to going to the *fiesta* in town tonight," Gordo said, picking corn.

"We're all going to have a good time," Pereza said, plucking tomatoes off the vine.

"Ah-ha!" Dinero said to himself. "I'll burn down the house while they are gone. Then they'll *have* to sell the land to me."

Wearing their best clothes, the brothers started walking toward town.

When they were out of sight, Dinero sneaked up to the adobe house. He lit a match and was ready to start the fire when a bright light shone in his face.

Dinero bellowed with frustration.

Key Vocabulary
<mark>frustration</mark> *n.*, a feeling of anger and confusion

In Other Words
flood plain valley
take it off their hands buy their land
sleazy dishonest
fiesta party (in Spanish)

"Hands up," a deep voice commanded.

Dinero turned around to see the Chicharrones with County Sheriff Sánchez.

"You've been cheating folks long enough, Dinero Martínez," Sheriff Sánchez said. "I'm going to see to it that you lose your **license** to do **business**. You won't be able to sell a *ratón* to a *gato*."

"Wait, let's talk," Dinero pleaded, **using his best salesman voice**. "I know about some great land in Florida."

Key Vocabulary
business *n.*, work someone does to earn money

In Other Words
license permission
ratón rat (in Spanish)
gato cat (in Spanish)
using his best salesman voice trying to get the sheriff to let him go by offering him something

The sheriff shook his head and led him away. "Say **adiós**."

Dinero knew he hadn't made a deal. "*Adiós*, Chicharrones."

"*Adiós*, Dinero." The Chicharrones waved goodbye.

After working hard and saving their pesos, the brothers decided to go into business for themselves. They started *Residencias* Chicharrones, which were homes for those just starting out in life. The houses they built weren't made of straw or *piñon* sticks, but of adobe bricks that were **sturdy** and would last. ❖

About the Author

As a little girl in Pueblo, Colorado, **Patricia Santos Marcantonio** loved to read fairy tales. She also enjoyed her parents' jokes and storytelling. Soon, she was writing stories of her own.

Marcantonio says she wanted the stories to honor her Mexican American heritage. So she decided to retell famous fairy tales in a creative new way. Her first book, *Red Ridin' in the Hood*, won the Américas Award.

In Other Words
adiós goodbye (in Spanish)
Residencias Homes, Residences (in Spanish)
sturdy strong

Before You Move On

1. **Confirm Prediction** Did Dinero **cheat** Astuto? Was your prediction correct?
2. **Summarize** How do the brothers work together to fool Dinero?
3. **Opinion** What do you think of the way the story ends? Explain.

Connect Reading and Writing

Vocabulary
advice
business
cheat
deal
deserve
fortune
frustration
property

CRITICAL THINKING

1. **SUM IT UP** Make a Cause-and-Effect Chart to tell what happens in the story and why. Use your chart to describe what happens to the brothers and their **fortunes** .

Cause-and-Effect Chart

What Happened?	Why?
brothers leave to make their fortunes	father sends them away

2. **Make Judgments** Do you think Astuto should have let his brothers live on his **property** with him? Why or why not?

3. **Synthesize** When Dinero tries to **cheat** the brothers, Astuto has a plan. Pereza says, "Of course you do" and "That's why we love you." Why does Pereza say this? Use details from the story to explain.

4. **Compare Across Texts** Which adaptations from "On the Menu" would have helped the pigs defend themselves against Dinero?

READING FLUENCY

Intonation Read the passage on page 638 to a partner. Assess your fluency.

1. I read
   a. great   **b.** OK   **c.** not very well

2. What I did best in my reading was _____ .

READING STRATEGY

Clarify Vocabulary
How did you figure out the definition of a new word? Share the steps you used with a partner. Explain how they helped you understand the meaning.

VOCABULARY REVIEW

Oral Review Read the paragraph aloud. Add the vocabulary words.

To make a _____ , you have to work hard. For example, you could start a _____ . You could buy _____ and then sell it to make money. Follow this _____ . Never _____ or lie. If you make a _____ with someone, you must keep it. Even when you experience _____ , keep working. Hard workers _____ to do well.

Written Review How can the brothers use the lessons they learned in their new **business** ? Write a journal entry about it. Use five vocabulary words.

WRITE ABOUT THE GUIDING QUESTION

Explore What It Takes to Survive

What **advice** did the three Chicharrones follow to survive Dinero? Explain. Read the selection again. Support your answers with examples from the text.

ELPS: 4.F.2 use visual and contextual support to enhance and confirm understanding

Literary Analysis

Analyze How Character Traits Affect Plot

> **Academic Vocabulary**
> • **affect** (u-**fekt**) *verb*
>   When you **affect** something, you change it in some way.

How Do Characters Change the Story? The plot, or the series of events in a story, includes the characters' actions. The way each character acts depends on his or her character traits, or special qualities. These character traits **affect** what happens in the story.

For example, Dinero Martínez is greedy. He wants what belongs to others:

> Dinero . . . looked not merely hungry to make a deal, but famished. . . . Dinero's eyes turned hard as rusty coins.

Because this character is greedy, he tries to take the Chicharrones' houses. What the other characters do in response to Dinero depends on their own character traits. Someone who is silly will act differently from someone who is mean. These character traits can **affect**, or change, the plot.

Practice Together

Use a Chart You can use the chart below to list the traits of characters in the story. Work with the class to add traits for Papá and Pereza. Discuss how the traits of each character **affect** what happens in the story. Briefly state what happens on the chart.

Character	Trait	What Happens
Dinero	Greedy	tries to take Chicharrones' land
Papá		
Pereza		

Try It!

Complete the Chart Work with a partner to finish the chart and confirm your understanding. Add two other characters. Analyze how the plot might be different if the characters had different traits. For example, what if the three pigs were all like Astuto? What if Dinero was helpful, lazy, or foolish?

Relate Words: Cognates

Academic Vocabulary
- **definition** (de-fu-**ni**-shun) *noun*
  The meaning of a word is its **definition**.

What Are Cognates? A cognate is a word that looks similar in two different languages. For example, the Spanish word *artista* looks like the English word *artist*. Both *artista* and *artist* mean "a person who creates art."

False cognates look similar but have different definitions. The Spanish word *ropa* looks like the English word *rope*, but *ropa* means "clothing."

Use Cognates You can use cognates to better understand what you read. For example, in "The Three Chicharrones," the name *Astuto* is a cognate of the word *astute*. *Astuto* and *astute* mean "smart." The character Astuto in the story is smart.

Analyze Cognates Study the Spanish words in the chart. With a partner, discuss what English words they are like. Then write a sentence to show what each English cognate means.

Spanish	English
familia	family
círculo	
danza	
acción	
gigante	

My parents, my brother, and I are a family.

ELPS: 3.B.2 expand and internalize initial vocabulary by retelling simple stories and basic information represented or supported by pictures

Make a Comic Book

ART

Academic Vocabulary
- **identify** (ī-**den**-tu-fī) *verb*
  When you **identify** something, you name it or tell what it is.

"The Three Chicharrones" is a modern fairy tale. The author told an old story in a new way. Dinero drives a sports car. The Chicharrones snack on salsa. These things are not part of the old story.

1 **Plan Your Story** Choose an old story to make modern. Decide how you might retell it to make the characters, setting, and events seem new.

2 **Draw a Comic Book** **Identify** the parts of your new story. Draw each part in a storyboard to make it look like a comic book. Use speech balloons to show the characters' speech and thoughts.

3 **Discuss with a Partner** Read your comic book aloud to a partner. Then compare your comic books. Explain what you changed to make your story modern.

Viewing/Speaking

Plan a Community

SOCIAL SCIENCE

> **Academic Vocabulary**
> • **plan** (plan) *noun*
>   A **plan** is a way of doing things.

What Is Next for the Chicharrones? Imagine that you will help the Chicharrones build a community. What are you going to put in it? There is room for several streets, buildings, and houses. How will you arrange them? Will there be green space around them? How will traffic move?

❶ Make a Plan Make a list of what you would like to put in the community. Do you want houses and apartments? Will there be parks and stores? After you've made your list, make a sketch to show your **plan**.

• Make a large square or rectangle for the property borders.
• Use simple shapes and lines for buildings, parks, and streets.
• Label streets, buildings, and other details in your **plan**.

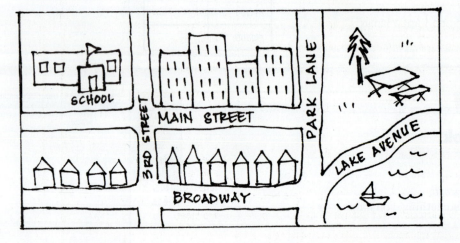

❷ Practice Your Presentation Practice presenting your **plan** to the class. Become familiar with your **plan** so you can quickly point out details. Use expression to show that you are interested. Ask a partner to listen and make suggestions.

❸ Present Your Plan Share your **plan** with the class. Speak in a loud, clear voice. Display your sketch so everyone can see it. Name each detail as you point it out. Invite students to ask questions. When listening to other presentations, monitor your understanding of the details discussed.

❹ Vote As a class, vote on which plan is the best community for the Chicharrones. Discuss what makes it the best plan.

ELPS: 4.G.2 demonstrate comprehension of increasingly complex English by retelling or summarizing material

Retell a Story

Group Talk With a group, make a plan for retelling "The Three Chicharrones." Decide which details to include and who will retell each part. Then do the retelling. Use correct forms of *be* and *have* in your story.

> Papá tells the three Chicharrones that it is time to go into the big world. Two of the pigs don't understand why they need to leave.

ELPS: ELPS: 1.E.2 internalize new basic language in writing activities; 5.D.1 edit writing for standard grammar and usage, including subject-verb agreement; 5.E employ increasingly complex grammatical structures in content area writing

Write About a Folk Tale

Study the Models When you write about stories and folk tales you have read, write clear and complete sentences so your reader will understand what you have to say. Remember that a complete sentence has both a subject and a predicate that go together.

▲ Brer Rabbit is a character from folk tales.

NOT OK

> Folk tales are fictional stories that often have children and animals in them. The animals have human traits—they talk and act like humans. Some animals is evil like the wolf in "Little Red Riding Hood." Other animals are clever like the rabbit in the "Brer Rabbit" tales. No matter what the animals are like, each folk tale have a lesson to teach.

The reader thinks: **"This isn't very clear. Is it one animal or some animals?"**

OK

> Folk tales are fictional stories that often have children and animals in them. The animals have human traits—they talk and act like humans. Some animals are evil like the wolf in "Little Red Riding Hood." Other animals are clever like the rabbit in the "Brer Rabbit" tales. No matter what the animals are like, each folk tale has a lesson to teach.

The subjects and verbs go together. Now the sentences are clear.

Add Sentences Think of two sentences to add to the OK model above. Use complete sentences. Make subjects and verbs agree, or go together.

✏ **WRITE ON YOUR OWN** Write about a favorite folk tale or other story that you know. Use forms of *be* and *have* in some of your sentences. Check your subjects and verbs to be sure they agree.

REMEMBER

Use the form of the verb that goes with your subject.

Forms of *Be*	Forms of *Have*
I + am	he she + has it
he she + is it	I you + have we they
we you + are they	

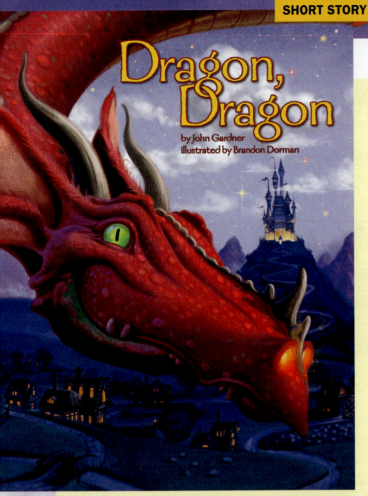

Dragon, Dragon

by John Gardner
illustrated by Brandon Dorman

Build Background

Discover Dragons

Dragons are imaginary creatures, but they hold real interest for people in every culture. They appear in art and literature all over the world.

Connect

Take a Vote What does it take to win against a rival? Do you need strength, wisdom, courage, luck, or love? Vote for one and defend your vote.

Digital Library

InsideNG.com
⬀ View the video.

▲ Dragons are a popular subject in art.

ELPS: 2.E.1 use visual support to enhance and confirm understanding of complex and elaborated spoken language; 2.G.5 understand the main points of spoken language regarding familiar to unfamiliar language

1 TRY OUT LANGUAGE
2 LEARN GRAMMAR
3 APPLY ON YOUR OWN

Engage in Conversation
CD

Listen to the song.
Sing along with the chorus.

SONG

The King's Plan

(sung to the tune of "When the Saints Go Marching In")

Chorus (*townspeople*)
> The dragon roars
> And scares the knights
> The wizard has no spells to cast.
> The king is mad
> At the destruction
> Someone must do something fast!

Verse 1 (*queen sings*)
> My husband dear
> I want to know
> When does the dragon leave our land?
> His roar is loud
> No one is happy
> It is worse than a rock band!

Verse 2 (*king sings*)
> My dearest queen
> I have a plan
> We will have dancing and a feast.
> I will give
> Our precious daughter
> To the one who kills the beast.

Chorus (*townspeople*)

Use Indefinite Pronouns

Use an **indefinite pronoun** when you are not talking about a specific person or thing.

- Some **indefinite pronouns** are always singular. They always need a **singular verb** that ends in -**s**.

  EXAMPLES **Everybody** **hates** the dragon.
  Nobody **likes** the dragon.

Singular Indefinite Pronouns

another	each	everything	nothing
anybody	either	neither	somebody
anyone	everybody	nobody	someone
anything	everyone	no one	something

- Some **indefinite pronouns** are always plural. They always need a **plural verb**.

  EXAMPLE **Many** of the townspeople **fear** the dragon.

Plural Indefinite Pronouns

both	many
few	several

Practice Together

Say each sentence. Use the correct form of the verb.

1. The king and queen are mad. Both (want/wants) the dragon dead.

2. No one (know/knows) how to kill the dragon.

3. Somebody (need/needs) to battle the beast.

4. Something (have/has) to be done about the monster.

Try It!

Read each sentence. Write the correct form of the verb on a card. Then say the sentence and add the correct form of the verb.

5. Each of the sons (try/tries) to kill the dragon.

6. Many of their ideas (sound/sounds) good.

7. Several of the townspeople (dream/dreams) of killing the dragon.

8. Nothing (seem/seems) to work.

▲ **Everyone wants the dragon dead!**

Talk with a Partner

ENGAGE IN CONVERSATION

Pretend you are a townsperson who wants to get rid of the dragon. With a partner, continue the conversation from the song.

Share your ideas and listen to your partner.

- Ask and answer questions.

  EXAMPLE

- Use words to show you are listening.

  EXAMPLE

- Use gestures to show you are listening.

  EXAMPLES   Nod your head. Smile at something funny. Make eye contact with your partner.

Now have a conversation with your partner about the dragon and the king's plan. Be sure to respond in ways that show you understand the main ideas and points your partner is making.

HOW TO ENGAGE IN CONVERSATION

1. Introduce a topic and comment on it.
2. Ask and answer questions about the topic.
3. Use words and gestures to show you are listening.

> I like dragons. How do you feel about them?

> I think dragons are scary. Don't you?

USE INDEFINITE PRONOUNS

Use **indefinite pronouns** when you talk about the other townspeople with your partner. Check your **verbs** to be sure they agree with your subjects.

Plural: **Many** of us **want** to kill the dragon.

Singular: **Everyone** **wonders** who will do it.

Prepare to Read

 **ELPS:** 1.F use accessible language and learn essential language in the process; 4.F.3 use visual and contextual support to develop vocabulary needed to comprehend increasingly challenging language

Learn Key Vocabulary

Rate and Study the Words Rate how well you know each word. Then:

1. Pronounce the word. Say it aloud several times. Spell it.
2. Study the example.
3. Tell more about the word.
4. Practice it. Make the word your own.

Rating Scale

1 = I have never seen this word before.

2 = I am not sure of the word's meaning.

3 = I know this word and can teach the word's meaning to someone else.

Key Words

bargain (bar-gen) *noun*
▶ page 146

A **bargain** is an agreement between people about what each person gives and receives. He made a **bargain** with the sales person for the car.

decent (dē-sent) *adjective*
▶ page 152

When you are **decent**, you are good and kind. A **decent** person welcomes a new neighbor.

kingdom (king-dum) *noun*
▶ page 142

A **kingdom** is a land or area ruled by a king or queen. The **kingdom** was made up of three countries.

nervous (ner-vus) *adjective*
▶ page 145

When you are **nervous**, you feel worried. The basketball player felt **nervous** before the game.

opinion (u-pin-yun) *noun*
▶ page 148

An **opinion** is a belief about something. Reporters ask people for their **opinions** about events in the news.

plague (plāg) *verb*
▶ page 142

When something really bothers you, it **plagues** you. The thought of the Monday morning math test **plagued** her all weekend.
Synonym: **bother**

quest (kwest) *noun*
▶ page 148

A **quest** is a journey or trip to find something. The knight is on a **quest** to find the dragon's cave.
Synonyms: **hunt, search**

recite (ri-sīt) *verb*
▶ page 148

When you **recite** something, you are speaking or reading something aloud in public. Every morning before class, we **recite** the Pledge of Allegiance.

Practice the Words Make a Study Card for each Key Word. Then compare your cards with a partner.

> **nervous**
>
> **What it means:** to feel scared or unsure
>
> **Example:** I was <u>nervous</u> about giving my speech.
>
> **Not an example:** I felt confident about the test.

Study Card

Reading Strategy: Monitor Your Reading

Make sure you understand what you read. Use these steps to figure out the meaning of unfamiliar words.

HOW TO CLARIFY VOCABULARY

1. Look for unfamiliar words in the story. Which words do you need to know to understand the story?
2. Have you seen the word before? Think about what you already know about the word.
3. Look at the text near the word. Does it help you understand the word's meaning?
4. Look at the parts of the word. Do they help you understand the whole word?
5. Do you still need to know more? Think about who or what can help you understand the word.

Strategy in Action

Here's how one student clarified vocabulary.

Look Into the Text

> I don't understand what "coward" means. I haven't seen the word before.

There was once a king whose kingdom was plagued by a dragon. The king did not know which way to turn. The king's knights were all cowards. They hid under their beds whenever the dragon came in sight. They were of no use to the king at all. And the king's wizard could not help either because, being old, he had forgotten his magic spells.

> If I look at the text near the word, I see that the knights hid under their beds. "Coward" must mean a person who is afraid.

Practice Together

Reread the passage from "Dragon, Dragon." Follow the steps in the How-To box to clarify the meaning of *either*.

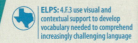

Focus on Genre

ELPS: 4.F.3 use visual and contextual support to develop vocabulary needed to comprehend increasingly challenging language

Short Story

A short story is a brief, made-up narrative. Every story has a **plot**, **setting**, and **characters**.

The **setting** is the time and place of the story. Sometimes, the setting can tell you what the characters will be like. For example, when you read that a story's setting is in a kingdom, you can expect to see certain kinds of characters, such as a king and queen.

> There was once a king whose kingdom was plagued by a dragon. The king's knights were all cowards. They hid under their beds . . .

Your Job as a Reader

Reading Strategy: Monitor Your Reading

As you read, if you see words you don't know, look for clues to help you figure out the meanings. Use the text around the word, the word itself, and sources outside of the text.

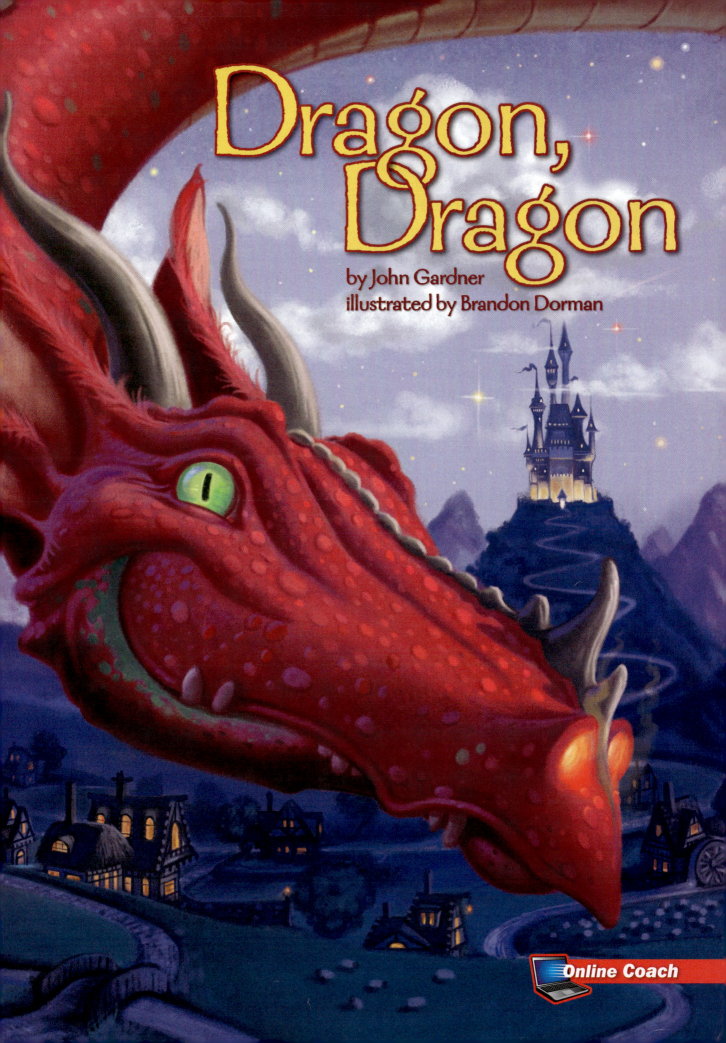

Dragon, Dragon

by John Gardner

illustrated by Brandon Dorman

Online Coach

There was once a king whose kingdom was **plagued** by a dragon. The king did not know **which way to turn**. The king's knights were all cowards. They hid under their beds whenever the dragon came in sight. They were of no use to the king at all. And the king's wizard could not help either because, being old, he had forgotten his magic spells. Nor could the wizard look up the spells that **had slipped his mind**. He had unfortunately misplaced his wizard's book many years before. The king **was at his wit's end**.

Every time there was a full moon the dragon came out of his **lair** and **ravaged** the countryside. He frightened maidens and stopped up chimneys. He broke store windows and set people's clocks back. He even made dogs bark until no one could hear himself think.

He tipped over fences and robbed graves and put frogs in people's drinking water and tore the last chapters out of novels.

He stole spark plugs out of people's cars and put firecrackers in people's cigars and stole the clappers from all the church bells. He sprung every bear trap for miles around so the bears could wander wherever they pleased.

And **to top it all off**, he changed around all the roads in the kingdom. People could not get anywhere except by starting out in the wrong direction.

"That," said the king in a fury, "is enough!" And he called a meeting of everyone in the kingdom.

Now it happened that there lived in the kingdom a wise old cobbler who had a wife and three sons. The cobbler and his family came to the king's meeting and stood way in back by the door. The cobbler had a feeling that since he was nobody important there had probably been some mistake. No doubt the king had intended the meeting for everyone in the kingdom except his family and him.

"Ladies and gentlemen," said the king when everyone was present, "I've **put up** with that dragon as long as I can. He has got to be stopped."

Key Vocabulary
kingdom *n.*, a land or area ruled by a king or queen
plague *v.*, to bother or make trouble again and again

In Other Words
which way to turn whom to ask for help
had slipped his mind he forgot
was at his wit's end did not know what to do
lair resting place; den
ravaged damaged, ruined
to top it all off even worse
put up been patient

All the people whispered amongst themselves. The king smiled, pleased with the impression he had made.

But the wise cobbler said gloomily, "It's all very well to talk about it—but how are you going to do it?"

And now all the people smiled and winked as if to say, "Well, King, he's **got you there**!"

The king frowned.

"It's not that His Majesty hasn't tried," the queen spoke up loyally.

"Yes," said the king. "I've told my knights again and again that they ought to slay that dragon. But I can't *force* them to go. I'm not a **tyrant**."

"Why doesn't the wizard say a magic spell?" asked the cobbler.

"He's done the best he can," said the king.

The wizard blushed and everyone looked embarrassed. "I used to do all sorts of spells and chants when I was younger," the wizard explained. "But I've lost my spell book. I begin to fear I'm losing my memory too. For **instance**, I've been trying for days to recall one spell I used to do. I forget,

just now, what the deuce it was for. It went something like—

> *Bimble,*
> *Wimble,*
> *Cha, Cha*
> CHOOMPF!

In Other Words

got you there made a good argument
tyrant cruel leader
instance example

Language Background

Among and **amongst** both mean "to be in a crowd" but each word is used in different areas of the world. **Among** is commonly used in American English while **amongst** is more often used in British English.

Suddenly, to everyone's surprise, the queen turned into a rosebush.

"Oh dear," said the wizard.

"Now you've done it," groaned the king.

"Poor Mother," said the princess.

"I don't know what can have happened," the wizard said **nervously**, "but don't worry, I'll have her changed back **in a jiffy**." He shut his eyes and **racked his brain for** a spell that would change her back.

But the king said quickly, "You'd better **leave well enough alone**. If you change her into a rattlesnake we'll have to chop off her head."

Key Vocabulary
nervous *adj.*, worried and afraid

In Other Words
in a jiffy quickly
racked his brain for tried to remember
leave well enough alone not do anything more

Meanwhile the cobbler stood with his hands in his pockets, sighing at the waste of time. "About the dragon…" he began.

"Oh yes," said the king. "I'll tell you what I'll do. I'll give the princess' hand in marriage to anyone who can make the dragon stop."

"It's not enough," said the cobbler. "She's a nice enough girl, you understand. But how would an ordinary person support her? Also, what about those of us that are already married?"

"In that case," said the king, "I'll offer the princess' hand or half the kingdom or both. Whichever is most convenient."

The cobbler scratched his chin and considered it. "It's not enough," he said at last. "It's a good enough kingdom, you understand, but it's too much responsibility."

"**Take it or leave it**," the king said.

"I'll leave it," said the cobbler. And he shrugged and went home.

But the cobbler's eldest son thought the <mark>bargain</mark> was a good one. The princess was very beautiful and he liked the idea of having half the kingdom to run as he pleased. So he said to he king, "I'll accept **those terms**, Your Majesty. By tomorrow morning the dragon will be slain."

"Bless you!" cried the king.

"Hooray, hooray, hooray!" cried all the people, throwing their hats in the air. The cobbler's eldest son **beamed with pride**, and the second eldest looked at him enviously. The youngest son said **timidly**,

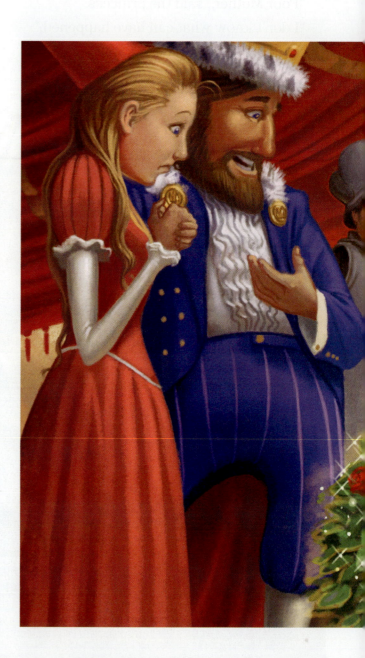

Key Vocabulary
<mark>bargain</mark> *n.*, agreement, deal

In Other Words
Take it or leave it Either accept my offer or don't
those terms your offer
beamed with pride looked very proud
timidly with fear

"Excuse me, Your Majesty, but don't you think the queen looks a little unwell? If I were you, I think I'd water her."

"**Good heavens**," cried the king, glancing at the queen who had been changed into a rosebush, "I'm glad you mentioned it!"

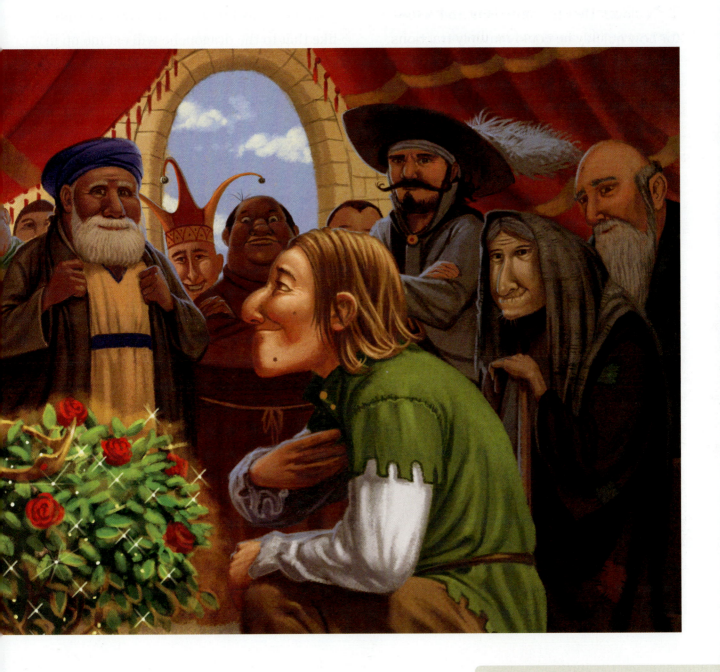

In Other Words
Good heavens Oh, no

Before You Move On

1. **Details** How does the dragon **plague** the kingdom? Why don't the knights kill the dragon?
2. **Summarize** Retell in your own words how the king tries to solve the problem with the dragon.
3. **Judgments** Is the **bargain** fair? Explain.

Can the eldest son or the middle son slay the dragon?

Now the cobbler's eldest son was very clever. He was known **far and wide** for how quickly he could multiply fractions in his head. He was perfectly sure he could slay the dragon by somehow or other playing a trick on him. He didn't feel that he needed his wise old father's advice. But he thought it was only polite to ask, and so he went to his father, who was working as usual at the cobbler's bench, and said, "Well, Father, I'm off to slay the dragon. Have you any advice to give me?"

The cobbler thought a moment and replied, "When and if you come to the dragon's lair, **recite** the following poem.

Dragon, dragon, how do you do?
I've come from the king to murder you.

Say it very loudly and firmly and the dragon will fall, God willing, at your feet."

"How curious!" said the eldest son.

Have you any advice to give me?

And he thought to himself, "The old man is not as wise as I thought. If I say something like that to the dragon, he will eat me up in an instant. The way to kill a dragon is to **out-fox** him." And keeping his **opinion** to himself, the eldest son **set forth** on his **quest**.

When he came at last to the dragon's lair, which was a cave, the eldest son slyly disguised himself as a peddler. He knocked on the door and called out, "Hello there!"

"There's nobody home!" roared a voice.

The voice was as loud as an earthquake. The eldest son's knees knocked together in terror.

"I don't come to trouble you," the eldest son said meekly. "I merely thought you might be interested in looking at some of our brushes. Or if you'd prefer," he added quickly, "I could leave our catalogue with you and I could drop by again, say, early next week."

Key Vocabulary
recite *v.*, to speak or read something aloud
opinion *n.*, a belief about something
quest *n.*, an adventurous journey

In Other Words
far and wide everywhere
out-fox be smarter than; trick
set forth went

"I don't want any brushes," the voice roared, "and I especially don't want any brushes next week."

"Oh," said the eldest son. By now his knees were knocking together so badly that he had to sit down.

Suddenly a great shadow fell over him. The eldest son looked up. It was the dragon.

The eldest son **drew** his sword, but the dragon lunged and swallowed him in a single gulp, sword and all. The eldest son found himself in the dark of the dragon's belly.

What a fool I was not to listen to my wise old father!" thought the eldest son. And he began to **weep bitterly**.

In Other Words
drew pulled out
weep bitterly get angry and cry

"Well," sighed the king the next morning, "I see the dragon has not been slain yet."

"I'm just as glad, personally," said the princess, sprinkling the queen. "I would have had to marry that eldest son, and he had warts."

Now the cobbler's middle son decided it was his turn to try. The middle son was very strong and was known far and wide for being able to lift up the corner of a church. He felt perfectly sure he could slay the dragon by simply **laying into him**. But he thought it would be only polite to ask his father's advice. So he went to his father and said to him, "Well, Father, I'm off to slay the dragon. Have you any advice for me?"

The cobbler told the middle son exactly what he'd told the eldest.

"When and if you come to the dragon's lair, recite the following poem.

Dragon, dragon, how do you do?
I've come from the king to murder you.

Say it very loudly and firmly, and the dragon will fall, God willing, at your feet."

"What an odd thing to say," thought the middle son. "The old man is not as wise as I thought. You have to **take these dragons by surprise**." But he kept his opinion to himself and set forth.

When he came in sight of the dragon's lair, the middle son **spurred his horse to a gallop**. He thundered into the entrance swinging his sword with all his **might**.

But the dragon had seen him while he was still a long way off. Being very clever, the dragon had crawled up on top of the door so that when the son came charging

In Other Words
laying into him using his strength
take these dragons by
surprise surprise a dragon
spurred his horse to a gallop made his horse run
might strength

in he went under the dragon and on to the back of the cave and slammed into the wall. Then the dragon chuckled and got down off the door, taking his time. He strolled back to where the man and the horse lay unconscious from **the terrific blow**. Opening his mouth as if for a yawn, the dragon swallowed the middle son in a single gulp and put the horse in the freezer to eat another day.

"What a fool I was not to listen to my wise old father," thought the middle son when he **came to** in the dragon's belly. And he too began to weep bitterly.

In Other Words
the terrific blow hitting the wall so hard
came to woke up

Before You Move On

1. **Confirm Prediction** What happened to the sons? Was your prediction correct?
2. **Character's Point of View** What opinion do the sons have of their wise father's advice? Why?
3. **Character** The middle son "felt perfectly sure he could slay the dragon." Why?

Dragon, Dragon **151**

That night there was a full moon. The dragon ravaged the countryside so terribly that several families moved to another kingdom.

"Well," sighed the king in the morning," still no luck **in this dragon business**, I see."

"I'm just as glad, myself," said the princess, moving her mother, pot and all, to the window where the sun could get at her. "The cobbler's middle son was a kind of humpback."

Now the cobbler's youngest son saw that his turn had come. He was very upset and nervous, and he wished he had never been born. He was not clever, like his eldest brother. He was not strong, like his second-eldest brother. He was a **decent**, honest boy who always **minded** his elders.

He borrowed a suit of armor from a friend of his who was a knight. When

> He wished he had never been born.

the youngest son put the armor on it was so heavy he could hardly walk. From another knight he borrowed a sword. It was so heavy that the only way the youngest son could get it to the dragon's lair was to drag it along behind his horse like a plow.

When everything was **in readiness**, the youngest son went for a last conversation with his father.

"Father, have you any advice to give me?" he asked.

"Only this," said the cobbler. "When and if you come to the dragon's lair, recite the following poem.

*Dragon, dragon, how do you do?
I've come from the king to murder you.*

Say it very loudly and firmly, and the dragon will fall, God willing, at your feet."

"Are you certain?" asked the youngest son uneasily.

"As certain as one can ever be in these

Key Vocabulary
decent *adj.*, good and kind

In Other Words
in this dragon business slaying the dragon
minded listened to
in readiness ready

matters," said the wise old cobbler.

And so the youngest son set forth on his quest. He traveled **over hill and dale** and at last came to the dragon's cave.

The dragon, who had seen the cobbler's youngest son while he was still a long way off, was seated up above the door, inside the cave. He was waiting and smiling to himself. But minutes passed and no one came thundering in. The dragon frowned, puzzled, and was tempted to peek out. However, **reflecting that patience seldom goes unrewarded**, the dragon kept his head up out of sight and went on waiting.

In Other Words
over hill and dale for a long time
reflecting that patience seldom goes unrewarded remembering that patience is a good thing

At last, when he could **stand it no longer**, the dragon **craned his neck** and looked. There at the entrance of the cave stood a trembling young man in a suit of armor twice his size. He was struggling with a sword so heavy he could lift only one end of it at a time.

At sight of the dragon, the cobbler's youngest son began to tremble so violently that his armor rattled like a house caving in. He heaved with all his might at the sword and got the handle up level with his chest, but even now the point was down in the dirt. As loudly and firmly as he could manage, the youngest son cried—

> *Dragon, dragon, how*
> *do you do?*
> *I've come from the king*
> *to murder you!*

"What?" cried the dragon, **flabbergasted**.

"You? *You? Murder Me???*" All at once he began to laugh, pointing at the little cobbler's son. "*He he he ho ha!*" he

roared, shaking all over, and tears filled his eyes. "*He he he ho ho ho ha ha!*" laughed the dragon. He was laughing so hard he had to hang onto his sides. He fell off the door and landed on his back, still laughing, kicking his legs helplessly, rolling from side to side, laughing and laughing and laughing.

The cobbler's son was annoyed. "I *do* come from the king to murder you," he said. "A person doesn't like to be laughed at for a thing like that."

"*He he he!*" wailed the dragon, almost sobbing, gasping for breath. "Of course not, poor dear boy! But really, *he he,* the *idea* of it, *ha ha ha*! And that simply ridiculous *poem*!" Tears streamed from the dragon's eyes and he lay on his back perfectly helpless with laughter.

"It's a good poem," said the cobbler's youngest son loyally. "My father made it up." And growing angrier he shouted, "I want you to stop that laughing, or I'll—I'll—" But the dragon could not stop for

In Other Words
stand it no longer not wait anymore
craned his neck bent his neck down
flabbergasted surprised

the life of him. And suddenly, in a terrific rage, the cobbler's son began flopping the sword end over end in the direction of the dragon. Sweat ran off the youngest son's forehead, but he **labored on**, blistering mad. At last, with one **supreme heave**, he had the sword standing on its handle a foot from the dragon's throat. **Of its own weight** the sword fell, slicing the dragon's head off.

"*He he ho huk*," went the dragon—and then he lay dead.

In Other Words
labored on kept trying to slay the dragon
supreme heave great push
Of its own weight Because it was so heavy

The two older brothers crawled out and thanked their younger brother for saving their lives. "We have learned our lesson," they said.

Then the three brothers gathered all the treasures from the dragon's cave and tied them to the back end of the youngest brother's horse. They tied the dragon's head on behind the treasures, and started home. "I'm glad I listened to my father," the youngest son thought. "Now I'll be the richest man in the kingdom."

There were hand-carved picture frames and silver spoons and boxes of jewels and chests of money and silver compasses and maps telling where there were more treasures buried when these ran out. There was also a curious old book with a picture of an owl on the cover. Inside the book were poems and odd sentences and recipes that seemed to make no sense.

When they reached the king's castle, the people all leaped for joy to see that the dragon was dead. The princess ran out and

kissed the youngest brother on the forehead, for secretly she had hoped it would be him.

"Well," said the king, "which half of the kingdom do you want?"

"My wizard's book!" exclaimed the wizard. "He's found my wizard's book!" He opened the book and **ran his fingers along under the words**. He then said in a loud voice, "Glmuzk, shkzmlp, blam!"

Instantly the queen stood before them **in her natural shape**. Except she was soaking wet from being sprinkled too often. She glared at the king.

"Oh, dear," said the king, hurrying toward the door. ❖

About the Author

John Gardner

John Gardner (1933–1982) grew up on a farm in Batavia, New York. He started writing stories when he was eight years old. His parents often read aloud Shakespeare's works to the family. This inspired him to write old-fashioned tales with a modern twist. Gardner's books on the craft of writing have had a strong influence on writers of all ages. *Dragon, Dragon and Other Tales* was named Outstanding Book of the Year by the *New York Times*.

In Other Words
ran his fingers along under the words started reading
in her natural shape and she was changed back into herself

Before You Move On

1. **Confirm Predictions** Was your prediction correct? In what ways did the youngest son's actions surprise you?
2. **Compare and Contrast** How is the youngest son different from his brothers?
3. **Conclusion** What lesson do the two older brothers learn?

Leapin' Lizards!
Is That a **Real** Dragon?

How would you feel if you came face to face with a dragon? Lucky for you, dragons are only make-believe.

But, wait. Here is a Komodo dragon and as you can see, it's real. How can that be?

Despite its name and scary appearance, the Komodo dragon is actually a lizard. In fact, it's the world's biggest lizard. The average Komodo weighs more than 150 pounds and can grow almost 10 feet long. Most Komodos are found today on the islands of Indonesia.

Unlike storybook dragons, Komodos don't breathe fire, but they sure like to eat. A Komodo can eat up to 80 percent of its own weight in one meal!

It can also swim, race up a tree, and run faster than 15 miles per hour. Now that's one creature that's not draggin' its feet.

Komodo dragon ▶

▲ Today, only 2,500–5,000 Komodos are left in the world, mostly in Indonesia.

Connect Reading and Writing

Vocabulary

bargain

decent

kingdoms

nervous

opinions

plague

quest

recite

CRITICAL THINKING

1. SUM IT UP Make a Sequence Chain. Write the events of the story in the order they happen. Then use your chart to tell what happens to the brothers on their **quest**.

Sequence Chain

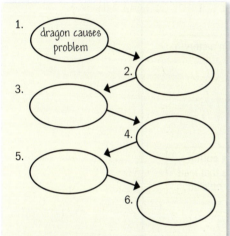

1. dragon causes problem
2.
3.
4.
5.
6.

2. Draw Conclusions What is the cobbler's **opinion** of the king's offer? What does this show about the king? Support your reasons with examples.

3. Compare "Dragon, Dragon" and "Leapin' Lizards!" are about different kinds of "dragons." Explain how both animals could make people **nervous**.

4. Analyze Which son was able to slay the dragon? Why?

READING FLUENCY

Expression Read the passage on page 639 to a partner. Assess your fluency.

1. I read
   a. great   **b.** OK   **c.** not very well

2. What I did best in my reading was _____.

READING STRATEGY

Clarify Vocabulary
Tell a partner about the strategy you used to figure out the meaning of new words. Give one step-by-step example.

VOCABULARY REVIEW

Oral Review Read the paragraph aloud. Add the vocabulary words.

When problems _____ kings and queens, they don't worry or feel _____. They just ask kind and _____ people to help them. Sometimes, rulers must go on a _____ all around their _____ to find wise people. They ask them to share their knowledge and _____. They may make a _____ to give gold for wise words. They may even _____ these wise words aloud to help them remember.

Written Review Imagine you are on a **quest** to find a dragon. What would you do? Write a journal entry about it. Use four vocabulary words.

REMEMBER
When a word begins with the letter "q," it is almost always followed by the letter "u." This creates the "kw" sound in *quest*.

WRITE ABOUT THE *GUIDING QUESTION*

Explore What It Takes to Win
Not all the sons had what it takes to win. Who did not? What should they have done differently? Support your opinion with examples from the text.

Connect Across the Curriculum

Analyze Plot and Setting

Academic Vocabulary
- **affect** (u-**fekt**) *verb*
  When you **affect** something, you change it in some way.

Review Plot

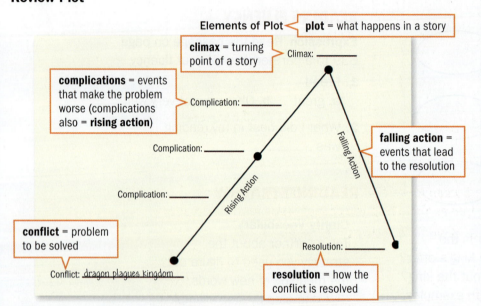

Elements of Plot

plot = what happens in a story

climax = turning point of a story

Climax: _____

complications = events that make the problem worse (complications also = **rising action**)

Complication: _____

Complication: _____

falling action = events that lead to the resolution

Falling Action

Rising Action

Complication: _____

conflict = problem to be solved

Conflict: _dragon plagues kingdom_

Resolution: _____

resolution = how the conflict is resolved

How Does Setting Affect Plot? Setting often **affects** the conflicts that the characters face. For example, the setting of "Dragon, Dragon" is a make-believe kingdom. Think about the people who live in a kingdom, like kings and magicians. What problems might these characters face in a make-believe kingdom that real people might not? What if you changed the setting of the story? Would they encounter the same problems?

Practice Together

Work with your class to analyze how setting **affects** the characters, conflict, rising action, and resolution in "Dragon, Dragon." Fill out a chart like this one:

Story Element	How Setting Affects the Element
Characters	Characters like kings, queens, wizards, and dragons exist in a make-believe kingdom.
Conflict	
Rising Action	
Resolution	

Try It!

Think About Setting Ask yourself how the story would change if it were set in the present and in a city. With a partner, make a new chart to show how this setting would **affect** the story. Share your ideas with the class. When other pairs present their ideas, listen closely to understand their main points.

Relate Words: Use Synonyms and Antonyms

> **Academic Vocabulary**
> • **scale** (skāl) *noun*
>   A **scale** is a graphic organizer that shows how a series of items are related.

Analyze Word Relationships A Synonym or Antonym **Scale** can help you think about how words relate to each other.

Beautiful is a stronger word than *pretty* to describe the way something looks. Where on the **scale** would you put the word *cute*?

This Synonym-Antonym **Scale** shows how the antonyms *polite* and *rude* relate.

Synonym Scale

As you move up the list, each word suggests more beauty.

Synonym-Antonym Scale

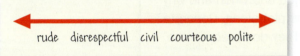

rude   disrespectful   civil   courteous   polite

The words at opposite sides of the scale are antonyms.

Make Synonym-Antonym Scales Make a **scale** for each of these words from the selection. Use a thesaurus to help you collect words for the **scales**.

1. coward   **2.** wise   **3.** timid   **4.** clever   **5.** weep

---

Explore Dragons Across Cultures

ART

ELPS: 3.E share information in cooperative learning interactions

> **Academic Vocabulary**
> • **symbol** (sim-bul) *noun*
>   A **symbol** is an object or idea that represents something else.

The dragon is a **symbol** in many cultures and stories.

❶ **Research Dragons** With a partner, find art of dragons from different cultures.

   Internet InsideNG.com
   Study illustrations of dragons.

❷ **Share Information** Answer these questions about the art and information you find. Then share your images and ideas with the rest of the class.

   • How are the dragons the same and different?

   • How does each dragon's appearance show what it represents?

▲ Throughout history, dragons have been important symbols.

ELPS: 3.H.1 narrate with increasing specificity and detail

Listening/Speaking

Deliver a Narrative Presentation

DRAMA

Academic Vocabulary
- **structure** (struk-chur) *noun*
  A **structure** is how parts are arranged or organized.

In "Dragon, Dragon," the dragon represented a challenge to each brother. Do you know a good story about facing a challenge? Tell an audience the story.

❶ Plan Your Narration To create the **structure** for your story, follow these steps:

- Plan an outline of the plot. Include what happened and when and why it happened. Use concrete language to move the plot along. Concrete language uses words that are direct and clear. They don't require the listener to interpret them.

- Consider how you will capture listeners' attention. You could start with a rhetorical device, such as a simile. For example: "Babysitting three-year-old Andrew was like trying to tame a lion."

- Use sensory details. Sensory details are words that appeal to listeners' senses, such as: *gurgling*, *mountain of bubbles*, *sweet vanilla perfume*, etc. Sensory details give listeners something interesting to visualize and make the story memorable.

NOT OK

I heard something. I took several slow steps toward the kitchen. Then I moved a little faster.

BETTER

I heard water gurgling and smelled a sweet vanilla perfume. What was Anthony doing? I ran into the kitchen.

❷ Practice Your Narration

- Think of different ways to introduce the narrative. Ask a friend which introduction is the most interesting and why.
- Use your voice and gestures to show time or mood changes.
- Practice until you are familiar with your story.

❸ Present Your Narrative Share your narrative with the class. Make eye contact. Stay relaxed but focused on the plot and important details. Speak loudly and clearly. Monitor your listeners' interest as you speak. Do you need to make more eye contact or use more energy?

Engage in Conversation

Role-Play With a partner, role-play a conversation between one of the sons and the dragon. Use some indefinite pronouns like *somebody* or *nobody* in your conversation.

> I am here to stop you, Dragon!

> Nobody talks to me like that.

ELPS: 1.B.2 monitor written language production and self-correct

Write About a Character in the Story

Study the Models When you write about a character, you want your sentences to make sense and to be clear to your reader. To avoid confusing your reader, be sure the subjects and verbs go together.

NOT OK

> The dragon scares everyone in the kingdom. The people know the dragon causes a lot of destruction and confusion. Several of the people <u>leaves</u> the kingdom. No one feels safe. Everyone <u>hope</u> that someone will finally stop the dragon.

The reader thinks: "How many people leave the kingdom?" It's hard to tell from this sentence.

OK

> The dragon scares everyone in the kingdom. The people know the dragon causes a lot of destruction and confusion. Several of the people <u>leave</u> the kingdom. No one feels safe. Everyone <u>hopes</u> that someone will finally stop the dragon.

The subjects and verbs now agree, and the meaning is clearer.

Add Sentences Think of two sentences to add to the OK model above. Use at least one indefinite pronoun. Check that your subjects and verbs agree.

✏️ **WRITE ON YOUR OWN** Write about a character in the story. Is the character brave? Is the character helpful? Review your writing and correct any verbs that do not agree with their subjects.

REMEMBER
These indefinite pronouns use a singular verb:

another	everybody	no one
anybody	everyone	nothing
anyone	everything	somebody
anything	neither	someone
each	nobody	something
either		

These indefinite pronouns use a plural verb:

both	few	many	several

These indefinite pronouns use either a singular or a plural verb:

all	most	some
any	none	

Compare Across Texts

Compare Characters, Settings, and Problems

"The Three Chicharrones" and "Dragon, Dragon" are tales about outwitting a rival. Compare the characters, settings, and problems in the two stories.

How It Works

Collect and Organize Ideas To compare the main characters in the stories, make a Venn Diagram like this one.

Venn Diagram

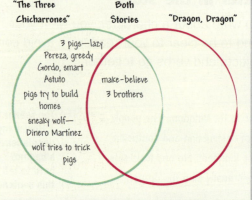

"The Three Chicharrones"

3 pigs—lazy
Pereza, greedy
Gordo, smart
Astuto

pigs try to build homes

sneaky wolf— Dinero Martínez

wolf tries to trick pigs

Both Stories

make-believe
3 brothers

"Dragon, Dragon"

Practice Together

Make Comparisons and Summarize Complete the "Dragon, Dragon" side of the diagram. Add more things that are **similar** about the characters in the middle. Then summarize. Here is a comparison and contrast paragraph for the characters of the two stories.

Summary

> The characters in both "The Three Chicharrones" and "Dragon, Dragon" are make-believe. The three Chicharrones are three pig brothers who must deal with a sneaky wolf. The three brothers in "Dragon, Dragon" are people, but there is a talking dragon. Although the characters are fictional, they often act like real people. In both stories, the characters use their wits to trick their enemies.

Try It!

Make a diagram to compare the settings of the stories, and another to compare the problems. Summarize them. You may want to use this frame.

Both "The Three Chicharrones" and "Dragon, Dragon," are set in a world that is _____. The time of "The Three Chicharrones" is _____, while "Dragon, Dragon" seems to take place _____. "The Three Chicharrones" takes place _____, while "Dragon, Dragon" happens in _____.

Stand or Fall

GUIDING QUESTION What happens when people come face-to-face with a rival?

Reflect on Your Reading

Think back on your reading of the unit selections. Discuss what you did to understand what you read.

Focus on Genre **Characters, Setting, Plot**
In this unit, you learned about three elements of fiction: characters, setting, and plot. Choose either "The Three Chicharrones" or "Dragon, Dragon" and write a brief summary of the elements.

Reading Strategy **Monitor Your Reading**
As you read the selections, you learned to monitor your reading. Explain to a partner how you will use this strategy in the future.

Explore the GUIDING QUESTION

Throughout this unit, you have been thinking about what it takes to survive a rival. Choose one of these ways to explore the Guiding Question:

- **Discuss** In these selections, it is not always the strongest who succeed. In a group, discuss what it really takes to win. Share examples from your life, and listen to the experiences of others.
- **Ask Questions** On a slip of paper, write the name of a character in one of the selections. Don't tell which one you have chosen. Take turns asking a partner questions to guess which character it is.
- **Write and Draw** Draw a real or made-up creature that has what it takes to survive. Add labels to identify and explain its special features.

Book Talk

Which Unit Library book did you choose? Explain to a partner what it taught you about how to survive a rival.

UNIT LIBRARY

Content Library

Amazing Animals

Leveled Library

Marching, 2005, Gil Mayers. Collage, private collection.

ELPS: 1.D speak using learning strategies; 2.F.2 listen to and derive meaning from a variety of media to build and reinforce language attainment; 2.G.2 understand the general meaning of spoken language regarding familiar to unfamiliar language; 2.H.2 understand implicit information in complex spoken language; 2.I.2 demonstrate listening comprehension of complex spoken English by retelling or summarizing spoken messages; 2.I.3 demonstrate listening comprehension of complex spoken English by responding to questions and requests; 2.I.5 demonstrate listening comprehension of complex spoken English by taking notes; 3.B.3 expand and internalize initial vocabulary by learning and using routine language needed for classroom communication; 3.C.1 speak using a variety of grammatical structures with increasing accuracy and ease; 3.F.1 ask (for) information; 3.H.2 describe with increasing specificity and detail; 4.C.4 comprehend English language structures used routinely in written classroom materials; 4.F.4 use visual and contextual support to develop grasp of language structures needed to comprehend increasingly challenging language; 4.F.9 use support from peers and teachers to develop grasp of language structures needed to comprehend increasingly challenging language

Making a Difference

GUIDING QUESTION

How can one individual make a difference?

Read More!

Content Library

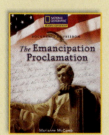

The Emancipation Proclamation
by Marianne McComb

Leveled Library

The House of Dies Drear
by Virginia Hamilton

Finding Miracles
by Julia Alvarez

The Bronx Masquerade
by Nikki Grimes

Internet
InsideNG.com

- View photos of people who made a difference during the Civil Rights Movement.

- Find out more about Dr. Martin Luther King, Jr.

- Discover how people work to improve their communities.

Focus on Genre

ELPS: 4.C.3 comprehend English vocabulary used routinely in written classroom materials

Organization of Ideas

▶ **Chronological Order**
▶ **Problem and Solution**

Writers **organize** information and ideas in different ways. You can better follow a writer's ideas and remember information if you see how it is **organized** .

How It Works

Before you read, preview the text to figure out the topic and see what kind of writing it is. Look for clues that tell you what the organization is.

Chronological Order A writer uses chronological, or time, order to help readers see how people, attitudes, and situations change over time. Study this example and look for **time words** .

Soccer for All

At an early age, Taylor Bell saw the need for more opportunities for disabled youth to play team sports. Taylor first researched soccer programs in other cities. Then, he scheduled a soccer camp to see how people would respond. Next, he trained coaches and found fields for the players. Finally, he created game schedules.

> **Time words help show the order of events. Some time words are:**
>
> | | |
> |---|---|
> | before | after |
> | next | soon |
> | then | finally |

Problem and Solution A writer who chooses **problem and solution** organization wants readers to learn about an issue, or problem, and how it could be solved. Study this passage to identify the **problem** and **solution** .

Soccer for All

Taylor Bell, an 18-year-old soccer player from Arkansas, saw a need for more activities for young people with disabilities. — **Problem**

Taylor decided to start a soccer program for disabled youth. He — **Solution**
researched soccer programs in other cities and met with soccer organizations to learn how to set up a soccer camp.

Academic Vocabulary

● **organize** (**or**-gu-nīz) *verb*
  To **organize** means to arrange things in a certain order.

Practice Together

Read the following passages aloud. As you read, listen for clues that show how each passage is organized. How does each organization affect the meaning of the passage?

Shaheen Mistri

While in college, Shaheen Mistri spent time with children in India's poorest areas. Shaheen learned that a major problem facing poor children was not having access to quality education. Shaheen wanted to help solve the problem. She gathered a group of her friends, and they began teaching children who lived in the slums. She later founded an organization that has expanded to help more than 4,500 children have access to quality education.

Shaheen Mistri

Shaheen Mistri was born in Mumbai, India. She lived in many places while growing up. Then, at the age of eighteen, she returned to Mumbai. She was surprised by the poor areas in the city. Soon Shaheen enrolled in college and worked with poor children to help them get a better education. In 1989, Shaheen founded an organization to provide better education to children. During the past fifteen years, the organization has helped thousands of children in India.

Try It!

Read the following passages aloud. How is each passage organized? How do you know? How does the organization affect the meaning of each?

Bring It On

Gangs and drugs were problems in teenager Geneva Johnson's New York neighborhood. Geneva decided to take action. She started "Bring It On!," an organization that offers young people a variety of volunteer activities. Geneva learned how to raise money and organize volunteers. Now her group organizes community projects that help kids practice leadership and make healthy choices.

Bring It On

To create her community service group "Bring It On!," teenager Geneva Johnson first learned how to raise money and set up a volunteer organization. Then, she found about 20 kids to become helpers. Next, the group worked on community service projects. Eventually, Geneva's organization helped more than 1,000 kids practice leadership and make healthy choices.

Focus on Vocabulary

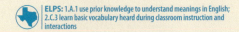ELPS: 1.A.1 use prior knowledge to understand meanings in English; 2.C.3 learn basic vocabulary heard during classroom instruction and interactions

Use Word Parts

Word parts include **base words**, **prefixes**, and **suffixes**. If you **focus** on word parts you already know, you can figure out the meanings of new words.

EXAMPLES

Word Parts			
Base Word **work** *verb* to make an effort at a task	**Prefix (*re-*)** **rework** *verb* to do something again	**Suffix (*-able*)** **workable** *adjective* something that is able to be done	**Prefix and Suffix** **unworkable** *adjective* something that is not able to be done

How the Strategy Works

When you read, you may come to a word you do not know. Check the word's parts to help you understand the word's meaning.

EXAMPLE The number of patients was **unmanageable** for one doctor.

1. Look closely at the word to see if you already know any of the parts.
2. Cover any prefixes and suffixes. **unmanageable**
3. Think about the meaning of the base word.
4. Uncover the prefixes and suffixes and determine their meanings.
5. Put the meanings of the word parts together to understand the whole word. Be sure the meaning makes sense in the passage.

Use the strategy to figure out the meaning of each underlined word.

> Do you agree that one person can make a difference? Or do you <u>disagree</u>? Rosa Parks, an African American seamstress in Alabama, made a <u>remarkable</u> difference with one action. In 1955, she refused to give up her seat on the bus to a white person. At that time in Alabama, African Americans were required by law to give up their seats to white people.

Strategy in Action

" I see the prefix *dis-*. I'll cover it. I already know the base word *agree*. I know *dis-* means 'the opposite of.' So *dis* + *agree* means the opposite of *agree*."

☑ **REMEMBER** You can figure out the meaning of an unknown word when you **focus** on the meanings of the word parts you already know.

Academic Vocabulary
- **focus** (fō-kus) *verb*
  When you **focus** on something, you pay attention to it.

Read this passage aloud. Look at each underlined word. Focus on the word parts, and put their meanings together to figure out the word.

History
A Day at a Time

▲ Peoples' choices change history.

Most people think history is a <u>retelling</u> of big events and famous people. But history is actually a <u>review</u> of everything that happens. History is always being made because of the choices people make. Change is <u>unavoidable</u>. Sometimes people are <u>unaware</u> of how <u>powerful</u> their choices can be. For example, Rosa Parks probably never thought that refusing to give up her bus seat would become such an important event in United States history. Look around you. Perhaps a choice you or a friend makes will show you a <u>preview</u> of history to come.

Some Word Parts
Prefix: *re-* means "again" (Latin)
Prefix: *un-* means "not" (Anglo-Saxon)
Prefix: *pre-* means "before" (Latin)
Prefix: *anti-* means "against" (Greek)
Suffix: *-able* means "can do" (Latin)
Suffix: *-ful* means "full of" (Anglo-Saxon)

Try It!

Read this passage aloud. What is the meaning of each underlined word? How do you know?

The 1960s: A Time of Change

The 1960s may seem like ancient times to you. Yet many people think the 1960s were the most amazing years in the United States. There were many changes during those years, and it was not a <u>peaceful</u> time. Four presidents held office in just ten years. The space program went from sending small rockets into space to sending men to the moon. Some people worked against <u>unjust</u> laws. Some tried to keep things the same.

Values changed, too. African Americans, young people, and women all became <u>forceful</u> voices for peace and against <u>unequal</u> treatment under the law. A war split the country into supporters and <u>antiwar</u> groups. New leaders arose. Some of them were killed in <u>unthinkable</u> acts of violence.

The challenges of the 1960s may seem far away today. Those years, though, prepared the way for the world you know today.

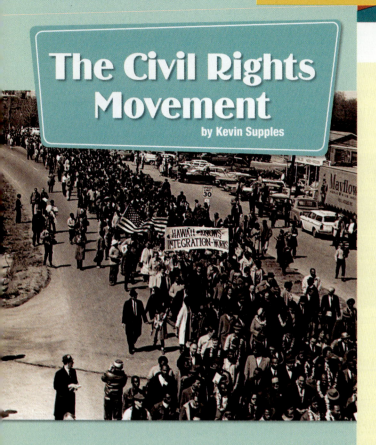

The Civil Rights Movement

by Kevin Supples

SELECTION 1 OVERVIEW

▶ **Build Background**

▶ **Language & Grammar**
Ask for and Give Information
Use Present and Past Tense Verbs

▶ **Prepare to Read**
Learn Key Vocabulary
Learn a Reading Strategy
Ask Questions

▶ **Read and Write**
Focus on Genre
History Article
Apply the Reading Strategy
Ask Questions
Critical Thinking
Reading Fluency
Read with Phrasing
Vocabulary Review
Write About the Guiding Question

▶ **Connect Across the Curriculum**
Literary Analysis
Analyze Text Structure: Chronological Order
Evaluate Informational Text
Analyze Tone
Vocabulary Study
Use Word Parts: Prefixes
Language and Grammar
Ask for and Give Information
Writing and Grammar
Write About a Past Event

Build Background

Discover Civil Rights

"The Civil Rights Movement" shows how individuals worked together to achieve fairness for all. Now meet the people who made the difference.

Connect

Group Discussion Imagine that your school made a rule that divided people: Students whose names begin with vowels are not allowed to use the main entrance. What would that be like? Discuss your ideas with the class.

Digital Library

InsideNG.com
↗ View the video.

▲ Rosa Parks acted on her beliefs.

Language & Grammar

ELPS: 2.H.2 understand implicit information in complex spoken language; 2.I.3 demonstrate listening comprehension of complex spoken English by responding to questions and requests; 3.F.1 ask [for] information; 4.F.4 use visual and contextual support to develop grasp of language structures needed to comprehend increasingly challenging language; 4.F.9 use support from peers and teachers to develop grasp of language structures needed to comprehend increasingly challenging language

1 TRY OUT LANGUAGE
2 LEARN GRAMMAR
3 APPLY ON YOUR OWN

Ask for and Give Information

CD

Look at the photograph and listen to questions and answers about the picture. Ask questions about any language you don't understand.

PICTURE PROMPT

From Selma to Montgomery

Student: What does this picture show?

Teacher: It shows people who participated in a march in the 1960s.

Student: Why did the people march?

Teacher: They marched to protest laws that made it hard for African Americans in Alabama to vote.

Use Present and Past Tense Verbs

The tense, or time, of a **verb** shows when an action happens.

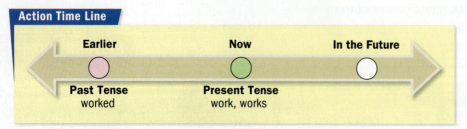

Action Time Line

Earlier   Now   In the Future

Past Tense
worked

Present Tense
work, works

- Use the **present tense** to tell about an action that happens now or often.

  EXAMPLES   Today, laws **treat** all people fairly. (*happens now*)

                  People **work** to protect our civil rights. (*happens often*)

The verb ends in **-s** only when it tells about one person, place, or thing.

  EXAMPLE   The government **protects** our civil rights.

- Use the **past tense** to tell about an action that has already happened.

  EXAMPLES   In the 1960s, many people **worked** to protect the civil rights of others.

                  Congress **passed** a voting rights law.

Add **-ed** to most verbs when you talk about a past action.

     work + -ed = worked   **pass + -ed = passed**

Practice Together

Change the verb in the box to the past tense. Say it. Then say the sentence and add the past tense verb.

1. | remember | Aunt Sally _____ the civil rights march.
2. | believe | She _____ in civil rights.
3. | want | She _____ everyone to be treated the same.
4. | help | The march _____ change the laws in her state.

▲ People marched for equal rights.

Try It!

Change the verb in the box to the past tense. Write the past tense verb on a card. Then say the sentence and add the past tense verb.

5. | listen | People _____ to what others said.
6. | march | They _____ for equal rights.
7. | pass | The government _____ civil rights laws.
8. | support | These laws _____ equality.

Learn About a Civil Rights March

ASK FOR AND GIVE INFORMATION

Look at the photograph. It shows protesters at the March on Washington. This famous civil rights march took place on August 28, 1963. What information does the photograph give you? What information about the march can you tell others?

Work with a small group to complete a Question-Answer Chart about the photograph. Give facts or details in your answers.

▲ Marchers protested at the March on Washington on August 28, 1963, in Washington, DC.

Question-Answer Chart

Question	Answer
1. Where did the people march?	The people marched in Washington, DC.
2. What was one thing the people wanted?	
3.	

Trade questions with another group. Answer their questions by giving information. Then trade roles.

HOW TO ASK FOR AND GIVE INFORMATION

1. Ask a question that starts with *Who, What, When, Where, Why, How, Are, Were, Can, Do,* or *Did.*

2. To answer, give facts or details.

> Why did this march happen?

> The people marched because they wanted to show their support for the passage of fair laws.

USE PRESENT AND PAST TENSE VERBS

When you give information, you may tell about something that happens now or often. If so, use a verb in the **present tense**. Or you may tell about something that already happened. If so, use a verb in the **past tense**.

In the Present: Why **do** people march today?
People **march** today for what they believe in.

In the Past: Why **did** people march in 1963?
People **marched** in 1963 for equal rights.

Prepare to Read

 ELPS: 3.A practice producing sounds of newly acquired vocabulary in a manner that is comprehensible; 4.D use prereading supports to enhance comprehension of written text; 4.F.6 use support from peers and teachers to read grade-appropriate content area text

Learn Key Vocabulary

Rate and Study the Words Rate how well you know each word. Then:

1. Pronounce the word. Say it aloud several times. Spell it.
2. Study the example.
3. Tell more about the word.
4. Practice it. Make the word your own.

Rating Scale

1 = I have never seen this word before.

2 = I am not sure of the word's meaning.

3 = I know this word and can teach the word's meaning to someone else.

Key Words

civil rights (siv-ul rīts) *noun*
▶ page 181

Your **civil rights** are the rights you have as a member of society. Many people marched to gain **civil rights** for all.

determined (dē-tur-mind) *adjective* ▶ page 181

When you are **determined** to do something, you work hard at it. The football team was **determined** to win.
Related Word: **determination**

equality (ē-kwal-i-tē) *noun*
▶ page 181

When you have the same rights as other people, you have **equality**. **Equality** is important within any group of people.
Related Words: **equal, equalize**

integrate (in-ti-grāt) *verb*
▶ page 184

When you **integrate** groups, you bring them together. Martin Luther King, Jr., worked to **integrate** schools.
Synonym: **combine**
Antonym: **segregate**

prejudice (prej-ū-dis) *noun*
▶ page 180

If you have **prejudice**, you judge things and people before you know about them. **Prejudice** is a form of ignorance.
Related Word: **judge**

protest (prō-test) *verb*
▶ page 191

To **protest** something means to show you are against it. Americans **protested** unfair treatment of African Americans.

segregation
(seg-ri-gā-shun) *noun* ▶ page 180

Segregation is when people are kept apart. The **segregation** of African American people in the 1950s was wrong.
Antonym: **integrate**

separate (sep-u-rut) *adjective*
▶ page 183

If you are **separate** from other people, you are not with them. It is not fun to feel **separate** from the group.
Antonym: **together**

Practice the Words Make a Study Card for each Key Word. Then compare your cards with a partner's.

---

determined

What it means: *to work hard for something*

Examples: *I was determined to get an A on the test, so I studied hard.*
She was determined to win the race.

Not examples: *I wanted an A, but I did not study.*
She didn't like to run races but thought she might win anyway.

Study Card

Reading Strategy: Ask Questions

Good readers stop and ask themselves questions as they read. This helps them check their understanding of the text.

Reading Strategy
Ask Questions

HOW TO SELF-QUESTION

1. Pause when you read. Ask yourself one of the 5Ws and H questions: *Who?, What?, Where?, When?, Why?,* and *How?*

2. Answer the question clearly in your own words.

3. If you can't answer a question on your own, go back and **reread** to find the answer.

Strategy in Action

Here's how one student asked questions.

Look Into the Text

America in 1950

A Divided Society

The 1950s were good years for many Americans. They had jobs that paid well, new homes in the suburbs, and good schools for their children. But African Americans were one group who did not share fully in all this. In the 1950s, prejudice against African Americans was widespread in the United States. One of the worst results of this prejudice was segregation, the practice of keeping people apart based on race.

Question-Answer Chart

Question	Answer
Why were the 1950s good years?	Many people had jobs, new homes, and their children went to good schools.
Who did not share in this?	African Americans were one group.

Practice Together

As you reread the passage, follow the steps in the How-To box to ask questions. Write them in a chart like the one above.

History Article

A history article tells about real events that happened in the past. Often, history articles include **photos** and details from news reports.

Photos and news reports give more information about historical events. Look at each photo **caption** to see what details it provides.

▲ Linda Brown and her family in the 1950s — caption

Many captions tell when the photo was taken.

Chronological, or time order, is important in history articles.

Your Job as a Reader

Reading Strategy: Ask Questions

As you read, ask yourself questions. Pay attention to the photos and captions to help find answers to your questions.

The Civil Rights Movement

by Kevin Supples

America in 1950

A Divided Society

The 1950s were good years for many Americans. They had jobs that paid well, new homes **in the suburbs**, and good schools for their children. But African Americans were one group who did not **share fully in all this**. In the 1950s, **prejudice** against African Americans was **widespread** in the United States.

One of the worst results of this prejudice was **segregation**, the practice of keeping people apart based on race.

Segregation was different in different parts of the United States. The South was home to more than half of African Americans. In the South, segregation was **enforced** by Jim Crow laws. These laws

▲ A child uses a drinking fountain outside of a North Carolina courthouse. In the 1950s, segregation controlled the everyday lives of most African Americans.

Key Vocabulary
prejudice *n.*, unfair opinions about a person, group, or race
segregation *n.*, the division of people into groups based on race

In Other Words
in the suburbs outside the city
share fully in all this have all of this
widespread very common
enforced supported; made legal

had controlled the lives of Southern blacks since the late 1800s. Jim Crow laws said that blacks and whites must use different schools, restaurants, hotels, theaters, parks, sections of trains and buses, and so on. Even funeral homes and cemeteries were segregated! In the few places where blacks and whites shared public services—such as post offices and banks—African Americans had to wait for all whites to be served first.

In the North, segregation happened by **practice and custom**. Many African Americans moved to Northern cities during the 1940s, and whites responded by moving to the suburbs. African Americans **found themselves trapped** in city slums—poor neighborhoods where housing and schools were bad and where there were few jobs.

Both Northern and Southern segregation were wrong and both forms of segregation denied black people an **equality** that they had a right to as Americans. In the 1950s, some African Americans were **determined** to change things. They started the **Civil Rights** Movement. This **movement** brought together many people and for some, the struggle to win equality became their life's work.

▲ Many white people moved out of Northern cities when African Americans moved in. Neighborhoods like Harlem, New York (pictured), suffered because of a lack of city services.

Key Vocabulary

equality *n.*, having the same rights as other people

determined *adj.*, working hard to make something happen

civil rights *n.*, basic rights and freedoms

In Other Words

practice and custom people's beliefs and not the law

found themselves trapped were left

movement organized effort for change

Before You Move On

1. **Cause and Effect** Why were African Americans **determined** to change things?
2. **Author's Point of View** How does the author feel about **segregation**? Support your answer with examples.

The Movement Begins

Thurgood Marshall

One group that fought for equality is the National Association for the Advancement of Colored People (NAACP). The NAACP was founded in 1909. Their goal was to obtain equal rights for all people and to **eliminate** racial hatred and discrimination.

The leader of the NAACP's efforts to end segregation was their top lawyer, Thurgood Marshall. He used the law to fight **injustice** against African Americans. Marshall argued thirty-two cases before the U.S. Supreme Court during his career, and he won twenty-nine of them. Some say that Marshall did more than any other **individual** to win civil rights for African Americans.

Marshall was born in Maryland in 1908. He was raised in a proud middle-class family. Smart and hard working, he was a fine student. Marshall went to college and later attended law school at Howard University in Washington, DC. Marshall graduated in 1933, first in his class.

Most of Marshall's clients were poor. Some couldn't even pay anything, but Marshall worked hard for them anyway. He usually won his cases. He became known as **the "little man's lawyer."** Marshall had a good sense of humor. He enjoyed jokes and often used humor to help him get through **hard times**.

Thurgood Marshall stands in front of the U.S. Supreme Court in 1954. Thirteen years later, he became the nation's first African American Supreme Court justice. ▶

In Other Words
eliminate end
injustice unfair treatment
individual person
the little man's lawyer a lawyer who helped the poor
hard times bad experiences

Government Background
The **U.S. Supreme Court** is the most important court in the nation. It has power over every court in each state. The U.S. Supreme Court is led by the Chief Justice of the United States, or the head of the court, and eight justices.

"Separate But Equal"

Throughout his career, Thurgood Marshall fought the "**separate** but equal" rule. This rule was created in 1896 by the Supreme Court. It said that states could offer separate services to African Americans and whites as long as the services were close to equal, but actually they often were not.

Many states passed laws saying that **local school districts** could decide whether to have separate schools for blacks and whites. The result was that all schools in the South were segregated. And there was nothing "equal" about the education black children were given in their poor, crowded schools.

After World War II, many Southern states tried to improve their blacks-only schools. They wanted to show that these schools were equal, but their efforts were **too little and too late**. By 1952, there were several court cases about segregated schools. The most famous case involved an eight-year-old girl named Linda Brown.

Linda's family lived close to a public school in Topeka, Kansas, but that school accepted only white students. So Linda had to travel by bus to a blacks-only school. To reach their bus stop, she and her sister

▲ Linda Brown (lower right) in a segregated classroom

had to walk through a dangerous railroad yard. Early in 1951, the Browns and some other African American families decided to take the local school district to **court**. In July, the local school board promised they would end segregation "as soon as possible." But that wasn't good enough for the Browns.

Key Vocabulary
separate *adj.*, apart

In Other Words
local school districts groups of schools in one area
too little and too late not enough and happened too slowly
court a place where a judge would hear their complaint

Historical Background
The U.S. Supreme Court ruled that **separate but equal** services were legal in the 1896 case of *Plessy v. Ferguson.* This decision allowed states and local governments to separate blacks and whites as long as they received similar services.

Brown v. Board of Education

The Browns' case became famous and Thurgood Marshall decided to use it to try to end segregated schools everywhere. He brought the case to the Supreme Court. The court decided to group the Browns' case with four others. Their case is known as *Brown v. Board of Education.*

Marshall argued the case **before** the Supreme Court. He argued that the Fourteenth Amendment of the U.S. Constitution said that states must treat all citizens alike, regardless of race. He said that black children did not receive schooling equal to that given to white children. He also said that black children thought less of themselves because they attended poor schools.

Almost three years after Linda Brown's family started the case, a final decision was reached. On May 17, 1954, the Supreme Court ruled that school segregation went against the Constitution.

After the ruling, the government made many school districts **redraw their borders**. Now white and black students would go to school together. This victory was an important step in the fight for civil rights. Many hoped that **integrating** schools would lead to integrating all of society. But there was still a long struggle ahead.

▲ African American children arrive for class. Segregated schools like this one led to the famous *Brown v. Board of Education* legal case.

Key Vocabulary
integrate *v.*, to bring together

In Other Words
v. (versus) against (in Latin)
before in front of
redraw their borders allow black students to attend

Historical Background
The **Fourteenth Amendment** of the U.S. Constitution was passed in June of 1866. The amendment was designed to grant citizenship for and protect the civil liberties of people who had recently been freed from slavery.

Linda Brown THEN

A young Linda Brown (left) stands with her younger sister Cheryl and her parents. Her father, Reverend Oliver Brown, asked "Why should my child walk four miles when there is a school only four blocks away? Why should I . . . explain to my daughter that she can't attend school with her neighborhood playmates because she is black?"

▲ Linda Brown and her family in the 1950s

Linda Brown TODAY

Today Linda Brown Thompson lives in Topeka, Kansas. She owns an educational consulting firm with her sister. Together, Linda and her sister have spoken about the court case and their experiences across the country. They have also appeared on television and were invited to the White House.

"We lived in the calm of the hurricane's eye, looking out at the storm and wondering how it would end," she recalled on the fiftieth anniversary of the Supreme Court decision to end segregation in public schools.

▲ Linda Brown Thompson, left, signs autographs at the University of Michigan in 2004.

Before You Move On

1. **Main Idea and Details** Thurgood Marshall fought hard for <mark>civil rights</mark>. Give two examples.
2. **Problem and Solution** Why did the Browns take the school district to court? What was the result?
3. **Conclusions** Why was the Browns' case important? Explain.

▲ National Guard troops stand outside Central High School in 1957.

The Little Rock Nine

Within a year, some school districts desegregated. **Here and there**, African American and white students attended school together. But many school districts, especially in the South, found ways to **resist** and delay the Supreme Court ruling.

Little Rock, Arkansas, became a test case for the new ruling because public schools there were ordered to desegregate in September 1957. The local school board agreed, but the governor of Arkansas, Orval Faubus, refused. He was **facing a tough re-election fight**, and he hoped

In Other Words
Here and there In some places
resist fight against
**facing a tough re-election
fight** trying to become governor
again, but had a stong opponent

Historical Background
The **National Guard** is one branch of the U.S. military. Its purpose is to help the nation in times of emergency or war.

to win the support of the many white Arkansas voters who still wanted segregated schools.

When school opened that September, Governor Faubus sent National Guard troops to Central High School. He ordered them to stop nine African American students from entering the newly integrated school. Elizabeth Eckford, one of the **"Little Rock Nine,"** arrived at school alone when **a white mob** began to scream at her.

For three weeks, the **crisis** continued. At this point, President Dwight Eisenhower **stepped in** by placing the Arkansas National Guard under federal control. The nine black students arrived at the school in a U.S. Army car. With soldiers protecting them, the students finally were integrated into the school. Eisenhower had shown that the federal government would protect civil rights.

Later, President Eisenhower wrote a message to parents of the Little Rock Nine. "In the course of our country's progress toward equality of opportunity, you have shown dignity and courage."

▲ Elizabeth Eckford had to walk past a crowd that shouted insults at her.

In Other Words
"Little Rock Nine" nine students whom Governor Faubus tried to stop from entering school
a white mob an angry group of white people
crisis trouble
stepped in helped

Before You Move On

1. **Cause and Effect** What did Governor Faubus do to fight against the Supreme Court ruling?
2. **Problem and Solution** How did President Eisenhower help to <mark>integrate</mark> Central High School?

The Struggle Continues

Martin Luther King, Jr.

The legal victory of *Brown v. Board of Education* was just one step in the fight against segregation. It did not change things as quickly as people had hoped. African Americans were ready to do more, and they began to organize. At this moment in history, a new leader arrived. He was a young minister named Martin Luther King, Jr.

King was born in 1929 in Atlanta, Georgia, to a middle class family. He was the son and grandson of Baptist ministers. His mother was a teacher. One of his grandfathers had been a slave. King **excelled at** school. He began college at the age of fifteen in a program for **gifted** students. He went to Morehouse College, a well-known all-black school in Atlanta. By the time King was eighteen, he had decided to **follow in his father's footsteps**.

While at Boston University finishing his studies to be a minister, King met Coretta Scott. She was studying voice and piano. The two were married in 1953 and the following year, Reverend King became pastor of a church in Montgomery, Alabama. He quickly became known for his wisdom and powerful preaching. Then in December 1955, an event **took place** that would make Martin Luther King, Jr., a leader of the Civil Rights Movement.

 Dr. Martin Luther King, Jr.

In Other Words
excelled at did really well in
gifted very smart or talented
follow in his father's footsteps
    be a minister like his father
took place happened

Changing the System

Rosa Parks

Montgomery, Alabama, was a segregated city in 1955. African Americans were treated **as second class citizens** there. The public bus system was a constant reminder of this.

As in many Southern cities, more blacks rode the city buses than whites. Even so, the first ten rows of every bus were reserved for white passengers only. If a bus was crowded and a white passenger needed a seat, blacks had to stand. Black passengers had to pay their **fares** at the front of the bus, but then they had to get off the bus and re-board by the back door. At busy times, the bus sometimes left before everyone who had paid got back on.

On December 1, 1955, Rosa Parks was riding the bus home from work. She was a **seamstress**, and she also worked at the local NAACP office. Parks had been on her feet all day, and she was tired. She was sitting in the eleventh row—the first row of seats set aside for African American passengers.

The bus was crowded and some black passengers were standing at the back. When a white man needed a seat, the bus driver ordered Parks and three African Americans in her row to stand. She refused to move and Parks was taken off the bus, arrested, and put in a jail cell.

News of Parks's arrest **shocked** the African American community. Civil rights supporters saw that this was their chance to change the rules. They asked Martin Luther King, Jr., to be their leader. That evening, Dr. King spoke to a cheering crowd of African Americans and he called for them to start a bus boycott, which meant they would not ride the buses.

▲ Rosa Parks is fingerprinted at the police station.

In Other Words
as second class citizens poorly
fares money
seamstress person who
  sews clothes
shocked surprised

Historical Background
The **bus boycott** led to the formation of the Montgomery Improvement Association, headed by Dr. Martin Luther King, Jr. The boycott lasted 381 days and made news around the world.

Before You Move On
1. **Sequence** Tell how Rosa Parks and the events in Montgomery changed history beginning on December 1, 1955.
2. **Summarize** Who was Martin Luther King, Jr.? How did he take part in the <mark>Civil Rights</mark> Movement?

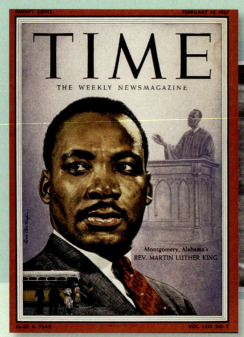

Martin Luther King, Jr., was featured on the cover of *Time* magazine in 1957.

The Montgomery Bus Boycott

For the next year, very few African Americans rode public buses in Montgomery, Alabama. Most **used car pools** to get to work. The boycott worked. The bus company lost a lot of money. The combination of the city's loss of money and a decision by the Supreme Court forced the Montgomery Bus Company to accept integration.

In June 1956, a federal court ruled that the bus segregation in Alabama was against the Constitution. The city of Montgomery did not **give in** easily. Lawyers for the city took the case to the Supreme Court, but that November, the Supreme Court agreed that segregation on buses was not lawful in the case of *Browder v. Gale*. A little over a year after the day that Rosa Parks refused to move, the Montgomery buses were integrated.

The Montgomery bus boycott was big news. It made Martin Luther King, Jr., famous. *Time* magazine put him on the cover. Requests to speak **poured in** from all over the country, and the **publicity** also led to boycotts in many other parts of the South.

The Protests

In February 1960, four African American college freshmen in Greensboro, North Carolina, decided to take another step toward equality. They sat down at the

In Other Words

used car pools rode together in cars
give in quit
poured in came in
publicity attention

Word History

In Ireland around 1880, landowner Charles Boycott refused to lower his high rents. To protest, renters and others stopped speaking to or working with him. Such planned inaction became known as a *boycott*.

▲ Thousands of African Americans walked to work during the Montgomery bus boycott.

whites-only lunch counter in a Woolworth's store and politely ordered coffee and donuts. The students were **refused service**. At that time, many department stores across the country had lunch counters, but most Southern lunch counters did not serve food to African Americans. Blacks were free to shop at the stores but could not eat there.

To <mark>protest</mark>, the four students sat at the counter for the rest of the afternoon. They returned the next day. This time, twenty more students came with them and each day, more people—both black and white—joined the "sit-in." By Saturday, hundreds **jammed** the lunch counters.

The events in Greensboro became news. At first, white business leaders refused to **bend to** the protest. But then black citizens set up a boycott of local stores. Stores began losing money and finally, on July 25, 1960, the first black person was served lunch at Woolworth's.

During the next eighteen months, thousands of people **staged** sit-ins all over the South. Most of those taking part were black students. Both Martin Luther King, Jr., and Thurgood Marshall supported these nonviolent protests. African Americans had found a new and powerful way to be heard.

In Other Words

refused service not served any food
jammed crowded
bend to change because of
staged held

Achieving the Dream

The Civil Rights Act

In the fall of 1960, John F. Kennedy was elected president of the United States. Kennedy won 70 percent of the **black vote**. He had shown that he would support ending segregation. Kennedy did not make changes quickly, but he did appoint more African Americans to high federal positions than any president before him. Kennedy appointed Thurgood Marshall to be a federal judge.

In June 1963, President Kennedy demanded that Congress pass a strong civil rights bill. In a speech to the nation he asked, "Are we to say to the world—and much more importantly to each other—that this is the land of the free, except for the Negroes?"

To persuade Congress to pass the bill, civil rights leaders A. Philip Randolph and Bayard Rustin organized a huge march on Washington, DC. On August 28, more than 250,000 people—both African Americans and whites—came together in the nation's capital. Labor unions and religious leaders joined the protest.

It was the largest show of support for the Civil Rights Movement so far.

The march ended at the Lincoln Memorial. For three hours, the crowd listened to a lot of speeches. People were getting sleepy and **restless** when the last speaker, Martin Luther King, Jr., came to the microphone. His famous "I Have a Dream"

In Other Words
black vote votes from African Americans
restless ready to leave

speech **electrified** the crowd.

A few months after the March on Washington, President Kennedy was **assassinated**. His vice-president, Lyndon Johnson, **succeeded him**. President Johnson passed the Civil Rights Act of 1964.

The new law **banned** segregation in public places, and it also banned unfair treatment of workers based on their color, sex, religion, or national origin. ❖

In Other Words

electrified excited
assassinated shot and killed
succeeded him became the
  next president
banned put a stop to

Before You Move On

1. **Main Idea and Details** How did President Kennedy affect the <mark>Civil Rights</mark> Movement?
2. **Summarize** In the 1960s, how did the Movement move forward?
3. **Judgment** In what ways did the Movement succeed? Explain.

Midway

by Naomi Long Madgett

I've come this far to freedom and I won't turn back.

I'm climbing to the highway from my old dirt track.

    I'm coming and I'm going

    And I'm stretching and I'm growing

5 And I'll reap what I've been sowing or my skin's not black.

I've prayed and slaved and waited and I've sung my song.

You've bled me and you've starved me but I've still grown strong.

    You've lashed me and you've treed me

    And you've everything but freed me

10 But in time you'll know you need me and it won't be long.

I've seen the daylight breaking high above the bough.

I've found my destination and I've made my vow;

    So whether you abhor me

    Or deride me or ignore me,

15 Mighty mountains loom before me and I won't stop now.

In Other Words

reap what I've been sowing get what I deserve

the daylight breaking high above the bough that there is hope

abhor me hate me

Or deride Disrespect

Before You Move On

1. **Interpret** What does the speaker mean by "I won't turn back"?
2. **Inference** What struggle does the speaker describe?
3. **Symbol** Reread the last line of the poem. What do the mountains symbolize?
4. **Explain** How is this poem similar to and different from a poem written in free verse? 4.A.1, 4.A.2

Connect Reading and Writing

CRITICAL THINKING

1. SUM IT UP Review the photos in "The **Civil Rights** Movement." Write new captions in your own words. Write a summary of the selection based on your captions.

▲ Rosa Parks was arrested for fighting against segregation.

2. Compare Compare the ways **segregation** was different for African Americans in the North and the South during the early 1960s.

3. Speculate What do you think life was like for students your age at the time of the **Civil Rights** Movement?

4. Compare Across Texts Explain how the poem "Midway" relates to the fight for **equality** in "The **Civil Rights** Movement."

READING FLUENCY

Phrasing Read the passage on page 640 to a partner. Assess your fluency.

1. I read
  a. great   **b.** OK   **c.** not very well

2. What I did best in my reading was _____ .

READING STRATEGY

Ask Questions
What were two literal questions you asked yourself as you read the selection? Explain to a partner how you answered them. RC-8.B.1

Vocabulary

Civil Rights

determined

equality

integrate

prejudice

protested

segregation

separate

VOCABULARY REVIEW

Oral Review Read the paragraph aloud. Add the vocabulary words.

In 1961, laws in the South enforced _____ that kept blacks and whites _____ . Supporters of the _____ Movement were _____ to change this. Black and white students got on buses to _____ public transportation. People who worked for racial _____ were called Freedom Riders. The Freedom Riders _____ unequal treatment and unfair opinions, or _____ .

Written Review Imagine you are a reporter during the **Civil Rights** Movement. Report on how one school **integrated** its students. Use five vocabulary words.

WRITE ABOUT THE GUIDING QUESTION

Reflect on Making a Difference
Which person in the selection made the biggest difference during the **Civil Rights** Movement? Support your opinion with examples.

Connect Across the Curriculum

ELPS: 2.C.4 learn academic vocabulary heard during classroom instruction and interactions; 4.F.1 use visual and contextual support to read grade-appropriate content area text; 4.F.2 use visual and contextual support to enhance and confirm understanding; 4.G.4 demonstrate comprehension of increasingly complex English by taking notes

Literary Analysis

Analyze Text Structure: Chronological Order

Academic Vocabulary
- **organize** (or-gu-nīz) *verb*
  To **organize** means to arrange things in a certain order.

How Is Writing Organized? Some writing is **organized** by time. Chronological order shows events in the order they happened. **Time words** give readers clues to when events happened.

Practice Together

Use Time Words As you read the passage, use the time words to follow chronological order.

> In February 1960, four African American college freshmen in Greensboro, North Carolina, decided to take another step toward equality. They sat down at the whites-only lunch counter in a Woolworth's store and politely ordered coffee and donuts. The students were refused service. . . . Then black citizens set up a boycott of local stores. Soon, the stores began losing money and finally, on July 25, 1960, the first black person was served lunch at Woolworth's.

Start a Time Line Make a time line to show the order of events.

Time Line

February 1960   July 1960

←————●————————●————————→

African American students sit at
a whites-only lunch counter.

Try It!

Finish the Time Line Reread the rest of "The Civil Rights Movement," starting at page 191. Use the time words to determine the order of events.

Internet InsideNG.com
🧭 Find out what happened in civil rights after the 1960s. Take notes and add to the time line.

Present Your Time Line Use your time line and time words to tell classmates about events after the 1960s. Then tell what you learned from seeing these events in chronological order.

Evaluate Informational Text

> **Academic Vocabulary**
> • **evidence** (e-vu-dents) *noun*
>   Evidence can be beliefs, proof, facts, or details that help support a conclusion.

How Do Writers Support Conclusions? We hear and read conclusions every day. For example: *This is the slowest bus in town!* If you read this in the newspaper, you would probably think the writer is just frustrated.

But what if you read this?: *I spent the entire month of April riding and timing every bus in town. The Main Street bus was always late by at least 15 minutes.* This is a conclusion supported with **evidence**.

What Makes Evidence Strong? Conclusions are most believable and effective when they are supported by **evidence** that is **adequate** and **appropriate**.

NOT OK

> The buses are probably always late, and I'm guessing that the downtown bus is the latest.

If there is not enough evidence or it is weak or incorrect, it is not adequate.

NOT OK

> Someone needs to clean up the bus stops!

If the evidence is not on topic, it is not appropriate.

Practice Together

Identify Conclusions and Evaluate Evidence When you read an informational article, such as a history article, identify the writer's conclusions. Then record the **evidence** that supports those conclusions on an Evidence Chart. Decide if the **evidence** is adequate and appropriate. Does the **evidence** support the writer's conclusion?

Evidence Chart

Conclusion	Evidence	Evaluation
Thurgood Marshall did more than any other person to win civil rights for African Americans.	He argued 32 cases before the U.S. Supreme Court and won 29 of them.	The writer used facts as evidence. The conclusion is valid.
Services for African Americans and whites were not equal.		

Try It!

Make an Evidence Chart In "The Civil Rights Movement," the writer makes other conclusions. Make a chart like the one above, and find the **evidence** that supports the writer's conclusion about unequal services. Is the **evidence** adequate and appropriate?

Vocabulary Study

Use Word Parts: Prefixes

Prefix	Meaning
dis-	the opposite of
un-	not
re-	again
non-	not
in-	not
de-	removal, reversal

Academic Vocabulary

● **analyze** (a-nu-līz) *verb*
When you **analyze**, you separate something into parts and examine, or study, it.

Many English words are made of different word parts. When you **analyze** the parts, you can figure out the meaning of the whole word. For example:

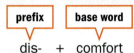

The prefix *dis-* means "the opposite of."   dis- + comfort

Discomfort means "the opposite of comfort," to not have comfort.

Find Word Parts Work with a partner. **Analyze** each of these words' parts. Put the meanings together to understand the whole word.

1. unfair   3. nonviolent   5. re-election
2. injustice   4. redraw   6. desegregate

Write Sentences Write a sentence for each word. Read your sentences aloud. Does the meaning you predicted make sense in the sentence?

ELPS: 2.C.4 learn academic vocabulary heard during classroom instruction and interactions

Literary Analysis

Analyze Tone

Academic Vocabulary

● **image** (im-ij) *noun*
An **image** is a mental picture of something.

The tone of a poem is the feeling it gives readers. Often tone is created by the sound of the words. When you read a poem aloud, notice the sounds. What **images** do they make you think of? What feeling do they give you? How a poem sounds can give you clues to a poem's tone, or feeling, and message.

Listen to the Sound Read these lines aloud. Notice how they sound. What do you think the speaker's attitude, or tone, is?

> I've come this far to freedom and I won't turn back.
> I'm climbing to the highway from my old dirt track.

Interpret the Poem With a partner, read the poem "Midway" aloud. What **images** do you see? What is the tone? What is the speaker saying?

ELPS: 2.C.4 learn academic vocabulary heard during classroom instruction and interactions; 4.G.1 demonstrate comprehension of increasingly complex English by participating in shared reading

Language and Grammar

Ask for and Give Information

Group Share Tell a small group the information you learned from reading the selection. Ask questions about your classmates' new knowledge. Use present and past tense verbs depending on the time of the action.

> What did you learn about schools during this time period?

> I learned that schools were segregated and that people tried to change them.

Writing and Grammar

Write About a Past Event

Study the Models When you write about an event that happened in the past, you need to be consistent so you don't confuse your readers. Choose verbs that make it clear that the events happened in the past, not in the present.

NOT OK

> In the 1950s, Linda Brown **walked** through a dangerous railroad yard on her way to the school bus stop. Then she **travels** by bus to a blacks-only school. Her family **decided** to take the school district to court. Three years later, the Supreme Court **rules** against school segregation.

The reader thinks: "Did these things all happen a long time ago or right now?" The time is not clear.

OK

> In the 1950s, Linda Brown **walked** through a dangerous railroad yard on her way to the school bus stop. Then she **traveled** by bus to a blacks-only school. Her family **decided** to take the school district to court. Three years later, the Supreme Court **ruled** against school segregation.

This writing is consistent. The time of the events is now clear.

Add Sentences Think of two sentences to add to the OK model above. Be consistent in showing that the events happened in the past.

WRITE ON YOUR OWN Imagine you are one of the "Little Rock Nine" and the year is 1957. Write about what your school day was like yesterday. Use words that make it clear that the events happened in the past.

REMEMBER

Check your past tense verbs for correct spelling.

- If a verb ends in silent **e**, drop the **e** before you add **-ed**.
  rul~~e~~ + **-ed** = rul**ed**

- If the verb has one syllable and ends in one vowel and one consonant, double the consonant.
  stop + **p** + **-ed** = stop**ped**

- If the verb ends in **y**, change the **y** to **i**. Then add **-ed**.
  tr~~y~~ + **-ed** = tr**ied**

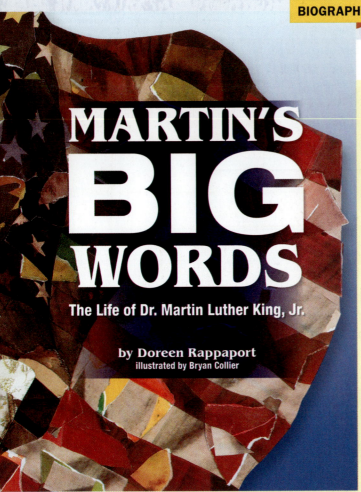

MARTIN'S BIG WORDS

The Life of Dr. Martin Luther King, Jr.

by Doreen Rappaport
illustrated by Bryan Collier

Build Background

Hear Powerful Words

Dr. Martin Luther King, Jr., used the power of language to speak up for civil rights. Forty years after his death, his speeches still inspire people today.

Connect

Quickwrite Words can be powerful. Recall words that have affected you. Perhaps it was advice that helped you, or words from a movie or a song that inspired you. Describe the effect these words had on your life.

Digital Library

InsideNG.com
⊘ View the video.

▲ Dr. Martin Luther King, Jr.

Language & Grammar

ELPS: 1.D speak using learning strategies; 2.F.2 listen to and derive meaning from a variety of media to build and reinforce language attainment; 3.B.3 expand and internalize initial vocabulary by learning and using routine language needed for classroom communication; 3.C.1 speak using a variety of grammatical structures with increasing accuracy and ease; 3.H.2 describe with increasing specificity and detail

Describe an Event
CD

Look at the photograph and listen to the song.
The song is about the March on Washington.

SONG

▲ Dr. Martin Luther King, Jr., gave a powerful speech at the March on Washington in 1963.

We're Marching for Freedom

We're marching for freedom.
Hear us now!
We're marching for freedom.
Hear us now!
We're marching for freedom.
Hear us now!
We want the rights that others have.

We want the right to vote.
Hear us now!
We want the right to vote.
Hear us now!
We want the right to vote.
Hear us now!
We want the rights that others have.

We want our education,
Hear us now!
We want our education,
Hear us now!
We want our education,
Hear us now!
We want the rights that others have.

We want to live in peace.
Hear us now!
We want to live in peace.
Hear us now!
We want to live in peace.
Hear us now!
We want the rights that others have.

Equal rights for all,
Hear us now!
Equal rights for all,
Hear us now!
Equal rights for all,
Hear us now!
We want the rights that others have.

Use Forms of *Be*

The verb **be** has special forms to tell about the present and the past.

Action Time Line

Earlier	Now	In the Future

Past Tense
I **was**
you **were**
he, she, or it **was**
we **were**
they **were**

Present Tense
I **am**
you **are**
he, she, or it **is**
we **are**
they **are**

- The verb *be* is irregular. An irregular verb does not follow the rules that regular verbs follow for making past tense forms.

  Past tense: Dr. Martin Luther King, Jr., **was** a great leader.
  Present tense: Today, he **is** a hero to many people.

- The verb form for *he*, *she*, or *it* is used with the name of a person or a thing, such as *Martin*, *Coretta*, or *the speech*.

  EXAMPLE   Martin **was** a minister like his father.

- The verb form for *they* is used for two or more people or things, such as *Martin and Coretta*, or *the speeches*.

  EXAMPLE   Martin and Coretta **were** husband and wife.

Practice Together

Change the verb in the box to the past tense. Say it. Then say the sentence and add the past tense verb.

1. | am | I _____ excited to hear Dr. Martin Luther King, Jr., speak.
2. | is | His wife _____ in a seat near us.
3. | are | His words _____ incredible.
4. | are | We _____ fortunate to hear him speak.

Try It!

Change the verb in the box to the past tense. Write the past tense verb on a card. Then say the sentence and add the past tense verb.

5. | is | Martin _____ an amazing man.
6. | are | His followers _____ very loyal.
7. | are | You _____ at the civil rights march.
8. | is | One man _____ there to march for equal job opportunities.

▲ Dr. Martin Luther King, Jr., was a famous leader who fought for equal rights.

Tell What Happened

DESCRIBE AN EVENT

We know about things that have happened in the past because people tell and write about the events. Choose an event from history or a past event in the news and describe it in your own words. Ask for help if you need it.

Read the directions in steps. Plan what you will say.

Steps	Example
1. Name the event.	Rosa Parks was arrested on a bus in Montgomery, Alabama.
2. Give details about what happened. Tell information that will answer questions that begin with *who, what, where, when, why,* and *how.* Use descriptive words.	She was on her way home after working all day as a seamstress. She was on the bus in the 11th row—the first row of seats set aside for African American passengers.
3. Use sensory words to describe the event. If possible, compare the event to something else.	Rosa's feet ached after standing all day. She was tired, like a runner who had just finished a race.

Now describe the event to a partner. Answer questions that your partner may ask. Trade roles.

HOW TO DESCRIBE AN EVENT

1. Name the event.

2. Give details. Use descriptive words.

3. Use sensory words. Compare people and things to something else.

What happened?

Rosa Parks had no energy after working hard all day. She was like a tired-out runner. She refused to give her bus seat to a white man.

USE PAST TENSE VERBS

The event you describe happened in the past. You will need to use past tense verbs when you talk about it. Remember that most **verbs** add **-ed** to show past time.

EXAMPLE   Police **arrested** Rosa Parks.

The irregular verb *be* has special forms to show the past.

EXAMPLE   Rosa **was** tired after a long day at work.

Prepare to Read

 ELPS: 1.C acquire basic and grade-level vocabulary; 2.B recognize elements of the English sound system in newly acquired vocabulary; 3.A practice producing sounds of newly acquired vocabulary in a manner that is comprehensible; 4.C.1 develop basic sight vocabulary used routinely in written classroom materials

Learn Key Vocabulary

Rate and Study the Words Rate how well you know each word. Then:

1. Pronounce the word. Say it aloud several times. Spell it.
2. Study the example.
3. Tell more about the word.
4. Practice it. Make the word your own.

Rating Scale

1 = I have never seen this word before.

2 = I am not sure of the word's meaning.

3 = I know this word and can teach the word's meaning to someone else.

Key Words

admire (ad-**mīr**) *verb*
▶ page 211

When you **admire** someone, you think highly of them. Many people **admire** Rosa Parks, who worked for civil rights.
Related Word: **admiration**

arrest (u-**rest**) *noun*
▶ page 210

An **arrest** is when a person is taken by a police officer. Police made many **arrests** of people during the Civil Rights Movement.

convince (kun-**vins**) *verb*
▶ page 210

When somebody **convinces** you of something, you think it's a good idea. He **convinced** her to agree with him.
Synonym: **persuade**

influence (**in**-flü-uns) *verb*
▶ page 208

When people **influence** you, they change the way you think. Dr. Martin Luther King, Jr., **influenced** people to work toward equality.
Synonyms: **affect, change**

movement (**müv**-munt) *noun*
▶ page 210

A **movement** is a group of people working together to make a change. People of all races took part in the Civil Rights **Movement**.

peace (**pēs**) *noun*
▶ page 208

Peace is freedom from war and fighting. Many people hope for **peace** in the world.
Antonym: **war**

preach (**prēch**) *verb*
▶ page 208

To **preach** is to tell people what you believe is right. The speaker **preached** the importance of kindness to all.
Related Word: **preacher**

problem (**prah**-blum) *noun*
▶ page 210

A **problem** is something you have to solve or fix. You can solve a math **problem**.
Synonym: **difficulty**

Practice the Words Work with a partner to write four sentences. Use at least two Key Words in each sentence.

EXAMPLE: My father always preaches to us that peace is better than war.

Reading Strategy: Ask Questions

When you read, ask questions about the way the author wrote the selection. This will help you better understand what you read. Asking questions also helps you decide if the author has communicated a clear message.

HOW TO QUESTION THE AUTHOR

1. Pause in your reading and ask these questions: What is the author trying to say? Why is the author telling me this?
2. State each answer clearly in your own words.
3. If you cannot answer your own questions, reread the text and think about the reasons for the author's decisions.

Strategy in Action

Here's how one student asked questions.

Look Into the Text

> Martin grew up. He became a minister like his father. And he used the big words he had heard as a child from his parents and from the Bible.
>
> "Everyone can be great."
>
> He studied the teachings of Mahatma Gandhi. He learned how the Indian nation won freedom without ever firing a gun. Martin said "love," when others said "hate."
>
> "Hate cannot drive out hate. Only love can do that."

> What does the author mean by "big words"?

> Maybe the author means that words like "hate" and "love" have a big impact.

Practice Together

Reread the passage above and ask two more questions. Follow the steps in the How-To box. Put your questions on sticky notes next to the passage.

Focus on Genre

Biography

In a biography, an author tells the story of a real person's life. The story is told from a third-person limited point of view. The events in a biography usually happen in **chronological**, or time, order. Look for **time words** that show when things happen.

> After ten years of protests, the lawmakers in Washington voted to end segregation.

Your Job as a Reader

Reading Strategy: Ask Questions

As you read, ask questions. Look for time words to help you make connections between the time and the events in the biography.

TEXT

"In the next ten years, black Americans all over the South protested for equal rights."

QUESTIONS

Why did people protest during this time?
What happened as a result of the protests?

MARTIN'S BIG WORDS

The Life of Dr. Martin Luther King, Jr.

by Doreen Rappaport
illustrated by Bryan Collier

Everywhere in Martin's hometown, he saw the signs, WHITE ONLY. His mother said these signs were in all Southern cities and towns in the United States. Every time Martin read the words, he felt bad, until he remembered what his mother told him: "You are as good as anyone."

In church Martin sang **hymns**. He read from the Bible. He listened to his father **preach**. These words made him feel good.

"When I grow up, I'm going to get big words, too."

Martin grew up. He became a minister like his father. And he used the big words he had heard as a child from his parents and from the Bible.

"Everyone can be great."

He studied the teachings of Mahatma Gandhi. He learned how the Indian nation won freedom without ever firing a gun. Martin said "love," when others said "hate."

"Hate cannot **drive out** hate. Only love can do that."

He said "together" when others said "separate." He said "**peace**" when others said "war."

"Sooner or later, all the people of the world will have to discover a way to live together."

Key Vocabulary
influence *v.*, to affect what someone thinks or does
preach *v.*, to urge people to believe something
peace *n.*, agreement among people

In Other Words
hymns religious songs
drive out stop

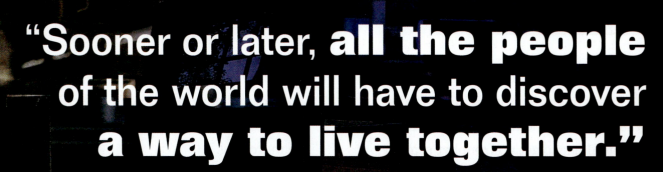

"Sooner or later, **all the people** of the world will have to discover **a way to live together.**"

Cultural Background

Mahatma Gandhi (1869–1948) was a political and spiritual leader of India and helped his country work for an end to British rule. He led the Indian Independence Movement by using peaceful protest.

Before You Move On

1. **Inference** What did Martin mean when he said he was "going to get big words"?
2. **Summarize** How did words **influence** Martin's beliefs?
3. **Cause and Effect** How did the teachings of Gandhi affect Martin?

In 1955 on a cold December day in Montgomery, Alabama, Rosa Parks was coming home from work. A white man told her to get up from her seat on the bus so he could sit. She said No, and was **arrested**.

Montgomery's black citizens learned of her arrest. It made them angry. They decided not to ride the buses until they could sit anywhere they wanted.

For 381 days they walked to work and school and church. They walked in rain and cold and in **blistering** heat. Martin walked with them and talked with them and sang with them and prayed with them until the white city leaders had to agree they could sit anywhere they wanted.

"When the history books are written, someone will say there lived black people who had the courage to **stand up** for their rights."

In the next ten years, black Americans all over the South protested for equal rights. Martin walked with them and talked with them and sang with them and prayed with them.

White ministers told them to stop. Mayors and governors and police chiefs and judges ordered them to stop. But they kept on marching.

"Wait! For years I have heard the word 'Wait!' We have waited more than three hundred and forty years for our rights."

They were jailed and beaten and murdered. But they kept on marching. Some black Americans wanted to fight back with their fists. Martin **convinced** them not to, by reminding them of the power of love.

"Love is the **key** to the **problems** of the world."

Many white Southerners hated and feared Martin's words. A few threatened to kill him and his family. His house was bombed. His brother's house was bombed. But he refused to stop.

"Remember, if I am stopped, this **movement** will not be stopped, because God is with this movement."

The marches continued. More and more Americans listened to Martin's words. He shared his dreams and **filled them with** hope.

Key Vocabulary
arrest *v.*, to be put under police control
convince *v.*, to make someone believe or agree
problem *n.*, a difficult situation
movement *n.*, an organized effort to reach a goal

In Other Words
blistering very great; extreme
stand up fight
key solution
filled them with gave people

"I have a dream that one day in Alabama little black boys and black girls will join hands with little white boys and white girls as sisters and brothers."

After ten years of protests, the lawmakers in Washington voted to end segregation. The WHITE ONLY signs in the South came down.

Dr. Martin Luther King, Jr., cared about all Americans. He cared about people all over the world. And people all over the world **admired** him.

In 1964, he won the Nobel Peace Prize. He won it because he taught others to fight with words, not fists.

Martin went wherever people needed help. In April 1968 he went to Memphis, Tennessee. He went to help garbage collectors who were on strike. He walked with them and talked with them and sang with them and prayed with them.

On his second day there, he was shot. He died.

His big words are alive for us today. ❖

Key Vocabulary

admire *v.*, to like and respect someone

Cultural Background
The **Nobel Peace Prize** is an international award given by the Nobel Foundation in Sweden. It honors those who work for world peace.

Before You Move On

1. **Main Idea and Details** What groups of people did Martin speak to? How did his words affect each group?
2. **Paraphrase** In your own words, explain one of Martin's teachings.
3. **Point of View** What point of view is used in the first paragraph? How does the point of view change after the first paragraph?

The power of Dr. King's words live on in his speeches, letters, and other writing. Here is an excerpt from a famous speech he gave on the steps of the Lincoln Memorial in 1963. Today many consider it to be one of the greatest speeches in human history.

▲ Martin Luther King, Jr., with his wife, Coretta, and two of their four children, Marty and Yoki.

from "I Have a Dream"

. . . I say to you today, my friends, so even though we face the difficulties of today and tomorrow, I still have a dream. It is a dream **deeply rooted in** the American dream.

I have a dream that one day this nation will rise up and **live out the true meaning of its creed**: "We hold these truths to be self-evident; that all men are created equal."

I have a dream that one day, on the red hills of Georgia, sons of former slaves and the sons of former slaveowners will be able to sit down together at the table of brotherhood. . . .

I have a dream that my four little children will one day live in a nation where they will not be judged by the color of their skin but by the content of their character.

In Other Words
deeply rooted in based on the beliefs of
live out the true meaning of its creed follow what is written as our country's beliefs

I have a dream today. . . .

This is our hope. This is the **faith** that I go back to the South with. With this faith we will be able to **hew** out of the mountain of despair a stone of hope. With this faith we will be able to transform the **jangling discords** of our nation into a beautiful **symphony** of brotherhood. With this faith we will be able to work together, to pray together, to struggle together, to stand up for freedom together, knowing that we will be free one day.

And this will be the day. This will be the day when all of God's children will be able to sing with new meaning "My country 'tis of thee, sweet land of liberty, of thee I sing. Land where my fathers died, land of the pilgrim's pride, from every mountainside, let freedom ring."

And if America is to be a great nation this must become true. So let freedom ring from the **prodigious** hilltops of New Hampshire. Let freedom ring from the mighty mountains of New York. Let freedom ring from the heightening **Alleghenies** of Pennsylvania!

Let freedom ring from the snowcapped Rockies of Colorado!

Let freedom ring from the curvaceous slopes of California!

But not only that; let freedom ring from Stone Mountain of Georgia! Let freedom ring from Lookout Mountain of Tennessee.

Let freedom ring from every hill and molehill of Mississippi. From every mountainside, let freedom ring.

And when this happens, and when we allow freedom to ring, when we let it ring from every village and every hamlet, from every state and every city, we will be able to speed up that day when all of God's children, black men and white men, Jews and Gentiles, Protestants and Catholics, will be able to join hands and sing in the words of that old Negro spiritual, "Free at last! Free at last! Thank God Almighty, we are free at last!"

August 28, 1963
Washington, DC

In Other Words
faith belief, confidence
hew carve
jangling discords loud differences of opinion
symphony agreement
prodigious enormous
Alleghenies Mountain ranges

Before You Move On
1. **Summarize** What was Martin Luther King, Jr's., dream?
2. **Repetition** How does Martin Luther King, Jr. use of repetition affect his speech?
3. **Personal Connection** Identify your favorite sentence in the speech. How do the words affect you?

About the Author

Doreen Rappaport

In the 1960s, **Doreen Rappaport** was a teacher in Mississippi. Rappaport's students changed her life. She describes them as "extraordinary ordinary people" whose courage inspired her. Her students' heroic struggle for their civil rights encouraged her to write about more "unknown heroes" who helped change history. Rappaport is an award-winning author of several other books, including *Escape from Slavery* and *Freedom River.* Today, she lives in New York and travels across the country to visit schools and talk with young people.

About the Speaker

Martin Luther King, Jr.

Time magazine named **Martin Luther King, Jr.**, (1929–1968) one of the 100 most important people of the twentieth century. "It is a testament to the greatness of Martin Luther King, Jr., that nearly every major city in the U.S. has a street or school named after him," wrote reporter Jack White. Throughout his life, King gave speeches, organized boycotts, and led marches. His birthday is a national holiday celebrated throughout the United States.

Connect Reading and Writing

Vocabulary
admire
arrest
convinced
influenced
movement
peace
preach
problems

CRITICAL THINKING

1. **SUM IT UP** Make a card for each vocabulary word. Use at least five words to explain how Martin used words to work for **peace**.

2. **Evaluate** Which words from "I Have a Dream" show that Martin got his own "big words"? Tell why you think these powerful words **influenced** his listeners so strongly.

3. **Speculate** Forty years after his death, people still **admire** and learn about Dr. King. Do you predict that in another 40 years children will still learn about him? Explain.

4. **Generalize** Martin said that African American people had the courage to stand up for their rights. Give several examples of this from the selection.

READING FLUENCY

Expression Read the passage on page 641 to a partner. Assess your fluency.

1. I read
   a. great   **b.** OK   **c.** not very well

2. What I did best in my reading was _____ .

READING STRATEGY

Ask Questions
What were two questions you asked the author while reading? Share with a partner.

VOCABULARY REVIEW

Oral Review Read the paragraph aloud. Add the vocabulary words.

> Young Martin Luther King, Jr., _____ people all over the world with his words. He faced risks for his work, including his _____ . But thanks to work like his, African Americans do not live separate lives. King did more than _____ . He started a _____ . He _____ people to solve their _____ with _____ , not violence. Today, people still _____ him.

Written Review Imagine you lived in the 1960s during the Civil Rights **Movement**. Write a letter about your experiences. Use five vocabulary words.

WRITE ABOUT THE ⟨GUIDING QUESTION⟩

Explore How Words Can Make a Difference

How did Martin Luther King, Jr., use words to **influence** others? Write a paragraph explaining the effect his words had. Include literary devices and specific phrases from the selection that support your explanation.

Connect Across the Curriculum

Literary Analysis

Evaluate a Biography

> **Academic Vocabulary**
> • **evidence** (e-vu-dents) *noun*
> **Evidence** can be beliefs, proof, facts, or details that help support a conclusion.

Biography writers provide **evidence** to support their conclusions about the people they write about. The reader's task is to decide whether or not the **evidence** really supports the writer's conclusions.

In "Martin's Big Words," the writer concludes that Martin believed in peaceful protests. The **evidence** below supports this conclusion because it tells how Martin studied the peaceful methods of protest used in India.

> He studied the teachings of Mahatma Gandhi. He learned how the Indian nation won freedom without ever firing a gun.

Practice Together

Use a T Chart This chart shows some conclusions the author makes in "Martin's Big Words" and the **evidence** she provides. Discuss whether the quotation is enough to prove the writer's conclusion.

T Chart

Conclusion	Evidence
Martin convinced others not to use violence.	Quotation: "Love is the key to the problems of the world."
Martin went wherever people needed his help.	

Read the second conclusion. Find **evidence** in the biography, such as details or quotations, to support this conclusion. Then, write the **evidence** you find in a copy of the T Chart and evaluate it.

Try It!

Make a T Chart Make a T Chart for the "I Have a Dream" speech. Find two conclusions Dr. King makes in his speech, and write the **evidence** he provides to support them. Decide whether the **evidence** is accurate and really supports Dr. King's conclusions.

ELPS: 2.C.4 learn academic vocabulary heard during classroom instruction and interactions

Vocabulary Study

Use Word Parts: Suffixes

Suffix	Meaning
-tion	condition or action
-or	one who does an action
-ness	state of
-ly	like; in the manner of
-ic	like; nature of

Academic Vocabulary
- **individual** (in-de-**vij**-yū-wul) *adjective*
  Something that is **individual** is separate from other things.

A word has **individual** parts. For example, a **suffix** is a word part added at the end of a base word. When you add a suffix to a base word, you create a new word. For example:

- *develop* is a verb that means "to grow."
- The suffix *-ment* means "instance or action."
- When you add *-ment* to *develop*, the new word *development* becomes a noun.
- What do you think *development* means?

> The base word is *develop*, which means "to grow." So *development* must mean "the action of growing."

Figure Out Word Meanings Work with a partner to identify the **individual** word parts. Cover the suffix and look at the base word. Then uncover the suffix. How does the suffix affect the base word? Write the meaning of the whole word.

1. movement   **3.** collectors   **5.** deeply

2. segregation   **4.** greatness   **6.** heroic

ELPS: 2.C.4 learn academic vocabulary heard during classroom instruction and interactions

Media/Viewing

Make a Collage

Academic Vocabulary
- **image** (im-ij) *noun*
  An **image** is a mental picture of something.

Use visual media to represent Dr. King's beliefs, words, and actions.

❶ **Select Images** Find pictures that show Dr. King's beliefs and actions. Look online or in magazines. Select and copy your favorite **images**. Then arrange them in a collage. Identify the source of the **images**.

▲ Dr. King used imagery in his speeches.

❷ **Plan Your Presentation** What powerful words can you use to present your collage to the class? Choose four or five key words that will help you explain how your **images** represent Dr. King's beliefs.

❸ **Present Your Collage** As you explain your collage, make eye contact with your audience. Use your body language to express your ideas.

SOCIAL SCIENCE

ELPS: 2.C.4 learn academic vocabulary heard during classroom instruction and interactions; 3.G.3 express feelings on a variety of social and grade-appropriate academic topics

Viewing/Speaking

Express Your Views

Academic Vocabulary
- **organize** (or-gu-nīz) *verb*
  To **organize** means to arrange things in a certain order.

Discover how others' views can inspire you to express your own views.

1 **Research** With a partner, search for speeches, songs, or poems from the civil rights era. Think about these questions as you search:

- How did people **organize** their views?
- What feelings did their words create?
- What sensory words and/or phrases are used to express the author's message?
- Does the author use certain literary devices to create an image or feeling?

Choose a speech, song, or poem that is meaningful to you and your partner. Use an Idea Web to **organize** your thoughts. Write the name of the song, poem, or speech in the center. In the outer circles, write the views that are expressed. Think about how these ideas affect you.

Idea Web

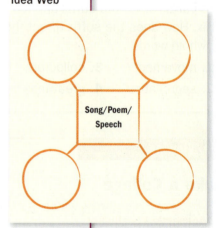

Song/Poem/ Speech

2 **Discuss Your Views** Talk with your partner about something you feel strongly about in your own life.

3 **Organize Your Views** Choose a way to **organize** your feelings, such as on an Idea Web. Then write a short speech, song, or poem to express your views. Think about

- the feelings you would like to express
- how you want people to feel about your views
- words that will affect people's feelings.

4 **Express Your Views** Share your views with the class. Explain where you got the ideas for your speech, song, or poem and why it is meaningful.

- Use facial expressions and gestures to show your emotions and convey the meaning of your speech, song, or poem.
- Make sure your posture and gestures match your feeling, tone, and pitch as you speak. For example, if you are excited, speak standing up straight rather than sitting in your seat.

Language and Grammar

Describe an Event

Quiz Your Partner With a partner, take turns asking questions and giving answers about events pictured in the selection. Use past tense verbs when you describe what happened in the picture or at the event.

> Why did the people march instead of fight?

> Dr. King convinced them that peaceful protests were better than violent ones.

Writing and Grammar

Write About the Past

Study the Models When you write about an event that already happened, be consistent and clear about when the events took place. Otherwise, you may confuse your readers.

NOT OK

> Dr. Martin Luther King, Jr., was a great man. He **believed** in peace instead of war. He **has** the courage to stand up for equal rights. He **walked** and **talks** with Americans all over the country. People **listen** to Martin's words.

The reader thinks: **"**Is the writer describing Dr. King today or in the past? This is confusing.**"**

OK

> Dr. Martin Luther King, Jr., was a great man. He **believed** in peace instead of war. He **had** the courage to stand up for equal rights. He **walked** and **talked** with Americans all over the country. People **listened** to Martin's words.

The reader thinks: **"**Now I can understand when the events happened.**"**

Add Sentences Think of two more sentences to add to the OK paragraph. Be sure to describe past events consistently.

WRITE ON YOUR OWN Describe an event that you heard or saw on the news recently. Use sentences that make it clear that the event happened in the past. Don't switch back and forth from the past to the present.

REMEMBER

Most **verbs** add **-ed** to make their past tense forms. The irregular verbs *be* and *have* use special forms to show the past tense.

Past Tense of *be*	I **was**	you **were**	he, she, or it **was**	we **were**	they **were**
Past Tense of *have*	I **had**	you **had**	he, she, or it **had**	we **had**	they **had**

Speaking Up

Read these news features about two teens who met very different challenges and made a difference by speaking up.

Build Background

Connect

Discussion Read the following statements:

1. If an individual wants to achieve his or her dream, he or she must first find others who share that dream.

2. One person, working alone, can achieve more than a group of people.

Which statement do you agree with? In a discussion with your classmates, present arguments to support your opinion.

See Leadership in Action

What does it mean to be a leader? Many teens have made a difference in their communities by speaking up and becoming involved.

Digital Library **InsideNG.com**
⬀ View the images.

▲ Teens discover their leadership skills.

Language & Grammar

ELPS: 2.G.2 understand the general meaning of spoken language regarding familiar to unfamiliar language; 2.I.2 demonstrate listening comprehension of complex spoken English by retelling or summarizing spoken messages; 2.I.5 demonstrate listening comprehension of complex spoken English by taking notes; 4.C.4 comprehend English language structures used routinely in written classroom materials

1 TRY OUT LANGUAGE
2 LEARN GRAMMAR
3 APPLY ON YOUR OWN

Summarize

CD

Look at the photograph and listen to a candidate's campaign speech. He explains why he should be elected class president. Then listen to a summary of the speech.

SUMMARY

I Will Make a Difference!

Summary of Hector's Speech:

Hector Espinosa wants to be our class president. In his campaign speech, he said that he was honest, fair, loyal, and a good leader.

He also said that he listens when others speak. He knew that we wanted an environmentally friendly, or green, cafeteria. As class president, he will try to make that happen.

Hector also said that he will talk to the teachers about limiting weekend homework and coordinating due dates for projects.

At the end of his speech, he promised to work hard and to make a difference.

Use Verbs in the Past Tense

A **past tense** verb shows an action that already happened. For most verbs, add **-ed** to show past tense.

> **EXAMPLE** The mayor **talked** about our community. (regular verb)

Use special past tense forms with **irregular verbs.**

> **EXAMPLE** He **gave** his speech yesterday. (irregular verb)

Each past tense form of an irregular verb must be memorized.

Examples of Irregular Verbs

Present	Past	Example in the Past
give	gave	I **gave** a letter to the mayor.
get	got	I **got** to see the mayor.
speak	spoke	The mayor **spoke** to us about improving our town.
see	saw	We **saw** photos of places in our community.
feel	felt	Everyone **felt** eager to help.
know	knew	The mayor **knew** my name!
tell	told	I **told** the mayor about some of my ideas.
think	thought	He **thought** my ideas were great.

Practice Together

Say each sentence with your class. Then say the sentence again, using the past tense form of the underlined verb.

1. The students <u>see</u> litter all over the park.
2. They <u>know</u> the problem.
3. They <u>think</u> about what they could do to clean up the area.
4. They <u>get</u> large trash bags.

Try It!

Say each sentence. Write the verb on a card. Then write the past tense form of the verb on the same card. Say the sentence again using the past tense form of the verb.

5. The teacher <u>gives</u> everyone gloves to wear.
6. She <u>tells</u> the students what to do.
7. She <u>speaks</u> to each group about their jobs.
8. Everyone <u>feels</u> good about helping the community.

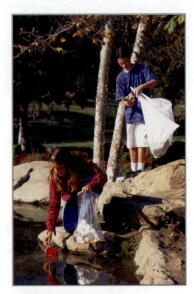

▲ These students helped their community.

Share How You Have Made a Difference

SUMMARIZE

How have you made a difference in someone's life or in your community? Share what you did with a partner, and summarize your partner's experience.

Follow these steps to create your summary.

1. Take notes as you listen to your partner speak. Decide what information is important to include in your summary and what information can be left out.

2. Just tell the main ideas or most important information. A good summary is shorter than the original telling or text.

3. Use your own words to summarize your partner's experience.

Listen to your partner tell about what he or she did to make a difference. Listen for the general meaning and the details. Summarize what your partner said. Trade roles.

HOW TO SUMMARIZE

1. Identify the main ideas or important information.
2. Leave out unimportant or repeated information.
3. Use your own words.

Original telling: Maria gave her neighbor some of the peas, carrots, corn, and broccoli that she grew in her garden.

Summary: Maria gave her neighbor some home-grown vegetables.

USE VERBS IN THE PAST TENSE

The event you summarize happened in the past. You will need to use **past tense verbs** when you talk about it. Remember that most **verbs** add **-ed** to make their past tense forms. **Irregular verbs** use special forms to show the past.

Irregular: Ike **knew** that his elderly neighbor **had** a doctor's appointment.

Regular: Ike **shoveled** the snow off his neighbor's sidewalk. Ike's neighbor **thanked** Ike for his thoughtfulness.

Prepare to Read

ELPS: 1.F use accessible language and learn essential language in the process; 3.A practice producing sounds of newly acquired vocabulary in a manner that is comprehensible; 4.K demonstrate and expand comprehension by employing analytical skills

Learn Key Vocabulary

Rate and Study the Words Rate how well you know each word. Then:

1. Pronounce the word. Say it aloud several times. Spell it.
2. Study the example.
3. Tell more about the word.
4. Practice it. Make the word your own.

Rating Scale

1 = I have never seen this word before.

2 = I am not sure of the word's meaning.

3 = I know this word and can teach the word's meaning to someone else.

Key Words

challenge (**chal**-unj) *noun*
▶ page 228

A **challenge** is something that is difficult to do. It is a **challenge** to climb a mountain.

contribute (kun-**trib**-yūt)
verb ▶ page 232

When you **contribute** to something, you give your time or money. The child **contributed** money to help people in need.
Synonyms: **give, provide, donate**

involved (in-**vahlvd**)
adjective ▶ page 228

To get **involved** is to become a part of something. Many people like to be **involved** in improving their communities.
Related Word: **involvement**

leadership (**lēd**-ur-ship)
noun ▶ page 230

Leadership means guiding others in what to do. A person who helps others shows **leadership**.
Related Words: **lead, leader**

negative (**neg**-u-tiv) *adjective*
▶ page 228

If you have a **negative** opinion about something, you don't like it. My sister was **negative** about my idea.
Antonyms: **positive, good**

overcome (**ō**-vur-**kum**) *verb*
▶ page 233

To **overcome** something is to succeed at something that was difficult. If you used to be afraid of dogs but now you like them, you have **overcome** your fear.

positive (**pahz**-u-tiv) *adjective*
▶ page 229

Positive means good or hopeful. If you have a **positive** attitude, you think things are good.
Antonyms: **negative, bad**

promote (pru-**mōt**) *verb*
▶ page 229

To **promote** something is to tell others that it is a good thing. The firefighters **promote** safety to the students.

Practice the Words Work with a partner to complete an Expanded Meaning Map for each Key Word.

> **What the Word Means**
> something difficult to do
>
> **Examples**
> climb mountain
> win a race
>
> **Word**
> challenge
>
> **What It Is Like**
> difficult
> not easy

Expanded Meaning Map

Reading Strategy: Ask Questions

It is important to ask literal and interpretive questions whenever you read something that you do not understand. Sometimes you will find the answer right in the same sentence. Other times you will need to search for the answer.

Reading Strategy
Ask Questions

HOW TO FIND ANSWERS

1. "Right There" Strategy
- Ask the question.
- See if the words that answer the question are directly stated.

2. "Think and Search" Strategy
- Ask the question.
- Find the answers in different sentences or paragraphs.
- Put the information you found together.

Strategy in Action

Here's how one student asked questions.

Look Into the Text

Why wasn't it easy for Eve's family?

Eve's parents expected her to do well in school, plus cook, clean, and help tutor her four younger siblings. It wasn't easy. Sometimes, the family lived on donated canned food and dry milk. "We've come a long, long way," Eve says.

Eve's parents came to Minnesota in the late 1970s from Laos in Southeast Asia. After years of hard work, they own a home and run a small business.

"The answer is right there!"

How has Eve's family come a long way?

"I'll get information from different sentences and put it together."

Practice Together

Reread the passage above and ask a question. Use the strategies in the How-To box to find answers. When you read the following two news features, search for answers to your questions.

News Features

News features give facts about real people and events. A **headline** in a news feature grabs your attention and gives you important information about the subject of the article.

> ### Student Gets Involved to Improve School's Reputation
>
> Arlington had a bad reputation. . . . At first, Eve didn't want to go there. "I hated Arlington until I got involved," she says.

Many news features explain a problem and how someone or a group of people worked together to solve the problem. Often headlines tell about the problem or the solution.

Your Job as a Reader

Reading Strategy: Ask Questions

As you read, ask questions. Look at the headlines. Put them together with other information from the article to find answers to your questions.

> HEADLINE
>
> "Student Gets Involved to Improve School's Reputation"
>
> QUESTION
>
> **What** does the student do to get involved?

Speaking Up

Read these news features about two teens who met very different challenges and made a difference by speaking up.

Online Coach

Student Gets Involved to Improve School's Reputation

by Jonathan Blum

What makes a good leader? For Eve Vang, her training started at home. She grew up as the oldest daughter in a large household. "You have to **play second mom** in a big family," says Eve, an 18-year-old student leader at Arlington High School in St. Paul, Minnesota.

"I hated Arlington until I got involved," recalls Eve Vang.

Eve's parents expected her to do well in school, plus cook, clean, and help tutor her four younger siblings. It wasn't easy. Sometimes, the family lived on donated canned food and dry milk. "We've come a long, long way," Eve says.

Eve's parents came to Minnesota in the late 1970s from Laos in Southeast Asia. After years of hard work, they own a home and run a small business. Eve's family is Hmong, a **close-knit Asian ethnic minority group**.

Like many Hmong, Eve's parents had to **flee** their homes during the Vietnam War. They survived by living in a refugee camp in Thailand. They often went hungry. Eventually, they came to the United States.

In junior high, Eve often felt like an outsider. There weren't many other minority students in her classes. Then, in 1999, she started at Arlington High. The school had many other Hmong students, which made her more comfortable. Yet there were new **challenges**.

Arlington had a bad reputation. Students performed low on standardized tests. Many people in the community had a **negative** image of the school. At first, Eve didn't want to go there. "I hated Arlington until I got **involved**," she says.

Then, Eve joined the freshman volleyball squad. She got to know some students and teachers. Soon, she saw that Arlington didn't deserve its bad reputation.

Key Vocabulary

challenge *n.*, a difficult or exciting problem to solve
negative *adj.*, bad, unpleasant
involved *adj.*, a part of something

In Other Words

play second mom be very responsible
close-knit Asian ethnic minority group group of people who share the same cultural background
flee quickly escape

Cultural Background

The Hmong are an ethnic group in China, Vietnam, Laos, and Thailand. Outside of Asia, the United States is home to the largest Hmong population in the world.

Sharing Her Pride

Eve **set out** to change the way people thought of her school.

She and other student leaders gave presentations at nearby middle schools, **promoting** Arlington. Eve also wrote **editorials** about Arlington High, which were published in *The St. Paul Pioneer Press* and the *Hmong Times*. "I wanted to share my pride, and I wanted to share what I love about Arlington High School," Eve says.

Eve also worked to improve the school. She **recruited** a group of student leaders. Together, they formed an organization called VOICE (Voicing Our Intelligence to Challenge Education). They started an annual carnival to promote the **rich mix of** cultures at the school. Eve thinks that cultural diversity is one of the best things about Arlington. Thirty-three different languages are spoken there!

Eve's efforts **sparked** change. In the past two years, **positive** articles on Arlington High School have appeared in the local media. Teachers and staff have started programs that have improved students' academic scores. More freshmen say they are excited to go to Arlington.

Eve Vang speaks to a group of students about school pride.

Key Vocabulary
promote *v.*, to add to the success of something
positive *adj.*, good, hopeful

In Other Words
set out made it her goal
editorials articles in which she gave her opinion
recruited got together
rich mix of large number of different
sparked caused

Before You Move On

1. **Problem and Solution** Why did Eve get **involved**? What did she discover?
2. **Details** How did Eve **promote** Arlington?
3. **Judgment** What makes Eve a good leader?

Eve organized a carnival, like this one, at her high school.

The annual carnival Eve helps organize has become a big success. More than 200 people participated last year, along with several area businesses. Other improvements in the school have been rewarded as well. Principal Bill Dunn has been named a Minnesota High School Principal of the Year.

Principal Dunn thinks that Eve's **leadership** skills will **take her far**. "If this young woman **set her mind to** being the mayor, that would happen," he says. "I hope that does happen. She's been a great student leader."

Eve, who stands 4 feet and 11 inches tall, says that it's not always easy being a leader. "People look at me and they **always underestimate me**. They say, 'Oh, this little girl can't do anything,'" Eve explains. "**I feed on that.** When people push you down, you've got to prove them wrong."

Sometimes Eve wants to run away from responsibility. But eventually, she remembers how much she likes making things better for others, especially at her school. ❖

Key Vocabulary
leadership *n.*, the ability to direct or guide other people

In Other Words
take her far help her in the future
set her mind to focused on
always underestimate me don't understand how much I can do
I feed on that. That motivates me.

Eve Vang Today

Today, Eve serves as an advisor to VOICE, the student-led activist group she founded at her high school in 1999. She works with the group to help the community and develop students' leadership skills. She also organized Operation Christmas Child, in which her school sent gifts to developing countries.

A past winner of the 2003 Yoshiyama Award for her service to the community, Eve continues to help others. After graduating from college in 2007, she was awarded a **prestigious** Fulbright U.S. Student Scholarship to teach English as a foreign language in Thailand.

Eve is the first student from her college to participate in the Fulbright program in Thailand. The program is the largest U.S. international exchange program.

Eve will teach English to middle school students outside Bangkok, Thailand.

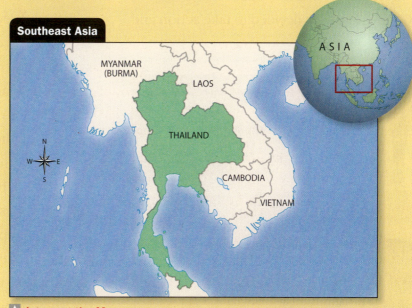

Interpret the Map Locate Thailand on the map. Which countries border Thailand?

Eve's decision to go to Thailand relates to her own cultural heritage. She says, "Personally, I am taking the journey to Thailand because I want to **immerse** myself back into my Hmong culture—its traditions, language and the people. Culture is a large part of my identity and without it, I could not be me."

In Other Words

prestigious respected, famous
immerse put

Before You Move On

1. **Cause and Effect** What **positive** differences has Eve made?
2. **Paraphrase** Explain in your own words what Eve means when she says, "I could not be me" without my culture.
3. **Generalization** What important message can you learn from Eve's story?

Student Works to End Bullying

by Genet Berhane

Matt Cavedon has been busy with a big job over the last few years—making the world a better place. Most recently, that has meant **doing his part** to stop bullying. Matt **witnessed** what it was like for some students to be bullied at his school in Berlin, Connecticut. He decided to take action and do something positive for people because he wanted everyone to be respected.

When national plans for an anti-bullying campaign recently began to **take shape**, Matt saw a cause to which he could **contribute**. While some schools have excellent prevention plans in place, they are often not enough. Even peer mediation systems, where kids meet to work through their problems with other students, do not completely stop the bullying.

One of the biggest problems is that a lot of bullying goes unreported. It's not just about the bullies and the victims, says Matt. Bystanders, the people who see bullying happen, have an important **role to play** in the situation.

"Anyone who sees something should do something," he says. "Don't just be bystanders; get involved."

Matt's contribution to the anti-bullying campaign is something he wanted to do simply because he understands how wrong

Teenager Matt Cavedon believes everyone needs to speak up about bullying.

Key Vocabulary
contribute *v.*, to help

In Other Words
doing his part offering his time and effort
witnessed saw
take shape form; get organized
role to play responsibility

bullying is. He understands that a problem, any problem, deserves attention.

"He wants to be involved," says his mom, Susan Cavedon. "He wants to help the next person."

It's important to remember that you have the power to make a difference, Matt says. Bystanders can get involved by speaking up for victims. He also has some advice for the kids who **have to put up with** bullying.

"No one can make you feel **inferior without your consent**," he says to the victims of bullying. "Keep your **self-esteem** high."

What does he have to say to the bullies?

"Why?" he says. "Why do you do it? Look at others who overcame their problems instead of **taking them out on** other people. Have the honor and respect not to take it out on others. You'll be stronger by not bullying."

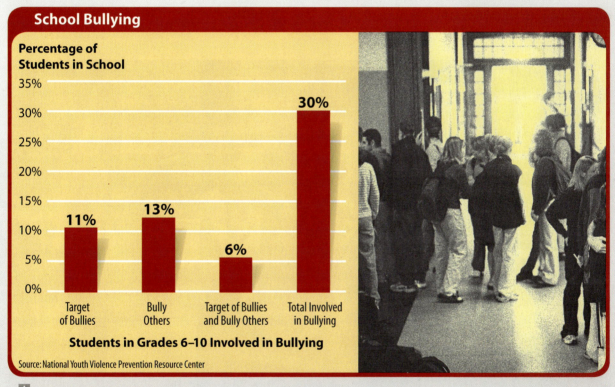

School Bullying

Percentage of Students in School

Students in Grades 6–10 Involved in Bullying

Source: National Youth Violence Prevention Resource Center

▲ **Interpret the Bar Graph** What does the graph reveal about problems of bullying in schools?

In Other Words
have to put up with experience
inferior without your consent bad unless you let them
self-esteem pride in yourself
taking them out on getting angry at

Making Change Happen

This isn't the first time Matt has done something to make life better for other kids. Even when he was younger, Matt was doing his part to make his community in Berlin, Connecticut, a better place.

"Anyone can make a difference," he says. "Age doesn't matter."

Age certainly never stopped Matt. While in elementary school, he worked with Boundless Playgrounds, an organization that creates play areas **accessible to** kids of all abilities. Matt uses a wheelchair because of a condition that keeps him from **extending his limbs**. He understands the importance of providing play spaces designed to fit everyone.

Matt developed equipment for Boundless Playgrounds and served as a co-chairman of the Jr. Advisory Board for the organization. He is proud of the positive responses his playgrounds have received.

"Everyone seems to love them," he says. ❖

Matt watches children play on equipment that he helped design for Boundless Playgrounds.

In Other Words
accessible to that can be used by
extending his limbs fully moving his arms and legs

Before You Move On
1. **Vocabulary** How does Matt **contribute** to his community?
2. **Summarize** What is Matt's message to bullies?

Connect Reading and Writing

Vocabulary
challenges
contributes
involved
leadership
negative
overcome
positive
promote

CRITICAL THINKING

1. SUM IT UP Choose two of the headlines in the selection. Use them to tell how either Eve Vang or Matt Cavedon show **leadership** in their communities.

2. Interpret Matt asks bullies, "Why do you do it? Look at others who **overcame** their problems instead of taking them out on other people." What does this mean to you? How does the bar graph on page 233 **contribute** support to Matt's ideas?

3. Evaluate Do you agree with Matt that no one can make you feel **negative** about yourself without your consent? Why or why not?

4. Compare Across Texts What **positive** characteristics do Eve Vang and Matt Cavedon have in common with Dr. Martin Luther King, Jr.?

READING FLUENCY

Intonation Read the passage on page 642 to a partner. Assess your fluency.

1. I read
a. great   b. OK   c. not very well

2. What I did best in my reading was _____.

READING STRATEGY

Ask Questions
How did you find the answer to a question you asked while reading? Tell a partner.

VOCABULARY REVIEW

Oral Review Read the paragraph aloud. Add the vocabulary words.

Sometimes in life there are _____. The best way to _____ problems in life is to have a _____ attitude. If a person gives, or _____, very little, then he or she will make situations _____. Even one person can make a difference, and when people work together, they can make life better. Either way, it is important to help, or _____, good _____ by becoming _____ in solving problems.

Written Review Write an e-mail to a friend. Describe a **challenge** you or someone you know faced. Use at least four vocabulary words in the e-mail.

 **WRITE ABOUT THE** **GUIDING QUESTION**

Explore How Words Can Make a Difference
Think about this question: Why did Eve Vang and Matt Cavedon get **involved** in their communities? What difference did their words and actions make? Show how they **contributed** their ideas to help others. Review the images from the Digital Library (p. 220) to inspire your thinking.

Connect Across the Curriculum

 ELPS: 2.C.4 learn academic vocabulary heard during classroom instruction and interactions; 4.F.1 use visual and contextual support to read grade-appropriate content area text; 4.F.2 use visual and contextual support to enhance and confirm understanding

Literary Analysis

Analyze Text Structure: Problem and Solution

> **Academic Vocabulary**
> • **organize** (or-gu-nīz) *verb*
>   To **organize** means to arrange things in a certain order.

How Are News Features Organized? Some news features are **organized** around a problem and a solution. A headline in a news feature often helps readers see what the problem and solution are.

Practice Together

Identify Problem and Solution As you read the passage, use the **headline** to help you **organize** the information in the news article. Identify the problem and solution.

> ### Student Works to End Bullying
>
> Matt Cavedon has been busy with a big job over the last few years—making the world a better place. Most recently, that has meant doing his part to stop bullying. . . . He decided to take action and do something positive for people because he wanted everyone to be respected.

Make a Problem-and-Solution Chart Reread the news feature about Matt Cavedon. Work with your class to complete the chart. Then discuss how the headline helps **organize** the information.

Problem-and-Solution Chart

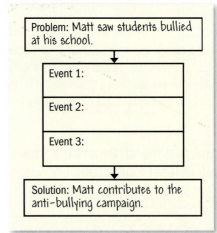

Try It!

Identify Problem and Solution Articles Use the Internet to research more articles. **Organize** the information you find in a new Problem-and-Solution Chart.

Internet InsideNG.com

🧭 Find out about others who are working to solve the problem of bullying.

Present the Problem-and-Solution Chart Use your chart to tell about other individuals or organizations that try to solve the problem of bullying. Discuss any headlines you found that helped you **organize** the information.

ELPS: 2.C.4 learn academic vocabulary heard during classroom instruction and interactions

Vocabulary Study

Use Word Parts

Academic Vocabulary

- **predict** (pri-**dikt**) *verb*
  When you **predict**, you guess about something or tell what will happen.

Word Part	Meaning
un-	not; the opposite of
-able	can be or is
re-	again
-ly	in this way; way of being
under-	below; not enough
-tion	the act of

Many English words are made up of a base word with prefixes and suffixes added. When you know the meaning of the parts, you can figure out the meaning of a whole word.

Figure Out Word Meanings Work with a partner. Break each of these words into word parts. Write the meaning of each word part. Then put the meanings together to **predict** the meaning of the word.

1. uncomfortable
2. uninvolved
3. reorganization
4. unorganized
5. underestimate
6. untruthfully

Write Sentences Use each word in a sentence. Trade sentences with a partner. Does the meaning you **predicted** make sense?

Viewing/Speaking

Distinguish Fact from Opinion

MEDIA & TECHNOLOGY

ELPS: 2.C.4 learn academic vocabulary heard during classroom instruction and interactions; 2.F.1 listen to and derive meaning from a variety of media to build and reinforce concept attainment; 2.F.2 listen to and derive meaning from a variety of media to build and reinforce language attainment; 2.I.5 demonstrate listening comprehension of complex spoken English by taking notes; 3.E share information in cooperative learning interactions

Academic Vocabulary

- **evidence** (e-vu-dents) *noun*
  Evidence can be beliefs, proof, facts, or details that help support a conclusion.

Writers may use facts or opinions as **evidence** . A fact is something that can be proved. An opinion is a belief that may or may not be true.

1 **Tell Fact from Opinion** Work with a partner. Tell whether each of the following statements is a fact or an opinion. Discuss why you think so.

Statement	Fact or Opinion
Eve lived in St. Paul, Minnesota.	
Arlington High is a fun place to go to school.	
Matt Cavedon tried to stop bullying at his school.	
Bullies can never change.	
Most bullying goes unreported.	

2 **Analyze News Reports** At home or at the library, find news reports online. Listen and watch for **evidence** on the topic. Identify the facts and any opinions. Take notes on a chart.

3 **Discuss Your Findings** Share the **evidence** you found with a partner. Discuss if most of the **evidence** in the news was fact or opinion.

ELPS: 2.C.4 learn academic vocabulary heard during classroom instruction and interactions

Listening/Speaking

Deliver a Problem-Solution Presentation

SOCIAL SCIENCE

> **Academic Vocabulary**
> • **convince** (kun-**vins**) *verb*
>   To **convince** means to persuade.

In "Speaking Up," Eve Vang and other student leaders gave presentations to help solve their problems. What if you had to **convince** your classmates that there was a problem to solve? Deliver a presentation to your class about a problem at school and share how you would solve the problem.

❶ Identify a Problem and Determine Solutions Think about a problem at your school or in your community that you want to see changed. Propose a solution. Now think of evidence that would **convince** your listeners that you have a good solution.

❷ Organize Your Presentation Use a Problem-Solution Chart to organize your ideas. For example:

Problem-Solution Chart

Problem	Solutions	Evidence
If the school band doesn't raise enough money, then it will not be able to go to the state music competition.	1. We should have a fundraiser to help raise the money. 2. We should speak to each class and ask them to help.	1. Last year the band's fundraiser earned $600. 2. If we have more people, we can do several fundraisers to earn more money.

❸ Practice Your Presentation Work with a partner and practice your presentation. Think of interesting ways to start so that you capture your audience's attention. For example, play a recording of the school band's music. Practice using your voice and gestures in a way that expresses your emotions. Speak with a convincing tone and use signal words such as *should*, *need*, and *if/then* to call attention to the problem and solutions. If possible, tell a story that illustrates the problem or supports a solution. Ask your partner for helpful suggestions. Was the problem clearly identified? How persuasive were you? Did the evidence you presented support your solutions?

❹ Give Your Presentation Share your presentation with the class. Keep your audience interested by making eye contact and speaking clearly and loudly. Look at your notes if you need to, but try to use them as little as possible.

Summarize

Pair Share With a partner, summarize either Eve's story or Matt's story. Remember to tell just the main ideas in your summary. Do not include unimportant details. Use past tense verbs in your summary.

> Eve changed the way people thought about her school.

> What were the main things she did to change people's opinions of her school?

Writing and Grammar

ELPS: 1.B.2 monitor written language production and self-correct

Write Consistently About the Past

Study the Models When you write a summary, monitor your writing so you do not switch to the present and then back to the past, or your reader will become confused about when events took place.

NOT OK

Matt **does** many things that made a difference in children's lives. When he was 14, Matt **tells** kids that bullying was wrong. He **spends** a lot of time talking to them. He also worked with an organization and **creates** play areas. He **makes** special playground equipment. Children of all abilities played at Matt's playgrounds.

> It is difficult to understand this writing because the writer switches between past and present.

OK

Matt did many things that made a difference in children's lives. When he was 14, Matt told kids that bullying was wrong. He spent a lot of time talking to them. He also worked with an organization and created play areas. He made special playground equipment. Children of all abilities played at Matt's playgrounds.

> The writer now sticks consistently with the past. The paragraph is much clearer.

WRITE ON YOUR OWN Think of an important or enjoyable event that happened at your school this year. Summarize the key points of the event. Do not switch back and forth between writing in the past and writing in the present. Review your writing and correct any errors in verb tense.

REMEMBER

Most **verbs** add **-ed** to make their past tense forms. The irregular verbs *be*, *have*, and *do* use special forms to show the past tense.

Past Tense of *be*	I **was**	you **were**	he, she, or it **was**	we **were**	they **were**
Past Tense of *have*	I **had**	you **had**	he, she, or it **had**	we **had**	they **had**
Past Tense of *do*	I **did**	you **did**	he, she, or it **did**	we **did**	they **did**

Compare Across Texts

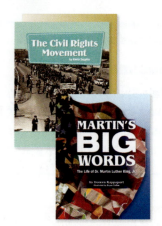

Compare Authors' Styles

"The Civil Rights Movement," "Midway," and "Martin's Big Words" all **focus** on an important time in U.S. history. Compare the authors' styles.

How It Works

Collect and Organize Ideas To compare authors' styles, list elements of style in a chart like this one.

Comparison Chart

Elements of Style Questions	"The Civil Rights Movement"	"Midway"	"Martin's Big Words"
What is the author's purpose?	to tell how the Civil Rights Movement started		
What genre and details does the author use to achieve this purpose?	nonfiction with historical facts, dates, and explanations of real events		
Paraphrase the main message of the selection	African-Americans begin to fight against racism and segregation in the United States		

Practice Together

Compare the Ideas Compare the answers for each question. Then summarize. Show how the authors' styles are similar and different.

Summary

> The authors of "The Civil Rights Movement," "Midway," and "Martin's Big Words" all write about the same topic. However, the author of "The Civil Rights Movement" uses a nonfiction genre, explains the time period, and gives facts.

Try It!

Add answers for "Midway" and "Martin's Big Words" to the chart. Compare and summarize them. Use a frame like this one to express your comparison.

Like the other two authors, the author of "_____" _____. Unlike them, the author _____.

Academic Vocabulary
- **focus** (fō-kus) *verb*
  When you **focus** on something, you pay attention to it.

Making a Difference

GUIDING QUESTION How can one individual make a difference?

Reflect on Your Reading

Think back on your reading of the unit selections. Discuss what you did to understand what you read.

Focus on Genre **Organization of Ideas**

In this unit, you learned about some ways writers organize ideas: chronological order and problem-and-solution. Draw a diagram that shows the organization of one of the selections from this unit. Use your drawing to explain the organization of the selection to a partner.

Reading Strategy **Ask Questions**

As you read the selections, you learned to ask and answer questions about the text. Explain to a partner how you will use this strategy in the future.

Explore the

Throughout this unit, you have been thinking about how one person can make a difference. Choose one of these ways to explore the Guiding Question:

- **Discuss** With a group, discuss ways an individual can make a difference. Listen to and share examples from life. What challenges may a person have to face to make a positive change?
- **Role-Play** Imagine that you know someone who is being bullied. One person can take that role, and another can offer advice. Be honest about the difficulty the person faces in dealing with the situation.
- **Write** Choose an issue or problem in your community or school that needs to be solved. Write a letter to the editor of a newspaper about the problem.

Book Talk

Which Unit Library book did you choose? Explain to a partner what you learned about individuals making a difference.

UNIT LIBRARY

Content Library

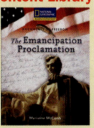

Leveled Library

Tar Beach 2, 1990, Faith Ringgold. Silk screen on silk, Philadelphia Museum of Art, Philadelphia.

▲ **Critical Viewing:** What is the artist saying about life in this location?

ELAR Focus: 2.C.1 learn new language structures heard during classroom instruction and interactions; 2.F.1 listen to and derive meaning from a variety of media to build and reinforce concept attainment; 2.F.2 listen to and derive meaning from a variety of media to build and reinforce language attainment; 2.G.2 understand the general meaning of spoken language regarding familiar to unfamiliar language; 2.I.4 demonstrate listening comprehension of complex spoken English by collaborating with peers; 3.B.1 expand and internalize initial vocabulary by learning and using high-frequency words necessary for identifying and describing people, places, and objects; 3.H.3 explain with increasing specificity and detail

Unit 4

At Home in the World

 **GUIDING QUESTION**

How can your location affect
the way you live?

Read More!

Content Library

The West Today

Leveled Library

Jane Eyre
by Charlotte Bronte,
adapted by Jane E. Gerver

Miracle's Boys
by Jacqueline Woodson

The Outsiders
by S.E. Hinton

Internet
InsideNG.com

- Explore our solar system.
- Discover what life is like for astronauts.
- Learn what it's like to live in two cultures.

Focus on Genre

Organization of Ideas

▶ **Comparison and Contrast**

Writers organize texts in a way that will explain facts and ideas
effectively . A writer who wants to show how things are alike and
different uses **comparison-and-contrast** organization.

How It Works

To **compare** things is to show how they
are similar. To **contrast** is to show how
they are different. As you read, look for
signal words that show similarities and
differences.

Words That Signal Similarities	Words That Signal Differences
like	but
both	unlike
also	although
too	different
similarly	in contrast
just as	on the other hand

A Moon and a Planet

Io is a moon that circles the
planet Jupiter. Although Io is a
moon and Earth is a planet, the
two are alike in some ways. For
example, Earth's oceans have
tides. That is, the level of the
ocean water along the shore rises
and falls regularly, pulled by the moon's gravity. Like Earth, Io also
has tides. But unlike Earth's ocean tides, Io's tides are in its solid
surface. Io's solid surface rises and falls, pulled by gravity from the
planet Jupiter and two other moons that orbit Jupiter.

While both Earth and Io have active volcanoes, Io has no water
and gets no rain. Unlike Earth, Io cannot support life as we know it.
In contrast to Io, Earth is a friendly habitat for many kinds of life.

▲ Io (left) has a temperature of
–230°F. Earth's most extreme
recorded low is –129°F.

**Contrast signal words
show how Io and Earth
are different.**

**Comparison signal
words show similarities
between Earth and Io.**

**Signal words help readers see
that the paragraph begins
with a comparison, then
continues with contrasts.**

Academic Vocabulary

• **effectively** (i-**fek**-tiv-lē) *adverb*
  Something that is done
  effectively is done in a way that
  works or gets results.

Practice Together

Read the following passage aloud with your class. As you read, listen for words that help signal comparisons and contrasts. What things are alike and what things are different?

Kinds of Galaxies

All galaxies are clusters of gases and millions of stars. Earth and its star, the Sun, are part of the Milky Way galaxy. Similar to many galaxies, the Milky Way is a spiral galaxy, which looks like a flat pinwheel of light. In contrast, some other galaxies are elliptical, looking almost like footballs. If a galaxy is neither spiral nor elliptical, it is called irregular.

▲ Milky Way's spiral arms hold billions of stars, just as other spiral galaxies do.

Try It!

Read the following passage. Which things are alike and which are different? How do you know?

Star Light, Star Bright

Stars come in many different sizes and colors. The sun's radius, or the distance from its center to its surface, is about 432,000 miles. In contrast, some stars have a radius that is about fifteen times that distance. Unlike those stars, a neutron star may have a radius of only about 6 miles.

Color is also a measure used for stars. Color indicates temperature. Green and blue stars are the hottest. Red stars, on the other hand, are very old and among the coolest. Betelguese and Antares are both red stars. Our sun is a yellow star. It has a temperature in between those of the blue and the red stars.

Focus on Vocabulary

ELPS: 1.H develop and expand repertoire of learning strategies; 4.F.3 use visual and contextual support to develop vocabulary needed to comprehend increasingly challenging language

Use Context Clues

When you read, you may come across words you don't know. In many cases, the meaning of an unknown word will become **obvious** if you use **context clues** to figure it out. Common types of context clues include definition, restatement, and examples. Signal words can help you find the clues.

Type of Clue	How It Works	Signal Words	Example Sentences
Definition or Restatement	The context tells the definition of the word or restates the meaning using other words.	*called, which is, or, in other words*	The rocket that lifts the shuttle toward space is *called* a **booster** rocket. The **circumference** of, *or* distance around, Earth is about 25,000 miles.
Examples	The unknown word may be listed as an example of something familiar. Or, you may find familiar examples of the unknown word.	*for example, like, such as, including*	Why are rocks interesting? Gases *such as* **hydrogen** are plentiful in the universe. Oxygen and iron are *examples* of chemical **elements** found in the universe.

How the Strategy Works

Use **context clues** to help make the meaning of new words **obvious**.

1. Use the topic of your reading to narrow down possible meanings for the unfamiliar word.
2. Reread the sentence where the word appears. Look for signal words or other patterns of language that point to a definition, a restatement, or an example.
3. Use the sentences around the word to help figure out its meaning.

Use the strategy to figure out the meaning of *moderate*.

> Most life on Earth needs a <u>moderate</u> climate, with temperatures neither too hot nor too cold. These middle temperatures, from around 30 degrees Fahrenheit to about 90 degrees, support life for many species of plants and animals.

Strategy in Action

" This paragraph describes the weather as 'neither too hot nor too cold.' It restates this as 'middle temperatures.' "

☑ **REMEMBER** You can use the context of a passage to figure out the meanings of new or unfamiliar words.

Academic Vocabulary
- **obvious** (ob-vē-us) *adjective*
  Something that is **obvious** is easily seen or understood.

Practice Together

Read the passage aloud with your class. Listen for context clues to help you figure out the meaning of each underlined word. How did context clues help?

Home, Sweet Home

The place where an animal lives, called its <u>habitat</u>, must supply the animal with what it needs to survive. Each habitat must provide <u>necessities</u> such as food, water, and shelter.

▲ Ants make complex tunnels part of their home.

One reason there are so many forms of life on Earth is that it offers so many different habitats. Some habitats are <u>harsh</u>, with difficult living conditions. For example, some animals can live in places with very little water. Others can live at ocean depths where the water pressure would crush even a submarine.

Many living beings <u>adapt</u>, or change and adjust, to the conditions around them. Some plants and animals live in places where most other living beings would not survive. These unusual habitats, or <u>niches</u>, allow creatures to survive in a sometimes dangerous world.

Try It!

Read the following passage. What do the underlined words mean? How do you know?

A Simple Life?

My visit to my grandfather's farm last summer surprised me. I had the idea, or <u>impression</u>, that Granddad led a quiet, simple life in the open air. I soon discovered that life on the farm was not so simple.

I usually think of noisy machinery as something you'd find mostly in the city, but Granddad had a different tool, or <u>implement</u>, for almost everything he did on the farm. He used <u>devices</u> such as an electric saw for cutting wood and a gas-powered machine for digging fence post holes. I expected quiet on a farm, but there was plenty of noise with all the machines.

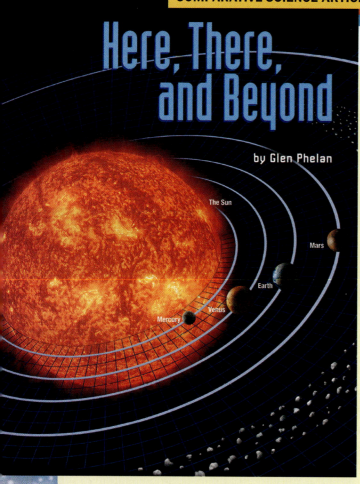

Here, There, and Beyond

by Glen Phelan

The Sun
Mars
Earth
Venus
Mercury

Build Background

Connect

KWL Chart With a partner, create a KWL Chart for the planets in our solar system.

KWL Chart

WHAT DO I KNOW?	WHAT DO I WANT TO LEARN?	WHAT DID I LEARN?
The planets in our solar system move around the sun.	Which planet is the biggest?	

The Solar System

Earth is just one of many objects in our solar system. What else is out there? In addition to eight planets, there are asteroids, comets, and hundreds of moons.

Digital Library

InsideNG.com
◯ View the video.

◀ There are eight planets in our solar system.

Language & Grammar

ELPS: 2.C.1 learn new language structures heard during classroom instruction and interactions; 2.F.1 listen to and derive meaning from a variety of media to build and reinforce concept attainment; 2.F.2 listen to and derive meaning from a variety of media to build and reinforce language attainment; 2.G.2 understand the general meaning of spoken language regarding familiar to unfamiliar language

1 TRY OUT LANGUAGE
2 LEARN GRAMMAR
3 APPLY ON YOUR OWN

Make Comparisons

CD

Study the photographs and listen to the conversation.
Listen for a comparison. When people compare things,
they tell how they are alike and how they are different.

PICTURE PROMPT

No Place Like Home

Jen: My family has lived in both a big city and a suburb.

Marcus: What were your homes like?

Jen: Well, our home in the suburb was a two-story house.
It had a backyard and lots of trees.

Marcus: So you had a lot of space in the suburb.

Jen: Yes. Our home in the city was an apartment.
The apartment was smaller than the house. It didn't
have a backyard, but there were many parks nearby.

Marcus: So you had less space in the city, but I bet
it was more interesting.

Use Nouns in the Subject and Predicate

A complete sentence has two parts: the **subject** and the **predicate** . The subject tells whom or what the sentence is about. The predicate often tells what the subject does.

> EXAMPLE   **People** **choose different places to live** .

- Nouns can be the **subject** of a sentence.

> EXAMPLE   **People** choose different places to live.
> subject

- Nouns can also be the **object** of an action **verb**. To find the object, turn the verb into a question like: "Choose what?" Your answer is the object.

> EXAMPLE   People **choose** different **places** to live.
> verb   object

- Many English sentences follow this pattern: subject ➔ verb ➔ object

> EXAMPLES   **People choose** different **places** to live.
> subject   verb   object

Practice Together

Say each sentence and tell the job of the <u>noun</u>. Is it a subject or an object noun?

1. The <u>man</u> lives in a desert climate.
2. The hot sun warms his <u>home</u> fast.
3. The heat creates a <u>challenge</u>.
4. <u>People</u> wear clothes to protect them from the sun.

Try It!

Say each sentence. Write the job of the <u>noun</u> on a card. Is it a subject or an object noun?

5. Some <u>astronauts</u> live on a space station.
6. They take <u>oxygen</u> with them to breathe.
7. Outer <u>space</u> does not support <u>life</u>.
8. Only <u>Earth</u> supports life.

▲ The man covers his head to protect it from the heat.

Compare Places to Live

MAKE COMPARISONS

What if you could choose any place in the world or universe as your home? What place would you choose? How does your choice compare to those of your classmates?

With a partner, make a list of places where people could live. Take a survey. Ask five other students which place they would choose to live. Make sure they understand the general meaning of your question. List their responses in a chart like this one. Then compare the results.

Place	Student 1	Student 2	Student 3	Student 4	Student 5
1. a big city					
2. a suburb					
3. a small town					
4. near an ocean					
5. near the mountains					
6. in a desert					
7. in a space station					
8.					
9.					
10.					

Share the results of your survey with another group. Make comparisons between your survey results and those of another pair of students.

HOW TO MAKE COMPARISONS

1. Tell how things are alike. Use words like *all*, *both*, and *too*.
2. Tell how things are different. Use words like *only* and *but*.

> Both Ana and Jen want to live in a big city, but Katrina prefers a small town.

> Tony prefers a small town, too. Only Jeff wants to live in a space station.

USE NOUNS IN THE SUBJECT AND PREDICATE

When you make comparisons, use **nouns** in the subjects and predicates of your sentences to tell how people, places, and things are alike or different.

In the Subject: Most **people** chose the big city as their favorite place to live.

In the Predicate: Both Rachel and Rosa chose the **mountains** as their favorite place to live.

Prepare to Read

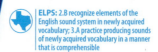 **ELPS:** 2.B recognize elements of the English sound system in newly acquired vocabulary; 3.A practice producing sounds of newly acquired vocabulary in a manner that is comprehensible

Learn Key Vocabulary

Rate and Study the Words Rate how well you know each word. Then:

1. Pronounce the word. Say it aloud several times. Spell it.
2. Study the example.
3. Tell more about the word.
4. Practice it. Make the word your own.

Key Words

atmosphere (at-mu-sfir)
noun ▶ page 257

The **atmosphere** is the air that surrounds the Earth. A spaceship can travel outside of Earth's **atmosphere**, but an airplane cannot.

energy (en-ur-jē) *noun*
▶ page 257

Energy is natural power that is used to make things work. We can turn the **energy** of the wind into electricity. *Synonyms:* **force, power**

feature (fē-chur) *noun*
▶ page 257

Features of something are its parts or details. Some of the **features** of Earth's surface include mountains, lakes, and trees.

measurement (mezh-ur-ment) *noun* ▶ page 262

A **measurement** is the size or quantity of something. I took **measurements** of the rock to find out how long it is.

rotation (rō-tā-shun) *noun*
▶ page 256

Rotation is the spinning of an object, such as a planet. Earth's **rotation** is what gives us night and day. *Related Word:* **rotate**

solar system (sō-lur sis-tem) *noun* ▶ page 256

Our **solar system** is made up of the sun and the objects that move around it. Earth's **solar system** includes eight planets.

solid (sah-led) *adjective*
▶ page 256

Something that is **solid** is hard or firm. Rocks are **solid** all the way through. *Antonym:* **soft**

surface (sur-fes) *noun*
▶ page 256

A **surface** is the outside or top layer of an object. The new road has a smoother **surface** than the old road.

Practice the Words Make a Study Card for each Key Word. Then compare your cards with a partner's.

---

feature

What it means: the details of something

Example: My eyes are my best feature.

Not an example: I am interested in hockey.

Study Card

Reading Strategy: Make Connections

When you read, make connections to things you already know about the subject. This will help you understand and remember new ideas and information.

HOW TO MAKE TEXT-TO-WORLD CONNECTIONS

1. Look at the title of the selection. Use a Connections Chart to record what you already know.
2. As you read, look for important facts and ideas. Explain the connections between the text and your prior knowledge.
3. After reading, think about the connections you made. How did they affect your reading?

Strategy in Action

Here's how one student made text-to-world connections.

Look Into the Text

You can think of Earth's neighbors as all the objects in our solar system. These objects include planets. A planet is a large object that moves around a star.

There are eight planets in our solar system. Scientists put these planets into groups. The four planets closest to the sun make up one group.

From Text	What I Know	Text-To-World Connections
There are eight planets in our solar system.	There are 8 planets, including Earth. I also know Mars, Venus, and Mercury.	I saw on TV that Pluto is no longer a planet. So the author says 8, not 9. I can name some planets. After all, I live on one!

Connections Chart

Practice Together

Reread the passage. Follow the steps in the How-To box to add on to a Connections Chart like the one shown.

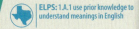
Comparative Science Article

A science article is expository nonfiction that gives information about the natural world.

Science writers often **compare** and **contrast** things they write about to help readers understand how things in the natural world are similar or different.

> . . . In addition, Earth and Mars spin at about the same rate—one rotation every twenty-four hours—but Mercury and Venus both take months to rotate just once.

Words such as *same* and *both* signal a similarity. The word *but* signals a difference.

Your Job as a Reader

Reading Strategy: Make Connections

As you read, think about what you already know about the subject. Make connections to important facts and ideas in the text. Note and explain each connection on your Connections Chart.

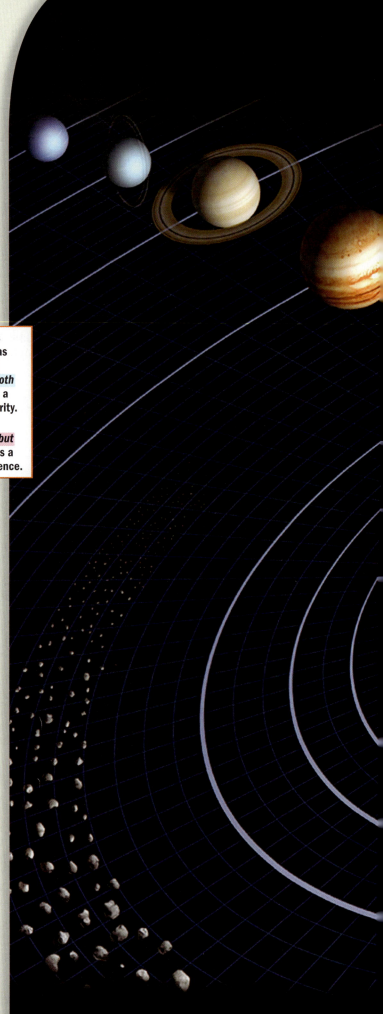

Here, There, and Beyond

by Glen Phelan

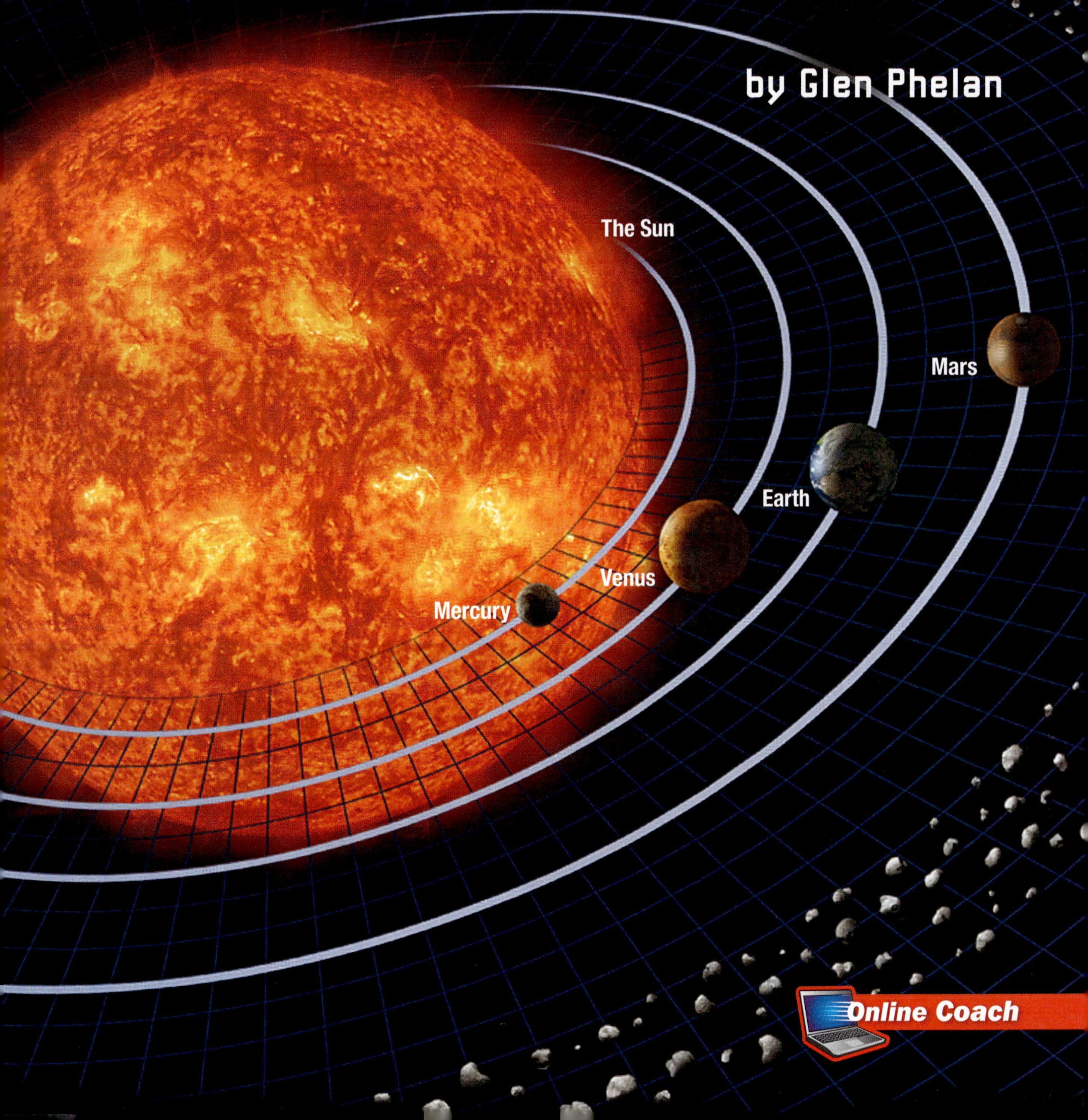

The Sun

Mercury

Venus

Earth

Mars

You probably know your neighborhood well. You know where your school is. You know how to get to the park. You know some nearby stores.

But how well do you know Earth's neighborhood? You can think of Earth's neighbors as all the objects in our <mark>solar system</mark>. These objects include planets. A planet is a large object that moves around a star.

There are eight planets in our solar system. Scientists put these planets into groups. The four planets closest to the sun make up one group.

Now do a shared reading of "Planets Closest to Our Sun"

▲ The Earth

Planets Closest to Our Sun

The four planets closest to the sun are Mercury, Venus, Earth, and Mars. These planets have a lot in common. They are mostly made up of rock and metal, so they all have hard, uneven <mark>surfaces</mark>.

Because of **their content**, the planets closest to the sun have high densities. This means that these planets are made up of condensed, or tightly packed, materials. They also share the qualities of having slow <mark>rotation</mark> and <mark>solid</mark> surfaces.

The rocky planets closest to the sun are also alike in other ways. They are small compared to most of the other planets in our solar system. These planets also do not have many moons, or objects that rotate, or move, around a planet.

▲ The rocky surface of Mars

Key Vocabulary

  solar system *n.*, the sun and the objects that move around it

  surface *n.*, the outside, or top layer, of an object

  rotation *n.*, the movement of one object around another object

  solid *adj.*, hard or firm

In Other Words

  their content what they have inside

On the other hand, each planet is also different from the others in its group. For example, each of the four rocky planets has a different kind of **atmosphere**. An atmosphere is a blanket of gas that covers a planet.

Different gases trap different amounts of heat from the sun, which means that each planet has a different temperature. For example, Venus is the hottest planet because it has a thick and heavy atmosphere covered with clouds. The clouds let in **energy** from the sun, and this makes Venus's surface temperature hotter than most ovens!

The rocky planets have many other differences. They are each different sizes, and they also have different **features** on their surfaces. In addition, Earth and Mars

spin at about the same **rate**—one rotation every twenty-four hours—but Mercury and Venus both take months to rotate just once.

▲ A detailed view of Venus's cloudy atmosphere

THE PLANETS **CLOSEST** TO THE SUN

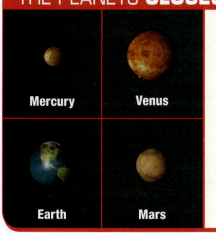

Mercury

Venus

Earth

Mars

How Are They Similar?

- **Surface** They are rocky and solid.
- **Rings** They do not have planetary rings.
- **Moons** They have few or no moons.
- **Size** They are small compared to other planets—less than 8,000 miles in **diameter**. Even so, Earth is more than 2.5 times bigger than Mercury!

How Are They Different?

- **Planet Life** Earth is the only planet known to have living things.
- **Temperatures** In this group, Venus is the hottest planet (average temperature: 867° F) while Mars is the coldest planet (average temperature: -85° F).
- **Locations** Mercury is closest to the sun, while Mars is farthest from the sun.

Key Vocabulary

atmosphere *n.*, air that surrounds a planet

energy *n.*, a source of usable power

feature *n.*, parts or details

In Other Words

rate time

diameter distance from one end of the planet to another through the center

Before You Move On

1. **Evidence and Conclusions** Give three details to support this conclusion: The planets closest to the sun have many similarities.
2. **Explain** How is Venus different from the other planets?
3. **Compare and Contrast** How does the rotation of the Earth compare to that of Mars and Mercury?

Planets Farthest from Our Sun

The next four planets are Jupiter, Saturn, Uranus, and Neptune. These planets are huge. Unlike the planets close to the sun, these planets are not **mainly composed** of rock or other solid **matter**. Their atmospheres are mostly made of gases. So, many scientists call these planets "gas giants."

Gas giants have many moons and rings. Their rings are made of dust and rocks. Some gas giants have rings that are hard to see, while others, such as Saturn, have rings that are easy to see from Earth.

Although the gas giants are alike in many ways, each planet is also different. Each gas giant has different features. Some of the gas giants have storms on their surface. For example, the orange-red oval on Jupiter is a storm. This storm has lasted more than 300 years.

Gas giants can also move through space in different ways. For example, Uranus spins differently than other planets. It spins on its side, moving like a rolling ball instead of a spinning top.

THE PLANETS **FARTHEST** FROM THE SUN

Jupiter

Saturn

Uranus

Neptune

How Are They Similar?

- **Rings** They are surrounded by rings.
- **Atmosphere** They have thick atmospheres made mostly of gases.
- **Movement** They travel around the sun in almost circular paths.
- **Moons** They have many moons.
- **Size** They are large compared to other planets—up to 88,900 miles in diameter.

How Are They Different?

- **Rings** Saturn's rings are the easiest to see from Earth.
- **Storms** Jupiter and Saturn have more storms than Uranus and Neptune.
- **Colors** Jupiter has shades of white, orange, brown, and red while Neptune is blue in color.
- **Temperatures** In this group, Neptune is the coldest planet (average temperature: -328° F) while Jupiter is the warmest planet (average temperature: -166° F).
- **Size** Jupiter is so large that all of the other planets could fit inside of it.

In Other Words
mainly composed made
matter materials

Science Background
Storms on planets are similar to hurricanes, or violent storms, on Earth. Jupiter's storms are twice as big as Earth's storms, and they have strong winds and heavy rain that can last for days.

Saturn's rings

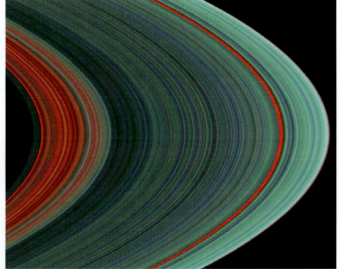

Uranus's rings

The storms of Saturn

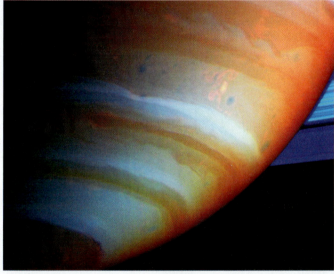

Jupiter's rising storm

▲ Each gas giant has rings, but only some gas giants have storms on their surfaces.

Before You Move On

1. **Cause and Effect** Why do scientists call Jupiter, Saturn, Uranus, and Neptune "gas giants"?

2. **Compare** How are the gas giants similar?

3. **Contrast** What are some of the ways that the gas giants differ from the planets closest to the sun?

Asteroids and Meteoroids

Earth has other neighbors in our solar system.

Asteroids are **chunks** of rock and metal. Like planets, asteroids move around our sun, and most are found between Mars and Jupiter. Some asteroids are as small as a house while others are as big as a city. One asteroid is the size of Texas!

Meteoroids are chunks of **debris** in space. They are smaller than asteroids, and some meteoroids are even smaller than an ant. Still, others are as big as a bus. Sometimes a meteoroid falls towards a planet. A meteoroid that hits a planet is called a meteorite.

▲ This large asteroid travels around the sun.

This crater, or large hole, in Arizona was created by a meteorite. ▶

In Other Words
chunks big pieces
debris pieces of rock

Icy Objects — Dwarf Planets and Comets

Pluto used to be considered the ninth planet in our solar system—but this has changed. Scientists have decided that Pluto is not a planet because it is too small. Pluto is now called a dwarf planet.

Pluto is not rocky, like Earth is, and it is not made of gas like Saturn. Pluto has a small, rocky center that is covered with ice. It is like a giant snowball in space. Pluto is farther from the sun than Neptune. It takes Pluto more than 248 years to travel once around the sun.

Pluto is not the only icy object that moves around the sun. Comets do, too. Comets are large chunks of ice, gas, dust, and rock.

Comets are found far from the sun most of the time. When a comet gets close to the sun, the ice on its surface becomes gas. The gas forms an atmosphere, called a coma, around the comet. Some of the gas is pushed from the comet into space, and this gas forms the tail of the comet.

▲ This image shows Pluto and its moons—Charon, Nix, and Hydra.

In Other Words
used to be considered was

Science Background
To be a planet, an object must: orbit around the sun, be large enough to have a round shape, and have an orbit which is free of rocky or icy objects. Pluto is a **dwarf planet** and not a planet, because it travels through an area called the Kuiper Belt, which is full of small icy objects.

Human and Nonhuman Observers

How do we know about objects in our solar system? Scientists use special tools to study them. One tool is the telescope. A telescope makes faraway objects look closer. Telescopes show detailed images of planets and other objects from space. Most telescopes are on Earth, however, some telescopes are in space. Space telescopes are large and can **reveal** important discoveries, such as **the collapse of a comet**.

Spacecraft also help scientists learn about our solar system. Some spacecraft allow scientists to fly into space. These spacecraft let people study the solar system from space. Other spacecraft do not have people on board. They are called probes. Probes take pictures, make **measurements**, and then send the information back to Earth. Spacecraft help us learn more about our neighbors in space. ❖

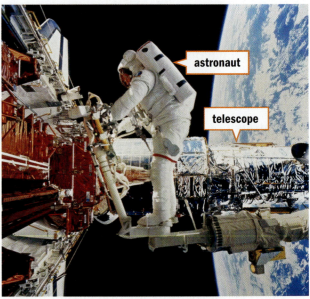

▲ An astronaut checks a telescope in space.

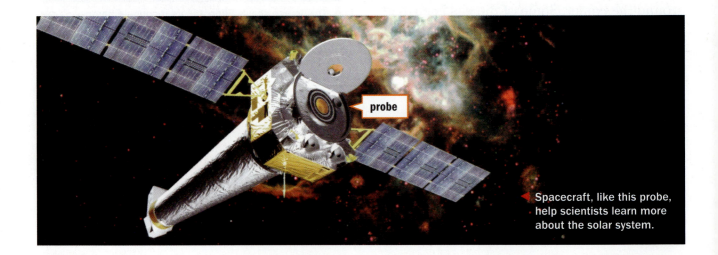

◀ Spacecraft, like this probe, help scientists learn more about the solar system.

Key Vocabulary
measurement *n.*, the size or quantity of something

In Other Words
reveal show
the collapse of a comet when a comet falls apart
Spacecraft Vehicles designed to travel in space

Before You Move On

1. **Contrast** How is Pluto different from both the Earth and Saturn?
2. **Summary** What are the main characteristics of asteroids?
3. **Conclusions** Why are telescopes and spacecraft important scientific tools?

Why the Sun and the Moon Live in the Sky

an adaptation of a Nigerian myth

Long before time began,

the Sun and the Moon met and got married. They created a home on Land and started their life together. They wanted to tell someone of their happiness, so they invited their friend the Ocean to visit.

"You are very kind to invite me," said the Ocean. "Unfortunately, I cannot accept your invitation."

"Oh dear!" cried the Moon. "You do not like us anymore."

The Ocean replied, "Of course I do. I just don't think I will fit inside your house."

"Aha!" blazed the Sun angrily. "You don't think our home is **fancy enough**."

"I do!" the Ocean insisted. "I'm sure it's **brilliant**, but—."

"Then come in," said the Moon and she opened the doors. The house was huge and stretched as far as the eye could see. The Ocean shyly **inched across the threshold**.

"Come on in, there's lots of space," laughed the Sun. So the Ocean began to flow in more rapidly.

Soon the entire floor was flooded in water. "See? There was nothing to worry about," said the Moon.

"Actually, I have only just begun to enter," said the Ocean and **with that**, a large wave rushed across the room and splashed against the walls. The Sun and the Moon rose higher and higher to avoid getting wet. Soon the

In Other Words
fancy enough nice
brilliant beautiful
**inched across the
   threshold** entered the house
with that after the Ocean spoke

fish and the other creatures of the sea began to swim around in the house. "I'm so sorry," said the Ocean but the Sun said, "**Think nothing of it**, there is room for all."

As the Ocean continued to pour into the house, the Sun and Moon were forced to rise higher and higher until at last they were up on the roof. "Tell me, Ocean," the Sun called down, "Are you almost in?"

"I am only halfway in," roared the Ocean. "You are so kind to invite me." The Sun and the Moon knew it would be impolite to take back their invitation so they just rose higher into the sky. Their lovely home floated upside down in the water below.

And that is why the Sun and the Moon **took up permanent residence** in the Sky and found harmony with the Land and the Ocean. To this day, they still watch the Earth and the Ocean with interest, but they have never again touched the ground.

Myths and Storytelling

A myth is a traditional story. Myths usually explain people's beliefs about why something in nature happens. These stories sometimes involve gods, heroes, or animals, and often focus on a life lesson. Myths are sources of how different cultures view the world.

Storytellers and those who pass along myths are known as the keepers of the people's wisdom and beliefs. Nigerian storytelling, for example, requires so much skill that it is considered a form of art. Traditionally, Nigerian storytellers have dramatically entertained their audiences. These storytellers have also tried to teach young people about important customs in Nigerian culture.

In Other Words
Think nothing of it Don't worry
took up permanent residence lived forever

Before You Move On
1. **Perspectives** Why doesn't the Ocean want to visit the Sun's and the Moon's house? How is this different from what the Sun thinks?
2. **Genre** What are some clues that show this selection is a myth?

Connect Reading and Writing

Vocabulary
atmosphere
energy
features
measurement
rotations
solar system
solid
surface

CRITICAL THINKING

1. SUM IT UP Use the headings and the main ideas of the selection to make an outline about our **solar system**.

> I. Planets Closest to Our Sun:
>   A. Mercury, Venus, Earth, Mars
>   B. They are made of rock and metal.
>   C. They have high density, slow rotation, and no rings.

2. Synthesize Complete the KWL Chart you began before reading the selection. Tell what you learned about **solid** planets and gaseous planets.

3. Compare How do the **features** of asteroids and meteoroids compare with planets?

4. Interpret How do the selection and the myth express the idea of being at home in the world?

READING FLUENCY

Phrasing Read the passage on page 643 to a partner. Assess your fluency.

1. I read
   a. great   **b.** OK   **c.** not very well

2. What I did best in my reading was _____.

READING STRATEGY

> **Make Connections**
> How did text-to-world connections help you understand the selection? Tell a partner.

VOCABULARY REVIEW

Oral Review Read the paragraph aloud. Add the vocabulary words.

> Beyond the _____ that surrounds Earth, there are seven other planets. All planets in our _____ revolve, or make _____ around the sun. All the planets get _____ from the sun. The _____ of planets differ in some ways. For example, the _____ of Mars is _____ and rocky, but Saturn is gaseous. There are also differences in size, or _____.

Written Review Imagine that your mission is to describe one of the planets as you explore its **surface** from a spacecraft. Use five vocabulary words.

 **WRITE ABOUT THE** (GUIDING QUESTION)

Explore Being at Home in the World
How do planets in the **solar system** compare to communities on Earth? Reread the selection to find **features** that support your ideas.

Connect Across the Curriculum

 ELPS: 2.C.4 learn academic vocabulary heard during classroom instruction and interactions; 2.G.9 understand the important details of spoken language regarding familiar to unfamiliar context

Literary Analysis

Analyze Text Structure: Compare and Contrast

> **Academic Vocabulary**
> • **compare** (**kum**-pair) *verb*
>   When you **compare**, you look closely at how things are alike or different.

How Is Nonfiction Organized? One way that writers organize information is by **comparing** and contrasting ideas.

These planets have a lot in common. They are mostly made up of rock and metal, so they all have hard, uneven surfaces.	This is a comparison. It tells about something that is alike on the planets— the surface. *Common* and *all* are key words.
On the other hand, each planet is also different from the others in its group. For example, each of the four rocky planets has a different kind of atmosphere.	This is a contrast. It tells about something that is different on the planets— the atmosphere. *On the other hand* and *different* are key words.

Practice Together

Use a Comparison Chart You can use a chart to help you **compare** and contrast information. Look back at the selection. Find two more comparisons and contrasts for the four planets closest to the sun. Remember to look for clue words.

The Four Planets Closest to the Sun

How They Are Alike	Signal Words from Text	How They Are Different	Signal Words from Text
have similar surfaces	"all have hard and uneven surfaces"	have different atmospheres	"different kind of atmosphere"

Try It!

Find Comparisons and Contrasts Review the text for the remaining four planets in "Here, There, and Beyond." Work with a partner to make a chart like the one above for the four planets farthest from the sun. Listen while another group reads their chart aloud to you. Do you agree?

ELPS: 2.C.4 learn academic vocabulary heard during classroom instruction and interactions

Vocabulary Study

Use Clues of Definition, Example, and Restatement

Academic Vocabulary
- **definition** (de-fu-**ni**-shun) *noun*
  The meaning of a word is its **definition**.

You can use context clues to figure out the meaning of a word or idea.

Type of Clue	Example
Definition clues make clear that a word or term is being explained.	The gas forms an atmosphere, called a coma, around the comet.
Example shows a case that makes the word or idea clear.	For example, Uranus spins differently from other planets because it spins on its side.
Restatement puts the idea another way so the reader understands.	It moves like a rolling ball instead of a spinning top.

Find Clues Use context clues to explain the underlined words.

These planets also do not have many moons or objects that <u>rotate</u>, or move, around a planet. . . . Different gases trap different amounts of heat from the sun, which means that each planet has a different <u>temperature</u>. For example, Venus is the hottest planet because it has a thick and heavy <u>atmosphere</u> covered with clouds.

ELPS: 2.C.4 learn academic vocabulary heard during classroom instruction and interactions

Media/Speaking

Choose Media Support

MEDIA & TECHNOLOGY

Academic Vocabulary
- **relate** (ri-**lāt**) *verb*
  When you **relate** things, you show how they are connected.

How do you select the appropriate media for a presentation? It depends on the purpose and the audience.

1 **Learn About Media** What is the purpose of your presentation? If it's to inform, you may want to use print media. If it's to entertain, nonprint media may add interest. Be sure your media choices are:

- **Accurate and Reliable** Check the source, especially when using the Internet. Who created the site? Can it be trusted? Check facts against a second source, such as an encyclopedia. Evaluate how the source creates a point of view, and the impact it will have on the audience.

- **Appropriate** Use only media that **relate** to the topic. Images and sounds can influence a presentation's message. Make sure the media used supports the purpose and/or position of the presentation.

- **Credited** Identify each reference. If it's music, identify the composer and performer. If it's an Internet image, provide the Web site address.

2 **Choose Media** What media would support a presentation on the planets? Share and explain your choices to the class.

ELPS: 2.C.4 learn academic vocabulary heard during classroom instruction and interactions; 5.G.1 narrate with increasing specificity and detail to fulfill content area writing needs

Literary Analysis

Analyze Myths

> **Academic Vocabulary**
> • **origin** (or-u-jin) *noun*
>   The **origin** of something is its source or beginning.

Learn About Myths Myths are one of the oldest forms of fiction. These stories began as tales told by people to explain the world around them. The **origins** of myths are usually unknown since the stories were told and retold over time, before they were written down. Some features of myths are:

• **Gods, goddesses, and heroes** Many myths focus on events between these figures and ordinary humans.

• **Causes of events** Most myths were created to explain why things happen. Other myths teach life lessons, such as the value of keeping promises.

• **Nonhuman things acting in human ways** Animals, monsters, and even natural features such as oceans and rocks may be personified, or given human qualities.

• **Values of society** Myths usually reflect the values and beliefs of a particular culture, such as strength in battle, bravery, or cleverness.

Practice Together

Create a Myth In "Why the Sun and the Moon Live in the Sky," the sun, moon, and ocean are given human qualities. Reread "Here, There, and Beyond." Choose one planet and write a myth about how it came to be or why it has a certain characteristic. For example, you could write a narrative about how Saturn got its rings. Start the story with your class.

> A long time ago before the Earth began, Saturn lived next to Jupiter. One day Jupiter and Saturn bumped into each other. "Saturn," Jupiter said, "why must you live so close to me? There is plenty of room in the sky."

▲ In myths, nonhuman objects often have the ability to speak.

Try It!

Present Your Myth Work with a partner to finish the myth. Then present your myth to the class. Compare your explanation for Saturn's rings with those of your classmates.

Make Comparisons

Group Share Work with a small group. Take turns making comparisons between the planets in our solar system. Use nouns in the subjects and predicates of your sentences.

> Venus is closer to the Sun than Saturn.

> Saturn and Neptune are both gas giants.

ELPS: 5.E employ increasingly complex grammatical structures in content area writing

Write About Astronomy

Study the Models When you write, you need to use naming words correctly in the different parts of your sentences. The correct use of words makes your writing clear and precise.

NOT OK

> My classmates and me visited an observatory. Us used a giant telescope to look at the stars and planets. Some of my classmates saw detailed images of the moon's surface. Them also saw a comet streaking through the sky. This trip inspired we to learn more about the solar system. They also inspired I to become an astronomer.

This writer uses naming words incorrectly so the ideas are confusing.

OK

> My classmates and I visited an observatory. We used a giant telescope to look at the stars and planets. Some of my classmates saw detailed images of the moon's surface. They also saw a comet streaking through the sky. This trip inspired us to learn more about the solar system. It also inspired me to become an astronomer.

This writer uses naming words correctly. The ideas are clear.

Add Sentences Add two sentences to the OK model above. Be sure to use naming words correctly.

✎ **WRITE ON YOUR OWN** Write about a time you observed the sky at night. What did you see? Use naming words correctly.

Subject Pronouns	I	you	he	she	it	we	you	they
Object Pronouns	me	you	him	her	it	us	you	them

REMEMBER

- A noun or pronoun used as a **subject** tells whom or what the sentence is about.
- A noun or pronoun used as an **object** tells who or what receives the action of the sentence.

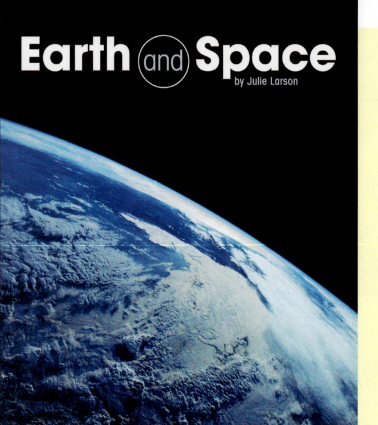

Earth (and) Space
by Julie Larson

Build Background

Connect

Question Brainstorm What questions do you have about what it's like to live in space? With a group, list questions you have about each category.

Food in Space Do astronauts have a stove or a refrigerator in space?	**Sleep in Space**
Gravity in Space	**Breathing in Space**

Living in Space

What is it like to live far from Earth? Astronauts get to experience life in space.

Digital Library InsideNG.com
↗ View the video.

▲ Working in space (left) is like and unlike working on Earth.

Language & Grammar

ELPS: 2.I.4 demonstrate listening comprehension of complex spoken English by collaborating with peers; 3.H.3 explain with increasing specificity and detail

1 TRY OUT LANGUAGE
2 LEARN GRAMMAR
3 APPLY ON YOUR OWN

Define and Explain

CD

Study the photo and listen to the explanation about gravity. Listen again and chime in.

RAP

▼ Dr. Mae Jemison floating in Spacelab

A Matter of Gravity

Mass is the measure of matter.
Matter
Is anything you can touch.
The more matter there is
The more mass there is.
That's why matter matters so much.

Gravity is a force.
Its force
Pulls masses of matter together.
The bigger the mass
The stronger the pull.
And the force will continue forever.

Distance is a factor.
It affects gravitational rules.
The longer the distance
Between two masses
The weaker is gravity's pull.

In the universe, gravity rules!
It holds the planets in place
As they orbit the stars
And everything, everything, everything
Continues to travel through space.

Gravity binds us to Earth,
And the Earth to the Sun's galaxy.
As we walk beneath stars,
When we rocket to Mars,
Without gravity, where would we be?

▲ Any ship in orbit around the Earth is actually falling slowly toward Earth. It never gets far enough away from Earth to escape Earth's gravitational pull. The astronauts inside the ship are falling at the same speed, so they feel weightless. Their falling motion in orbit creates this effect. It is the same sensation you would have in a free-falling elevator ride.

Use Prepositions

Prepositions are words that help add details to sentences. They can show location, direction, time, and origin.

Meaning	Prepositions
Direction	across, down, into, through, to, up
Location	above, at, behind, below, beside, in, in back of, in front of, inside, next to, on, on top of, over, under
Origin	from
Time	after, at, before, during, in, until

- Use a preposition of **location** to tell where someone or something is.

    EXAMPLES   The astronaut floated **beside** the space shuttle. He checked the heat tiles **under** its wing.

- Use a preposition of **direction** to tell where someone is going.

    EXAMPLES   The astronaut floated **across** the cabin **to** the computer.

- Use a preposition of **time** to tell when something happens.

    EXAMPLE   **After** breakfast, the astronaut exercised.

- Use a preposition of **origin** to tell where someone or something is from.

    EXAMPLE   The astronaut received an e-mail **from** her family.

Practice Together

Say each sentence with the correct preposition.

1. A lack of gravity allows objects to float (in/under) space.
2. If objects are not tied down, they can float (inside/to) the ceiling.
3. (After/At) eating, an astronaut must secure food packets.
4. Crumbs (from/behind) floating food can damage equipment.

Try It!

Read each sentence. Write the correct preposition on a card. Then say the sentence with the correct preposition.

5. The rocket blasted (into/under) space.
6. The astronaut wore her spacesuit (after/during) the flight.
7. The astronaut sat (next to/on top of) the window.
8. The light in the cabin came (beside/from) the sun.

▲ The rocket launched after several delays.

Tell About Your World

DEFINE AND EXPLAIN

Many inventions, such as MP3 players, cell phones, and computers, make our lives easier. It can be hard to remember a time without them.

Work with a small group. Define and explain a gadget or invention you use all the time. Tell why you feel it is important.

First, use a Word Web to collect the important words that go with your invention. Here is a Word Web about a cell phone. Decide which words you may need to define for your group. Use a dictionary if necessary.

Word Web

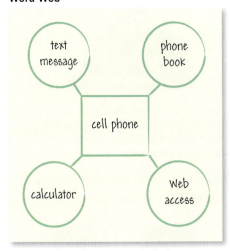

Present your gadget to another group. When you give your explanation, define at least one word. Answer questions they may have. Trade roles.

HOW TO DEFINE AND EXPLAIN

1. **Define:** Tell what the word means.
2. **Explain:** Give details and examples to make the definition more clear.

> A cell phone is a mobile telephone. I can talk to people from wherever I am. This helps me stay in touch with my family and friends.

USE PREPOSITIONS

When you define and explain, you may tell details or give examples to illustrate what you're talking about. Use **prepositions** to tell location, direction, time, and origin.

Location: I can use my laptop **in** the car.
Direction: I scroll **through** the menu for help.
Time: **After** school, I send text messages to my friends.
Origin: I like to receive e-mails **from** my friends.

Prepare to Read

ELPS: 1.A.1 use prior knowledge to understand meanings in English; **1.F** use accessible language and learn essential language in the process; **3.A** practice producing sounds of newly acquired vocabulary in a manner that is comprehensible

Learn Key Vocabulary

Rate and Study the Words Rate how well you know each word. Then:

1. Pronounce the word. Say it aloud several times. Spell it.
2. Study the example.
3. Tell more about the word.
4. Practice it. Make the word your own.

Key Words

astronaut (**as**-tre-not) *noun*
▶ page 278

An **astronaut** is a person trained to travel to space. **Astronauts** need special equipment to travel in space.

element (**e**-lu-munt) *noun*
▶ page 280

An **element** is something that is part of a whole. Copper is one of the **elements** used to make pennies.
Synonym: **part**

essential (i-**sen**-shul)
adjective ▶ page 286

Something that is **essential** is needed for survival. Food and water are **essential** for living beings.
Synonym: **necessary**

experience (ik-**spir**-ē-ens)
verb ▶ page 278

To **experience** something is to go through it yourself. I want to **experience** a ride on a roller coaster.

process (**prah**-ses) *noun*
▶ page 280

A **process** is a series of actions that lead to a result. The **process** of building the house took a year.

routine (rü-**tēn**) *noun*
▶ page 288

A **routine** is a normal series of actions that you repeat. As part of my daily morning **routine**, I brush my teeth.
Synonym: **habit**

similarity (si-mu-**lair**-u-tē)
noun ▶ page 278

A **similarity** is something that makes things alike. The **similarity** between the cars is their color.
Related Word: **similar**
Antonym: **difference**

universe (**yu-nu**-vers) *noun*
▶ page 278

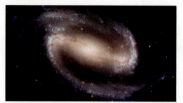

The **universe** is everything that exists, including all of space. Our solar system is just one part of the whole **universe**.
Related Word: **universal**

Practice the Words Make an Expanded Meaning Map for each Key Word. Then compare your maps with a partner.

What the Word Means
actions you repeat

Examples
an evening routine
a cheerleader's routine

Word
routine

What It Is Like
a habit, or something you always do

Expanded Meaning Map

Reading Strategy: Make Connections

Making connections between a new text and something you have already read helps you understand and remember new ideas.

HOW TO MAKE TEXT-TO-TEXT CONNECTIONS

1. As you read, think about what you have read on the Internet or in books, magazines, and other writing.
2. Explain the connections you make on sticky notes.

Strategy in Action

Here's how one student made text-to-text connections.

Look Into the Text

> I read about gravity in my science textbook.

On Earth, we experience a force that pulls us to the ground. That force is called gravity. It is probably not something that you think about too much. Yet without gravity, we would all float away into the atmosphere. Everything from walking, riding a bike, driving a car, or sleeping in a bed is possible because of gravity. Our strong skeletons support our bodies against the pull of Earth's gravity.

> Rockets must overcome gravity to get into space.

Practice Together

Read the passage again and make your own connection from other reading. Follow the steps in the How-To box.

ELPS: 1.A.1 use prior knowledge to understand meanings in English;
4.F.1 use visual and contextual support to read grade-appropriate
content area text; 4.F.2 use visual and contextual support to enhance
and confirm understanding

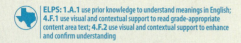

Focus on Genre

Science Article and Journal

When scientists write about topics that may be unfamiliar to the reader, they often compare and contrast the new information with something more familiar.

▲ On Earth, we sometimes sleep in sleeping bags—but they are always on the ground.

> This photo and caption describe the familiar first.

▲ In space, astronauts sleep in sleeping bags, too. The sleeping bags have to be . . . attached to the wall so they don't fly away!

> The second photo and caption contrast a familiar use with a less familiar one.

Your Job as a Reader

Reading Strategy: Make Connections

As you read, make connections to other texts you have read about the topic.

Earth (and) Space

by Julie Larson

"Our endeavors in space are so special and essential," says Peggy Whitson. She and other astronauts have compared firsthand the many differences between living on Earth and living in space.

From the beginning of time, humans have been asking questions about our **universe**. For centuries, scientists have wondered how Earth might compare to other planets. More than fifty years ago in the United States, the National Aeronautics and Space Administration (NASA) began planning the first explorations of space.

Today, **astronauts** from many different countries work together on the International Space Station (ISS). It is a huge research facility in space where astronauts work to improve life on Earth and learn about our solar system.

Life in space is very different from life on Earth. Many activities that we **take for granted** on Earth, including eating, sleeping, and even breathing, work differently in space. Some NASA astronauts have written journal entries for their families and friends back home about their life in space. These true **accounts** describe what astronauts **experience** in space.

Compare life in space and on Earth as you get facts and read journal entries from astronauts. You might even discover some **similarities**.

Key Vocabulary
universe *n.*, the world
astronaut *n.*, a person who travels to space
experience *v.*, to live through an event
similarity *n.*, way in which things are alike

In Other Words
take for granted don't think about
accounts stories

On **Earth** and In **Space**

How Strong is the Gravity?

On Earth, we experience a force that pulls us to the ground. That force is called gravity. It is probably not something that you think about too much. Yet without gravity, we would all float away into the atmosphere. Everything from walking, riding a bike, driving a car, or sleeping in a bed is possible because of gravity. Our strong skeletons support our bodies against the pull of Earth's gravity.

In space, the force of gravity is so weak that a feeling of **weightlessness** results. Astronauts use the word *microgravity* to describe this lack of gravity in space. Here's how one NASA astronaut **recounts** the experience.

▶ From the Journal of **Ed Lu**

"You fly everywhere. You don't walk. *That* is a lot of fun! But we do spend a lot of time exercising since microgravity has eliminated the need for crew members to walk. Our muscles and bones would **atrophy** during a six month **tour of duty** because of lack of use. While I am doing all of this exercising, I enjoy listening to music from the space station's large CD collection."

Many different things happen to the human body while in space because of microgravity. Blood shifts from the lower body up to the top. Because of this, astronauts may appear to have **puffy** heads! Fortunately, their heads go back to normal size upon returning to Earth. Astronauts also get a little bit taller during long stays in space. The absence of gravity allows the spine to stretch slightly.

In Other Words
weightlessness weighing nothing
recounts tells about
atrophy lose all of their strength
tour of duty trip to space
puffy large and swollen

Historical Background
The National Aeronautics and Space Administration (NASA) is an organization funded by the United States government. **NASA's** mission is to research and explore space, and to apply this knowledge to improve life on Earth.

Before You Move On

1. **Cause and Effect** Why do astronauts go to space?
2. **Details** What are three things that happen because of microgravity in space?
3. **Fact and Opinion** Identify one fact and one opinion from the Journal of Ed Lu. 26.C.3

Where's the Oxygen?

On Earth, our environment is made up of the perfect mixture of **elements** to **sustain** life. Oxygen is one of the most important of those elements. When you take in a breath, what happens? You can feel air going into your body through your nose or mouth. You can't see it, but it's there in the air. We breathe because our bodies need oxygen in the air. Oxygen is like food for our blood. We need it to survive.

In space, there is no oxygen. Because of this, astronauts do not breathe the same as they do on Earth. They have to breathe with the help of a protective spacesuit that supplies them with oxygen. A human being would not survive on a spacewalk for more than a minute or two without a spacesuit.

Compared to getting dressed on Earth, which takes just a few minutes, putting on a spacesuit takes 45 minutes. The astronauts must then spend lots of time breathing only pure oxygen before going outside the space station. This **process** is called prebreathing.

Without a protective space suit, astronauts would not be able to survive on space stations. ▶

Key Vocabulary
> **element** *n.*, something that is
> part of a whole
> **process** *n.*, a series of actions
> that lead to a result

In Other Words
sustain support

On Earth as in space, people have oxygen in their blood. People also have another element in their blood called nitrogen. On Earth, nitrogen **takes up** 78 percent of the air we breathe. This gas is harmless when we breathe it on Earth.

In space, however, breathing nitrogen would cause air bubbles in the blood and be very painful. The pure oxygen that astronauts **take in** during prebreathing flushes all of the nitrogen out. Sunita Williams explains this process in her journal.

▶ From the Journal of **Sunita Williams**

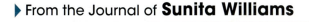

"In order to go out the door of the ship safely, we go through a **pretty thorough process** called pre-breathe. In space, if you have nitrogen in your blood, it creates air bubbles. This can cause serious pain. To breathe safely in a spacesuit, there can only be oxygen in the blood. To do this, we spend time breathing in only pure oxygen. We can't get medical care to help us out. So, in this **line of work**, we need to try to eliminate this kind of pain caused by air bubbles in the blood."

In Other Words
takes up is in
take in breathe
pretty thorough process
    complete set of steps
line of work job

Before You Move On

1. **Explain** Why is oxygen so important to humans on Earth and in space?
2. **Summarize** Why do astronauts go through the process of prebreathing?

What's the Food Like?

Whether in space or on Earth, food is necessary for life—it gives a person's body the nutrients needed to be strong and healthy. The difference between food on Earth and in space is the way it is stored and prepared.

On Earth, food is prepared to be delicious. Think of all of your favorite foods. On Earth we store our food in a freezer, refrigerator, or cupboard. Some foods, such as bowls of fresh fruit, can be set on the counter.

In space, foods are individually packaged for easy handling in microgravity. Most food is **precooked or processed**. It requires no refrigeration and is either ready to eat or can be prepared simply by adding water or by heating it. The only exceptions are the fresh fruit and vegetables **stowed** in the fresh food locker. Without refrigeration, many of these must be eaten within the first two days of the flight or they will **spoil**.

In his journal, astronaut Michael Lopez-Alegria explains more about food in space.

▸ From the Journal of **Michael Lopez-Alegria**

"The food aboard the International Space Station (ISS) is plentiful and tasty, considering the **obstacles in our paths**. We have no refrigerator, we go long periods of time without being able to refill our pantry, and everything we eat is by necessity pre-cooked.

Food comes in a variety of forms. Dehydrated food, or food that is dried out, is packaged in plastic containers or bags. The containers or bags are made so that we can easily add hot or cold water. Once you add the water, you shake up the container. Next thing you know, you have a plate of good food in front of you.

Another form is called thermo-stabilized. This just means that it is packed in a foil pouch. This type of food is like canned food you might find in any grocery store."

In Other Words

precooked or processed already cooked or does not need to be cooked
stowed kept
spoil be ruined
obstacles in our paths challenges

Labels on packaged meals (visible):
- Mixed Fruit Pandowdy — 75 ml Cold Water *5-10 Minutes
- Spicy Green Beans with Garlic — 75 ml Hot Water *5-10 Minutes
- Kicked Up Bacon Cheese Mashed Potatoes — 100 ml Hot Water *10-15 Minutes
- Mardi Gras Jambalaya — 100 ml Hot Water *10-15 Minutes

▲ A well-known chef created and packaged these meals for the astronauts. They are shown here next to the same meal freshly prepared to be eaten on Earth.

Science Background

Each meal prepared for space costs an average of $100, mostly due to packaging and testing. It can take six to eight months for food scientists in the lab to develop and test a new food item.

Before You Move On

1. **Compare and Contrast** What is food like in space compared to on Earth?
2. **Inference** What do you think it is like to prepare a meal in space?

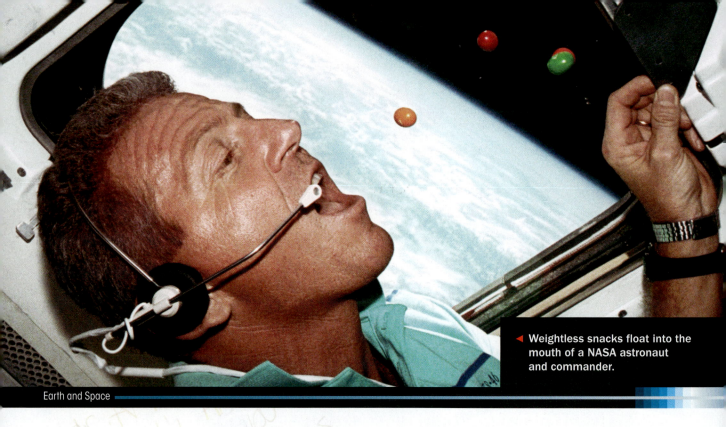

Weightless snacks float into the mouth of a NASA astronaut and commander.

When is Dinner?

Mealtimes on Earth are often special times. When families or friends gather together to share a meal, they are able to relax, have fun, and share stories about life. Your family might share a holiday dinner, or you might meet your friends in the school cafeteria for lunch. Meals are a great way to **connect** with each other. Here's what Michael Lopez-Alegria writes about mealtimes in space.

▶ From the Journal of **Michael Lopez-Alegria**

"We usually pause for about one hour midday to have our meal together and almost always have dinner together. Meals are our **primary** social time.

One truly **bright spot in** our menu is food that is sent up from our families or friends in **'bonus' containers or care** packages—it's just as you might see it in the store."

In Other Words

connect talk and have fun
primary biggest or main
bright spot in great part about
'bonus' containers or care special

There is one big difference between mealtimes in space and on Earth. On Earth, the plates stay on the table! Compare this to what Ed Lu writes about eating in microgravity.

▶ From the Journal of **Ed Lu**

"We don't have a real kitchen up here, but we do have a kitchen table. You might wonder what use a table is if you can't set anything down on it. But we have **bungee straps and Velcro** on the tabletop so you can keep your food containers, spoon, napkins, **etc.** from floating away."

▲ A family shares a meal on Earth.

▲ Astronauts share a meal on the International Space Station (ISS).

Before You Move On

1. **Compare and Contrast** How are mealtimes on Earth and in Space similar? How are they different?
2. **Visualize** Describe what you think a typical meal in space would be like.

Time to Sleep!

On Earth, we need to go to sleep every night to rest our bodies and gain energy for a new day. Getting **a good night's** sleep is **essential** to our health and **well being**. On Earth, most people sleep in a bed that is soft and comfortable.

In space, it is still necessary for astronauts to go to sleep every night in order to rest their bodies and stay healthy. Most astronauts even sleep about the same amount of time in space as they do on Earth. But because of microgravity, the way astronauts sleep is very different from the way we sleep on Earth.

There is nothing weighing down the astronauts' bodies in space because there is very little gravity. That's why astronauts have to strap themselves into special sleeping bags that hang from the wall! The sleeping bags have straps that press astronauts to a soft surface and to a pillow. Yet, most astronauts actually like to sleep floating in the air, with only a couple of straps to keep them from bouncing around the cabin. In addition to special sleeping bags, astronauts may need to wear blindfolds to protect them from the strong sunlight that **streams in** the windows during orbit in space.

In her journal, Joan Higginbotham explains how sleeping in space is different from sleeping at home on Earth.

▶ From the Journal of **Joan Higginbotham**

"Everyone thinks that it must be difficult to sleep in space because they imagine there to be a lot of noise. There is a lot of noise on the shuttle, but not so much that it makes it uncomfortable to sleep. You can hear the **fans whirling**—the cabin fans that actually help clean the air. I actually sleep without earplugs. Some of my crewmates did use earplugs. But it wasn't noisy enough that it disturbed their sleep."

Key Vocabulary
essential *adj.*, necessary for success or survival

In Other Words
a good night's enough
well being happiness
streams in comes through
fans whirling loud noise from the fans

On Earth, we sometimes sleep in sleeping bags—but they are always on the ground. ▶

In space, astronauts sleep in sleeping bags, too. The sleeping bags have to be strapped in and attached to the wall so they don't fly away! ▶

As you can see, astronauts move, breathe, sleep, and eat differently in space than they do on Earth. Astronauts are willing to trade the **routines** they are used to on Earth to travel in space because they have an important job. Astronauts are exploring an unknown world so **future generations** can benefit from what they learn. This special mission outweighs some of the dangers and difficulties astronauts experience in space.

No Place Like Home

Exploring the unknown world of space is an exciting adventure. **On the other hand**, most astronauts will tell you how excited they are to go home to Earth after their mission is over. Clayton Anderson explains.

▶ From the Journal of **Clayton Anderson**

"I am often asked just what it is I miss the most up here. **First and foremost**, of course, is my wonderful family. ... I also miss some significant physical things. ... For example, sometimes as I daydream I **envision** a soft breeze from Galveston Bay and the warm rays of the summer sun, or the smell of freshly cut grass amid the sound of all the neighborhood lawn mowers." ❖

Key Vocabulary
routine *n.*, a normal process

In Other Words
future generations people years from now
On the other hand While astronauts enjoy being in space
First and foremost Most important
envision imagine

Before You Move On

1. **Compare and Contrast** How is sleeping on Earth and in space different?
2. **Opinion** Do you think it's worth the difficulties **astronauts** go through to explore space? Why or why not?

Connect Reading and Writing

Vocabulary
astronaut
element
essential
experience
process
routine
similarity
universe

CRITICAL THINKING

1. SUM IT UP Make a card for each vocabulary word. Use five words to compare the **routine** of an **astronaut** in space to your daily routine on Earth.

experience

routine

similarity

2. Compare Compare the **astronauts'** journal entries. Why do you think the entry of Clayton Anderson is included?

3. Conclusion **Astronauts** may spend months on a space station. What traits are **essential** to live in space for that long? Review the photos and journal entries for ideas.

4. Infer Why is it valuable for **astronauts** to record what they **experience** in journal entries like those in the selection?

READING FLUENCY

Intonation Read the passage on page 644 to a partner. Assess your fluency.

1. I read

    a. great   **b.** OK   **c.** not very well

2. What I did best in my reading was _____ .

READING STRATEGY

Make Connections
How did text-to-text connections help you understand the article? Tell a partner.

VOCABULARY REVIEW

Oral Review Read the paragraph aloud. Add the vocabulary words.

    Would you like to explore the _____ as an _____ ? To _____ life in space, it is _____ that you follow a new daily _____ . It may have some _____ to your daily schedule on Earth. However, the _____ by which you eat, sleep, or even breathe, is quite different. For example, you need special equipment to breathe because oxygen, an important _____ of air, is not found in space.

Written Review Imagine you can travel anywhere in the **universe**. Describe what you **experience**. Use four vocabulary words.

WRITE ABOUT THE GUIDING QUESTION

Explore Being at Home in the World
Astronauts practice space tasks in an underwater lab. How are the features of living in space **similar** to being in water? Reread the selection to find examples that support your ideas.

Connect Across the Curriculum

ELPS: 2.C.4 learn academic vocabulary heard during classroom instruction and interactions; 3.D.2 speak using content area vocabulary in context to build academic language proficiency

Literary Analysis

Compare Genres

> **Academic Vocabulary**
> • **purpose** (pur-pus) *noun*
>   A **purpose** is a reason for doing something.

What Are Some Different Kinds of Writing? Different forms of writing are called genres. Writers select a genre based on their **purpose** for writing.

FICTION

Imaginary characters

Once, the Moon and his friend the Sun chased each other in the sky. Then Sun needed to light up the day and could no longer play with the Moon. So the Sun sent little stars to be with the Moon at night.

> **Purpose:**
> **to entertain**

NONFICTION

Fact

By measuring the ages of lunar rocks, we know that the moon is about 4.6 billion years old.

> **Purpose:**
> **to inform**

POETRY

Moonlight, summer moonlight, **Line breaks**
All soft and still and fair; **Rhyme**
The solemn hour of midnight
Breathes sweet thoughts everywhere

> **Purpose:**
> **to express**

Practice Together

Analyze Genres Review "Earth and Space." Identify the topic and analyze the genre. List the ways you can tell what kind of writing it is. What is the **purpose** of the selection? Give examples that show its **purpose**. How does the genre fit the **purpose**? What would change if this selection was fiction?

Title	Topic	Genre	Ways to Tell	Purpose	Examples That Show Purpose
"Earth and Space"					
"Moonlight"					

Try It!

Compare Genres Work with a partner. Make a chart like this one to analyze the poem. How does the genre fit the **purpose**? Speak to the class about your ideas.

ELPS: 2.C.4 learn academic vocabulary heard during classroom instruction and interactions; 4.F.3 use contextual support to develop vocabulary needed to comprehend increasingly challenging language

Vocabulary Study

Understand Jargon and Specialized Language

Academic Vocabulary

- **unique** (yü-nēk) *adjective*
  Something that is **unique** is different or special.

Language that is **unique** to certain fields of work is called **jargon**. It may not appear in everyday language. Use context to figure out its meaning.

> In space, the force of gravity is so weak that a feeling of weightlessness results. Astronauts use the word *microgravity* to describe this lack of gravity in space.

The context shows that *microgravity* is what astronauts feel in space.

Use Context Clues Discuss the meanings of the underlined jargon.

1. The astronauts must spend lots of time breathing only pure oxygen before going outside the space station. This is a process called <u>prebreathing</u>.

2. Most food is either <u>precooked</u> or processed. It requires no refrigeration and is either ready to eat or can be prepared simply by adding water or by heating it.

3. <u>Dehydrated</u> food, or food that is dried out, is packaged in plastic containers or bags.

Listening/Speaking

Role-Play an Interview

SOCIAL SCIENCE

ELPS: 2.C.4 learn academic vocabulary heard during classroom instruction and interactions; 2.G.6 understand the main points of spoken language regarding familiar to unfamiliar contexts; 3.C.3 speak using a variety of sentence types with increasing accuracy and ease

Academic Vocabulary

- **plan** (plan) *noun*
  A **plan** is a way of doing things.

What would reporters ask if they interviewed astronauts about their experiences in space? Role-play an interview with an astronaut.

1 **Make a Plan** With a partner, make a **plan** for the interview. List questions that a news reporter might ask an astronaut. Then answer each question as you think the astronaut would.

Question	Answer
What is microgravity like?	You fly everywhere. You don't walk.

2 **Act Out Your Interview** Decide who will play the news reporter and who will play the astronaut. Use your list of questions and answers as you role-play the interview. Perform your role-play for the class.

Research/Writing

Make a Technical Manual

MEDIA & TECHNOLOGY

ELPS: 2.C.4 learn academic vocabulary heard during classroom instruction and interactions; **2.G.9** understand the important details of spoken language regarding familiar to unfamiliar context; **5.G.3** explain with increasing specificity and detail to fulfill content area writing needs

> **Academic Vocabulary**
> * **technical** (tek-ni-kal) *adjective*
>   Something that is **technical** is based on scientific knowledge.

A **technical** manual is a document that explains how to do something or how something works. In "Earth and Space," the astronauts used **technical** manuals to use the equipment and tools on the space station. Now create a **technical** manual of your own.

1 **Choose Your Process** With a partner, list tasks that would need instructions, for example, how to program a VCR, how to use a camera, or how to change a flat bicycle tire.

2 **Research Steps in the Process** Use books, magazines, or the Internet to find out what steps are involved in the process. Write each step on a separate note card.

3 **Organize the Information** Put the steps on the note cards in the order in which they happen. Organize the steps in groups. Use these groups to organize the information in a flow chart.

First Step	Pull out the old tube with your hand.

↓

Next Step	With a bicycle pump, put one or two strokes of air into the new tube.

↓

Next Step	Put the new tube in the bicycle tire.

↓

Last Step	Check that there is enough air in the tire.

4 **Create a Manual** Using your flow chart as a guide, write the sections of your **technical** manual. Briefly explain every step in the process. Be sure there is no missing or unnecessary information. Add diagrams or photos to illustrate the different steps.

Internet InsideNG.com
See examples of technical manuals.

5 **Share Your Manual** Share your manual with your classmates. Ask a volunteer to follow your instruction independently and report back on whether they were effective. Do they understand the important details?

▲ A technical manual can explain how to change a tire.

Language and Grammar

Define and Explain

Role-Play With a group, act out a classroom visit by astronauts from the International Space Station. Some of you ask questions. The astronauts answer by defining and explaining their experiences in space. Use prepositions and prepositional phrases to add details to your questions and answers. Trade roles.

> Does noise on the space shuttle keep you awake?

> Before bed, I put earplugs in my ears. Earplugs really help muffle the sound.

Writing and Grammar

Write About an Adventure

Study the Models When you write, you can use words and phrases to add descriptive details and information to your sentences. Some phrases add meaning to your writing by showing location, direction, time, and origin.

OK

There is no gravity **in space**. Astronauts and objects float if they are not anchored. Some astronauts strap themselves down so that they do not float. Some astronauts use straps to secure their food packets when they eat.

> This writer needs to add details and information to the paragraph.

BETTER

There is no gravity **in space**. Astronauts and objects float **around a space station** if they are not anchored. **Before going to sleep**, some astronauts strap themselves **into special sleeping bags** so that they do not float **around the cabin during sleep**. **During mealtimes**, some astronauts use straps **on the tabletop** to secure their food packets.

> This writer uses prepositional phrases to add descriptive details and information to the paragraph.

WRITE ON YOUR OWN Write about an adventure you'd like to take. Use descriptive words and phrases in your writing to add detailed information.

REMEMBER
- A prepositional phrase starts with a preposition.
- A prepositional phrase ends with a noun or a pronoun.

Prepositions	
Show location	above, at, behind, below, beside, in, in back of, in front of, next to, on, on top of, over, under
Show direction	across, down, into, through, to, up
Show time	after, before, during, until
Show origin	from

Indian Summer Sun
by Carmen T. Bernier-Grand

Juanita IV, 2004, Lou Wall, Oil on canvas.

Build Background

At Home in the World

"Indian Summer Sun" is about a girl from Puerto Rico who moves to Connecticut. Connecticut is in the northeastern United States near the Atlantic Ocean. Puerto Rico is southeast of the U.S. near the Caribbean Ocean.

Connect

Quickwrite Have you or someone you know ever moved to a new place? What makes a new place feel like home? Do a Quickwrite of your ideas.

Digital Library

InsideNG.com
◉ View the images.

▲ There are many places people call home.

Language & Grammar

ELPS: 2.C.1 learn new language structures heard during classroom instruction and interactions; 2.G.2 understand the general meaning of spoken language regarding familiar to unfamiliar language; 3.B.1 expand and internalize initial vocabulary by learning and using high-frequency words necessary for identifying and describing people, places, and objects

1 TRY OUT LANGUAGE
2 LEARN GRAMMAR
3 APPLY ON YOUR OWN

Clarify and Verify

CD

Listen to a conversation between two students. How does the boy make sure he understands what was said? Role-play the conversation.

PICTURE PROMPT

Home Sweet Home

Use Pronouns in the Subject and Predicate

A **pronoun** refers to a noun. You can use pronouns in the subject or the predicate of a sentence.

Subject Pronouns	I	you	he	she	it	we	you	they
Object Pronouns	me	you	him	her	it	us	you	them

- Use a **subject pronoun** as the subject of a sentence.

    EXAMPLE **Some students** are new to our school. **They** moved to new homes recently.

- Use an **object pronoun** as the object of the verb.

    EXAMPLE The principal greeted the new **students**. He gave **them** a warm welcome.

- When you talk about yourself, use the pronouns **I** and **me**. Use the pronoun **I** in the subject of a sentence. Use the pronoun **me** as the object in the predicate of a sentence.

    EXAMPLES **I** met Roberto yesterday. He told **me** about his old home.

> Many statements follow the pattern:
> subject → verb → object
>
> | She | likes | them. |
> |---|---|---|
> | subject | verb | object |
>
> In questions, the subject often comes after the first word of the sentence.
>
> | Do | they | like | her? |
> |---|---|---|---|
> | | subject | verb | object |

Practice Together

Say each pair of sentences. Add the correct pronoun from the chart and tell what it refers to.

1. Julia had a problem when she moved homes. She could not solve _____ easily.
2. The English language is sometimes difficult for my friends and me. _____ sounds strange to us.
3. I do not understand the directions. My teacher explains _____ to me.
4. A new situation makes some people uncomfortable. _____ don't know what to do.

Try It!

Say each pair of sentences. Write the correct pronoun and what it refers to on a card. Then say the sentence and add the pronoun.

5. Moving to a new town affected my family. It brought _____ closer together.
6. My family met the neighbors. We told _____ about our move.
7. My brother found the post office. _____ mailed a letter to an old friend.
8. I have many good memories of my old town. _____ comfort me.

▲ I talk to my friends. They understand how I feel.

Follow the Rules

CLARIFY AND VERIFY

What school or classroom rules are important for new students to know?

With a small group of students, role-play explaining and clarifying a classroom or school rule to a new student. Tell how you could clarify or verify the information.

First, think of some rules and questions about them that a new student might ask. Make a chart like this one.

Classroom/School Rule	Questions the New Student Might Ask
Do not interrupt others while they are speaking.	Could you tell me what "interrupt" means?
	Could you repeat that, please?

Take turns role-playing the new student and the informed student. As the new student, clarify and verify new ideas and information to understand the general meaning. As the veteran student, clarify and verify the rule.

How To CLARIFY AND VERIFY

1. To get clarification, ask a question about what is unclear.
2. To clarify, restate using new words. Define confusing words. Give examples or compare to something else.
3. To verify, ask for repetition, restate what you heard, or check a trusted source.

> Could you tell me what "interrupt" means?

> When you interrupt, you stop someone from talking. It is considered rude. This rule is posted on the bulletin board in our classroom.

USE PRONOUNS IN THE SUBJECT AND THE PREDICATE

When you clarify and verify information, you may need to ask questions or restate information in a way that makes the general meaning clear. If you use pronouns in the subject or the predicate of your sentences, remember that the pronoun has to match the noun it refers to.

In the Subject: **Students** must be in their seats when the bell rings.
They must get to class on time.

In the Predicate: Why do **students** have to follow rules?
Rules help **them** learn better.

Prepare to Read

ELPS: 3.A practice producing sounds of newly acquired vocabulary in a manner that is comprehensible; 4.J demonstrate and expand comprehension by employing inferential skills

Learn Key Vocabulary

Rate and Study the Words Rate how well you know each word. Then:

1. Pronounce the word. Say it aloud several times. Spell it.
2. Study the example.
3. Tell more about the word.
4. Practice it. Make the word your own.

Key Words

adjustment (u-**just**-ment)
noun ▶ page 302

An **adjustment** is the way you go along with, or get used to a change. It takes a while to make an **adjustment** to moving to a new home.
Related Word: **adjust**

concentrate (**kon**-sen-trāt)
verb ▶ page 306

To **concentrate** means to focus on something. Students have to **concentrate** when studying.
Related Word: **concentration**

couple (**kup**-ul) *noun*
▶ page 303

A **couple** is two people who are together. My grandparents are a happy **couple**.
Synonym: **pair**
Antonym: **single**

ignore (ig-**nor**) *verb*
▶ page 302

To **ignore** means to pay no attention to something. It is best to **ignore** people who are bullies.

opportunity
(op-ur-**tü**-ni-tē) *noun* ▶ page 303

An **opportunity** is a chance to do something. My teacher gave me the **opportunity** to tell my ideas to the other students.

perspective (pur-**spek**-tiv)
noun ▶ page 304

A **perspective** is a way of thinking about something. My teacher's **perspective** on music is that everyone should learn to play.

refuse (ri-**fūz**) *verb*
▶ page 306

To **refuse** means to choose not to do something. The child **refused** to eat any more food.
Antonyms: **agree, obey**

remind (ri-**mīnd**) *verb*
▶ page 304

To **remind** is to help someone remember something or tell them again. As I left for school, my mom **reminded** me to take my lunch.

Practice the Words Make a Definition Map for each Key Word. Then compare your maps with a partner.

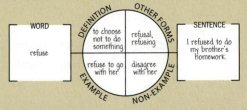

Definition Map

Reading Strategy: Make Connections

When you read, some details may remind you of your own experiences. Making connections can give a text more meaning.

Reading Strategy
Make Connections

HOW TO MAKE TEXT-TO-SELF CONNECTIONS

1. As you read, notice details that stand out or have meaning for you.

2. At the end of a page or section, think about each connection. How does it help you make inferences about the text?

3. Explain the connection in a Text-to-Self Connections Chart.

Strategy in Action

Here's how one student made text-to-self connections.

Look Into the Text

The morning wind felt like a sharp knife on my legs, like it was carving me. How could it be so cold when the sun was shining?

Would I get used to this and would I ever get to like Connecticut? I doubted it, but here I was, on my first day in an American high school and I had to make the best of it.

I went from class to class trying to be ignored. I was mostly successful, except for algebra.

This reminds me of when my family moved to California.

I remember a sunny day when I felt cold, too!

Text-to-Self Connections Chart

The text says . . .	This reminds me of . . .	The connection helps because . . .
How could it be so cold when the sun is shining?	I stood in mountain snow but the day was very warm.	I understand why the character is puzzled by new and different weather.

Practice Together

Reread the passage. Follow the steps in the How-To box to make your own text-to-self connections.

Short Story

A short story is a brief, fictional narrative.

Many short story writers use dialogue, or speech between characters, to show what the characters are like and to move the plot along.

> When I went to the Latino table, Sergio was talking about salsa.
>
> "I bet you're a good dancer," he said.
>
> "I'm not," I answered. "I don't even know how to dance."
>
> "You're Puerto Rican and you don't know how to dance!" That was Norma.
>
> "Exactly," I said . . .

Dialogue between characters helps develop them and moves the plot forward.

Your Job as a Reader

Reading Strategy: Make Connections

As you read, make connections between ideas in the text and your own life. Record your connections on a Text-to-Self Connections Chart.

Indian Summer Sun

by Carmen T. Bernier-Grand

Juanita IV, 2004, Lou Wall. Oil on canvas.

 **Critical Viewing: Effect** What do you notice about the details in this painting? What mood or feeling does this create?

Online Coach

The morning wind felt like a sharp knife on my legs, like it was **carving** me. How could it be so cold when the sun was shining?

Would I get used to this and would I ever get to like Connecticut? I doubted it, but here I was, on my first day in an American high school and I had to **make the best of it**.

I went from class to class trying to be <mark>ignored</mark>. I was mostly successful, except for algebra. In that class, I sat in the second row, and, without thinking, rested my feet on the metal basket of the desk in front of me.

This cute guy (Jerry, the teacher later called him) moved the front desk forward and my feet suddenly dropped.

"Oh, I'm sorry," he said and pushed the desk back so I could comfortably rest my feet on the basket again.

The thank-you didn't come out of my mouth and I wondered what he thought of me.

Lunchtime came after algebra class and I sat all by myself at a cafeteria table, looking out the window. Glass windows! This surprised me because there was no glass in the windows in my school in Puerto Rico.

The Connecticut trees were **dressed-up**, as if they were going to the carnival. There were yellow, orange, purple, red, and bright, bright leaves.

I noticed, however, that there were no palm trees anywhere.

I'd made a mistake. Actually, I'd made a huge mistake! I'd left Puerto Rico and my

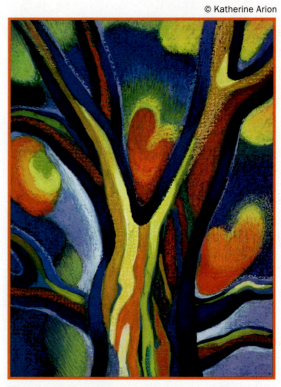

© Katherine Arion

▲ **Critical Viewing: Plot** How do the shapes in this image relate to what the narrator describes?

Key Vocabulary
   adjustment *n.*, a change in situation
   <mark>ignore</mark> *v.*, to give little or no attention to

In Other Words
   carving cutting
   make the best of it try to like it
   dressed-up colorful

father to live with my mother. I missed him but I'd missed her just as much. This was my chance to be with her and it also was an **opportunity** to learn to speak English better. The problem was that all I wanted now was to get out of here.

A group of students I'd seen in algebra came by my table, food trays in hand. "Please, God," I thought in Spanish, "don't let them sit by me."

They sat three tables ahead.

I knew English. My mother is American and she always spoke to me in English. She knew Spanish, but even when she was married to my father and we lived together in Puerto Rico, she'd spoken to me in English. Although I knew English, I always answered in Spanish.

Jerry came in and whispered something to a blonde girl the algebra teacher had called Kathy. I thought that she was probably his girlfriend. They seemed like the perfect **couple** to me and they even looked alike.

Kathy must have noticed my staring because she waved and said, "Come, sit with us."

I looked out the window, pretending I hadn't heard her.

Even my friends in Puerto Rico had laughed at my accent and teased me when I spoke English.

There was no way I was going to join Jerry and Kathy and all those other algebra students because they would laugh at my accent, too.

The guy behind me was wearing earphones, his music was so loud that I could hear it. I recognized that rhythm. Salsa!

Two girls joined him. "Sergio!" one said, "*Baja esa música.*"

He obeyed and after turning the music down, he turned it off and took off his earphones.

"*¿Hablan español?*" This was a stupid question because I'd heard them speaking in Spanish.

"*Sí. ¿Y tú?*" the other girl asked.

I nodded.

"*Pues, siéntate con nosotros,*" said the girl, her eyes so dark I couldn't even see her pupils.

I sat with them.

Norma was from Cuba, Sergio from the Dominican Republic; Minerva with those beautiful dark eyes was from Mexico. They were not new to the school, but they hung out together. I felt like I had friends! I began to think that I was going to like it here.

Key Vocabulary

opportunity *n.*, a good chance

couple *n.*, two people together, a pair

In Other Words (all in Spanish)

Baja esa música Lower the volume of the music
¿Hablan español? Do you all speak Spanish?
Sí. ¿Y tú? Yes, and you?
Pues, siéntate con nosotros Well, sit with us

Before You Move On

1. **Explain** Why does the narrator experience an **adjustment**?
2. **Contrast** What are some differences between the narrator's experience in Puerto Rico and her experience in Connecticut?
3. **Cause and Effect** Why doesn't the narrator want to sit with the algebra students?

That evening at dinner, when I told my mother about my day, she said, "Cristina, I thought you came to learn English."

The spaghetti I'd rolled around the fork fell off and I didn't want to talk about my English.

"*Vine para estar contigo*," I <mark>reminded</mark> her.

"It is nice that you came to be with me," my mother said. "I love having you here but you also came to **become fluent** in English, or at least that's what you told me before you came. Have you changed your mind?"

I shook my head.

My mother continued. "I'm glad you found somebody to talk to but don't talk just to people who speak Spanish. If that girl from algebra class invites you again, you should join her!"

"*Se van a reír de mi inglés.*"

"So what if they laugh at your English? If I'd worried about Puerto Ricans laughing at my Spanish, would I have learned the language?"

This was easy for her to say. Everybody thought she sounded cute when speaking Spanish but she didn't have to go to a high school where students might have teased her.

The next morning, I prepared myself for the cold. I put on three pairs of socks so that my shoes hardly fit with so many socks. I put on my heavy coat, hat, gloves, and scarf and headed to school. The sun had fooled me the day before, but it wouldn't fool me again.

I was almost at the school entrance when I heard a girl behind me saying, "Johnny, isn't it hot today?"

She and the guy she was with walked by me. He turned and fanned himself. "It sure is," he said.

He was wearing short pants and she had on a short skirt. Other students were wearing tank tops and sandals. I guess I was the only one who was cold.

I went in, opened my locker and threw in my hat, scarf, and gloves and with tears in my eyes, I told Minerva what had happened.

"This is what we call Indian Summer," she explained in Spanish. "It lasts a week or two and then it gets really cold."

Key Vocabulary

<mark>perspective</mark> *n.*, a way of thinking about something
<mark>remind</mark> *v.*, to tell someone something again

In Other Words

Vine para estar contigo I came here to be with you (in Spanish)
become fluent learn to speak more
Se van a reír de mi inglés. They are going to laugh at my English. (in Spanish)

Science Background

Indian summer is a brief period of warm, dry weather that occurs late in the season of fall, or autumn. Indian summer is a temporary and warm break from colder temperatures.

Muchacha en la Ventana (Girl in the Window), 2000, Graciela Genoves. Oil on canvas, Zurbaran Gallery, Buenos Aires, Argentina.

▲ **Critical Viewing: Character** How would you describe the girl's mood in this painting?
How might she be similar to Cristina?

You mean it gets really cold? Even colder than this? **No way!**

Everything went wrong that day. The English teacher asked me to read aloud, and I **refused**. I'd probably flunk the class if I continued doing this.

In algebra Jerry moved his desk toward me so I could rest my feet on the metal basket. That was pretty neat but then I caught Kathy staring at my feet because my socks were **bulging** out of my shoes. How embarrassing!

And then the algebra teacher called on me. "Cristina, could you, please, come up and solve this problem?"

All eyes were on me, but I walked to the board and tried to **concentrate** on the problem.

$(3x + 5)(2x + 7)$

I remembered what the teacher had said the day before, the word **FOIL** would help solve this problem.

F for first. Multiply the first two terms.
$(3x)(2x) = 6x^2$

Everything went wrong that day.

O for outside. Multiply the outside terms.
$3x \times 7 = 21x$

I for inside. Multiply the inside terms.
$5 \times 2x = 10x$

L for last. Multiply the last terms.
$5 \times 7 = 35$

So, I came up with: $6x^2 + 21x + 10x + 35$
I almost sat down, but the teacher stopped me. "Wait a minute, Cristina. You need to finish it."

I looked back at the board, and saw what she meant. I needed to add the **common terms** to finish the problem.
$6x^2 + 31x + 35$
"Perfect," the teacher said.

That should have made me feel good, but when I was walking back to my desk, I overheard Jerry whispering to Kathy, "I told you! She understands English."

Kathy didn't answer and instead, she stared at my socks.

When the bell rang, I packed my books in a hurry to go to the bathroom and take off at least one pair of socks.

Key Vocabulary
refuse *v.*, to choose not to do something
concentrate *v.*, to focus on something

In Other Words
No way! I can't believe it!
bulging coming
All eyes were on me Everyone was looking at me
common terms numbers that were similar

Language Background
An acronym (ak-ruh-nim), like **FOIL**, is a word formed from the first letter of each word in a phrase. Acronyms can be helpful in remembering long rules and names.

On my way out, Kathy stopped me and I was sure she'd tell me about my socks—as if I didn't know. But that is not what she did.

Instead, she said, "Tomorrow is a **half-day**. After class a bunch of us are going to my house to eat lunch and party." She paused and looked straight to my eyes. "Do you understand what I'm saying?"

Of course, I did!

I just nodded to show that I understood.

"I hope you can come," she said.

I knew the answer. No, thank you. I just smiled and ran to the bathroom where I took off all of my socks, thinking that I'd rather be cold than look **like an alien**.

Lunch break wasn't much fun either.

When I went to the Latino table, Sergio was talking about salsa.

"I bet you're a good dancer," he said.

"I'm not," I answered. "I don't even know how to dance."

"You're Puerto Rican and you don't know how to dance!" That was Norma.

"Exactly," I said, louder than I had to, because I was feeling as if I didn't **fit in** with this group either.

If I only dared to go to Kathy's party—but what would I do there, just sit and watch? If only she would invite my Latino friends, but they were not in my algebra class.

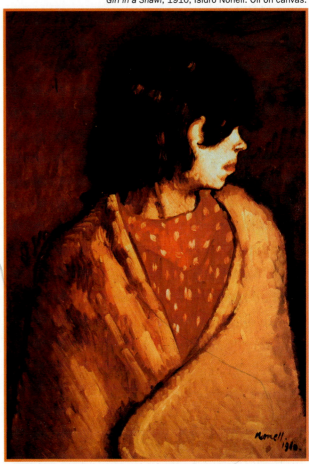

Girl in a Shawl, 1910, Isidro Nonell. Oil on canvas.

▲ **Critical Viewing: Character** How does the girl in this image represent Cristina?

In Other Words
half-day school day that ends early
like an alien different from everyone else
fit in belong

Before You Move On

1. **Character's Point of View** How is Cristina feeling? Why?
2. **Perspectives** Why does Cristina's mom <mark>remind</mark> her to make friends with people who speak English?
3. **Visualize** How do you imagine that Cristina is dressed in comparison to the other students?

It was an accident, a pure accident. The next day I stood by the door after algebra class, and couldn't go through, too many students in my way and of course, I didn't dare say "Excuse me."

Then I felt a hand on my shoulder. "Cristina, good!" It was Kathy. "Jeremy asked me to make sure you were coming."

Jeremy? Who was that?

Soon I **found myself** walking to Kathy's house with the rest of the class because I just wasn't brave enough to say that I wasn't going to the party.

Mistake, mistake, or so I thought during the first few minutes at Kathy's party. We'd come in and gone straight to the finished basement of the house where there was an entertainment room. I guessed it was an entertainment room because it had a big screen TV and a CD player with speakers almost as tall as I was. I sat on a black leather **recliner** that a guy had moved to a corner so they could have space to dance.

Kathy came down with chips and salsa, put them on the table in front of me and began to dance with the guy who had moved the recliner. How would Jerry feel about this and where was he, anyway?

Everybody joined Kathy, dancing.

Nobody asked me to dance, thank God and nobody made me speak, thank God.

State of My Heart, 2005, Elizabeth Rosen. Mixed media collage, collection of the artist, courtesy of Morgan Gaynin, New York.

▲ **Critical Viewing: Plot** What connection can you make between this image and the story?

In Other Words
found myself was
Mistake, mistake It was not a good idea to go to the party
recliner chair

I felt stupid but then, Jerry came down. He looked like he had just taken a shower. I could tell because his hair was wet. He had on a blue shirt with its long sleeves rolled up to his elbows and he came directly to me and sat by me.

"Hi," he said.

I smiled. "Jerry?" It came out as Yerry, but it was too late to **take it back**.

"My parents and my sister," his chin pointed to Kathy, "call me Jeremy, my real name, but almost everybody else calls me Jerry. You can call me whatever is easier for you."

Jeremy! Kathy's brother— not her boyfriend.

"Why are you always so quiet?" he asked.

"*¿Hablas español?*"

He made a 0 with his fingers. "Zero."

"I have an accent." **That came out** without warning.

"What are you talking about?" he said, almost yelling because the music was loud. "It's cute!"

Why are you always so quiet?

I turned and pretended to be interested in the dancers but all I could feel were his eyes on me. His eyes felt warm and they were full of hazel light as he looked at me. His glance was so powerful that it made my whole inside smile.

"Do you dance?" he asked.

Did a piano fall on me? Not only did I feel weight on my back, but his words **sounded like scratchy music to my ears**.

Why did he have to ask me that?

I had to say the truth, so I shook my head no.

He wiped his forehead with his fingers, and then sighed. "I don't either."

I put my hand on my heart and sighed, too.

We both laughed.

As if we were too shy to look at each other, we turned to watch the dancers.

But a few seconds later, he said, "This music is too loud to talk. Would you like to take a walk?"

In Other Words

take it back change what I had said
That came out I said that
sounded like scratchy music to my ears did not sound good

Spring Thaw, 2005, Elizabeth Rosen. Acrylic on canvas, private collection, courtesy of Morgan Gaynin, New York.

▲ **Critical Viewing: Effect** How does the mood of the painting compare to Cristina's feelings at the end of the story?

I nodded and stood up.

He held my upper arm and guided me out.

We could still hear the music, but near us the only sound was that of our feet **crunching** leaves.

Was he waiting for me to speak? I had to say something—but what?

A **grove of dark green pines** was before us.

"*¿Cambian de color?*" I thought I could ask but how would it sound?

I practiced it in my head. *Do dose trees . . .* those, *Cristina, like the z in Spanish.*

"Do those trees change color?" I pointed with my chin at the pines.

"No, they're evergreens."

"Like palm trees," I said.

"Do you miss Puerto Rico?" he asked.

"A little," I caught myself saying.

It was then I realized I wasn't cold. And I wasn't wearing a coat. ❖

About the Author

Carmen T. Bernier-Grand

Carmen T. Bernier-Grand (1947–) is the author of many books for young adults. Bernier-Grand writes most of her books in English, her second language. She grew up in Puerto Rico speaking Spanish. Bernier-Grand says that she "thinks, writes, and dreams" in both languages. Her experience of living in different places plays an important part in the creativity of her writing. Today, Bernier-Grand lives in Portland, Oregon.

In Other Words

crunching walking on the
grove of dark green pines group of trees
¿Cambian de color? Do the trees change color? (in Spanish)

Before You Move On

1. **Confirm Prediction** Was your prediction right? What happened that you didn't expect?
2. **Paraphrase** In your own words, explain what Cristina means when she says, "I realized I wasn't cold."

Almost Evenly Divided
by Emma Suárez-Báez

My life
almost evenly divided
17½ years Puertorican
20½ years New Yorker

5 I've lost
a land that felt mine
flamboyanes, canarias
going to the bank con papi
learning to cook like mami
10 las parrandas
the sun that warms up the chickens
el campo en Lajas
mi prima Adira
la vida lenta
15 ser mujer puertorriqueña
ser mujer puertorriqueña

Almost evenly divided
but half lost

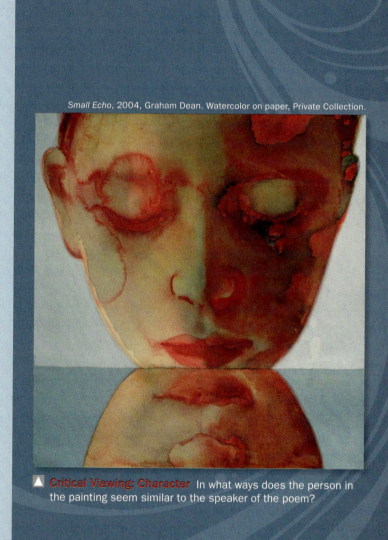

Small Echo, 2004, Graham Dean. Watercolor on paper, Private Collection.

▲ **Critical Viewing: Character** In what ways does the person in the painting seem similar to the speaker of the poem?

In Other Words (all in Spanish)

flamboyanes, canarias trees and canary birds
con papi with daddy
mami mommy
las parrandas the street celebrations

el campo en Lajas the countryside around Lajas in Puerto Rico
mi prima my cousin
la vida lenta the slow life
ser mujer puertorriqueña being a Puerto Rican woman

Before You Move On

1. **Compare and Contrast** How does Cristina's experience in "Indian Summer Sun" compare to the experience of the speaker of this poem?
2. **Paraphrase** In your own words, explain what the speaker in the poem means when she says her life is "almost evenly divided".

Connect Reading and Writing

Vocabulary
- adjustment
- concentrate
- couple
- ignore
- opportunity
- perspective
- refuse
- remind

CRITICAL THINKING

1. **SUM IT UP** Use the Text-to-Self Connections Chart you made to sum up the selection and tell about Cristina's **adjustment** to the United States.

Text-to-Self Connections Chart

The text says . . .	This reminds me of . . .	The connection helps because . . .

2. **Analyze** What is the turning point of the story? Explain how Cristina's **perspective** on her new home changes as a result.

3. **Speculate** What might have happened if Cristina had **refused** to go to the party? Base your answer on events in the story.

4. **Interpret** How are the **perspectives** of the poem and the short story similar and different?

READING FLUENCY

Expression Read the passage on page 645 to a partner. Assess your fluency.

1. I read
   a. great   **b.** OK   **c.** not very well

2. What I did best in my reading was _____.

READING STRATEGY

Make Connections
How did making text-to-self connections help you? Tell a partner about two of your connections.

VOCABULARY REVIEW

Oral Review Read the paragraph aloud. Add the vocabulary words.

Moving to a new place can be a big _____. You can't simply _____ to change, but you can still be you. Open your mind to the _____ that this is a great _____ to be at home in a new location. _____ on what is positive about the experience and _____ the rest. If you feel alone and everyone seems to be a _____ or in a group, don't worry. _____ yourself that you will soon make new friends.

Written Review Imagine you are Cristina's father. Write a letter to **remind** her how she can make a positive **adjustment** to her new home. Use five vocabulary words.

WRITE ABOUT THE GUIDING QUESTION

Explore Being At Home in the World
Choose a character from the story. How did he or she affect Cristina's **adjustment** to her new location? How does this remind you of a situation in your own life? Give examples from the text and your own experience.

Connect Across the Curriculum

ELPS: 2.C.4 learn academic vocabulary heard during classroom instruction and interactions; 4.F.8 use support from peers and teachers to develop vocabulary needed to comprehend increasingly challenging language

Literary Analysis

Analyze Realistic Fiction

Academic Vocabulary
- **element** (e-lu-munt) *noun*
  An **element** is one part of a whole.

What Makes Fiction Seem Real? Realistic fiction is about people, relationships, and problems like those in real life. The **elements** that make realistic fiction true to life are the **characters**, **setting**, **dialogue**, and **plot**. Realistic fiction has a conflict, or problem, that might be found in real life. The characters may deal with issues or feelings that readers can relate to.

> **Characters are like real people you know.**

When I went to the Latino table, Sergio was talking about salsa.

"I bet you're a good dancer," he said.

"I'm not," I answered. "I don't even know how to dance."

> **Dialogue sounds natural and real.**

"You're Puerto Rican and you don't know how to dance!" That was Norma.

"Exactly," I said, louder than I had to, because I was feeling as if I didn't fit in with this group either.

> **The conflicts characters face are like those people face in real life.**

Practice Together

Analyze Elements Look at the passage above to identify the realistic story **elements**. With the class, review a different passage from "Indian Summer Sun." Identify the **elements** that seem realistic in that passage.

Try It!

Select another passage from "Indian Summer Sun" to review. Analyze the passage, and identify the **elements** that make it seem realistic. How do you know? Discuss your ideas with a partner.

▲ The characters in realistic fiction are like those in real life.

ELPS: 2.C.4 learn academic vocabulary heard during classroom instruction and interactions; 2.H.1 understand implicit ideas in complex spoken language

Vocabulary Study

Understand Denotation and Connotation

Academic Vocabulary
- **connotation** (con-ō-tā-shun) *noun*
  The **connotation** of a word is the set of feelings that is associated with it.

Denotation is the exact dictionary meaning of a word. **Connotation** involves the feelings associated with a word. **Connotations** of words may be positive, negative, or neutral. We usually admire someone who is *determined*. This word has a positive **connotation**. We are less likely to admire someone who is *stubborn*, a word with a negative **connotation**. The synonym *persistent* is neutral in feeling.

Identify Connotation Read the sentences aloud with a partner. Decide which underlined words have positive, negative, and neutral **connotations**. Use a dictionary to check your ideas.

1. The new student was <u>intelligent</u> and could solve math problems easily.
2. The new student was <u>brilliant</u> and won the school math competition.
3. That car was on sale, so it was <u>inexpensive</u>.
4. The <u>cheap</u> car lost its hubcap after we bought it.

Listening/Speaking

Perform a Poem

DRAMA

ELPS: 1.E.3 internalize new academic language in speaking activities; 2.C.4 learn academic vocabulary heard during classroom instruction and interactions

Academic Vocabulary
- **effect** (i-fekt) *noun*
  An **effect** is the result or an action or cause.

Two elements that make up the rhythm of poetry are **repetition** and **cadence**. **Repetition** refers to repeated words, lines, phrases, and other patterns in writing. **Cadence** refers to the flow of language. It is a mixture of speed, rhythm, and the rise and fall of voice.

❶ **Read the Poem** The poem "Almost Evenly Divided" repeats a pattern in lines 3 and 4, using different numbers. What **effect** does the repetition have? What other repetitions can you find?

❷ **Practice the Poem** Recite the poem "Almost Evenly Divided" from memory or brief notes. Emphasize the rhythm and stress important words to show the emotions of the poem.

❸ **Perform the Poem** Present the poem to the class. Recite the poem in a way that will keep your audience interested. Make eye contact and look around the room as you speak.

ELPS: 2.C.4 learn academic vocabulary heard during classroom instruction and interactions

Listening/Speaking

Deliver an Entertaining Speech

Academic Vocabulary
- **location** (lo-kā-shun) *noun*
  The **location** is the site or place where a person lives.

How did Cristina feel in "Indian Summer Sun"? Imagine you are a new student at school. Create a speech that describes your old home to your class in an entertaining way.

1 **Research a Location** Choose the **location** you "moved" from in your imaginary role as a new student. Pick a specific town or city that you want to learn more about. Use the Internet, books, or magazines to find fun and interesting facts to share about your **location**. What information will entertain your audience in your speech? Find out about the traditions, culture, and climate of your old **location**.

2 **Write Your Speech** As you write, choose your words carefully so that they carry the connotations you want them to. Create an interesting introduction that will grab your audience's attention. Include rhetorical devices such, as similes and metaphors, that effectively develop your speech. Fill out a Main-Idea Diagram to help you organize your speech.

Main-Idea Diagram

Main Idea:
Detail:
Detail:
Detail:

3 **Practice Your Speech** As you practice, work on speaking clearly and using a tone of voice that matches the material. Plan for pauses, repetitions, and rises and falls in your voice that match the subject. Practice facial expressions and gestures that help express your meaning and entertain your audience.

4 **Deliver Your Speech** Present your speech to the class. Relax and be as natural as you can. Speak loudly and clearly. When it is your turn to listen, respect the work others have done.

5 **Ask for Feedback** Work with a partner and summarize each other's presentations. Be sure to evaluate the main ideas for clarity.

Clarify and Verify

Pair Talk With a partner, talk about things Cristina may have missed after she went to live with her mother. Clarify your ideas by explaining them or comparing them to something else. Verify your ideas with examples from the story. Use pronouns in subjects and predicates.

> Cristina missed palm trees.

> She mentioned them to Jerry when she asked about evergreens.

ELPS: 5.D.2 edit writing for standard grammar and usage, including pronoun agreement

Write About Fitting In

Study the Models When you write, you want to avoid confusing your reader. Using the correct forms of pronouns will make your writing clear and easy to understand.

NOT OK

> Me see Kathy in the lunchroom. Her is talking to Jerry. Them are sister and brother. She waves to I. Then me see Sergio. He and me are in the same English class. I go and sit with he. Us speak Spanish together. I tell he and his friends about my school in Puerto Rico.

This writer confuses the reader by using pronouns incorrectly.

OK

> I see Kathy in the lunchroom. She is talking to Jerry. They are sister and brother. She waves to me. Then I see Sergio. He and I are in the same English class. I go and sit with him. We speak Spanish together. I tell him and his friends about my school in Puerto Rico.

This writing makes much more sense.

Add Sentences Write two more sentences to add to the OK model that add detail and explain more of the events.

✏ **WRITE ON YOUR OWN** Write about a situation when a friend did not feel comfortable. Tell how that person felt and what happened. Be sure to use correct pronouns in your sentences.

REMEMBER

- Subject pronouns include: **I, you, he, she, it, we, you, they**
- Object pronouns include: **me, you, him, her, it, us, you, them**

Compare Across Texts

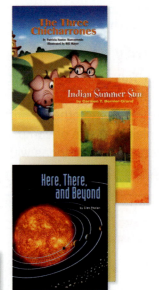

Compare and Contrast Forms of Fiction

Compare the **characteristics** of these selections.

How It Works

Organize Ideas Use a chart to compare the **characteristics** of three forms of fiction.

Comparison Chart

Comparison Questions	Realistic Fiction such as "Indian Summer Sun"	Myths such as "Why the Sun and the Moon Live in the Sky"	Fairy Tales/Fables such as "The Three Chicharrones"
1. What things are similar about these forms of fiction?	made up (fiction) has a setting has characters has a theme	made up (fiction) has a setting has characters has a theme	made up (fiction) has a setting has characters has a theme
2. What things are different?			
3. Paraphrase plot to illustrate form characteristics.			

Practice Together

Compare and Contrast the Ideas To write your comparison, look for how the ideas are alike and explain the connection. Here is a summary for question 1.

Summary

> Realistic fiction, myths, and fairy tales are similar because they are all made up from the writers' imagination. They each have characters, settings, and a theme, or message.

Try It!

Make a chart to record your answers to question 2. You may want to use this frame to write your comparison and contrast summary.

All fiction is made up from a writer's imagination. In realistic fiction, characters _____. Settings in realistic fiction _____. The ideas in realistic fiction _____. In myths, the settings _____. Characters are _____. Myths show _____. In fairy tales and fables, settings _____. Characters are _____. Fairy tales and fables make a point by _____.

Academic Vocabulary

- **characteristic** (kair-ik-tu-**ris**-tik)
  noun
  A **characteristic** is a specific feature or trait that helps you identify something.

At Home in the World

 GUIDING QUESTION How can your location affect the way you live?

UNIT LIBRARY

Content Library

Leveled Library

Reflect on Your Reading

Think back on your reading of the unit selections. Discuss what you did to understand what you read.

Focus on Genre **Comparing and Contrasting**

In this unit, you learned about comparison and contrast. Choose two selections from the unit. Explain to a partner the similarities and differences between the two selections.

Reading Strategy **Make Connections**

As you read the selections, you learned how making connections helps you understand what you read. Explain to a partner how you will use this strategy in the future.

Explore the GUIDING QUESTION

Throughout this unit, you have been thinking about how people's locations affect the way they live. Choose one of these ways to explore the Guiding Question:

- **Discuss** With a group, discuss the Guiding Question. Listen and learn from your classmates' responses. Discuss examples from the selections that support your ideas.

- **Write** Write a letter to, or as, one of the people in this unit. Compare your location to that of the person you're writing to.

- **Draw** Create a visual response to the Guiding Question. It could be a drawing of your community, state, country, or Earth. Show how this location affects the way you live.

Book Talk

Which Unit Library book did you choose? Explain to a partner what it taught you about feeling at home in the world.

The Tiger's Garden, 2006, Alfredo Arreguin. Oil on canvas, private collection.

 **Critical Viewing:** How do the details in this image show that our environment is valuable?

ELPS Focus: 2.H.2 understand implicit information in complex spoken language; 2.I.4 demonstrate listening comprehension of complex spoken English by collaborating with peers; 3.B.1 expand and internalize initial vocabulary by learning and using high-frequency words necessary for identifying and describing people, places, and objects; 3.C.1 speak using a variety of grammatical structures with increasing accuracy and ease; 3.H.2 describe with increasing specificity and detail; 4.C.4 comprehend English language structures used routinely in written classroom materials

Unit 5

Our Precious World

GUIDING QUESTION

What makes the environment so valuable?

Read More!

Content Library

Ecosystems
by Nancy Finton

Leveled Library

The Summer of the Swans
by Betsy Byars

And the Earth Did Not Devour Him
by Tomás Rivera

Left Behind
by Velma Wallis

Internet
InsideNG.com

- Learn more about our environment.
- Read about the efforts to save endangered species.
- Discover the work of National Geographic explorers.

Focus on Genre

 ELPS: 1.A.1 use prior knowledge to understand meanings in English; 4.C.3 comprehend English vocabulary used routinely in written classroom materials; 4.F.1 use visual and contextual support to read grade-appropriate content area text; 4.F.2 use visual and contextual support to enhance and confirm understanding; 4.F.6 use support from peers and teachers to read grade-appropriate content area text

Text Features in Nonfiction

▶ **Features That Organize**
▶ **Features That Show Information**

Nonfiction text gives information about real events, issues, people, and ideas. Writers use text **features** to help readers locate, use, and analyze the information they need.

How It Works

Writers use text **features** to organize information.

- **Headings and subheadings** and **boldface** and **italic type** help you see the organization of a text. In longer works, **tables of contents** and **indexes** help you locate specific information.

Writers also use text **features** to show information.

- **Charts**, **diagrams**, **graphs**, **sidebars**, and **maps**, as well as **illustrations** and **photographs** show specific information visually instead of in words.

Here is an example of how text **features** can help organize and present information in nonfiction.

Classroom Words

This lesson contains several words that are routinely used in written classroom materials, no matter what the subject.

information
practice
organize

Forests of the World
Location Matters

All forests have trees, but not all forests are alike. Forests can be very different, depending on where they are found in the world.

Central American Tropical Forest

North American Mountain Forest

▲ A tropical forest in Central America (left) gets warmer than an evergreen forest in North America (right).

> **Main heading**

> **Each subheading gives the main idea of the section that follows.**

> **Labels identify what is shown.**

> **Photos present information at a glance.**

> **Captions give more details about photos and other visuals.**

Academic Vocabulary

- **feature** (fē-chur) *noun*
  A **feature** is part of something that stands out or is noticeable.

Practice Together

Read the passage below aloud with your class to see how the text features help organize the text and provide additional information.

The American Alligator ← Main heading

Endangered

People once made shoes and bags from alligator skins. Such fashions and human destruction of alligators' **habitat**, or places to live, were serious threats to these reptiles. In 1967, alligators were listed as **endangered**—that is, in danger of becoming extinct.

> Boldface type indicates important terms or vocabulary.

Recovered ← Subheading

By working together, the government and other groups were able to save alligators. The species is now doing well. It was removed from the endangered list in 1987, although the U.S. Fish and Wildlife Service still watches it closely.

Habitat of the American Alligator

> The map title tells what the map shows.

Pacific Ocean

> Color coding shows where to focus attention.

N

> A compass rose points north to show direction.

> A caption gives more information about the map.

▲ As a cold-blooded reptile, the American alligator lives in warm climates, shown here in yellow.

▲ American alligator

Practice Together

Read the passage aloud with your class. What informational text features are here? What does each one do?

Saved from Extinction

The bald eagle is a triumph of wildlife conservation. By the middle of the 1900s, very few bald eagles existed in the United States. Hunting, loss of habitat to humans, and the use of pesticides, or chemicals used to protect crops from insect pests, had nearly wiped out the bald eagle population . . . .

▲ Bald eagles are known for their white heads and tails. Birds are about five years old when their head and tail feathers become white.

National Bird

In 1782, the bald eagle was selected to be the national bird of the new United States. At that time, the bald eagle population was about 100,000 nesting eagles. By 1963, there were only about 400 breeding pairs. Thanks to the work of conservationists, there are now at least 7,500 breeding pairs of bald eagles in most of the United States, not counting Alaska and Hawaii.

Facts About the Bald Eagle	
Food	Fish, small mammals
Life span	Can live about 50 years
Number of eggs	2–3 eggs per year
Wingspan	6–7 ½ feet

BALD EAGLE HABITAT

▲ The red area shows the bald eagle's habitat.

Read the following passage and text features aloud. What are the text features in this example? How does each one help a reader understand the text? How do you know?

Falcons Saved Just in Time

▲ peregrine falcon

Falcon Populations Drop

Peregrine falcons are **raptors**, or birds of prey. They eat smaller animals. The populations of these raptors in the United States dropped dangerously low from the 1940s to the 1970s.

Effects of DDT

DDT is a chemical used to control insects. From 1939 to 1972, it was used widely on crops. Then scientists proved it was harmful to wildlife.

Small levels of DDT got into the bodies of small animals. Peregrine falcons ate the animals, and the DDT collected in the falcons' bodies. It caused falcons to lay thin eggs that broke before the babies could hatch.

DDT affected many animals. In 1962, Rachel Carson published *Silent Spring* to make the public aware of the problem. Finally, the Environmental Protection Agency banned the general use of DDT.

Range of the Peregrine Falcon

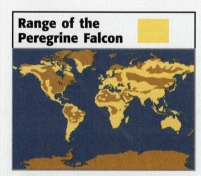
▲ Peregrine falcons are again one of the most common birds of prey, living everywhere but Antarctica.

Number of Falcon Pairs

Pairs

Year

Source: The U.S. Department of Environmental Protection

▲ From 1940–1975 the number of nesting pairs of peregrine falcons dropped from over 3,000 to under 400.

Focus on Vocabulary

ELPS: 1.A.1 use prior knowledge to understand meanings in English; 4.F.3 use visual and contextual support to develop vocabulary needed to comprehend increasingly challenging language; 4.F.8 use support from peers and teachers to develop vocabulary needed to comprehend increasingly challenging language

Use Context Clues: Multiple-Meaning Words

Some words in English have multiple, or more than one, meaning. For instance, the word *well* has more than one meaning.

Rosa felt **well** enough to go to the concert. (*well* = not sick)

My uncle gets water from a **well**. (*well* = a deep hole in the ground)

As you read, if you come to a word you know but that doesn't make sense in the text, the word is probably a multiple-meaning word.

How the Strategy Works

When you come to a word that has more than one meaning, use its <mark>context</mark>, or surrounding text, to figure out which meaning the writer used.

EXAMPLE   Jan is ready to **present** her report.

1. Read the entire sentence or paragraph to find other words that might be clues to the word's meaning.
2. Decide if the word names an action, a thing, or describes something. In this example, Jan is about to do something, so *present* names an action.
3. Try to see how the word affects the rest of the sentence. Jan is ready to do something with her report. What might she do?
4. Restate the sentence. "Jan is ready to *give* her report."
5. Decide the meaning of the word that makes sense. In this example, *present* means "to give or to share."

Use the strategy to figure out the meaning of *close*.

> Are there more kinds of animals now than 100 years ago, or are there fewer? Answering that kind of question is not easy. Scientists spend years of <u>close</u> study to find the answers. They take careful notes and measurements and compare them over time.

☑ **REMEMBER** You can often use <mark>context</mark> to figure out the meaning of a word that has more than one meaning.

Strategy in Action

" The word *close* here describes how scientists study, so it cannot be an action, like closing a book. It might mean 'nearby,' but that doesn't make sense. I think that *close* here means 'careful and exact.'"

Academic Vocabulary

- **context** (**kon**-tekst) *noun*
  Context is the surrounding text near a word or phrase that helps explain the meaning of the word.

Practice Together

Read the passage aloud. As you read, listen for context that helps you figure out the correct meaning of each underlined word.

What's the Good News?

Television, radio, newspapers, and the Internet tell us news about the environment. Sometimes their stories give a <u>dim</u> view of things.

Sometimes, however, bad news can lead to action. One good example is California Coastal Cleanup Day.

News reports about the amount of garbage along California's <u>coast</u> caused people to take action. Now more than 50,000 people come together each year on the third Saturday of September to clean up the coast. Since the <u>program</u> began in 1985, more than three <u>quarters</u> of a million volunteers have removed over 12 million pounds of <u>waste</u> and garbage from California shores.

Try It!

Read the following passage. What is the correct meaning of each underlined word? How do you know?

One Person

How can one person help the natural world? Perhaps you don't live in a rain forest or can't do research at the South <u>Pole</u>. But if you <u>long</u> to help the planet, you can make choices that make a difference. Use less water. Use fewer plastics. Recycle whenever it's possible. Keep your home a little cooler in winter and a little warmer in summer. Use batteries that you can recharge. Avoid driving when you can walk. Dispose of trash properly.

None of these <u>tips</u> is new. Think, though, about the difference it would make if the <u>rest</u> of us, all 250 million Americans, followed your <u>lead</u>.

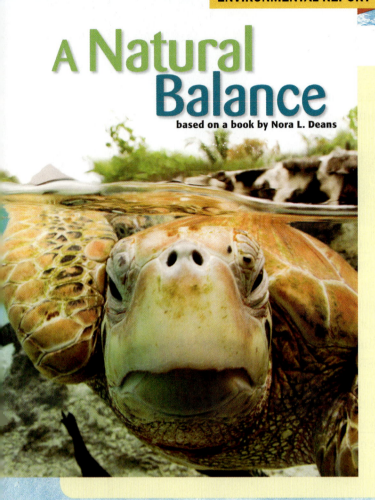

A Natural Balance

based on a book by Nora L. Deans

Build Background

See How Humans Affect the Environment

How do humans affect the environment? Our actions can make the world better or worse. We may not know that some of the things we do harm plants and animals.

Connect

Habitat Drawing Brainstorm what wild animals need to survive. Then draw a habitat, such as the mountains, desert, or forest. What if people built a town on that land? Discuss with a partner how it would affect the animals.

Digital Library

InsideNG.com
⊘ View the video.

▲ Like many plants and animals, gray wolves face danger from humans.

ELPS: 3.C.1 speak using a variety of grammatical structures with increasing accuracy and ease; 3.H.2 describe with increasing specificity and detail

1 TRY OUT LANGUAGE
2 LEARN GRAMMAR
3 APPLY ON YOUR OWN

Describe Animals and Things

CD

Listen to the rap that describes an animal. Then listen again and chime in. If you don't understand what is being said, ask for clarification.

RAP

The Okapi

You rarely see an okapi.
She lives quietly and alone
In dense African forests.
For years she was unknown.
Now that we have found her,
She may soon be gone.

She is a funny creature
With a lo-o-ong and clever tongue,
A tongue that is unique among
Her African animal peers.
She uses it to wash her eyelids
And to clean her ears.

She has an awkward body.
It makes you want to laugh.
Her legs are zebra-striped.
That's just her bottom half.
Sitting on her short, thick neck
Is the head of a giraffe.

You may never see an okapi,
And that would be a shame,
Except in a zoo, but you know it's true,
A zoo is not the same
As seeing the okapi
Or any animal you name
Living and free, alive and free
Within its own domain.

▲ The okapi lives in the African rain forest. It is one of the few animals that can lick its own ears with its long tongue. This animal, or species, is in danger of disappearing.

Use Adjectives That Describe

You can describe people, places, or things with **adjectives**. They answer the question: *What is the person, place, or thing like?*

EXAMPLES   The **blue whale** makes **deep sounds**.

Adjectives help the reader imagine people, places, or things.

Use adjectives to describe:	Examples
how something looks	beautiful, huge, long, red, tiny
how something sounds	deep, loud, quiet, rumbling, squeaky
how something feels, tastes, or smells	bitter, cold, salty, slimy, smooth
a person's mood	angry, fearful, helpful, kind, timid
how many	many, plentiful, rare, ten

Often the adjective comes before the **noun** you are describing.

EXAMPLES   This **large mammal** is a **fast swimmer**.

If your verb is a form of **be**, you can put the adjective after the verb.
The forms of *be* are *am*, *is*, *are*, *was*, and *were*.

EXAMPLES   The bats' cave **is dark**. Attacks on humans **are rare**.

Practice Together

Say each sentence. Choose an adjective from the box to describe the noun.
Then say the sentence again with the adjective.

| colorful   graceful   loud   slimy   tiny |

1. The bat made a _____ sound as it flew out of the cave.
2. The parrot's feathers are bright and _____.
3. The _____ worm slipped out of my hand.
4. The _____ mouse scampered through the leaves.
5. The _____ eagle soared easily through the air.

Try It!

Say each sentence. Choose an adjective from the box, and
write it on a card. Then say the sentence with the adjective.

| dark   endangered   huge   many   strong |

6. The gray bat lives in _____ caves.
7. The blue whale is _____.
8. Gray wolves travel _____ miles a day to hunt for food.
9. The jaguar is a _____ swimmer.
10. Many animals are _____.

▲ Bats help control insect populations. Some
bats are endangered.

Describe an Endangered Animal

DESCRIBE ANIMALS

Many animals are in danger of vanishing from the world. Find out about an endangered animal, and describe what it looks like and where it lives to the class.

Choose an animal from this list or another endangered animal that you know.

Ozark big-eared bat	West Indian manatee	pygmy rabbit
American black bear	Pacific pocket mouse	black rhinoceros
Key deer	ocelot	Hawaiian monk seal
black-footed ferret	northern sea otter	bighorn sheep
jaguar	Florida panther	blue whale

Internet InsideNG.com

⚲ Go online to learn what your animal looks like and other interesting information about it. Take notes.

Questions	Answers	Adjectives to Use
What does my animal look like?	glossy fur, black ears	glossy, black
Where does my animal live?		
What does my animal eat?		
What other interesting information do I know?		
Why is my animal endangered?		

Now describe your animal to a group.

HOW TO DESCRIBE ANIMALS AND THINGS

1. Tell how things look, sound, smell, taste, and feel.

2. Use adjectives to help others picture what you're describing.

The jaguar is a solitary animal that lives in Central and South America. It has a tan coat with large, black spots. This huge cat is an excellent swimmer, too.

USE ADJECTIVES THAT DESCRIBE

Use **adjectives** in your description. Remember that the adjectives you choose should help readers or listeners form pictures in their minds.

Often, the adjective comes before the noun you are describing. If two adjectives both describe the noun, separate them with a comma (,).

EXAMPLES The **gray** bat has **glossy** fur and **long** , **black** ears. **Gray** bats live in **limestone** caves. Their **summer** caves are **warm** , and their **winter** caves are **cold** .

Prepare to Read

ELPS: 1.A.1 use prior knowledge to understand meanings in English; 3.A practice producing sounds of newly acquired vocabulary in a manner that is comprehensible; 4.F.3 use visual and contextual support to develop vocabulary needed to comprehend increasingly challenging language; 4.F.6 use support from peers and teachers to read grade-appropriate content area text; 4.F.8 use support from peers and teachers to develop vocabulary needed to comprehend increasingly challenging language; 4.I.2 expand reading skills

Learn Key Vocabulary

Rate and Study the Words Rate how well you know each word. Then:

1. Pronounce the word. Say it aloud several times. Spell it.
2. Study the example.
3. Tell more about the word.
4. Practice it. Make the word your own.

Key Words

classified (klas-u-fīd) *verb*
▶ page 340

To be **classified** means to be arranged or put into groups. Scientists have **classified** many plants and animals.
Related Word: **classify**

endangered (en-dān-jurd) *adjective* ▶ page 338

To be **endangered** means to be at risk of disappearing forever. The ivory-billed woodpecker is an example of an **endangered** animal.

environment (en-vī-run-ment) *noun* ▶ page 337

The **environment** is all of the living and nonliving things that surround a person, animal, or plant. Every **environment** affects the things that live in it.

extinct (ik-stingt) *adjective*
▶ page 340

Something that is **extinct** is no longer living. The dodo bird became **extinct** because people hunted too many over time.
Related Word: **extinction**

illegal (i-lē-gul) *adjective*
▶ page 340

Something that is **illegal** is against the law. It is **illegal** to park in some areas.
Antonyms: **legal, lawful**

pollution (pul-lü-shun) *noun*
▶ page 338

Pollution is waste, chemicals, and gases that have a harmful effect. Air and water **pollution** hurt living things.

population
(pop-yu-lā-shun) *noun* ▶ page 338

Population is the total number of plants or animals in a group. The human **population** of Earth is more than six billion.

species (spē-shēz) *noun*
▶ page 338

A **species** is a related group of animals or plants. Lions and tigers are different **species**. African lions and Asian lions are the same **species**.

Practice the Words Work with a partner to complete an Expanded Meaning Map for each Key Word.

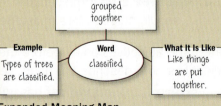

Expanded Meaning Map

Reading Strategy: Visualize

Nonfiction texts are filled with facts. When you create mental pictures as you read, you can better understand and remember information.

Reading Strategy
Visualize

HOW TO RECORD MENTAL IMAGES

1. Preview before you read. Look at the photos and graphics. Use these as a starting point to create your own mental images.
2. Look for words that explain. Use the words to form pictures in your mind. Ask: *What would this look like?*
3. Add what you know from your own life. Use your own experiences to add to your mental images.
4. Note important details and visualize the words. Sketch images you form in your mind.

Visualization Chart

Words in the Text	My Own Experiences	What I Visualize
Suppose you put seeds out for the birds in your area. Then, the bird population might get larger, too.	My father puts out seeds for sparrows and other birds in winter.	I picture more birds making nests in spring because of the food supply.

Strategy in Action

Here's how one student visualized a passage.

Look Into the Text

Sometimes our actions benefit the environment because we might help a certain plant or animal population get larger. For example, imagine that you plant tulips in your neighborhood. This action helps the tulip population grow in your area. Suppose you put seeds out for the birds in your area. Then, the bird population might get larger, too.

To visualize, look for words that explain. "I picture more birds coming to our yard."

Use your own experience to form images. "I've seen Dad put out seeds for birds in our yard."

Practice Together

With a partner, read the passage again and create your own mental images. Follow the steps in the How-To box to make a Visualization Chart.

ELPS: 4.F.1 use visual and contextual support to read grade-appropriate content area text; 4.F.2 use visual and contextual support to enhance and confirm understanding; 4.I.2 expand reading skills

Green sea turtles swim off the coast of Bora Bora Island. These turtles are endangered in many countries. ▶

Focus on Genre

Environmental Report

A report is expository nonfiction that provides detailed information about a particular topic. Many reports have **text features** like diagrams, photos, and charts that explain information in a visual way.

Diagram

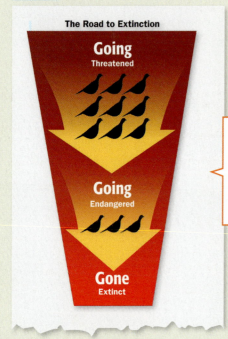

The Road to Extinction

Going
Threatened

Going
Endangered

Gone
Extinct

Arrows and images illustrate stages of a process described in the text.

Your Job as a Reader

Reading Strategy: Visualize

As you read, use words that explain or describe to create mental images. Take notes.

> Boys in Miami Beach, Florida, gather the eggs of sea turtles to protect them from other animals.

"In my mind, I can visualize boys walking on the beach, picking up eggs."

A Natural Balance

Balance

based on a book by Nora L. Deans

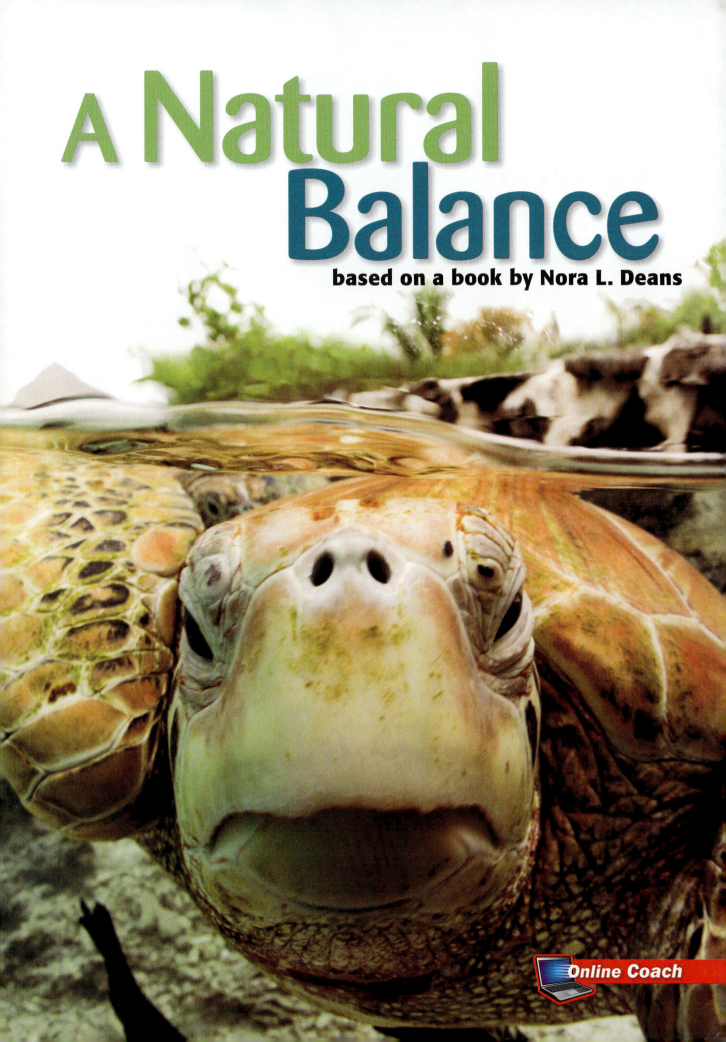

Boys in Miami Beach, Florida, gather the eggs of sea turtles to protect them from other animals. ▶

Our Effect on the Environment

Beep! Beep! Beep! Your alarm goes off and you hop out of bed. You wash your face, chat with your family, eat your breakfast, and take the bus to school. Even before you go to school, you have connected with many people and things. All of the things you do affect the **environment.**

Your environment is all of the living and nonliving things around you. All across Earth, humans are changing the environment in different ways. For example: we cut down trees to build houses, **plow fields** to grow crops, build roads and parking lots, and empty **waste** into rivers, lakes, and oceans. We also use large nets and boats to catch huge amounts of fish. Activities like these greatly affect plants and animals in our environment.

▲ A kayaker passes by trash along the shore of the Anacostia River.

Key Vocabulary
environment *n.*, everything that surrounds you

In Other Words
plow fields clear land
waste garbage

Are We Helping or Harming?

The way we live our lives can affect our environment in both positive and negative ways. Sometimes our actions **benefit** the environment because we might help a certain plant or animal **population** get larger. For example, imagine that you plant tulips in your neighborhood. This action helps the tulip population grow in your area. Suppose you **put seeds out for** the birds in your area. Then, the bird population might get larger, too.

On the other hand, our activities can also harm plant and animal populations. Think about all of the plants and animals in neighborhood parks. What happens to the population of these plants and animals if the parks turn into apartment buildings? These plants and animals might die or move someplace else because of increased development. As a result, the area's plant and animal population decreases.

Over-hunting, **pollution**, and other activities can also decrease the population of a **species**. The population may become so small that it is in danger of dying out. When a species is in danger of dying out, it is called an **endangered** species.

▲ Florida's black bears need more protection as development moves in.

The Road to Extinction

An easy way to remember the threats facing plants and animals today is HIPPO. It stands for:

- **H**abitat loss—cutting down trees, tearing up the land; such activities often leave plants and animals with no place to live

- **I**ntroduced species—bringing in new life-forms that crowd out or feed on the ones that were there

- **P**ollution—chemicals and wastes that damage or even kill living things

- **P**opulation growth—more and more people who need more food and more land

- **O**ver-consumption—hunting and fishing and harvesting too many plants or animals

What's Harming the Habitat?

The way we use or pollute natural resources like water or land affects the environment. Several factors contribute to the loss of habitat, the areas that support plant and animal populations.

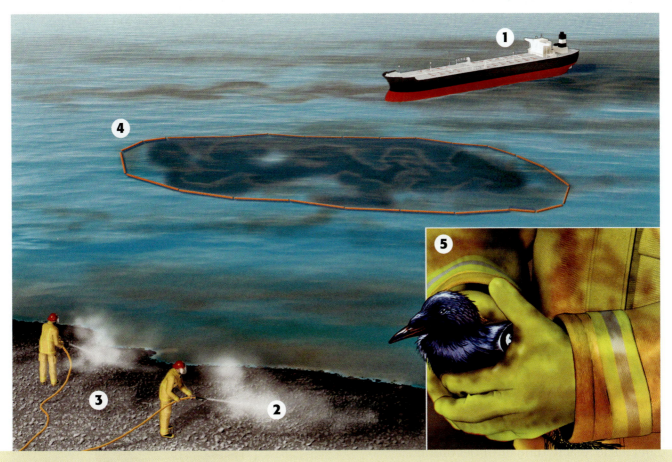

Oil spill emergency

Oil spills are major ocean disasters. An oil spill is what happens when a tanker, or large ship, carrying oil gets a hole in it and leaks the oil.

1 A large tanker gets stuck on shallow land. When crew members start to drive the tanker again, they can put a hole in it, leaking the oil.

2 As part of the clean-up effort, oily shore rocks and sand are rinsed with very hot water.

3 Thousands of workers help clean up the spill.

4 Containment booms surround large areas of oil.

5 Oil-soaked birds are cleaned with absorbent pads. Some survive but hundreds of thousands die. Sea otters, whales, and schools of fish also die.

Before You Move On

1. **Explain** How might buildings that replace parks affect plant and animal **populations**?
2. **Paraphrase** Tell in your own words what threats plants and animals face today.
3. **Evaluate** Is the illustration clear? What purpose does it achieve?

Are We Solving the Problem?

The problem of the endangered environment is not new, and over time large groups of plants and animals quickly began to disappear. So, people began to look for ways to protect these important species. In the early 1900s, laws were passed to protect certain animals, but the biggest change came many years later. In 1973, the U.S. government passed the Endangered Species Act. This act lists species that are in danger of becoming **extinct**, or lost forever. The act makes it **illegal** to **collect** or harm any of the species on the list and it also protects the areas where the listed species live.

There is only one way that a species can be added to or removed from the list. Congress must agree to the change. In other words, state representatives must meet, vote, and pass a law or an act.

Many species are already on the list and they can be **classified** as either "threatened" or "endangered." A threatened species is less in danger of becoming extinct. An endangered species is most in danger of becoming extinct. A threatened species could, however, become endangered without protection.

Many more plants are endangered than animals. About one out of every ten plants may become extinct.

About 75 percent of the world's bird species are endangered. More than 60 percent of primates, such as apes and monkeys, are also endangered. Some scientists think as many as 100 species become extinct each day.

The Road to Extinction

Going Threatened

Going Endangered

Gone Extinct

▲ A threatened species can become endangered without protection. An endangered species can become extinct.

Key Vocabulary
extinct *adj.*, no longer living
illegal *adj.*, against the law
classified *v.*, placed into groups

In Other Words
collect take

Science Background
You rely on plants for food, shelter, clothing, medicines, and the air you breathe. Yet, a very large number of plant species are endangered. You can help save these plants by starting your own garden or joining a program in your community.

Endangered Animals

▲ **Black rhinoceros**

▲ **Mitchell's satyr butterfly**

▲ **Golden-shouldered parrot**

▲ Habitat loss is the most serious threat facing manatees today.

Before You Move On

1. **Main Idea and Details** List three ways the Endangered Species Act helps protect species that are threatened or endangered.
2. **Compare and Contrast** The U.S. government labels **species** as either threatened or **endangered**. Explain the difference.

The U.S. Fish and Wildlife Service (FWS) is the government agency **in charge of** enforcing the Endangered Species Act. Many of the scientists at FWS study threatened and endangered plants and animals by **tracking** the populations of the species on the list.

For example, the bald eagle used to be listed as an endangered species. In 1963, there were only 400 pairs left. By 1995, after many **recovery efforts**, the bald eagle population increased enough for the FWS to reclassify the bald eagle from "endangered" to "threatened." Due to government and volunteer efforts, there are about 10,000 pairs today. Thus, the bald eagle has now been removed from the endangered and threatened species list.

The scientists at FWS have a challenging job. They need to protect all the species on the list. Even so, there are always more species in need of protection.

Organizations and individuals try to protect endangered species as well. Zoos and aquariums often work together. They breed and raise rare and endangered animals. Botanical gardens and other groups raise rare and endangered plants. They also save their seeds. In this way, the plants won't disappear.

Not everyone agrees on the best way to help endangered species, especially when people's jobs or way of life may be threatened. Like so many cases involving endangered species, survival means balancing the protection of endangered species with people's way of life. ❖

◄ On June 28, 2007, the bald eagle was taken off the Federal List of Endangered and Threatened Wildlife and Plants. The bald eagle will still be protected by the Bald and Golden Eagle Protection Act.

In Other Words
in charge of responsible for
tracking watching and researching
recovery efforts efforts to save the
   birds

Endangered Plants

▲ The aloe's habitat is affected by burning and other kinds of habitat destruction.

▲ Orchid smuggling is leading to the loss of many kinds of wild orchids.

▲ The government began protecting the saguaro cactus when it started to disappear. This has prevented it from becoming endangered.

▲ A worker arranges seed plantings in a laboratory in China. These plants will grow fast to create new forests to keep up with China's growing demand for paper, which is made from trees.

Before You Move On

1. **Sequence** Tell what happened to the bald eagle **population** from 1963 to today.
2. **Problem and Solution** Why are scientists still concerned? What is being done to help?

In My Dreams

by Francisco X. Alarcón

buffaloes roam
free once again
on the plains

whales become
5 opera singers
of the sea

dolphins are
admired by all for
their smarts and joy

10 in my dreams
there is no word
for "war"

all humans
and all living
15 beings

come together
as one big family
of the Earth

△ Critical Viewing: Theme How does this painting connect to the unit theme "Our Precious World"?

Science Background

A whale song is the sound made by whales to communicate with each other. Sound travels much more quickly under water than above ground.

Before You Move On

1. **Visualize** Find words and lines that help you see, hear, or feel. How do they help you understand the poem?
2. **Inference** What do you think the speaker dreams will happen? Why is it just a dream?

Connect Reading and Writing

Vocabulary
classified
endangered
environment
extinct
illegal
pollution
population
species

CRITICAL THINKING

1. **SUM IT UP** Use the Visualization Chart you created to sum up the main ideas in "A Natural Balance."

Visualization Chart

Words in the Text	My Own Experiences	What I Visualize
HIPPO: The first letter stands for habitat loss—such as clearing forests where animals live.	A new mall was built near my home. My mom and I saw deer wander into a parking lot.	I picture a forest being cut down and animals having to move on.

2. **Speculate** How might the future change if certain plants and animals become **extinct**? Use examples from the text.

3. **Conclusion** **Populations** of wildlife can be **classified** as " **endangered** " or "threatened." Why is the difference important?

4. **Interpret** Are the speaker of the poem "In My Dreams" and the author of "A Natural Balance" hopeful about the **environment**? Explain.

READING FLUENCY

Intonation Read the passage on page 646 to a partner. Assess your fluency.

1. I read
   a. great   **b.** OK   **c.** not very well

2. What I did best in my reading was _____.

READING STRATEGY

Visualize
Share the Visualization Chart you made with a partner. Tell how the strategy helped you.

VOCABULARY REVIEW

Oral Review Read the paragraph aloud. Add the vocabulary words.

> In Washington, there are now very few pygmy rabbits, a special type or _____ of rabbit. Once, there were thousands, but now the _____ is decreasing. The U.S. Fish and Wildlife Service has _____ the pygmy rabbit as _____ . It is _____ to hunt it. Air and water _____ are not the main problems. Instead, the rabbit is losing its natural _____ . This animal is in danger of becoming _____ .

Written Review Imagine you are a scientist working to save **endangered** species. Write a brief report to describe the problems and suggest a solution. Use five vocabulary words.

WRITE ABOUT THE GUIDING QUESTION

Explore Our Valuable Environment
In your opinion, why is the **environment** so valuable? Reread the selection to find information that supports your ideas.

Connect Across the Curriculum

Literary Analysis

Use Text Features: Diagrams

Academic Vocabulary
- **interpret** (in-**tur**-prut) *verb*
  When you **interpret** something, you explain or tell the meaning of it.

Learn About Diagrams

A diagram is a picture or drawing that helps you **interpret** the information in nonfiction texts. Look at the diagram. Read the caption and the labels. The labels tell you what the layers of the Earth are, and the picture shows what the layers look like.

Crust

Mantle

Outer Core

Inner Core

▲ The Earth is made of many layers.

Practice Together

Identify Information Look at the diagram on page 339 of "A Natural Balance." This diagram shows what happens to a habitat when there is an oil spill. The labels identify the different parts of the diagram. Look at the first label, and answer these questions:

1. What is a tanker?

2. What causes a tanker to leak oil?

How does the first label help you understand the information about oil spills? How does the diagram and all its parts help you understand the main message in the selection?

Try It!

Interpret the Diagram Use the diagram in "A Natural Balance" to help you answer the following questions:

1. What is one cause of an oil spill?

2. How many workers helped clean up the oil spill?

3. What parts of the oil spill cleanup does the diagram show?

4. How are birds affected by the oil spill?

What other information do you get from the diagram that is not in the text? How do the diagram and the text work together to give you a clearer understanding of what harms a habitat? Does the diagram have any missing or unnecessary information? Discuss your ideas with a partner. Be sure you listen to the important details in each other's ideas.

ELPS:4.F.3 use visual and contextual support to develop vocabulary needed to comprehend increasingly challenging language

Use Context Clues: Multiple-Meaning Words

> **Academic Vocabulary**
> • **context** (**kon**-tekst) *noun*
>   **Context** is the surrounding text near a word that helps explain the meaning of the word.

Many words have more than one meaning. For example, a *bank* may be a place to put your money, or it may be the edge of a river. You can use **context** to choose the right meaning.

EXAMPLE   Eddie keeps his money in a **bank**.

Does Eddie dig a hole by the side of a river? No, it is most likely that he keeps his money at a business that protects it.

Think About Multiple Meanings Work with a partner. Read these sentences from the selection. Use **context** to figure out the correct meaning of each underlined word. Then, for each underlined word, write a sentence using a different meaning of the word.

1. Humans often empty <u>waste</u> into rivers, lakes, and oceans.

2. Imagine that you <u>plant</u> tulips in your neighborhood.

3. Think about all of the plants and animals in neighborhood <u>parks</u>.

4. Scientists <u>track</u> the populations of the endangered species on the list.

5. The Endangered Species <u>Act</u> makes it illegal to harm any of the species.

Analyze Imagery in Poetry

> **Academic Vocabulary**
> • **image** (**im**-ij) *noun*
>   An **image** is a mental picture of something.

Poets choose words carefully to create **images** in a reader's mind. These "word **images**" are called **imagery**. Do you "see" any special **image** when you read this? *Animals walked on the land again*. Compare that line to these lines from "In My Dreams."

> buffaloes roam
> free once again
> on the plains

Analyze Imagery With a partner, discuss **images** you "see" when you read "In My Dreams." Which examples of imagery are the most powerful? What message is the speaker trying to give?

ELPS: 5.G.3 explain with increasing specificity and detail to fulfill content area writing needs

Listening/Speaking

Give a Presentation on Endangered Species

HEALTH & SCIENCE

> **Academic Vocabulary**
> • **effect** (i-fekt) *noun*
>   An **effect** is the result of an action or cause.

In "A Natural Balance," you learned about problems that cause the extinction of plants and animals. Review the sidebar on page 338. Each of the "**HIPPO**" problems has a negative **effect** on plants and animals.

> **HIPPO** stands for
> **H**abitat loss
> **I**ntroduced species
> **P**ollution
> **P**opulation growth
> **O**ver-consumption

1 **Study Causes** What causes each of the five **HIPPO** problems? Work with a group to study and discuss the causes of each problem. For example: The problem of habitat loss is caused by trees being cut down and land being torn up.

2 **Think of Solutions** Choose one of the **HIPPO** problems. Discuss possible solutions with your group. Sometimes the cause or **effect** of the problem can help you think of solutions. Be sure to:

- Identify the problem.
- Explain why it is a problem.
- Tell what causes it.
- Suggest ideas that can help solve the problem.

3 **Prepare a Presentation** As a group, plan a problem-solution presentation to share with your class. Set goals and deadlines for completing your presentation. Use an outline like this to help organize your ideas:

> I. Problem: Habitat loss
>   A. threatens animals
>   B. threatens plants
> II. Causes
>   A. cutting down trees
>   B. tearing up land
> III. Effects
>   A. leaves plants and animals with no place to live
>   B. plants and animals become endangered
> IV. Solutions
>   A. plant more trees
>   B. preserve specific habitats

4 **Give Your Presentation** Write a draft of your presentation and share it with the class. Plan for each group member to speak for a certain amount of time. Make sure to explain your group's ideas clearly.

ELPS: 3.H.2 describe with increasing specificity and detail

Describe Animals and Things

Group Game Write names of common objects or familiar animals on index cards. Take turns choosing a card and adding an adjective or two to describe the noun. Then, the group members decide if the adjective accurately describes the noun.

> whale

> enormous whale

> enormous, blue whale

ELPS: 5.E employ increasingly complex grammatical structures in content area writing; 5.G.2 describe with increasing specificity and detail to fulfill content area writing needs

Write About an Animal

Study the Models Descriptive details add a lot of interest to your writing. Words that tell how things look, sound, smell, taste, and feel help readers see and experience what you are writing about.

JUST OK

> Manatees are endangered. These large mammals are related to the elephant. Manatees live in the waters around Florida. Algae often grow on their skin. Manatees use their flippers to steer and their tails to push themselves through water. These animals are playful.

This writer gives few descriptive details.

BETTER

> Manatees are endangered. These large, gentle mammals are related to the elephant. They live in the warm, coastal waters around Florida. Algae often grow on their thick, wrinkled skin. Manatees use their front flippers to steer and their powerful, flat tails to push themselves through shallow water. These slow-moving animals are playful.

This writer adds descriptive details by using effective adjectives. These words help readers picture a manatee more clearly.

Revise It Look back at the JUST OK model above. Work with a partner to improve it. Add different colorful details to help readers see, hear, feel, and smell the things that are described.

✏ **WRITE ON YOUR OWN** Write a descriptive paragraph about an animal you know well. Use colorful adjectives to help the reader imagine the animal's appearance and behavior.

▲ The playful manatee is an endangered species.

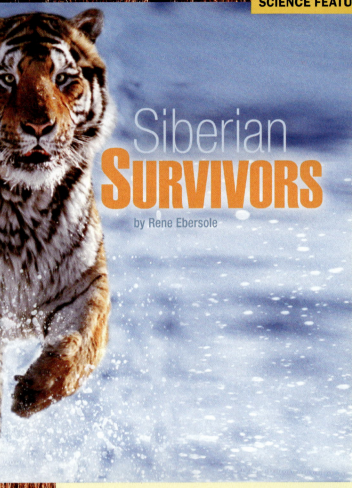

Siberian SURVIVORS

by Rene Ebersole

SELECTION 2 OVERVIEW

▶ **Build Background**

▶ **Language & Grammar**
Make Comparisons
Use Adjectives
That Compare

▶ **Prepare to Read**
Learn Key Vocabulary
Learn a Reading
Strategy
Visualize

▶ **Read and Write**
Focus on Genre
Science Feature
Apply the
Reading Strategy
Visualize
Critical Thinking
Reading Fluency
Read with Phrasing
Vocabulary Review
Write About the
Guiding Question

▶ **Connect Across the Curriculum**

Literary Analysis
Text Structure:
Use Text Features to
Make Comparisons

Vocabulary Study
Use Context Clues:
Multiple-Meaning Words
Across Content Areas

Research/Speaking
Give an Informative
Report

Listening/Speaking
Listen to a Report

Language and Grammar
Make Comparisons

Writing and Grammar
Write to Compare Tigers

Build Background

See Efforts to Save Our Environment

What is being done to protect wild animals and their habitats? Scientists from many countries are working together to save Siberian tigers.

Connect

Quickwrite What is your favorite animal? Describe it in a Quickwrite. Tell what you know about its appearance, its behavior, and its environment.

Digital Library

InsideNG.com
➤ View the images.

▲ Tigers are in more danger than other kinds of cats.

Language & Grammar

ELPS: 2.H.2 understand implicit information in complex spoken language; 3.B.1 expand and internalize initial vocabulary by learning and using high-frequency words necessary for identifying and describing people, places, and objects; 4.C.4 comprehend English language structures used routinely in written classroom materials

1 TRY OUT LANGUAGE
2 LEARN GRAMMAR
3 APPLY ON YOUR OWN

Make Comparisons

CD

Study the photographs and listen to this comparison.
How would you compare the two cats? Find one more way.

PICTURE PROMPT

▼ **Siberian tiger**

domestic cat ▶

It's All in the Family

The Siberian tiger and the domestic cat are relatives. Both belong to the cat family. However, the tiger lives in the wild and is much larger than the domesticated house cat. Large, wild cats like lions and tigers are often called "big cats."

All cats are natural hunters. They have sharp claws, strong jaws, and thirty sharp teeth. They have powerful bodies with padded feet. The tiger is more powerful and more ferocious than the house cat.

Cats can sneak up and suddenly pounce on their prey. They use their long tails for balance as they jump and leap. They use their rough, moist tongues for cleaning meat from animal bones and for grooming themselves.

All cats have the ability to see well in the dark. They have very good hearing, too. Both big cats and domestic cats mark their territories with their scents. This informs others of their home range. A tiger has a wider home range than a house cat.

Use Adjectives That Compare

Use a **comparative adjective** to compare two people, places, or things. Comparative adjectives are used routinely in written classroom materials.

EXAMPLES   The tiger is **fast,** but the cheetah is **faster** .

The tiger is **more powerful than** a house cat.

There are two ways to turn an adjective into a comparative adjective:

1. If the adjective has one syllable, add **-er**.	green cold large heavy green**er** cold**er** larg**er** heav**ier**
If it ends in silent **e**, drop the **e**. Then add **-er**.	The tiger is **larger than** the house cat.
If it ends in **y**, change the **y** to **i** before you add **-er**.	The lion is **heavy**, but the tiger is **heavier** .
2. If the adjective has three or more syllables, use **more** before the adjective.	curious threatening **more** curious **more** threatening Many cats are **curious**, but our cat Fluffy is **more curious than** most.

If an adjective has two syllables, sometimes you can use either form.

EXAMPLES   friendly   fearless
friendl**i er** or **more** friendly   **more** fearless

Practice Together

Change the adjective in the box to a comparative adjective. Say it. Then say the sentence with the comparative adjective.

1. | colorful | The tiger is colorful, but the parrot is _____.
2. | heavy | The rhinoceros is _____ than the tiger.
3. | fast | The cheetah is _____ than the tiger.
4. | dangerous | A tiger is _____ than a cheetah.
5. | sensitive | A cat's hearing is _____ than a dog's hearing.

▲ A cheetah is faster than a tiger.

Try It!

Change the adjective in the box to a comparative adjective. Write it on a card. Then say the sentence and add the comparative adjective.

6. | interested | I am _____ in learning about tigers than cows.
7. | cuddly | I think my cat is _____ than your cat.
8. | small | Your cat is small, but my hamster is _____.
9. | pretty | My cat's eyes are _____ than my dog's eyes.
10. | soft | My cat's fur is _____ than my pillow.

Tell How Animals Are Alike and Different

MAKE COMPARISONS

What is your favorite animal? Return to the Quickwrite you did on page 350. Compare your choice of animal to a partner's choice.

Share what you know about your animal with a partner. Tell your partner what your animal looks like, where it lives, what it eats, and other interesting facts that you know. Then have your partner share information about his or her animal. Make sure each of you understands the information presented.

	My Animal: Jaguar	My Partner's Animal: Amazon Parrot
Appearance	tan or orange fur with black spots, large paws, sharp claws	green, yellow, and blue feathers, big beak, long claws
Habitat	Central and South America	Central and South America
Diet	eats meat and fish	eats vegetables, fruit, seeds, grains, and nuts
Other facts	strong swimmer, hunter	can talk and sing

Now compare your animal to your partner's animal. Talk about the things that are the same and the things that are different. Trade roles.

> Both the jaguar and the parrot live in Central and South America. The parrot is more colorful than the jaguar. The jaguar and the parrot have very different diets and abilities.

HOW TO MAKE COMPARISONS

1. Tell how things are alike.
2. Tell how things are different.
3. Use comparison words to compare details about the two things.

USE ADJECTIVES THAT COMPARE

When you make comparisons, you describe how things are alike and different. Use **adjectives** that compare details about the two things.

Add **-er** to the end of one-syllable adjectives.

> EXAMPLE   The jaguar is **faster** than the parrot.

If the adjective has three or more syllables, use **more** before the adjective.

> EXAMPLE   The parrot is **more colorful** than the jaguar.

If the adjective has two syllables, you can sometimes use either form.

> EXAMPLE   The jaguar is a **more skillful** hunter.

Prepare to Read

 ELPS: 1.C acquire basic and grade-level vocabulary; 3.A practice producing sounds of newly acquired vocabulary in a manner that is comprehensible; 4.C.1 develop basic sight vocabulary used routinely in written classroom materials; 4.D use prereading supports to enhance composition of written text; 4.F.1 use visual and contextual support to read grade-appropriate content area text; 4.I.2 expand reading skills

Learn Key Vocabulary

Rate and Study the Words Rate how well you know each word. Then:

1. Pronounce the word. Say it aloud several times. Spell it.
2. Study the example.
3. Tell more about the word.
4. Practice it. Make the word your own.

Rating Scale

1 = I have never seen this word before.

2 = I am not sure of the word's meaning.

3 = I know this word and can teach the word's meaning to someone else.

Key Words

biologist (bī-**ol**-u-jist) *noun*
▶ page 358

A **biologist** is a person who studies living things. **Biologists** study how living things grow and where they are found.
Related Word: **biology**

expert (e-**kspurt**) *noun*
▶ page 360

An **expert** is a person who knows a lot about a subject. A ranger is an **expert** about wildlife in the area.

habitat (**hab**-i-tat) *noun*
▶ page 360

A **habitat** is the place where a plant or an animal naturally lives. The **habitat** of polar bears is the cold Arctic.

increase (in-**krēs**) *verb*
▶ page 363

To **increase** means to become larger in number or size. The size of my family **increased** when my brother was born.
Synonym: **grow**

poacher (**pō**-chur) *noun*
▶ page 360

A **poacher** is a person who hunts plants or animals illegally. The **poacher** saw the "no hunting" sign but hunted animals anyway.

shrink (shringk) *verb*
▶ page 363

To **shrink** means to become smaller. The forests that animals need are **shrinking** as people cut down trees.
Past tense: **shrank**
Past participle: **shrunk**

thrive (thrīv) *verb*
▶ page 363

To **thrive** means to grow strong and healthy. With lots of care, plants can **thrive**.

wildlife (**wīld**-līf) *noun*
▶ page 360

Wildlife means animals and plants that live freely outdoors without human care. Bears and moose are examples of **wildlife**.

Practice the Words Work with a partner. Write a question using two Key Words. Answer your partner's question. Use at least one Key Word in your answer. Keep going until you have used all the words twice.

EXAMPLE: What is required for wildlife to thrive?
A safe and healthy habitat.

Reading Strategy: Visualize

Sensory images are details that help you experience a piece of writing through all five senses: sight, sound, smell, taste, and touch.

Reading Strategy Visualize

HOW TO USE SENSORY IMAGES

1. Look for words that tell you how things look, sound, smell, taste, and feel.

> Howard Quigley has been stalked by a jaguar, charged by a black bear, and bitten by parasites.

2. Visualize the scene.

I see: a man followed closely by a big cat, then with a scary black bear running at him.

I hear: the bear growling as it charges.

I smell: woods and green plants.

I feel: the sting of the parasites' bites.

Strategy in Action

Here's how one student used sensory images.

Look Into the Text

First Meeting

"If I don't see details for all five senses, I use my own experiences."

Shivers rolled down Quigley's spine as Olga bellowed a fierce roar. He wasn't sure what the angry cat would do next. Would she stand still? Would she run off? Or would she pounce?

The biologist remained calm as he carefully aimed his tranquilizer gun at the tiger. Then he squeezed the trigger and a dart soared through the air toward the cat.

My Responses to the Text

I see a man trying to stay calm.
I hear a loud roar from the cat.
I see the cat's sharp teeth and big claws.

Using my experiences, I smell the outdoors. I feel a cat's fur.

Practice Together

Reread the passage. Then follow the steps in the How-To box to use sensory images and visualize the scene.

Focus on Genre

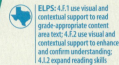

ELPS: 4.F.1 use visual and contextual support to read grade-appropriate content area text; 4.F.2 use visual and contextual support to enhance and confirm understanding; 4.I.2 expand reading skills

Science Feature

A science feature is expository nonfiction about the study of the natural world. Many science features include graphs, charts, maps, and other **text features** that show information visually. **Graphs** show how two or more things are related.

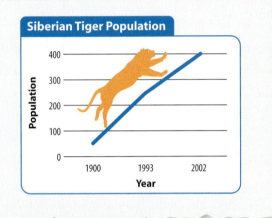

Siberian Tiger Population

This graph shows how the number of Siberian tigers (Population) changed over time (Year). Points on the line show the tiger population in a particular year.

Your Job as a Reader

Reading Strategy: Visualize

As you read, make notes about sensory details. Use them to help you visualize.

Siberian
SURVIVORS

by Rene Ebersole

Howard Quigley has been stalked by
a jaguar, charged by a black bear, and
bitten by parasites. But he was most
scared when he came face-to-face
with Olga, a female Siberian tiger.

Online Coach

First Meeting

Shivers rolled down Quigley's spine as Olga bellowed a fierce roar. He wasn't sure what the angry cat would do next. Would she stand still? Would she run off? Or would she **pounce**?

The **biologist** remained calm as he carefully aimed his tranquilizer gun at the tiger. Then he squeezed the trigger and a dart soared through the air toward the cat.

Bull's eye! The dart struck Olga in her shoulder. She staggered and slowly slumped to the ground–asleep.

As the cat slept, Quigley and his team of scientists went to work. They had to be careful; a female tiger can weigh 370 pounds. They wanted to finish their work before the cat woke up.

The scientists took blood samples, checked Olga's heartbeat, and measured her body from head to tail.

They also put a radio collar around her neck. The collar sends a radio signal–a series of beeps–that helps scientists track an animal's movements.

collar

radio tracking device

◀ Radio collars like this one help scientists track a wild animal's movements. Each collar is specially designed for a particular species, or kind, of animal.

Key Vocabulary
biologist *n.*, a scientist who studies living things

In Other Words
Shivers rolled down Quigley's spine Quigley was scared
pounce suddenly jump at him
Bull's eye! Quigley made a good shot.

Science Background
Howard Quigley started and co-directed the Siberian Tiger Project. He is a specialist in the research and protection of carnivores, or meat-eating animals, like tigers.

A scientist places a radio collar on a tiger. Olga was the first tiger to be fitted with a radio collar.

Cat Tracks

Quigley hoped Olga's collar would help him learn more about Siberian tigers. The speed of the beeps from her collar would tell him about the tiger's habits. It would also tell Quigley when she was sleeping, hunting, moving to a new **territory**–or dead.

Quigley needed to learn all he could about Olga's habits. His goal is to keep tigers like her from disappearing from the forest forever, or from becoming extinct.

Quigley wants to protect Siberian tigers because he knows what has happened to other tigers. In the last century, three species, or kinds, of tigers have died out. Only five species, including Siberian tigers, are left.

In Other Words
territory area of land

Before You Move On

1. **Paraphrase** In your own words, tell how the radio collar works. What information does it provide about Olga?
2. **Problem and Solution** What problem is the **biologist** trying to solve? How is he hoping to accomplish this?

Poaching and Potions

By the time Quigley first saw Olga, many **wildlife experts** worried that Siberian tigers were about to become extinct. Their **habitat**, or home, had almost disappeared.

The big cats once **roamed** the area from eastern Russia to South Korea but by the early 1900s, overhunting had **wiped out** most of them. Fewer than fifty were left!

By 1947 laws were passed to protect the tigers. The laws have helped a little, but Olga and other tigers still face serious threats.

Some people in Asia believe that tiger parts can be used to improve health. Almost every body part is used to make some kind of **potion**. Brains, tails, and whiskers, for instance, are used to treat everything from pimples to toothaches to **paralysis**.

Poachers, people who hunt illegally, can make $15,000 from selling just one dead tiger. That's more money than most Asian families make in several years.

Siberian Tigers' Habitat: Then and Now

SIBERIA RUSSIA
MONGOLIA
CHINA
NORTH KOREA
SOUTH KOREA
JAPAN

KEY
- Where Siberian tigers live today
- Where Siberian tigers lived 100 years ago

▲ **Interpret the Map** How has the location of Siberian tigers changed over the last 100 years?

Large numbers of trees in the Russian taiga forest are being cut down to make timber. This is destroying tiger habitat.

Key Vocabulary

wildlife *n.*, animals living in the wild
expert *n.*, a person who knows a lot about a subject
habitat *n.*, the place where a plant or an animal normally lives
poacher *n.*, a person who hunts animals illegally

In Other Words

roamed lived in
wiped out killed
potion drink used to treat disease
paralysis the inability to move
timber wood used for building

Dangers in the Wild

Poaching isn't the only danger tigers face. The cats are losing their forest habitat.

The Russian taiga is the largest forest on the planet. Scientists say a third of all trees in the world grow there. Many Siberian tigers and their prey—elk, wild boar, and deer—also live there.

But animals aren't alone in the forest. Many people are moving in. They're cutting down trees and tiger habitat.

High climber. Like house cats, Siberian tigers can climb trees.

Before You Move On

1. **Explain** Laws have been passed to help protect tigers. Why are tigers still in danger?
2. **Cause and Effect** Why do people cut down the trees?

Snow covers the taiga in the harsh winter. Siberian tigers need their thick fur to stay warm in their habitat.

Tiger Protection

Tiger habitat doesn't have to be destroyed. Quigley thinks people can find a way to **balance their needs with those of** the tiger. "It's hard to tell the Russians that they can't sell their natural resources," says Quigley. "It's important to find a way to manage forests so tigers and their prey can continue to have a place to live."

Many experts say we can manage forests **in a cat-friendly way**. Some trees can be cut down, while others are left standing. This could allow people and tigers to use the same forests.

Protecting tiger habitat could even help people who live nearby make money. Tourists could travel there to see tigers. Tourism would create jobs for the local people. People with jobs that pay well are less likely to poach tigers.

In Other Words
balance their needs with those of share the forests with
in a cat-friendly way without disturbing tigers

Tiger Triumph?

Scientists are finding ways to protect Olga and other tigers. So far, they've helped set up anti-poaching **squads** to keep poachers out of the forest.

The squads look for signs that poachers have been in the forest. If they spot gun shells or traps, they know to look for poachers. Their work **is paying off**. They have helped make several arrests.

Some tigers still get poached, and their habitat is still **shrinking** but Siberian tiger numbers are **on the rise**. Nearly 400 may now roam the wild. Some are even moving into areas where they haven't been seen in years.

Four hundred tigers may not sound like a lot. It isn't. But it's a start. There are more tigers today than there were 100 years ago. And their numbers are **increasing**.

In May 2002, Olga gave birth to her sixth litter of cubs. In many ways, she was **thriving** and helping the endangered cats to make an amazing **comeback**. However, Olga's story also shows why poaching remains a serious threat to Siberian tigers.

In January 2005, Olga suddenly disappeared. Officials who were tracking Olga believe she is the victim of poachers. Staff of the Siberian Tiger Project have seen many cases in which poachers first kill the tiger and then destroy its collar. That's why scientists today are more determined than ever to protect endangered tigers, like Olga, from the continued threats to their survival. ❖

Siberian Tiger Population

Population / Year
(400, 300, 200, 100, 0 — 1900, 1993, 2002)

Before You Move On

1. **Summarize** How can people work together to protect tigers and their **habitats**?
2. **Cause and Effect** Why has the Siberian tiger population **increased**?

Key Vocabulary

shrink *v.*, to become smaller in size
increase *v.*, to become greater in number
thrive *v.*, to grow strong and healthy

In Other Words

squads groups of skilled people working together
is paying off has been successful
on the rise getting larger
comeback return, recovery

Tigers in the Wild

Five Species of tigers are still alive today. They live in the wild only in Asia.

Bengal

Population: Scientists believe there are between 3,000-5,000 tigers in the wild.

Indochinese

Population: Scientists believe there are fewer than 2,000 tigers in the wild.

Sumatran

Population: Scientists believe there are about 400 tigers in the wild.

Siberian

Population: Scientists believe there are fewer than 400 tigers in the wild.

South China

Population: Scientists believe there are no tigers left in the wild.

Tiger Facts

- The Siberian tiger is the largest type of tiger. An adult male can grow to be more than 10 feet long and weigh more than 600 pounds.

- Female tigers usually give birth to two or three cubs at a time.

- A newborn cub weighs between two and three pounds.

- Big cats such as tigers can roar, but they can't purr.

- Tigers are one of the few cats that like to swim in water.

Connect Reading and Writing

Vocabulary

biologists

experts

habitats

increase

poachers

shrink

thrive

wildlife

CRITICAL THINKING

1. SUM IT UP Make a card for each vocabulary word. Use at least five words to tell how **experts** help tigers.

2. Describe and Explain Tell a partner about the tools and steps that **experts** use to help animals like Olga.

3. Make Judgments What has the most harmful effect on tigers and their **habitat**? Give reasons from the text.

4. Compare What is the effect of **shrinking habitat** on Bengal tigers compared with Siberian tigers?

READING FLUENCY

Phrasing Read the passage on page 647 to a partner. Assess your fluency.

1. I read
   a. great   **b.** OK   **c.** not very well

2. What I did best in my reading was _____.

READING STRATEGY

Visualize
What effect did using sensory images have on your reading? Tell a partner about two images you visualized.

VOCABULARY REVIEW

Oral Review Read the paragraph aloud. Add the vocabulary words.

_____, scientists who study _____, including tigers, are worried. They want to save endangered animals and give them what they need to _____ so that the animal population will _____. The threats to animals include _____ who illegally hunt them. When people move into new areas, it can hurt the animals' _____. _____ say that if such places _____, some animals will become extinct.

Written Review Imagine you are a **biologist** who protects tigers. Write a journal entry about one day's work. Use five vocabulary words.

WRITE ABOUT THE **GUIDING QUESTION**

Explore How People Help Animals
How can people everywhere help protect **wildlife**? Reread the selection to find information people should have. Explain which actions have a harmful or helpful effect.

Connect Across the Curriculum

ELPS: 4.F.1 use visual and contextual support to read grade-appropriate content area text; 4.F.2 use visual and contextual support to enhance and confirm understanding

Literary Analysis

Text Structure: Use Text Features to Make Comparisons

Academic Vocabulary
- **feature** (fē-chur) *noun*
  A **feature** is part of something that stands out or is noticeable.

Why Do Writers Use Text Features? Nonfiction text **features** help readers understand what they read. Read the passage and look at the photo and labels.

They also put a radio collar around her neck. The collar sends a radio signal—a series of beeps—that helps scientists track an animal's movement.

◀ radio collar

Venn Diagram

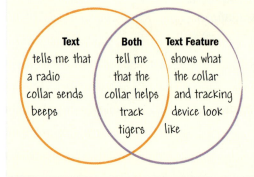

Text	Both	Text Feature
tells me that a radio collar sends beeps	tell me that the collar helps track tigers	shows what the collar and tracking device look like

The Venn Diagram compares the information in the text to the information in the text **feature**.

Practice Together

Compare Information Read the passage and look at the map on page 360.

The big cats once roamed the area from eastern Russia to South Korea but by the early 1900s, overhunting had wiped out most of them. Fewer than fifty were left!

With your class, compare the information in a Venn Diagram.

Try It!

Compare Information Make a Venn Diagram that compares the text and the graph on page 363. How is the information different? How is it the same?

Use Context Clues: Multiple-Meaning Words Across Content Areas

Academic Vocabulary

- **context** (**kon**-tekst) *noun*
  Context is the surrounding text near a word or phrase that helps explain the meaning of the word.

Words have different meanings in different subject, or content, areas. For instance, the word *product* in social science means "something that is made." The same word in math means "the result of multiplying two numbers."

Think About Context These words have more than one meaning. Work with a partner to find each word in the selection. Use **context** to determine which meaning makes sense in each instance.

1. poach (p. 362)   a. to cook   b. to steal
2. resources (p. 362)   a. a supply   b. money, property, or wealth

Write Sentences Write a sentence for each meaning of the words above. Do any of your sentences seem like they belong to a particular content area?

ELPS: 1.D speak using learning strategies

HEALTH & SCIENCE

Give an Informative Report

Academic Vocabulary

- **research** (**rē**-surch) *noun*
  Research is a collection of information about something.

Learn more facts about tigers and share the information with your class.

1. **Conduct Research** Pick one of the five tigers from "Tigers in the Wild" on page 364. Use resources such as the Internet, books, and magazines to do **research** . Take notes about an aspect of the tiger that interests you.

   Internet InsideNG.com
   Use an online search engine to find information about the tiger you selected.

2. **Organize Your Report** Review your notes and decide which facts you will tell about and how you will organize them. Include an introduction and a conclusion.

3. **Give Your Report** Summarize your findings and tell your classmates what you learned. If you don't know the word for something when you're speaking, use hand gestures or familiar words to describe what you mean.

> The Sumatran tiger has lived only in Sumatra, Indonesia, for over a million years.

ELPS: 2.6.4 understand the main points of spoken language regarding familiar to unfamiliar topics

Listening/Speaking

Listen to a Report

SOCIAL SCIENCE

> **Academic Vocabulary**
> • **focus** (fō-kus) *verb*
>   When you **focus** on something, you pay attention to it.

How Can You Listen and Understand More? Do you think you are a good listener? Good listeners hear many details but also **focus** on the main point. Good listeners can **paraphrase**, or tell in their own words, what they have heard. Review these listening strategies, and then test your skills.

1 **Set a Purpose for Listening** Decide whether you are listening to be entertained or to get information.
  • If you are listening to an entertaining story, **focus** on the main events or problems, the main characters, and important dialogue.
  • If you are listening to an informative report or speech, **focus** on main ideas, which usually come first. Then listen for details that support the main ideas.

2 **Listen Quietly** You cannot listen carefully if you are making noise. Be quiet during the speaker's presentation. You will hear and understand more. It is also important to **focus** on the speaker's pauses or stops. These brief silences usually let you know that a main idea has ended and a new main idea is going to start. Take notes to remind you of the speaker's main points.

3 **Summarize** Use your own words to tell the main ideas you heard. Does everything make sense?

> You said that the Sumatran tiger has been around for a really long time.

Test Your Listening Skills

4 **Listen to a Report** Listen to a partner read his or her tiger report from the Research/Speaking activity or a short report on tigers that has been downloaded from the Internet. Follow the listening strategies in Steps 1–3 above.

5 **Get Feedback** Have your partner tell you if you heard the main points correctly. Did you miss anything? If so, repeat Steps 1–3.

Make Comparisons

Question Quiz Go back to the selection and look for ways to make three comparative statements about the Siberian tiger. Use comparative adjectives in your statements. They may be true or false. Quiz your partner. Trade roles.

> The Siberian tiger population is smaller than it used to be.

> False. The Siberian tiger population is larger than it used to be.

ELPS: 5.E employ increasingly complex grammatical structures in content area writing

Write to Compare Tigers

Study the Models When you write, you can use comparisons to add details and make your writing more interesting. When you make comparisons, be sure the words show the comparison clearly so your reader can understand them.

NOT OK

> The biologist was more fearless than the expedition leader. He bent over the tranquilized Siberian tiger and discovered that it was <u>more large</u> than the one he had examined yesterday. As he ran his hand through the big cat's fur, the biologist realized that its coat was <u>more thicker</u> than any other kind of tiger. The biologist thought that the tiger was <u>beautifuler</u> than any cat he'd seen.

The reader thinks: **"What exactly is 'beautifuler'?"**

OK

> The biologist was more fearless than the expedition leader. He bent over the tranquilized Siberian tiger and discovered that it was <u>larger</u> than the one he had examined yesterday. As he ran his hand through the big cat's fur, the biologist realized that its coat was <u>thicker</u> than any other kind of tiger. The biologist thought that the tiger was <u>more beautiful</u> than any cat he'd seen.

The comparisons are now correct and clear.

Add Sentences Think of two sentences to add to the OK model above. Look for more ways that the people or animals are similar or different.

WRITE ON YOUR OWN Write to compare the Siberian tigers in Russia with the Bengal tigers in India. Which tigers are larger? Which tigers are safer from poachers? Be sure to use the correct comparison words to make your writing clear.

REMEMBER

- Add **-er** to one-syllable adjectives.
  A tiger's tail is long**er** than a cat's tail.

- If the adjective ends in **y**, change the **y** to **i**. Then add **-er**.
  A tiger is heav**ier** than a house cat.

- Add **more** before adjectives with three or more syllables.
  A tiger's roar is **more ferocious** than a house cat's meow.

- Never use **more** and **-er** together.

Mireya Mayor
Explorer/Correspondent

Build Background

See an Explorer in Action

What does it feel like to explore the world and learn about the environment? Mireya Mayor knows. Her discovery of a tiny animal made a big difference in protecting the environment.

Digital Library

InsideNG.com
➤ View the video.

◀ Mireya Mayor travels the world to protect the environment.

Connect

Team Brainstorm Imagine that you are in the rainforest with Mireya Mayor, and you are trying to learn about a tiny animal called a mouse lemur. Brainstorm a list of questions to start your science log.

Questions for Nature Journey
1. What are some facts about the rainforest?
2. What is a mouse lemur?
3. Does it look like a mouse?

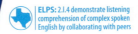
Elaborate

CD

Study the photos and listen for the differences between the main idea and the elaboration of the main idea. What details do you learn? If you don't understand something, ask for clarification.

PICTURE PROMPT

Outfoxing a Predator

Main Idea: These scientists are examining a type of fox that is in danger. By capturing and counting the foxes, they are trying to help them survive.

Elaboration: These biologists are examining the island fox, a type of fox that lives on islands near the coast of California. The island fox faces danger from predators that have been introduced to the islands. The biggest threat to the foxes is the golden eagle. It is mostly responsible for the recent decrease in the island fox population.

The island fox is about the size of a house cat. It does not mind being handled by humans. This makes it easier for scientists to capture island foxes, count them, release them, and help them. Scientists hope to increase the number of island foxes by giving them safe places to breed and moving the golden eagle back to its original habitat.

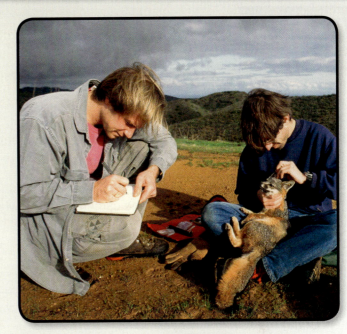

island fox ▶

golden eagle ▶

Use Adverbs

Adverbs are words that describe verbs, adjectives, or other adverbs. Adverbs can tell *how*, *when*, or *where*.

- Use an adverb to describe a verb. Many adverbs end in **-ly**.

  EXAMPLE   The animal **suddenly** makes a noise. (how)
                              verb

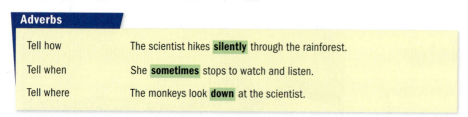

Adverbs	
Tell how	The scientist hikes **silently** through the rainforest.
Tell when	She **sometimes** stops to watch and listen.
Tell where	The monkeys look **down** at the scientist.

- Use an adverb to make an adjective or another adverb stronger.

  EXAMPLES   The rainforest is **unusually** quiet.
                                    adjective

  The scientist raises the camera **very** slowly.
                                         adverb

Practice Together

Say each adverb in the box with your class. Then say each sentence. Choose an adverb from the box to describe the underlined word. Say the sentence with the adverb.

| again   carefully   peacefully   very |

1. Walk _____ through the rainforest.
2. Be _____ respectful of the environment.
3. Look at the monkey sleeping _____ in that tree.
4. We will come _____ to see the monkey.

Try It!

Choose an adverb from the box to describe the underlined word. Then say and write each sentence with the adverb.

| loudly   slowly   suddenly   very |

5. The scientist _____ sees a snake in a tree.
6. The snake is lying _____ still on a branch.
7. It hisses _____.
8. The scientist moves _____ away.

▲ Scientists study wildlife closely.

Share an Experience

ELABORATE

Tell a partner about a hike or trip that you've taken or would like to take.

Begin by writing down the main points you want to share. Then think of ways you can elaborate on them. Elaborate by adding details, examples, and explanations.

Topic: Trip to Miller's Falls

Main Point	Elaboration
We climbed a hill to get to the waterfall.	We carefully climbed a rocky hill to get to the waterfall. The hill was very steep. We had to hold on tightly to the trees that lined the trail.
The waterfall was powerful.	The waterfall rushed powerfully to the river below. The water crashed down hard. Mist and spray from the waterfall filled the air.

Now share information about your hike or trip with your partner. Add details, examples, and explanations to elaborate. Trade roles. Be sure to listen closely so you understand the information about each other's trip.

HOW TO ELABORATE

1. Tell the topic or main point of discussion.
2. Add details. Give background information, examples, or explanations.
3. Tell *when*, *where*, and *how* events happened.

> What was the waterfall like?

> It was absolutely beautiful! The water moved quickly but very gracefully.

USE ADVERBS

When you tell about an experience, add details that tell *when*, *where*, and *how* things happened. Use **adverbs** to add interest and detail.

EXAMPLES   We hiked the trail **slowly**. It was **very** steep and rocky. At the top, we **finally** stopped and **gratefully** watched the waterfall plummet **swiftly** to the bottom.

▲ The waterfall rushed swiftly to the river.

Prepare to Read

 ELPS: 1.C acquire basic and grade-level vocabulary; 3.A practice producing sounds of newly acquired vocabulary in a manner that is comprehensible; 4.C.1 develop basic sight vocabulary used routinely in written classroom materials; 4.I.2 expand reading skills

Learn Key Vocabulary

Rate and Study the Words Rate how well you know each word. Then:

1. Pronounce the word. Say it aloud several times. Spell it.
2. Study the example.
3. Tell more about the word.
4. Practice it. Make the word your own.

Rating Scale

1 = I have never seen this word before.

2 = I am not sure of the word's meaning.

3 = I know this word and can teach the word's meaning to someone else.

Key Words

awareness (u-**wair**-nes)

noun ▶ page 379

Awareness is having knowledge of something. To protect the Earth, it is important to have an **awareness** of things that could harm the planet.
Related Word: **aware**

conservation

(kon-sur-**vā**-shun) *noun* ▶ page 379

Conservation is careful protection of something. **Conservation** efforts protect national parks.

discovery (dis-**kuv**-ur-ē)

noun ▶ page 379

A **discovery** is the act of seeing or finding something for the first time. The hikers made an interesting **discovery** and took a closer look.
Plural: **discoveries**

document (**dok**-yu-ment)

verb ▶ page 380

To **document** something is to provide facts about it. A research study must be **documented** carefully with facts.

ensure (en-**shur**) *verb*
▶ page 378

To **ensure** is to make sure or certain. Humans should **ensure** that rainforests are protected.

establish (i-**stab**-lish) *verb*
▶ page 380

To **establish** something is to start it. My friends and I **established** a yearly food collection for families in need.

expedition

(ek-spu-**di**-shun) *noun* ▶ page 378

An **expedition** is a trip or journey made for a particular purpose. This is an **expedition** through the desert.

explorer (ek-**splor**-ur) *noun*
▶ page 378

An **explorer** goes to a place that is new to him or her to find information about it. Astronauts are **explorers** of our universe.
Related Words: **explore, exploration**

Practice the Words Tell a story that uses the Key Words. Partner 1 uses the first word. Partner 2 uses the next word to continue the story. Continue until you have used all the Key Words.

PARTNER 1: Juana and Hyo have a new awareness of endangered wildlife.

PARTNER 2: They want to learn more about conservation of animal habitats.

Reading Strategy: Visualize

As you read, you create mental images. When you combine these images with your own imagination, you experience different reactions to what you read. These reactions, or emotional responses, can deepen your understanding of the text.

Reading Strategy
Visualize

HOW TO IDENTIFY EMOTIONAL RESPONSES

1. As you read, use a chart like the one shown. Record words and phrases that create images in your mind.
2. Describe what you "see" and "hear" in your mind.
3. Combine the mental image with your personal experience to identify how you feel. Note the specific words that led to your reaction.

Strategy in Action

Here's how one student identified emotional responses.

Look Into the Text

Mireya Mayor has slept in the rainforest among poisonous snakes . She has been chased by gorillas, elephants, and leopards. She even swam with great white sharks! Mayor is a city girl and a former NFL cheerleader. How does she find herself as an explorer in situations like this?

> I remember scenes like these from wildlife programs on TV.

Visualization Chart

Words or Phrases	I Visualize . . .	I Feel . . .
slept in the rainforest	wet, rocky ground and darkness.	uncomfortable and nervous.
among poisonous snakes	dangerous snakes trying to get into a tent.	scared of the snakes and amazed by Mayor's bravery.

Practice Together

Reread the passage. Follow the steps in the How-To box to identify your own emotional responses.

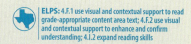
ELPS: 4.F.1 use visual and contextual support to read grade-appropriate content area text; 4.F.2 use visual and contextual support to enhance and confirm understanding; 4.I.2 expand reading skills

Focus on Genre

Online Article

Nonfiction online articles may have the same text features as printed articles. They also may contain **links** that lead to other Web pages that have expanded illustrations, more details about specific topics, and related information.

Web site heading

Emerging Explorers
National Geographic's Next Generation

OUR EXPLORERS | ABOUT THE PROGRAM

menu of places on this Web site

2007 2008 2009

» John Bul Dau
**HUMANITARIAN/
SURVIVOR**

» David de Rothschild
**ENVIRONMENTAL
STORYTELLER**

» MIREYA MAYOR
**EXPLORER/
CORRESPONDENT**

» Roshini Thinakaran
**FILMMAKER/
GLOBALIST**

links to other Web sites

Your Job as a Reader

Reading Strategy: Visualize

As you read, make notes about words and phrases that create emotional responses.

Mireya Mayor in Madagascar, where she discovered a rare species of mouse lemur. ▶

Mireya Mayor

Explorer/Correspondent

Online Coach

MIREYA MAYOR
EXPLORER/CORRESPONDENT

2007	2008	2009

» John Bul Dau
HUMANITARIAN/ SURVIVOR

» David de Rothschild
ENVIRONMENTAL STORYTELLER

» MIREYA MAYOR
EXPLORER/ CORRESPONDENT

» Roshini Thinakaran
FILMMAKER/ GLOBALIST

"The rainforest appears to be a **gigantic, green mishmash** of unknowns. We are still discovering new species and who knows what else might be out there. But we do know that every tree and creature in it plays a vital role in our existence. **Ensuring** their survival helps to ensure ours."

Mireya Mayor has slept in the rainforest among poisonous snakes. She has been chased by gorillas, elephants, and leopards. She even swam with great white sharks! Mayor is a city girl and a former NFL cheerleader. How does she find herself as an **explorer** in situations like this?

It all began in college. Mayor began studying **primates**. "I was **seized by** the fact that some of these incredible animals are **on the verge of** extinction. And they had never been studied. In some cases, not even a mere photograph existed to show their existence. I asked more questions. It became clear to me that much about our natural world still remained a mystery." Mayor decided to dedicate her life to solving that mystery.

Today, Mayor is a Fulbright scholar and a National Science Foundation Fellow. She also appears as a **correspondent** on the National Geographic Ultimate Explorer television series. Each **expedition** allows Mayor to teach viewers about a different species of animal that needs our help.

◄ Page 1 of 5 ►

Go to page: [ ] Go

Key Vocabulary

ensure *v.*, to make sure that something happens
explorer *n.*, someone who travels around the world to discover new information
expedition *n.*, a trip

In Other Words

gigantic, green mishmash big, green mixture
primates apes, gorillas, and other animals like them
seized by completely focused on
on the verge of close to
correspondent reporter

OUR EXPLORERS | ABOUT THE PROGRAM

MIREYA MAYOR
EXPLORER/CORRESPONDENT

Click on map for detail

For example, one of Mayor's Ultimate Explorer TV expeditions allowed her to go to the Gulf of California. Her goal there was to research the powerful six-foot-long Humboldt Squid. It was a time of personal **discovery** that gave Mayor the opportunity to climb rocky cliffs and look at untouched tropical ecosystems.

An expedition led Mayor to Namibia. She went into a veterinarian's haven, or safe place, for leopards. "While caring for the leopards," Mayor explains, "the vet accidentally discovered a cure for fluid in the brain. It is a disease that also occurs in human infants. As a result of our film and the media attention it received, new studies are now taking place in children's hospitals. That is why I consider my television work just as important as my **conservation** field work," she notes. "The TV series sheds light on the **plight** of endangered species and animals around the world. Television has the power to help people know and connect with these animals and habitats that are disappearing. We may be facing the largest mass extinction of our time. **Awareness** is crucial. If we don't act now, it will be too late."

Mayor went to Madagascar on another of her Ultimate Explorer expeditions. On that expedition, she discovered a new species of mouse

◄ Page 2 of 5 ►   Go to page: [   ] Go

Key Vocabulary

discovery *n.*, something that is seen and made known for the first time

conservation *n.*, a careful protection of something

awareness *n.*, having knowledge of

In Other Words

plight difficult situation

Before You Move On

1. **Fact and Opinion** What is one fact and one opinion that Mayor expresses?

2. **Personal Connection** Which of Mayor's **expeditions** seems the most exciting or interesting to you? Why?

Emerging Explorers

National Geographic's Next Generation

OUR EXPLORERS   ABOUT THE PROGRAM

MIREYA MAYOR
EXPLORER/CORRESPONDENT

"I had to get that documentation because only then was I able to lobby to have its (the lemur's) habitat fully protected," said Mayor.

lemur. This discovery brought everyone's attention to Mayor's work. She had to **document** it. Once it was documented, she could try to obtain protection for the animal's habitat. This required **grueling** field work during the **monsoon** season. "There we were, tromping through remote areas of jungle, rain pouring, tents blowing. We were looking for **a nocturnal animal**. One that happens to be the smallest primate in the world," she says. Her careful research and documentation were important. She was able to convince Madagascar's president to declare the species' habitat a national park. He also agreed to triple the number of protected areas in the nation. In addition, he **established** a $50 million conservation fund. As Mayor reports, one tiny discovery became "a huge **ambassador for** all things wild in Madagascar."

Mayor believes that local support for conservation is a key factor in bringing about change.

Mouse lemur

Key Vocabulary

document *v.*, to provide facts
establish *v.*, to create or setup

In Other Words

grueling very hard and tiring
monsoon rainy
a nocturnal animal an animal that stays awake at night and sleeps during the day
ambassador for way to bring attention to

OUR EXPLORERS ABOUT THE PROGRAM

MIREYA MAYOR
EXPLORER/CORRESPONDENT

Related NEWS

» Emerging Explorers News

» Photo Gallery: Best Mountain Photographs of 2008 Announced

» What Triggers Tornadoes? New Season May Hold Answers

"The local people are **the very core** of effective conservation. Without their support, the 'dream' of saving the planet can never become a reality. The rainforest is **literally their backyard**. Yet many Malagasy kids have never even seen a lemur. So I organize lots of field trips into the forest. Only by seeing how amazing these creatures are, will kids want to protect them." Mayor stresses the importance of providing education and opportunities for local communities to learn about the threats to animals and how they can help. She believes it will be critical to protecting the planet.

Healthy Rainforest

Destroyed Rainforest

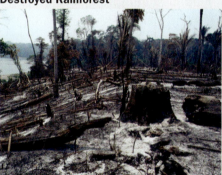

Mayor's conservation work makes locals aware that the destruction of the rainforest threatens the lives of plants and animals.

◀ Page 4 of 5 ▶

Go to page: [ ] Go

In Other Words

the very core the most important part

literally their backyard so close by

Before You Move On

1. **Conclusion** Why was it important for Mayor to **document** her **discovery**?
2. **Cause and Effect** Name two things Madagascar's president **established** as a result of Mayor's work.
3. **Paraphrase** Tell in your own words why Mayor organizes field trips.

MIREYA MAYOR
EXPLORER/CORRESPONDENT

Baobab tree in Madagascar

Mayor **circles the globe** on television expeditions, but her heart remains in the rainforests of Madagascar. As she describes it, "This phenomenal natural laboratory could vanish in our lifetime. It could become **the stuff of history books, not science books**. Until I can walk away . . . and know it's going to be okay, I just can't leave." ❖

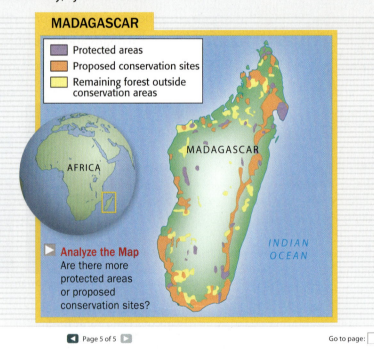

MADAGASCAR

- ■ Protected areas
- ■ Proposed conservation sites
- ■ Remaining forest outside conservation areas

AFRICA

MADAGASCAR

INDIAN OCEAN

▶ **Analyze the Map**
Are there more protected areas or proposed conservation sites?

◀ Page 5 of 5 ▷   Go to page: [   ] Go

In Other Words

circles the globe travels around the world

the stuff of history books, not science books something that is gone forever

Before You Move On

1. **Conclusion** Why are the **conservation** efforts of people like Mayor important? Support your answer.

2. **Fact and Opinion** State one fact that increased your **awareness** about the environment. Give one opinion of your own about Mayor's work.

Connect Reading and Writing

Vocabulary
awareness
conservation
discovery
document
ensure
establish
expedition
explorer

CRITICAL THINKING

1. SUM IT UP Interview a partner about the events that led to Mayor's first **expedition** in Namibia. Then switch roles and answer questions about her work in Madagascar. Summarize the importance of each **expedition**.

T Chart

Question	Answer
Why did Mayor become interested in conservation?	Mayor wanted to solve mysteries of the natural world.

2. Classify Mayor is an **explorer** and a correspondent. First, classify her audience into different groups. Then, classify the different ways she communicates to each group.

3. Explain During her Madagascar **expedition**, Mayor had to **document** a **discovery**. Explain this process, using details from the text.

4. Evaluate Why is it important to **ensure** that Malagasy kids and other young people develop an **awareness** of animals in their local environment?

READING FLUENCY

Expression Read the passage on page 648 to a partner. Assess your fluency.

1. I read
   a. great   **b.** OK   **c.** not very well

2. What I did best in my reading was _____.

READING STRATEGY

Visualize
Share the emotional responses you recorded on your chart with a partner. How did the strategy improve your understanding of the text?

VOCABULARY REVIEW

Oral Review Read the paragraph aloud. Add the vocabulary words.

When an _____ goes on an _____ somewhere, he or she always hopes to make an important _____. To _____ that the facts are correct, this person must _____ what he or she finds. The work of _____ includes developing public _____ of local environments. This can lead governments to _____ funds and laws to help protect the environment.

Written Review Imagine you are an **explorer** who wants to raise **awareness** about **conservation**. Write a letter that expresses your opinion about conservation and encourages people to learn about their environment. Use five vocabulary words.

WRITE ABOUT THE GUIDING QUESTION

Explore Our Precious World
What traits should an **explorer** who makes **expeditions** around the world have? Reread the selection to find examples that support your ideas.

Connect Across the Curriculum

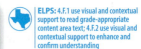
ELPS: 4.F.1 use visual and contextual support to read grade-appropriate content area text; 4.F.2 use visual and contextual support to enhance and confirm understanding

Literary Analysis

Use Text Features: Graphics

Academic Vocabulary
- **image** (im-ij) *noun*
  An **image** is a mental picture of something.

Learn About Graphics Graphics, such as charts and photos, often provide additional information that may not be in the text. Read the passage below. If you had only this text, what **image** might you have of this scientist?

> The scientist studied her subject over time. She took detailed notes. She kept good records and published her results. One of her discoveries led to an important cure for an illness.

When you read this text, you probably get an **image** of a scientist in a laboratory or at a desk. How would that **image** change if there were photos of the scientist sitting in a rainforest taking notes with a lemur in her hand?

Practice Together

Interpret Graphics Photos are **images** that make text come alive, or seem real. Photo captions are text features that give more information about graphics.

You may know more than you think you do about Mireya Mayor. Study the photos in the selection. Answer the following questions.

▲ Photos tell you more about people, places, and events.

1. How comfortable is the place where Mayor works?
2. How does Mayor keep records?
3. How does Mayor feel about the animals she studies?

Explain why you answered each question as you did. What in the photos gave you the ideas?

Try It!

Learn More from Graphics With a partner, look at another online article. Think about the information the photos provide. What meaning do the graphics communicate? What specific purpose do they achieve? Write a list of questions about the article. See if you can answer your partner's questions using the photos or other graphics.

Use Context Clues: Jargon

> **Academic Vocabulary**
> • **specific** (spi-**sif**-ik) *adjective*
>   When something is **specific**, it is definite or particular.

Words and phrases that have special meanings related to a **specific** subject or job are called **jargon**. You can use **context**, or the words around the jargon, to figure out its meaning. For example, you may know that *cell* means "a small room." But if you are reading about cellular telephones, you can figure out that *cell* is jargon for *cell phone*.

Use Context Find each of these jargon words in the selection. Use context to figure out the meaning. Use a dictionary for more information, such as determining part of speech.

1. haven (p. 379)   **3.** field (p. 379)

2. habitats (p. 379)   **4.** document (p. 380)

How is the **specific** meaning different from other meanings of each word?

Conduct Career Interviews

> **Academic Vocabulary**
> • **focus** (fō-kus) *verb*
>   When you **focus** on something, you pay attention to it.

CAREER STUDY

ELPS: 2.1.5 demonstrate listening comprehension of complex spoken English by taking notes

Mireya Mayor has had several jobs. Many people change careers several times in their lives. What causes people to change careers?

1 **Plan Interviews** Choose several adults to interview about their careers. Before you begin your interviews, **focus** your questions to make them specific. For example:

Unfocused Question: What jobs have you had?

Focused Question: What is the best job you have had?

2 **Conduct Interviews** Have your list of questions ready. Make eye contact as you ask questions to show your interest in what the person says. Ask the person to explain any information that you don't understand. Use a chart to take notes and keep your information **focused** . Thank each person for his or her time.

3 **Present Interviews** Summarize your interviews for the class. Tell what you discovered about why people change careers.

Research/Speaking

Learn About Primates

HEALTH & SCIENCE

ELPS: 2.G.4 understand the main points of spoken language regarding familiar to unfamiliar topics; 2.G.7 understand the important details of spoken language regarding familiar to unfamiliar topics

Academic Vocabulary

- **research** (rē-surch) *noun*
  Research is a collection of information about something.

What if you could report on a specific primate to help protect its habitat? What information would you need? Select a primate to study, and deliver an informative presentation to your class.

❶ **Conduct Research** Use books, periodicals, or the Internet to conduct **research** on a primate. Compare your sources with a partner, and determine which sources are the most useful and relevant, and why. A source that ends in *.edu* is usually reliable and valid because it is from a school or university. Write a research plan in the form of relevant, or appropriate, questions about the primate. For example:

- Where does the primate live?
- What are the primate's habits and behaviors?

Narrow or broaden your questions as needed.

❷ **Focus Your Ideas** Make notes to guide your **research**. Look for photos, too. Categorize information into three or four important themes, and write facts and examples for each theme. Have relevant reasons for drawing conclusions and deciding what to include and what to leave out. Record bibliographic information about each source using a standard format. Be sure your sources are valid and reliable.

▲ A chimpanzee is a primate; so are humans.

❸ **Prepare the Presentation** Write an informative presentation based on your **research**. Organize your paragraphs by main idea and supporting details. Follow the proper format for integrating citations into your written text. Practice giving your presentation. Ask a friend to listen to it and ask you questions. Are the details clear? Is your presentation informative?

❹ **Give Your Presentation** Explain the information in a way your audience will understand. Details and examples will help your listeners visualize the information in your presentation. As you listen to other presentations, pay attention to the main points and important details.

Elaborate

Role-Play With a partner, act out an interview with Mireya Mayor. One partner plays the role of a news reporter and asks questions about Mayor's work and discoveries. The other partner plays Mayor and gives detailed answers. Be sure to listen for important details in each other's answers. Use adverbs to elaborate. Trade roles.

> What did you recently discover in Madagascar?

> I recently discovered a very small primate. It is the smallest primate in the world!

 ELPS: 2.G.8 understand the important details of spoken language regarding familiar to unfamiliar language; 2.I.4 demonstrate listening comprehension of complex spoken English by collaborating with peers

 ELPS: 5.E employ increasingly complex grammatical structures in content area writing

Write About a Discovery

Study the Models When you write about events, you want to keep your readers interested in your writing. A key way to hold their interest is to elaborate and add colorful details about *when*, *where*, and *how* the events happen. You can provide comparisons to elaborate even more.

NOT OK

> Of all endangered species, Mireya studied primates the most <u>serious</u>. She <u>skillful</u> investigated the jungles of Madagascar. The wind blew <u>fierce</u> in her face as she walked deeper into the underbrush. Then she saw it—a new species of mouse lemur. She held the small primate <u>gentle</u>. Then she documented her discovery <u>carefuller</u> than ever before. The expedition was a success.

The reader thinks: "**I don't understand the details.**"

OK

> Of all endangered species, Mireya studied primates the most <u>seriously</u>. She <u>skillfully</u> investigated the jungles of Madagascar. The wind blew <u>fiercely</u> in her face as she walked deeper into the underbrush. Then she saw it—a new species of mouse lemur. She held the small primate <u>gently</u>. Then she documented her discovery <u>more carefully</u> than ever before. The expedition was a success.

The adverbs are correct, so the details are clear.

Add Sentences Think of two sentences to add to the OK model above. Look for more ways to add details to your sentences.

WRITE ON YOUR OWN Write a description of a time you discovered something new. Use colorful details that tell *when*, *where*, and *how*. Help the reader see and experience the event you are writing about.

REMEMBER

- Many adverbs end in **-ly**: **slowly, carefully, playfully**

- Use **-er** with one-syllable adverbs to compare two actions: **faster, softer**

- Use **more** with two- or three-syllable adverbs: **more slowly, more carefully, more playfully**

Compare Across Texts

Compare Topics

"A Natural Balance," "Siberian Survivors," and "Mireya Mayor: Explorer/
Correspondent" all tell about our **effect** on the environment. Compare
the different ways the authors treat this topic.

How It Works

Organize and Compare Ideas To compare the way the three authors
approach the same topic, use a chart. What information do the text
features tell you about the topic?

Comparison Chart

Selection	Topic	Text Features Used	Author's Purpose
"A Natural Balance"	humans' effects on the environment	photos, captions, diagrams	
"Siberian Survivors"	humans' effects on the environment	photos, captions, maps, graphs	
"Mireya Mayor Explorer/Correspondent"	humans' effects on the environment	photos, captions, online links, maps	

Practice Together

Summarize the Ideas Compare the information in the chart and then
summarize. Here is the beginning of a summary comparing all three texts.

Summary

> "A Natural Balance," "Siberian Survivors," and "Mireya Mayor Explorer/
> Correspondent" all show humans' effects on the environment. Each author has
> different ideas and uses text features to support them. In "A Natural Balance,"
> the writer uses a diagram to show the effects of an oil spill. . . .

Try It!

Copy the chart and fill in the empty boxes. Summarize the ideas that are
explained. You may want to use this frame to help you write your summary.

The selections all give different pictures of the same _____ . "A Natural Balance" uses
_____ . "Siberian Survivors" uses _____ . "Mireya Mayor" shows _____ . All three
selections offer suggestions on how we can _____ .

Academic Vocabulary

• **effect** (i-**fekt**) *noun*
  An **effect** is the result of an action
  or cause.

Our Precious World

GUIDING QUESTION What makes the environment so valuable?

UNIT LIBRARY

Content Library

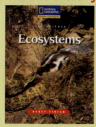

Leveled Library

Reflect on Your Reading

Think back on your reading of the unit selections. Discuss what you did to understand what you read.

Focus on Genre | **Text Features in Nonfiction**
In this unit, you learned how text features such as charts, graphs, and online links help you gain information. Choose a feature from one of the selections that was most helpful to you. Discuss with a partner why it was useful.

Reading Strategy | **Visualize**
As you read the selections, you learned to visualize what you were reading. Explain to a partner how this strategy will help you in the future.

Explore the

In this unit, you have been reading about our precious world. Choose one of these ways to explore the Guiding Question:

- **Discuss** With a group, discuss the Guiding Question. What makes our environment so valuable? How can we solve its problems? Share your ideas with classmates and give examples from the selections to support them.
- **Role-Play** Imagine that Howard Quigley and Mireya Mayor meet to talk about the Guiding Question. With a partner, role-play their discussion. To help you create the discussion, think of two questions they might ask each other.
- **Draw** Create a drawing to answer to the Guiding Question. Your drawing could be anything that shows your view about the value of our environment.

Book Talk

Which Unit Library book did you choose? Explain to a partner what it taught you about the environment.

Tree, 1994, Ron Waddams. Acrylic on board, private collection.

 **Critical Viewing:** What is the mood, or feeling, of this image? Tell why you think so.

ELPS: 2.C.1 learn new language structures heard during classroom instruction and interactions; 2.E.1 use visual support to enhance and confirm understanding of complex and elaborated spoken language; 2.G.3 understand the general meaning of spoken language regarding familiar to unfamiliar contexts; 2.G.5 understand the main points of spoken language regarding familiar to unfamiliar language; 2.I.4 demonstrate listening comprehension of complex spoken English by collaborating with peers; 3.C.2 speak using a variety of sentence lengths with increasing accuracy and ease; 3.C.4 speak using a variety of connecting words with increasing accuracy and ease; 3.G.1 express opinions on a variety of social and grade-appropriate academic topics

CONFLICT AND RESOLUTION

GUIDING QUESTION

How can people overcome conflict?

Read More!

Content Library

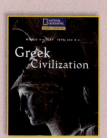

Greek Civilization

Leveled Library

I Will Plant You a Lilac Tree
by Laura Hillman

The Other Side of the Sky
by Farah Ahmedi and Ansary Tamim

Navajo Code Talkers
by Andrew Santella

Internet
InsideNG.com

- Learn how people resolve conflicts fairly.

- Find out about people who risk their lives to save others.

- See pictures of Sarajevo, where Zlata Filipović lived.

Author's Purpose and Word Choice

▶ **Author's Purpose**
▶ **Word Choice**

An author's <mark>purpose</mark> is his or her reason for writing. It may be to entertain, inform, express ideas and feelings, or to persuade readers.

How It Works

Recognizing an author's <mark>purpose</mark> for writing can help you understand what the author wants you to know or think. The genre is one clue that can help you figure this out.

Genre	Purposes
Short stories, fables, other fiction	to entertain; to communicate a message
Expository nonfiction	to inform; to express feelings and ideas
Advertisements, other persuasive writing	to convince you to act or think a certain way

The author's **word choices** also provide clues.

- Words that create a funny, sad, angry, or other kind of mood suggest that the <mark>purpose</mark> is to entertain or persuade.
- Positive words that describe one idea and negative words that describe another idea could show you the author's attitude.
- Words that emphasize fact signal that the <mark>purpose</mark> is to inform.

Study the passage below to discover the author's <mark>purpose</mark>.

The Daydreamer and the Baker

Once there lived a pleasant young man who spent his time daydreaming about the delicious smells from the bakery next door. The stingy baker grew annoyed that the young man enjoyed the aromas but never bought a single thing.

"The title sounds like a folk tale."

Positive words describe the young man.

Negative words describe the baker.

Academic Vocabulary

- **purpose** (**pur**-pus) *noun*
  A **purpose** is a reason for doing something.

Practice Together

Read the following passages aloud with your class. Identify the author's purpose in each. How do the word choices fit the purpose?

Mistaken Identity

Liza storms into the room. "Dad, my boyfriend is such a jerk! I was at the mall with Shannon, and we saw him there with another girl."

They hear a knock at the door. "Maybe that's Richard now," says Dad.

Richard enters with a girl. "Hi! This is my favorite cousin, Sarah, from Arizona. Sarah, this is Liza, my girlfriend."

Liza blushes. Dad chuckles.

Cesar Chavez

During grape harvest season in 1965, grape growers in the U.S. cut back on how much they paid the farm workers. To fight the pay cut, the farm workers developed a new and effective plan. Under the leadership of Cesar Chavez, the workers went directly to people and asked them to stop buying grapes. Over time, the plan worked. In 1969, the grape growers signed a contract with farm workers promising better pay and fair treatment.

Try It!

Read the following passage aloud. What is the author's purpose? How do you know?

Internment in America

In 1942 the United States and Japan were at war. The President of the U.S. issued an Executive Order that said Japanese Americans on the west coast had to leave their homes and live in government camps. Families were forced to move to terrible, overcrowded camps guarded by soldiers. Many of these people were good citizens, and not one had been proved to be a spy.

▲ Thousands of Japanese Americans were forced into internment camps like this one at Gila River, Arizona.

After the war, Japanese Americans spent years working to get an apology from the U.S. government. Finally, Congress passed the Civil Liberties Act of 1988. The Act formally admitted the suffering and losses of the Japanese Americans during World War II. Their honor

Focus on Vocabulary

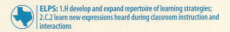ELPS: 1.H develop and expand repertoire of learning strategies; 2.C.2 learn new expressions heard during classroom instruction and interactions

Go Beyond the Literal Meaning

Sometimes writers use words to mean exactly what they say and nothing else. These exact meanings are called **literal** meanings. **Figurative language** goes beyond the **literal** meanings of the words and creates images in the reader's mind. Many common sayings and expressions are examples of figurative language.

Types of Figurative Language

Definitions	Examples	Explanations
A **simile** compares two things, usually using *like*, *as*, or *than*.	A spring breeze arrived **like** a joyful dancer.	The simile compares a spring breeze to a joyful dancer.
A **metaphor** says one thing *is* another.	A spring breeze **was** a gift after the long winter.	This metaphor compares a spring breeze to a gift.
Personification gives human qualities to things that aren't human.	A spring breeze **smiled** on us after the long winter.	A breeze cannot smile; this is a human trait.
In an **idiom**, the words mean something different from their dictionary meanings.	Jon stopped singing when his friends said to **cool it**.	The literal meaning of *cool it* is "to make something colder." The idiom means to stop.

How the Strategy Works

Use context to help you figure out language that is not **literal** .

1. Decide whether a **literal** meaning could be correct.
2. Look at the figurative language to see what is being compared.
3. Think about what the comparison could mean.
4. Decide what feeling or image the writer is trying to create.

Follow the strategy to figure out the meanings of the underlined phrases.

Marie was new in our school that year. She had lived in many places and was <u>as bright as a new penny</u>. Her mind was <u>a present waiting to be opened</u>. Her stories <u>handed me the world</u>.

Strategy in Action

" The friend is bright, which also means smart. A new penny is shiny and seems special. The new friend is smart and special. "

☑ **REMEMBER** **Literal** meanings are the exact meanings of words. **Figurative language** extends beyond the exact meanings of words.

Academic Vocabulary
• **literal** (lit-ur-al) *adjective*
The **literal** meaning of a word is its exact meaning.

Practice Together

Read the passage aloud. Figure out the meaning of each underlined phrase.

A Nation Rises

In December of 1941, enemy aircraft attacked the U.S. Naval Base at Pearl Harbor, Hawaii. The attack struck the American people like a thunderbolt. War had been going on in Europe and in Asia for more than two years, but the United States had stayed out.

Many Americans thought war could never reach them. It was a distant buzz, troublesome but far away. That way of thinking soon ended.

Protected by oceans on either side, few Americans imagined the country being attacked. The events of Pearl Harbor woke up the nation.

At first angry, then with determination like steel, America went to work. Millions joined the Army. Factories produced war supplies around the clock. Everyone did what he or she could. A spirit of purpose gripped the nation.

Try It!

Read the following passage. Look at each underlined phrase. What does it mean? How do you know?

GOAL!

Tina raced like the wind down the sidelines of the soccer field. No defenders were nearby. Looking back up the field, she saw that luck was her friend. Her teammate had broken loose with the ball. Tina cut to the center to get the pass.

She was alone no longer. A hawk of a defender was on her. Tina got the pass and then dribbled left and quickly back right. The defender stayed with her at first, then stumbled and fell back like a confused kitten. With a mind of its own, Tina's foot hammered the ball toward the net. Goal!

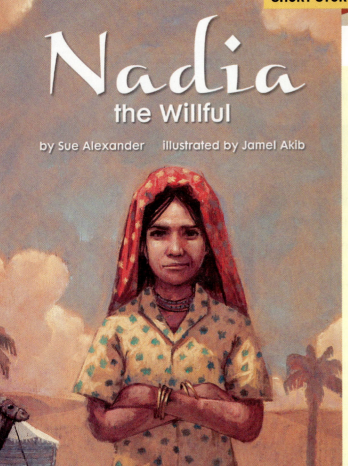

SHORT STORY

Nadia
the Willful

by Sue Alexander   illustrated by Jamel Akib

SELECTION 1 OVERVIEW

▶ **Build Background**

▶ **Language & Grammar**
Express Opinions
Use Complete Sentences

▶ **Prepare to Read**
Learn Key Vocabulary
Learn a Reading Strategy
Make Inferences

▶ **Read and Write**
Focus on Genre
Short Story
Apply the
Reading Strategy
Make Inferences
Critical Thinking
Reading Fluency
Read with Phrasing
Vocabulary Review
Write About the
Guiding Question

▶ **Connect Across the Curriculum**
Literary Analysis
Evaluate Literature:
Imagery
Evaluate Characters
Interpret Metaphor
Vocabulary Study
Use Simile, Metaphor, and
Personification
Language and Grammar
Express Opinions
Writing and Grammar
Write About Conflicts

Build Background

Connect

Anticipation Guide Conflict is difficult. Read the statements below and tell whether you agree or disagree with them.

Anticipation Guide

	Agree	Disagree
1. You should not talk about problems or feelings.	_____	_____
2. You should never change your mind.	_____	_____
3. If you know something is right, act on your belief.	_____	_____

Bedouin Culture

"Nadia the Willful" takes place in the Bedouin culture of the Arabian Peninsula. Find out more about the lives of Bedouin people today.

Digital Library

InsideNG.com
↻ View the images.

Bedouin people have their own unique culture. ▶

396 Unit 6 Conflict and Resolution

Language & Grammar

ELPS: 2.C.1 learn new language structures heard during classroom instruction and interactions; 2.E.1 use visual support to enhance and confirm understanding of complex and elaborated spoken language; 2.I.4 demonstrate listening comprehension of complex spoken English by collaborating with peers; 3.G.1 express opinions on a variety of social and grade-appropriate academic topics

1 TRY OUT LANGUAGE
2 LEARN GRAMMAR
3 APPLY ON YOUR OWN

Express Opinions

Study the image below. Look at the people's expressions. Listen to the song. What opinion is expressed in this song? Listen again and sing along.

SONG

I've Been Thinking

Mother, Father, I've been thinking
There are times we don't agree,
Still I think it's good to follow
Family rules and policy.

"Do your schoolwork. Clean your bedroom.
Exercise! Watch less TV."
Such advice is beneficial
Even when I disagree.

But here's a little brief opinion:
We could have more harmony
If you take this small suggestion—
Just a little tip from me.

Doing chores and all my schoolwork
Pleases you and pleases me.
I deserve a small allowance.
That's my view. Do you agree?

Use Complete Sentences

You can express a complete thought with a simple sentence. A simple sentence has one **subject** and one **predicate**. In statements, the subject usually comes before the predicate.

Simple Sentences

Subject	Predicate
The **subject** is the person or thing that is doing the action or is being described. The **noun** is the most important word in the subject.	The **predicate** tells what the person or thing *does*, *has*, or *is*. The **verb** is the most important word in the predicate.
Parents	**make** many rules.
Some **children**	**disagree** with the rules.
Arguments about rules	**develop**.
Some **people**	**get** upset.
Solutions	**create** peace again.

Practice Together

Say each group of words. Add subjects to turn numbers 1–3 into complete sentences. Add predicates to turn numbers 4–6 into complete sentences. Say each new sentence.

1. _____ know the importance of kindness.
2. _____ makes people happy.
3. _____ hurts people's feelings.
4. Arguments _____.
5. A peaceful home _____.
6. Kindness _____.

Try It!

Say each group of words. Write subjects on a card to turn numbers 7–8 into complete sentences. Write predicates on a card to turn numbers 9–10 into complete sentences. Say each new sentence.

7. _____ solve problems.
8. _____ makes things worse.
9. Resolutions _____.
10. People _____.

▲ Discussions help people solve conflicts.

What Do You Think?

EXPRESS OPINIONS

When you express an opinion, you tell what you think or how you feel about something. Read this story. How do you think Rico should solve his problem?

> Rico looked forward to the football game on Saturday night. The teams were cross-town rivals, and excitement had been building for weeks.
>
> On Saturday morning, Rico's mom told him that she needed him to babysit his five-year-old sister. Their regular sitter had canceled, and Rico's parents had to go to a business dinner.
>
> When Rico protested, his mom told him that there was nothing else they could do.

First, gather your opinions in a list, like this example.

My Opinions:

I think Rico should try to go to the game.

In my opinion, his parents are being unfair.

They could try to find another babysitter.

Then use your list to express your opinions with a group.

HOW TO EXPRESS OPINIONS

1. Tell what you think or believe.
2. Use opinion words like *I think, I don't think, I believe, I don't believe, in my opinion.*
3. Give reasons for your opinions. Then people will take them more seriously.

> I don't think Rico should have to babysit. He's been planning on going to the game for weeks.

USE COMPLETE SENTENCES

When you tell your opinions, use complete sentences to express yourself. Make sure there is a **subject** and a **verb** in each sentence.

EXAMPLE   **I** **think** Rico is right.

Prepare to Read

**ELPS:** 3.A practice producing sounds of newly acquired vocabulary in a manner that is comprehensible; 4.J demonstrate and expand comprehension by employing inferential skills

Learn Key Vocabulary

Rate and Study the Words Rate how well you know each word. Then:

1. Pronounce the word. Say it aloud several times. Spell it.
2. Study the example.
3. Tell more about the word.
4. Practice it. Make the word your own.

Key Words

banish (ban-ish) *verb*
▶ page 410

To **banish** means to send away or punish by making someone leave. The referee **banished** the player from the game.

forbid (fur-bid) *verb*
▶ page 410

To **forbid** means to order not to do something. The sign **forbids** anyone to swim in this area.
Related Word: **forbidden**

grief (grēf) *noun*
▶ page 406

To feel **grief** is to feel very sad. My friend felt **grief** when her dog died.
Antonym: **happiness**

memory (me-mu-rē) *noun*
▶ page 406

A **memory** is something remembered. Looking through family photographs can bring back **memories** of good times.

obey (ō-bā) *verb*
▶ page 406

To **obey** is to follow an order. If your parents tell you to clean your room, you must **obey** them.

punishment
(pun-ish-ment) *noun* ▶ page 406

A **punishment** is a penalty for doing something bad. When Dad was a kid, the **punishment** for late homework was to write lines on the chalkboard.
Related Word: **punish**

recall (rē-kawl) *verb*
▶ page 410

To **recall** means to remember. The student tries to **recall** the answer to a test question.
Synonym: **remember**

willful (wil-ful) *adjective*
▶ page 404

Someone who is **willful** refuses to change. A **willful** child only does what he wants, not what others tell him.

Practice the Words Make a Synonym–Antonym Chart for each Key Word.

Word	Synonyms	Antonyms
banish	expel, send away	welcome, invite
forbid		
grief		

Synonym–Antonym Chart

Reading Strategy: Make Inferences

An author often gives clues about characters and events instead of telling readers the information directly. When this happens, you have to make inferences, or "read between the lines."

HOW TO MAKE INFERENCES

1. As you read, look for clues and details the author gives you about the characters.
2. Use what you know about people to make sense of the story. Connect details to your own experience. What new ideas can you put together?
3. Track your thoughts on an Inference Chart like the one below.

Strategy in Action

Here's how one student made inferences.

Look Into the Text

Nadia's father, the sheik Tarik, whose kindness and graciousness caused his name to be praised in every tent, did not know what to do with his willful daughter.

Only Hamed, the eldest of Nadia's six brothers and Tarik's favorite son, could calm Nadia's temper when it flashed. "Oh, angry one," he would say, "shall we see how long you can stay that way?" And he would laugh and tease and pull at her dark hair until she laughed back. Then she would follow Hamed wherever he led.

Inference Chart

What I Read	What I Already Know
Tarik **did not know what to do with his daughter**.	Parents try but don't always understand us.
Only Hamed could calm Nadia's temper.	I admire my older brother and sister.

What I Can Infer: Nadia feels close to her brother because they understand each other.

Practice Together

Reread the passage from "Nadia the Willful." Then, follow the steps in the How-To box to make an inference of your own.

ELPS: 4.J demonstrate and expand comprehension by employing inferential skills

Short Story

Authors write short stories to help readers imagine different experiences and to communicate **themes**, or messages, about life. The author's **word choices** bring imaginary people, places, and events to life.

> In the land of the drifting sands where the Bedouin move their tents to follow the fertile grasses, there lived a girl whose stubbornness and flashing temper caused her to be known throughout the desert as Nadia the Willful.

Your Job as a Reader

Reading Strategy: Make Inferences

As you read, use the clues and details the author gives you to make inferences about the characters and events.

Nadia
the Willful

by Sue Alexander   illustrated by Jamel Akib

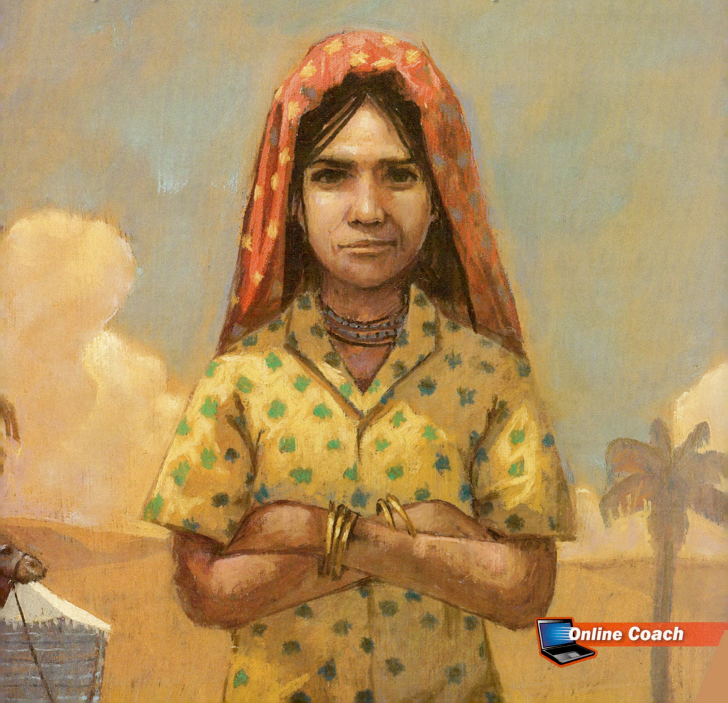

Online Coach

Discover the difficulties that Nadia experiences.

In the land of the drifting sands where the Bedouin move their tents to **follow the fertile grasses**, there lived a girl whose stubbornness and **flashing temper** caused her to be known throughout the desert as Nadia the <mark>Willful</mark>.

Nadia's father, the **sheik** Tarik, whose kindness and graciousness **caused his name to be praised** in every tent, did not know what to do with his willful daughter.

Only Hamed, the eldest of Nadia's six brothers and Tarik's favorite son, could calm Nadia's temper when it flashed. "Oh, angry one," he would say, "shall we see how long you can stay that way?" And he would laugh and tease and pull at her dark hair until she laughed back. Then she would follow Hamed wherever he led.

▲ **Critical Viewing: Character** Which characters does the artist portray in this painting?

Key Vocabulary

willful *adj.*, doing things your own way

In Other Words

follow the fertile grasses find food for their animals
flashing temper bursts of anger
sheik old and wise man
caused his name to be praised made him well-liked

Cultural Background

Many **Bedouin** people live in the deserts of the Arabian Peninsula. They move from place to place with their flocks to find food, water, and shelter.

One day before dawn, Hamed mounted his father's great white stallion and rode to the west to seek new grazing ground for the sheep. Nadia stood with her father at the edge of the oasis and watched him go.

Hamed did not return.

Nadia rode behind her father as he traveled across the desert **from oasis to oasis**, seeking Hamed.

Shepherds told them of seeing a great white stallion fleeing before the pillars of wind that stirred the sand. And they said that the horse carried no rider.

Passing merchants, their camels laden with spices and sweets for the **bazaar**, told of the emptiness of the desert they had crossed.

Tribesmen, strangers, everyone whom Tarik asked, sighed and gazed into the desert, saying, "**Such is the will of Allah.**"

At last Tarik knew in his heart that his favorite son, Hamed, had been claimed, as other Bedouin before him, by the drifting sands. And he told Nadia what he knew—that Hamed was dead.

Nadia screamed and wept and stamped the sand, crying, "Not even Allah will take Hamed from me!" until her father could bear no more and **sternly bade her to silence**.

▲ **Critical Viewing: Design** How does the artist capture the pain of Tarik?

In Other Words
from oasis to oasis stopping at places to get water and shelter
bazaar market
Such is the will of Allah It is meant to be
sternly bade her to silence angrily told her to be quiet

Nadia's **grief knew no bounds**. She walked blindly through the oasis neither seeing nor hearing those who would **console her**. And Tarik was silent. For days he sat inside his tent, speaking not at all and barely tasting the meals set before him.

Then, on the seventh day, Tarik came out of his tent. He called all his people to him, and when they were assembled, he spoke. "From this day forward," he said, "let no one **utter** Hamed's name. **Punishment** shall be swift for those who would remind me of what I have lost."

Hamed's mother wept at the **decree**. The people of the clan looked at one another uneasily. All could see the hardness that had settled on the sheik's face and the coldness in his eyes, and so they said nothing. But they **obeyed**.

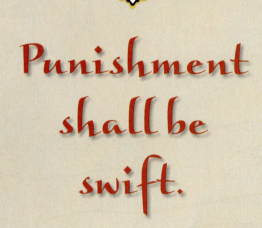

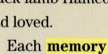

Nadia, too, did as her father decreed, though each day held something to remind her of Hamed. As she passed her brothers at play, she remembered games Hamed had taught her. As she walked by the women weaving patches for the tents, and heard them talking and laughing, she remembered tales Hamed had told her and how they had made her laugh. And as she watched the shepherds with their flock, she remembered the little black lamb Hamed had loved.

Each **memory** brought Hamed's name to Nadia's lips, but she **stilled the sound**. And each time that she did so, her unhappiness grew until, finally, she could no longer contain it. She wept and raged at anyone and anything that crossed her path. Soon everyone at the oasis fled at her approach. And she was more lonely than she had ever been before.

Key Vocabulary

grief *n.*, great sadness
punishment *n.*, the suffering received for doing wrong
obey *v.*, to do as you are told
memory *n.*, something you remember from the past

In Other Words

knew no bounds did not stop
console her try to make her feel better
utter say
decree order
stilled the sound did not say his name

Before You Move On

1. **Cause and Effect** What difficulties does Nadia experience? How do they affect her?
2. **Character's Motive** What does Tarik forbid his people to say out loud? Why?
3. **Conflict** How do the people react to Tarik's order? Explain.

One day, as Nadia passed the place where her brothers were playing, she stopped to watch them. They were playing one of the games that Hamed had taught her. But they were playing it wrong.

Without thinking, Nadia called out to them. "That is not the way! Hamed said that first you jump this way and then you jump back!"

Her brothers stopped their game and looked around in fear. Had Tarik heard Nadia say Hamed's name? But the sheik was **nowhere to be seen**.

"Teach us, Nadia, as our brother taught you," said her smallest brother.

And so she did. Then she told them of other games and how Hamed had taught her to play them. And as she spoke of Hamed she felt **an easing of the hurt within her**.

In Other Words
nowhere to be seen not there
an easing of the hurt within her her pain begin to go away

So she went on speaking of him.

She went to where the women sat at their loom and spoke of Hamed. She told them tales that Hamed had told her. And she told how he had made her laugh as he was telling them.

At first the women were afraid to listen to the willful girl and covered their ears, but after a time, they listened and laughed with her.

"Remember your father's promise of punishment!" Nadia's mother warned when she heard Nadia speaking of Hamed. **"Cease, I implore you!"**

Nadia knew that her mother had reason to be afraid, for Tarik, in his grief and **bitterness**, had grown quick-tempered and **sharp of tongue**. But she did not know how to tell her mother that speaking of Hamed eased the pain she felt, and so she said only, "I will speak of my brother! I will!" And she ran away from the sound of her mother's voice. She went to where the shepherds tended the flock and spoke

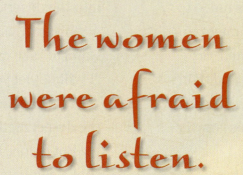

The women were afraid to listen.

of Hamed. The shepherds ran from her in fear and hid behind the sheep. But Nadia went on speaking. She told of Hamed's love for the little black lamb and how he had taught it to leap at his whistle. Soon the shepherds left off their hiding and came to listen. Then they told their own stories of Hamed and the little black lamb.

The more Nadia spoke of Hamed, **the clearer his face became in her mind**. She could see his smile and the light in his eyes. She could hear his voice. And the clearer Hamed's voice and face became, the less Nadia hurt inside and the less her temper flashed. At last, she was filled with peace.

But her mother was still afraid for her willful daughter. Again and again she sought to quiet Nadia so that Tarik's bitterness would not be turned against her. And again and again Nadia tossed her head and went on speaking of Hamed.

Soon, all who listened could see Hamed's face clearly before them.

In Other Words

"Cease, I implore you!" Stop, I beg you!
bitterness anger
sharp of tongue said mean things
the clearer his face became in her mind the more she could remember him

Before You Move On

1. **Confirm Prediction** Was your prediction correct? What happens after Nadia begins to talk about Hamed?

2. **Foreshadowing/Prediction** Why does Nadia's mother warn her? What do you think might happen? Discuss your ideas with a partner.

Will Tarik punish those who talk about Hamed?

One day, the youngest shepherd came to Nadia's tent calling, "Come, Nadia! See Hamed's black lamb, it has grown so big and strong!"

But it was not Nadia who came out of the tent.

It was Tarik.

On the sheik's face was a look **more fierce than that of a desert hawk**, and when he spoke, his words were as **sharp as a scimitar**.

"I have **forbidden** my son's name to be said. And I promised punishment to whoever disobeyed my command. So shall it be. Before the sun sets and the moon casts its first shadow on the sand, you will be gone from this oasis—never to return."

"No!" cried Nadia, hearing her father's words.

"I have spoken!" roared the sheik. "It shall be done!"

Trembling, the shepherd went to gather his possessions. And the rest of the clan looked at one another uneasily and muttered among themselves.

In the hours that followed, fear of being **banished** to the desert made everyone turn away from Nadia as she tried to tell them of Hamed and the things he had done and said.

And the less she was listened to, the less she was able to **recall** Hamed's face and voice. And the less she recalled, the more her temper raged within her, destroying the peace she had found.

By evening, she could stand it no longer. She went to where her father sat, staring into the desert, and stood before him.

"You will not **rob me** of my brother Hamed!" she cried, stamping her foot. "I will not let you!"

Tarik looked at her, his eyes colder than the desert night.

But before he could utter a word, Nadia spoke again. "Can you recall Hamed's face? Can you still hear his voice?"

Tarik started in surprise, and his answer seemed to come **unbidden to his lips**. "No, I cannot! Day after day I have sat in this spot where I last saw Hamed, trying to remember the look, the sound, the happiness that was my beloved son—but I cannot."

Key Vocabulary

forbid *v.*, to not allow
banish *v.*, to send away
recall *v.*, to remember

In Other Words

more fierce than that of a desert hawk that was extremely scary
sharp as a scimitar painful as a sword
rob me take away the memory
unbidden to his lips without thinking

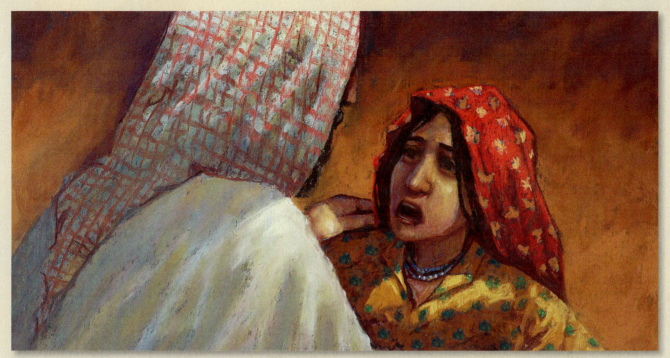

And he wept.

Nadia's **tone** became gentle. "There is a way, honored father," she said. "Listen."

And she began to speak of Hamed. She told of walks she and Hamed had taken, and of talks they had had. She told how he had taught her games, told her tales and calmed her when she was angry. She told many things that she remembered, some happy and some sad.

And when she was done with the telling, she said gently, "Can you not recall him now, Father? Can you not see his face? Can you not hear his voice?"

Tarik nodded through his tears, and for the first time since Hamed had been gone, he smiled.

"Now you see," Nadia said, her tone more gentle than the softest of the desert breezes, "there is a way that Hamed can be with us still."

The sheik **pondered** what Nadia had said. After a long time, he spoke, and the sharpness was gone from his voice.

"Tell my people to come before me,

In Other Words
tone voice
pondered thought about

Nadia," he said. "I have something to say to them."

When all were assembled, Tarik said, "From this day forward, let my daughter Nadia be known not as Willful, but as Wise. And let her name be praised in every tent, for she has given me back my beloved son."

And so it was. The shepherd returned to his flock, kindness and graciousness returned to the oasis, and Nadia's name was praised in every tent. And Hamed lived again—in the hearts of all who remembered him. ❖

About the Author

Sue Alexander

Sue Alexander (1933–) loves to write stories and is the author of more than twenty books for young people. Alexander wrote *Nadia the Willful* because she had a similar experience. When her brother died, her father found it painful to talk about him. Alexander needed to talk about her brother and did not know how to explain this to her father. She decided to write a story about it. Because Alexander had always had an interest in the Bedouin culture, she set her story in the desert.

About the Illustrator

Jamel Akib

Jamel Akib (1965–) is an award-winning illustrator of English and Malaysian ancestry. His work has been shown in museums and galleries. Akib's style includes both chalk pastels and digital artwork. Akib lives in Essex, England with his family.

Before You Move On

1. **Confirm Prediction** Was your prediction correct? What <mark>punishment</mark> does Tarik give to the shepherd? How does Nadia change his mind?

2. **Theme** How does Nadia's behavior reflect the theme of conflict and resolution?

3. **Interpret** What does the simile "sharp as a scimitar" tell you about Tarik's feelings?

Quilt

by Janet S. Wong

Our family
is a quilt

of odd **remnants**
patched together

5 in a strange
pattern,

threads fraying, fabric
wearing thin—

but made to keep
10 its warmth

even in bitter
cold.

▲ **Critical Viewing: Design** How does this image show that a quilt or other object can also be art?

In Other Words
remnants unused pieces of cloth
wearing thin old, used

Before You Move On

1. **Paraphrase** Using your own words explain what "Our family is a quilt" means.
2. **Compare and Contrast** How does Nadia's family compare to the family in "Quilt"?

Chief Koruinka's Song

a traditional poem from Chile

Face in Landscape, John Martin.

The entire earth is one soul
to which we belong.
Our souls will not die.
Change they might,
5   go out they will not.
We are one soul,
there is just one world.

▲ **Critical Viewing: Design** How does the artist create more than one image?

Before You Move On

1. **Mood** What is the mood or feeling of this poem?
2. **Perspectives** How would Nadia in "Nadia the Willful" feel about this poem? Why do you think so?

Connect Reading and Writing

Vocabulary
banish

forbidden

grief

memory

obey

punishment

recall

willful

CRITICAL THINKING

1. SUM IT UP Make a card for each vocabulary word. Use at least five vocabulary words to **recall** the story events that led Nadia the **Willful** to become known as Nadia the Wise.

2. Infer Why might Tarik have **forbidden** people to talk about Hamed?

3. Compare Use a line in "Quilt" or "Chief Koruinka's Song" to express an idea about Nadia's family.

4. Analyze Look again at the Anticipation Guide on page 396. Do you want to change any responses? With a group, discuss when you should or should not change your mind in a conflict.

READING FLUENCY

Phrasing Read the passage on page 649 to a partner. Assess your fluency.

1. I read

   a. great   **b.** OK   **c.** not very well

2. What I did best in my reading was _____.

READING STRATEGY

Make Inferences
Show your Inference Chart to a partner. Explain two inferences you made.

VOCABULARY REVIEW

Oral Review Read the paragraph aloud. Add the vocabulary words.

> The mayor said she will _____ people from the park if they do not _____ the rules. I _____ what happened last year when my brother tried to climb the tallest tree. The sign said, "Climbing is _____." But he is _____ and never fears _____. He almost got hurt. My family would have felt such _____. That awful event is just a _____ now, but one that we will never forget.

Written Review Imagine you are Tarik. Write a journal entry to tell how your feelings have changed about **forbidding** people's actions. Use four vocabulary words.

REMEMBER
If a word ends in a consonant, double the consonant when adding a suffix.

WRITE ABOUT THE **GUIDING QUESTION**

Explore Conflict and Understanding
Tell how conflict can hurt or help a family. Can it ever do both? Reread "Nadia the Willful" to find examples that support your opinion.

Connect Across the Curriculum

ELPS: 2.C.4 learn academic vocabulary heard during classroom instruction and interactions

Literary Analysis

Evaluate Literature: Imagery

> **Academic Vocabulary**
> • **image** (im-ij) *noun*
>   An **image** is a mental picture of something.

Learn About Imagery Writers use descriptive words and phrases to give readers strong **images** . These words are called "imagery." Imagery helps readers "see, taste, smell, feel, and hear" what they are reading. Then readers understand better how characters feel, what a place is like, and so on.

Think About Imagery In "Nadia the Willful," the writer uses imagery to help readers understand the feelings and emotions that Nadia and her family experience and to show what life was like in the desert. What mental **image** do you see when you read the sentence below? How does this **image** help you "see" what is being described?

> In the land of the drifting sands where the Bedouin move their tents to follow the fertile grasses . . .

> I picture a desert with sand blowing across it, lots of tents, and some green grass. This helps me picture where the story takes place.

Practice Together

Analyze Imagery Read these words and phrases from "Nadia the Willful." What sense do they appeal to? What effect do the underlined words or phrases have on your understanding of the scene and the characters?

Imagery Chart

Imagery	Sense	Effect
". . . for Tarik, in his grief and bitterness, had grown quick-tempered and <u>sharp of tongue</u>."	sight, touch, sound	I understand that Tarik feels upset and because he is hurt, he gets angry easily.
"She could see his smile and <u>the light in his eyes</u>."		

Try It!

With a partner, find three more examples of descriptive phrases in "Nadia the Willful." Create an Imagery Chart to record examples of imagery in the selection. Discuss how the **images** help you understand and relate to the text.

ELPS: 2.C.4 learn academic vocabulary heard during classroom instruction and interactions

Simile, Metaphor, and Personification

Academic Vocabulary

- **compare** (kum-**pair**) *verb*
  When you **compare**, you look closely at how things are alike or different.

Review Figurative Language Writers use figurative language to create mental images and express ideas beyond the literal meaning of the words.

- A **simile** uses the words *like, as,* or *than* to **compare** things.
  . . . his words were as sharp as a scimitar.
- A **metaphor** **compares** things without using *like* or *as*.
  The entire earth is one soul.
- **Personification** gives human qualities to non-human things.
  . . . her temper raged within her . . .

Analyze Figurative Language Work with a partner to identify the type of figurative language and the meaning of these phrases from "Nadia the Willfull."

  1. Nadia's grief knew no bounds. . .
  2. . . . a look more fierce than that of a desert hawk . . .
  3. She could see his smile and the light in his eyes.

ELPS: 2.C.4 learn academic vocabulary heard during classroom instruction and interactions; 2.H.1 understand implicit ideas in complex spoken language

Evaluate Characters

Academic Vocabulary

- **evaluate** (i-**val**-yu-wāt) *verb*
  To **evaluate** is to decide on the quality of something.

What Makes a Character Believable? Use what you know about characters' traits to **evaluate** if their actions are believable. Make an Idea Web like this one. Nadia disobeys her father by speaking Hamed's name. Because she is willful, this action is believable.

Evaluate Believability Nadia persuades her father to let people speak of Hamed. Which of Nadia's traits make this believable? Discuss your Idea Web and Nadia's character traits with a partner.

Idea Web

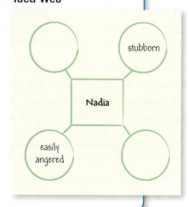

ELPS: 2.C.4 learn academic vocabulary heard during classroom instruction and interactions; 4.F.2 use visual and contextual support to enhance and confirm understanding

Literary Analysis

Interpret Metaphor

Academic Vocabulary
- **interpret** (in-**tur**-prut) *verb*
  When you **interpret** something, you explain or tell the meaning of it.

What Is a Metaphor? A metaphor makes a comparison by saying that one thing is another thing. For example: *The desert sun is a ball of fire*.

"Quilt" and "Chief Koruinka's Song" are poems that use **metaphors** to express ideas. When you **interpret** the metaphors, you can better understand the meanings of the poems.

Practice Together

Analyze Metaphor With the class, reread the poem "Quilt" aloud. Follow these steps to **interpret** the metaphor and understand the meaning of the poem:

- Identify the two things being compared. In this poem, the speaker says her *family* is a *quilt*.

- Ask questions about what is being compared. For example: *How is a family like a quilt?*

- Look closely at each line and word of the poem to answer your questions.

- To **interpret** the poem's meaning, examine the effect of comparing family to a quilt. What idea is the poet expressing about her family?

The speaker talks about a quilt being made up of odd remnants but that also keeps you warm, even when it's cold outside. I think she means that her family members are all different but they come together to comfort each other, especially in hard times.

Try It!

With a partner, reread the poem "Chief Koruinka's Song." Follow the steps explained above to **interpret** the metaphor. How does the metaphor help enhance and confirm your understanding of the poem.

ELPS: 3.6.1 express
opinions on a variety of
social and grade-appropriate
academic topics

Language and Grammar

Express Opinions

Group Share With a group, express your opinions about the decree, or order, that Tarik made. Give reasons for your opinions. Use complete sentences.

> I think Tarik's decree was too harsh. His daughter suffered because of it.

Writing and Grammar

Write About Conflicts

Study the Models When you write about real and fictional conflicts, you want readers to understand. Use complete sentences to show what the conflict is and how it affects people.

NOT OK

> The **people** in front of Tarik's tent. They looked at one another uneasily. They saw the hardness. **Tarik** his people to speak Hamed's name. **Wept** at the decree. **Walked** blindly through the oasis. Remembering things about Hamed. **Brought** Hamed's name to her lips.

The reader thinks: "**What is this story about? I don't understand!**"

OK

> The **people** **assembled** in front of Tarik's tent. They looked at one another uneasily. They saw the hardness **on the sheik's face. Tarik** **forbade** his people to speak Hamed's name. **Hamed's mother** **wept** at the decree. **Nadia** **walked** blindly through the oasis, **remembering things about Hamed.** Each **memory** **brought** Hamed's name to her lips.

This writer uses complete sentences, combines ideas, and adds detail to the paragraph.

Add Sentences Think of three sentences to add to the OK model above. Be sure your sentences are complete.

🖊 **WRITE ON YOUR OWN** Write about a time when someone you know did not want to follow a rule. Did he or she think the rule was unfair or unreasonable? Why? Check your sentences to be sure they are complete.

REMEMBER

How do you know if a sentence is complete?
- It has a **subject** and a **predicate**.

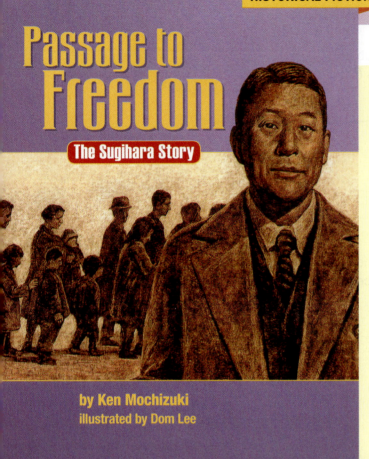

Passage to Freedom

The Sugihara Story

by Ken Mochizuki
illustrated by Dom Lee

Build Background

Overcoming Conflict

How do people overcome a conflict that affects thousands of people? Meet Chiune Sugihara of Japan who faced a life and death conflict in 1940.

Connect

Brainstorm Make a list of people who have risked their lives to save others. Think of movies you have seen, books you have read, or other sources. Describe what one person on your list did to save others.

Digital Library | InsideNG.com
🔵 View the video.

▲ Chiune Sugihara (top left) and his family helped thousands of Jews escape the Nazis during World War II.

Language & Grammar

ELPS: 2.E.1 use visual support to enhance and confirm understanding of complex and elaborated spoken language; 2.G.5 understand the main points of spoken language regarding familiar to unfamiliar language; 3.C.2 speak using a variety of sentence lengths with increasing accuracy and ease; 3.C.4 speak using a variety of connecting words with increasing accuracy and ease

1 TRY OUT LANGUAGE
2 LEARN GRAMMAR
3 APPLY ON YOUR OWN

Engage in Discussion

CD

Look at the photo and listen to the discussion.

PICTURE PROMPT and DISCUSSION

What Would You Do?

Daniel: My history teacher says that wherever there are people, there will be conflicts.

Martina: Why can't people get along?

Fred: That's a good question, but I don't have the answer. People don't get along for a lot of reasons. There are disagreements between friends or neighbors, and there are disagreements between countries. Some are little problems, and some are huge issues.

Daniel: Sometimes people are afraid to speak up. Everyone should be willing to say what they think is right, wouldn't you agree?

Fred: True, but I would not risk my life needlessly.

Martina: No, but you probably would be willing to take a risk if it was important to your life or a loved one's life.

Daniel: Lots of people risk their lives defending their countries and helping people. I'm sure most of them don't even think about the risks because it's their job. Wouldn't it be easier if people everywhere just got along?

Fred: It sure would!

▲ Conflicts take place in everyday life, even in sports.

Use Compound Sentences

- A **clause** contains a subject and a verb. An **independent clause** contains a subject and a verb and can stand alone as a sentence.

    EXAMPLES   **Some people risk their lives.**
    independent clause

    Their efforts help others.
    independent clause

- A **compound sentence** contains at least two independent clauses joined by **and**, **but**, or **or**.

- The words **and**, **but**, and **or** are **conjunctions**, or connecting words. They join two independent clauses to form a compound sentence. A comma (**,**) always comes before the conjunction. ELPS 3.C.4

    EXAMPLE   Some people risk their lives**,** **but** their efforts help others.
    independent clause   independent clause

Conjunction	Independent Clauses	Compound Sentence
Use **and** to join similar ideas.	Soldiers protect our country. They keep us safe.	Soldiers protect our country, **and** they keep us safe.
Use **but** to join different ideas.	Soldiers help people. Sometimes they get hurt.	Soldiers help people, **but** sometimes they get hurt.
Use **or** to show a choice.	People can become soldiers. They can choose another career.	People can become soldiers, **or** they can choose another career.

Practice Together

Say each pair of sentences. Choose *and*, *but*, or *or* to combine them. Say each new compound sentence and add the correct word.

   1. Fires can be big. Fires can be small.

   2. Firefighters use safety equipment. Sometimes they get hurt.

   3. Firefighters know how to put out fires. They know how to save lives.

Try It!

Say each pair of sentences. Choose *and*, *but*, or *or* to combine them. Write each compound sentence on a card. Include the comma.

   4. People can choose to help others. They can choose not to get involved.

   5. Many people assist others. They do these things without being asked.

   6. People are not always recognized for their help. They should be.

▲ People care about others, and they help them.

Share Your Ideas About Heroes

ENGAGE IN DISCUSSION

Look at the photo. What do you think is happening? What makes a person a hero? Does a person have to save lives to be a hero, or can a person be heroic in an everyday situation?

Discuss the questions above in a small group. Ask questions to help clarify ideas that might seem confusing. Express your opinions and listen to others' opinions. Be sure you understand each person's main points. ELPS 2.G.5

Take turns talking. Make sure everyone in the group has the chance to speak.

HOW TO ENGAGE IN DISCUSSION

1. Focus on the discussion topic. Listen for key ideas. Summarize for yourself what others are saying.
2. Ask and answer questions.
3. Tell your point of view or opinion.
4. Respect others' ideas.

> What do you think makes someone a hero? In my opinion, a hero saves someone's life and risks his or her own life to do so.

> That's an interesting idea, but I don't really agree. I think a person can be a hero without risking his or her life.

USE COMPOUND SENTENCES

In your discussion, ask questions and use a variety of sentence lengths. Include simple and compound sentences. Combine your ideas into compound sentences.

Simple Sentences: Heroes are brave. Heroes think about others' safety first.

Compound Sentence: Heroes are brave, and they think about others' safety first.

Prepare to Read

 ELPS: 3.A practice producing sounds of newly acquired vocabulary in a manner that is comprehensible

Learn Key Vocabulary

Rate and Study the Words Rate how well you know each word. Then:

1. Pronounce the word. Say it aloud several times. Spell it.
2. Study the example.
3. Tell more about the word.
4. Practice it. Make the word your own.

Rating Scale

1 = I have never seen this word before.

2 = I am not sure of the word's meaning.

3 = I know this word and can teach the word's meaning to someone else.

Key Words

agreement (a-**grē**-ment) *noun* ▸ page 436

To have an **agreement** is to have an understanding with people about something. My aunt signed an **agreement** to buy a car.
Related Word: **agree**

approach (u-**prōch**) *verb* ▸ page 437

To **approach** means to come closer or near. The diver **approached** the dolphin.

diplomat (**dip**-lō-mat) *noun* ▸ page 428

A **diplomat** is a person who represents his or her government. To do his or her job, a **diplomat** lives in another country.
Related Word: **diplomatic**

insist (in-**sist**) *verb* ▸ page 436

To **insist** means to demand or to keep saying. The child **insisted** on walking the other direction.

issue (i-**shü**) *verb* ▸ page 432

To **issue** means to give or hand out. The agent **issued** tickets to the passengers.
Antonym: **take**

permission (pur-**mish**-un) *noun* ▸ page 432

When you have **permission**, you are allowed to do something. You must ask **permission** to go onto private property.
Related Word: **permit**

refugee (**ref**-yu-jē) *noun* ▸ page 432

A person who must leave his or her home or country to be safe is a **refugee**. A **refugee** may have to live with just a few belongings.
Related Word: **refuge**

translate (trans-**lāt**) *verb* ▸ page 430

To **translate** means to explain in another language. The sign **translates** information into English.
Related Word: **translation**

Practice the Words Make an Expanded Meaning Map for each Key Word. Compare with a partner.

┌─ **What the Word Means** ─┐
person who represents the government

Example
ambassador

Word
diplomat

What It Is Like
always polite and respectful

Expanded Meaning Map

Reading Strategy: Make Inferences

When you read historical fiction, you can add information from your own knowledge and experiences. Use this information to make inferences that help you better understand the text.

Reading Strategy
Make Inferences

HOW TO **MAKE INFERENCES**

1. As you read, look for details from the text that help you understand the characters and the events.
2. Use your own experience and knowledge to make sense of the story.
3. Track your thoughts in a chart like the one below.

Strategy in Action

Here's how one student made inferences.

Look Into the Text

At a store, my father saw a young Jewish boy who didn't have enough money to buy what he wanted. So my father gave the boy some of his. That boy looked into my father's eyes and, to thank him, invited my father to his home.

That is when my family and I went to a Hanukkah celebration for the first time. I was five years old.

In 1940, my father was a diplomat, representing the country of Japan.

" The father was kind and generous to the boy. "

I Read . . .	I Know . . .	And So . . .
"So my father gave the boy some of his [money]."	To give without being asked is kind and generous.	The father cares about other people.
"In 1940, my father was a diplomat . . . ."	Diplomats do important work for their countries in times of war.	The father must be smart and powerful.

" The father had an important job around the time of World War II. "

Practice Together

Reread the excerpt from "Passage to Freedom." Follow the steps in the How-To box to make an inference.

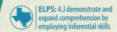
Historical Fiction

Historical fiction is based on **real historical events** or on **real historical people**, or on both. The author's purpose is to both inform and entertain.

The author may create dialogue and tell the story from the point of view of a real person or a fictional character.

> In 1940, my father was a diplomat, representing the country of Japan. Our family lived in a small town in the small country called Lithuania. . . .
>
> Then one early morning in late July, my life changed forever.

Real dates and other details provide factual information.

Suspense makes the story entertaining.

Your Job as a Reader

Reading Strategy: Make Inferences

As you read, add your own knowledge to important details to create meaning.

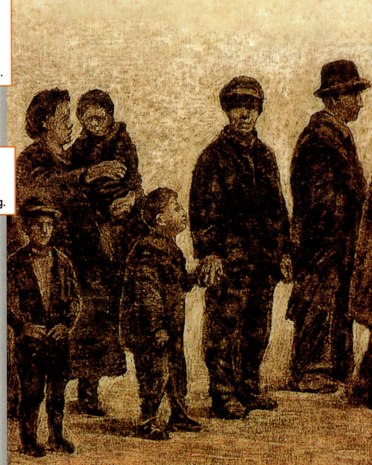

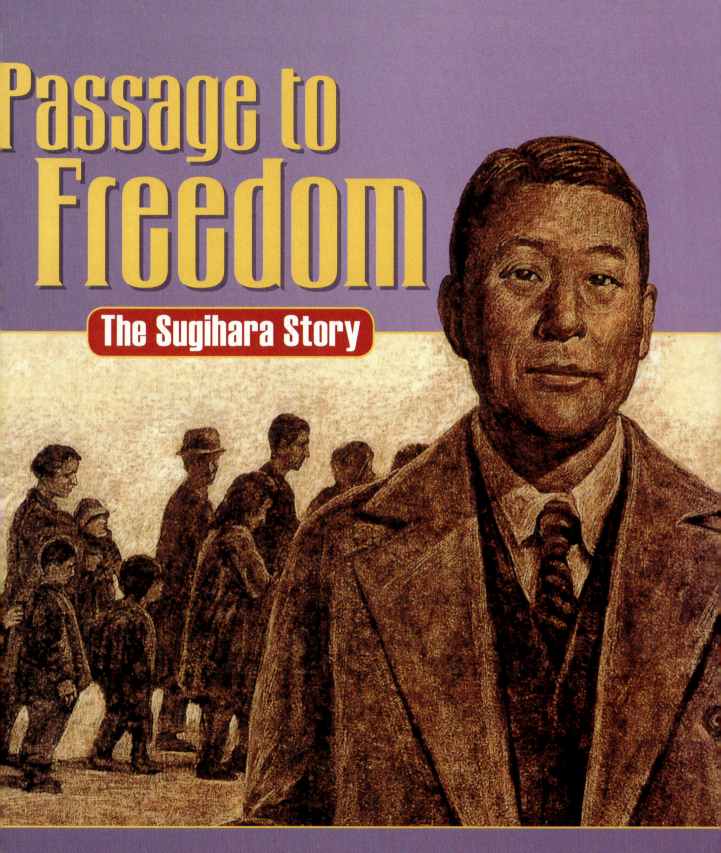

Passage to Freedom
The Sugihara Story

by Ken Mochizuki

illustrated by Dom Lee

There is a **saying that the eyes tell** everything about a person.

At a store, my father saw a young Jewish boy who didn't have enough money to buy what he wanted. So my father gave the boy some of his. That boy looked into my father's eyes and, to thank him, invited my father to his home.

That is when my family and I went to a Hanukkah celebration for the first time. I was five years old.

In 1940, my father was a diplomat, representing the country of Japan. Our family lived in a small town in the small country called Lithuania. There was my father and mother, my Auntie Setsuko, my younger brother Chiaki, and my three-month-old baby brother, Haruki. My father worked in his office downstairs.

In the mornings, birds sang in the trees. We played with girls and boys from the neighborhood at a huge park near our home. Houses and churches around us were hundreds of years old. In our room, Chiaki and I played with toy German soldiers, tanks, and planes. **Little did we** know that the real soldiers were coming our way.

Then one early morning in late July, my life changed forever.

My mother and Auntie Setsuko woke Chiaki and me up, telling us to get dressed quickly. My father ran upstairs from his office.

"There are a lot of people outside," my mother said. "We don't know what is going to happen."

In the living room, my parents told my brother and me not to let anybody see us looking through the window. So, I **parted** the curtains a tiny bit. Outside, I saw hundreds of people **crowded around the gate** in front of our house.

> ❴ My life changed forever. ❵

Key Vocabulary
diplomat *n.*, a person who represents his or her government

In Other Words
saying that the eyes tell belief that a person's eyes show
Little did we We did not
parted opened
crowded around the gate waiting closely together

Cultural Background
Hanukkah is an eight-day Jewish holiday, also called the Festival of Lights. People eat special foods, light candles, and play games to celebrate the miracle of freedom.

⚠ **Critical Viewing: Effect** What part of the selection goes with this image? Why did the artist place the boy's eyes in the center?

The grown-ups shouted in Polish, a language I did not understand. Then I saw the children. They stared at our house through the iron bars of the gate. Some of them were my age. Like the grown-ups, their eyes were red from not having slept for days. They wore heavy winter coats—some wore more than one coat, even though it was

Language Background
Here is how to pronounce the names of family members in the selection:
    Setsuko (set-sü-kō)
    Chiaki (chē-ah-kē)
    Haruki (hah-ru-kē)
    Sugihara (sü-gē-hah-rah)

warm outside. These children looked as though they had dressed in a hurry. But if they came from somewhere else, where were their suitcases?

"What do they want?" I asked my mother.

"They have come to ask for your father's help," she replied. "**Unless we** help, they may be killed or taken away by some bad men."

Some of the children held on tightly to the hands of their fathers, some **clung** to their mothers. One little girl sat on the ground, crying.

I felt like crying, too. "Father," I said, "please help them."

My father stood quietly next to me, but I knew he saw the children. Then some of the men in the crowd began climbing over the fence. Borislav and Gudje, two young men who worked for my father, tried to keep the crowd calm.

My father walked outside. **Peering** through the curtains, I saw him standing on the steps. Borislav **translated** what my father said: He asked the crowd to choose five people to come inside and talk.

▷ **Critical Viewing: Effect** How do you think the people in this image feel? How does the artist create this mood?

Key Vocabulary
translate *v.*, to explain in another language

In Other Words
Unless we If we do not
clung stayed very close
Peering Looking secretly

Before You Move On

1. **Paraphrase** Retell in your own words what changes the boy's life. How does he feel?

2. **Foreshadowing** What is the narrator suggesting when he says on p. 428, "Little did we know that the real soldiers were coming our way"?

My father met downstairs with the five men. My father could speak Japanese, Chinese, Russian, German, French, and English. At this meeting, everyone spoke Russian.

I couldn't help but stare out the window and watch the crowd, while downstairs, for two hours, my father listened to frightening stories. These people were **refugees**—people who ran away from their homes because, if they stayed, they would be killed. They were Jews from Poland, escaping from the Nazi soldiers who had taken over their country.

The five men had heard my father could give them visas—**official** written **permission** to travel through another country. The hundreds of Jewish refugees outside hoped to travel east through the Soviet Union and end up in Japan. Once in Japan, they could go to another country. Was it true? the men

{ **Would he put our family in danger?** }

asked. Could my father **issue** these visas? If he did not, the Nazis would soon **catch up with** them.

My father answered that he could issue a few, but not hundreds. To do that, he would have to ask for permission from his government in Japan.

That night, the crowd stayed outside our house. Exhausted from the day's excitement, I slept soundly. But it was one of the worst nights of my father's life. He had to make a decision. If he helped these people, would he put our family in danger? If the Nazis found out, what would they do?

But if he did not help these people, they could all die.

My mother listened to the bed squeak as my father **tossed and turned** all night.

The next day, my father said he was going to ask his government about the visas. My mother agreed it was the right thing to do.

Key Vocabulary

refugee *n.*, someone who must leave his or her country for safety

permission *n.*, allowing something to happen

issue *v.*, to give or hand out

In Other Words

official the government's
catch up with find
tossed and turned moved and did not sleep

▲ **Critical Viewing: Design** Describe this image. What details does the artist use to show emotion?

My father sent his message by **cable**. Gudje took my father's written message down to the telegraph office.

I watched the crowd as they waited for the Japanese government's reply. The five representatives came into our house several

In Other Words
cable a mechanical method that turns words into signals

times that day to ask if an answer had been received. Any time the gate opened, the crowd tried to **charge** inside.

Finally, the answer came from the Japanese government. It was "no." My father could not issue that many visas to Japan. For the next two days, he thought about what to do.

Hundreds more Jewish refugees joined the crowd. My father sent a second message to his government, and again the answer was "no." We still couldn't go outside. My little brother Haruki cried often because we **were running out of** milk.

I grew tired of staying indoors. I asked my father **constantly**, "Why are these people here? What do they want? Why do they have to be here? Who are they?"

My father always took the time to explain everything to me. He said the refugees needed his help, that they needed permission from him to go to another part of the world where they would be safe.

"I cannot help these people yet," he calmly told me. "But when the time comes, I will help them all that I can."

My father **cabled his superiors yet a third time**, and I knew the answer by the look in his eyes. That night, he said to my mother, "I have to do something. I may have to disobey my government, but if I don't, I will be disobeying God."

{ **The refugees needed his help.** }

In Other Words
charge run
were running out of did not have enough
constantly all the time
cabled his superiors yet a third time sent another message to his bosses

Before You Move On

1. **Summarize** Tell what the **refugees** want from the **diplomat** and why.
2. **Conclusion** Why is the **diplomat's** decision so difficult?

**The diplomat faces a hard choice.
What will he decide to do?**

The next morning, he brought the family together and asked what he should do. This was the first time he ever asked all of us to help him with anything.

My mother and Auntie Setsuko **had already made up their minds**. They said we had to think about the people outside before we thought about ourselves. And that is what my parents had always told me—that I must think as if I were in someone else's place. If I were one of those children out there, what would I want someone to do for me?

In Other Words
had already made up their minds knew what they wanted

I said to my father, "If we don't help them, won't they die?"

With the entire family in **agreement**, I could tell **a huge weight was lifted off my father's shoulders**. His voice was firm as he told us, "I will start helping these people."

Outside, the crowd went quiet as my father spoke, with Borislav translating.

"I will issue visas to **each and every one of you to the last**. So, please wait patiently."

The crowd **stood frozen** for a second. Then the refugees burst into cheers. Grown-ups embraced each other, and some reached to the sky. Fathers and mothers hugged their children. I was especially glad for the children.

My father opened the garage door and the crowd tried to rush in. To keep order, Borislav handed out cards with numbers. My father wrote out each visa by hand. After he finished each one, he looked into the eyes of the person receiving the visa and said, "Good luck."

Refugees **camped out** at our favorite park, waiting to see my father. I was finally able to go outside.

Chiaki and I played with the other children in our toy car. They pushed as we rode, and they rode as we pushed.

We chased each other around the big trees. We did not speak the same language, but that didn't stop us.

For about a month, there was always a line leading to the garage. Every day, from early in the morning till late at night, my father tried to write three hundred visas. He **watered down** the ink to make it last. Gudje and a young Jewish man helped out by stamping my father's name on the visas.

My mother offered to help write the visas, but my father **insisted** he be the only

---

Key Vocabulary

agreement *n.*, an understanding between people

insist *v.*, to keep saying or repeating something

In Other Words

a huge weight was lifted off my father's shoulders my father felt better

each and every one of you to the last everyone

stood frozen stopped moving

camped out waited

watered down mixed water with

one, so no one else could get into trouble. So my mother watched the crowd and told my father how many were still in line.

One day, my father pressed down so hard on his fountain pen, the tip broke off. During that month, I only saw him late at night. His eyes were always red and he could hardly talk. While he slept, my mother massaged his arm, **stiff and cramped** from writing all day.

Soon my father grew so tired, he wanted to quit writing the visas. But my mother encouraged him to continue. "Many people are still waiting," she said. "Let's issue some more visas and save as many lives as we can."

While the Germans **approached** from the west, the Soviets came from the east and took over Lithuania. They ordered my father to leave. So did the Japanese government, which **reassigned him** to Germany. Still, my father wrote the visas until we **absolutely**

Key Vocabulary
approach *v.*, to come closer

In Other Words
stiff and cramped hurt
reassigned him moved his work
absolutely finally

Government Background
In order to enter some countries, visitors from other countries must have a **visa** stamped in or attached to their passports. Today, Japan has seven types of visa, and the time it takes to get a visa depends on the person's reason for travel to Japan.

had to move out of our home. We stayed at a hotel for two days, where my father still wrote visas for the many refugees who followed him there.

Then it was time to leave Lithuania. Refugees who had slept at the train station crowded around my father. Some refugee men surrounded my father to protect him. He now just issued permission papers— blank pieces of paper with his signature.

As the train pulled away, refugees ran alongside. My father still handed permission papers out the window. As the train **picked up speed**, he threw them out to waiting hands. The people in the front of the crowd looked into my father's eyes and cried, "We will never forget you! We will see you again!"

I **gazed** out the train window, watching Lithuania and the crowd of refugees **fade away**. I wondered if we would ever see them again.

"Where are we going?" I asked my father.

"We are going to Berlin," he replied.

Chiaki and I became very excited about going to the big city. I had so many questions for my father. But he fell asleep as soon as he settled into his seat. My mother and Auntie Setsuko looked really tired, too.

Back then, I did not fully understand what the three of them had done, or why it was so important.

I do now. ❖

In Other Words
picked up speed went faster
gazed looked
fade away appear smaller as we
  rode away

Before You Move On

1. **Confirm Predictions** Was your prediction correct? What happened that you didn't expect?

2. **Personal Connection** What would you have done if you were the diplomat?

3. **Paraphrase** Tell in your own words what happened to the family at the train station.

A Message from Hiroki Sugihara

Each time that I think about what my father did at Kaunas, Lithuania, in 1940, my appreciation and understanding of the incident continues to grow. In fact, it makes me very emotional to realize that his deed saved thousands of lives, and that I had the opportunity to be a part of it.

I am proud that my father had the courage to do the right thing. Yet, his superiors in the Japanese government did not agree. The years after my family left Kaunas were difficult ones. We were imprisoned for eighteen months in a Soviet internment camp; and when we finally returned to Japan, my father was asked to resign from diplomatic service. After holding several different jobs, my father joined an export company, where he worked until his retirement in 1976.

My father remained concerned about the fate of the refugees, and at one point left his address at the Israeli Embassy in Japan. Finally, in the 1960s, he started hearing from "Sugihara survivors," many of whom had kept their visas, and considered the worn pieces of paper to be family treasures.

▲ Japanese Emperor Akihito visits a monument dedicated to Chiune Sugihara in Vilnius, Lithuania. Several monuments around the world honor Sugihara.

In 1969, my father was invited to Israel, where he was taken to the famous Holocaust memorial, Yad Vashem. In 1985, he was chosen to receive the "Righteous Among Nations" Award from Yad Vashem. He was the first and only Asian to have been given this great honor.

Historical Background
The **Holocaust** (1933-1945) was the organized mass murder of millions of European Jews and other groups viewed as inferior, or of less worth, by Germany's Nazi party.

In 1992, six years after his death, a monument to my father was dedicated in his birthplace of Yaotsu, Japan, on a hill that is now known as the Hill of Humanity.

In 1994, a group of Sugihara survivors traveled to Japan to re-dedicate the monument in a ceremony that was attended by several high officials of the Japanese government.

The story of what my father and my family experienced in 1940 is an important one for young people today. It is a story that I believe will inspire you to care for all people and to respect life. It is a story that proves that one person can make a difference.

About the Author

Ken Mochizuki

To write *Passage to Freedom*, **Ken Mochizuki** had to gather as much factual information as possible. To do this, he worked closely with the Sugihara family. He also decided to write the account in the first person, as if he was Hiroki, the son of Sugihara. Mochizuki wrote the book in honor of those who have put the safety of others before themselves.

About the Author

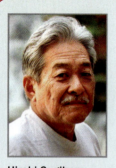
Hiroki Sugihara

Hiroki Sugihara has honored his father's memory in many ways. He donated hundreds of family photos to the Bay Area Holocaust Oral History Project. This helped create "Visas for Life," a photo exhibit that appeared in over 100 museums worldwide. Sugihara has helped to honor diplomats like his father who helped save the lives of Jewish people during World War II.

Before You Move On

1. **Determine Importance** What important information does the Afterword add?
2. **Inference** Why do you think the government's treatment of Sugihara's father changed?

Connect Reading and Writing

Vocabulary
agreement
approached
diplomats
insist
issue
permission
refugees
translate

CRITICAL THINKING

1. SUM IT UP Fill out a 5Ws Chart for the story. Use the chart to give a short news report about the **diplomat** .

5Ws Chart

| Who? Mr. Sugihara |
| What? |
| Where? |
| When? |
| Why? |

2. Speculate Many **refugees** **approached** Mr. Sugihara for visas. Why do countries have to give people **permission** to enter?

3. Infer Why did Mr. Sugihara ask his family if he should act without his government's **permission** ?

4. Evaluate Reread the last paragraph of the Afterword on page 440. Hiroki Sugihara **insists** that his father's story will inspire young people. Do you agree with him? Explain.

READING FLUENCY

Intonation Read the passage on page 650 to a partner. Assess your fluency.

1. I read
   a. great   **b.** OK   **c.** not very well

2. What I did best in my reading was _____.

READING STRATEGY

Make Inferences
Share with a partner two inferences you made. How did making a chart help you?

VOCABULARY REVIEW

Oral Review Read the paragraph aloud. Add the vocabulary words.

_____, or people who represent a country, usually speak two or more languages. This helps them _____ communications between countries. They also make an _____ to follow certain rules. To do otherwise, they must ask the government for _____. Even then, the government may _____ that they follow the rule. Sometimes, they are asked to _____ visas. For example, they may be _____ by _____ who ask for their government's protection.

Written Review Write a news report about Mr. Sugihara and the Lithuanian **refugees** . Use five vocabulary words.

WRITE ABOUT THE **GUIDING QUESTION**

Explore Conflict and Bravery
If Mr. Sugihara had known what would happen, would he have made the same decision? Read the selection again to find support for your opinion.

Connect Across the Curriculum

ELPS: 2.C.4 learn academic vocabulary heard during classroom instruction and interactions

Literary Analysis

Evaluate Historical Fiction

> **Academic Vocabulary**
> • **evaluate** (i-**val**-yu-wāt) *verb*
>   To **evaluate** is to decide on the quality of something.

Historical fiction, like "Passage to Freedom," is made up, but based on true events. For example, the setting is a real place during a real time (Lithuania during World War II), but the events are told like a story. The story has a narrator, dialogue, and some made-up details.

Evaluate Story Elements The **credibility** of a story is how believable it seems. To **evaluate** historical fiction, ask:

• **Setting** Are the places real or made up?
• **Characters** Is the story about a real person? Who is telling the story?
• **Events** Did the story events actually happen? What details tell if events are fact or fiction?

Practice Together

Evaluate Credibility Which details in "Passage to Freedom" are facts? Which details are probably fiction? Reread the selection. Make a T Chart to record the details. How credible is the story?

T Chart

Fact	Fiction
Mr. Sugihara was a real person. His son, Hiroki Sugihara, is also a real person.	Ken Mochizuki wrote the story from the son's point of view. Mochizuki made up the dialogue.

Try It!

Work with a partner to add more details to the chart. Then look up details in history books and online. How many can you prove are facts? Based on the information you find, how credible is the story?

Internet InsideNG.com
 Learn more about World War II.

ELPS: 1.H develop and expand repertoire of learning strategies; 2.C.4 learn academic vocabulary heard during classroom instruction and interactions; 2.H.1 understand implicit ideas in complex spoken language

Vocabulary Study

Idioms

Academic Vocabulary
- **literal** (lit-ur-al) *adjective*
  The **literal** meaning of a word is its exact meaning.

An **idiom** is a group of words that together mean something different than their **literal** meaning. "It's raining cats and dogs" does not mean that animals are falling from the sky. This idiom means "It is raining hard."

Interpret Idioms With a partner, interpret these idioms from "Passage to Freedom."

1. My father *tossed and turned* all night.
2. We *were running out* of milk.
3. The crowd *stood frozen* for a second.

ELPS: 2.C.4 learn academic vocabulary heard during classroom instruction and interactions; 2.G.7 understand the important details of spoken language regarding familiar to unfamiliar topics

Research/Writing

Report on Lithuania

HISTORY

Academic Vocabulary
- **focus** (fō-kus) *verb*
  When you **focus** on something, you pay attention to it.

The Sugiharas lived in Lithuania during the time of "Passage to Freedom." Research and report on Lithuania.

Focus Your Research Set a purpose for your report by asking questions. What do you want to know? Create a chart like this one to **focus** your topic.

Questions	Where can I find the answer?
1. Where is it located?	a map or globe
2. What landforms are in Lithuania?	an atlas, map, or encyclopedia

Prepare Your Report To find facts and details about your topic, choose sources such as encyclopedias, atlases, books, and the Internet. Use your questions and answers to organize the main ideas and details of your report.

Present Your Report As you give your report to the class, speak slowly and clearly. Listen to the reports of others. Note new information. Interpret the speaker's purpose by explaining the content of the presentation to a partner.

Writing/Speaking

Deliver an Oral Response to Literature

DRAMA

ELPS: 2.C.4 learn academic vocabulary heard during classroom instruction and interactions; 3.G.3 express feelings on a variety of social and grade-appropriate academic topics

Academic Vocabulary

• **response** (ri-**spons**) *noun*
   A **response** is an answer or reply to something that has happened or has been said.

"Passage to Freedom" shows what some people did to overcome a conflict. How did the Sugiharas deal with a difficult situation? What did they do to help resolve the conflict? Tell your class what you think and why. Give your **response** to the story.

❶ **Plan Your Oral Response** Follow these steps:

- Read the story several times. Get to know it well. What is the story about?
- Think about your reaction to the story. How did it make you feel? What did you learn from it? What message do you think the author wants to convey?
- Look at the different elements of the story—the plot, the characters, the setting, and the theme. Decide which part you like most.
- Make notes about your **response** to the story.

❷ **Practice Your Oral Response** Practice giving your **response** to a partner who knows the story.

- Give a short summary of the main events and details in the story.
- Tell what you learned from the story and what you think it means.
- Explain how the characters overcame the conflict.
- Include several examples from the text to support your ideas.
- Ask your partner what you could do to make your **response** better.

❸ **Present Your Oral Response** Follow these steps to keep your oral **response** focused and clear:

- Let your feelings about the story show in your words, tone of voice, facial expressions, and gestures.
- Make eye contact with your audience. Look at your notes occasionally but not too often.
- Speak clearly and loudly so your audience can understand everything you say.

❹ **Listen Attentively** Work with a partner to summarize each other's presentations to show your understanding.

Unsupported response

> I learned that even though a problem might seem big, one person can do a lot to help solve it. The father's actions did a lot to help other people.

Supported response

> After reading "Passage to Freedom," I learned that one person really can make a difference. The father issued visas to help Jewish refugees travel to a safe country. He helped save many people's lives.

ELPS: 1.E.1 internalize new basic language in speaking activities; 3.C.2 speak using a variety of sentence lengths with increasing accuracy and ease; 3.C.4 speak using a variety of connecting words with increasing accuracy and ease

Language and Grammar

Engage in Discussion

Group Talk With a small group, discuss what Chiune Sugihara did and the risks he took. Was he wise to do what he did? Listen attentively to others' opinions. Use a variety of sentence lengths, including compound sentences, to present some of your ideas. Also use connecting words *and*, *but,* and *or*.

> Mr. Sugihara was a hero, but he took some big risks.

> Mr. Sugihara helped many people, and he wasn't afraid of the consequences.

ELPS: 5.F.2 write using a variety of grade-appropriate sentence patterns; 5.F.3 write using a variety of grade-appropriate connecting words to combine phrases, clauses, and sentences

Writing and Grammar

Write About a Heroic Action

Study the Models You can make your writing more interesting by using a variety of sentences. You can also make your writing easier to read by combining your ideas into longer, more interesting sentences. Longer sentences show how ideas relate to each other.

NOT OK

> My father looked out the window. He saw many people. They were crowded around the gate in front of the house. My father read the government's answer. He knew in his heart it was wrong. He could obey the government. He could do what he thought was right. It was a difficult decision. It was worth it.

The reader thinks: "**This writing does not flow. It's hard to see how the ideas relate.**"

OK

> My father looked out the window, and he saw many people. They were crowded around the gate in front of the house. My father read the government's answer, and he knew in his heart it was wrong. He could obey the government, or he could do what he thought was right. It was a difficult decision, but it was worth it.

This writing combines some ideas into smoother, more connected sentences.

 WRITE ON YOUR OWN Write a short personal narrative about a time when you helped someone. What did you have to risk or give up? Use a variety of sentences in your writing. Keep your narrative focused on this topic, and be sure to state the reasons for your actions.

REMEMBER

When you join your ideas, use the connecting word that shows what you mean.

- Use **and** to join like ideas.
- Use **but** to join different ideas.
- Use **or** to show a choice.

Don't put too many ideas together with commas or **and**. If your sentences are too long, the reader can't understand them.

Zlata's Diary

by Zlata Filipović

Build Background

Connect

Word Webs What comes to mind when you think of the words *peace* and *war*? Create a web for each word to show your ideas.

Word Web

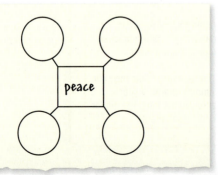

The Effects of War

Zlata Filipović lived through a war. When she decided to keep a personal diary about the conflict, she had no idea that it would become famous around the world.

Digital Library

InsideNG.com
➤ View the video.

Zlata Filipović ▶

Language & Grammar

ELPS: 2.C.1 learn new language structures heard during classroom instruction and interactions; 2.E.1 use visual support to enhance and confirm understanding of complex and elaborated spoken language; 2.G.3 understand the general meaning of spoken language regarding familiar to unfamiliar contexts; 3.C.4 speak using a variety of connecting words with increasing accuracy and ease; 3.G.1 express opinions on a variety of social and grade-appropriate academic topics

Justify

Look at the photo and listen to the discussion. Think about the reason Laila gives to justify, or explain, her view.

1 TRY OUT LANGUAGE
2 LEARN GRAMMAR
3 APPLY ON YOUR OWN

DISCUSSION

A Little Effort **Goes a Long Way**

Laila: Did you read this article about refugees in some parts of Africa?

Tony: No, what does it say?

Laila: Daily life is getting worse for people who have lost their homes because of war and other conflicts. Not only are people losing their homes and towns, but now food is in short supply. In addition, there isn't enough clean water for people to drink. If these people need food, then I'm going to help!

Tony: How? What could you do to help?

Laila: I could start a food drive to donate food. It will take some work, but it will be worth it because this is an important cause.

Use Complex Sentences

A **complex sentence** is a sentence with two kinds of clauses—an independent clause and a dependent clause.

- A clause has a **subject** and a **verb**. An **independent clause** can stand alone as a sentence.

    EXAMPLE   **We learn about current events.**
    independent clause

- A **dependent clause** also has a subject and a verb. However, it cannot stand alone because it begins with a **conjunction** like **when**.

    EXAMPLE   **when we read a newspaper**
    dependent clause

- You can use the **subordinating conjunction** to "hook" the dependent clause to an independent clause. The new sentence is complete, and it is called a **complex sentence**.

    EXAMPLE   **We learn about current events when we read a newspaper.**
    independent clause   dependent clause

> Conjunctions that can connect dependent clauses to independent clauses are called **subordinating conjunctions.** Some of these include:
>
> | | |
> |---|---|
> | after | since |
> | although | unless |
> | as | until |
> | because | when |
> | before | whenever |
> | even though | wherever |
> | if | while |
> | only if | |

Practice Together

Match each independent clause on the left to a dependent clause on the right. Add punctuation. Say the new complex sentence.

1. It is important to follow the news

2. I listen to the news on the radio

3. I get my news on the Internet

4. I watch the nightly news on television

a. whenever I am at my computer

b. unless I am not home

c. when I am in the car

d. because the news affects our opinions

Try It!

Match each independent clause on the left to a dependent clause on the right. Write the complex sentence on a card. Say the new sentence.

5. There may be a war

6. Some people are starving

7. We must do our part to help others

8. We can make a difference

e. even if our effort seems small

f. although there is enough food

g. if we work together

h. unless we sign a peace treaty

▲ News reporters cover world events wherever they happen.

What's Your Position?

JUSTIFY

There are at least two sides or approaches to every issue. Read the following statements. Choose one and justify your thoughts in a group.

First, choose a statement.

1. There will always be conflict in the world.
2. Peace is possible in our lifetime.

Then organize your thoughts in a T Chart like this one:

T Chart

Opinion	Reason
I think there will always be conflict in the world.	People don't always agree with each other.
I believe that conflicting ideas can be good.	Different ideas can lead to new solutions.

Now justify your opinions to a group. Listen to the positions of other group members and be sure you understand their general meaning.

HOW TO JUSTIFY

1. State an opinion or idea.
2. Give logical reasons for it.
3. Combine your ideas to make the logic clear.

> A little conflict can be good because it leads to new ideas.

> Peace is possible if we respect others' ideas.

USE COMPLEX SENTENCES

When you justify your position, choose connecting words like *if* or *because* to show a condition or logical reason for your idea. Such words will "hook" the condition or reason to your idea or opinion. The new complex sentence will explain the relationship.

Condition Words	Reason Words
if, if only, as long as, unless, until	because, since, therefore

Simple Sentences: Peace is possible. People listen to each other.

Complex Sentence: Peace is possible **if** people listen to each other.

Prepare to Read

 ELPS: 1.A.2 use prior experiences to understand meanings in English; 3.A practice producing sounds of newly acquired vocabulary in a manner that is comprehensible; 4.J demonstrate and expand comprehension by employing inferential skills

Learn Key Vocabulary

Rate and Study the Words Rate how well you know each word. Then:

1. Pronounce the word. Say it aloud several times. Spell it.
2. Study the example.
3. Tell more about the word.
4. Practice it. Make the word your own.

Rating Scale

1 = I have never seen this word before.

2 = I am not sure of the word's meaning.

3 = I know this word and can teach the word's meaning to someone else.

Key Words

conflict (kon-flikt) *noun*
▶ page 454

A **conflict** is a fight between two people or groups of people. My friend and I got into a **conflict** over a book she borrowed from me.

desperate (des-pu-rit) *adjective* ▶ page 455

Someone who is **desperate** has lost hope. The **desperate** team tried hard but lost.
Related Word: **desperation**

destroy (di-stroi) *verb*
▶ page 455

To **destroy** means to completely ruin. The house was **destroyed** by a fire.
Antonym: **create**

humanity (hū-man-i-tē) *noun* ▶ page 456

Humanity is kindness and caring about the suffering of others. Firefighters show **humanity** by doing what they must to save others.
Related Word: **human**

impact (im-pakt) *verb*
▶ page 459

To **impact** means to have an effect. The new sales people will continue to **impact** the sales numbers, pushing them up.

innocent (in-u-sent) *adjective*
▶ page 457

Someone who is **innocent** is without guilt. The puppy looks **innocent** and sweet.
Related Words: **innocence, innocently**

politics (pol-i-tiks) *noun*
▶ page 458

Politics are people's beliefs about government and its plans. People with similar **politics** came to the convention.
Related Words: **political, politician**

reality (rē-a-lu-tē) *noun*
▶ page 458

Reality is what people actually experience in life. I wish I could have whatever I liked, but the **reality** is that I must work to pay for things.

Practice the Words Complete a Vocabulary Example Chart. Connect your prior experiences with each Key Word.

Word	Definition	Example from My Life
innocent	free from guilt	My baby sister is innocent.

Vocabulary Example Chart

Reading Strategy: Make Inferences

Notice the kinds of words the writer uses to give information. Try this strategy to find and track clues as you read.

HOW TO MAKE INFERENCES

1. Notice *what* the narrator says and *how* she says it.
2. Think about your own experiences. Use them to make an inference.
3. Write your ideas on a sticky note and put it next to the text.
4. Notice how your ideas about the narrator change as you read on.

Strategy in Action

Here's how one student made inferences.

Look Into the Text

Dear Mimmy,

I'm trying to concentrate so I can do my homework (reading), but I simply can't. Something is going on in town. You can hear gunfire from the hills. Columns of people are spreading out from Dobrinja. They're trying to stop something, but they themselves don't know what. You can simply feel that something is coming, something very bad. On TV I see people in front of the B-H parliament building. The radio keeps playing the same song: "Sarajevo, My Love."

> Zlata names her diary. I think it's like a trusted friend.

> Zlata repeats the word "something." I can tell she's confused and worried.

Practice Together

Reread the passage from "Zlata's Diary." Follow the steps in the How-To box to make an inference.

Focus on Genre

 **ELPS:** 4.J demonstrate and expand comprehension by employing inferential skills

Diary

A diary is a daily account of the events, thoughts, and feelings in a person's life. Most diaries are kept private.

Some writers publish their diaries with the **purpose** of telling about history and sharing their feelings and opinions about their experiences.

> **Date of entry**
>
> Tuesday, September 15, 1992
> Dear Mimmy,
>
> I have another sad piece of news for you. A boy from my drama club got KILLED! . . . A shell fell in front of the community center and a horrible piece of shrapnel killed him.

Many people write diary entries like letters to a friend.

Capital letters show strong feelings.

Your Job as a Reader

Reading Strategy: Make Inferences

As you read, notice *what* the narrator says and *how* she says it.

> Mimmy, I'm afraid of WAR!!!

The way Zlata writes the word "war" shows how big and frightening it is to her.

Zlata's Diary

by Zlata Filipović

War has many effects that go beyond the battlefield. In 1992, the city of Sarajevo was attacked. What was this experience like for a young person who lived through it?

In 1992, **shells rocked** the city of Sarajevo in the former republic of Yugoslavia. The cause of this attack was a **conflict** among the three main ethnic groups who lived in the area—the Serbs, the Croats, and the Muslims.

Eleven-year-old Zlata Filipović and her parents were witnesses to the **destruction** of Sarajevo. Zlata wrote about the effects of the war in her diary until her family was able to escape to Paris, France, in 1993. When her diary was **published** it became **an international bestseller** and was translated into thirty-six languages.

The following is a brief excerpt from her diary, which she called "Mimmy."

▼ This is a view of downtown Sarajevo through a shattered window, in 1994.

Key Vocabulary
conflict *n.*, a fight or disagreement

In Other Words
shells rocked bullets and explosives damaged
destruction damage, ruin
published made into a book
an international bestseller popular all over the world

from *Zlata's Diary*

Sunday, April 5, 1992
Dear Mimmy,

I'm trying to concentrate so I can do my homework (reading), but I simply can't. Something is going on in town. You can hear gunfire from the hills. **Columns** of people are spreading out from **Dobrinja**. They're trying to stop something, but they themselves don't know what. You can simply feel that something is coming, something very bad. On TV I see people in front of the B-H parliament building. The radio keeps playing the same song: "Sarajevo, My Love." That's all very nice, but **my stomach is still in knots** and I can't concentrate on my homework anymore.

Mimmy, I'm afraid of WAR!!!

~Zlata

Monday, April 6, 1992
Dear Mimmy,

Yesterday the people in front of the parliament tried peacefully to cross the Vrbanja bridge. But they were shot at. Who? How? Why? A girl, a medical student from Dubrovnik, was KILLED. Her blood spilled onto the bridge. In her final moments all she said was: "Is this Sarajevo?" HORRIBLE, HORRIBLE HORRIBLE!

NO ONE AND NOTHING HERE IS NORMAL!

The **Baščaršija** has been **destroyed**! Those "fine gentlemen" from Pale fired on Baščaršija!

Since yesterday people have been inside the B-H parliament. Some of them are standing outside, in front of it. We've moved my television set into the living room, so I watch Channel 1 on one TV and "Good Vibrations" on the other. Now they're shooting from the Holiday Inn, killing people in front of the parliament. And Bokica is there with Vanja and Andrej. Oh, God!

Maybe we'll go to the **cellar**. You, Mimmy, will go with me, of course. I'm **desperate**. The people in front of the parliament are desperate too. Mimmy, war is here. PEACE, NOW!

They say they're going to attack RTV Sarajevo [radio and TV center]. But they haven't. They've stopped shooting in our neighborhood. KNOCK! KNOCK! (I'm knocking on wood for good luck.)

WHEW! It was tough. Oh, God! They're shooting again!!!

~Zlata

Key Vocabulary

destroy *v.*, to ruin or to damage
desperate *adj.*, loss of hope

In Other Words

Columns Groups
Dobrinja a nearby part of town
my stomach is still in knots I am so nervous
Baščaršija main street
cellar basement

Before You Move On

1. **Paraphrase** Tell in your own words how the war is affecting Zlata. Why is she **desperate**?
2. **Inference** What did the medical student mean when she said, "Is this Sarajevo?"

Sunday, April 12, 1992

Dear Mimmy,

The new sections of town—Dobrinja, Mojmilo, Vojničko polje—are being badly shelled. Everything is being destroyed, burned, the people are in **shelters**. Here in the middle of town, where we live, it's different. It's quiet. People go out. It was a nice warm spring day today. We went out too. Vaso Miškin Street was full of people, children. It looked like a peace march. People came out to be together, they don't want war. They want to live and enjoy themselves the way they used to. That's only **natural**, isn't it? Who likes or wants war, when it's the worst thing in the world?

I keep thinking about the march I joined today. It's bigger and stronger than war. That's why it will win. The people must be the ones to win, not the war, because war has nothing to do with **humanity**. War is something inhuman.

~Zlata

▼ **Sarajevo in peacetime** Several bridges were destroyed during the war.

Key Vocabulary

humanity *n.*, kindness and compassion for others

In Other Words

shelters temporary homes
natural normal

Tuesday, September 15, 1992
Dear Mimmy,

I have another sad piece of news for you. A boy from my drama club got KILLED! . . . A shell fell in front of the community center and a horrible piece of **shrapnel** killed him. His name was Eldin and he was a **refugee** from Grbavica.

Another **innocent** victim of this disgusting war, another child among the thousands of other children killed in Sarajevo. I feel so sorry, he was a sweet, good boy. Oh, God, what is happening here? Hasn't there been enough!?

~Zlata

Thursday, September 17, 1992
Dear Mimmy,

Today is Alma's birthday. We gave her two herbal shampoos. We had a super time, but . . . I looked out the window and saw a flash. I thought it was somebody signaling, that's not unusual in war time. But . . . BOOM!! Shattered glass, falling plaster. A shell fell in front of the shop next door and I saw it all from the fourth floor. We rushed over to Nedo's apartment and watched TV.

The birthday party wasn't bad, but it would have been even better if that shell hadn't spoiled it.

~Your Zlata

▲ A building in Sarajevo burns after being hit by shells.

Thursday, November 19, 1992
Dear Mimmy,

Nothing new on the political front. **They are adopting some resolutions, the "kids" are negotiating**, and we are dying, freezing, starving, crying, parting with our friends, leaving our loved ones.

Key Vocabulary
innocent *adj.*, without guilt

In Other Words
shrapnel the shell's metal
refugee person who had to leave his country for safety
They are adopting some resolutions, the "kids" are negotiating The government is deciding what to do

Before You Move On

1. **Compare and Contrast** Describe how the new sections of town are different from where Zlata lives.
2. **Details** What happened at the community center and next door to Zlata's house?

I keep wanting to explain these stupid **politics** to myself, because it seems to me that politics caused this war, making it our everyday **reality**. War has crossed out the day and replaced it with horror, and now horrors are unfolding instead of days. It looks to me as though these politics mean Serbs, Croats and Muslims. But they are all people. They are all the same. They all look like people, there's no difference. They all have arms, legs and heads, they walk and talk, but now there's "something" that wants to make them different.

Among my girlfriends, among our friends, in our family, there are Serbs and Croats and Muslims. It's a mixed group and I never knew who was a Serb, a Croat or a Muslim. Now politics has started **meddling around**. It has put an "S" on Serbs, an "M" on Muslims and a "C" on Croats, it wants to separate them. And to do so it has chosen the worst, blackest pencil of all—the pencil of war which spells only misery and death.

Why is politics making us unhappy, separating us, when we ourselves know who is good and who isn't? We mix with the good, not with the bad. And among the good there are Serbs and Croats and Muslims, just as there are among the bad. I simply don't understand it. Of course, I'm "young," and politics are **conducted** by "grown-ups." But I think we "young" would do it better. We certainly wouldn't have chosen war.

The "kids" really are playing, which is why us kids are not playing, we are living in fear, we are suffering, we are not enjoying the sun and flowers, we are not enjoying our childhood, WE ARE CRYING.

A bit of philosophizing on my part, but I was alone and felt I could write this to you, Mimmy. You understand me. Fortunately, I've got you to talk to.

And now,

Love,

Zlata ❖

Key Vocabulary

politics *n.*, relating to government activities and policy

reality *n.*, what people actually experience

In Other Words

meddling around getting involved
conducted lead, directed
A bit of philosophizing on my part This is only what I think

Zlata Filipović Today

As a twelve-year-old girl, Zlata Filipović never knew how much her diary would **impact** her life. Her diary not only helped her get through the emotional pain of war, it also helped her escape.

Many people were interested in publishing Filipović's diary. Her family chose a French publisher with connections to the French government. In exchange, the publisher promised to help Filipović and her parents escape the fighting.

In 1993, the publisher kept the promise and Filipović and her family were flown to Paris in safety. After years of living without electricity, not going to school, and not having enough to eat, Zlata was finally free. To her great surprise, she was also famous.

"I had no idea of the impact the diary had, because we had no TV, no newspapers, no way to see what all these journalists coming to interview me had done," she says. "We thought we'd come to France

and be regular refugees, start our life again, but coming out of the plane there were cameras, photographers . . . people who could pronounce my name and had a sense of who I was based on the **scribbles** I'd done for myself as a twelve-year-old girl."

For the next four months, Filipović shared her book and met with students around the world. Sometimes she felt guilty because she was one of the few people to get out of Sarajevo.

"There was a level of guilt because my best friend stayed behind. Why was I different from another thirteen-year-old girl in Bosnia?" she remembers asking herself. "My responsibility was to use this in some kind of way for all those who remained. If people were willing to listen, I'd tell them about it."

Today, in her twenties, Filipović is still sharing her voice and experiences. She lives in Ireland and has a college degree in International Peace Studies. Filipović teamed up with another writer to edit a book titled *Stolen Voices*, a collection of young people's diaries written during wars—from World War I to the Iraq War. As she explains, when you study history there are "all the names and dates that you forget . . . but with a diary or an individual story . . . you connect."

Key Vocabulary
impact *v.*, to affect in an important way

In Other Words
scribbles writing

Before You Move On

1. **Summarize** Describe what Zlata could not understand about war.
2. **Explain** How did Zlata's diary help her escape? Why did Zlata become famous?
3. **Personal Connection** What **impact** did Zlata's diary have on you?

Last Night I Had the Strangest Dream

by Ed McCurdy

Chorus

Last night I had the strangest dream,

I'd ever dreamed before,

I dreamed the world had all agreed

To put an end to war.

I dreamed I saw a mighty room,

Filled with women and men

And the paper they were signing said

They'd never fight again.

And when the paper was all signed,

And a million copies made,

They all joined hands and bowed their heads

And grateful pray'rs were prayed.

And the people in the streets below

Were dancing 'round and 'round,

And swords and guns and uniforms

Were scattered on the ground.

Chorus

Last night I had the strangest dream,

I'd ever dreamed before,

I dreamed the world had all agreed

To put an end to war.

©Joel Nakamura, 2001.

▲ **Critical Viewing: Design** What details do you see in this image? How do they relate to the song's message?

Words and Music by Ed McCurdy. TRO–© Copyright 1950 (Renewed), 1951 (Renewed), 1955 (Renewed) Folkways Music Publishers, Inc., New York, NY. Used by Permission.

Historical Background

Ed McCurdy (1919-2000) wrote this famous song in 1950 when he wished for peace in the world. The song has been recorded in many different languages and covered by well-known singers, including Simon and Garfunkel.

Before You Move On

1. **Explain** What is the singer's dream?
2. **Opinion** Do you think the singer's dream can become a **reality**? Why or why not?

Connect Reading and Writing

Vocabulary

conflict

desperate

destroy

humanity

impacted

innocent

politics

reality

CRITICAL THINKING

1. SUM IT UP List important details from each diary entry on a Tree Diagram like the one shown. Use your entries to summarize how the war **impacted** Zlata's **reality**.

Tree Diagram

Sunday
April 5, 1992

- I can't concentrate on homework.
- I can hear gunfire.
- I'm afraid of war.

2. Interpret Zlata writes that people feel **desperate**. What does she mean? Give an example from the text.

3. Infer Do you think that Zlata feels **desperate** or hopeful about **humanity** today? Support your inference with examples from the text.

4. Speculate If Zlata could read "Last Night I Had the Strangest Dream," which stanza would most remind her of her diary? Why?

READING FLUENCY

Expression Read the passage on page 651 to a partner. Assess your fluency.

1. I read
   a. great   **b.** OK   **c.** not very well

2. What I did best in my reading was _____.

READING STRATEGY

Make Inferences
What inferences did you make while reading? Explain two of them to a partner.

VOCABULARY REVIEW

Oral Review Read the paragraph aloud. Add the vocabulary words.

Throughout history, war has _____ people's lives. Today, TV news lets us see the harsh _____ of war. It has the power to _____ buildings, countries, and, worst of all, _____ children and adults. The _____ behind war can be confusing. War makes people feel _____. To end such a terrible _____, we must respect all of _____ around the world.

Written Review Write an ad or a book review for "Zlata's Diary." Imagine that your audience is young people. Why is it important for young people to read about the terrible **reality** that Zlata experienced? Use four vocabulary words. ELAR 14.A.1

WRITE ABOUT THE GUIDING QUESTION

Explore Living with Conflict
How does writing about **conflict** help a person live with it? Reread "Zlata's Diary" and look for details that support your ideas.

Connect Across the Curriculum

Literary Analysis

Evaluate Literature: Word Choice

Academic Vocabulary
- **effect** (i-**fekt**) *noun*
  An **effect** is the result of an action or cause.

How Do Words Matter? Writers carefully choose words to convey specific meanings or feelings. In her diary, Zlata uses specific words that let you feel her emotions.

A word's **connotation** is the feeling or idea that the word suggests. One word might have a stronger **effect** than another. In "Zlata's Diary," she says war is "the worst thing in the world." Would you feel the same way if she had said, "War is wrong"? Which word choices create a stronger **effect**? Why?

▲ An author's word choices create images in the reader's mind.

Practice Together

Analyze Word Choice Reread "Zlata's Diary" to find examples of thoughtful word choices. Tell the **connotation** of the words. Then discuss the **effect** of the words and how they make you feel.

Word Choice	Connotation	Effect of the Words
"the worst thing in the world"	the horror of war	It sounds like the war was really horrible. I feel sad reading about what she went through.
"I'm desperate."	the feeling of fear	It sounds like she is really afraid and not sure what to do.

Try It!

Respond to Word Choice Work with a partner to finish the chart. Which word choices have the greatest **effect** on you? Explain.

ELPS: 2.C.4 learn academic vocabulary
heard during classroom instruction and
interactions

Vocabulary Study

Shades of Meaning and Word Choice

Academic Vocabulary
● **scale** (skāl) *noun*
  A **scale** is a graphic organizer that shows how
  a series of items are related.

You already know that words that share the same meaning are called
synonyms. But even among words that mean the same thing there are
shades of meaning, or slightly different meanings. When writers choose
among these shades of meaning, they look for a word that says just
want they want.

Analyze a Scale of Meaning You can arrange synonyms on a **scale** to
examine their different meanings. A **scale** might show weaker to stronger,
funny to serious, simple to complex, or many other ranges of meaning.

Zlata thinks war is bad. She also thinks it is "disgusting" and "horrible."
This is how those shades of meaning might look on a **scale** :

bad   disgusting   horrible

Weaker Meaning   Stronger Meaning

Make Word Choices Find each word below in the selection. See how it
is used. Create a **scale** for each word. Use a thesaurus or dictionary to
help you.

  1. nice (p. 455)   **2.** tough (p. 455)   **3.** freezing (p. 457)

Trade **scales** with other students. Discuss how you placed the words.

Viewing/Writing

Create Original Art

ART

ELPS: 2.C.4 learn academic vocabulary
heard during classroom instruction and
interactions

Academic Vocabulary
● **plan** (plan) *noun*
  A **plan** is a way of doing things.

Create a work of art to show your response to Zlata's life. Reread "Zlata's
Diary" to recall your strongest ideas, images, or feelings.

❶ **Plan Your Work** Make a **plan** to list steps in making a drawing,
painting, collage, or sculpture. Write a brief statement about your work
to read to the class. Then, create your art.

❷ **Present Your Art** Share your art with the class. Invite people to ask
questions.

Literary Analysis

Analyze Song Lyrics

> **Academic Vocabulary**
> • **element** (el-u-munt) *noun*
>   An **element** is one part of a whole.

Song lyrics are words that are set to music and sung. In a poem, a group of lines that form a unit is called a **stanza**. In a song, a stanza is called a **verse**. Like poetry, lyrics have **elements** that help convey meaning. For example:

- **Repetition** Words that repeat stay in your mind.
- **Rhyme** Rhyming words have the same or similar ending sounds, such as *day, say,* and *weigh.* Notice that rhyming sounds can have different spellings.
- **Rhythm** Rhythm is the natural rise and fall, or "beat" of language. For example, read aloud the following song lyric: *Last night I had the strangest dream.* You probably stressed the underlined syllables.

Practice Together

With the class, read aloud the following verse from "Last Night I Had the Strangest Dream."

> Last night I had the strangest dream,
> I'd ever dreamed before,
> I dreamed the world had all agreed
> To put an end to war.

Analyze the Verse To better understand these lyrics, notice how they bring together repetition, rhyme, and rhythm. Here's how:

1. Listen for repetition. This verse uses a form of the word *dream* three times. Do you think the speaker believes that war can end? Why?
2. Look for words that have the same ending sound, such as *before* and *war.* Sometimes rhyme calls attention to key words. Which word in this rhyming pair do you think the speaker wants to emphasize? Why?
3. Notice which syllables are stressed and which are unstressed. Count the stressed syllables, or beats. What does the rhythm remind you of— dancing, marching, or something else?

Try It!

With a small group, apply Steps 1–3 to another verse in the song. Then, discuss your ideas with the rest of the class. Use what you have discovered to plan a class read-aloud of the song lyrics.

Justify

Group Talk Take turns talking about what you would and would not write about in a diary. Justify your opinions and ideas. Use a variety of sentence lengths, including complex sentences.

I would write about my family because they are important to me.

I would write in a diary only if I knew others would not read my words.

ELPS: 2.C.4 learn academic vocabulary heard during classroom instruction and interactions; 3.C.2 speak using a variety of sentence lengths with increasing accuracy and ease; 3.G.1 express opinions on a variety of social and grade-appropriate academic topics

ELPS: 2.C.4 learn academic vocabulary heard during classroom instruction and interactions; 5.F.2 write using a variety of grade-appropriate sentence patterns; 5.F.3 write using a variety of grade-appropriate connecting words to combine phrases, clauses, and sentences

Writing and Grammar

Write About Your Opinion

Study the Models When you write, use a variety of sentences to make your writing more interesting. Use longer sentences with connecting words that show reasons, conditions, and other explanations for your ideas and opinions. Then your reader will understand why you believe something.

JUST OK

I ate lunch with the new student today and he told me what life was like in his homeland it was scary to hear about the danger his family was in. Don't blame him for wanting a better life. If I had to decide whether to stay or leave, I'd leave. Because living in a place where everyone is fighting is not good. Even if you have to leave your friends and neighbors behind.

The reader thinks: "**This writer just rambles on. The ideas don't connect very well.**"

BETTER

I ate lunch with the new student today, and he told me what life was like in his homeland. It was scary to hear about the danger his family was in. Who could blame him for wanting a better life? If I had to decide whether to stay or leave, I'd leave. Living surrounded by fighting is not good, even if you must leave friends and neighbors behind.

This writer uses sentences that are varied and more smoothly connected.

WRITE ON YOUR OWN Write about a current event in the news. Tell what you think of the event. Give reasons for your thinking. Use a variety of sentences, including complex sentences. Combine ideas smoothly to explain your opinions. Then read what you wrote aloud. Make sure it makes sense to your reader.

REMEMBER

Don't string together too many ideas in one sentence. It can confuse the reader.

▲ **People have many different opinions of current events.**

Compare Across Texts

Compare Themes

"Nadia the Willful," "Passage to Freedom," and "Zlata's Diary" all focus on people facing problems in different cultures and time periods.

How It Works

Collect and Organize Ideas Compare themes across selections.

Comparison Chart

Questions	"Nadia the Willful"	"Passage to Freedom"	"Zlata's Diary"
1. What are the beliefs and values?	Nadia values memories of her brother.	The family values helping Jewish refugees escape from Nazis.	Zlata values peace and freedom.
2. What does the story say about difficult times?			
3. Paraphrase one thing that the narrator of each story says.			

Practice Together

Compare Ideas Compare the answers for question 1, and then summarize.

Summary

> "Nadia the Willful," "Passage to Freedom," and "Zlata's Diary" are set in different times and cultures. However, all the characters value freedom. Nadia values the freedom to speak of her brother. The Sugiharas value the freedom of the Jewish people, and Zlata values freedom from the dangers of war.

Try It!

Make a chart to answer question 2. Compare and contrast ideas and explain their **connection** to the unit theme. Use this frame.

"Nadia the Willful," "Passage to Freedom," and "Zlata's Diary" all show people dealing with _____. However, _____. Nadia teaches _____. Mr. Sugihara faces _____. Zlata expresses _____. All three selections show that _____.

Academic Vocabulary
- **identify** (ī-**den**-tu-fī) *verb*
  When you **identify** something, you name it or tell what it is.
- **connection** (ku-**nek**-shun) *noun*
  The **connection** between two things is something they have in common.

CONFLICT AND RESOLUTION

GUIDING QUESTION How can people overcome conflict?

UNIT LIBRARY

Content Library

Greek Civilization

Leveled Library

Navajo Code Talkers
BY ANDREW SANTELLA

Reflect on Your Reading

Think back on your reading of the unit selections. Discuss what you did to understand what you read.

Focus on Genre   **Author's Purpose and Word Choice**
In this unit, you learned that authors use word choice to support their purpose for writing. Choose a selection from the unit. Then, list words and phrases that show why the author wrote that selection. Trade lists with a partner, and explain how each word choice supports the author's purpose.

Reading Strategy   **Make Inferences**
As you read the selections, you made inferences based on the text and your own experiences. Explain to a partner how you will use this strategy in the future.

Explore the

Throughout this unit, you have considered how people overcome conflict.

- **Discuss** With a group, discuss the Guiding Question. Use quotations, dialogue, photographs, and events from the selection to support your answer.

- **Write** Imagine that one of the characters or people in the selections is facing a new and different conflict. Write a story about it. Sustain reader interest with well-paced action and an engaging story line. Describe the setting using sensory details.

- **Reflect** Think about a conflict that people often face in real life. With a partner, brainstorm the best ways to overcome the conflict.

Book Talk

Which Unit Library book did you choose? Discuss with a partner what you learned about people in conflict.

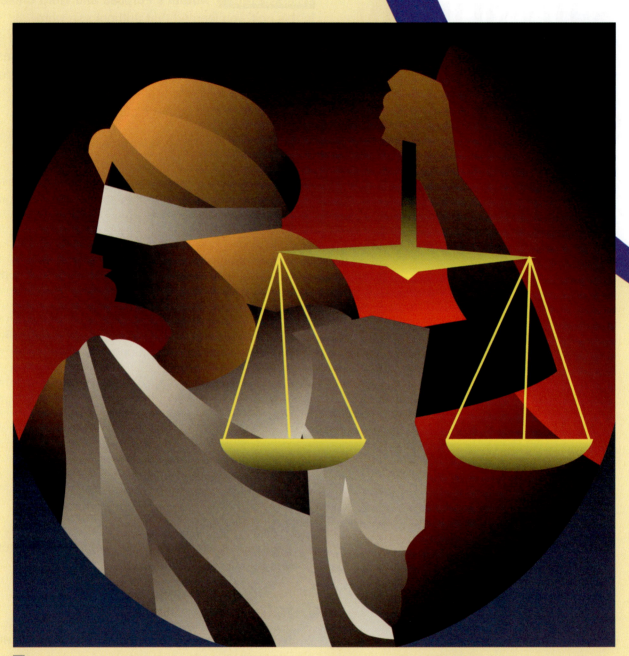

▲ **Critical Viewing:** This image presents justice as if it were a living being. Why do you think the eyes of justice are covered?

ELPS Focus: 2.C.1 learn new language structures heard during classroom instruction and interactions; 2.F.1 listen to and derive meaning from a variety of media to build and reinforce concept attainment; 2.F.2 listen to and derive meaning from a variety of media to build and reinforce language attainment; 2.G.2 understand the general meaning of spoken language regarding familiar to unfamiliar language; 2.I.4 demonstrate listening comprehension of complex spoken English by collaborating with peers; 3.B.1 expand and internalize initial vocabulary by learning and using high-frequency words necessary for identifying and describing people, places, and objects; 3.H.3 explain with increasing specificity and detail;

Unit 7

Fair Is Fair

GUIDING QUESTION

What can you do when life is unfair?

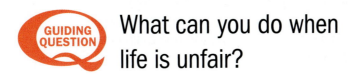

Read More!

Content Library

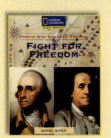

Fight for Freedom
by Daniel Rosen

Leveled Library

Alia's Mission
by Mark Alan Stamaty

Esperanza Rising
by Pam Muñoz Ryan

Out of War
by Sara Cameron

Internet
InsideNG.com

🔹 Find out what judges do.

🔹 Take a closer look at Washington, D.C., where the original Constitution is on display.

🔹 Discover how kids take positive action in their community.

Focus on Genre

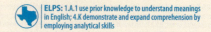**ELPS:** 1.A.1 use prior knowledge to understand meanings in English; 4.K demonstrate and expand comprehension by employing analytical skills

Organization of Ideas

▶ **Logical Order**
▶ **Cause and Effect**

When writers want to inform readers, they think about their purpose and choose a <mark>logical</mark> organization—that is, an organization that makes sense.

How It Works

As you read, look for clues to the organization of the text. Knowing how a text is organized will help you find and remember important information.

Logical Order A logical way to organize expository nonfiction is by <mark>main idea</mark> and supporting details. Writers might state a main idea and then provide details that explain it. If you don't see the main idea right away, look at how the details fit together. The details should all point to one main idea. Study this example that shows a <mark>logical</mark> order of ideas.

Consequence Fits the Crime

Stevenson High School has an interesting way to enforce the school's no-gum-chewing rule. Students who chew gum during class must stay after school to clean desks—even the undersides where chewed gum may be found. Cleaning desks convinces students that chewing gum outside of school is a better choice.

> The <mark>main idea</mark> is the point the writer wants to make in the paragraph.
>
> Details help explain, or support, the main idea.

Cause and Effect Writers may organize ideas in a <mark>cause-and-effect</mark> structure to explain the reasons something happens. They may give a cause and then show the effects, or they may first state a result, and then explain its causes. Study this passage to learn about cause-and-effect structure.

Messy Situation Solved

Due to the large amount of litter on school grounds, Central Middle School held a volunteer clean-up event. As a result of this event, Central soon became a cleaner school.

> The following <mark>signal words</mark> help show a cause-and-effect text structure.
>
> | | |
> |---|---|
> | because | due to |
> | since | therefore |
> | so | as a result |
> | thus | consequently |

Academic Vocabulary
• **logical** (**lah-ji-kul**) *adjective*
When something is **logical**, it makes sense or is reasonable.

Practice Together

Read the following passages aloud with your class. As you read, listen for clues to identify how each is organized.

One Teen Makes Change

Over the last two years, middle school student Natalie Simmons has changed her community for the better. Tired of seeing cars speed down her residential street, Natalie convinced officials at city hall to put up more stop signs in her neighborhood. But she didn't stop there. Natalie's civic pride has also led her to volunteer every Saturday, picking up trash in the neighborhood park. Natalie uses her power as a citizen to improve the place where she lives.

One Teen Makes Change

Because she has younger brothers who play outside, middle school student Natalie Simmons wanted cars to stop speeding on her street. Due to her efforts, new stop signs were posted in her neighborhood. As a result, there have been fewer speeding cars.

Try It!

Read the following passage. How is it organized? What is the main idea? How do you know?

Keeping the Peace

▲ Family meetings encourage fairness and help end fights.

My family has a good way to settle arguments—we hold family meetings. Any time there is a disagreement between family members, one of us can call a family meeting. At the meeting, we each share our side of the story and listen to each other's ideas. We are careful not to choose sides during a family meeting. Instead, we focus on how to solve the problem and try to be as fair as possible. Most of the time, we all work together to resolve the conflict. Family meetings help us keep the peace.

Focus on Vocabulary

ELPS: 1.A.1 use prior knowledge to understand meanings in English; 1.H develop and expand repertoire of learning strategies; 4.F.3 use visual and contextual support to develop vocabulary needed to comprehend increasingly challenging language

Use Word Origins

Many English words have their **origins** in other languages, like Greek, Latin, and Anglo-Saxon. Certain roots and affixes help form many words.

Some Common Roots and Affixes for English Words

Word Part	Source and Meaning	Example
bio-	Greek, *bios* (life), of or about living things	biology—study of life
cred-	Latin, *credere* (to believe), about beliefs	incredible—unbelievable
divi-	Latin, *dividere* (to separate), in parts or disconnected	divide—to separate
leg-	Latin, *lex* (law), of or about the law	legal—according to law
mis-	Anglo-Saxon, *missan* (to miss), badly or wrongly	misjudge—judge wrongly
-ology	Greek, *logos* (word), the study or science of	geology—study of Earth
psych-	Greek, *psyche* (spirit), of or about the mind or emotions	psychology—study of the mind
posi-	Latin, *positus* (place), put in place or set down	deposit—to put down
uni-	Latin, *unus* (one), one, or singular	unite—to bring together

How the Strategy Works

Use **origins** to figure out the meanings of unfamiliar words.

> EXAMPLE   We don't give much **credence** to her statement.

1. Study the word. Look for a root or affix. (*cred-*)
2. Think of a word you already know that has a similar word part. (*incredible*)
3. Use this similarity to figure out the meaning of the unfamiliar word. (*cred-* means "*believe*")

Follow the strategy to figure out the meanings of the underlined words:

> What causes conflict between people? <u>Psychologists</u> and <u>biologists</u> have studied the role of conflict in human life. Out of their many different questions and ideas, scientists hope to find a <u>universal</u> answer.

Strategy in Action

" I know *bio* means life and *–ology* means the study of something. A *biologist* must study life."

☑ **REMEMBER** You can use roots and affixes to figure out many new words.

Academic Vocabulary
- **origin** (or-u-jin) *noun*
  The **origin** of something is its source or beginning.

Practice Together

Read the passage aloud with your class. Find the familiar word part in each underlined word. Use it to help you figure out the meaning of the underlined word.

A House Divided

The future of the <u>United</u> States was in question in 1861. As President Abraham Lincoln took office, some southern states were thinking of <u>dividing</u> the <u>Union</u>. Leaders of those states <u>mistrusted</u> the U.S. government.

They wanted to quit the nation and start a new one. Lincoln's view was clear. The United States was <u>indivisible</u>. Every action Lincoln took as president was meant to end <u>division</u> and <u>unify</u> the country.

▲ Our sixteenth president struggled to save the Union.

Try It!

Read the following passage. What does each underlined word mean? How do you know?

The Voice of the People

You don't need to be elected to office to take part in government. In many states, people can take <u>legislative</u> action in other ways. In California, citizens can suggest ideas for new laws, taxes, and other state changes. They state their ideas in a <u>proposition</u> for voters to decide on. If enough voters <u>unite</u> to pass the proposition, it can become law.

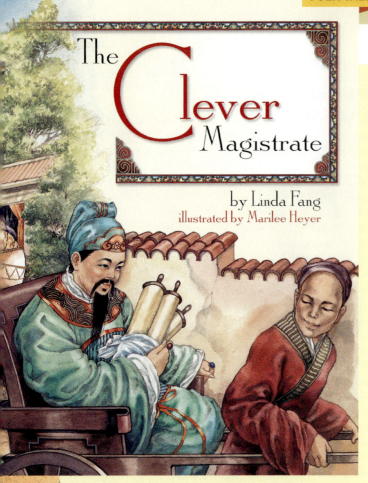

The **Clever** Magistrate

by Linda Fang
illustrated by Marilee Heyer

SELECTION 1 OVERVIEW

▶ **Build Background**

▶ **Language & Grammar**
Tell an Original Story
Use Possessive Adjectives

▶ **Prepare to Read**
Learn Key Vocabulary
Learn a Reading Strategy
Determine Importance

▶ **Read and Write**
Focus on Genre
Folk Tale
Apply the Reading Strategy
Determine Importance
Critical Thinking
Reading Fluency
Read with Expression
Vocabulary Review
Write About the Guiding Question

▶ **Connect Across the Curriculum**
Literary Analysis
Analyze Theme in Folk Tales
Vocabulary Study
Use Word Origins: Borrowed Words
Listening/Speaking
Read a Poem Aloud
Give a Narrative Presentation
Language and Grammar
Tell an Original Story
Writing and Grammar
Write Clear Stories

Build Background

Connect

Quickwrite What's the best way to settle an argument? Write down your thoughts in a Quickwrite. Share your ideas with classmates.

See Fairness in Action

How do you decide what is fair? A judge makes that decision every day.

Digital Library

InsideNG.com
⬇ View the images.

▲ In a trial, a judge listens to an argument and decides what is fair.

ELPS: 2.E.2 use contextual support to enhance and confirm understanding of complex and elaborated spoken language; 3.H.1 narrate with increasing specificity and detail; 4.C.4 comprehend English language structures used routinely in written classroom materials; 4.F.4 use visual and contextual support to develop grasp of language structures needed to comprehend increasingly challenging language; 4.F.9 use support from peers and teachers to develop grasp of language structures needed to comprehend increasingly challenging language

1	TRY OUT LANGUAGE
2	LEARN GRAMMAR
3	APPLY ON YOUR OWN

Tell an Original Story CD

Look at the pictures and think about the context of the story. Then listen to the story.

STORY

It was time to rake the leaves. The boys' mother was working inside the house while they worked outside.

The older brother relaxed while the younger brother was busy raking.

The mother gave each son a small payment for a job well done.

The older son knew he did not do his share of the work. Later, he felt guilty, and gave most of his payment to the real worker, his younger brother.

Use Possessive Adjectives

How do you show who owns or has something? You use **possessive** words. The language structures described below are used routinely in classroom materials.

- Use a **possessive adjective** to tell who has or owns something. Put the possessive adjective before the **noun**.

  EXAMPLES   The leaves covered the yard. **Their colors** looked like a rainbow on the grass.

  The mother told **her sons** to rake the leaves.

- Match the possessive adjective to the **noun** or **pronoun** it goes with.

  EXAMPLES   Lou opened the tool shed. **He** grabbed **his rake** from the hook.

  └ pronoun

  └ noun

  Lou thought **life** was unfair. **Its demands** ruined his day.

Subject Pronoun	Possessive Adjective
I	my
you	your
he	his
she	her
it	its
we	our
they	their

Practice Together

Read the passage. Choose the correct form.

> The older brother felt bad. (He/His) guilt made him pay his
> brother. The mom did not know what happened. (She/Her)
> paid both sons equally. "You have done (you/your) job well,"
> said (they/their) mom.

Try It!

Read the passage. Write each correct form on a card.
Read the passage and add the correct forms.

> The class listened while (we/our) teacher read the
> folk tale. (It/Its) main characters were a crow and a fox.
> (They/Their) friendship was put to a test. The fox was
> being unfair. However, the crow was smart. (She/Her)
> cleverness taught the fox a lesson.

▲ The fox tried to trick his friend.

Create a Story

TELL AN ORIGINAL STORY

A good story holds people's attention. It makes them want to hear more. What story do you want to tell? To whom will you tell it? With a group, discuss your ideas for a story to tell a small child.

With your group, think about the characters and the setting. Discuss a conflict or problem and its complications. Decide how it will be resolved. Fill out a chart like this one to help your group plan its story.

Story Element	Group Choice
Characters (who is in the story)	a polar bear and a seal
Setting (where and when the story happens)	an icy island in the Arctic Ocean
Conflict (the problem and complications the characters face)	
Plot (the events that happen as the characters try to solve the conflict)	
Resolution (how the conflict is solved)	

Work with your group to improve the story. Add details. Tell the new story to another group.

HOW TO TELL AN ORIGINAL STORY

1. Introduce the characters and setting.
2. Tell about the problem.
3. Describe how characters try to solve the problem.
4. Tell how the story ends.

> Once upon a time, a hungry polar bear sat on the tip of a huge iceberg in the Arctic Ocean. The iceberg was his home.

USE POSSESSIVE ADJECTIVES

When you tell a story, use **possessive adjectives** to tell who has or owns something. Match the possessive adjective to the **noun** it goes with.

EXAMPLES   The sad **seal** swam in circles. **His** life was lonely.
The **polar bear** watched the seal. **His** stomach rumbled.

Both **animals** had problems. As time passed, **their** problems grew.

Prepare to Read

 ELPS: 1.A.2 use prior experiences to understand meanings in English; 3.A practice producing sounds of newly acquired vocabulary in a manner that is comprehensible; 4.G.2 demonstrate comprehension of increasingly complex English by retelling or summarizing material

Learn Key Vocabulary

Rate and Study the Words Rate how well you know each word. Then:

1. Pronounce the word. Say it aloud several times. Spell it.
2. Study the example.
3. Tell more about the word.
4. Practice it. Make the word your own.

Key Words

argument (ar-gyu-munt)
noun ▶ page 482

An **argument** is a strong disagreement. My friend and I got into an **argument** because he was late.
Related Word: **argue**

---

complaint (kum-**plānt**) *noun*
▶ page 484

> YOUR VIEWS ■ LETTERS TO THE EDITOR
>
> To the Editor:
> I have a complaint. Elm Park is not big enough for our town. It gets crowded. We need another park so all kids have room to play.

To give a **complaint** is to tell others that you are unhappy about something. I sent my **complaint** in a letter to the editor.
Antonym: **praise**

---

damage (dam-ij) *noun*
▶ page 482

Damage means harm that is done. I threw a baseball, which caused **damage** to the window.
Antonym: **repair**

---

furious (fyur-ē-us) *adjective*
▶ page 482

Someone who is **furious** is very angry. The man was **furious** when his car was hit.
Related Word: **fury**
Synonym: **angry**

---

inevitable (i-**nev**-i-tu-bul)
adjective ▶ page 486

Something that is **inevitable** will happen no matter what. If you throw a ball up, it is **inevitable** that it will come down.

---

mercy (mur-sē) *noun*
▶ page 484

Mercy is kindness to someone in trouble. My mom showed **mercy** when I spilled food on the floor.
Related Word: **merciful**

---

plead (plēd) *verb*
▶ page 483

To **plead** means to strongly ask for something. Children might **plead** for a larger allowance.

---

relent (ri-lent) *verb*
▶ page 483

To **relent** means to stop. After flooding the town, the rain finally **relented**.

Practice the Words Complete a Vocabulary Example Chart. Connect your own experiences with each Key Word.

Word	Definition	Example from My Life
relent	to stop trying	My cousin wanted to borrow money from me, but he finally relented.

Vocabulary Example Chart

Reading Strategy: Determine Importance

A story includes all kinds of details. When you read, you decide which ones are the most important. This helps you focus on what the story is all about.

HOW TO SUMMARIZE

1. As you read each part of the story, pay close attention to characters and plot. Notice *who* does *what*.
2. Take notes about the most important events.
3. In your own words, summarize each part of the story.

Strategy in Action

Here's how one student summarized part of a story.

Look Into the Text

One cold winter day, a farmer was carrying two buckets of spoiled food from a restaurant to his pigsty. As he was passing a coat shop, he accidentally spilled some of the slop on the ground. Sour cabbage, rotten eggs, and fish bones scattered all over the ground. Ugh! Ugh! What a smell!

The shopkeeper, who happened to be standing inside the door, saw this and was furious. He rushed out, grabbed the man, and shouted, "You dirty beggar!"

> A farmer carrying spoiled food made a smelly mess outside a shop.

> "It's probably not important to remember exactly how many buckets the farmer is carrying."

> The shopkeeper was angry.

> "This part has many actions, so I focus on the most important event."

Practice Together

As you read "The Clever Magistrate," follow the steps in the How-To box to summarize the story.

Focus on Genre

ELPS: 4.6.2 demonstrate comprehension of increasingly complex English by retelling or summarizing material

Folk Tale

Folk tales are short fictional narratives that typically explain a wise action or how things came to be. Folk tales were originally told orally and then handed down from one generation to the next.

Some folk tales use **cause-and-effect** organization to express their message.

> One cold winter day, a farmer was carrying two buckets of spoiled food from a restaurant to his pigsty. As he was passing a coat shop, he accidentally spilled some of the slop on the ground. . . .
>
> The shopkeeper, who happened to be standing inside the door, saw this and was furious.

Often the characters do not have names.

A cause leads to an effect.

An effect results from the cause.

As you read folk tales, look for familiar themes, or messages, that appear in tales from many cultures.

Your Job as a Reader

Reading Strategy: Determine Importance

As you read, decide which details are most important and take notes about them. After reading, use your notes to summarize the story.

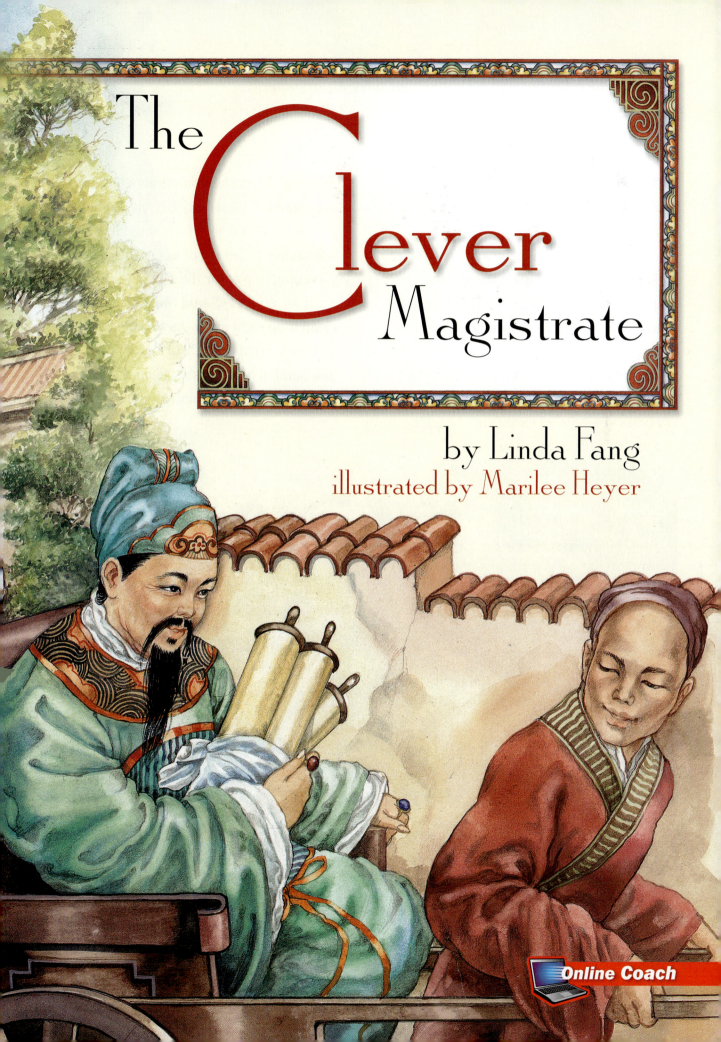

The Clever Magistrate

by Linda Fang

illustrated by Marilee Heyer

Online Coach

Find out why a farmer and a shopkeeper have an <mark>argument</mark>.

One cold winter day, a farmer was carrying two buckets of **spoiled** food from a restaurant to **his pigsty**. As he was passing a coat shop, he accidentally spilled some of the slop on the ground. Sour cabbage, rotten eggs, and fish bones scattered all over the ground. Ugh! Ugh! What a smell!

The shopkeeper, who happened to be standing inside the door, saw this and was <mark>furious</mark>. He rushed out, grabbed the man, and shouted, "You dirty beggar! Look what you've done in front of my shop! It will be impossible to get rid of the smell! How are you going to pay for the <mark>damage</mark>?"

"I am so sorry," said the farmer. "I will clean it up right away. As for the damage, all I have is this coin." He took out a coin and handed it to the shopkeeper.

The shopkeeper snatched the coin,

Key Vocabulary

argument *n.*, disagreement, fight
furious *adj.*, extremely angry
damage *n.*, the result of an accident

In Other Words

spoiled rotten
his pigsty where he kept his pigs

Science Background

Silver and gold are very soft metals. In the past, it was common for people to bite into coins to find out if they were made from real silver or gold. If the coins were real, the bite would leave tooth marks.

put it between his teeth, and bit down on it. The metal was soft, which proved that it contained silver. He thrust it into his pocket and said, "All right, I will take it. But you still need to clean up the mess."

"Let me go and get some rags and a mop," said the farmer. "I will be right back."

"No," said the shopkeeper. "I want you to clean it up right away. It smells so bad that I am going to be sick. Take off your coat and wipe up the mess."

"Please don't ask me to do that!" cried the farmer. "This is the only **quilted** coat I have, and if I use it to wipe up the mess, it will be ruined. I won't be able to wear it anymore."

"That's your problem, not mine!" said the shopkeeper. "In fact, the coat you are wearing is no better than rags. If you don't do what I say, I am going to take you to court."

The farmer **pleaded** with him to reconsider, but the shopkeeper would not **relent**.

Just then they heard, "**Make way for the magistrate**! Make way for the magistrate!"

Key Vocabulary
plead v., to ask for something in an emotional way
relent v., to stop trying

In Other Words
quilted padded and warm
Make way for the magistrate! The judge is coming!

Before You Move On

1. **Summarize** What was the **argument** about? Explain.
2. **Details** How did the farmer offer to repay the shopkeeper for the **damage**?
3. **Judgment** Was the shopkeeper's reaction fair? Why or why not?

The county magistrate was coming down the road in his sedan chair. When he saw the **commotion**, he ordered his guards to put down the chair and bring the two men before him.

"What is the matter?" he asked.

The shopkeeper quickly replied, "*Ta-jen*, this man made a mess in front of my shop. He gave me a coin to pay for the damage, but when I asked him to wipe up the mess, he wouldn't do it."

The magistrate stepped down from his chair and went over to look at the mess. Sour cabbage, rotten eggs, and fish bones were scattered all over the place. Ugh! Ugh! What a smell!

"Why don't you clean up the mess?" asked the magistrate.

"He wants me to wipe up the mess with my coat," said the farmer. "It will be ruined if I do so. And this is the only coat I have."

"Is that what you want?" the magistrate asked the shopkeeper.

"Yes, that is exactly what I want."

"And you will not **settle for less**?"

"No, I will not settle for anything less."

"Well," said the magistrate to the farmer, "if that is what he wants, you'd better do it."

"*Ta-jen*, have **mercy**! I can't do that!" cried the farmer. "Without the coat I will **freeze to death**."

"I am sorry," said the magistrate. "But that doesn't change anything. If you don't do it, I will have to put you in jail."

"That is not **just**!" cried the farmer.

"Hmm…" said the magistrate. He looked angry.

"*Ouh! Ouh! Ouh!*" cried the guards. "*Ouh! Ouh! Ouh!*" They looked threatening.

The farmer realized that there was no way out. **Reluctantly, he used** his coat to clean up the mess. Sour cabbage, rotten eggs, and fish bones. Ugh! Ugh! What a smell! He threw the coat into one of his buckets and stood shivering in front of the magistrate.

The shopkeeper laughed. "Ha, ha, ha!"

"Well," said the magistrate to the shopkeeper, "are you satisfied now?"

"Yes, *Ta-jen*, I am completely satisfied."

"No more **complaints**?"

Key Vocabulary

mercy *n.*, kindness shown to someone in trouble

complaint *n.*, an expression of unhappiness about something

In Other Words

commotion confusion, excitement
Ta-jen Your Excellency (in Chinese)
settle for less agree to anything else
freeze to death be too cold
just fair
Reluctantly, he used He had no choice but to use

"No more complaints!" said the shopkeeper.

"**Case closed**," said the magistrate.

"Case closed."

"But his case against you is now open."

"What!" said the shopkeeper, stunned.

"Well, you see, he is now freezing without a coat. In such weather he could catch a cold. Is that not possible?" asked the magistrate.

"Yes, *Ta-jen*."

"His cold could develop into pneumonia. Is that not possible?"

"Yes, *Ta-jen*."

In Other Words
Case closed The problem has been solved

Cultural Background
A **magistrate** is a person elected to enforce laws. In the past, a magistrate might have traveled in a **sedan chair**— a covered chair that is carried on poles by two people. This showed power and authority.

"Then he could die. His family could sue you for murder, and if **you are convicted**, you would be put to death. Isn't that almost **inevitable**?"

"Yes, *Ta-jen*."

"Well, I don't think you can **afford** that, can you?"

"Oh, no, *Ta-jen*. I cannot afford that. What shall I do?"

"Well, it would be better to settle this out of court."

"Yes, yes, we'd better settle this out of court. But how?"

"We should get him a coat so he won't catch a cold."

"But where can we get one?"

"Right here, from your coat shop."

The shopkeeper looked **as if he had swallowed a fly alive**. He yelled at the farmer, "Go get a coat and be gone!"

The farmer went into the shop, picked out a very cheap coat, and came out. The magistrate stopped him.

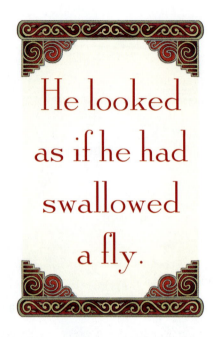

He looked as if he had swallowed a fly.

"You poor thing!" he said. "Look at the coat you've got. It is so thin. You could still catch a cold, isn't that so?"

"Yes, *Ta-jen*."

"You might get pneumonia, isn't that so?"

"Yes, *Ta-jen*."

"You might even die, isn't that so?"

"Yes, *Ta-jen*."

"And then your family could come and **harass** this nice gentleman. I know all your tricks!" The magistrate turned to one of his guards. "Go into the shop and get him the warmest coat you can find."

So the guard went into the shop and picked out the warmest coat he could find for the farmer. As you might guess, the warmest coat happened to be the most expensive.

When the farmer left, the magistrate smiled at the shopkeeper. "Well, what do you think about the way I settled this case? Didn't I handle it very well?"

"Yes, *Ta-jen*," the shopkeeper said **glumly**. "There is no question about that."

"I am glad I was able to take care of this case," said the magistrate. "You have to watch out for these troublemakers. Next time, if you have a case like this, don't try to settle it yourself. Be sure to let me handle it for you." ❖

About the Author

Linda Fang

Linda Fang grew up in Shanghai, China. As a child, Fang was extremely shy. A teacher who wanted to help her overcome her shyness gave Fang a special assignment. The teacher gave her a book to read at home and said, "Come back tomorrow and see if you can tell it to me." This helped Fang discover her talent for storytelling. Fang went on to win storytelling competitions and became a professional storyteller whose tales delight both children and adults.

In Other Words
glumly sadly, unhappily

Before You Move On

1. **Confirm Predictions** Was your prediction correct? If so, what evidence did you use? If not, what happened that you did not expect?
2. **Explain** Why does the Magistrate say, "his case against you is now open"?
3. **Opinion** Do you think the magistrate's decisions are fair?

The Clever Old Woman

In ancient days, a farmer and his clever old mother lived in a village ruled by an **ignorant** young chief. The chief believed that old people were useless, so he ordered that everyone over seventy be taken to the mountains and **abandoned**. Away went the clever old judges, the knowledgeable old doctors, and the wise old teachers, up to the mountains.

The good farmer could not bear to do such a **heartless** thing. Instead, he hid his mother in a cave that he dug under his house.

One day, powerful Lord Higa and his warriors rode into the village and threatened to conquer it. The ignorant chief begged for mercy, although he himself had never shown mercy to others. "Set us any task," he pleaded, "and it shall be done."

"Any task?" said Lord Higa. "I am fair and I do admire cleverness, so let's see if there is any cleverness in this village."

He ordered the villagers to complete three impossible tasks.

"But no one can do what is impossible!" protested the chief.

"Fair is fair," replied Lord Higa. "You did say 'any task.' Now then, first you must make a rope out of ashes. Next, run a thread through a crooked log. Lastly, make a drum that plays without being tapped on top." With that, Lord Higa and his warriors galloped away, vowing to come back before it was fully dark. Already the light was fading from the sky.

With no time to lose, the chief asked all the people in the village for their advice, but they didn't **have a clue**. "If only the elders were still living among us!" they all cried. "Think of how clever they were and all that they had learned over the years."

When the clever old woman heard the chatter of confusion above her, she

---

In Other Words
ignorant uncaring
abandoned left alone
heartless mean
have a clue know what to do

Language Background
Lord and **Chief** are titles for leaders who have control, or authority, over others.

couldn't take it any longer and dared to step out among them.

"How dare you!" **bellowed** the ignorant chief, but the clever old woman ignored him and quickly set to work. First, she soaked rope in salt water and then dried it. When the villagers set the rope on fire, it burned away, but the ash remained in the shape of a rope. Next, she put honey at one end of a log and an ant tied with silk thread at the other end. The ant raced through the log, pulling the thread behind it. Lastly, she opened one side of a drum and **sealed** a bumblebee inside. As the bee beat against the sides of the drum to escape, the drum played without being tapped on top.

When the ignorant chief saw how clever the old woman was, he hung his head in

How dare you!

shame for having treated old people so unfairly. By then, darkness had fallen and Lord Higa and his warriors returned, ready to destroy the village. But when they saw that all three impossible tasks had been completed, they were **astonished**.

"Fair is fair," said Lord Higa. "Clearly everyone in this village deserves to be treated with respect."

"Yes, everyone deserves to be treated with respect," said the clever old woman **firmly**, as she stared **intently** at the chief.

So Lord Higa left and never again bothered the village, the ignorant chief changed his ways, and the old people came back down from the mountain. As for the clever old woman, she went on being clever for many, many years.

Before You Move On

1. **Compare** How are "The Clever Old Woman" and "The Clever Magistrate" alike and different?
2. **Speculate** How would the story change if the farmer had not helped his mother?
3. **Judgment** Which characters in the two stories are the most fair? Why do you think so?

Argument

by Eve Merriam

Good morning.
   Hmm.
Nice day.
   Dim.
5 Sorry.
   Glad.

Hadn't.
   Had.
Go.
10   Stay.
   Work.
Play.
Pro.
   Con.
15 Off.
   On.
Front.
   Back.
   Taut.
20 Slack.
Open.
   Shut.
And.
   But.
25 Over.
   Under.
Cloudless.
   Thunder.
Detour.
30   Highway.
New way.
   Thruway.
Byway...?
   MY WAY!

Connect Reading and Writing

Vocabulary
- argument
- complaint
- damage
- furious
- inevitable
- mercy
- pleaded
- relented

CRITICAL THINKING

1. SUM IT UP Review the notes you took as you read. Use them to make a Cause-and-Effect Chain about the story events.

Cause-and-Effect Chain

Original Cause	First Effect
farmer spills smelly garbage outside a shop	shopkeeper makes farmer clean it up

2. Explain Why does the shopkeeper **relent** and give the farmer what is fair?

3. Compare How are characters in "The Clever Magistrate" like those in "The Clever Old Woman"?

4. Generalize In both the folk tales and the poem, **arguments** take place. Are arguments an **inevitable** part of people's lives? Explain.

READING FLUENCY

Expression Read the passage on page 652 to a partner. Assess your fluency.

1. I read
    a. great   **b.** OK   **c.** not very well

2. What I did best in my reading was _____.

READING STRATEGY

Determine Importance
Show a partner the notes you took to help you summarize. Tell why those details are important.

VOCABULARY REVIEW

Oral Review Read the paragraph aloud. Add the vocabulary words.

My older sister and I got into an _____ when she accidentally drove over my bike. When I saw the _____ this caused, I felt _____. She _____ with me to be fair. After all, I had left the bike lying in the garage, hidden behind the car. So it was _____ that someone would drive over it. I felt sorry about making a _____, so I _____. Out of kindness and _____, my sister replaced the wheel.

Written Review Write a diary entry to tell how you feel about **arguments**. Use four vocabulary words.

WRITE ABOUT THE GUIDING QUESTION

Explore Fairness
Write as the shopkeeper or the farmer in "The Clever Magistrate." Judge if the magistrate was fair when he settled each **complaint**. Support your judgment with examples from the text.

Connect Across the Curriculum

Analyze Theme in Folk Tales

> **Academic Vocabulary**
> - **culture** (kul-chur) *noun*
>   **Culture** includes the beliefs, attitudes, and behaviors shared by a group of people.

A **folk tale** is a simple story that has been shared and told to many people over the years. Folk tales generally reflect the **culture** they come from. The plot of a folk tale involves simple events and problems. The setting and the events reflect the traditions of the tale's **culture** .

Folk tales often share a life lesson. The theme of a folk tale is usually a timeless and universal message that relates to most people. In fact, the same theme may appear in tales from different **cultures** .

What is the theme of "The Clever Magistrate"? One way to identify the theme is to look for clues in the title, the setting, the thoughts and actions of the characters, and the plot.

Practice Together

Begin a Theme Chart Use a Theme Chart to collect the clues you discover. Copy the chart below. Then think about the title of the folk tale. What message does the title hint at? Talk with a partner and find one more clue from the characters, setting, or plot.

Theme Chart

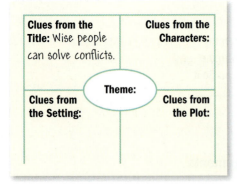

Try It!

Complete the Theme Chart Add more clues from the setting, the characters, and the plot that lead to the main message, or theme, of the folk tale. Then write a sentence that tells the theme of the tale. How does the theme relate to your experience? What life lesson do you think the folk tale conveys? Discuss your ideas with a partner.

Use Word Origins: Borrowed Words

Academic Vocabulary
- **definition** (de-fu-**ni**-shun) *noun*
  The meaning of a word is its **definition**.

How are *zero* and *giraffe* alike? They are both **borrowed words**, or English words taken from another language. Borrowed words keep the same **definition** and sounds from their original language. Here are some examples from "The Clever Magistrate."

Word	Source
coat	Old French *kotta*, coarse cloth, or German *kotze*, a rough overcoat
egg	Old Norse, *ey*, from Anglo-Saxon *æg*, an egg
pocket	Old French *poquette*, a little pouch

Learn More About Borrowed Words Read the following borrowed words. Use a dictionary to find each word's **definition** and country of origin. Which ones surprise you? With a partner, take turns reading what you found out.

1. banana   **3.** parka   **5.** canyon   **7.** sofa

2. mosquito   **4.** chef   **6.** bagel   **8.** diesel

Read a Poem Aloud

DRAMA

Academic Vocabulary
- **structure** (**struk**-chur) *noun*
  A **structure** is how parts are arranged or organized.

The **structure** of the poem "Argument" (line length, word placement, and punctuation) expresses ideas and creates a mood. You can use the **structure** to plan a read-aloud of the poem.

❶ Find Clues in the Poem Reread "Argument." Note clues in the **structure** that tell you how to read the poem.
- The lines are staggered. Some start to the left. Some start to the right. I think this means _____.
- The lines are really short. I think I should read them _____.
- Most lines end with a period, but the last two lines _____.
- The mood of the poem is _____.

❷ Do a Poetry Reading Work with a partner. Decide who will read which lines. Practice reading with facial expression. Vary your pace and volume. Create several versions and choose your favorite to present to your classmates. Listen attentively and respectfully while your classmates present their readings.

Listening/Speaking

Give a Narrative Presentation

DRAMA

ELPS: 3.H.1 narrate with increasing specificity and detail

> **Academic Vocabulary**
> • **characteristic** (kair-ik-tu-**ris**-tik) *noun*
>   A **characteristic** is a specific feature or trait that helps you identify something.

What Makes a Good Story? Some of the **characteristics** of a good story are vivid descriptions, interesting events, and an expressive reading.

When you give a **narrative** presentation, you tell a story. It may be fictional or true. Here is one way to tell a story:

> The magistrate arrived in front of the shop. He looked at the mess and asked why it wasn't cleaned up.

Here is the same part of the story, told another way:

> The magistrate stepped down from his chair and went over to look at the mess. Sour cabbage, rotten eggs, and fish bones were scattered all over the place. Ugh! Ugh! What a smell!
> "Why don't you clean up the mess?" asked the magistrate.

Both passages have a setting, characters, and a plot. But the second one includes more sensory detail.

❶ Plan Your Presentation Follow these steps:
- Choose a topic. What kind of stories do you like? Make sure it's a story that will interest others, too.
- Identify the story elements. Think about the plot, characters, and setting of your story.
- Include specific details that will make the story real.
- Write an outline of the story before you tell it.
- Include time words such as *first*, *next*, and *then* so listeners can follow the story. Look for places to use sensory language.
- Practice telling your story so it becomes natural for you.

❷ Give Your Narrative Presentation Present your narrative to the class. As you speak, make eye contact with your audience. Use expression and gestures to help them "see" the story. As an audience member, listen attentively.

ELPS: 2.G.8 understand the important details of spoken language regarding familiar to unfamiliar language

Tell an Original Story

Group Tale With a group, create a new story to tell. First, brainstorm the topic of the story. Then, one person starts the story with a sentence or two. When that person stops, the next person continues the story to tell what happens next. Continue around the group several times until you create an end to the story. Use possessive words correctly. Review the story as a group, and make sure that everyone understands the important details.

> One day a shopkeeper stepped out of his store. What he saw surprised him.

> The shopkeeper shouted, "Who left this mess at my door?"

ELPS: 1.E.2 internalize new basic language in writing activities; 5.G.1 narrate with increasing specificity and detail to fulfill content area writing needs

Write Clear Narratives

Study the Models When you write, make sure your reader can understand who is doing what. Make it clear who has or owns something. Be sure to include specific details. This helps the reader follow the plot.

NOT OK

> The shopkeeper was furious. <u>He</u> rage showed on <u>he</u> red face. The farmer's slop was scattered all over the ground. <u>It</u> smell was horrible. "This coin is <u>my</u> now," shouted the shopkeeper. "It will help pay for the damage done to <u>me</u> shop. This slop is <u>your</u>. Clean up <u>you</u> mess now!"

The reader thinks, **"Whose face is the writer talking about? This is really confusing."**

OK

> The shopkeeper was furious. <u>His</u> rage showed on <u>his</u> red face. The farmer's slop was scattered all over the ground. <u>Its</u> smell was horrible. "This coin is <u>mine</u> now," shouted the shopkeeper. "It will help pay for the damage done to <u>my</u> shop. This slop is <u>yours</u>. Clean up <u>your</u> mess now!"

This writer uses correct possessive words to make the meaning clear.

 WRITE ON YOUR OWN Write a narrative about an argument between two friends who accuse each other of breaking one of their possessions. Make it clear who owns what and what happens.

REMEMBER

Possessive Adjectives	my	your	his	her	our	their
Possessive Pronouns	mine	yours	his	hers	ours	theirs

THE CONSTITUTION
by Paul Finkelman

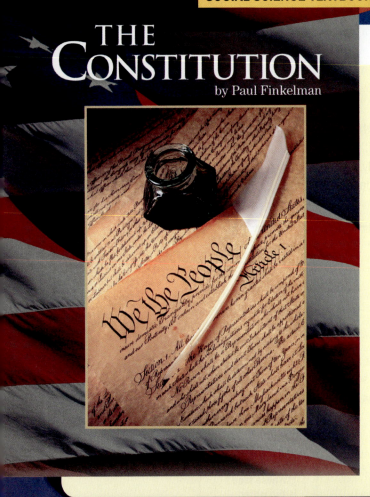

Build Background

Connect

KWL Chart Create a KWL Chart about the Constitution. After you read the selection, you will record what you have learned.

KWL Chart

WHAT I KNOW	WHAT I WANT TO KNOW	WHAT I LEARNED
Sets up branches of government	Which branch of government is most important?	

Explore the Constitution

How did our nation create a system of fairness for all? In 1787, 55 people met in Philadelphia to write a plan of government.

Digital Library

InsideNG.com
◿ View the video.

◀ Benjamin Franklin is one of the best known signers of the U.S. Constitution.

Language & Grammar

 **ELPS:** 2.E.2 use contextual support to enhance and confirm understanding of complex and elaborated spoken language; 4.G.2 demonstrate comprehension of increasingly complex English by retelling or summarizing material

1 TRY OUT LANGUAGE
2 LEARN GRAMMAR
3 APPLY ON YOUR OWN

Summarize

CD

Look at the picture and think about its context. Then listen to the speech and to a summary of the speech. A summary contains only the most important ideas and details of a longer work.

PICTURE PROMPT

Washington as Statesman at the Constitutional Convention, 1856, Junius Brutus Stearns. Oil on canvas, Virginia Museum of Fine Arts, Richmond, Virginia.

Summary

Benjamin Franklin wanted to persuade delegates at the Convention to sign the completed Constitution. Even though Franklin didn't agree with everything in the document, he believed that having a central government for the United States was necessary. He felt that the Constitution they wrote was as good as possible.

He urged the delegates to talk positively about the Constitution when they presented it to the voters in their states. He also urged those delegates who were unsure about the document to support it for the good of the country.

1 TRY OUT LANGUAGE
2 LEARN GRAMMAR
3 APPLY ON YOUR OWN

Use Participles as Adjectives

Verbs have **four principal parts**. For example:

Present	Present Participle	Past	Past Participle
write	writing	wrote	written
satisfy	satisfying	satisfied	satisfied

- Sometimes a **participle** is part of a verb phrase. A verb phrase contains a **helping verb** and a **participle**.

  Present Participle: The people **were** **writing** laws for the new country.

  Past Participle: The people **had** **written** many important documents.

- Sometimes a **participle** acts as an adjective to describe a **noun** or **pronoun**.

  EXAMPLES   **Writing**, **they** worked hard for many months.

  Their **written** **works** are still important today.

- Sometimes you can combine sentences using participles.

  EXAMPLE   The writer looked for two pages. Two pages were **missing**.

  The writer looked for two **missing** pages.

Practice Together

Combine each pair of sentences. Move the <u>participle</u> to tell about a noun or a pronoun in the first sentence. Say the new sentence.

   1. The writers read the words out loud. They were <u>satisfied</u>.
   2. The words were impressive. They had <u>spoken</u> the words.
   3. The writers admired their work. They were <u>smiling</u>.

Try It!

Combine each pair of sentences. Move the <u>participle</u> to tell about a noun or a pronoun in the first sentence. Write the new sentence on a card. Say it.

   4. The sun lit up the room. The sun was <u>shining</u>.
   5. The writers signed their names to the document. They were <u>exhausted</u>.
   6. The writers took turns admiring their work. They were <u>amazed</u>.

▲ The Constitution is a written document.

Tell About Ben

SUMMARIZE

You are exposed to lots of information every day. It's impossible to remember everything you read and hear. How do you share what's important with others? Summarize! You don't need to remember everything. Many details are fun and interesting but not all that important.

With a partner, read this passage about Benjamin Franklin.

> Benjamin Franklin once said, "If you would not be forgotten as soon as you are dead and rotten, either write things worth reading, or do things worth the writing." He followed his own advice and did both. Today, Ben Franklin is remembered as one of our Founding Fathers. He helped write both the Declaration of Independence and the Constitution of the United States. He is also remembered as an inventor. Some of his inventions include bifocal glasses, the lightning rod, and the Franklin stove. Franklin was also a skilled printer. He printed paper money and helped begin our paper currency system. Did you know that his face appears on a hundred-dollar bill?

Now decide with your partner what information is important to remember. List just the most important or main ideas. Create a summary of the passage in your own words.

Main Ideas

Franklin was a Founding Father of the U.S.
He was an inventor.

Read your summary to a small group.

HOW TO SUMMARIZE

1. Identify the main ideas and important information.
2. Leave out less important information and most details and examples that are used to illustrate the main ideas.
3. Use your own words to tell about what you heard or read.

> Franklin was a Founding Father of this country. He helped write the Constitution. He was also an inventor.

USE PARTICIPLES AS ADJECTIVES

When you write a summary, you may want to use **participles** as adjectives to describe the people or things you are telling about.

Past Participle: Franklin was a **skilled** printer.

Present Participle: His **smiling** face appears on paper money.

Prepare to Read

 **ELPS:** 3.A practice producing sounds of newly acquired vocabulary in a manner that is comprehensible; 4.F.6 use support from peers and teachers to read grade-appropriate content area text

Learn Key Vocabulary

Rate and Study the Words Rate how well you know each word. Then:

1. Pronounce the word. Say it aloud several times. Spell it.
2. Study the example.
3. Tell more about the word.
4. Practice it. Make the word your own.

Rating Scale

1 = I have never seen this word before.

2 = I am not sure of the word's meaning.

3 = I know this word and can teach the word's meaning to someone else.

Key Words

amend (u-mend) *verb*
► page 509

To **amend** means to change or to improve. I **amended** the sentence to make it complete.
Related Word: **amendment**
Synonym: **improve**

---

delegate (del-i-get) *noun*
► page 510

A **delegate** is a person who has the power to act and speak for others. The **delegates** met to talk about laws that would help people.

---

democracy (di-**mok**-ru-sē)
noun ► page 517

In a **democracy**, people have the power to vote for what they believe. The United States is a **democracy**.
Related Word: **democratic**

---

government
(**guv**-urn-ment) *noun* ► page 504

A **government** is a group of people who are in charge of a country, state, or city. The U.S. **government** is run by many people.

---

independence
(in-di-**pen**-duns) *noun* ► page 505

Independence means freedom from control by others. The U.S. celebrates its **independence** with fireworks on the Fourth of July.
Related Word: **independent**

---

interpret (in-**tur**-prut) *verb*
► page 512

To **interpret** means to explain the meaning of something. A judge **interprets** the meanings of laws.

---

justice (**jus**-tis) *noun*
► page 504

Justice means fairness. Our court system is set up to give everyone an opportunity for **justice**.
Related Word: **just**

---

represent (rep-ri-**zent**) *verb*
► page 510

To **represent** means to speak or act for a person or group. The president **represents** all of the people of his or her country.
Related Word: **representative**

Practice the Words Make an Expanded Meaning Map for each Key Word. Then compare your maps with a partner.

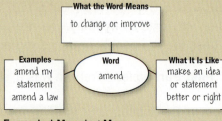

Expanded Meaning Map

Reading Strategy: Determine Importance

Section headings divide a nonfiction selection into its most important, or main, ideas. The supporting details in each section are clues that can help you identify the main idea.

HOW TO IDENTIFY MAIN IDEA AND DETAILS

1. As you read each section, look for clues about its main idea. Sometimes, the author states the idea directly. Sometimes, you must figure it out from the details.
2. Look for details that support the main idea. Record what you find.
3. Look at your notes. Do the details support the most important idea, or the main idea, of this section?
4. After reading, review all the main ideas that you recorded. Summarize them into one main idea statement about the text.

Strategy in Action

This shows how a student identified main idea and details.

Look Into the Text

What would it be like if our government had no president or any one leader? What if the government could not collect taxes to pay its bills? What if each state had its own kind of money? You would have to change your Pennsylvania money into Virginia money as you traveled south. What if a criminal only had to slip out of state to escape justice? That is what the United States was like before the Constitution was written.

"Every detail seems to lead up to the last sentence."

"The main idea was not stated directly. I used details to identify it."

Practice Together

As you read each section of "The Constitution," follow the steps in the How-To box to identify the main ideas and details. With a partner, record them on a chart like this one.

Main-Idea Diagram

Main Idea: The Constitution changed the U.S. for the better.

Detail: Before the Constitution, there was no president or leader.

Detail: The government could not collect taxes to pay its bills.

Detail: Money was different in each state.

Detail: Criminals could escape justice.

Social Science Textbook

A social science textbook presents information about real people, real events, and real conditions in the world.

Textbooks present information in **logical** order with **headings** that organize the text. Photos, captions, sidebars, and other **graphics** illustrate important ideas and provide more information.

> This sidebar illustrates how the branches of government are organized.

Three Branches of Government

The Constitution created a government with three separate branches, or divisions. They are the legislative, executive, and judicial branches.

Legislative Branch	Executive Branch	Judicial Branch
★ called Congress	★ includes the President, government agencies, and the military	★ includes the Supreme Court and other federal courts
★ includes the House of Representatives and the Senate	★ carries out our laws	★ hears cases and interprets our laws
★ makes our laws		

> Headings give you information about each branch.

> Bulleted lists provide specific information about each branch.

Your Job as a Reader

Reading Strategy: Determine Importance

As you read each section, look for details that give clues to its main ideas.

Main Idea:

Detail: A new nation needs a written plan of government.

Detail: The U.S. needed a new government.

Detail: The Constitution is a model for governments around the world.

> "The main idea must be: The U.S. Constitution is a written plan of government."

THE CONSTITUTION

by Paul Finkelman

Introduction

What would it be like if our **government** had no president or any one leader? What if the government could not collect taxes to pay its bills? What if each state had its own kind of money? You would have to change your Pennsylvania money into Virginia money as you traveled south. What if a criminal only had to **slip out of** state to escape **justice**? That is what the United States was like before the Constitution was written.

Key Vocabulary
government *n.*, people who rule a country or state
justice *n.*, equality or fairness

In Other Words
slip out of leave a

A new nation needs a written plan of government. When the United States declared its **independence** from Britain, it needed a new government. Its first plan created a weak national government that did not work well. So, Americans wrote a second plan, the U.S. Constitution. This new plan worked, and it has become a model for governments around the world! What does the U.S. Constitution say and what does it mean in our lives? Let's find out.

The Constitution is at work when a President makes the annual State of the Union Address to the three branches of government.

Key Vocabulary
independence *n.*, freedom from the control of others

Before You Move On

1. **Explain** What is the Constitution? Why does a new nation need one?
2. **Inference** Describe what life in the United States would be like without the U.S. Constitution.

On Display

The original Constitution was written in 1787 on four sheets of parchment, a heavy kind of paper. It was kept in various cities until 1952, when it was placed in the National Archives Building in Washington, D.C. In 2003, a major **renovation** of the National Archives was completed. The entire Constitution is now on display.

First of Its Kind

The U.S. Constitution has about 4,500 words. It is the oldest and the shortest written constitution of any government in the world today.

Who Signed It?

Thirty-nine men signed the Constitution. The oldest was 81-year-old Benjamin Franklin of Pennsylvania. The youngest was Jonathan Dayton of New Jersey, who was 26.

The Clerk's Fee

The clerk who wrote out the Constitution was paid $30 for the job. That is worth about $575 today.

Visitors look at the original Constitution at the National Archives Building in Washington, DC.

In Other Words

renovation repair and update

Historical Background

The **National Archives Building** holds our nation's most important documents including the Bill of Rights and The Declaration of Independence. The building looks like a temple and covers two city blocks.

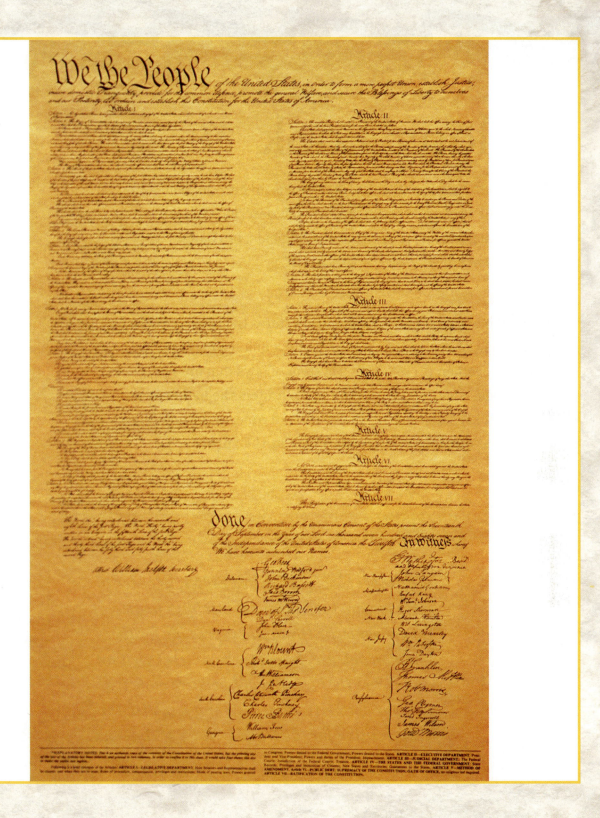

Before You Move On

1. **Details** Describe the Constitution. How is it different from other countries' constitutions?
2. **Opinion** What do you think of the way the Constitution is displayed?

A Closer Look

The Constitution has three parts. There is an introduction called the Preamble, seven articles that describe the plan of the national government, and the amendments, or changes to the Constitution.

The Preamble

The first paragraph of the Constitution states the basic purposes of the new plan of government: (1) to create a union where the states work together; (2) to create a system of laws that are fair; (3) to keep peace within the country; (4) to protect the nation from **outside attack**; (5) to improve the lives of all Americans; and (6) to make sure that **our free society survives in the future**.

Preamble

We the people of the United States, in order to form a more perfect union, establish justice, insure domestic tranquility, provide for the common defense, promote the general welfare, and secure the blessings of liberty to ourselves and our posterity, do ordain and establish this Constitution for the United States of America.

In Other Words
outside attack an attack by another country
our free society survives in the future we always have freedom

The Articles

The seven articles **set out** the powers of Congress, the President, and the federal courts. The articles also explain how the states are to relate to the national government and how the Constitution can be <mark>amended</mark>, or changed. Most importantly, the articles declare that the Constitution and all laws made by Congress will be the "supreme law of the land." All states must obey the national laws and follow the Constitution.

The Amendments

The amendments, or changes to the Constitution, were not written at the Constitutional Convention. They were added later, when changing conditions showed a need for a change to our plan of government. Changing the Constitution is not easy. There have been only twenty-seven amendments in more than 200 years.

"We the people"

The Constitution begins with the famous words, "We the people of the United States." This means that the government is our government. It is established by "the people," not by a king or any other authority.

The Constitutional Convention took place in Philadelphia in 1787 and lasted four months. During this time, fifty-five delegates met to create the Constitution of the United States.

Key Vocabulary
amend *v.*, to make changes or improvements

In Other Words
set out describe

Before You Move On

1. **Paraphrase** In your own words, tell one purpose of the Preamble.
2. **Cause and Effect** Why are amendments necessary?

Three Branches of Government

The Constitution created a government with three separate branches, or divisions. They are the legislative, executive, and judicial branches.

Legislative Branch

★ called Congress
★ includes the House of Representatives and the Senate
★ makes our laws

Executive Branch

★ includes the President, government agencies, and the military
★ carries out our laws

Judicial Branch

★ includes the Supreme Court and other federal courts
★ hears cases and interprets our laws

The Legislative Branch

The Constitution begins with the Congress. The **delegates** started here because this branch passes the laws. It is the most important branch. It is also the part of government that is closest to the people. This branch **represents** the people of each state. Article I sets up the House of Representatives and the Senate. It says how the members of **each body** will be chosen, who can be a member, and how many members each body will have. The most important part of Article I tells what kinds of laws Congress can pass and what kinds it cannot pass. Among other things, Congress can enact taxes, borrow money, and declare war.

A serious responsibility of Congress is to declare war at the request of the President.

Key Vocabulary

delegate *n.*, a person chosen to speak for U.S. citizens
represent *v.*, to serve a group and present their beliefs

In Other Words

each body the House of Representatives and the Senate

Congress cannot favor one state over another or grant titles of nobility, such as duke or earl. Finally, Article I says Congress also can make any laws "necessary and proper" to carrying out its powers. This **elastic** clause was a way for future Americans to expand the meaning of the Constitution.

The Executive Branch

Article II describes the office of the President and who can **fill the office**. It also tells what powers and duties that person has. The President serves as commander-in-chief of the military. With Senate approval, the President also makes treaties and **appoints** ambassadors and judges. One of the President's most important duties is to give Congress information about the State of the Union. This means the President reports on how the United States is doing and urges Congress to pass laws that the country needs.

Today, the executive branch of government is huge. It employs millions of people. The delegates never imagined how our government would grow. They gave the President enough power, however, to carry out Congress's laws. As our society **grew and became more complex**, so did our government.

The President leads the government from his office in the White House.

In Other Words
elastic changing, flexible
fill the office become the President
appoints decides who will be
grew and became more complex became larger and more difficult to manage

Before You Move On

1. **Summarize** How does the Legislative Branch **represent** the people?
2. **Details** What are the duties of the Executive Branch?

The Judicial Branch

This branch consists of the Supreme Court and other federal courts. This branch **interprets** the law. That means these courts hear cases to decide how the Constitution and other national laws apply to them. Article III creates the office of Chief Justice of the United States and tells Congress to create a Supreme Court. The Constitution also allows Congress to create other federal courts. Today, we have federal courts for trials, appeals, and special areas of the law, such as immigration. An appeal means a transfer of a legal case from a lower to a higher court for a new hearing.

The Supreme Court building

Justices of the U.S. Supreme Court in 2007

Key Vocabulary
interpret *v.*, to explain

Checks and Balances

Government needs to have power to do its job. However, it may use this power to do wrong. Governments have used the police to take away the rights of the people. Officials have used tax money to make themselves rich. Governments have gone to war when many citizens believed it was wrong.

The delegates wanted to control the power they gave to our government. To do this, they built into the Constitution a system of **checks and balances.** They created three separate branches of government. They wanted each branch to help control the power of the others.

To take one example, Congress passes laws, but the President signs the laws. The President can veto, or reject, a law. However, if two-thirds of the members of the House and the Senate then vote for the law, **they can override** the President's veto. Later, if a legal case results from the law, the Supreme Court can decide whether the law is unconstitutional. In this way, all three branches of government have a role in seeing that our laws are fair.

If Congress believes a President has seriously misused power, it can impeach, or formally charge, him or her with misconduct. The Senate puts the President on trial. If found guilty, the President can be removed from office. In U.S. history, two Presidents, Andrew Johnson and William Jefferson Clinton, have been impeached and brought to trial. Neither was found guilty.

A political cartoon in 1833 portrays President Andrew Jackson as a king stepping on the Constitution. Critics felt he wanted too much power.

In Other Words
checks and balances fairness
they can override their vote will
   be used instead of

Before You Move On

1. **Vocabulary** How does the Judicial Branch **interpret** the law?
2. **Explain** Tell how the system of checks and balances works.

The Amendments

The delegates in Philadelphia knew that they were not perfect. They understood that the Constitution might have to be changed.

The delegates wanted the Constitution changed only when it was very important and when most of the people in the country agreed. So, they made changing the Constitution a difficult process. Two-thirds of each house of Congress must vote for an amendment. After that, three-quarters of the states must **ratify** the amendment. Only then does the amendment become part of the Constitution.

Americans celebrate the passage of the 13th Amendment, which ended slavery in 1865.

In Other Words
ratify approve

The Bill of Rights

At first, the Constitution did not include a bill of rights. Many people thought it was a mistake that the Constitution did not have one. That problem was fixed by the first ten amendments, our Bill of Rights. The amendments of the Bill of Rights protect the basic freedoms of individuals. These include freedom of religion, freedom of speech, freedom to protest government actions peacefully, and the right to a fair trial.

These amendments guarantee that people accused of crimes will have a lawyer. They are guaranteed that they will be given a trial held in the open—not in secret. People convicted of a crime are guaranteed they will not receive "cruel and unusual punishment." These amendments also guarantee a free government and an open society. Sometimes we may have to listen to people whose ideas we do not share. This is part of living in a free country. Freedom, as protected by the Bill of Rights, means we must **tolerate** those who disagree with us. It also means we respect those who have a different religion from ours or no religion at all.

The Bill of Rights allows people to peacefully fight for what they think is fair.

◁ **Critical Viewing: Environmental Print** What do the signs tell you about the firefighters?

In Other Words
tolerate respect

Before You Move On

1. **Describe** What process is used to <mark>amend</mark> the Constitution?
2. **Make a Connection** List the freedoms that the Bill of Rights protects. Which freedom is the most important to you? Why?

Later Changes

After the Bill of Rights was ratified, the Constitution was still not perfect. So, we have added another seventeen amendments since 1791. Some amendments were needed to fix things that did not work well. Here is an example. At first, a new President was elected in November, but did not **take office** until March. This made sense in an age of horses and sailing ships. It took time to get the news from one place to the other. It took time for people to get to the national capital. Now, in an age of trains, cars, and planes, this no longer makes sense. In 1933, the 20th Amendment changed the date the new President takes office to January 20.

Women celebrate passage of the 19th Amendment in 1920.

In Other Words
take office begin the job as President

Some of the most important amendments have created more freedom, liberty, and political opportunity for all Americans. The Constitution could not solve the problem of slavery. In the end, a very bloody Civil War was needed to end slavery. After the war, we added the 13th, 14th, and 15th amendments to end all slavery and make the former slaves full citizens of the United States.

Other amendments have **expanded** American **democracy**. The 15th Amendment allowed all adult men, including former slaves, to vote. The 19th Amendment allowed women to vote. The 24th Amendment says states cannot discriminate against poor people by making people pay a tax if they want to vote. The 26th Amendment allowed 18-year-olds to vote.

In 1987, people celebrate the 200th anniversary of the signing of the Constitution at Independence Hall, in Philadelphia.

200 Years Old—and Still Working

Our Constitution has been **in operation** for more than 200 years. It is the oldest working constitution in the world. It is not perfect. We have changed it twenty-seven times. Yet, for all its faults and problems, it has brought more **liberty** to more people than any other system of government in the history of the world. Over the years, millions of immigrants have come to the United States. One reason they came was because they understood that this nation had a strong Constitution. It guaranteed them a voice to say what they want, and the right to vote for their leaders.

The delegates in Philadelphia said in the Preamble that they wanted to create "a more perfect Union." They wanted to "establish Justice" and "secure the Blessings of Liberty" to the American people. They succeeded remarkably well. ❖

Preamble, 1987, Mike Wilkins. Painted metal on vinyl and wood, Smithsonian American Art Museum, Washington DC.

This 1987 work by American sculptor Mike Wilkins uses license plates to celebrate the U.S. Constitution on its 200th birthday. What do the words on the plates spell out?

In Other Words
in operation used
liberty freedom

Before You Move On

1. **Cause and Effect** Describe two improvements that have resulted from amendments.
2. **Main Idea and Details** How does the Constitution make people's lives better? Give an example.

The Star-Spangled Banner

by Francis Scott Key

This is the original flag seen by Francis Scott Key flying over Fort McHenry, in Maryland.

O! say, can you see by the dawn's early light,

What so proudly we **hail'd** at the twilight's last gleaming;

Whose broad stripes and bright stars through the **perilous** fight

O'er the ramparts we watched were so gallantly streaming;

And the rocket's red glare, the bombs bursting in air,

Gave proof through the night that our flag was still there;

O! say, does the star-spangled banner yet wave,

O'er the land of the free and the home of the brave!

In Other Words
hail'd saw
perilous dangerous
O'er the ramparts we watched The stars and stripes waving over the fort

Historical Background
The British attacked Fort McHenry on September 13, 1814. The next morning, Francis Scott Key saw that the flag was still flying above the fort. This inspired him to write "The Star-Spangled Banner," the national anthem, or song of the U.S.

Before You Move On
1. **Conclusion** What symbols does the flag represent?
2. **Judgment** In what ways is the flag a good representation of the United States?

The Flag We Love

by Pam Muñoz Ryan

When people come to our great country
Aboard ships that cross the sea
They are welcomed to our harbors
By the flags of liberty.

5 Citizens march for freedom
With action, faith, and **word**.
A righteous banner guarantees
Their voices will be heard.

Celebrate the flag we love
10 **A majesty** in the sky
And feel the pride that swells inside
As our banner goes streaming by.

In Other Words
Aboard On
word through the words they speak
A majesty Greatness

Before You Move On

1. **Paraphrase** In your own words, explain what "A righteous banner guarantees their voices will be heard" means.

2. **Theme** How do *The Star-Spangled Banner* and the poem relate to this unit's theme?

Connect Reading and Writing

Vocabulary
amend
delegates
democracy
government
independence
interpret
justice
represent

CRITICAL THINKING

1. SUM IT UP Complete column three of the KWL Chart you started on page 496. Use your chart to summarize the article.

KWL Chart

The Constitution		
WHAT I KNOW	WHAT I WANT TO LEARN	WHAT I LEARNED
Sets up branches of government	Which branch of government is most important?	

2. Analyze Use examples in the selection to explain what **independence** meant to the **delegates**.

3. Evaluate In a **democracy** how important is one branch of **government** compared to the other two branches? Give examples from the text.

4. Compare Use details from the poems and the selection to tell how the Constitution and the U.S. flag are alike and how they are different.

READING FLUENCY

Phrasing Read the passage on page 653 to a partner. Assess your fluency.

1. I read
   a. great   **b.** OK   **c.** not very well

2. What I did best in my reading was _____.

READING STRATEGY

Determine Importance
How did you determine what was most important as you read this selection? Show a partner.

VOCABULARY REVIEW

Oral Review Read the paragraph aloud. Add the vocabulary words.

When the U.S. declared _____ from Britain and became a _____, it needed a new plan of _____. Without the Constitution, who would _____ the laws and _____ the people? The _____ who wrote the Constitution could not think of everything. Over time, it became necessary to change, or _____ the Constitution. These changes helped bring liberty and _____ to all.

Written Review Imagine that you view the original Constitution. Write a brief message about what it **represents** to you. Use four vocabulary words.

 **WRITE ABOUT THE** **GUIDING QUESTION**

Explore Fairness for All
The Constitution was written more than 200 years ago. Why do you think people still follow this plan of **government** today? Read the selection to find information that supports your ideas.

Connect Across the Curriculum

ELPS: 2.G.7 understand the important details of spoken language regarding familiar to unfamiliar topics; 4.F.2 use visual and contextual support to enhance and confirm understanding; 4.I.2 expand reading skills

Literary Analysis

Analyze Text Structure: Logical Order

Academic Vocabulary
- **logical** (lah-ji-kul) *adjective*
  When something is **logical**, it makes sense or is reasonable.

Main Idea and Details Writers may organize their writing in a **logical** order. One common way to organize nonfiction is to use **main idea and details**. In this type of organization, the main idea is given and the writer includes details that explain, show, or support the main idea. Think of it this way:

Main-Idea Diagram

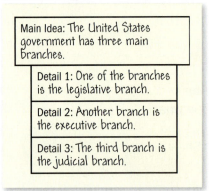

Main Idea: The United States government has three main branches.

Detail 1: One of the branches is the legislative branch.

Detail 2: Another branch is the executive branch.

Detail 3: The third branch is the judicial branch.

Do you see how each of the **details** explains and gives more information about the **main idea**? These four sentences are organized in a **logical** order.

Practice Together

Use a Main-Idea Diagram Copy this diagram. Look back at the selection. Find details that support this main idea and fill in the chart with your class to confirm your understanding.

Main-Idea Diagram

Main Idea: The judicial branch interprets the law.

Detail 1:

Detail 2:

Detail 3:

Try It!

Analyze Logical Order With a partner, choose a paragraph from "The Constitution." Take turns reading the paragraph aloud and listening. Find the main idea and important supporting details. Create a Main-Idea Diagram to show the **logical** order of the paragraph.

Use Word Origins: Greek, Latin, and Anglo-Saxon Roots

Academic Vocabulary

- **origin** (**or**-u-jin) *noun*
  The **origin** of something is its source or beginning.

Many English words have their **origins** in ancient languages.

Root	Meaning	Related English Word
dem, Greek	people	democracy
chron, Greek	time	chronological
popul, Latin	people	population

Identify Word Origins Match each word from the selection with its correct **origin** . Then work with a partner to say a sentence using each word.

1. legislative
2. judicial
3. constitution
4. right

A. *constitutere*, Latin; to set up

B. *riht*, Anglo-Saxon; straight, direct

C. *jud*, Latin; judge

D. *legis*, Latin; law

Compare Texts Across Time

Academic Vocabulary

- **characteristic** (kair-ik-tu-**ris**-tik) *noun*
  A **characteristic** is a specific feature or trait that helps you identify something.

Content Area Vocabulary: Social Science

Word Bank
preamble
constitution

ELPS: 3.D.2 speak using content area vocabulary in context to build academic language proficiency

How Has Writing Changed? Read the Preamble to the Constitution on page 508. Compare it to this preamble, written in 2008.

Preamble for the Constitution of the Westview Chess Club

> The Westview Chess Club is a club for all who believe in fair play. Our mission is to create a community that has fun and treats all players with respect.

❶ Compare Text List the **characteristics** of both preambles. Discuss their similarities and differences with a partner.

❷ Rewrite Text Work with a partner to rewrite the Preamble in a more modern style. Take turns reading your versions of the Preamble to the class.

Literary Analysis

ELPS: 2.C.4 learn academic vocabulary heard during classroom instruction and interactions

Analyze Poetry: Symbol

Academic Vocabulary
- **symbol** (sim-bul) *noun*
  A **symbol** is an object or idea that represents something else.

Symbol is an element of poetry that writers use to express their ideas. A **symbol** is something that represents something other than itself, such as a dove as a **symbol** for peace.

The same **symbol** can be used across history. In the two poems "The Star-Spangled Banner" and "The Flag We Love," the flag is a **symbol**. What is it a **symbol** of? Even though these poems were written over a hundred years apart, both use the flag to convey a universal theme, or message.

▲ A flag represents many things to the people of its country.

Practice Together

Compare Poems Reread "The Star-Spangled Banner" and "The Flag We Love." One way to identify the meaning of the **symbol** is to look at the writer's word choice and descriptive language. Notice how both writers use words that appeal to your senses. For example, in "The Star-Spangled Banner," the speaker describes the scene as "by the dawn's early light." You can picture when the scene takes place—early in the morning.

Make a Venn Diagram like this one and list a word or phrase in each poem that stands out to you. Compare the words and phrases used in both poems. Do they tell you what the flag symbolizes?

Venn Diagram

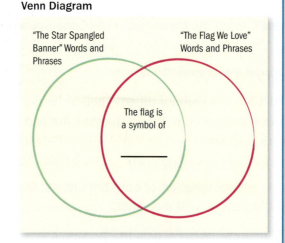

"The Star Spangled Banner" Words and Phrases

"The Flag We Love" Words and Phrases

The flag is a symbol of

_____

Try It!

Work with a partner to come up with at least two more descriptive words or phrases from each poem. Write them on your diagram. Discuss how the poems are different and how they are alike. Decide what you think the flag symbolizes, and share your ideas with the class. What message, or theme, is the writer trying to convey?

Summarize

Group Share Work in a group. Take turns summarizing different sections of the selection. Identify and tell just the main ideas and important details, using your own words. Use participles as adjectives in some of your sentences.

> The U.S. Constitution is the shortest written constitution of any government in the world today. A few chosen people wrote the Constitution.

ELPS: 2.G.8 understand the important details of spoken language regarding familiar to unfamiliar language; 4.G.2 demonstrate comprehension of increasingly complex English by retelling or summarizing material

ELPS: 5.E.1 employ increasingly complex grammatical structures in content area writing

Write to Add Details to Sentences

Study the Models When you write about a famous person or event, be sure to add descriptive details and interest to your sentences. Combine ideas to create smoother, richer sentences.

OK

> The writer looked at the tip of his quill pen. It was broken. He had been writing all night. He rubbed his eyes. He was tired. Then he listened to the rain hitting the roof. The rain was pouring. He realized the importance of his work. He was smiling. He grabbed a new quill pen and continued to write. The words were powerful. They were written.

This writing is choppy and does not add descriptive details smoothly to the sentences.

BETTER

> The writer looked at the tip of his <u>broken</u> quill pen. He had been writing all night. <u>Tired</u>, he rubbed his eyes. Then he listened to the <u>pouring</u> rain hitting the roof. <u>Smiling</u>, he realized the importance of his work. He grabbed a new quill pen and continued to write. The <u>written</u> words were powerful.

This writer adds descriptive details and combines ideas to make sentences less choppy.

WRITE ON YOUR OWN Choose a famous document that you have read about. Describe what you know about it. Add details and avoid choppy sentences.

REMEMBER

Verb forms change depending on how they are used.

Present	Present Participle	Past	Past Participle
impress	impressing	impressed	impressed
write	writing	wrote	written

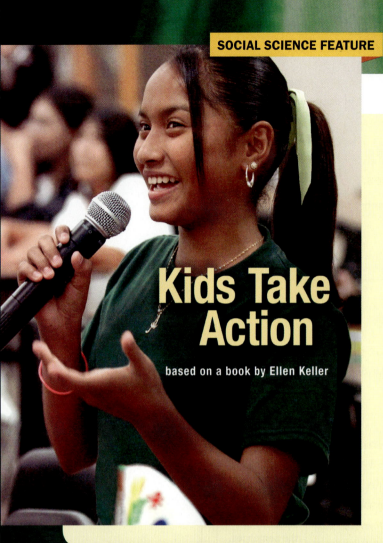

Kids Take Action

based on a book by Ellen Keller

Build Background

Connect

Anticipation Guide Tell whether you agree or disagree with these statements. Compare your answers with a partner.

Anticipation Guide

	Agree	Disagree
1. It is important to speak out against unfairness.	_____	_____
2. Not everyone should get involved in their community.	_____	_____
3. There is no way for students to make their voices heard.	_____	_____

See a Campaign in Action

What is it like to get involved in a campaign? These students know. We can all create positive change in our communities.

Digital Library

InsideNG.com
◗ View the video.

◀ Kids can help in their communities.

Language & Grammar

ELPS: 2.H.2 understand implicit information in complex spoken language; 2.I.1 demonstrate listening comprehension of complex spoken English by following directions

1 **TRY OUT LANGUAGE**
2 **LEARN GRAMMAR**
3 **APPLY ON YOUR OWN**

Give and Follow Directions

CD

Look at the photograph and listen to the directions.
Follow along carefully to understand each step.

PICTURE PROMPT

In our state, citizens use electronic voting machines to cast their ballots.

How do I use the machine?

How to Use a Voting Machine

1. *First, enter the voting machine booth.*

2. *Then, read each item that you are voting on.*

3. *Next, press the X next to the candidate or item you wish to select. The X will light up.*

4. *To change a selection, press the button next to the X that is lighted. The light will go out. Then make another selection.*

5. *To write in a candidate's name, press the WRITE–IN button. Then use the keypad at the bottom of the machine to enter the person's name, one letter at a time.*

6. *Review all your selections after you make your choices. Changes can only be made before you press the large VOTE button.*

7. *Finally, press the large VOTE button to cast your ballot.*

8. *Exit the voting machine booth.*

Use Participial Phrases to Combine Sentences

A **participle** is a verb form that sometimes acts as an adjective. A **participial phrase** begins with a participle. Participles and participial phrases describe nouns and pronouns.

- A participle ends in **-ing** or **-ed**, or it has a special form. It can stand alone, or it can come at the start of a group of words called a **participial phrase**.

    EXAMPLES   **Caring** citizens vote in elections.

    Showing concern for the issues, they first listen to what the candidates say.

    The candidates often have many **heated** debates.

    Seen by many people, the debates help people understand the issues.

- You can use participial phrases to combine or expand sentences.

    EXAMPLE   These elections are important. They are **covered by many reporters**.

    Covered by many reporters, these elections are important.

Practice Together

Use a participial phrase to combine each pair of sentences. Say each new sentence.

1. Many people campaign for the candidate. They are working as a team.
2. The candidate has many good ideas. He is admired for his honesty.
3. People ask the candidate lots of questions. The questions are written on note cards.

Try It!

Use a participial phrase to combine each pair of sentences. Write each new sentence on a card. Then say each new sentence.

4. The candidate speaks with voters. The candidate knows what our town needs.
5. The candidate will be a strong contender. She is praised for her knowledge.
6. I cast my vote. I think carefully about the issues.

▲ Speaking about the issues, the candidate made her ideas known.

Make a Campaign Sign

GIVE AND FOLLOW DIRECTIONS

Campaign signs are everywhere before an election. Candidates use them to advertise their names and the offices they seek. Signs come in all sizes and colors, with different wording. How would you make a campaign sign?

With a partner, create step-by-step directions for making a campaign sign. Use words that tell the sequence, or the order, of the steps.

▲ Campaign signs help candidates get votes.

> **How to Make a Campaign Sign**
>
> 1. First, find your materials: poster board, markers, etc.
> 2. Next, decide what information to put on the sign.
> 3. Then,
> 4. After that,
> 5. Finally,

Read your directions to another group. Have them repeat your directions to make sure they understand the information. If they don't, make changes.

HOW TO GIVE AND FOLLOW DIRECTIONS

1. Give directions in steps. Use sequence words.
2. Use simple vocabulary and speak clearly and concisely. Use gestures when appropriate.
3. Ask the people receiving the directions to repeat them back to you in their own words to make sure they understand.

> Next, plan the information you will include on the sign. Then, make sure the words are printed clearly.

> OK. The next thing I should do is plan what to put on the sign. Then, I need to make sure the words are easy to read.

USE PARTICIPLES TO COMBINE SENTENCES

When you give directions, you can use **participles** to combine sentences. You can add details with a **participial phrase** to make your writing more interesting.

EXAMPLES   **Printing the words neatly**, you carefully letter the sign.
Seen by many, the campaign sign tells people to vote for your candidate.

Prepare to Read

ELPS: 3.A practice producing sounds of newly acquired vocabulary in a manner that is comprehensible; 5.A learn relationships between sounds and letters to represent sounds when writing in English

Learn Key Vocabulary

Rate and Study the Words Rate how well you know each word. Then:

1. Pronounce the word. Say it aloud several times. Spell it. Write it.
2. Study the example.
3. Tell more about the word.
4. Practice it. Make the word your own.

Rating Scale

1 = I have never seen this word before.

2 = I am not sure of the word's meaning.

3 = I know this word and can teach the word's meaning to someone else.

Key Words

campaign (kam-**pān**) *noun*
▶ page 534

A **campaign** is a series of actions by an individual or a group working toward a goal. John F. Kennedy led a **campaign** to become president in 1960.

citizen (**sit**-u-zen) *noun*
▶ page 539

A **citizen** is a person who was born in a country or becomes a member of a country. All American **citizens** share the same rights.
Related Word: **citizenship**

debate (di-**bāt**) *verb*
▶ page 539

To **debate** means to discuss different views of something. In a **debate**, two or more people tell why they have different opinions or ideas.

informed (in-**formd**)
adjective ▶ page 536

To be **informed** is to have knowledge. It is our duty to be **informed** about issues.
Related Word: **information**
Synonym: **aware**

persuade (pur-**swād**) *verb*
▶ page 538

To **persuade** means to try to make others agree. The student **persuaded** us by giving a strong speech with good ideas.
Synonym: **convince**

petition (pu-**tish**-un) *noun*
▶ page 534

A **petition** is a written request for a government or leader to take action. If enough people sign our **petition**, it may convince the mayor to do what we ask.

support (su-**pōrt**) *noun*
▶ page 534

To have **support** means that people help you. Students need the **support** of their teachers.
Related Word: **supportive**
Synonym: **help**

volunteer (vol-en-**tēr**) *verb*
▶ page 535

To **volunteer** means to work without pay. One way I can help others is to **volunteer** at the soup kitchen.

Practice the Words Work with a partner to write four sentences. Use at least two Key Words in each sentence.

EXAMPLE: I volunteer at a park after school to support the community soccer program.

Reading Strategy: Determine Importance

We all respond to a text in different ways. If a text relates to our lives and experiences, it will be more important to us.

Reading Strategy
Determine Importance

HOW TO DETERMINE WHAT'S IMPORTANT TO YOU

1. Use a Personal Reading Journal to note what each part is about.
2. Write down ideas you think are most important to remember.
3. Write down what has personal meaning to you and why.

Strategy in Action

Here's how one student determined what was important to her.

Look Into the Text

These are important ideas to me.

    The teens in Burnsville, Minnesota, had no place to skateboard. They were getting in trouble for skateboarding in public places, and they thought that was unfair. So they met with the mayor and suggested that the city build a skateboarding park. Because the mayor liked the idea, she told the teens they needed to go to the City Council to get it approved and funded.

Practice Together

Reread the passage and start your own Personal Reading Journal.

Personal Reading Journal

This part is mostly about . . .	The important details include . . .
Taking action to change something in our community	• The teens had no place to skateboard. • They talked to the mayor about building a skateboarding park.

The most important idea to me is . . .
Kids like me can take positive action in our communities.

Focus on Genre

Social Science Feature

Social science features often tell about people getting involved in the world around them.

Many articles use a **cause-and-effect organization** to show why people get involved and the results of their actions. Headings help you follow the text structure.

> **Persuading the City Council**
>
> The teens worked on a speech to give before the City Council. . . . They got people to agree with their point of view and to volunteer to talk for them before the City Council. The mayor also said she would support them. . . .
>
> All the hard work paid off— the City Council voted in favor of the park. The teens' reward for all their effort was a brand-new skateboarding park.

causes

An effect can also be a cause.

effect

Your Job as a Reader

Reading Strategy: Determine Importance

As you read, take notes of ideas that are personally important to you.

A student expresses her opinion about an after-school program at her school. ▶

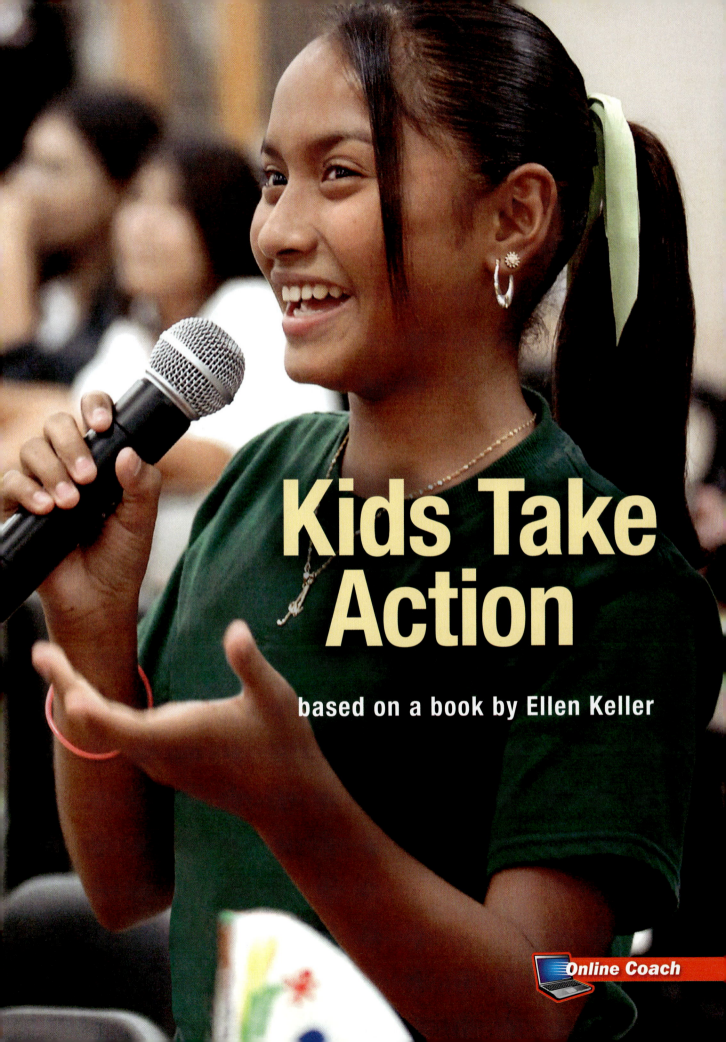

Kids Take
Action

based on a book by Ellen Keller

Online Coach

The teens in Burnsville, Minnesota, had no place to skateboard. They were getting in trouble for skateboarding in public places, and they thought that was unfair. So they met with the mayor and suggested that the city build a skateboarding park. Because the mayor liked the idea, she told the teens they needed to go to the City Council to get it approved and **funded**. She advised them on what steps they should take.

▲ Students in Burnsville, Minnesota helped construct a public skateboard park.

Campaign Skateboard Park

The teens started a **campaign** to get **support** for a skateboarding park. First, they contacted local business people, met with them in person, and explained what they were trying to do.

Then, they wrote letters to the business people asking for money to help build their skateboarding park. They pointed out that the park would help them by **eliminating** skateboarding in front of their buildings and by offering advertising space. Everyone would gain something. Many businesses gave money to show their support.

Getting Local Support

In the next step, the teens met with the people who lived in the area. They explained how the skateboarding park would help the residents: there would no longer be skateboarding on sidewalks or in public places. The local people were convinced to sign **petitions** showing their support for the park.

Now the teens had local support and some of the money to build the park. However, they still had one more step to take: they had to present their plan to the City Council. The City Council would

Key Vocabulary
campaign *n.*, an organized effort by people working towards the same goal
support *n.*, help or funding
petition *n.*, a formal written request

In Other Words
funded paid for
eliminating stopping

then vote on whether or not to support the skateboarding park and to give the rest of the money needed to build the park.

Persuading the City Council

The teens worked on a speech to give before the City Council. They practiced it until they knew it **by heart**. They got people to agree with their point of view and to **volunteer** to talk for them before the City Council. The mayor also said she would support them.

In their speech, the teens explained why the skateboarding park was important to them. They described the benefits, or good things, that a park would create and used examples from their own lives to personalize the speech.

Finally, it was time for the City Council to vote. All the hard work **paid off**—the City Council voted **in favor of** the park. The teens' reward for all their effort was a brand-new skateboarding park.

Before You Move On

1. **Sequence** What did the teens want to accomplish? What steps did they take?
2. **Judgment** Which part of the process got the most **support**? Explain your answer.

Making Your Voice Heard

The students in Burnsville, Minnesota, **made their voices heard**. They had an opinion, and then made sure it was an **informed** opinion. An informed opinion is based on facts that can be checked. It reflects careful thinking about all sides of an issue. There are millions of people in this country with their own **points of view on** issues. Expressing your own point of view can seem like a Herculean effort.

Even if you yelled very loudly, would the government hear you and listen to your point of view?

Making your voice heard does not mean speaking loudly. It means getting others to listen to you and getting **a majority of** people to agree with what you're saying.

How do you make your voice heard? How do you get the government and other people to hear you?

◄ A member of the Chicago Bulls raised his voice to encourage people to volunteer in a Hurricane Relief event. Many students responded.

Key Vocabulary
informed *adj.*, having information and knowledge

In Other Words
made their voices heard expressed their beliefs
points of view on beliefs about
a majority of most

Language Background
Hercules is a hero from Greek mythology. He is known for his strength, courage, and kindness. To say that something is **"Herculean"** means that it is a big job that requires a lot of strength or work.

Writing Letters

One way to express your beliefs is to write a letter. If you write it to the editor of your local newspaper it might be published. Then everyone in your community can read it.

Carl Franklin wrote this letter to his local paper after deciding that his school needed a new community teen center.

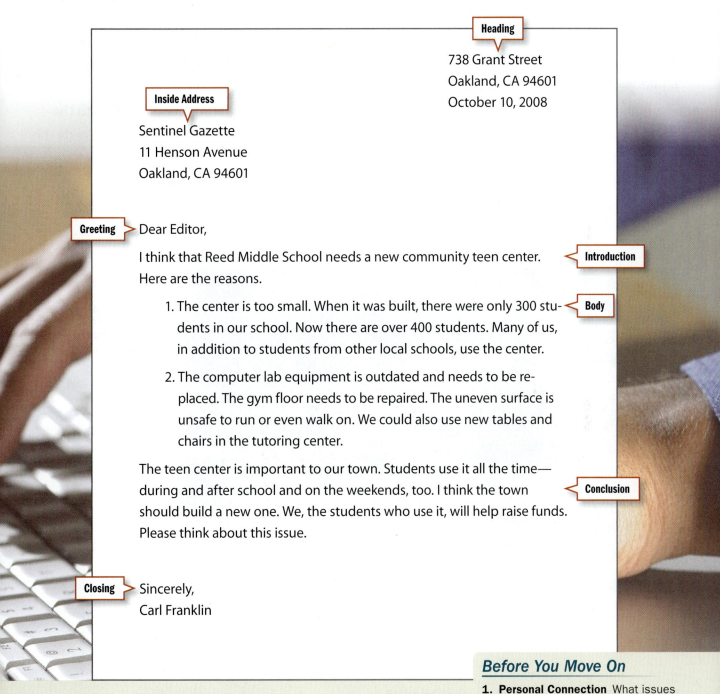

Heading

738 Grant Street
Oakland, CA 94601
October 10, 2008

Inside Address

Sentinel Gazette
11 Henson Avenue
Oakland, CA 94601

Greeting

Dear Editor,

Introduction

I think that Reed Middle School needs a new community teen center. Here are the reasons.

Body

1. The center is too small. When it was built, there were only 300 students in our school. Now there are over 400 students. Many of us, in addition to students from other local schools, use the center.

2. The computer lab equipment is outdated and needs to be replaced. The gym floor needs to be repaired. The uneven surface is unsafe to run or even walk on. We could also use new tables and chairs in the tutoring center.

Conclusion

The teen center is important to our town. Students use it all the time—during and after school and on the weekends, too. I think the town should build a new one. We, the students who use it, will help raise funds. Please think about this issue.

Closing

Sincerely,
Carl Franklin

Before You Move On

1. **Personal Connection** What issues in your community would you write a letter about?
2. **Judgment** What details in the letter might help **persuade** others?

Starting a Petition

Another way that you can make your voice heard is to start a petition. A petition is a formal document, or paper, that tells what you want. People who agree with your request sign your petition. The signed petition is presented to an official, a person who makes decisions. A petition with a lot of signatures might **persuade** that official to support what you want.

Let's say that you think that your community should have an arts center. You and your friends see that the library has a room that is often empty so you talk with the librarian who agrees that the room could be turned into an arts center. How can you get the town to support your idea?

You and your friends decide to start a petition. With the help of others, you collect as many signatures as possible. Soon the town is talking about what a good idea it would be to have an arts center.

Finally, you present your petition to the local government. The town council reads the petition and **acts on it**. A few months later, the arts center opens!

◄ Students urge people to protect the environment by adding their signatures to a petition.

Key Vocabulary
persuade *v.*, to try to make others agree

In Other Words
acts on it decides to do something

Creating a Campaign

A campaign, or series of planned actions, is another way to call attention to a problem or **issue**. In a campaign, you use the tools you just read about to make your voice heard. For example, in a presidential election, candidates start a campaign to get people to vote for them. The candidates write letters, make speeches, and work with others to win the election. Another example of a campaign is the Civil Rights Movement, which focused on ending racial segregation. Dr. Martin Luther King, Jr., helped lead the campaign by giving speeches, writing letters, and working with others.

Giving a Speech

Freedom of speech is an important right that you have as a **citizen** of the United States. You have the right to say what you want as long as it doesn't harm another person. Giving a speech is one way you can share your point of view and try to persuade others to agree with you.

During an election, candidates **running for office** give speeches and **debate** each other. In their speeches and debates, they tell how they feel about issues and try to get people to vote for them.

Many famous people have used speeches to make their points heard and understood.

A good speech stays in people's minds and can even earn a place in history. For example, here are memorable lines from speeches given by famous leaders.

Memorable Voices

"The only thing we have to fear is fear itself."

–Franklin D. Roosevelt

"Government of the people, by the people, for the people, shall not perish from the earth."

–Abraham Lincoln

"My fellow Americans, ask not what your country can do for you. Ask what you can do for your country."

–John F. Kennedy

Key Vocabulary

citizen *n.*, a person who lives in a country and has certain rights and duties

debate *v.*, to discuss different views about an issue

In Other Words

issue a topic of strong interest to people

running for office who are trying to get elected

Staying Involved

Good citizens are involved in their communities. They care about what happens and take action to change things that need changing. Sometimes they work with others and sometimes they work alone. But they make their voices heard. ❖

► People gather in support of a campaign.

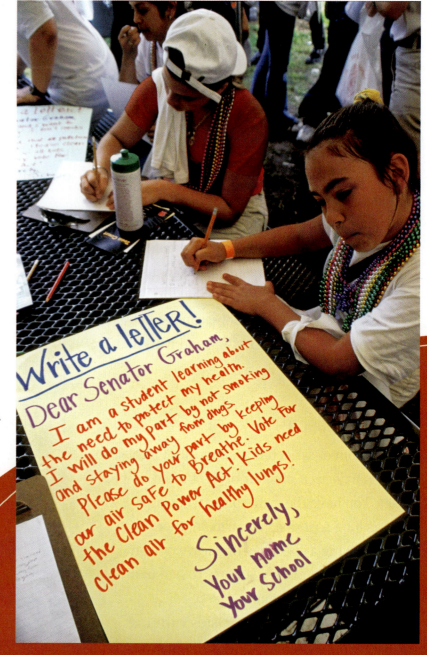

Before You Move On

1. **Steps in a Process** Describe the process of starting a **petition**.
2. **Paraphrase** In your own words, describe what a campaign is.

Connect Reading and Writing

Vocabulary

campaign

citizen

debate

informed

persuade

petition

support

volunteers

CRITICAL THINKING

1. SUM IT UP Create a Main-Idea Diagram to show what you personally find important about this topic. Use the chart to summarize the selection.

Main-Idea Diagram

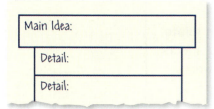

Main Idea:

Detail:

Detail:

2. Paraphrase In your own words, tell how skateboarders took action to **persuade** their city to build a park.

3. Make Judgments In your judgment, which of the skateboarders' actions would help win the most **support** for an issue? Why?

4. Evaluate Review the Anticipation Guide on page 526. Now that you are more **informed** about the way kids take action, do you want to change your responses? **Persuade** a partner to agree with you.

READING FLUENCY

Intonation Read the passage on page 654 to a partner. Assess your fluency.

1. I read

   a. great   **b.** OK   **c.** not very well

2. What I did best in my reading was _____.

READING STRATEGY

Determine Importance
How did you determine which ideas were most important to you? Tell a partner.

VOCABULARY REVIEW

Oral Review Read the paragraph aloud. Add the vocabulary words.

> Suppose you want to change something in your state. What actions can you take to _____ the public to agree with you? First, create a _____ to bring attention to the issue. Ask _____ to sign a _____ to show their _____. If people disagree with you, invite them to _____ the issue. The more you share facts and opinions, the more it will help every _____ make an _____ decision.

Written Review Create a **petition** for an issue you would like changed at school. Describe the purpose. Use four vocabulary words.

WRITE ABOUT THE GUIDING QUESTION

Explore Taking Action
How important is it for people to **volunteer** in their communities? Why? Support your opinion with examples from the selections.

Connect Across the Curriculum

Analyze Text Structure: Cause and Effect

> **Academic Vocabulary**
> • **relate** (ri-lāt) *verb*
>   When you **relate** things, you show how they are connected.

How Are Events Related? As you read, think about how some events **relate** to other events in the text. When writers want to explain how one thing affects another, they often use a cause-and-effect structure to organize their writing.

- A cause is *why* something happens. An effect is *what* happens.
- Sometimes a cause has more than one effect, or an effect has more than one cause.
- Sometimes one effect can be the cause of another effect.

Practice Together

Relate Causes and Effects Read the passage and **relate** a **cause** with an **effect**.

> The teens in Burnsville, Minnesota, had no place to skateboard. They were getting in trouble for skateboarding in public places. So they met with the mayor and suggested that the city build a skateboarding park.

A Cause-and-Effect Chain shows how one event **relates** to another. Reread the passage. Find a second effect. Add it to the chain.

Cause-and-Effect Chain

Original Cause	First Effect	Second Effect
The teens in Burnsville, Minnesota, had no place to skateboard.	They got in trouble for skateboarding in public places.	

Try It!

Make a Cause-and-Effect Chain With a partner, create another Cause-and-Effect Chain. Reread the section titled "Campaign Skateboard Park" on page 530. Find an effect for this cause: "The teens started a campaign to get support for a skateboarding park." Then find a second effect that results from the first effect. Add both effects to the chain.

Use Word Origins: Greek and Latin Mythology

Academic Vocabulary
- **origin** (or-u-jin) *noun*
  The **origin** of something is its source or beginning.

A myth is a story with gods, goddesses, heroes, and great deeds. Some words we use today have their **origins** in mythology.

> Changing your community can take a **Herculean** effort.

Herculean refers to Hercules, a hero in a Greek myth, who performed twelve difficult tasks. To make a *Herculean effort* is to try extremely hard.

Mentor	a trustworthy and wise character in ancient Greek myth
Vulcan	ancient Roman god of fire
Achilles	Greek soldier whose only weak spot was his heel

Use Word Origins Work with a partner. Use the chart and a dictionary to discuss the meanings of these sentences.

1. Ms. Alvarez is a great teacher who has been a **mentor** to me.
2. There are still active **volcanoes** in Hawaii.
3. Not doing her homework has been her **Achilles heel**.

Give an Informative Speech

SOCIAL SCIENCE

ELPS: 2.G.6 understand the main points of spoken language regarding familiar to unfamiliar contexts; 3.D.1 speak using content area vocabulary in context to internalize new English words

Academic Vocabulary
- **organize** (or-gu-nīz) *verb*
  To **organize** means to arrange things in a certain order.

Think of something that has changed for the better in your community. Write and deliver a speech to explain how the change came about.

① **Organize Information** To **organize** your speech, use a cause-and-effect structure to explain what happened. To research your topic, interview people in the community or read local newspaper articles. Take notes.

② **Prepare Your Speech** Write a strong introduction that makes your subject clear. As you conclude, restate your topic. Practice your speech.

③ **Present Your Speech** Make eye contact with your audience. Speak clearly and loudly.

④ **Listen** Listen for the main points of other speeches. Identify the main points to show your understanding.

Media/Writing

Complete a Membership Form

CAREER STUDY

> **Academic Vocabulary**
> • **issue** (i-shü) *noun*
>   An **issue** is a problem or a concern.

If you volunteer to support an **issue** that matters to you, most organizations ask you to fill out a **membership form**.

1 **Find a Group** Use these steps to find a group you want to support.

- Think about what matters to you. What would you like to see changed in your community? Is there an **issue** that is important to you, such as keeping your parks clean or encouraging people to vote?
- Check your local newspaper. What group supports this **issue**?
- Look up information about the group online, or call the organization to talk to someone about what it does.
- Choose a group and get a membership form.

2 **Read the Membership Form** What information do you get from the membership form? What information do you have to give?

3 **Complete the Form** Follow instructions closely. Write as neatly as possible or type the information. Fill out every part of the form. If you do not understand something, ask for help.

4 **Return the Form** Return the completed form to the volunteer organization as instructed.

Kids in Action!
Monterey, CA 93940

MEMBERSHIP FORM

Kids in Action helps the local environment.

Personal Information
Name: _____   Phone Number: _____
Address: _____   E-mail Address: _____
Date of Birth: _____

Education and Experience
Name of School: _____   Grade: _____

Volunteer Experience: _____
_____

Areas of Interest (check the areas that interest you)
____ distribute posters   ____ write letters
____ event planning   ____ fundraising

Why do you want to be a member of our organization?
_____

Note: Mail your form to the street address on the back.
No e-mails, please.

ELPS: 2.I.1 demonstrate listening comprehension of complex spoken English by following directions

Give and Follow Directions

Pair Share Work with a partner. Give directions to your partner on how to write a letter to the editor to change the name of a street in your town. Tell about the parts of a letter, where in the letter the parts are placed, and any special punctuation that is needed. Use participles to combine some of the sentences in your directions. Have your partner repeat your directions in his or her own words. Trade roles.

> Ending with a closing, you are now ready to sign your name.

> OK. The closing is the last thing I write before I sign my name.

ELPS: 5.F.2 write using a variety of grade-appropriate sentence patterns; 5.F.3 write using a variety of grade-appropriate connecting words to combine phrases, clauses, and sentences

Write to Elaborate

Study the Models When you write, you can add interest and details to your sentences by using participial phrases to elaborate on nouns and pronouns. You can use a participial phrase to put two ideas together for writing that flows.

NOT OK

The teens wanted a skateboard park. They talked with the mayor. They knew she supported their idea. Now they needed the City Council to approve the plan. They met first with local business people **starting a campaign for the park**. Then they wrote letters. They asked for money to help build the skateboard park. Many businesses gave money to the project. They wanted to show their support. Next, the teens got the support of the local homeowners. They were ready to present their plan to the City Council.

The reader thinks: **"This is confusing. I don't know who is starting a campaign for the park."**

OK

The teens wanted a skateboard park. **Talking with the mayor**, they knew she supported their idea. Now they needed the City Council to approve the plan. **Starting a campaign for the park**, they met first with local business people. Then they wrote letters and asked for money to help build the skateboard park. **Showing their support**, many businesses gave money to the project. **Getting local homeowners' support next**, the teens were ready to present their plan to the City Council.

This writer moved the misplaced words to correctly describe the teens. The writer combined some ideas, too.

✎ **WRITE ON YOUR OWN** Write about a global or community issue you feel strongly about. Combine ideas so your writing flows.

REMEMBER

Use participial phrases to add detail to your sentences or to combine ideas. For example:
- **Showing interest in their community**, the teens took action.
- **Forming a committee**, they made a plan.
- **Working together**, they reached their goal.

Compare Across Texts

Compare Literary Elements

The selections in this unit all have messages about justice and freedom. Compare their imagery and symbolism and **analyze** how these elements express the authors' ideas.

How It Works

Collect and Organize Ideas To compare literary elements in more than one selection, organize the words and phrases in a chart like this one.

Comparison Chart

Selection	Imagery	Symbol	How Images and Symbols Express the Main Idea
"The Clever Magistrate"	sights, sounds, smells of a Chinese village	coat	The images make you feel as if you are there. The coat is a symbol of justice.
"The Flag We Love"	ships arriving, marches for freedom, patriotic parade		
"The Star-Spangled Banner"	explosions in the dawn air, flag streaming		

Practice Together

Analyze and Compare Ideas Compare the information you collected. Then summarize the way each selection uses imagery. Give examples.

Summary

"The Clever Magistrate," "The Flag We Love," and "The Star-Spangled Banner" all use imagery to make the writing come alive. In "The Clever Magistrate," readers experience the sights, sounds, and smells of the village. . . .

Try It!

Complete the chart. Compare how the selections use symbols to express ideas. You may want to use this frame to write your summary.

The symbols in all three selections _____. In "The Clever Magistrate," the _____ symbolizes _____. In "The Flag We Love," the _____ symbolizes _____. In "The Star-Spangled Banner," the _____ is a symbol of _____.

Academic Vocabulary
- **analyze** (a-nu-līz) *verb*
  When you **analyze**, you separate something into parts and examine, or study, it.

Fair Is Fair

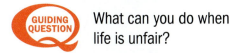

 GUIDING QUESTION What can you do when life is unfair?

Reflect on Your Reading

Think back on your reading of the unit selections. Discuss what you did to understand what you read.

Focus on Genre **Organization of Ideas**

In this unit, you learned about some ways writers organize ideas. Choose "The Constitution" or "Kids Take Action" and draw a diagram that shows how the text is organized. Use your drawing to explain the text organization to a partner.

Reading Strategy **Determine Importance**

As you read the selections, you learned how to determine importance. Explain to a partner how you will use this strategy in the future.

Explore the **GUIDING QUESTION**

Throughout this unit, you have been thinking about fairness.

Write Write a poem that expresses your ideas about fairness. As you write, consider these poetic elements:

- What will be your rhyme scheme? Will lines rhyme by twos, by every other line, or some other way?
- What figurative language will you use? Consider personification or idioms.
- What will your poem look like on the page? Will it have certain shape? Will some lines be indented?

Book Talk

Which Unit Library book did you choose? Explain to a partner what it taught you about fairness.

UNIT LIBRARY

Content Library

Leveled Library

Bowl of Life, 2004, Jose Ramirez.
Mixed media on wood, private collection, Los Angeles.

△ **Critical Viewing:** Why do you think the artist called this image "Bowl of Life"?

Food for Thought

GUIDING QUESTION

How can people provide for our communities?

ELPS Focus: 2.E.2 use contextual support to enhance and confirm understanding of complex and elaborated spoken language; 2.E.3 use linguistic support to enhance and confirm understanding of complex and elaborated spoken language; 2.G.3 understand the general meaning of spoken language regarding familiar to unfamiliar contexts; 2.G.5 understand the main points of spoken language regarding familiar to unfamiliar language; 3.A practice producing sounds of newly acquired vocabulary in a manner that is comprehensible; 3.J.1 respond orally to information presented in a wide variety of media to build and reinforce concept attainment; 3.I.1 adapt spoken language appropriately for formal purposes; 3.I.2 adapt spoken language appropriately for informal purposes; 4.F.9 use support from peers and teachers to develop grasp of language structures needed to comprehend increasingly challenging language

Read More!

Content Library

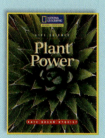

Plant Power
by Kate Boehm Nyquist

Leveled Library

The Code
by Mawi Asgedom

Dr. Jenner and the Speckled Monster
by Albert Marrin

Spike Lee
by James Haskins

Internet
InsideNG.com

- See how farms provide food.
- Find out how to make healthy choices about what you eat.
- Explore the Abenaki culture — its customs, food, and traditions.

Focus on Genre

Persuasive Writing

▶ **Argument**
▶ **Support**

In persuasive writing, an author tries to convince the reader to agree with his or her **position**, or viewpoint, on an issue. Persuasive writing includes essays, speeches, newspaper editorials, and advertisements.

How It Works

The writer's position and the **support** he or she gives is called the **argument**. Different writers use different kinds of appeals , or ways of persuading readers.

- **Appeals to logic** make sense, relate to the topic, and include support that can be proved. Such evidence includes facts, statistics, opinions of experts, and details from personal experience.

- **Appeals to ethics** speak to the reader's sense of right and wrong.

- **Appeals to emotions** focus on readers' feelings.

Study this passage to learn more about persuasive appeals .

Logical and Rhetorical Fallacies:
Unsupported Inferences: conclusions that aren't supported by the evidence
Fallacious Reasoning: an argument based on a **fallacy**—that is, an idea that is misleading or false
Propaganda: persuasion based on faulty reasoning, stereotypes, and emotional appeals
Commonplace Assertions: oversimplified arguments that may or may not be true

---

Nutrition First

Teens need nutritious diets, but vending machines tempt them to make bad food choices. Our schools should get rid of their vending machines. ◁ **Writer's position**

The typical vending machine offers too much of a bad thing. Most snacks offered are high in sugar and fats. Candy bars, chips, and cookies make up 80% of the snack choices.

> **Propaganda uses a stereotype to turn readers against something.**
>
> **Facts and statistics** as evidence

According to Lee Oto, Nutrition Director, "School meals help meet the required daily servings of fruits and vegetables, but students don't choose the school meal if they pass a vending machine."

> **Opinion of a reliable expert as evidence**

Isn't the health of our children more important than profit? We need to do the right thing. Remove the machines!

> **Ethical and emotional appeals call for action.**

Academic Vocabulary
- **appeal** (a-pēl) *noun*
An **appeal** is a request for a response.

Practice Together

Read the following passage aloud with your class. As you read, identify the argument, the type of evidence, and the appeals the author uses.

Food Fight

Vending machines help students get through the long day, so they must stay. It takes too long to stand in the cafeteria line during our short lunch periods, and grabbing something from a vending machine is quicker. We need vending machines for after-school events like sports practices, too. Without them we would starve! Coach Mathis agrees. "Many of our sports activities are funded by vending machine profits." We students want vending machines to stay. They fill a gap in our need for nutrition during the day.

Try It!

Read the following passage. What is the writer's argument? What types of evidence and appeals does the writer use? How do you know?

Change for Vending Machines

Schools depend on profits from vending machines, but poor food quality is a health problem. Students cannot learn properly with only junk food in their systems. The School Board, therefore, demands more nutritious foods in vending machines rather than removing the machines.

Superintendent Kacy Miles states, "Student success depends on good health." We don't want students relying on high-fat snacks and sugary beverages. We'll require more drinks and snacks like milk, vegetable juices, water, fruits, salads, yogurt, and granola bars. If necessary, we'll insist on newer models of vending machines to handle these foods. Students can still use vending machines but will have healthier choices. "We know our responsible students will appreciate and grow to love the new vending machines," Miles states. "They won't even miss the junk food."

Focus on Vocabulary

Use Context Clues: Specialized Language and Vocabulary

Many words in English have several meanings, depending on the context, or the place where the word is used. Specialized language and vocabulary includes **technical** terms, jargon, and special cultural references.

How the Strategy Works

When you come to a specialized word you don't know, use the language around it to figure out its meaning.

1. Read the entire sentence. Try to understand the main idea.
2. See how the word fits into the sentence. Does the word seem like jargon or a **technical** term?
3. Think about the topic of the piece and the subject area it covers.
4. Use the information to figure out a meaning that makes sense in the context. Check the word in a dictionary to be sure.

Use the strategy to figure out the meaning of the underlined words.

A key issue in the quest to feed the world is water use. You can't grow plants without water. Surface water in lakes, rivers, and streams supplies about three-fourths of the fresh water in the United States. Ground water in sand or gravel beneath the earth's surface supplies much of the nation's drinking water. Almost all of the drinking water in rural areas comes from such aquifers. However, some areas may be losing their ground water. Many places report that their aquifers are drier than in the past. In other areas, well diggers must bore much deeper to reach water. Protecting water reserves is increasingly important, now and into the future.

Strategy in Action

" **This passage is about water. Since it lies underground and some of it comes from *aquifers*, they must be underground water sources.** "

☑ **REMEMBER** You can use context to help you figure out the meaning of specialized language.

Academic Vocabulary
- **technical** (tek-ni-kul) *adjective*
  Something that is **technical** is based on scientific knowledge.

Practice Together

Read the passage aloud with your class. Listen to each underlined word.
Use context to figure out its meaning.

The Changing Farm

Farming has changed with the rest of the world. The simple image of a farmer in a field is outdated. Farming is a business, and <u>agribusiness</u> is a huge industry. It takes complicated equipment and larger and larger <u>acreages</u> to farm today.

The tools of farming have changed, too. Almost all farms today use computers to plan and keep records. The Internet is also important because farmers check markets, weather, and crop conditions <u>online</u>.

▲ Farming equipment is changing with the times.

Some tractor models include air-conditioned <u>operator stations</u>, self-steering ability, and a <u>global positioning</u> satellite system (GPS) to guide the machines.

Try It!

Read the passage. What do the underlined words mean? How do you know?

The Price of Change

Probably the biggest change in society in the last 25 years has been the growth of the personal computer. <u>PCs</u> were once not much more than toys. Now they help us do everything. <u>Networks</u> link computers to other computers and help people share information freely.

Technology can come with a price, though. All that information is stored on other computers. Anything you enter on a <u>search engine</u>, any <u>Web site</u> you visit on the Internet, or any <u>data</u> about you creates a record somewhere. If someone uses a computer to <u>hack</u> into a <u>database</u>, your personal information could be stolen. Although technology can solve problems, it also creates new ones.

Feeding the World

by Peter Winkler

Build Background

Connect

Quickwrite In your opinion, why is there hunger in the world? Do a Quickwrite about two possible causes of this problem.

Explore an Issue

Some people argue that we should use science to improve the foods people eat. Others say that such changes could be unsafe. People on both sides of the issue agree that world hunger is a problem. Now find out why they disagree about how to solve it.

Digital Library
InsideNG.com
◉ View the video.

▲ Is it helpful or harmful to make scientific changes to food?

Language & Grammar

ELPS: 2.E.1 use visual support to enhance and confirm understanding of complex and elaborated spoken language; 2.G.3 understand the general meaning of spoken language regarding familiar to unfamiliar contexts; 3.G.1 express opinions on a variety of social and grade-appropriate academic topics

1 **TRY OUT LANGUAGE**
2 **LEARN GRAMMAR**
3 **APPLY ON YOUR OWN**

Persuade

CD

Study the photo, and listen to the conversation. Listen to how one friend persuades another friend to volunteer. When you persuade someone, you convince that person to do something.

PICTURE PROMPT

Help End Hunger

Emilio: I can't help out today because I planned to see a movie.

Sarah: I think you should volunteer today instead. I volunteer because many people in our community do not have enough food to feed their families. We can help.

Emilio: That is a good reason.

Sarah: In fact, about 25,000 people in the *world* are in great danger every day because of hunger! It is very important that we give some of our time to do something.

Emilio: Well, you convinced me! I can see a movie anytime. I want to volunteer today, too. How can I help?

Sarah: We are collecting canned food for a food drive at school. You can help collect canned food.

Use Verbs in the Present, Past, and Future Tense

The tense, or time, of a **verb** shows when an action happens.

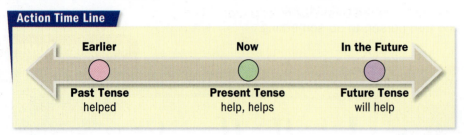

Action Time Line

Earlier	Now	In the Future
Past Tense	**Present Tense**	**Future Tense**
helped	help, helps	will help

- Use the **present tense** to tell about an action that happens now or often.

  EXAMPLE   Today, the volunteers **help** with food. *(happens now)*

  Use **-s** at the end of a verb that tells what one other person or thing does.

  EXAMPLE   My friend **helps** many people every day. *(happens often)*

- Use the **past tense** to tell about an action that already happened.

  EXAMPLES   Volunteers **helped** many people last year. They **gave** them food.

  Add **-ed** to show the past: **help + -ed = helped.** Or use the correct form of an irregular verb.

Present Tense	am, is	are	have, has	give, gives	feed, feeds	make, makes
Past Tense	was	were	had	gave	fed	made

- **Future tense** verbs tell about actions that haven't happened yet.

  EXAMPLES   Volunteers **will help** many people next year.
  They **will give** people food and clothing.

Practice Together

Say each sentence. Then say it again and change the <u>verb</u> to the past tense and the future tense. Say both new sentences.

1. Many people <u>need</u> food.

2. Many people <u>want</u> to volunteer.

3. They <u>collect</u> food for the hungry.

Try It!

Say each sentence. Write the past tense and the future tense of each <u>verb</u> on a card. Then say both new sentences.

4. My family <u>donates</u> canned food at the food drive.

5. The food <u>feeds</u> many people.

6. The people <u>are</u> thankful.

Feed the World

PERSUADE

World hunger is a serious problem. What is the best way to help feed the world?

Work with a group to write three ways to help feed the world. Use persuasive language to make your argument more convincing.

> **Proposition:** We should volunteer our time.
>
> **Support**
> 1. If we collect food, we can do our part to help people locally.
> 2.
> 3.

Present your proposition and support to another group. Then listen to their arguments. Make sure you understand each argument's general meaning. Which group was more persuasive? Why?

HOW TO PERSUADE

1. Tell your opinion, or proposition.

2. Give support for your opinion.

3. Use persuasive language and emotional words, or appeals.

> We should help feed the world. We can do our part by starting locally. We help many people when we collect food.

USE VERBS IN THE PRESENT, PAST, AND FUTURE TENSE

When you make persuasive arguments, you may need to change the tense of the verb to show when an action happens.

In the Present: Hunger **is** a problem in our world now.

In the Past: We **helped** many people last year.

In the Future: We **will do** something to help next year, too.

▲ People give food to help t...

557

Language &

Learn Key Vocabulary

Rate and Study the Words Rate how well you know each word. Then:

1. Pronounce the word. Say it aloud several times. Spell it.
2. Study the example.
3. Tell more about the word.
4. Practice it. Make the word your own.

Key Words

agricultural
(ag-ri-**kul**-chur-ul) *adjective* ▶ page 565

Something that is **agricultural** is related to farms or farming. Growing vegetables to sell as food is one kind of **agricultural** business.

gene (jēn) *noun*
▶ page 562

A **gene** is a physical unit that controls what a living cell is like. The color of your hair depends on your **genes**.
Related Word: **genetics**

mission (mish-un) *noun*
▶ page 564

ELPS 3.G.1

A **mission** is the goal of someone's work. An astronaut's **mission** is to explore space.
Synonyms: **aim, purpose**

modified (mod-u-fīd)
adjective ▶ page 563

5 Minute Chili Con Queso Dip
Ingredients:
1 can (15.5 ounces) chili with beans
2 bags 1 jar (15.5 ounces) processed cheese
1 bag of tortilla or corn chips
Directions:
In microwavable bowl, mix chili and cheese. Heat 2 or 3 minutes, or until cheese melts. Stir. Serve with chips.

Something that has been **modified** has been changed. We **modified** the recipe to feed more people.

technique (tek-**nēk**) *noun*
▶ page 563

Technique is a skilled way of doing something. My serving **technique** improved after taking tennis lessons.

technology (tek-**nol**-u-jē)
noun ▶ page 563

Technology is the use of knowledge to do a task or to improve how the task is done. Because of new **technology**, computers are faster and smaller than they once were.

viewpoint (vyü-point) *noun*
▶ page 563

...ewpoint is the way a person ...about things. My friends and ...different **viewpoints** about ...to go.

virus (vī-rus) *noun*
▶ page 562

A **virus** is a tiny particle that can cause disease in people, plants, and animals. My brother had a **virus** so he couldn't go to school.

Practice the Words Make a Study Card for each Key Word. Then compare your cards with a partner's.

agricultural

What it means: related to farming

Example: California has large areas of agricultural land.

Not an example: the beach

Study Card

...r Thought

Reading Strategy: Synthesize

When you read persuasive writing by more than one writer, evaluate each writer's argument. Then compare the evidence across texts.

**Reading Strategy
Synthesize**

HOW TO COMPARE ARGUMENTS AND EVIDENCE

1. Make a Comparison Chart. Record examples of effective evidence used by each writer.
2. Note what type of evidence it is. Is it a fact, a personal experience, or an expert opinion?
3. Express your own understanding of the issue based on your evaluation of both writers' arguments.

Strategy in Action

Here's how one student compared two arguments.

Look Into the Text

"Wambugu's **argument** is for genetically modified food."

Yes, new technology can help protect against hunger.

Florence Wambugu, *The Washington Post*

African growers. . .need better seeds and biotechnology. . . . Crop production is. . .the lowest in the world. . .

"Bloch's **argument** is against genetically modified food."

No, genetically modified food is a risky form of technology.

Michael Bloch, *Oak High School Gazette*

Genetically modified (GM) food is. . . harmful and risky. . . . A study. . .showed that 44% of caterpillars. . .died when fed large amounts of pollen. . .from GM corn. . . .

Comparison Chart

Should we use GM food to feed the world?

Wambugu	Type of Evidence	Bloch	Type of Evidence
Yes. Africa has the lowest crop production in the world.	Fact	No. Bugs died after eating GM pollen.	Fact

My understanding: Some countries can't grow enough food. GM food may help or put human health at risk.

Practice Together

When you read "Feeding the World," follow the steps in the How-To box. Evaluate the evidence each writer presents.

Persuasive Article

Writers of persuasive articles choose words and evidence that will get readers to agree with them about a position on an issue.

> **Yes, new technology can help protect against hunger.**
>
> . . . I learned firsthand about the enormous challenge of breaking the cycle of poverty and hunger in rural Africa. . . .
>
> African growers desperately need access to the best management practices . . .

Positive words show the writer's confidence.

The writer uses her personal experience.

Emotional language affects readers.

Your Job as a Reader

Reading Strategy: Synthesize

Note the types of evidence used in each writer's argument. Make a chart to help you evaluate each argument.

Should we use GM food to feed the world?

Wambugu	Type of Evidence	Bloch	Type of Evidence
Yes. She knows firsthand the cycle of poverty, hunger, and suffering.	Personal Experience		

My understanding: _____

Feeding the World

by Peter Winkler

Scientist Florence Wambugu wants to help farmers grow more food.

How much food do people need?

The average adult needs between 2,200 and 2,900 calories each day, and also requires a variety of vitamins, minerals, and other nutrients to stay healthy. For many people, having enough food to meet these requirements isn't a problem; for others it is.

Poverty, war, and poor farming practices are among the reasons that people go hungry. In some parts of the world there are millions of hungry people. According to the United Nations, Asia has the largest number of underfed people—about half a billion. Africa comes next with about 200,000,000 hungry people.

Scientists, politicians, and citizens around the world disagree about how to solve the problem of world hunger. Scientists have discovered new technology to create more food, but many people disagree that it's a good method. The one thing everyone agrees on is that no one in the world should have to go hungry.

The Need for Food

Scientist Florence Wambugu works with farmers in Kenya. Kenya is a country in East Africa. She helps farmers grow bigger and better crops. Wambugu is interested in finding simple ways to **raise** more food. In the past ten years, Wambugu has spent a lot of time studying sweet potatoes. Sweet potatoes are an important food in her part of Kenya. A **virus** kept attacking the plants. It stopped the sweet potatoes from growing properly. Some farmers, says Wambugu, lost three-quarters of their crops because of the virus.

Wambugu **went to war against** the virus. Her search for a **weapon that could** save the sweet potatoes led to a **laboratory** in St. Louis, Missouri. Scientists there are studying new ways to create better plants.

The lab's work focuses on genes. **Genes** are the chemical "computer programs" found

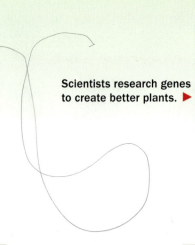

Scientists research genes to create better plants.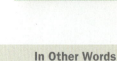

in the cells of living things. Genes tell a plant to produce pink flowers. Genes tell an animal to grow black hair. Now scientists move genes from one living thing to another. That process is called genetic engineering.

Wambugu spent three years at the lab. She created a sweet potato plant using the **techniques** of genetic engineering. This sweet potato plant could actually fight off the virus. Wambugu tested her research in Kenya. Her plants produced magnificent sweet potatoes.

Wambugu believes that's just the beginning. Genetically **modified** foods, she argues, could help farmers in poor countries grow desperately needed crops. "What farmers need," Wambugu says, "is **technology** that is **packaged in** the seed." She believes expensive chemicals and machines aren't needed. Further, she argues that by creating strong plants that farmers can raise simply, fewer people will go hungry.

Scientists disagree about genetically modified food and the question of how to feed the world is widely debated. Now read different **viewpoints**—one pro and one con—about this new technology.

▲ A worker checks genetically modified rice in Africa.

Key Vocabulary

technique *n.*, a skilled way of doing something

modified *adj.*, changed

technology *n.*, a process or invention based on scientific knowledge

viewpoint *n.*, a way of thinking about something

In Other Words
packaged in inside

Before You Move On

1. **Cause and Effect** Why did Wambugu spend three years working at a lab in St. Louis? What **techniques** did she learn?

2. **Problem and Solution** What does Wambugu think will help farmers in poor countries grow crops?

PRO

Supporters of genetic engineering argue that high-tech foods are a safe way to improve farming. They point to the fact that genetically modified corn and soybeans have been used in the United States since 1996 and say that no one has suffered as a result. Florence Wambugu supports this view on the issue in the following editorial.

▲ Biotechnology is used to create important crops in Ibaden, Nigeria. Scientists store the plants in test tubes to keep them strong and free of pests.

Is genetically modified food a good way to feed the world?

Yes, new technology can help protect against hunger.

Florence Wambugu, *The Washington Post*

I was one in a family of nine children growing up on a small farm in Kenya's **highlands**. I learned firsthand about the enormous challenge of **breaking the cycle of** poverty and hunger in rural Africa. In fact, the reason I became a plant scientist was to help farmers like my mother. My mother sold the only cow our family owned to pay for my secondary education. This was a **sacrifice** because I, like most children in Kenya, was needed on the farm.

I have since made it my **mission** to alert others to the urgent need for new technology in Africa. New technology can help protect against hunger, environmental damage, and poverty. African growers desperately need access to the best **management practices and fertilizer**. They need better seeds and biotechnology to help improve crop production. Crop production is currently the lowest in the world per unit area of land.

Key Vocabulary

mission *n.*, the goal of someone's work

In Other Words

highlands mountains
breaking the cycle of ending
sacrifice loss
management practices and fertilizer ways to plant the land and enrich the soil

Science Background

Biotechnology is a specific kind of science. Scientists who study biotechnology change the genetic materials of living organisms. They make different products, such as crops that cannot be damaged by pests.

ELPS 4.G.2

▲ A farmer plows a field in Kenya.

Traditional **agricultural** practices continue to produce only **low yields** and poor people. These practices will not be **sufficient** to feed the additional millions of people who will live on the continent fifty years from now. So the question becomes, why aren't these types of biotechnology applications more readily available to African farmers?

The priority of Africa must be to feed its people and to **sustain** agricultural production and the environment.

The people of Africa cannot wait for others to debate the **merits of** biotechnology. America and other developed nations must act now to **allocate** technologies that can prevent suffering and starvation.

Key Vocabulary
agricultural *adj.*, farming

In Other Words
low yields small amounts of food
sufficient enough
sustain support
merits of good and bad points about
allocate give other countries

Before You Move On

1. **Fact and Opinion** Find two facts and one opinion in Wambugu's article. Why do you think she includes her opinions?

2. **Summarize** According to Wambugu, why do African growers need new **technology**?

CON

Some scientists and other critics of genetic engineering argue that we do not know the effects of this technology. We do not know how mixing genes will affect plants and animals in the future. Michael Bloch supports this view in the following editorial.

▲ Activists unite in Greece to protest against genetically modified food.

Is genetically modified food a good way to feed the world?

No, genetically modified food is a risky form of technology.

Michael Bloch, *Oak High School Gazette*

Genetically modified (GM) food is not the best way to feed the world. In my opinion, genetically modified food is a harmful and risky form of technology.

I do not think we should genetically modify our food because it harms plant and animal life. GM plants can accidentally mix with wild plants. When this happens, superweeds, or giant weeds, grow. Farmers need to use stronger forms of **pesticide** to kill superweeds. Stronger pesticides are bad for other plants and for the air we breathe.

Animals are also affected by GM foods. Some GM corn crops are a major health risk to animals that eat them. A **study** done in the U.S. showed that 44% of caterpillars of the monarch butterfly died when fed large amounts of pollen, or powder, from GM corn.

We know that GM foods negatively affect plant and animal life. It is important to think

In Other Words
pesticide chemicals
study reseach project

Science Background
The **monarch butterfly** is a flying insect, with vivid orange and black markings, commonly found in North America. Caterpillars transform into adult butterflies in about two weeks.

about the risks GM foods pose to humans as well. Many experts caution against GM foods. Ronnie Cummins of the Organic Consumers Association warns, "We are rushing **headlong** into a new technology. **We are courting disaster if we don't look before we leap.**" Furthermore, Dr. Mae-Wan Ho, a geneticist and physicist, cautions that, "Genetic engineering is **inherently** dangerous."

Since nearly half the U.S. corn and soybean crops are now genetically modified, we must act now. We do not know the health effects of these foods. Until we do, it is in everyone's interest to find better ways of feeding the world.

▼ Protesters fight for labels on genetically modified foods.

In Other Words
headlong too fast
We are courting disaster if we don't look before we leap. We should think more about the risks of GM food.
inherently basically

Before You Move On

1. **Evaluating Sources** How do the experts quoted support Bloch's arguments?
2. **Compare and Contrast** How are Wambugu's and Bloch's calls to action similar and different?
3. **Opinion** What is your view on genetically **modified** food?

Market Women

by Daisy Myrie

Down from the hills, they come
With swinging hips and steady **stride**
To feed the hungry Town
They **stirred the steep dark land**
5 To place within the growing seed.
And in the rain and sunshine
Tended the young green plants,
They **bred, and dug and reaped.**
And now, as Heaven has blessed their **toil,**
10 They come, bearing the fruits,
These **hand-maids** of the Soil,
Who bring full baskets down,
To feed the hungry Town.

The Marketplace, 1988, Carlton Murrell. Oil on canvas, private collection.

▲ **Critical Viewing: Design** What details in the artwork remind you of details in the poem?

In Other Words
stride walk
stirred the steep dark farmed the
bred, and dug and reaped cared
   for the plants and harvested them
toil work
hand-maids women

Before You Move On
1. **Inference** Do the farmers in the poem care about the food they grow? How do you know?
2. **Mood** What is the feeling at the end of the poem?

Connect Reading and Writing

agricultural

genes

mission

modified

techniques

technology

viewpoint

viruses

CRITICAL THINKING

1. SUM IT UP Create a Comparison Chart to summarize each writer's **viewpoint** on **modified** food.

Comparison Chart

Should we use GM food to feed the world?			
Wambugu	**Type of Evidence**	**Bloch**	**Type of Evidence**
Viruses won't kill GM plants.	Fact	GM plants can create superweeds.	Fact

2. Interpret Why does Wambugu say, "Africa cannot wait for others to debate the merits of biotechnology?"

3. Infer Soybeans and corn have had **modified genes** since 1996. Why do you think Bloch says "We do not know the health effects of these foods"?

4. Compare Compare the feelings of the speaker in "Market Women" with each writer's **viewpoint** in "Feeding the World."

READING FLUENCY

Intonation Read the passage on page 655 to a partner. Assess your fluency.

1. I read
   a. great   **b.** OK   **c.** not very well

2. What I did best in my reading was _____ .

READING STRATEGY

Synthesize
How did synthesizing arguments and evidence help you understand the text? Discuss with a partner.

VOCABULARY REVIEW

Oral Review Read the paragraph aloud. Add the vocabulary words.

Modern _____ can protect crops from harmful _____ . For example, the _____ in the plant cells can be _____ in a lab. Some people who do _____ work say this is helpful. But other people look at the issue from a different _____ . Although people disagree on which _____ to use in growing food, everyone agrees that feeding the world is an important _____ .

Written Review Write a paragraph to describe **techniques** people might use to feed the world. Use five vocabulary words.

WRITE ABOUT THE **GUIDING QUESTION**

Explore Feeding the World
Which writer makes the stronger argument about the best way to feed the world? Support your **viewpoint** with examples from the selection.

Connect Across the Curriculum

Literary Analysis

Analyze Arguments in Persuasive Text

> **Academic Vocabulary**
> • **appeal** (a-pēl) *noun*
>   An **appeal** is a request for a response.

In persuasive nonfiction, writers use **arguments** to convince readers. An argument is a statement about the author's position, or viewpoint.

Types of Appeals An author uses different types of **appeals** to convince readers.

- **Appeal to Logic**: The argument makes sense. It is based on facts. Watch out for logical fallacies, which contain facts that are used incorrectly.
- **Appeal to Ethics**: The argument seems like the right way to behave or think. It's what most people would say is good or right.
- **Appeal to Emotions**: The argument makes you feel a certain way.
- **Multiple Appeals**: Often one argument has one or more appeals. This one is logical, ethical, and emotional:

> Since all children deserve good nutrition, a school meals program would insure that no child went hungry.

Practice Together

Analyze an Argument Work with your class to analyze this argument from the pro viewpoint in "Feeding the World" (page 564).

> Supporters of genetic engineering argue that high-tech foods are a safe way to improve farming. They point to the fact that genetically modified corn and soybeans have been used in the United States since 1996 and say that no one has suffered as a result.

1. Restate the argument.
2. What **appeals** does this argument use?

Reread the first paragraph of the con viewpoint on page 566. Restate the arguments and tell what **appeals** they use.

Try It!

Analyze More Arguments Reread "Feeding the World." Identify as many arguments as you can. Restate the arguments and tell what **appeals** they use. Do any of the arguments contain logical fallacies?

ELPS: 4.F.3 use visual and contextual support to develop vocabulary needed to comprehend increasingly challenging language

Vocabulary Study

Use Context Clues: Technical Vocabulary

Academic Vocabulary
- **technical** (tek-ni-kul) *adjective*
  Something that is **technical** is based on scientific knowledge.

Recognize Technical Terms **Technical** terms are words used in different ways for particular subjects. You can use context clues to help understand their meanings. Reread "The Need for Food" on pages 562–563. Answer the questions, using context clues to understand the term *genetic engineering*.

1. What is a gene?
2. What do genes do in living things?
3. What can scientists now do with genes?

Literary Analysis

Analyze Support in Persuasive Text

Academic Vocabulary
- **evidence** (e-vu-dents) *noun*
  Evidence can be beliefs, proof, facts, or details that help support a conclusion.

Persuasive arguments use **evidence** as **support** to convince the reader.

Facts	Dates, names of people and places, other things that can be proved
Statistics	Measurements, numbers, percentages
Quotations	Exact words from interviews or documents
Expert Opinions	Ideas from people who know a lot about the topic
Personal Experience	Details the author gives about his or her experience with the topic

The **argument** below uses a fact as **support**. The reader is meant to infer that because no one has suffered from genetically modified corn and soybeans, genetic engineering is not dangerous.

> Supporters of genetic engineering argue that high-tech foods are a safe way to improve farming. They point to the fact that genetically modified corn and soybeans have been used in the United States since 1996 and . . . no one has suffered . . . .

Identify and Evaluate Support Make a list of the arguments in "Feeding the World." Look for support for each. What logical inferences can you make?

ELPS: 2.C.4 learn academic vocabulary heard during classroom instruction and interactions

Literary Analysis

Identify Propaganda

Academic Vocabulary

•**propaganda** (prop-u-**gan**-da) *noun*
Propaganda is the use of faulty methods to persuade an audience.

What Is Propaganda? Writers use many techniques to persuade their readers. Some of these methods, however, are kinds of rhetorical fallacy. They may be unsupported by facts, not related to the issue, or simply not true. These methods are called **propaganda** .

The most common place you see **propaganda** is in advertising. Companies want to persuade you to buy. Here are some common types of **propaganda** :

Propaganda Type	Example
Glittering generality uses impressive words that may skip past the truth.	"Try the **new** and **improved** Sudso, a more **modern** way to clean your floors."
Transfers use appealing ideas or symbols to get your support, but the ideas are not actually related.	"Our candidate was **born in the shadow of the Statue of Liberty** and raised by **good parents.** She will make a **caring** and **patriotic** mayor."
Testimonials use famous people to try to persuade you.	"The **world's greatest soccer player** wears an Exacta watch off the field. You should, too."
Circular reasoning means to argue that something is true by simply restating what you're arguing about.	"**Everybody should buy** this product because this product is something **everybody should have.**"
Bandwagon appeals claim that everyone else is doing something, so you should, too.	"The Guzzler is the **number one selling SUV** in the country. It must be the best for you."
Name calling makes negative claims or attacks on a person or product.	"My opponent in this election is **just a rich city boy.** Who wants **that kind of person** for this office?"

Practice Together

Analyze Propaganda Look at the photo on page 567. Dr. Frankenstein was a character in a story who created a monster. The photo shows a person holding a sign that says "Dr. Frankenfood." What point is the person trying to make? What kind of **propaganda** is this?

Try It!

Find Propaganda Collect examples of **propaganda** from newspapers, magazines, radio, and television. Discuss whether they are effective. Explain.

Language and Grammar

Persuade

Group Debate Work in a group. Divide into two teams. Take turns debating the pros and cons of genetically modified food. Then take a class vote on whether it is good or bad. Use present tense, past tense, and future tense verbs in your arguments.

> I think genetically modified food will help solve the world's hunger problem.

> I think genetically modified food may be dangerous. We don't know the effects of eating some of these foods.

Writing and Grammar

ELPS: 5.D.3 edit writing for standard grammar and usage, including appropriate verb tenses

Write Effectively About Events

Study the Models When you write, make sure your readers can understand what you want to say. Choose verbs carefully to make it clear when events happen.

NOT OK

A virus **hurts** the sweet potato plants, and the plants **died**. Some farmers **lose** most of their crop because of the virus. Then scientists **studied** ways to grow better plants. They **focused** on genes and **create** a strong plant. The plants **produced** magnificent sweet potatoes.

> This writer confuses the reader by switching between what happened in the **past** and what is happening now in the **present**.

OK

A virus **hurt** the sweet potato plants, and the plants **died**. Some farmers **lost** most of their crop because of the virus. Then scientists **studied** ways to grow better plants. They **focused** on plant genes and **created** a strong plant. The plants **produced** magnificent sweet potatoes.

> This writer sticks to the **past**.

Add Sentences Think of two sentences to add to the OK model above. Be sure to use words correctly as you tell when events occur.

WRITE ON YOUR OWN Think about a time when you helped prepare a meal. Describe the events. Be careful to choose words that make it clear when the events happened.

REMEMBER

- **Present tense** verbs tell about actions that happen now or on a regular basis.
- **Past tense** verbs tell about an action that already happened.
- **Future tense** verbs tell about actions that haven't happened yet.

Soup for the Soul

by Kristin Donnelly

SELECTION 2 OVERVIEW ELPS 3.J.1

▶ **Build Background**

▶ **Language & Grammar**
Negotiate
Use Verbs in the Present Perfect Tense

▶ **Prepare to Read**
Learn Key Vocabulary
Learn a Reading Strategy
Synthesize

▶ **Read and Write**
Focus on Genre
Interview
Apply the Reading Strategy
Synthesize
Critical Thinking
Reading Fluency
Read with Phrasing
Vocabulary Review
Write About the Guiding Question

▶ **Connect Across the Curriculum**

Literary Analysis
Analyze Persuasive Language

Vocabulary Study
Use Context Clues: Jargon

Listening/Speaking
Analyze Food Commercials
Deliver a Persuasive Speech

Language and Grammar
Negotiate

Writing and Grammar
Write About Helping Others

Build Background

Providing for the Community

Mary Ellen Diaz decided to cook delicious, healthy food for the homeless.

Digital Library
InsideNG.com
◉ View the video.

▲ Everyone needs to eat healthy foods.

Connect

Anticipation Guide Tell whether you agree or disagree with these statements.

Anticipation Guide

	Agree	Disagree
1. One person can't help feed a community.	_____	_____
2. It doesn't matter to hungry people what they eat.	_____	_____
3. Sharing good meals can change people's lives.	_____	_____

Language & Grammar

ELPS: 2.C.2 learn new expressions heard during classroom instruction and interactions; 2.E.1 use visual support to enhance and confirm understanding of complex and elaborated spoken language; 2.E.2 use contextual support to enhance and confirm understanding of complex and elaborated spoken language; 2.E.3 use linguistic support to enhance and confirm understanding of complex and elaborated spoken language; 2.G.5 understand the main points of spoken language regarding familiar to unfamiliar language

1 TRY OUT LANGUAGE
2 LEARN GRAMMAR
3 APPLY ON YOUR OWN

Negotiate CD

Study the photo and think about the context. Listen to the conversation as a teenager negotiates with her parents. When people negotiate, they try to reach an agreement with each other.

PICTURE PROMPT

Work for Change

Alexis: Mom, Mrs. Park needs a babysitter so she can volunteer at the soup kitchen. You know Mrs. Park. She lives on the corner. She has a little girl and needs a sitter on Tuesdays after school and on Saturday mornings. Babysitting would be a great job for me.

Mother: Yes, babysitting can be good experience, Alexis, but it is also hard work and a big responsibility. I don't think it's a good idea because you won't have time for your homework.

Alexis: I understand what you're saying, Mom, but I really want this job. I can do my homework in study hall.

Father: I have an idea. How about if you babysit just on Saturday morning? If you help Mrs. Park one morning a week, it will give you valuable experience and leave enough time for homework, chores, and other activities.

Alexis: That sounds like a great idea, Dad. I'll get experience and make a little spending money, and I won't have a conflict with school work.

Use Verbs in the Present Perfect Tense

- If you know when an action happened in the past, use a **past tense** verb.

    EXAMPLE   I **helped** last week.

- If you're not sure when a past action happened, use a **verb** in the **present perfect tense** .

    EXAMPLE   Volunteers **have helped** people in the past.

- You can also use the present perfect tense to show that an action began in the past and may still be happening now.

    EXAMPLES   Mrs. Park and other volunteers **have served** many meals to the homeless. (And they are probably still serving meals.)

    Mrs. Park **has served** meals at the soup kitchen every Saturday. (And she is probably still serving meals on Saturdays.)

- To form the present perfect, use the helping verb **have** or **has** plus the **past participle** of the main verb. For regular verbs, the past participle ends in -**ed**.

Verb	Past Tense	Past Participle
help	helped	helped
serve	served	served
try	tried	tried

Practice Together

Say each sentence. Choose the correct form of the verb.

1. Last year, Mr. Lopez (opened/has opened) a soup kitchen.
2. He (tried/has tried) opening a soup kitchen in our neighborhood for a long time.
3. People in the community (wanted/have wanted) to help the homeless for a while.

Try It!

Say each sentence. Write the correct form of the verb on a card. Then say the sentence with the correct verb.

4. Many teens (babysat/have babysat) at neighbors' homes before.
5. Alexis (agreed/has agreed) to babysit one day a week.
6. She always (enjoyed/has enjoyed) the chance to help others.

▲ The chef has cooked many meals at the soup kitchen.

Reach an Agreement

NEGOTIATE

People negotiate when they try to reach an agreement with each other. When they negotiate, they often compromise, or agree to a type of change.

Work with a partner to role-play a teen and his or her parent negotiating one of these issues: getting an after-school job, an increase in allowance, or extending a weekend curfew. Use calm and polite language when you negotiate.

Polite Words and Phrases		
please	I understand	let's try
may I	I guess	how about if we
can I	could you	why don't we

One important word in negotiations is *but*. When you use it, it means there is a certain condition to remember.

EXAMPLE   You can get an allowance, but you must earn it.

Negotiate an issue with your partner, then act out your negotiation in front of a small group. Talk about the compromise that you reached. Identify strengths and weaknesses in the negotiation. Then listen to another pair negotiate.

HOW TO NEGOTIATE

1. State the issue and your opinion in a calm and polite way.
2. Listen respectfully to other's main points. Restate what you heard.
3. Calmly state your side.
4. Make a compromise.

> I really want to buy that hat. Can I babysit to earn money?

> You can babysit, but only on the weekend.

USE VERBS IN THE PRESENT PERFECT TENSE

When you negotiate, you may tell about an action that started in the past and is still going on. If so, use the **present perfect tense** when you talk about these actions.

EXAMPLES   I **have wanted** to babysit for a long time.

I **have planned** to work on the weekend for a while.

Prepare to Read

ELPS: 3.A practice producing sounds of newly acquired vocabulary in a manner that is comprehensible; 5.A learn relationships between sounds and letters to represent sounds when writing in English

Learn Key Vocabulary

Rate and Study the Words Rate how well you know each word. Then:

1. Pronounce the word. Say it aloud several times. Spell it. Write it.
2. Study the example.
3. Tell more about the word.
4. Practice it. Make the word your own.

Rating Scale

1 = I have never seen this word before.

2 = I am not sure of the word's meaning.

3 = I know this word and can teach the word's meaning to someone else.

Key Words

benefit (ben-e-fit) *noun*
▶ page 586

A **benefit** is something that is good for people, places, or things. One **benefit** of exercise is that it makes you strong.
Antonyms: **damage, hurt**

career (ku-rear) *noun*
▶ page 583

A **career** is a job that someone does for a long time. For 20 years, my aunt has had a **career** as a doctor.
Synonyms: **job, work**

donate (dō-nāt) *verb*
▶ page 585

To **donate** means to give to people in need. I always try to **donate** some of my spending money to help others.
Related Word: **donation**

founder (fown-der) *noun*
▶ page 582

A **founder** is a person who starts something. My uncle is the **founder** of his own company.

ingredient (in-grē-dē-unt) *noun* ▶ page 582

An **ingredient** is something that is part of a mixture. These **ingredients** are used to make cookies.
Synonyms: **part, piece**

inspiration (in-spu-rā-shun) *noun* ▶ page 583

An **inspiration** is a reason for doing or creating something. Artists often find their **inspiration** in the beauty of nature.

organic (or-gan-ik) *adjective*
▶ page 582

Organic refers to a type of food that is all natural. **Organic** fruits and vegetables are grown without chemicals.

organization (or-gu-nu-zā-shun) *noun* ▶ page 582

An **organization** is a group of people who work toward a common goal. The Red Cross is an **organization**.
Related Word: **organize**

Practice the Words Make an Example Web for each Key Word. Then compare your webs with a partner's.

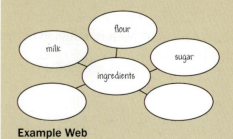

flour

milk

sugar

ingredients

Example Web

Reading Strategy: Synthesize

When you draw conclusions, you develop judgments, or opinions, about the author's message. When you synthesize, you put together these conclusions and other ideas to form a new overall understanding.

Reading Strategy
Synthesize

HOW TO DRAW CONCLUSIONS

1. Look for several facts or details the author provides about the topic.

2. Use logic and what you already know to form a judgment that makes sense.

3. As you continue reading, check to see if additional details cause you to rethink your conclusions.

Strategy in Action

Here's how one student drew conclusions as she read.

Look Into the Text

Diaz is the founder of an innovative Chicago soup kitchen called First Slice. "This organization gives the first slice to people who rarely get anything special." A former chef at Chicago's acclaimed North Pond restaurant, Diaz feeds 400 homeless people each week, preparing delicious meals with fresh, locally grown, mostly organic ingredients.

"A chef at a well-known restaurant makes special dishes."

"That's a lot of people in need of food."

Practice Together

Read the passage and follow the steps in the How-To box. Draw a conclusion of your own, based on what you have read.

Evidence in the Text	What I Already Know	My Conclusion
Diaz is a skilled chef who feeds the homeless.	It takes money and effort to cook for so many people.	Diaz cares about people, not about being famous or rich.

Focus on Genre

Interview

An interview is a type of writing in which one person questions someone else about a topic. The **interviewer** asks questions, and the **interviewee** responds with answers.

A printed interview is a series of questions and answers. As you read, try to "hear" two voices asking and answering.

Q: What's the biggest lesson you've learned since starting First Slice?

Q is for Questions the interviewer asks.

A: The smallest things can help change somebody's life. Saying hello to a homeless person instead of looking away.

A is for Answers the interviewee gives.

Your Job as a Reader

Reading Strategy: Synthesize

As you read, notice the details. Use what you already know to draw conclusions about them. Then use your conclusions to form a new understanding of the text.

Evidence in the Text	What I Already Know	My Conclusion
"The smallest things can change someone's life."	Homelessness is a big problem that some people say can't be solved.	Diaz shows that every effort does help.

Chef Mary Ellen Diaz prepares food in the First Slice kitchen. ▶

Soup for the Soul

by Kristin Donnelly

Mary Ellen Diaz's food is good enough for Chicago's best restaurants. Instead, she gives meals away to people in need.

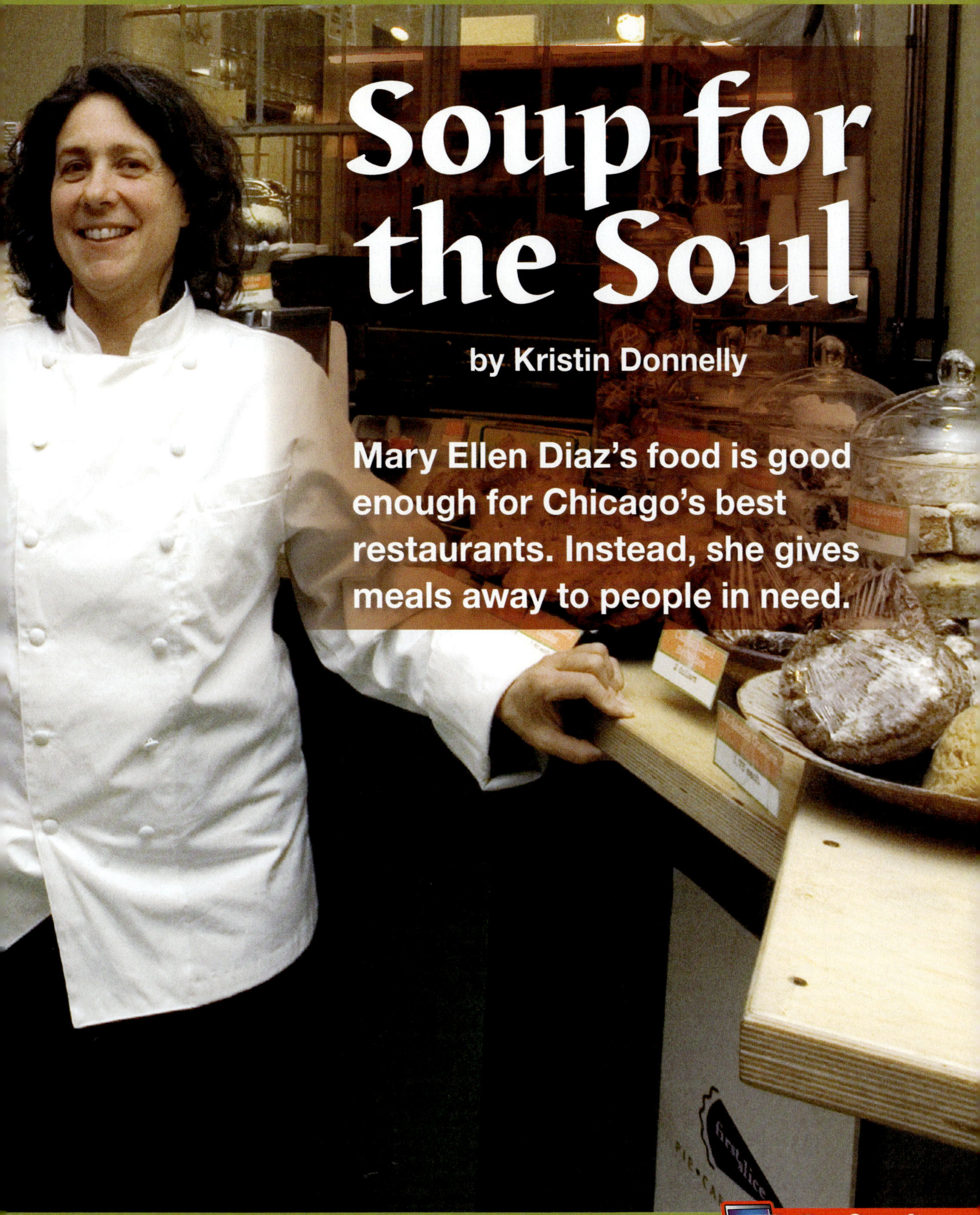

Online Coach

▲ Mary Ellen Diaz uses her skills as a chef to help people.

"Pie is a symbol of community, and giving the first slice is like giving the best," says Mary Ellen Diaz.

Diaz is the **founder** of **an innovative** Chicago soup kitchen called First Slice. "This **organization** gives the first slice to people who rarely get anything special." A former chef at Chicago's **acclaimed** North Pond restaurant, Diaz feeds 400 homeless people each week, preparing delicious meals with fresh, locally grown, mostly **organic ingredients** —dishes like butternut squash soup or spicy multigrain-vegetable soup.

First Slice soup kitchen is successful partly because of generous people who work as volunteers, donate money, or become customers. Diaz opened a restaurant called First Slice Pie Café. It serves a seasonal menu including **made-from-scratch** pies. Diaz also started a program that allows busy families to help the hungry. At the same time, they are making their own schedule a little bit easier. Families may sign up to receive three gourmet meals a week. Every meal is nourishing, balanced, and prepared from local organic ingredients. Profits from both the private chef service and the café go toward the soup kitchen.

Key Vocabulary

founder *n.*, a person who forms an organization or group
organization *n.*, a group of people working toward a common goal
organic *adj.*, naturally grown
ingredient *n.*, a part of a mixture

In Other Words

an innovative a new and creative
acclaimed award-winning, famous
made-from-scratch fresh, homemade

Q: What inspired you to leave your job as a chef and launch First Slice?

A: I had a great restaurant **career**, but I felt like I had to make a choice about whether or not to stay. I wanted to be home at night reading books to my little girl instead of **slaving away** in the kitchen. I was also reading a lot about Jane Addams. She ran her own community kitchen that served food to people living on the street. She also helped women who were trying to **enter the workforce**. Jane Addams is still very much the **inspiration** for First Slice. I also started volunteering in soup kitchens, and I realized feeding forty to fifty people takes talent. I never thought of using my skills that way until then.

Q: What kind of food do you cook at First Slice?

A: Last year we made a lot of Cajun food to feed **displaced victims** of Hurricane Katrina. We also get a lot of requests for food with Latin flavors, dishes that might use tortillas. Smothered pork chops are really popular. A pot of greens is definitely a big thing, because most people on the street don't have access to farm-fresh produce. It's interesting: A lot of **our clientele** grew up in rural communities, and they know more about growing fruit and vegetables than I do. They ask really specific questions about the soil and the farming methods. It's wonderful that we can make that fresh-from-the-farm connection.

▲ A student volunteer helps prepare a meal at First Slice.

Key Vocabulary

career *n.*, a job that you do for a long time

inspiration *n.*, reason for doing something

In Other Words

slaving away working too much
enter the workforce get jobs
displaced victims the people who had to leave their homes because
our clientele the people we cook for

Before You Move On

1. **Problem and Solution** How does Diaz's **organization** help feed the homeless?

2. **Cause and Effect** What **inspired** Diaz to start First Slice?

3. **Recall and Interpret** Think about the food served at First Slice. What is important to Diaz? Explain.

Q: *Where do most of your ingredients come from?*

A: I use a lot of the same local suppliers that I did when I was a restaurant chef. The farmers I work with are community-based and **a bit quirky and anti-establishment**, like me.

Q: *Is soup a big part of your program?*

A: Definitely. In the fall and winter we serve soup on a street corner every Tuesday night to homeless youth. We probably have thirty different recipes. We hide a lot of vegetables in our soups—I **play the same game** with the kids on the streets that I do with my own two kids. They might think they're eating just cheddar cheese soup but it's been thickened with vegetables like butternut squash.

Q: *What's the biggest lesson you've learned since starting First Slice?*

A: The smallest things can help change somebody's life. Saying hello to a homeless person instead of looking away. Or cooking something really simple and giving it to a homeless person so she feels good.

Q: *How do you work with volunteers?*

A: There's a food writer who comes in four hours a week and all she does is roll pie dough for us. She just loves pie dough. We serve a lot of pie, and making pie dough is really **therapeutic**. There's a man who comes in and just wants to chop onions. He recently applied for a job at a new **gourmet** store. He didn't get it, but I was thrilled that chopping onions gave him the confidence to start looking for a job; he's been out of work for so many years.

In Other Words

a bit quirky and anti-establishment like to do things differently
play the same game do the same thing
therapeutic relaxing
gourmet high-quality food

Q: *What's the best way for people to help feed the homeless?*

A: Make a connection with a **food pantry** and find a way to **donate** nutritious food. Fresh fruit and vegetables are always appreciated. Canned beans are always great to have around. Rice, dried grains, canned tomatoes and jarred salsa are also good to have. I have issues with the fact that the first thing I see in most food pantries are overstarched, oversugared things. Homeless people need nutritious food as much as anyone, even more.

Q: *What do you eat to stay healthy?*

A: A lot of salads, like one with carrots from the farm, radishes, organic greens, blue cheese, spiced pecans and pepitas [pumpkin seeds]—with bacon on the side.

Q: *How do you find balance in your life between work and family?*

▲ Mary Ellen Diaz encourages students of all ages to get involved with feeding the world.

A: What's neat is that I can bring my kids to anything we do at First Slice; they love what I do and they love to come with me. The people **get a kick out of** them, and **vice versa**. My daughter mentioned to me this morning that when it's her birthday, she is going to have a party and ask people to bring her a toy that she can donate to kids in need. How great is that? ❖

Key Vocabulary
donate *v.*, to give something to a person in need

In Other Words
food pantry place that collects food for the homeless
get a kick out of enjoy
vice versa they enjoy the people

Before You Move On
1. **Explain** Who else does Diaz help besides the homeless?
2. **Personal Connection** Do you volunteer in your community? Explain.

Would it be fun to run a restaurant?

Running a restaurant is a lot of fun.

YES!

Wouldn't it be great to have a job that you really like? My aunt does. She runs a restaurant.

I think working in a restaurant is a lot of fun. For **one thing**, you get to be creative. According to the National Restaurant Association, culinary creativity plays a key role in the restaurant business. When I help out my aunt in her restaurant, we create many recipes for each night's menu. The menu creativity and effort inspires restaurant employees and makes customers feel special.

A second **benefit** of running a restaurant is that you get to make other people happy. According to the National Restaurant Association, four out of five people think going out to a restaurant is a better use of their time than cooking and cleaning up. I know that my aunt feels good about making the quality of people's lives better.

Finally, the most important reason that running a restaurant is an enjoyable job is because you get to be a part of the community. My aunt is involved in many community groups and a lot of meetings are held at her restaurant. The restaurant is a great space to relax and **socialize**.

If you want a great job, I urge you to consider working in a restaurant. You can develop important skills, be creative, and meet many different people.

Key Vocabulary
benefit *n.*, positive result, advantage

In Other Words
one thing example
socialize talk with other people

Would it be fun to run a restaurant?

Running a restaurant is no fun.

Do you want to feel stress and pressure every day at your job? Of course not! If you don't want a stressful job, you probably should not work in a restaurant.

Running a restaurant can be a very tiring job because it is so much work. My cousin, Steve, is the manager of a large restaurant. Steve often has to work up to fourteen hours per day! A recent article in the *San Francisco Chronicle* supports Steve's experience by stating that, "restaurants **are among the most labor-intensive of businesses**." Furthermore, having this much responsibility at work means you don't have much free time to do the other things you like to do.

Another problem with running a restaurant is the possibility of losing your job. Everyone knows that the restaurant business is very risky. According to a study by Cornell University and Michigan State, a quarter of all new restaurants in the U.S. go out of business in the first year. That number rises to 50 percent after three years and 70 percent after ten years. That risk puts pressure and stress on workers who may have to worry about losing their jobs.

For all these reasons, I strongly believe that running a restaurant is not much fun. If you want to enjoy your free time, avoid stress, and have greater security, you may want to consider another job.

In Other Words

are among the most labor-intensive of businesses require a lot of hard work

Before You Move On

1. **Compare and Contrast** What are the **benefits** of and problems with running a restaurant?
2. **Opinion** Do you think it would be fun to run a restaurant? Explain.

Holding Up the Sky

a tale from China

One day an elephant saw a hummingbird lying on the ground with its tiny feet up in the air. "Why are you doing that?" the elephant asked.

"I heard that the sky might fall today," the hummingbird replied. "I am going to help hold it up."

The mighty elephant made fun of the little bird. "Do you think," he **sneered**, "that those tiny feet could hold up the sky?"

The hummingbird kept his feet up in the air as he replied, "Not alone. But everyone must do whatever he can. And this is what I can do."

Science Background
Hummingbirds are very small birds found in North and South America. They are named for the hum, or sound, that their wings make when they move.

In Other Words
sneered said meanly

Before You Move On

1. **Conclusions** What is the implicit message of this folk tale?
2. **Compare** How are the actions of the hummingbird and Mary Ellen Diaz similar?

Connect Reading and Writing

Vocabulary
benefits
career
donate
founder
ingredients
inspiration
organic
organization

CRITICAL THINKING

1. **SUM IT UP** Work with a partner to role-play an interview with Diaz. Ask about her **career** and her **organization** .

Ms. Diaz, what is First Slice?

It is an organic soup kitchen.

2. **Analyze** Review the Anticipation Guide on page 574. Do you have new ideas? With a group, discuss the **benefits** of an **organization** like First Slice.

3. **Draw Conclusions** Why does Diaz put so much thought into choosing **ingredients**? Support your conclusion with evidence from the text.

4. **Speculate** If Diaz read the essays and the poem, which might give her **inspiration**? Explain.

READING FLUENCY

Phrasing Read the passage on page 656 to a partner. Assess your fluency.

1. I read
   a. great   **b.** OK   **c.** not very well

2. What I did best in my reading was _____ .

READING STRATEGY

Synthesize
Show a partner how you drew conclusions from the text.

VOCABULARY REVIEW

Oral Review Read the paragraph aloud. Add the vocabulary words.

One way to help your community is to support an _____ that feeds the hungry. Meet with the _____ who started it, or share ideas with other members. For example, you could cook, buy, or even grow _____ vegetables and other healthy _____ . If you have a busy job or _____ , you can _____ money instead. The _____ of helping include new friendships, as well as more hope and _____ for everyone.

Written Review Imagine you had an **organic** garden. Write a diary entry to tell how you would use it to provide food for your community. Use five vocabulary words.

WRITE ABOUT THE GUIDING QUESTION

Explore Feeding Our Communities
What advice would you give to the **founder** of an **organization** to feed people in need? Use examples from the selections to support your advice.

Connect Across the Curriculum

ELPS: 2.C.4 learn academic vocabulary heard during classroom instruction and interactions

Literary Analysis

Analyze Persuasive Language

> **Academic Vocabulary**
> ● **appeal** (a-**pēl**) *noun*
>   An **appeal** is a request for a response.

How Does Language Persuade? As you read persuasive writing, you may find that some **appeals** are more persuasive than others.

- **Details** Good writers use details to make **appeals** easier to understand. The writers of both of these sentences want you to save water:

> A. Leaking faucets waste lots of water.
> B. That little drip, drip, drip sends hundreds of gallons down the drain.

Specific details bring the second sentence to life.

- **Word Choice** Choosing the right words can make a difference:

> A. Our school is too warm. We are hot in our classroom.
> B. Our school is overheated. We roast in our classroom.
> C. Our school is sweltering. We are all going to suffer heat exhaustion.

Which sentence is the most persuasive? Different words have shades of meaning that can strengthen or weaken an argument. However, sometimes writers use words that are too strong for the situation. This is a type of rhetorical fallacy that is meant to evoke strong emotions from the reader without providing solid evidence.

Practice Together

Improve Sentences Work with a partner. Suggest ways to improve each of the following sentences from "Soup for the Soul."

1. *Provide Details*: "For one thing, you get to be creative."
2. *Word Choice*: "I know that my aunt feels good about making the quality of people's lives better."

Try It!

Strengthen Writing Revise these sentences to make them more persuasive.

3. *Word Choice*: "I think working in a restaurant is a lot of fun."
4. *Provide Details*: "The restaurant is a great space to relax and socialize."

ELPS: 4.F.3 use visual and contextual support to develop vocabulary needed to comprehend increasingly challenging language

Vocabulary Study

Use Context Clues: Jargon

Academic Vocabulary
- **technical** (tek-ni-kal) *adjective*
  Something that is **technical** is based on scientific knowledge.

I just got three four-tops down.

> The server is saying that three tables of four people just sat down.

Do you know what this sentence means? It is an example of **jargon**, a special language that is part of a particular setting. Jargon may consist of **technical** terms or slang.

Use Context Clues Read each sentence. Discuss with a partner how context helps you understand each term.

1. Rather than just buying desserts for First Slice, Diaz spends hours preparing <u>made-from-scratch</u> pies.
2. Many homeless people would have a hard time feeding themselves if they could not get supplies that are donated to local <u>food pantries</u>.

Listening/Speaking

Analyze Food Commercials

MEDIA & TECHNOLOGY

ELPS: 2.F.1 listen to and derive meaning from a variety of media to build and reinforce concept attainment; 2.F.2 listen to and derive meaning from a variety of media to build and reinforce language attainment; 2.G.3 understand the general meaning of spoken language regarding familiar to unfamiliar contexts

Academic Vocabulary
- **media** (mē-dē-u) *noun*
  Television, radio, newspapers, magazines, and the Internet make up the **media**.

Advertising is a form of persuasion. You can analyze **media** persuasion the same way you analyze persuasive writing.

1 **Analyze Media** Make a chart to analyze the persuasive elements in ads. At home or at the library, look online for videos of food commercials. Listen for words that encourage you to buy a product or believe a message, to build your understanding of the concept of persuasion.

Commercial or Ad	Sounds and Images	Appeals	Persuasive Language	Propaganda	Evidence
Jo's Pizza	pizza slices, happy customers	"Aren't you hungry?"	"finest cheeses"	"Everyone loves Jo's Pizza"	"voted #1 five years running"

2 **Discuss Media Persuasion** As a group, discuss what you discover about food advertising. Take a vote: Which are the most effective ads? Why?

Listening/Speaking

Deliver a Persuasive Speech

SOCIAL SCIENCE

ELPS: 2.6.3 understand the general meaning of spoken language regarding familiar to unfamiliar contexts

> **Academic Vocabulary**
> ● **position** (pu-zi-shun) *noun*
>   A **position** is a viewpoint, side, or placement.

1 **Pick a Position** Reread the persuasive essays about running a restaurant (pages 586–587). Now think about a job you would be great at. Write a **position** statement on a notecard.

> Position Statement
> I would be a great filmmaker.

2 **Gather Evidence** What if you had to persuade someone to give you this job? What is the main reason you would be great at it? What evidence, or proof, could you give that would support your **position**? Remember that evidence such as facts, statistics, quotations, and expert opinions are very persuasive. Add some notes about evidence to your notecard. You can also tell a story to help support your position.

> Position Statement
> I would be a great filmmaker.
> * I know how to use a video camera already.
> * I made four short films last year.
> *My best friend's mother teaches a film class. She once said, "Your films are really creative."

3 **Give Your Presentation** Use this checklist to help you.

> **✔** **Speaking Skill**
> ☐ Stand up straight. Show interest in your topic.
> ☐ Make eye contact with your audience.
> ☐ Speak slowly and clearly. Don't rush. Speak loudly enough to be heard.
> ☐ Introduce your topic clearly at the beginning.
> ☐ Speak with expression. Let your voice rise and fall with the flow of ideas.
> ☐ Use words like "first," "also," and "in addition" to make points of support clear.
> ☐ Use gestures and body motions where you can.
> ☐ Conclude by restating your position and the support.

4 **Listen to Others** Take notes to help you identify your classmates' **positions** and points of support as they present. Show respect for their opinions and their efforts. Use the rubric to evaluate the delivery of the presentation and interpret the speaker's purpose.

Language and Grammar

Negotiate

Role-Play With a group, act out a negotiation between volunteers at a soup kitchen and local farmers. Listen to the other group members to be sure you understand the main points of their opinions. Use present perfect tense verbs.

> We have needed more vegetables for some time now.

> We have given you extra corn for over a month.

Writing and Grammar

Write About Helping Others

Study the Models When you write, make sure your readers can follow the action without confusion. Use the correct verbs depending on when the action happens.

NOT OK

> Raul has wanted to help people for a long time, so he **has volunteered** at a shelter last week. Yesterday, he **has learned** that this shelter **has opened** its doors five years ago. Hundreds of people **received** hot meals since the shelter opened. The director of the shelter has served food to anyone in need. She has donated her time and talents to those less fortunate.

> **This writer uses the present perfect to tell about an action that happened last week. The reader is confused.**

OK

> Raul has wanted to help people for a long time, so he **volunteered** at a shelter last week. Yesterday, he **learned** that this shelter **opened** its doors five years ago. Hundreds of people **have received** hot meals since the shelter opened. The director of the shelter has served food to anyone in need. She has donated her time and talents to those less fortunate.

> **This writer makes it easier to follow the action.**

Add Sentences Think of two sentences to add to the OK model above. Be sure to make it clear whether the action already happened or may still be going on.

WRITE ON YOUR OWN Write a personal narrative about something you have done in the past to help someone. Tell why you did it. Be sure to use words correctly to show when action happens.

REMEMBER
- Use the **past tense** if you know when a past action happened.
- Use the **present perfect tense** to tell about a past action that may still be going on now.

THE GIRL AND THE CHENOO

by **Joseph Bruchac**

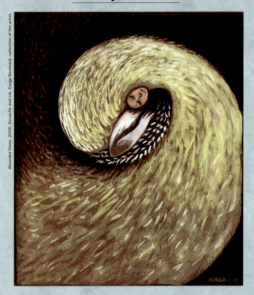

Wounded Sleep, 2006, Gouache and ink. Durga Bernhard, collection of the artist

Build Background

Learn About the Abenaki

"The Girl and the Chenoo" is a Native American play in the Abenaki tradition. It takes place in the northeast of what is now the United States. The Chenoo is a legendary monster who appears in the stories of many Native American cultures.

Connect

Brainstorm and Role-Play How does food connect people? With a group, brainstorm ways that people have found, prepared, and shared food throughout time. Choose one idea to role-play for the class.

Digital Library

InsideNG.com
➔ View the images.

▲ Abenaki people today

ELPS: 1.G.2 demonstrate knowledge of when to use formal and informal English; 2.C.1 learn new language structures heard during classroom instruction and interactions; 3.I.1 adapt spoken language appropriately for formal purposes; 3.I.2 adapt spoken language appropriately for informal purposes

1 **TRY OUT LANGUAGE**
2 **LEARN GRAMMAR**
3 **APPLY ON YOUR OWN**

Use Appropriate Language

CD

Listen to the two raps. Then listen again and chime in. How do the words in each rap fit with the place and the occasion?

RAP

Dinner at a Fancy Restaurant

Good evening.
Welcome to the *Tropical Bay*.
My name is Robert,
And I'll be your server today.
I'll leave while you look at the menu,
But first allow me to say,
We have some very nice specials,
Which I'll tell you about if I may.

Pizza Lunch

Hi! What can I get you?
Do you need more time to decide?
OK, I hear you.
One pepperoni pizza
With a salad on the side.
Right! One pizza coming up!
It'll be ready in a little bit.
In the meantime, while you are waiting,
Why don't you just sit?

1 TRY OUT LANGUAGE
2 LEARN GRAMMAR
3 APPLY ON YOUR OWN

Use Verbs in the Past Perfect Tense

The **past perfect tense** of a verb shows that one action in the past happened before another past action.

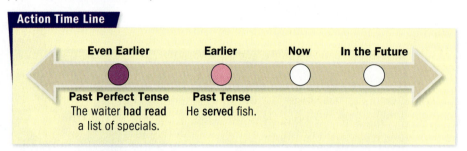

Action Time Line

Even Earlier   Earlier   Now   In the Future

Past Perfect Tense
The waiter **had read** a list of specials.

Past Tense
He served fish.

- Use the **past tense** of a verb to tell about an action that was completed in the past.

    EXAMPLE Yesterday, the waiter **served** fish.

- If you want to show that one past action happened before another, use the **past perfect tense** for the action that happened first.

    EXAMPLE The waiter **had read** the specials before he **served** the fish.

- To form the past perfect tense, use **had** plus the **past participle** of the main verb.

    EXAMPLES The waiter **had served** the salad before he served the main dish.
    The waiter **had read** the specials before he took the order.

Practice Together

Change the verb in the box to the past perfect tense. Say it. Then say the sentence and add the past perfect tense verb.

1. | read | Before he took the order, the waiter _____ the specials.

2. | order | The people _____ their salads first.

3. | hear | After they _____ the specials, the diners decided what to order.

▲ The waiters had set the tables before the diners arrived.

Try It!

Change the verb in the box to the past perfect tense. Write the past perfect tense verb on a card. Then say the sentence and add the past perfect tense verb.

4. | set | Before we arrived, the waiters _____ the tables.

5. | see | The waiters placed extra napkins on the table because they _____ the soup bowls were full.

6. | agree | Before dinner was over, the diners _____ that the restaurant was excellent.

Place an Order

USE APPROPRIATE LANGUAGE

Our body language and the language, tone, and volume of our voices all change depending on the social situation. For example, formal language is appropriate to use in presentations, interviews, and other formal or academic settings. Informal, or relaxed, language is appropriate to use when talking with friends and family.

With a partner, role-play how you would order from a waiter at a fancy restaurant. Then role-play how you would order from a neighbor who works at a casual restaurant. Use verb tenses correctly. Trade roles.

Language Type	Formal	Informal
Body Language	make eye contact, stand or sit up straight	relaxed
Tone	serious	relaxed
Volume	loud, clear	varies with the situation (can range from a whisper to a shout)
Example	I would like to order the steak, please.	How's it going? I'll have a slice of pepperoni, please.

Have other students listen to your role-play and note what they think is appropriate in each situation, such as the words you use or the tone of your voice.

HOW TO USE APPROPRIATE LANGUAGE

1. Use words that match the audience and the occasion.
2. Use appropriate tone, volume, and body language.

> Formal:
> I'd like to order a salad, please.

> Informal:
> Hey, Miguel, can I get a slice of cheese pizza?

USE VERBS IN THE PAST PERFECT TENSE

If you are speaking about actions that have already happened, you may want to show that one past action happened before another. You can use the past perfect tense for the action that happened first.

EXAMPLES   After I **had ordered** a slice of pizza, I **bought** a can of soda pop.

After I **had talked** to Miguel, I **ate** my pizza.

Prepare to Read

ELPS: 3.A practice producing sounds of newly acquired vocabulary in a manner that is comprehensible; 4.F.8 use support from peers and teachers to develop vocabulary needed to comprehend increasingly challenging language; 4.K demonstrate and expand comprehension by employing analytical skills; 5.B.2 write using content-based grade-level vocabulary

Learn Key Vocabulary

Rate and Study the Words Rate how well you know each word. Then:

1. Pronounce the word. Say it aloud several times. Spell it.
2. Study the example.
3. Tell more about the word.
4. Practice it. Make the word your own.

Rating Scale

1 = I have never seen this word before.

2 = I am not sure of the word's meaning.

3 = I know this word and can teach the word's meaning to someone else.

Key Words

brag (brag) *verb*
▶ page 603

To **brag** means to show too much pride about doing something well. The fisherman **bragged** that he caught more fish than anyone else.

confident (kon-fi-dent) *adjective* ▶ page 603

A **confident** person is someone who is sure of his or her abilities. You have to be **confident** to succeed.

engage (en-gāj) *verb*
▶ page 603

To **engage** means to take part or get involved in an activity. She **engaged** her friends in a conversation.

hesitant (hez-i-tent) *adjective*
▶ page 604

A **hesitant** person feels unsure, or not ready to do something. The boy is **hesitant** to pet the rabbit.
Related Word: **hesitate**

modest (mod-ist) *adjective*
▶ page 604

A **modest** person does not act overly proud of an accomplishment or success. The girl was **modest** about winning first prize.

react (rē-akt) *verb*
▶ page 614

To **react** means to show your feelings about something. A person may **react** in fear to a scary movie.
Related Word: **reaction**
Synonym: **respond**

relative (rel-u-tiv) *noun*
▶ page 615

A **relative** is a family member. I love my **relatives**, and I am especially close with my grandmother.
Synonym: **family**

talented (tal-en-tid) *adjective*
▶ page 602

A **talented** person is good at doing one or more activities. They are very **talented** musicians.
Base Word: **talent**

Practice the Words Work with a partner. Write a question using one Key Word. Answer your partner's question. Use at least one Key Word in your answer. Keep going until you have used all of the words twice.

EXAMPLE: Are you <u>hesitant</u> to run in the race?

No, I feel <u>confident</u> I will win!

Reading Strategy: Synthesize

A generalization is a broad statement that applies to many people, ideas, or events. To form a generalization, analyze what such things have in common.

Reading Strategy
Synthesize

HOW TO FORM GENERALIZATIONS

1. As you read, note details that are about the same idea.

2. Add examples about this idea by using your own experience or knowledge.

3. Make a generalization that seems true for both the author's examples and your own examples.

Strategy in Action

Here's how one student made generalizations.

Look Into the Text

"Getting **food** seems important to the story."
ELPS 3.A

UNCLE MUSKRAT. My **fish** trap was good to us today. . . . Where are my nephews? Have they not come back from their **hunt**?

LITTLE LISTENER. No, uncle. My brothers have not yet returned. I am sure they will arrive soon and tell us of their adventures.

UNCLE MUSKRAT. Adventures? Well, adventures won't **feed** our village, so I hope they come back with more than stories!

LITTLE LISTENER. My brothers are great **hunters**. Don't worry, Uncle. I am sure they will bring us more **food**.

Forming Generalizations

Details in Text: Most of the details are about food.

What I Know: Early people like Native Americans, settlers, and trappers had to hunt for food to eat.

Generalization: Long ago **most** people had to hunt for food.

"Signal words like **most** and **many** leave room for exceptions."

Practice Together

Read "The Girl and the Chenoo." Follow the steps in the How-To box to make generalizations as you read.

Focus on Genre

Play

A play is a story written to be performed by actors for an audience. Most plays are divided into sections called **acts**. Acts are divided into **scenes**. Each scene is a change in time or place.

The **lines**, or words characters speak, are arranged in sequence and signaled by the character's name in bold type.

> **MOOSBAS**. [*snatching food from a young child*] Give me some of that.
> [*The young child looks upset but does not say anything.*]
> **LITTLE LISTENER**. Moosbas, there's enough food for everyone.

Stage directions in italics tell actors how to move and talk.

Your Job as a Reader

Reading Strategy: Synthesize

As you read, record important details in your chart. Then add examples from your own knowledge to form generalizations.

Forming Generalizations

Details: Moosbas takes food away. He upsets a child. Little Listener tells Moosbas that there is enough food for all.

What I Know: My parents taught me that it's important to share with others.

Generalization: People should share food with others.

THE GIRL AND THE CHENOO

by Joseph Bruchac

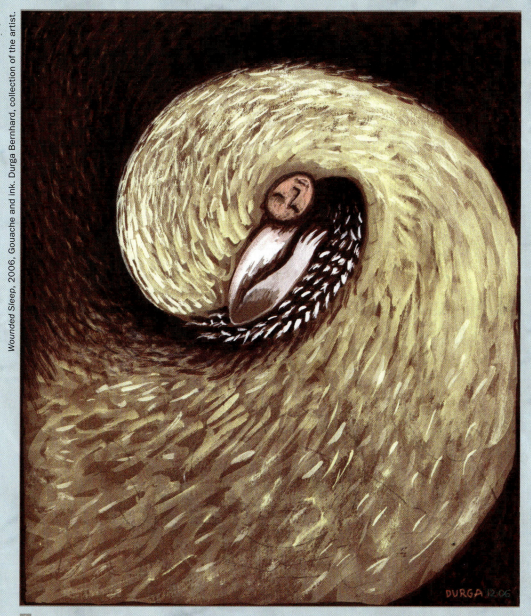

▲ **Critical Viewing: Effect** What feeling or mood does the painting create? What details help the artist create that mood?

Online Coach

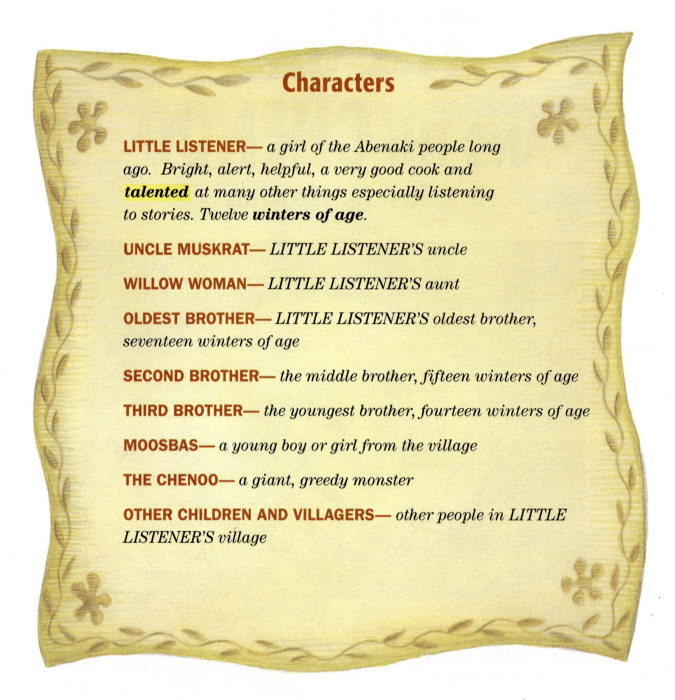

Characters

LITTLE LISTENER— *a girl of the Abenaki people long ago. Bright, alert, helpful, a very good cook and* <mark>**talented**</mark> *at many other things especially listening to stories. Twelve* **winters of age**.

UNCLE MUSKRAT— *LITTLE LISTENER'S uncle*

WILLOW WOMAN— *LITTLE LISTENER'S aunt*

OLDEST BROTHER— *LITTLE LISTENER'S oldest brother, seventeen winters of age*

SECOND BROTHER— *the middle brother, fifteen winters of age*

THIRD BROTHER— *the youngest brother, fourteen winters of age*

MOOSBAS— *a young boy or girl from the village*

THE CHENOO— *a giant, greedy monster*

OTHER CHILDREN AND VILLAGERS— *other people in LITTLE LISTENER'S village*

Key Vocabulary
talented *adj.*, good at doing things

In Other Words
winters of age years old

ACT 1: **In The Village**

SETTING. *Several wigwams are in the background. Wigwams are dome shaped and covered with birch bark. Villagers are* **engaged** *in various activities. Two wigwams are set to the front. Between them* LITTLE LISTENER *stirs a pot over the cooking fire.* WILLOW WOMAN *adds wood to the fire.*

ACT 1, SCENE 1 UNCLE MUSKRAT *comes in carrying a string of fish.*

WILLOW WOMAN. Husband, you've done well!

UNCLE MUSKRAT. My fish trap was **good to us** today, my wife. There's more than enough for us and our niece and our three hungry nephews. With these fish and your big stew of vegetables, we can feed the whole village. Where are my nephews? Have they not come back from their hunt?

LITTLE LISTENER. No, uncle. My brothers have not yet returned. I am sure they will arrive soon and tell us of their adventures.

UNCLE MUSKRAT. Adventures? Well, adventures won't feed our village, so I hope they come back with more than stories!

LITTLE LISTENER. My brothers are great hunters. Don't worry, uncle. I am sure they will bring us more food.

WILLOW WOMAN. And even more stories! [*She and the uncle look at each other and* **chuckle**.] Look, here they are now.

[*The three brothers of* LITTLE LISTENER *enter, each holding a small bag. First, there is* OLDEST BROTHER *who is seventeen winters of age. Then* SECOND BROTHER *enters. He is fifteen winters of age. The* THIRD BROTHER *is fourteen winters of age. They are good hunters, but their imagination is greater than their hunting skills. They walk over to the fire, looking* **confident** *and proud. As they walk over, they are talking among themselves and* **bragging** *about their day of hunting.*]

Key Vocabulary
engage *v.*, to be involved in an activity
confident *adj.*, sure of oneself
brag *v.*, to express too much pride

In Other Words
good to us successful
chuckle laugh

ALL THREE BROTHERS. [*talking in unison*]
What a great day of hunting we had. Yes,
probably the best day ever!

OLDEST BROTHER. Is the food ready?

SECOND BROTHER. It smells good.

THIRD BROTHER. Oooh, oooh! Fish stew!
I can't wait!

UNCLE MUSKRAT. How was your hunting?
I see you brought something back. What
did you bring? [*He looks over at his wife
and* LITTLE LISTENER *and winks.*]

[*The three brothers stop what they are
doing and act* **hesitant**. *Not wanting to
appear as if they are bragging, they act*
modest *and wait for encouragement to
share their stories.*]

LITTLE LISTENER. Yes, brothers. How was
the hunting? Please tell us your stories.

OLDEST BROTHER. Ah, I had a very good
day hunting.

UNCLE MUSKRAT. Really?

OLDEST BROTHER. Today I shot a very
big deer.

WILLOW WOMAN. Where is it?

OLDEST BROTHER. Ah, it fell into the
river and was swept away. [*He reaches into*

his **game bag**.] But I did catch
this squirrel.

SECOND BROTHER. And today was a fine
day for me, too. I shot two deer. [*He* **mimes**
pulling a bow and arrow.]

UNCLE MUSKRAT. Two deer?

SECOND BROTHER. Believe me uncle.
And these were really big ones. Bigger
than the one that Oldest Brother shot.

WILLOW WOMAN. [*aside to the uncle*] Any
deer is bigger than no deer! [*She turns to*
SECOND BROTHER.] And where are those
two big deer?

SECOND BROTHER. I didn't bring them
back with me.

UNCLE MUSKRAT. I can see that.
But why?

SECOND BROTHER. [*hesitating*] Why?

LITTLE LISTENER. Yes, brother.
Why did you not bring back those
two deer?

SECOND BROTHER. Because there
was this mountain lion, actually, two
mountain lions. Yes! They grabbed my
two deer and carried them off before
I could stop them. Two mountain lions.
Imagine that!

Key Vocabulary

hesitant *adj.*, feeling unsure,
or not ready to do something
modest *adj.*, quiet and
selfless, or shy

In Other Words

in unison at the same time
game bag bag that holds the
animals he hunted
mimes acts like he is
Imagine that! Can you believe it?

Aurochs and Deer, 2004, Cecilia Henle. Oil on canvas, collection of the artist.

▲ **Critical Viewing: Effect** Describe the shapes you see in this image. What effect does the artist create by overlapping these shapes?

UNCLE MUSKRAT. Yes, indeed.

SECOND BROTHER. But I did bring this. [*He reaches into his game bag.*] This very fat rabbit.

UNCLE MUSKRAT. [*to THIRD BROTHER, who is leaning over the cooking pot and reaching in to pull out a bit of fish*] And what about you, nephew?

THIRD BROTHER. What?

WILLOW WOMAN. How was your hunting today?

THIRD BROTHER. Today was a good day. It was very good indeed, better than my brothers. I shot three moose!

UNCLE MUSKRAT. [*holding out his hands and looking up at the sky*] Three moose!

THIRD BROTHER. With one arrow.

WILLOW WOMAN. One arrow?

THIRD BROTHER. I waited till they were all lined up so that my arrow went through them one after another.

UNCLE MUSKRAT. Of course. Why waste arrows?

WILLOW WOMAN. I hate to ask this.

THIRD BROTHER. Ask what?

WILLOW WOMAN. Those three moose. Where are they?

THIRD BROTHER. Oh, right. Well, what happened was that . . .

LITTLE LISTENER. Go on, brother. I am listening.

THIRD BROTHER. I went to try to find my brothers so they could help me skin those moose and bring the meat back to camp. But while I was gone a group of bears came and they dragged all three moose away. [*He reaches into his game bag.*] But I did get this fat **pheasant**.

LITTLE LISTENER. Brothers, you did well. We can add the game you brought back to what we have. We will share our **feast** with the whole village.

END OF ACT 1, SCENE 1

In Other Words
pheasant wild bird
feast food

ACT 1, SCENE 2 *The people of the village are all sitting around eating. They are talking happily, sharing food with each other. But one child in a circle of children around* LITTLE LISTENER *does not want to share.*

MOOSBAS. [*snatching food from a young child*] Give me some of that.

[*The young child looks upset but does not say anything.*]

LITTLE LISTENER. Moosbas, there's enough food for everyone.

MOOSBAS. But I wanted that piece of fish. It was a very good piece of fish.

LITTLE LISTENER. That's all the more reason to share. You know, if you are too greedy and selfish, you might turn into a Chenoo.

MOOSBAS. What is a Chenoo?

LITTLE LISTENER. Are you sure you want to know? It's getting dark and this is a scary story.

MOOSBAS. Tell me. I won't be afraid.

OTHER CHILDREN. Tell us. Please, please.

LITTLE LISTENER. I can see that you are all brave, so I'll tell you. A Chenoo is a huge monster whose hunger is never satisfied.

Its stomach hurts all the time because it is so hungry. And do you know what a Chenoo looks like?

MOOSBAS. [*hesitating before he speaks*] No.

OTHER CHILDREN. Tell us, tell us.

LITTLE LISTENER. It looks like a giant person, but it is covered with **shaggy** hair like a great bear. It has sharp teeth like those of the wolf. It has long claws like a mountain lion and red, **piercing** eyes. Long ago, it was once a human being. But it was a greedy, selfish human being who would never share his food.

OTHER CHILDREN. Didn't he remember to give thanks to the plants and animals for **providing food for** him? Didn't he help to provide for his village?

LITTLE LISTENER. No, he forgot to give thanks. He kept everything for himself. He forgot everything except for satisfying his own hunger. He became so greedy and selfish that one day his human heart

In Other Words
snatching taking
shaggy lots of
piercing scary, frightening
providing food for feeding

froze into ice and he turned into a horrible monster. Now the Chenoo wanders through the forest always looking for food. It eats anything it finds, even human beings! And if the Chenoo sees you, you cannot escape. It has a terrible cry, so loud and piercing that anything close to it that hears the cry will drop dead! Soooo . . . unless you want to become a Chenoo, too, you must always share your food with others.

UNCLE MUSKRAT. [*leaning over* MOOSBAS *from behind*] ARRRGGHH!

MOOSBAS. [*falling over in fright*] EEEEEYYY!

LITTLE LISTENER. [*helping* MOOSBAS *sit back up*] It's all right. It's only my uncle being silly.

MOOSBAS. I wasn't really scared.

LITTLE LISTENER. I can see that.

MOOSBAS. [*looking down at his bowl and then turning to the younger child*] Red Bird, would you like some more of this fish? This is the best part.

[LITTLE LISTENER'S *three brothers have entered from stage left while this is going on. They've been engaging in conversation with each other and now come over to* LITTLE LISTENER.]

OLDEST BROTHER. Sister, the three of us have come to a decision.

SECOND BROTHER. The hunting is no longer good around here.

THIRD BROTHER. We need to travel to the north where the hunting is much better. We will go far into the forest and camp. Because you love to hear our stories, we would be happy to have you come along.

OLDEST BROTHER. If you choose to come along, as the youngest, you will need to stay behind and take care of our camp. While we are out **on the game trails**, you will need to repair the bark-covered lodge, gather plants for food, and dry wood for the fire. Then, near the end of the day, you will need to cook our meal in the big pot.

SECOND BROTHER. Will you come with us on our hunting trip?

LITTLE LISTENER. [*She looks thoughtfully at the three of them.*] Thank you, my brothers. I will travel with you.

END OF ACT 1, SCENE 2

In Other Words
on the game trails hunting

Before You Move On

1. **Recall and Interpret** What kind of stories do the brothers tell? Why do they decide to travel?
2. **Explain** What is a Chenoo? Describe how a person could become a Chenoo.
3. **Inference** Why do the brothers ask Little Listener to go with them? Discuss with a partner.
ELPS 4.F.7

ACT 2: **In The Forest to The North**

SCENE 1 *A hunting camp deep in the forest with a river nearby. Show trees around a single wigwam covered with birchbark. LITTLE LISTENER sits by the fire outside the wigwam stirring a cooking pot. Each night, when her three brothers return from their hunting, they all sit around the fire and speak of what happened to them that day. On this day, her three brothers came back from hunting, entering from stage left, with even more exciting stories to tell.*

LITTLE LISTENER. Welcome back, brothers. How was your day?

ALL THREE BROTHERS. [*talking at once and over each other*] Good. Very good. A great day. I have a great story to tell. Me, too. As do I.

LITTLE LISTENER. And how did your hunting go?

OLDEST BROTHER. Today, I found the tracks of a great moose and followed them across the hills. At last I caught up with the moose **by the fork in the crooked stream**. But when I saw how big it was, I knew that if I killed it, it would be hard to carry it back to our camp. And I already had caught enough game for the day. So I let it go.

SECOND BROTHER. Today, I found the den of a big bear. Just as I looked inside for it, I heard a sound behind me. There was that bear! But when I saw it was a mother with cubs, I knew it would not be right to kill it. I had to run for my life to escape.

THIRD BROTHER. Today, I was on the track of two deer. I had one arrow, so I waited until they were standing right next to each other. When I shot, my arrow went through the first deer and also killed the second one. Why have I brought home only one deer? After I put down my bow, a great mountain lion dropped from a tree branch. I picked up a stick and fought for a long time. See the scratch here on my hand? When it saw it could **now defeat me**, it grabbed the bigger deer and ran off.

In Other Words
by the fork in the crooked stream where the stream went in two directions
now defeat me win

[*The three brothers continue to brag about their day and their "great" deeds as hunters. After much laughing and sharing, they turn their attention to their sister.*]

OLDEST BROTHER. How was your day, sister?

SECOND BROTHER. Yes, tell us about your day, sister. What did you do?

LITTLE LISTENER. My day was quiet. I gathered wood, food, and plants. I made a fire and cooked our meal. Now let us eat.

END OF ACT 2, SCENE 1

Indian Camp, Eanger Irving Couse (1866–1936), oil on canvas.

▲ **Critical Viewing: Setting** How does the setting of this painting compare to how you imagine the setting of the play?

ACT 2, SCENE 2 *At the hunting camp the following day. LITTLE LISTENER is waiting as always for her brothers.*

[*The three brothers come running on from stage right, **stumbling**, looking back over their shoulders, breathing hard from running. All three of them seem to be badly frightened and **shaken up**.*]

LITTLE LISTENER. What is wrong?

OLDEST BROTHER. I have seen strange tracks to the north, like those of a man but much larger.

SECOND BROTHER. I have also seen those tracks, but I saw them to the west.

THIRD BROTHER. I have seen such tracks, too. I found those tracks to the south.

LITTLE LISTENER. I have gathered berries and firewood, and I have made our meal. Now let us eat.

[*The three brothers dish out food for themselves and start eating. They all sit quietly around the fire. Finally the oldest brother speaks.*]

OLDEST BROTHER. Brothers, I think we were mistaken. I think those were only the tracks of bears.

SECOND BROTHER. Yes, I think you are right, Oldest Brother.

THIRD BROTHER. Ooh, ooh! I am sure you are right. Those footprints I saw were just bear prints that looked bigger than usual because they were in such soft earth.

[*The brothers **gradually act relieved**. They laugh and joke about being frightened by mere bear tracks. LITTLE LISTENER continues to eat her dinner and doesn't say anything. She is **deep in thought**.*]

LITTLE LISTENER. [*out loud but to herself; her brothers continue eating, laughing, and talking, and they don't hear what she says*] I, too, have seen those tracks. They were very close to the edge of the hill by our camp. And I know that those were not bear tracks. There is only one creature that could make such tracks. But I mustn't speak the name out loud, or I will invite it into our camp. I will remain quiet, but I must make a plan.

END OF ACT 2, SCENE 2

In Other Words
stumbling almost falling down
shaken up upset
gradually act relieved slowly start to relax
deep in thought thinking about something

ACT 2, SCENE 3 *In the forest. Actor dressed as* DEER *grazes peacefully in the foreground. All seems peaceful and quiet.*

DEER. [*quietly grazing on some leaves*] Munch, chew, swallow. Munch, chew, swallow. Munch, chew, chew, chew.

[*The Chenoo enters from stage left.*]

CHENOO. [*making grunting and grumbling sounds*] Garrnh. Garg. Arrk. Grrr.

[*The Chenoo then sees* DEER, *but* DEER *is looking in the other direction. The Chenoo* **creeps up on** DEER, *raises his big hands high in the air.*]

CHENOO. [*heads toward deer and lets out a loud howling sound*] YAAAAAAAAARRRRRRRHHHHHH.

[*This loud howl could be done by the actor or come from an amplified sound source. It should be very loud and piercing.*]

DEER. Yeeep!

[DEER *falls over dead. Other small animals, such as birds and squirrels, drop onto the stage as if falling out of the air and treetops. The Chenoo gathers up the birds and animals.*]

END OF ACT 2, SCENE 3

In Other Words
grazes eats
creeps up on slowly moves towards

Before You Move On

1. **Confirm Prediction** Was your prediction correct? What did the brothers encounter on their trip?
2. **Character** Describe Little Listener. How do you know that she loves her brothers?
3. **Character's Motive** Why does Little Listener stay quiet about the bear tracks?

Mountain Buck, 2000, Durga Bernhard. Gouache on paper collage, Michael Densmore collection.

▲ **Critical Viewing: Effect** How does the artist create a sense of motion and other effects in this image?

ACT 3: **At The Camp**

SCENE 1 *The next morning the three brothers set out to hunt as usual, leaving their sister behind to care for the camp.* LITTLE LISTENER *is cooking by the fire. But this time she has a much larger cooking pot than usual. She does not do her usual chores. Instead she cooks up a big batch of stew. She gathers bearskin robes and spreads them out behind the lodge to make a* **place of honor** *as if for an expected guest.*

LITTLE LISTENER. I think this may be enough food. [*She gets up and looks behind the wigwam.*] And I have spread out all of our blankets to make a resting place back here. Yes, I think everything is ready. [*She looks toward stage left and cups her hand over her ear to listen.* LITTLE LISTENER *sits down with her back toward stage left.*]

[*Boom, boom. BOOM, BOOM. The sound comes closer until the Chenoo appears at stage left, walking heavily. It* **stalks** *forward slowly, lifting a foot and* **thudding** *it down.* LITTLE LISTENER *does not seem to hear it or move. The Chenoo seems*

puzzled by that, lifts another foot and thuds it down. Still, LITTLE LISTENER *doesn't* **react**.]

CHENOO. Garrnh. Garg. Arrk. Grrr?

[*The Chenoo stalks closer until he is standing right over* LITTLE LISTENER. *He raises his arms up as if to grab her. Suddenly* LITTLE LISTENER *turns around and smiles up at the Chenoo in delight.*]

LITTLE LISTENER. Grandfather! I am glad you have come to visit me. [*She stands up and wraps her arms around the monster in a big hug.*] Oh, grandfather!

CHENOO. [*snarls*] Garrh! Garg! Grrrrrannnnndfatherrrr?

Key Vocabulary
react *v.*, to show your feelings about something

In Other Words
place of honor special place to sleep
stalks moves
thudding loudly putting
puzzled confused

LITTLE LISTENER. Yes, grandfather. Welcome to our camp. [*She takes the* Chenoo *by the hand.*] Come over here, sit down, grandfather. I have cooked a special meal for you.

[*The* Chenoo *looks confused but takes her hand and follows her. They sit by the fire.*]

CHENOO. [*in a **rumbling** voice*] Grrrrranddaughter, I accept your invitation.

LITTLE LISTENER. Here, grandfather, you must be hungry. Have some of this stew. This food is for you to eat.

[Chenoo *takes some of the stew, eats it, likes it. Then picks up the pot and swallows down all of the rest of the stew.*]

CHENOO. Gooood [*he rumbles*]. Granddaughterrrrrr, I am glad you **greeted** me and invited me to your camp. I was about to eat you. But now that I have learned you are my relative, I will not hurt you or the others who live at this camp. Tell me what I can do to help you.

LITTLE LISTENER. Grandfather, I am glad you have recognized me. There may indeed be some things that you can do to help. Now, though, all I want you to do is rest. I know you must be tired, grandfather. [*She takes him by the hand and leads him behind the wigwam.*] I have made a place for you to sleep with these bear robes. You can rest until your grandsons come back.

CHENOO. Grrr. Grrrranndsons? I have grrrrrrandsons?

LITTLE LISTENER. Shhh, grandfather. Go to sleep.

CHENOO. Granddaughter, I am tired indeed. I will do as you say, and I will rest. [*She covers him with blankets and soon the* Chenoo *is asleep.*]

[LITTLE LISTENER *goes back to the fire and sits in front of the wigwam with a smile on her face. The three brothers enter from stage right, excited and happy, carrying what they have caught. They are eager to share their stories.*]

OLDEST BROTHER. Today, I have hunted well. Look at these rabbits I have brought back.

SECOND BROTHER. Today, I, too, have hunted well. See the fine goose I have here.

THIRD BROTHER. Ah, brothers, I have also had a successful day. I have brought home this fine deer that I killed with one arrow.

[LITTLE LISTENER *sits smiling in front of the wigwam, saying nothing.*

Key Vocabulary
relative *n.*, a family member

In Other Words
rumbling loud
greeted said hello to; welcomed

The brothers pause, surprised that she is not more excited. They notice the empty stew pot and that there is no food cooking. They look at each other, puzzled.]

THIRD BROTHER. Tell us about your day, sister. What did you do?

LITTLE LISTENER. My day was quiet. I gathered berries and firewood. I made a big stew and invited our grandfather into our camp.

OLDEST BROTHER. Grandfather? Our grandfather is here?

SECOND BROTHER. What grandfather?

THIRD BROTHER. Do we have a grandfather?

LITTLE LISTENER. Indeed. He is sleeping now. I will wake him, but you must promise me to greet him as your relative when he comes outside.

OLDEST BROTHER. Of course we will greet him. Wake him up.

[LITTLE LISTENER *stands up and taps on the side of the lodge.*]

LITTLE LISTENER. Grandfather, your three grandsons are here. They wish to greet you.

[Chenoo *sits up and then stands, looming over the three brothers who are* **paralyzed with terror**. *They stare at the Chenoo, so frightened that they cannot speak.*]

CHENOO. Garrrh?

LITTLE LISTENER. [*nudges* OLDEST BROTHER] Greet our grandfather.

OLDEST BROTHER, SECOND BROTHER, and THIRD BROTHER. [*together in shaking voices*] Welcome, grandfather.

CHENOO. Grrrranndsooons?

OLDEST BROTHER. [*still shaking but steps forward to greet the* Chenoo] We are glad to see you. It has been so long since we have seen you that you appear new to us.

SECOND BROTHER and THIRD BROTHER. [*standing behind* OLDEST BROTHER, *nodding their heads in unison*] Unh-hunnh.

CHENOO. Grrr, grandsons, I am glad you have greeted me as a relative. I see you have gotten food for my dinner.

[*The* Chenoo *reaches out to take the rabbit, goose, and deer from the three brothers, and stuffs the food into his mouth.*]

In Other Words
paralyzed with terror very afraid

LITTLE LISTENER. Grandfather, now that you have eaten, we have nothing for our own meal. Can you bring us some food?

CHENOO. Grrr? Yes, whatever you ask, I will do. [*The* Chenoo *goes off stage.*]

LITTLE LISTENER. Brothers, try to remember to be more friendly to our grandfather when he returns.

[***No sooner has she finished speaking than*** the Chenoo *comes **striding** back, **dragging** several large animals.*]

CHENOO. Here is a herd of moose. Is that gooood?

END OF ACT 3, SCENE 1

Teepees in the Moonlight, Ralph Albert Blakelock (1847–1919), oil on canvas.

🔺 **Critical Viewing: Setting** Describe how this image suggests peace.

In Other Words
No sooner has she finished speaking than Just when she finished speaking
striding walking
dragging carrying

ACT 3, SCENE 2 *The camp in the forest. Now, though, there are piles of tanned skins and much meat hanging on the drying racks. Another wigwam, this one shaped like a dome and covered with blankets, has been built to stage left of the fire.* LITTLE LISTENER, *her brothers, and the* Chenoo *are all sitting together around the fire.*

LITTLE LISTENER. Grandfather, you have helped my brothers with their hunting. We now have many skins **for trade** and have dried much meat to share with our people in the village. It is time for us to say good-bye. We must go back to our village now. Thank you for working so hard with us to provide for our village.

CHENOO. Granddaughter, I wish to come with you.

OLDEST BROTHER. Grandfather, you have been good to us and . . .

SECOND BROTHER. Grandfather, we have enjoyed being with you, but . . .

THIRD BROTHER. Grandfather, you will scare the other people in our village.

CHENOO. Grrrr, I fear you are right. I do not wish to frighten the people. Although I may not appear fearsome to you, my grandchildren, some people may be afraid of the way I look. Will you help me?

LITTLE LISTENER. Yes, grandfather. Tell me what we must do.

CHENOO. Make for me a sweat lodge and make it very hot.

[LITTLE LISTENER *and her three brothers make a big sweat lodge.*]

[*When it is ready, the* Chenoo *goes inside by himself and closes the door of the lodge. The three brothers use forked branches to lift the heated stones from the fire and hand them in through the door of the lodge.*]

CHENOO. Now pour the waterrrrr.

[LITTLE LISTENER *hands him a big pot of water.*]

CHENOO. Close the dooorrrr.

[*They cover the opening with blankets. Some time passes.*]

CHENOO. [*from inside the lodge*] Not hot enough.

In Other Words
for trade to exchange for other goods

[LITTLE LISTENER *opens the door, and her brothers pass along more hot stones. They repeat this three more times. During this time, inside the lodge, the* Chenoo *begins to sing.*]

CHENOO. GRRR-AH, WAY YA, GRRR-AH WAY YAH.

[*The hissing sound of water poured over hot rocks follows his chant.*]

CHENOO. RRR-AH, WAY YA! RRR-AH WAY YAH! [*His voice is loud, but not as loud as before. Hissing sound of steam again.*]

CHENOO. Rah-way yah, rah way yah. [*Now his voice is almost normal. Steam sound.*]

CHENOO. Ah way yah, ah way yah. [*His voice is very different now, like that of an old man. Suddenly it is very quiet and a long time seems to pass.*]

LITTLE LISTENER. Grandfather, are you all right?

CHEÑOO. [*in a small, weak voice*] Open the door. I am ready.

[*They open the door of the lodge and out steps not the giant* Chenoo *but an old man, no larger than any other* **elderly** *man. His* hair is long and white. He holds his hands out to show them something.]

CHENOO (NOW GRANDFATHER).
Granddaughter, that is the icy heart of a greedy monster. Throw it into the fire, and I will be able to remain a human being as you see me now.

In Depth, 2006, Carmen Hathaway. Acrylic on canvas, collection of the artist.

▲ **Critical Viewing: Plot** How does this image relate to the Chenoo changing?

In Other Words
elderly old

Cultural Background
Sweat lodges are used during traditional Native American rituals. Sweat lodges are small structures heated with hot rocks and water to create a warm, steamy room. The lodges are seen as a place that gives healing and life.

ELPS 5.B.1

[*The brothers are too afraid to touch it but* LITTLE LISTENER *uses two sticks to pick up the ice heart and throws it into the fire. From offstage the scream of the* Chenoo *is heard—but at a much lower volume than before.*]

CHENOO (NOW GRANDFATHER). Thank you, granddaughter. Now I can go with you and truly be your grandfather.

LITTLE LISTENER AND BROTHERS.
Grandfather!

[LITTLE LISTENER *and her three brothers all join together in a big hug with their grandfather who had been a* Chenoo.]

CURTAIN

About the Author

Joseph Bruchac

Joseph Bruchac (1942–) grew up listening to customers' stories in his grandparents' general store. Bruchac's grandparents raised him, and they were important influences in his life. His grandfather was an Abenaki Indian. His grandmother was an avid reader. Most of Bruchac's writing is about his childhood and his Abenaki ancestry. "I wanted to share those stories with my sons," he says, "so I started to write them down." Bruchac became the storyteller instead of the listener. He has written more than seventy books, hundreds of poems and articles, and several plays. He has been honored with the Lifetime Achievement Award from the Native Writers Circle of the Americas.

Before You Move On

1. **Confirm Prediction** Was your prediction correct? What happened that you didn't expect?
2. **Theme** What is the theme of this play?
3. **Judgment** Do you think Little Listener chose the best way to deal with the Chenoo? Why or why not?

Connect Reading and Writing

Vocabulary
brag
confident
engages
hesitant
modest
react
relative
talented

CRITICAL THINKING

1. **SUM IT UP** Create a Story Plan and use it to sum up the events of the play.

Story Plan

SOMEBODY Character Who?	WANTED Goal What were they trying to do?	BUT Conflict What got in their way?	SO Resolution How did they reach their goal?

2. **Describe** Describe the Chenoo before and after he becomes a **relative**. What does his appearance represent?

3. **Generalize** Recall how Little Listener **engages** Chenoo and how he **reacts**. Add examples of your own to form a generalization.

4. **Interpret** Explain the real **talents** of **modest** Little Listener and her **bragging** brothers.

READING FLUENCY

Expression Read the passage on page 657 to a partner. Assess your fluency.

1. I read
   a. great   **b.** OK   **c.** not very well

2. What I did best in my reading was _____ .

READING STRATEGY

Synthesize
How did making generalizations help you understand the play? Tell a partner.

VOCABULARY REVIEW

Oral Review Read the paragraph aloud. Add the vocabulary words.

Everyone is gifted, or _____ , in some way. For example, you might be good at cooking or singing. Perhaps your parents or another _____ taught you how to fish or draw. It's good to feel _____ about your skills, but don't _____ about them. Likewise, don't be so shy and _____ that you are _____ to say anything. If an activity _____ your interest, say so. Others will _____ to that with interest, too.

Written Review Write a brief comparison of two **relatives** in the play. Use five vocabulary words.

WRITE ABOUT THE GUIDING QUESTION

Consider How People Provide Food

In "The Girl and the Chenoo" who is the most **talented** at providing food for the community? Use examples from the selection to support your opinion.

Connect Across the Curriculum

ELPS: 2.C.4 learn academic vocabulary heard during classroom instruction and interactions

Literary Analysis

Analyze Drama

> **Academic Vocabulary**
> • **characteristic** (kair-ik-tu-**ris**-tik) *noun*
>   A **characteristic** is a specific feature or trait that helps you identify something.

Learn About Drama Dramas are stories that are meant to be performed for an audience. Like short stories, dramas have characters, a setting, and a plot. The conflict drives the plot.

An important **characteristic** of drama is its use of dialogue to tell the story. Plays are mostly dialogue, or conversations between characters. Dialogue, not description, moves the plot forward. The writer does not use "he said" or "she said," but presents all dialogue in a script for actors to say aloud.

Practice Together

Study a Script Read the passage below. In drama, you learn about events through the characters' dialogue:

> Little Listener: Moosbas, there's enough food for everyone.
> Moosbas: But I wanted that piece of fish. It was a very good piece of fish.

In a short story, the writer might describe the event like this:

> Suddenly, Moosbas reached over and grabbed a piece of fish off a young girl's plate.
>
> "Moosbas, there's enough food for everyone," Little Listener said.
>
> "But I wanted that piece of fish," Moosbas replied. "It was a very good piece of fish." He looked upset.

Compare both versions of the same event. What is different about them? What is the same? Use a Venn Diagram to record your notes.

Try It!

Analyze Drama Work with a partner. Choose a scene from the play to rewrite in the style of a short story. With the class, discuss the difference between the two versions.

ELPS: 4.F.3 use visual and contextual support to develop vocabulary needed to comprehend increasingly challenging language

Use Context Clues: Specialized Language

> **Academic Vocabulary**
> - **culture** (**kul**-chur) *noun*
>   **Culture** includes the beliefs, attitudes, and behaviors shared by a group of people.

Specialized language consists of words or phrases used in a certain place or situation. In some cases, specialized language may be related to a particular setting or **culture**, as it is in "The Girl and the Chenoo."

> [*He reaches into his game bag.*] But I did catch this squirrel.

In this example, you can tell from the context that a *game bag* is a place to keep things caught on a hunt.

Use Context Clues Use context clues to predict the meaning of each example of specialized language in the selection. Share your thoughts with a partner.

1. wigwam (page 603, top)

2. game trails (page 608, col. 2)

3. bearskin robes (page 614, top)

4. sweat lodge (page 618, col. 2)

ELPS: 2.C.4 learn academic vocabulary heard during classroom instruction and interactions

DRAMA

Readers Theater

> **Academic Vocabulary**
> - **interpret** (in-**tur**-prut) *verb*
>   When you **interpret** something, you explain or tell the meaning of it.

Onstage, actors give life to the characters in a drama. They move, speak, and **interpret** the characters' actions according to a script. Each actor's performance is different. With a group, take turns reading aloud an act from the play.

1 **Practice** Decide who will read which part. Practice reading your part. Think about your character's personality, voice, and motives.

2 **Present** As a group, rehearse the act and present it to your classmates. Speak clearly and loudly so the audience can understand you. Use gestures and expressions to keep the audience's attention.

3 **Discuss** Take turns reading with other groups. Notice how others say their lines. Discuss what each person does well. What delivery techniques did the speakers use to achieve their purpose? How is each group's reading different?

ELPS: 2.C.4 learn academic vocabulary heard during classroom instruction and interactions

Media/Writing

Complete an Application

CAREER STUDY

> **Academic Vocabulary**
> * **application** (ap-lu-kā-shun) *noun*
>   An **application** is a form used for filling out a request.

In addition to actors, a play needs stagehands. Stagehands work backstage, or behind the scenes, to set up scenery, lights, sound, and props. To decide if a job like this is for you, use the **description** of the job and the **application** .

❶ **Read the Description**

> Wanted: Stagehands for "The Girl and the Chenoo"
> Applicants must be available weekends in April and be able to:
>   * help paint scenery and organize props
>   * follow directions from the stage manager
>   * move scenery quickly and quietly

❷ **Read the Application** What information do you get from the **application** ? What information do you have to give?

❸ **Make a Decision** Does the job interest you? Do you have the necessary experience? Are you available to work the times requested?

❹ **Complete the Application** Follow instructions closely and write as neatly as possible. Fill out every part of the **application** . Role-play with a partner. One of you will be the stage manager giving the instructions to fill out the **application** , and one of you will apply for the job. Then switch roles. What did you learn about completing an **application** ?

Position Applied For: _____

Personal Information
First Name: _____ Last Name: _____
Address: _____
City: _____ State: _____ Zip Code: _____
Phone: _____ E-mail Address: _____
Date of Birth: _____

Education
School Name: _____
School Address: _____

What skills do you have that will help you meet the goals of this position? _____
_____

What skills do you want to learn? _____
_____
_____

Use Appropriate Language

Act It Out With a partner, role-play Little Listener talking with another young girl in the tribe. Then role-play Little Listener talking to the Chenoo. Use appropriate formal or informal language in each situation. Use past tense and past perfect tense verbs to show the order of past actions. Trade roles.

> Before I started dinner, I had collected berries.

> Grandfather, I was happy that you had come to our camp.

ELPS: 1.G.2 demonstrate knowledge of when to use formal and informal English; 3.I.1 adapt spoken language appropriately for formal purposes; 3.I.2 adapt spoken language appropriately for informal purposes

ELPS: 5.E.1 employ increasingly complex grammatical structures in content area writing

Write About a Memory

Study the Models When you write, you want to make sure your readers can understand the order in which actions happen. Use words correctly to show how actions are related in time.

NOT OK

> Since Little Listener was young, she **performed** the task of collecting firewood. Just this morning, she **has gathered** dry wood for the fire before she picked berries. As she worked, she thought of her three brothers. After she **has returned** to camp, she looked at the dinner pot. It sat empty on the ground. She hoped that her brothers had caught something for her to cook.

This writer confuses the reader by shifting back and forth in time.

OK

> Since Little Listener was young, she **has performed** the task of collecting firewood. Just this morning, she **had gathered** dry wood for the fire before she picked berries. As she worked, she thought of her three brothers. After she **had returned** to camp, she looked at the big dinner pot. It sat empty on the ground. She hoped that her brothers had caught something for her to cook.

This writer correctly uses words that make it clear when the actions happen.

Add Sentences Think of two sentences to add to the OK model above. Be sure to use words that make it clear when actions happened.

WRITE ON YOUR OWN Write a paragraph about a memory you have of your family working together. Use correct verbs to show when actions happened.

Compare Across Texts

Compare Persuasive Texts

The Pro/Con essays in "Feeding the World" and the Yes!/No! essays in "Would It Be Fun to Run a Restaurant?" are persuasive texts. Compare their persuasive techniques. Then **evaluate** how effective the texts are.

How It Works

Collect and Organize Ideas Make a chart like this one. List each selection on your chart. **Evaluate** the writers' arguments, support, and word choice. Do they **convince** you? Do the logic and rhetoric make sense or are there errors in reasoning? Under *Is It Effective?,* write "Yes" or "No," and then give reasons for your opinion.

Comparison Chart

Title	Argument and Support	Persuasive Language	Is It Effective?
Genetically Modified Food: Pro	GM food is a good way to feed the world. New technology improves crops so there is more food.	"I learned firsthand about. . .poverty and hunger" "urgent need for new technology"	

Practice Together

Compare Ideas Identify the persuasive elements in each essay. Note each argument and its support. Then compare the two essays. Tell which essay **convinced** you. Explain.

Try It!

Complete the chart for the two essays about running a restaurant. Then summarize. Which essay persuaded you? Why? You may want to use a frame like this one to help you write your comparison.

In "_____," the writer argues that _____. The writer supports the argument by saying _____. In "_____," the writer argues that _____. The writer supports the argument by saying _____. The more persuasive of these two essays is _____ because _____.

Food for Thought

How can people provide for our communities?

UNIT LIBRARY

Content Library

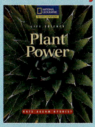

Plant Power

Leveled Library

Reflect on Your Reading

Think back on your reading of the unit selections. Discuss what you did to understand what you read.

Focus on Genre — **Persuasive Writing**

In this unit, you learned how writers try to persuade readers. Choose the selection from the unit that you thought was most persuasive. List reasons that support your opinion. Trade lists with a partner.

Reading Strategy — **Synthesize**

As you read the selections, you learned to synthesize. Explain to a partner how this skill could be useful in the future.

Explore the

Throughout this unit, you have explored how people provide food for their communities. Choose one of these ways to explore the Guiding Question:

- **Discuss** With a group, discuss the Guiding Question. Remember, there can be many answers. Use details from the selections to support your ideas.
- **Interview** Conduct an interview with a partner. Take turns role-playing a character or person in one of the selections. Ask questions to find out the best ways to help end hunger.
- **Write a Story** Write an interesting story about a person who does something to help his or her community. Be sure to include all the elements of a story, including well-paced action, an engaging plot, a detailed setting, and interesting characters. Try to use literary strategies to make your tone and style unique.

Book Talk

Which Unit Library book did you choose? Explain to a partner what it taught you about the ways people provide for or help their communities.

READING FLUENCY

What Is Reading Fluency?

Reading fluency is the ability to read smoothly and expressively with clear understanding. Fluent readers are able to better understand and enjoy what they read. Use the strategies that follow to build your fluency in these four key areas:

- accuracy and rate
- phrasing
- intonation
- expression

How to Improve Accuracy and Rate

Accuracy is the correctness of your reading. Rate is the speed of your reading.

How to read accurately:

- Use correct pronunciation.
- Emphasize correct syllables.
- Recognize most words.

How to read with proper rate:

- Match your reading speed to what you are reading. For example, if you are reading an exciting story, read slightly faster. If you are reading a sad story, read slightly slower.
- Recognize and use punctuation.

Test your accuracy and rate:

- Choose a text you are familiar with, and practice reading it aloud or silently multiple times.
- Keep a dictionary with you while you read, and look up words you do not recognize.
- Use a watch or clock to time yourself while you read a passage.
- Ask a friend or family member to read a passage for you, so you know what it should sound like.

Use the formula below to measure a reader's accuracy and rate while reading aloud. For passages to practice with, see **Reading Fluency Practice**, pp. 634–657.

Accuracy and Rate Formula

_____	−	_____	=	_____
words attempted in one minute		number of errors		words correct per minute (wcpm)

How to Improve Intonation

Intonation is the rise and fall in the pitch or tone of your voice as you read aloud. Pitch and tone both mean the highness or lowness of the sound.

How to read with proper intonation:

- Change the sound of your voice to match what you are reading.
- Make your voice flow, or sound smooth while you read.
- Make sure you are pronouncing words correctly.
- Raise the sound of your voice for words that should be stressed, or emphasized.
- Use proper rhythm and meter.
- Use visual clues. (see box below)

Visual Clue and Meaning	Example	How to Read It
Italics: draw attention to a word to show special importance	She is *smart*.	Emphasize "smart."
Dash: shows a quick break in a sentence	She is—smart.	Pause before saying "smart."
Exclamation: can represent energy, excitement, or anger	She is smart!	Make your voice louder at the end of the sentence.
All capital letters: can represent strong emphasis, or yelling	SHE IS SMART.	Emphasize the whole sentence.
Bold facing: draws attention to a word to show importance	She is **smart**.	Emphasize "smart."
Question mark: shows curiosity or confusion	She is smart?	Raise the pitch of your voice slightly at the end of the sentence.

Use the rubric below to measure how well a reader uses intonation while reading aloud. For intonation passages, see **Reading Fluency Practice**, pp. 634–657.

Intonation Rubric

1	2	3
The reader's tone does not change. The reading all sounds the same.	The reader's tone changes sometimes to match what is being read.	The reader's tone always changes to match what is being read.

ELPS 1.B.1

How to Improve Phrasing

Phrasing is how you use your voice to group words together.

How to read with proper phrasing:

- Use correct rhythm and meter by not reading too fast or too slow.
- Pause for key words within the text.
- Make sure your sentences have proper flow and meter, so they sound smooth instead of choppy.
- Make sure you sound like you are reading a sentence instead of a list.
- Use punctuation to tell you when to stop, pause, or emphasize. (see box below)

Punctuation	How to Use It
. period	stop at the end of the sentence
, comma	pause within the sentence
! exclamation point	emphasize the sentence and pause at the end ELPS 2.A.2; 4.F.2
? question mark	emphasize the end of the sentence and pause at the end
; semicolon	pause within the sentence between two related thoughts
: colon	pause within the sentence before giving an example or explanation

One way to practice phrasing is to copy a passage, then place a slash (/), or pause mark, within a sentence where there should be a pause. One slash (/) means a short pause. Two slashes (//) mean a longer pause, such as a pause at the end of a sentence.

Read aloud the passage below, pausing at each pause mark. Then try reading the passage again without any pauses. Compare how you sound each time.

There are many ways / to get involved in your school / and community. // Joining a club / or trying out for a sports team/ are a few of the options. // Volunteer work can also be very rewarding. // You can volunteer at community centers, / nursing homes, / or animal shelters. //

Use the rubric below to measure how well a reader uses phrasing while reading aloud. For phrasing passages, see **Reading Fluency Practice**, pp. 634–657.

Phrasing Rubric		
1	2	3
Reading is choppy. There are usually no pauses for punctuation.	Reading is mostly smooth. There are some pauses for punctuation.	Reading is very smooth. Punctuation is being used properly.

How to Improve Expression

Expression in reading is how you use your voice to express feeling.

How to read with proper expression:

- Match the sound of your voice to what you are reading. For example, read louder and faster to show strong feeling. Read slower and quieter to show sadness or seriousness.
- Match the sound of your voice to the genre. For example, read a fun, fictional story using a fun, friendly voice. Read an informative, nonfiction article using an even tone and a more serious voice.
- Avoid speaking in monotone, which is using only one tone in your voice.
- Pause for emphasis and exaggerate letter sounds to match the mood or theme of what you are reading.

Practice incorrect expression by reading this sentence without changing the tone of your voice: *I am so excited!*

Now read the sentence again with proper expression: *I am so excited!* The way you use your voice while reading can help you to better understand what is happening in the text.

For additional practice, read the sentences below aloud with and without changing your expression. Compare how you sound each time.

- I am very sad.
- That was the most *boring* movie I have ever seen.
- We won the game!

Use the rubric below to measure how well a reader uses expression while reading aloud. For expression passages, see **Reading Fluency Practice**, pp. 634–657.

Expression Rubric

1	2	3
The reader sounds monotone. The reader's voice does not match the subject of what is being read.	The reader is making some tone changes. Sometimes, the reader's voice matches what is being read.	The reader is using proper tones and pauses. The reader's voice matches what is being read.

Practice Intonation: "American Names"

Intonation is the rise and fall in the pitch or tone of your voice as you read aloud. Use this passage to practice reading with proper intonation. Print a copy of this passage from **InsideNG.com** to help you monitor your progress.

My name's Arturo, "Turo" for short. For my father, and my grandfather, and *his* father, back and back. Arturos—like stacks of strong adobe bricks, forever, my grandmother says.

Really, my name *was* Arturo. Here's why: Three years ago our family came up from Mexico to L.A. From stories they'd heard, my parents were worried for our safety in "that hard-as-a-fist Los Angeles." But Papi needed better work.

Rosa, my little sister, wailed, "'Nighted States, no! Too dark!" My brother, Luis, and I pretty much clammed up. I guess numbed by the thought of leaving our home, and a little scared, too, about the tough barrio.

Like some random, windblown weeds, we landed in L.A., home to movie stars and crazies and crazy movie stars.

From "American Names," page 12

Practice Expression: "A Lion Hunt"

Expression in reading is how you use your voice to express feeling. Use this passage to practice reading with proper expression. Print a copy of this passage from InsideNG.com to help you monitor your progress.

Everyone was in a trance.

I felt that something inside me was about to burst, that my heart was about to come out. I was ready. Then we came face-to-face with the lions. The female lion walked away, but the male stayed. We formed a little semicircle around the male, with our long spears raised. We didn't move. The lion had stopped eating and was now looking at us. It felt like he was looking right at me. He was big, really big. His tail was thumping the ground.

He gave one loud roar to warn us. Everything shook. The ground where I was standing started to tremble. I could see right into his throat, that's how close we were. His mouth was huge and full of gore from the cow. I could count his teeth. His face and mane were red with blood. Blood was everywhere.

From "A Lion Hunt," page 36

Practice Phrasing: "*from* The House on Mango Street"

Phrasing is how you use your voice to group words together. Use this passage to practice reading with proper phrasing. Print a copy of this passage from **InsideNG.com** to help you monitor your progress.

We didn't always live on Mango Street. Before that we lived on Loomis on the third floor, and before that we lived on Keeler. Before Keeler it was Paulina, and before that I can't remember. But what I remember most is moving a lot. Each time it seemed there'd be one more of us. By the time we got to Mango Street we were six—Mama, Papa, Carlos, Kiki, my sister Nenny and me.

The house on Mango Street is ours, and we don't have to pay rent to anybody, or share the yard with the people downstairs, or be careful not to make too much noise, and there isn't a landlord banging on the ceiling with a broom. But even so, it's not the house we'd thought we'd get.

From "*from* The House on Mango Street" page 60

Practice Phrasing: "On the Menu"

Phrasing is how you use your voice to group words together. Use this passage to practice reading with proper phrasing. Print a copy of this passage from InsideNG.com to help you monitor your progress.

Cats arch their backs to look big and scary. Green grasshoppers blend into grass. Claws and teeth help animals fight.

These adaptations, or useful traits, are quite different. Yet they share one purpose. They all keep an animal from landing on the menu.

Camouflage helps animals hide from hungry predators. Did you know that it also helps predators hide from their prey? Why would predators need to hide? Sometimes they need help finding—and catching—dinner.

Some predators are awfully slow, and they can't run as fast as their prey. Camouflage lets them sneak up at their own pace.

Other predators are quick but sneaky. Clever coloring helps them hide from view. They lie in wait, hoping a meal will wander by. Surprise! The predator snaps up its prey.

From "On the Menu," page 92

Practice Intonation: "The Three Chicharrones"

Intonation is the rise and fall in the pitch or tone of your voice as you read aloud. Use this passage to practice reading with proper intonation. Print a copy of this passage from **InsideNG.com** to help you monitor your progress.

"Pereza, Gordo, and Astuto, it's time for you to go into the world and make your fortunes."

He handed them each little bags. "You'll receive the same number of *pesos* I received from my *papá* when I was your age."

They opened their bags and found two hundred coins.

"Can't we stay here a little longer, *Papá*?" drawled Pereza, yawning, for he was lazy.

"This is impossible. How can we make our way in the world like this?" whined Gordo, who always looked for the quickest way to everything.

"I'll do my best, *Papá*," said Astuto, who always worked hard.

"With two hundred *pesos* and a lot of work, I did well for myself." Their father spread his arms out, indicating his large house. "Now, get packed, *hijos*."

From "The Three Chicharrones," page 116

Practice Expression: "Dragon, Dragon"

Expression in reading is how you use your voice to express feeling. Use this passage to practice reading with proper expression. Print a copy of this passage from InsideNG.com to help you monitor your progress.

"Ladies and gentlemen," said the king when everyone was present, "I've put up with that dragon as long as I can. He has got to be stopped."

All the people whispered amongst themselves. The king smiled, pleased with the impression he had made.

But the wise cobbler said gloomily, "It's all very well to talk about it—but how are you going to do it?"

And now all the people smiled and winked as if to say, "Well, King, he's got you there!"

The king frowned.

"It's not that His Majesty hasn't tried," the queen spoke up loyally.

"Yes," said the king. "I've told my knights again and again that they ought to slay that dragon. But I can't *force* them to go. I'm not a tyrant."

From "Dragon, Dragon," page 140

Practice Phrasing: "The Civil Rights Movement"

Phrasing is how you use your voice to group words together. Use this passage to practice reading with proper phrasing. Print a copy of this passage from **InsideNG.com** to help you monitor your progress.

In the South, segregation was enforced by Jim Crow laws. These laws had controlled the lives of Southern blacks since the late 1800s. Jim Crow laws said that blacks and whites must use different schools, restaurants, hotels, theaters, parks, sections of trains and buses, and so on. Even funeral homes and cemeteries were segregated! In the few places where blacks and whites shared public services—such as post offices and banks—African Americans had to wait for all whites to be served first.

In the North, segregation happened by practice and custom. Many African Americans moved to Northern cities during the 1940s, and whites responded by moving to the suburbs. African Americans found themselves trapped in city slums—poor neighborhoods where housing and schools were bad and where there were few jobs.

From "The Civil Rights Movement," page 178

Practice Expression: "Martin's Big Words"

Expression in reading is how you use your voice to express feeling. Use this passage to practice reading with proper expression. Print a copy of this passage from **InsideNG.com** to help you monitor your progress.

After ten years of protests, the lawmakers in Washington voted to end segregation. The WHITE ONLY signs in the South came down.

Dr. Martin Luther King, Jr., cared about all Americans. He cared about people all over the world. And people all over the world admired him.

In 1964, he won the Nobel Peace Prize. He won it because he taught others to fight with words, not fists.

Martin went wherever people needed help. In April 1968 he went to Memphis, Tennessee. He went to help garbage collectors who were on strike. He walked with them and talked with them and sang with them and prayed with them.

On his second day there, he was shot.

He died.

His big words are alive for us today.

From "Martin's Big Words," page 206

Practice Intonation: "Speaking Up"

Intonation is the rise and fall in the pitch or tone of your voice as you read aloud. Use this passage to practice reading with proper intonation. Print a copy of this passage from **InsideNG.com** to help you monitor your progress.

Principal Dunn thinks that Eve's leadership skills will take her far. "If this young woman set her mind to being the mayor, that would happen," he says. "I hope that does happen. She's been a great student leader."

Eve, who stands 4 feet and 11 inches tall, says that it's not always easy being a leader. "People look at me and they always underestimate me. They say 'Oh, this little girl can't do anything,'" Eve explains. "I feed on that. When people push you down, you've got to prove them wrong."

Sometimes Eve wants to run away from responsibility. But eventually, she remembers how much she likes making things better for others, especially at her school.

From "Speaking Up," page 226

Practice Phrasing: "Here, There, and Beyond"

Phrasing is how you use your voice to group words together. Use this passage to practice reading with proper phrasing. Print a copy of this passage from **InsideNG.com** to help you monitor your progress.

The four planets closest to the sun are Mercury, Venus, Earth, and Mars. These planets have a lot in common. They are mostly made up of rock and metal, so they all have hard, uneven surfaces.

Because of their content, the planets closest to the sun have high densities. This means that these planets are made up of condensed, or tightly packed, materials. They also share the qualities of having slow rotation and solid surfaces.

The rocky planets closest to the sun are also alike in other ways. They are small compared to most of the other planets in our solar system. These planets also do not have many moons, or objects that rotate, or move, around a planet.

From "Here, There, and Beyond," page 254

Practice Intonation: "Earth and Space"

Intonation is the rise and fall in the pitch or tone of your voice as you read aloud. Use this passage to practice reading with proper intonation. Print a copy of this passage from **InsideNG.com** to help you monitor your progress.

We breathe because our bodies need oxygen in the air. Oxygen is like food for our blood. We need it to survive.

In space, there is no oxygen. Because of this, astronauts do not breathe the same as they do on Earth. They have to breathe with the help of a protective spacesuit that supplies them with oxygen. A human being would not survive on a spacewalk for more than a minute or two without a spacesuit.

Compared to getting dressed on Earth, which takes just a few minutes, putting on a spacesuit takes 45 minutes. The astronauts must then spend lots of time breathing only pure oxygen before going outside the space station. This process is called prebreathing.

From "Earth and Space," page 276

Practice Expression: "Indian Summer Sun"

Expression in reading is how you use your voice to express feeling. Use this passage to practice reading with proper expression. Print a copy of this passage from **InsideNG.com** to help you monitor your progress.

"Hi," he said.

I smiled. "Jerry?" It came out as Yerry, but it was too late to take it back.

"My parents and my sister," his chin pointed to Kathy, "call me Jeremy, my real name, but almost everybody else calls me Jerry. You can call me whatever is easier for you."

Jeremy! Kathy's brother—not her boyfriend.

"Why are you always so quiet?" he asked.

"*¿Hablas español?*"

He made a 0 with his fingers. "Zero."

"I have an accent." That came out without warning.

"What are you talking about?" he said, almost yelling because the music was loud. "It's cute!"

From "Indian Summer Sun," page 300

Practice Intonation: "A Natural Balance"

Intonation is the rise and fall in the pitch or tone of your voice as you read aloud. Use this passage to practice reading with proper intonation. Print a copy of this passage from InsideNG.com to help you monitor your progress.

Beep! Beep! Beep! Your alarm goes off and you hop out of bed. You wash your face, chat with your family, eat your breakfast, and take the bus to school. Even before you go to school, you have connected with many people and things. All of the things you do affect the environment.

Your environment is all of the living and nonliving things around you. All across Earth, humans are changing the environment in different ways. For example: we cut down trees to build houses, plow fields to grow crops, build roads and parking lots, and empty waste into rivers, lakes, and oceans. We also use large nets and boats to catch huge amounts of fish. Activities like these greatly affect plants and animals in our environment.

From "A Natural Balance," page 334
ELAR 1.A.2

Practice Phrasing: "Siberian Survivors"

Phrasing is how you use your voice to group words together. Use this passage to practice reading with proper phrasing. Print a copy of this passage from **InsideNG.com** to help you monitor your progress.
ELPS 2.A.2

The biologist remained calm as he carefully aimed his tranquilizer gun at the tiger. Then he squeezed the trigger and a dart soared through the air toward the cat.

Bull's eye! The dart struck Olga in her shoulder. She staggered and slowly slumped to the ground—asleep.

As the cat slept, Quigley and his team of scientists went to work. They had to be careful; a female tiger can weigh 370 pounds. They wanted to finish their work before the cat woke up.

The scientists took blood samples, checked Olga's heartbeat, and measured her body from head to tail.

They also put a radio collar around her neck. The collar sends a radio signal—a series of beeps—that helps scientists track an animal's movements.

From "Siberian Survivors," page 356
ELPS 2.A.2

Practice Expression: "Mireya Mayor Explorer/Correspondent"

Expression in reading is how you use your voice to express feeling. Use this passage to practice reading with proper expression. Print a copy of this passage from InsideNG.com to help you monitor your progress.

Mayor believes that local support for conservation is a key factor in bringing about change. "The local people are the very core of effective conservation. Without their support, the 'dream' of saving the planet can never become a reality. The rainforest is literally their backyard. Yet many Malagasy kids have never even seen a lemur. So I organize lots of field trips into the forest. Only by seeing how amazing these creatures are, will kids want to protect them." Mayor stresses the importance of providing education and opportunities for local communities to learn about the threats to animals and how they can help. She believes it will be critical to protecting the planet.

From "Mireya Mayor Explorer/Correspondent," page 376

Practice Phrasing: "Nadia the Willful"

Phrasing is how you use your voice to group words together. Use this passage to practice reading with proper phrasing. Print a copy of this passage from **InsideNG.com** to help you monitor your progress.

ELAR 1.A.2

Nadia rode behind her father as he traveled across the desert from oasis to oasis, seeking Hamed.

Shepherds told them of seeing a great white stallion fleeing before the pillars of wind that stirred the sand. And they said that the horse carried no rider.

Passing merchants, their camels laden with spices and sweets for the bazaar, told of the emptiness of the desert they had crossed.

Tribesmen, strangers, everyone whom Tarik asked, sighed and gazed into the desert, saying, "Such is the will of Allah."

At last Tarik knew in his heart that his favorite son, Hamed, had been claimed, as other Bedouin before him, by the drifting sands. And he told Nadia what he knew—that Hamed was dead.

From "Nadia the Willful," page 402
ELAR 1.A.2

Practice Intonation: "Passage to Freedom"

Intonation is the rise and fall in the pitch or tone of your voice as you read aloud. Use this passage to practice reading with proper intonation. Print a copy of this passage from **InsideNG.com** to help you monitor your progress.

I said to my father, "If we don't help them, won't they die?"

With the entire family in agreement, I could tell a huge weight was lifted off my father's shoulders. His voice was firm as he told us, "I will start helping these people."

Outside, the crowd went quiet as my father spoke, with Borislav translating.

"I will issue visas to each and every one of you to the last. So, please wait patiently."

The crowd stood frozen for a second. Then the refugees burst into cheers. Grown-ups embraced each other, and some reached to the sky. Fathers and mothers hugged their children. I was especially glad for the children.

From "Passage to Freedom," page 426

Practice Expression: "Zlata's Diary"

Expression in reading is how you use your voice to express feeling. Use this passage to practice reading with proper expression. Print a copy of this passage from **InsideNG.com** to help you monitor your progress.

Thursday, September 17, 1992

Dear Mimmy,

Today is Alma's birthday. We gave her two herbal shampoos. We had a super time, but . . . I looked out the window and saw a flash. I thought it was somebody signaling, that's not unusual in war time. But . . . BOOM!! Shattered glass, falling plaster. A shell fell in front of the shop next door and I saw it all from the fourth floor. We rushed over to Nedo's apartment and watched TV.

ELPS 2.A.2

The birthday party wasn't bad, but it would have been even better if that shell hadn't spoiled it.

–Your Zlata

From "Zlata's Diary," page 452
ELPS 2.A.2

Practice Expression: "The Clever Magistrate"

Expression in reading is how you use your voice to express feeling. Use this passage to practice reading with proper expression. Print a copy of this passage from **InsideNG.com** to help you monitor your progress.
ELAR 1.A.2

One cold winter day, a farmer was carrying two buckets of spoiled food from a restaurant to his pigsty. As he was passing a coat shop, he accidentally spilled some of the slop on the ground. Sour cabbage, rotten eggs, and fish bones scattered all over the ground. Ugh! Ugh! What a smell!

The shopkeeper, who happened to be standing inside the door, saw this and was furious. He rushed out, grabbed the man, and shouted, "You dirty beggar! Look what you've done in front of my shop! It will be impossible to get rid of the smell! How are you going to pay for the damage?"

"I am so sorry," said the farmer. "I will clean it up right away. As for the damage, all I have is this coin."

From "The Clever Magistrate," page 480
ELAR 1.A.2

Practice Phrasing: "The Constitution"

Phrasing is how you use your voice to group words together. Use this passage to practice reading with proper phrasing. Print a copy of this passage from **InsideNG.com** to help you monitor your progress.
ELAR 1.A.2

The Constitution has three parts. There is an introduction called the Preamble, seven articles that describe the plan of the national government, and the amendments, or changes to the Constitution.

The first paragraph of the Constitution states the basic purposes of the new plan of government: (1) to create a union where the states work together; (2) to create a system of laws that are fair; (3) to keep peace within the country; (4) to protect the nation from outside attack; (5) to improve the lives of all Americans; and (6) to make sure that our free society survives in the future.

From "The Constitution," page 502
ELAR 1.A.2

Practice Intonation: "Kids Take Action"

Intonation is the rise and fall in the pitch or tone of your voice as you read aloud. Use this passage to practice reading with proper intonation. Print a copy of this passage from **InsideNG.com** to help you monitor your progress.

Freedom of speech is an important right that you have as a citizen of the United States. You have the right to say what you want as long as it doesn't harm another person. Giving a speech is one way you can share your point of view and try to persuade others to agree with you.

During an election, candidates running for office give speeches and debate each other. In their speeches and debates, they tell how they feel about issues and try to get people to vote for them.

Many famous people have used speeches to make their points heard and understood.

A good speech stays in people's minds and can even earn a place in history.

From "Kids Take Action," page 532

Practice Intonation: "Feeding the World"

Intonation is the rise and fall in the pitch or tone of your voice as you read aloud. Use this passage to practice reading with proper intonation. Print a copy of this passage from **InsideNG.com** to help you monitor your progress.
ELPS 2.A.2

I was one in a family of nine children growing up on a small farm in Kenya's highlands. I learned firsthand about the enormous challenge of breaking the cycle of poverty and hunger in rural Africa. In fact, the reason I became a plant scientist was to help farmers like my mother. My mother sold the only cow our family owned to pay for my secondary education. This was a sacrifice because I, like most children in Kenya, was needed on the farm.

I have since made it my mission to alert others to the urgent need for new technology in Africa. New technology can help protect against hunger, environmental damage, and poverty.

From "Feeding the World," page 560
ELPS 2.A.2

Practice Phrasing: "Soup for the Soul"

Phrasing is how you use your voice to group words together. Use this passage to practice reading with proper phrasing. Print a copy of this passage from **InsideNG.com** to help you monitor your progress.
ELPS 2.A.2

Q: *What kind of food do you cook at First Slice?*

A: Last year we made a lot of Cajun food to feed displaced victims of Hurricane Katrina. We also get a lot of requests for food with Latin flavors, dishes that might use tortillas. Smothered pork chops are really popular. A pot of greens is definitely a big thing, because most people on the street don't have access to farm-fresh produce. It's interesting: A lot of our clientele grew up in rural communities, and they know more about growing fruit and vegetables than I do. They ask really specific questions about the soil and the farming methods. It's wonderful that we can make that fresh-from-the-farm connection.

From "Soup for the Soul," page 580
ELPS 2.A.2

Practice Expression: "The Girl and the Chenoo"

Expression in reading is how you use your voice to express feeling. Use this passage to practice reading with proper expression. Print a copy of this passage from **InsideNG.com** to help you monitor your progress.

MOOSBAS. [*snatching food from a young child*] Give me some of that.

[*The young child looks upset but does not say anything.*]

LITTLE LISTENER. Moosbas, there's enough food for everyone.

MOOSBAS. But I wanted that piece of fish. It was a very good piece of fish.

LITTLE LISTENER. That's all the more reason to share. You know, if you are too greedy and selfish, you might turn into a Chenoo.

MOOSBAS. What is a Chenoo?

LITTLE LISTENER. Are you sure you want to know? It's getting dark and this is a scary story.

MOOSBAS. Tell me. I won't be afraid.

OTHER CHILDREN. Tell us. Please, please.

LITTLE LISTENER. I can see that you are all brave, so I'll tell you. A Chenoo is a huge monster whose hunger is never satisfied. Its stomach hurts all the time because it is so hungry. And do you know what a Chenoo looks like?

MOOSBAS. [*hesitating before he speaks*] No.

From "The Girl and the Chenoo," page 602

Glossary

The definitions in this glossary are for words as they are used in the selections in this book. Use the Pronunciation Key below to help you use each word's pronunciation. Then read about the parts of an entry.

Pronunciation Key

Symbols for Consonant Sounds				Symbols for Short Vowel Sounds		Symbols for R-controlled Sounds		Symbols for Variant Vowel Sounds	
b	box	p	pan	a	hat	ar	barn	ah	father
ch	chick	r	ring	e	bell	air	chair	aw	ball
d	dog	s	bus	i	chick	ear	ear	oi	boy
f	fish	sh	fish	o	box	ir	fire	ow	mouse
g	girl	t	hat	u	bus	or	corn	oo	book
h	hat	th	earth			ur	girl	ü	fruit
j	jar	th	father	**Symbols for Long Vowel Sounds**					
k	cake	v	vase					**Miscellaneous Symbols**	
ks	box	w	window	ā	cake			shun	fraction
kw	queen	wh	whale	ē	key			chun	question
l	bell	y	yarn	ī	bike			zhun	division
m	mouse	z	zipper	ō	goat				
n	pan	zh	treasure	yū	mule				
ng	ring								

•Academic Vocabulary

Certain words in this glossary have a red dot indicating that they are academic vocabulary words. These are the words that you will use as you study many different subjects in school.

Parts of an Entry

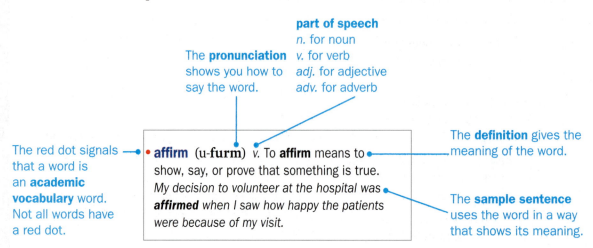

part of speech
n. for noun
v. for verb
adj. for adjective
adv. for adverb

The **pronunciation** shows you how to say the word.

The red dot signals that a word is an **academic vocabulary** word. Not all words have a red dot.

•**affirm** (u-**furm**) *v.* To **affirm** means to show, say, or prove that something is true. *My decision to volunteer at the hospital was affirmed when I saw how happy the patients were because of my visit.*

The **definition** gives the meaning of the word.

The **sample sentence** uses the word in a way that shows its meaning.

A

- **adaptation** (a-dap-**tā**-shun) *n.* An **adaptation** is a feature or behavior that helps animals survive. *The cat's arched back is an adaptation that protects it.*

- **adjustment** (u-**just**-ment) *n.* An **adjustment** is the way you go along with or get used to a change. *It takes a while to make an adjustment to a new home.*

admire (ad-**mīr**) *v.* When you **admire** someone, you think highly of them. *Many people admire Rosa Parks, who worked for civil rights.*

advantage (ad-**van**-tij) *n.* When you have an **advantage**, you have a better chance to succeed than others. *If you are stronger or faster, it is an advantage.*

advice (ad-**vīs**) *n.* To give **advice** means to share wise words. *Parents give advice to their children.*

- **affect** (u-**fekt**) *v.* When you **affect** something, you change it in some way. *The rain will affect the water level in the lake.*

agreement (a-**grē**-ment) *n.* To have an **agreement** is to have an understanding with people about something. *We made an agreement to follow the rules of the school.*

agricultural (ag-ri-**kul**-chur-ul) *adj.* Something that is **agricultural** is related to farms or farming. *Growing vegetables to sell as food is one kind of agricultural business.*

- **amend** (u-**mend**) *v.* To **amend** means to change or to improve. *I amended the sentence to make it complete.*

- **analyze** (**a**-nu-līz) *v.* When you **analyze**, you separate something into parts and examine, or study, it. *Rey has to analyze the stem of the flower.*

- **appeal** (u-**pēl**) *n.* An **appeal** is a request for a response. *The school made an appeal to the community for more textbooks.*

- **application** (ap-lu-**kā**-shun) *n.* An **application** is a form used for filling out a request. *The job application was one page.*

- **appreciate** (u-**prē**-shē-āt) *v.* When you **appreciate** something, you understand its importance. *You appreciate an umbrella when it rains.*

- **approach** (u-**prōch**) *v.* To **approach** means to come closer or near. *The diver approached the dolphin.*

argument (ar-**gyū**-ment) *n.* An **argument** is a strong disagreement. *My friend and I got into an argument because he was late.*

arrest (u-**rest**) *n.* An **arrest** is when a person is taken by a police officer. *Police made many arrests of people during the Civil Rights Movement.*

astronaut (**as**-tre-not) *n.* An **astronaut** is a person trained to travel to space. *Astronauts need special equipment to travel in space.*

atmosphere (**at**-mu-sfir) *n.* The **atmosphere** is the air that surrounds Earth. *A spaceship can travel outside of Earth's atmosphere, but an airplane cannot.*

- **awareness** (u-**wair**-nes) *n.* **Awareness** is having knowledge of something. *To protect Earth, it is important to have an awareness of things that could harm the planet.*

B

banish (**ban**-ish) *v.* To **banish** means to send away or punish by making someone leave. *The referee banished the player from the game.*

bargain (**bar**-gen) *n.* A **bargain** is an agreement between people about what each person gives and receives. *He made a bargain with the salesperson for the car.*

- **benefit** (**ben**-e-fit) *n.* A **benefit** is something that is good for people, places, or things. *One benefit of exercise is that it makes you strong.*

biologist (bī-**ol**-u-jist) *n.* A **biologist** is a person who studies living things. *Biologists study how living things grow and where they are found.*

brag (**brag**) *v.* To **brag** means to show too much pride about doing something well. *The fisherman bragged that he caught more fish than anyone else.*

bravery (**brā**-vu-rē) *n.* **Bravery** means courage, or not being afraid. *Firefighters show bravery when they put out fires.*

brotherhood (**bruth**-ur-hood) *n.* A **brotherhood** is a close group of people. *A sports team can be a brotherhood.*

business (**biz**-nis) *n.* A **business** is where you do work for money. *Some people's place of business is in an office.*

- **Academic Vocabulary**

Glossary

C

camouflage (kam-a-flazh) *n.* **Camouflage** is a color or pattern that helps people or animals hide. *People use camouflage to help them hide when they hunt.*

campaign (kam-pān) *n.* A **campaign** is a series of actions by an individual or a group working toward a goal. *John F. Kennedy led a campaign to become President in 1960.*

career (ku-rear) *n.* A **career** is a job that someone does for a long time. *For twenty years, my aunt has made a career as a doctor.*

• **challenge** (chal-unj) *n.* A **challenge** is something that is difficult to do. *It is a challenge to climb a mountain.*

• **characteristic** (kair-ik-tu-ris-tik) *n.* A **characteristic** is a specific feature or trait that helps you identify something. *A loud roar is one characteristic of a lion.*

cheat (chēt) *v.* When you **cheat**, you act unfairly. *It is wrong to cheat on a test.*

citizen (sit-i-zun) *n.* A **citizen** is a person who was born in a country or becomes a member of a country. *All American citizens share the same rights.*

civil rights (siv-ul rīts) *n.* Your **civil rights** are the rights you have as a member of society. *Many people marched to gain civil rights for all.*

classified (klas-u-fīd) *v.* To be **classified** means to be arranged or put into groups. *Scientists have classified many plants and animals.*

• **community** (ku-myū-nu-tē) *n.* A **community** is a group of people in a specific area. *Our community started a recycling program.*

• **compare** (kum-pair) *v.* When you **compare**, you look closely at how things are alike. *We have to compare the two houses.*

complaint (kum-plānt) *n.* To give a **complaint** is to tell others that you are unhappy about something. *I sent my complaint in a letter to the editor.*

• **compound** (kahm-pownd) *adj.* Something that is **compound** is made up of two or more parts. *The x-ray showed a compound fracture in her arm.*

• **concentrate** (kon-sen-trāt) *v.* To **concentrate** means to focus on something. *Students have to concentrate when studying.*

• **Academic Vocabulary**

confident (kahn-fi-dent) *adj.* A **confident** person is someone who is sure of his or her abilities. *You have to be confident to succeed.*

• **conflict** (kahn-flikt) *n.* A **conflict** is a fight between two people or groups of people. *My friend and I got into a conflict over a book she borrowed from me.*

• **connection** (ku-nek-shun) *n.* The **connection** between two things is something they have in common.

• **connotation** (con-ō-tā-shun) *n.* The **connotation** of a word is the set of feelings that is associated with it. *One connotation of the word "waterfall" can be "peaceful".*

conservation (kon-sur-vā-shun) *n.* **Conservation** is careful protection of something. *Conservation efforts protect national parks.*

• **context** (kon-tekst) *n.* **Context** is the surrounding text near a word or phrase that helps explain the meaning of the word. *The context of the sentence helps you understand what a new word means.*

contribute (kun-trib-yūt) *v.* When you **contribute** to something, you give your time or money. *The child contributed money to help people in need.*

• **convince** (kun-vints) *v.* When somebody **convinces** you of something, you think it's a good idea. *He convinced her to agree with him.*

• **couple** (kup-ul) *n.* A **couple** is two people who are together. *My grandparents are a happy couple.*

• **culture** (kul-chur) *n.* A **culture** is a set of beliefs and customs that a group of people share. *Dancing is a custom found in many cultures.*

D

damage (dam-ij) *n.* **Damage** means harm that is done. *I threw a baseball, which caused damage to the window.*

deal (dēl) *n.* A **deal** is an agreement. *If you agree to mow your neighbor's lawn for money, you have made a deal with your neighbor.*

• **debate** (di-bāt) *v.* To **debate** means to discuss different views of something. *In a debate, two or more people tell why they have different opinions or ideas.*

decent (**dē**-sent) *adj.* When you are **decent**, you are good and kind. *A decent person welcomes a new neighbor.*

• **decision** (dē-**si**-zhun) *n.* A **decision** is a choice. *You make a decision when you choose clothes to wear each day.*

defend (dē-**fend**) *v.* When you **defend** something, you protect it. *A mother animal defends its young.*

• **definition** (de-fu-**ni**-shun) *n.* The meaning of a word is its **definition**. *Please look up the definition of five new words in the dictionary.*

delegate (**del**-i-get) *n.* A **delegate** is a person who has the power to act and speak for others. *The delegates met to talk about laws that would help people.*

democracy (di-**mok**-ru-sē) *n.* In a **democracy**, people have the power to vote for what they believe. *The United States is a democracy.*

deserve (di-**zurv**) *v.* When you **deserve** something it means you have worked hard to earn it. *If you study hard for a test, you deserve a good grade.*

desperate (**des**-pu-rit) *adj.* Someone who is **desperate** has lost hope. *The desperate team tried hard but lost.*

• **despite** (di-**spīt**) *prep.* **Despite** means even though or without regard to. *The man felt cold, despite his warm jacket.*

destroy (di-**stroi**) *v.* To **destroy** means to completely ruin. *The house was destroyed by a fire.*

determined (dē-**tur**-mind) *adj.* When you are **determined** to do something, you work hard at it. *The football team was determined to win.*

diplomat (**dip**-lō-mat) *n.* A **diplomat** is a person who represents his or her government. *To do his or her job, a diplomat lives in another country.*

discovery (dis-**kuv**-ur-ē) *n.* A **discovery** is the act of seeing or finding something for the first time. *The teen made an interesting discovery and took a closer look.*

disfavor (dis-**fā**-vor) *n.* When you show **disfavor**, you show that you don't like something. *A thumbs down is one way to show disfavor about something.*

disguise (dis-**gīz**) *n.* When you wear a **disguise**, you try to look different from what you normally look like. *A disguise can help people or animals hide.*

disgusted (di-**skus**-tid) *adj.* To be **disgusted** means that you dislike something. *Some people are disgusted by frogs.*

document (**dok**-yu-ment) *v.* To **document** something is to provide facts about it. *A research study must be documented carefully with facts.*

donate (**dō**-nāt) *v.* To **donate** means to give to people in need. *I always try to donate some of my money to help others.*

doubt (**dowt**) *n.* When you feel **doubt**, you are not sure. *The girl had doubts about the food after she saw how it was cooked.*

E

• **effect** (e-**fekt**) *n.* An **effect** is the result of an action or cause. *The coach's positive attitude has had a good effect on the team.*

• **effectively** (i-**fek**-tiv-lē) *adv.* Something that is done **effectively** is done in a way that works or gets results. *The teacher effectively taught us how to add and subtract.*

• **element** (**e**-lu-munt) *n.* An **element** is something that is part of a whole. *Copper is one of the elements use to make pennies.*

endangered (en-**dān**-jurd) *adj.* To be **endangered** means to be at risk of disappearing forever. *The ivory-billed woodpecker is an example of an endangered animal.*

• **energy** (**en**-ur-jē) *n.* **Energy** is natural power that is used to make things work. *We can turn the energy of the wind into electricity.*

engage (en-**gāj**) *v.* To **engage** means to take part or get involved in an activity. *She engaged her friends in a conversation.*

• **ensure** (en-**shur**) *v.* To **ensure** is to make sure or certain. *Humans should ensure that rainforests are protected.*

• **environment** (en-**vī**-run-ment) *n.* The **environment** is all of the living and nonliving things that surround a person, animal, or plant. *People plant trees to improve the environment.*

equality (ē-**kwal**-i-tē) *n.* When you have the same rights as other people, you have **equality**. *Equality is important within any group of people.*

• **Academic Vocabulary**

erase (e-**rās**) *v.* When you **erase** something, you make it go away. *We can **erase** mistakes when we write.*

essential (e-**sen**-shul) *adj.* Something that is **essential** is needed for survival. *Food and water are **essential** for living beings.*

• **establish** (es-**tab**-lish) *v.* To **establish** something is to start it. *My friends and I **established** a yearly food collection for families in need.*

• **evaluate** (i-**val**-yū-wāt) *v.* To **evaluate** is to decide on the quality of something. *The test will **evaluate** how well the students are doing.*

• **evidence** (**e**-vi-dents) *n.* **Evidence** can be beliefs, proof, facts, or details that help support a conclusion. *The police need **evidence** to solve the crime.*

excessive (ik-**ses**-iv) *adj.* When something is **excessive**, it is too much. *That is an **excessive** number of pancakes for one person.*

expectation (eks-pek-**tā**-shun) *n.* An **expectation** is something you look forward to or have ideas about. *We had great **expectations** about our project.*

expedition (eks-pe-**dish**-un) *n.* An **expedition** is a trip or journey made for a particular purpose. *The explorer led an **expedition** through the desert.*

experience (eks-**pēr**-ē-ens) *v.* To **experience** something is to go through it yourself. *My first **experience** on a roller coaster was scary but fun.*

• **expert** (**eks**-purt) *n.* An **expert** is a person who knows a lot about a subject. *A ranger is an **expert** about wildlife in the area.*

explorer (eks-**plor**-er) *n.* An **explorer** goes to a place that is new to him or her to find information about it. *Astronauts are **explorers** of our universe.*

extinct (eks-**stingt**) *adj.* Something that is **extinct** is no longer living. *The dodo bird became **extinct** because people hunted too many over time.*

F

• **feature** (**fē**-chur) *n.* **Features** of something are its parts or details. *Some of the **features** of Earth's surface include mountains, lakes, and trees.*

• **focus** (**fō**-kus) *v.* When you **focus** on something, you pay attention to it. *You must **focus** all your attention to hear what the speaker is saying.*

• **Academic Vocabulary**

forbid (for-**bid**) *v.* To **forbid** means to order not to do something. *The sign **forbids** anyone to swim in this area.*

fortune (**for**-chun) *n.* A **fortune** is a large amount of money or a lot of good things. *The woman worked hard to earn her **fortune**.*

founder (**fown**-der) *n.* A **founder** is a person who starts something. *My uncle is the **founder** of his own company.*

frustration (frus-**trā**-shun) *n.* When you feel **frustration**, you feel angry because you cannot do something. *If you do not understand your homework, you may feel **frustration**.*

furious (**fyur**-ē-us) *adj.* Someone who is **furious** is very angry. *The man was **furious** when his car was hit.*

G

gene (**jēn**) *n.* A **gene** is a physical unit that controls what a living cell is like. *The color of your hair depends on your **genes**.*

government (**guv**-urn-ment) *n.* A **government** is a group of people who are in charge of a country, state, or city. *The U.S. **government is run by many people.***

grief (**grēf**) *n.* To feel **grief** is to feel very sad. *My friend felt **grief** when her dog died.*

H

habitat (**hab**-i-tat) *n.* A **habitat** is the place where a plant or an animal naturally lives. *The **habitat** of polar bears is the cold Arctic.*

hesitant (**hez**-i-tunt) *adj.* A **hesitant** person feels unsure, or not ready to do something. *The boy was **hesitant** to pet the rabbit for fear that it would bite.*

humanity (hū-**man**-i-tē) *n.* **Humanity** is kindness and caring about the suffering of others. *Firefighters show **humanity** by doing what they must to save others.*

I

• **identify** (ī-**den**-ti-fī) *v.* When you **identify** something, you name it or tell what it is. *Can you **identify** which jacket is yours?*

ignore (ig-**nor**) *v.* To **ignore** means to pay no attention to something. *It is best to **ignore** people who are bullies.*

illegal (i-**lē**-gul) *adj.* Something that is **illegal** is against the law. *It is illegal to hunt in some areas.*

• **image** (**im**-ij) *n.* An **image** is a mental picture of something. *Moira has a mental image of her grandmother baking cookies.*

• **impact** (**im**-pakt) *v.* To **impact** means to have an effect. *The new salespeople will continue to impact the sales numbers, pushing them up.*

increase (in-**krēs**) *v.* To **increase** means to become larger in number or size. *The size of my family increased when my brother was born.*

independence (in-di-**pen**-duns) *n.* **Independence** means freedom from control by others. *The U.S. celebrates its independence with fireworks on the Fourth of July.*

• **individual** (in-de-**vij**-yū-wul) **1** *adj.* Something that is individual is separate from other things. *Most students like to receive individual attention from their teacher.* **2** *n.* An **individual** is one person. *Only one individual can sit on the chair.*

• **inevitable** (i-**nev**-i-tu-bul) *adj.* Something that is **inevitable** will happen no matter what. *If you throw a ball up, it is inevitable that it will come down.*

influence (**in**-flü-uns) *v.* When people **influence** you, they change the way you think. *Martin Luther King, Jr. influenced people to work toward equality.*

informed (in-**formd**) *adj.* To be **informed** is to have knowledge. *It is our duty to be informed about issues.*

ingredient (in-**grē**-dē-unt) *n.* An **ingredient** is something that is part of a mixture. *Flour, sugar, and butter are ingredients used to make cookies.*

innocent (**in**-u-sent) *adj.* Someone who is **innocent** is without guilt. *The puppy looks innocent and sweet.*

insist (in-**sist**) *v.* To **insist** means to demand or to keep saying. *The child insisted on walking the other direction.*

inspiration (in-spu-**rā**-shun) *n.* An **inspiration** is a reason for doing or creating something. *Artists often find their inspiration in the beauty of nature.*

• **integrate** (**in**-te-grāt) *v.* When you **integrate** groups, you bring them together. *Martin Luther King, Jr. worked to integrate schools.*

• **interpret** (in-**tur**-prut) *v.* To **interpret** means to explain the meaning of something. *A judge interprets the meanings of laws.*

• **involved** (in-**vahlvd**) *adj.* To get **involved** is to become a part of something. *Many people are involved in improving their communities.*

• **issue** (**i**-shü) *v.* To **issue** means to give or hand out. *The agent issued tickets to the passengers.*

J

• **judgment** (**juj**-ment) *n.* **Judgment** is the ability to make good decisions. *He used good judgment by coming home before it started to rain.*

justice (**jus**-tis) *n.* **Justice** means fairness. *Our court system is set up to give everyone an opportunity for justice.*

K

kingdom (**king**-dum) *n.* A **kingdom** is a land or area ruled by a king or a queen. *The kingdom was made up of three countries.*

L

landlord (**land**-lawrd) *n.* A **landlord** is a person who owns land or buildings. *My landlord always makes sure the building is clean.*

leadership (**lēd**-ur-ship) *n.* **Leadership** means guiding others in what to do. *A person who helps others shows leadership.*

• **literal** (**lit**-ur-al) *adj.* The **literal** meaning of a word is its exact meaning. *Always use literal words when explaining things to children.*

• **location** (lō-**kā**-shun) *n.* The **location** is the site or place where a person lives. *She lives in a location close to the beach.*

• **logical** (**lah**-ji-kul) *adj.* When something is **logical**, it makes sense or is reasonable. *It is logical to close the windows when it rains.*

M

measurement (**mezh**-ur-ment) *n.* A **measurement** is the size or quantity of something. *I took measurements of the rock to find out how long it is.*

- **media** (mē-dē-u) *n.* Television, radio, newspapers, magazines and the Internet make up the **media**. *The media can spread information to millions of people.*

memory (mem-e-rī) *n.* A **memory** is something remembered. *Looking through family photographs can bring back memories of good times.*

mercy (mur-sē) *n.* **Mercy** is kindness to someone in trouble. *My mom showed mercy when I spilled food all over the floor.*

mission (mish-un) *n.* A **mission** is the goal of someone's work. *An astronaut's mission is to explore space.*

modest (mod-ist) *adj.* A **modest** person does not act overly proud of an accomplishment or success. *The girl was modest about winning first prize.*

- **modified** (mod-i-fīd) *adj.* Something that has been **modified** has been changed. *We modified the recipe to feed more people.*

movement (müv-ment) *n.* A **movement** is a group of people working together to make a change. *People of all races took part in the Civil Rights Movement.*

N

- **negative** (neg-u-tiv) *adj.* If you have a **negative** opinion about something, you don't like it. *My sister was negative about my idea.*

nervous (ner-vus) *adj.* When you are **nervous**, you feel worried. *The basketball player felt nervous before the game.*

O

obey (ō-bā) *v.* To **obey** is to follow an order. *If your parents tell you to clean your room, you must obey them.*

- **obvious** (ob-vē-us) *adj.* Something that is **obvious** is easily seen or understood. *It was obvious he was sick because he had a fever.*

opinion (ō-pin-yun) *n.* An **opinion** is a belief about something. *Reporters ask people for their opinions about events in the news.*

opportunity (op-ur-tü-ni-tē) *n.* An **opportunity** is a chance to do something. *My teacher gave me the opportunity to tell my ideas to the other students.*

organic (or-gan-ik) *adj.* **Organic** refers to a type of food that is all natural. *Organic fruits and vegetables are grown without chemicals.*

organization (or-ge-nī-zā-shun) *n.* An **organization** is a group of people who work toward a common goal. *The Red Cross is an organization.*

- **organize** (or-ge-nīz) *v.* To **organize** means to arrange things in a certain order. *Please organize the students by height.*

- **origin** (or-u-jin) *n.* The **origin** of something is its source or beginning. *The map shows the origin of the river.*

overcome (ō-vur-kum) *v.* To **overcome** something is to succeed at something that is difficult. *If you used to be afraid of dogs but now you like them, you have overcome your fear.*

P

pact (pakt) *n.* A **pact** is a promise between people. *Friends might make a pact to always help each other.*

peace (pēs) *n.* **Peace** is freedom from war and fighting. *Many people hope for peace in the world.*

permission (pur-mish-un) *n.* When you have **permission**, you are allowed to do something. *You must ask permission to go onto private property.*

- **perspective** (pur-spek-tiv) *n.* A **perspective** is a way of thinking about something. *My teacher's perspective on music is that everyone should learn to play.*

persuade (pur-swād) *v.* To **persuade** means to try to make others agree. *The student persuaded us by giving a strong speech with good ideas.*

petition (pe-tish-un) *n.* A **petition** is a written request for a government or leader to take action. *If enough people sign our petition, it may convince the mayor to do what we ask.*

plague (plāg) *v.* When something really bothers you, it **plagues** you. *The thought of the Monday morning math test plagued her all weekend.*

- **plan** (plan) *n.* A **plan** is a way of doing things. *The building has an escape plan in case of a fire.*

plead (plēd) *v.* To **plead** means to strongly ask for something. *A student might plead for a larger allowance.*

- **Academic Vocabulary**

poacher (pō-chur) *n.* A **poacher** is a person who hunts plants or animals illegally. *Poachers are a problem to endangered wildlife.*

politics (pol-i-tiks) *n.* **Politics** are people's beliefs about government and its plans. *People with similar politics came to the convention.*

pollution (pul-lü-shun) *n.* **Pollution** is waste, chemicals, and gases that have a harmful effect. *Air and water pollution hurt living things.*

population (pop-yū-lā-shun) *n.* **Population** is the number of plants or animals in a group. *The human population of Earth is more than six billion.*

• **position** (puh-zi-shun) *n.* A **position** is a viewpoint, side, or placement. *His position is against serving hot lunches at school.*

• **positive** (pahz-u-tiv) *adj.* **Positive** means good or hopeful. *If you have a positive attitude, you think things are good.*

preach (prēch) *v.* To **preach** is to tell people what you believe is right. *The speaker preached the importance of kindness to all.*

predator (pre-duh-tur) *n.* A **predator** is an animal that eats other animals for food. *Lions and tigers are predators.*

• **predict** (prē-dikt) *v.* When you **predict**, you guess about something or tell what will happen. *We will predict what happens next in the story.*

prejudice (prej-ū-dis) *n.* If you have **prejudice**, you judge things and people before you know about them. *Many people fought to end prejudice.*

prey (prā) *n.* **Prey** is an animal that other animals eat. *A mouse is prey for a snake.*

pride (prīd) *n.* When you feel **pride**, you feel good about something you or someone else does. *The boy felt pride when he graduated from high school.*

problem (prahb-lum) *n.* A **problem** is something you have to solve or fix. *You can solve a math problem.*

• **process** (präs-es) *n.* A **process** is a series of actions that lead to a result. *The process of building the house took a year.*

• **promote** (prō-mōt) *v.* To **promote** something is to tell others that it is a good thing. *The firemen promote safety to the students.*

• **Academic Vocabulary**

• **propaganda** (prop-u-gan-da) *n.* **Propaganda** is the use of faulty methods to persuade an audience. *The report was propaganda and not based on facts.*

property (prop-er-tē) *n.* **Property** is what someone owns, like a house or land. *People can sell their property to someone else.*

protest (prō-test) *v.* To **protest** something means to show you are against it. *Americans protested unfair treatment of African Americans.*

punishment (pun-ish-ment) *n.* A **punishment** is a penalty caused by doing something bad. *We were noisy during class, so as punishment we had to stay after school.*

• **purpose** (pur-pus) *n.* A **purpose** is a reason for doing something. *His purpose for going to the store was to buy milk.*

Q

quest (kwest) *n.* A **quest** is a journey or trip to find something. *The knight is on a quest to find the dragon's cave.*

R

• **react** (rē-akt) *v.* To **react** means to show your feelings about something. *A person may react in fear to a scary movie.*

reality (rē-al-it-ē) *n.* **Reality** is what people actually experience in life. *I wish I could have whatever I liked, but the reality is that I must work to pay for things.*

recall (rē-kawl) *v.* To **recall** means to remember. *The student tried to recall the answer to a test question.*

recite (ri-sīt) *v.* When you **recite** something, you are speaking or reading something aloud in public. *Every morning before class, we recite the Pledge of Allegiance.*

refugee (ref-yu-jē) *n.* A person who must leave his or her home or country to be safe is a **refugee**. *A refugee may have to live with just a few belongings.*

refuse (ri-fūz) *v.* To **refuse** means to choose not to do something. *The child refused to eat any more food.*

• **relate** (ri-lāt) *v.* When you **relate** things, you show how they are connected. *The report should relate how ice and water are alike.*

relative (rel-u-tiv) *n.* A **relative** is a family member. *I love my relatives, but I am especially close with my grandmother.*

relent (ri-lent) *v.* To **relent** means to stop. *After flooding the town, the rain finally relented.*

remind (ri-mīnd) *v.* To **remind** is to help someone remember something or tell them again. *As I left for school, my mom reminded me to take my lunch.*

rent (rent) *n.* When you pay **rent**, you pay money to the owner of a property to live there. *The mother paid rent for the family's apartment every month.*

represent (rep-ri-zent) *v.* To **represent** means to speak or act for a person or group. *The president represents all of the people of his or her country.*

• **research** (rē-surch) *n.* **Research** is a collection of information about something. *There is a lot of research on the solar system.*

• **response** (ri-spons) *n.* A **response** is an answer or reply to something that has happened or has been said. *The fireman had a quick response to the alarm bell.*

rotation (rō-tā-shun) *n.* **Rotation** is the spinning of an object, such as a planet. *Earth's rotation is what gives us night and day.*

routine (rü-tēn) *n.* A **routine** is a normal series of actions that you repeat. *As part of my daily morning routine, I brush my teeth.*

S

• **scale** (skāl) *n.* A **scale** is a graphic organizer that shows how a series of items are related. *The scale on the map measures distance in miles.*

scrape (skrāp) *v.* When you **scrape** something, you damage it. *Did you scrape your knee when you fell?*

segregation (seg-ri-gā-shun) *n.* **Segregation** is when people are kept apart. *The segregation of African American people in the 1950s was wrong.*

separate (sep-u-rut) *adj.* If you are **separate** from other people, you are not with them. *It is not fun to feel separate from the group.*

shame (shām) *n.* When you feel **shame**, you feel badly about something you did. *She felt shame about the mistake she made.*

shrink (shringk) *v.* To **shrink** means to become smaller. *The forests that animals need are shrinking as people cut down trees.*

• **similar** (si-mu-lur) *adj.* Things that are nearly alike are **similar**. *The brothers are very similar in appearance.*

similarity (sim-e-lār-et-ē) *n.* A **similarity** is something that makes things alike. *The similarity between the cars is their color.*

society (so-sī-e-tē) *n.* A **society** is a group of people who share beliefs and goals. *The historical society met to find out about our town's history.*

solar system (sō-lur sis-tem) *n.* Our **solar system** is made up of the sun and the objects that move around it. *Earth's solar system includes eight planets.*

solid (säl-ed) *adj.* Something that is **solid** is hard or firm. *Rocks are solid all the way through.*

species (spē-shēz) *n.* A **species** is a related group of animals or plants. *Lions and tigers are different species. African lions and Asian lions are the same species.*

• **specific** (spe-sif-ik) *adj.* When something is **specific**, it is definite or particular. *Follow the specific directions to do the experiment correctly.*

strength (strength) *n.* **Strength** is the quality of being powerful. *The strength of the storm destroyed many homes.*

• **structure** (struk-chur) *n.* A **structure** is how parts are arranged or organized. *The structure of the bridge is very solid.*

• **summarize** (sum-u-rīz) *v.* When you **summarize** something, you cover the main points briefly. *Please summarize the book in less than a hundred words.*

• **support** (su-pōrt) *n.* To have **support** means that people help you. *Students need the support of their teachers.*

surface (sur-fes) *n.* A **surface** is the outside or top layer of an object. *The new road has a smoother surface than the old road.*

• **Academic Vocabulary**

- **survive** (sur-vīv) *v.* When you **survive**, you stay alive. *In cold weather, you need warm clothes to* ***survive***.
- **symbol** (sim-bul) *n.* A **symbol** is an object that stands for something else. *In the U.S., the Bald Eagle is a* ***symbol*** *of power.*

T

talented (tal-en-tid) *adj.* A **talented** person is good at doing one or more activities. *They are very* ***talented*** *musicians.*

- **technical** (tek-nih-kal) *adj.* Something that is **technical** is based on scientific knowledge. *The science textbook is written in* ***technical*** *terms.*
- **technique** (tek-nēk) *n.* **Technique** is a skilled way of doing something. *My serving* ***technique*** *improved after taking tennis lessons.*
- **technology** (tek-nol-uj-ē) *n.* **Technology** is the use of knowledge to do a task or to improve how the task is done. *Because of new* ***technology***, *computers are faster and smaller than they once were.*
- **temporary** (tem-pō-rair-ē) *adj.* When something is **temporary**, it lasts only a short time. *They had* ***temporary*** *housing.*

threat (thret) *n.* A **threat** is a danger. *Clouds show the* ***threat*** *of a storm.*

thrive (thrīv) *v.* To **thrive** means to grow strong and healthy. *With lots of care, plants can* ***thrive***.

translate (trans-lāt) *v.* To **translate** means to explain in another language. *The sign* ***translates*** *information into English.*

U

- **unique** (yū-nēk) *adj.* Something that is **unique** is different or special. *The giraffe has a* ***unique*** *neck.*

universe (yu-nu-vers) *n.* The **universe** is everything that exists, including all of space. *Our solar system is just one part of the whole* ***universe***.

V

viewpoint (vyū-point) *n.* A **viewpoint** is the way a person thinks about things. *My friends and I had different* ***viewpoints*** *about which way to go.*

virus (vī-rus) *n.* A **virus** is a tiny particle that can cause disease in people, plants, and animals. *My brother had a* ***virus*** *so he couldn't go to school.*

volunteer (vol-en-tēr) *v.* To **volunteer** means to work without pay. *One way I can help others is to* ***volunteer*** *at the soup kitchen.*

W

warrior (wor-ē-yur) *n.* A **warrior** is someone who protects his people. *Some* ***warriors*** *hunt animals for food.*

wildlife (wīld-līf) *n.* **Wildlife** means animals and plants that live freely outdoors without human care. *Bears and moose are examples of* ***wildlife***.

willful (wil-ful) *adj.* Someone who is **willful** refuses to change. *A* ***willful*** *child only does what he wants, not what others tell him.*

- **Academic Vocabulary**

• Academic Vocabulary Master Word List

adaptation	convince	globe	reflect
adjust	couple	identify	region
adjustment	create	illustrate	relate
affect	credit	image	release
aid	culture	immigrant	report
amend	data	impact	research
analyze	debate	individual	resource
appeal	decision	inevitable	response
application	define	integrate	result
apply	definition	interpret	role
appreciate	demonstrate	interview	route
approach	describe	involve	scale
appropriate	design	issue	section
area	despite	job	select
arrange	device	judgment	sequence
assignment	discover	literal	series
assist	discuss	locate	similar
associate	distinguish	location	situation
assume	effect	logical	solve
attach	effectively	media	source
available	element	migrate	space
awareness	emerge	model	specific
belief	encounter	modify	structure
benefit	energy	negative	style
bond	ensure	obvious	summarize
capable	environment	organize	support
category	equipment	origin	survive
challenge	establish	original	symbol
chapter	evaluate	outcome	team
characteristic	evidence	perspective	technical
classic	exact	plan	technique
collapse	experiment	position	technology
collect	expert	positive	temporary
communicate	explain	predict	theme
community	explanation	presentation	topic
compare	express	process	tradition
compound	fact	professional	trait
concentrate	feature	promote	unique
conflict	focus	propaganda	vary
connect	force	purpose	
connotation	freedom	react	
context	goal	record	
contrast	generate	refer	

• Words in red appear in Level E.

Literary Terms

A

Alliteration The repetition of the same sounds (usually consonants) at the beginning of words that are close together. **Example:** Molly makes magnificent mousse, though Pablo prefers pecan pie.

> *See also* **Repetition**

Allusion A key form of literary language, in which one text makes the reader think about another text that was written before it. Allusion can also mean a reference to a person, place, thing, or event that is not specifically named. **Example:** When Hannah wrote in her short story that vanity was the talented main character's "Achilles heel," her teacher understood that Hannah was referring to a character in a Greek myth. So, she suspected that the vanity of the main character in Hannah's short story would prove to be the character's greatest weakness.

> *See also* **Connotation; Literature; Poetry**

Article A short piece of nonfiction writing on a specific topic. Articles appear in newspapers and magazines.

> *See also* **Expository nonfiction; Nonfiction**

Autobiography The story of a person's life, written by that person. **Example:** Mahatma Gandhi wrote an autobiography titled *Gandhi: An Autobiography: The Story of My Experiments With Truth*.

> *See also* **Diary; Journal; Personal narrative**

B

Biographical fiction A fictional story that is based on real events in the life of a real person. **Example:** Although the book *Farmer Boy* by Laura Ingalls Wilder is about her husband's childhood, the conversations between characters are from the author's imagination. They are based on what she thought the characters might have said at the time.

> *See also* **Biography; Fiction**

Biography The story of a person's life, written by another person.

> *See also* **Autobiography; Biographical fiction**

C

Character A person, an animal, or an imaginary creature in a work of fiction.

> *See also* **Characterization; Character traits**

Characterization The way a writer creates and develops a character. Writers use a variety of ways to bring a character to life: through descriptions of the character's appearance, thoughts, feelings, and actions; through the character's words; and through the words or thoughts of other characters.

> *See also* **Character; Character traits; Motive**

Character traits The special qualities of personality that writers give their characters.

> *See also* **Character; Characterization**

Climax The turning point or most important event in a plot.

> *See also* **Falling action; Plot; Rising action**

Complication *See* **Rising action**

Conflict The main problem faced by a character in a story or play. The character may be involved in a struggle against nature, another character, or society. The struggle may also be between two elements in the character's mind.

> *See also* **Plot**

Connotation The feelings suggested by a word or phrase, apart from its dictionary meaning. **Example:** The terms "used car" and "previously owned vehicle" have different connotations. To most people, the phrase "previously owned vehicle" sounds better than "used car."

> *See also* **Denotation; Poetry**

D

Denotation The dictionary meaning of a word or phrase. Denotation is especially important in functional texts and other types of nonfiction used to communicate information precisely.

> *See also* **Connotation; Functional text; Nonfiction**

Descriptive language Language that creates a "picture" of a person, place, or thing—often using words that appeal to the five senses: sight, hearing, touch, smell, and taste. **Example:** The bright, hot sun beat down on Earth's surface. Where once a vibrant lake cooled the skin of hippos and zebras, only thin, dry cracks remained, reaching across the land like an old man's fingers, as far as the eye could see. The smell of herds was gone, and only silence filled the space.

> *See also* **Imagery**

Dialogue What characters say to each other. Writers use dialogue to develop characters, move the plot forward, and add interest. In most writing, dialogue is set off by quotation marks; in play scripts, however, dialogue appears without quotation marks.

Diary A book written by a person about his or her own life as it is happening. Unlike an autobiography, a diary is not usually meant to be published. It is made up of entries that are written shortly after events occur. The person writing a diary often expresses feelings and opinions about what has happened.

> *See also* **Autobiography; Journal**

Drama A kind of writing in which a plot unfolds in the words and actions of characters performed by actors.

> *See also* **Genre; Play; Plot**

Literary Terms

E

Essay A short piece of nonfiction, normally in prose, that discusses a single topic without claiming to do so thoroughly. Its purpose may be to inform, entertain, or persuade.

    See also **Nonfiction; Photo-essay; Topic**

Exaggeration Figurative language that makes things seem bigger than they really are in order to create a funny image in the reader's mind. **Example:** My eyes are so big they pop out of my face when I get surprised or angry.

    See also **Figurative language; Hyperbole**

Exposition The rising action of a story in which characters and the problems they face are introduced.

    See also **Rising action**

Expository nonfiction Writing that gives information and facts. It is usually divided into sections that give information about subtopics of a larger topic.

    See also **Article; News feature; Nonfiction; Report; Textbook; Topic**

F

Fable A brief fictional narrative that teaches a lesson about life. Many fables have animals instead of humans as characters. Fables often end with a short, witty statement of their lesson. **Example:** "The Tortoise and the Hare" is a famous fable in which a boastful, quick-moving hare challenges a slow-moving tortoise to a race. Because the overconfident hare takes a nap during the race, the tortoise wins. The moral of the fable is that slow and steady wins the race.

    See also **Fiction; Folk tale;**

Fairy tale *See* **Fantasy; Folk tale**

Falling action The actions and events in a plot that happen after the climax. Usually, the major problem is solved in some way, so the remaining events serve to bring the story to an end.

    See also **Climax; Conflict; Plot, Rising action**

Fantasy Fiction in which imaginary worlds differ from the "real" world outside the text. Fairy tales, science fiction, and fables are examples of fantasy.

    See also **Fable; Fiction**

Fiction Narrative writing about imaginary people, places, things, or events.

    See also **Biographical fiction; Fable; Fantasy; Folk tale; Historical fiction; Myth; Novel; Realistic fiction; Short story**

Figurative language The use of a word or phrase to say one thing and mean another. Figurative language is especially important in literature and poetry because it gives writers a more effective way of expressing what they mean than using direct, literal language. **Example:** Upon receiving her monthly bills, Victoria complained that she was "drowning in debt."

    See also **Exaggeration; Hyperbole; Idiom; Imagery; Literature; Metaphor; Personification; Poetry; Simile; Symbol**

Folk tale A short, fictional narrative shared orally rather than in writing, and thus partly changed through its retellings before being written down. Folk tales include myths, legends, fables, ghost stories, and fairy tales.

    See also **Fable; Legend; Myth**

Folklore The collection of a people's beliefs, customs, rituals, spells, songs, sayings, and stories as shared mainly orally rather than in writing.

    See also **Folk tale; Legend; Myth**

Functional text Writing in which the main purpose is to communicate the information people need to accomplish tasks in everyday life. **Examples:** résumés, business letters, technical manuals, and the help systems of word-processing programs.

G

Genre A type or class of literary works grouped according to form, style, and/or topic. Major genres include fictional narrative prose (such as short stories and most novels), nonfiction narrative prose (such as autobiographies, diaries, and journals), drama, poetry, and the essay.

    See also **Essay; Fiction; Literature; Nonfiction; Poetry; Prose; Style; Topic**

H

Hero or **Heroine** In myths and legends, a man or woman of great courage and strength who is celebrated for his or her daring feats.

    See also **Legend; Myth**

Historical fiction Fiction based on events that actually happened or on people who actually lived. It may be written from the point of view of a "real" or an imaginary character, and it usually includes invented dialogue.

    See also **Fiction**

Hyperbole Figurative language that exaggerates, often to the point of being funny, to emphasize something. **Example:** When his mother asked how long he had waited for the school bus that morning, Jeremy grinned and said, "Oh, not long. Only about a million years."

    See also **Exaggeration; Figurative language**

I

Idiom A phrase or expression that means something different from the word or words' dictionary meanings. Idioms cannot be translated word for word into another language because an idiom's meaning is not the same as that of the individual words that make it up. **Example:** "Mind your p's and q's" in English means to be careful, thoughtful, and behave properly.

Imagery Figurative language that communicates sensory experience. Imagery can help the reader imagine how people, places, and things look, sound, taste, smell, and feel. It can also make the reader think about emotions and ideas that commonly go with certain sensations. Because imagery appeals to the senses, it is sometimes called *sensory language*.

> *See also* **Descriptive language; Figurative language; Symbol**

Interview A discussion between two or more people in which questions are asked and answered so that the interviewer can get information. The record of such a discussion is also called an interview.

J

Jargon Specialized language used by people to describe things that are specific to their group or subject. **Example:** *Mouse* in a computer class means "part of a computer system," not "a rodent."

Journal A personal record, similar to a diary. It may include accounts of actual events, stories, poems, sketches, thoughts, essays, a collection of interesting information, or just about anything the writer wishes to include.

> *See also* **Diary**

L

Legend A very old story, usually written about a hero or heroine or to explain something in nature. Legends are mostly fiction, but some details may be true.

> *See also* **Folk tale; Hero or Heroine; Myth**

Literature Works written as prose or poetry.

> *See also* **Poetry; Prose**

M

Metaphor A type of figurative language that compares two unlike things by saying that one thing is the other thing. **Example:** Dhara says her grandfather can be a real mule when he doesn't get enough sleep.

> *See also* **Figurative language; Simile; Symbol**

Meter The patterning of language into regularly repeating units of rhythm. Language patterned in this way is called *verse*. By varying the rhythm within a meter, the writer can heighten the reader's attention to what is going on in the verse and reinforce meaning.

> *See also* **Poetry; Rhythm**

Mood The overall feeling or atmosphere a writer creates in a piece of writing.

> *See also* **Tone**

Motive The reason a character has for his or her thoughts, feelings, actions, or words. **Example:** Maria's motive for bringing cookies to her new neighbors was to learn what they were like.

> *See also* **Characterization**

Myth A fictional narrative, often a folk tale, that tells of supernatural events as a way of explaining natural events and their relation to human life. Myths commonly involve gods, goddesses, monsters, and superhuman heroes or heroines.

> *See also* **Folk tale; Hero** or **Heroine; Legend**

N

Narrative writing Writing that gives an account of a set of real or imaginary events (the story), which the writer selects and arranges in a particular order (the plot). Narrative writing includes nonfiction works such as news articles, autobiographies, and journals, as well as fictional works such as short stories, novels, and plays.

> *See also* **Autobiography; Fiction; Journal; Narrator; Nonfiction; Plot; Story**

Narrator Someone who gives an account of events. In fiction, the narrator is the teller of a story (as opposed to the real author, who invented the narrator as well as the story). Narrators differ in how much they participate in a story's events. In a first-person narrative, the narrator is the "I" telling the story. In a third-person narrative, the narrator is not directly involved in the events and refers to characters by name or as *he*, *she*, *it*, or *they*. Narrators also differ in how much they know and how much they can be trusted by the reader.

> *See also* **Character; Point of view**

News feature A nonfiction article that gives facts about real people and events.

> *See also* **Article; Expository nonfiction; Nonfiction**

Nonfiction Written works about events or things that are not imaginary; writing other than fiction.

> *See also* **Autobiography; Biography; Diary; Essay; Fiction; Journal; Personal narrative; Photo-essay; Report; Textbook**

Novel A long, fictional narrative, usually in prose. Its length enables it to have more characters, a more complicated plot, and a more fully developed setting than shorter works of fiction.

> *See also* **Character; Fiction; Plot; Prose; Setting; Short story**

O

Onomatopoeia The use of words that imitate the sounds they refer to. **Examples:** *buzz*, *slam*, *hiss*

Literary Terms

P

Personal narrative An account of a certain event or set of events in a person's life, written by that person.
See also **Autobiography; Diary; Journal**

Personification Figurative language that describes animals, things, or ideas as having human traits.
Examples: In the movie *Babe* and in the book *Charlotte's Web*, the animals are all personified.
See also **Figurative language**

Persuasive writing Writing that attempts to get someone to do or agree to something by appealing to logic or emotion. Persuasive writing is used in advertisements, editorials, and political speeches.

Photo-essay A short nonfiction piece made up of photographs and captions. The photographs are as important as the words in presenting information.
See also **Essay; Nonfiction**

Play A work of drama, especially one written to be performed on a stage. **Example:** Lorraine Hansberry's *A Raisin in the Sun* was first performed in 1959.
See also **Drama**

Plot The pattern of events and situations in a story or play. Plot is usually divided into four main parts: *conflict* (or *problem*), *rising action* (or *exposition* or *complication*), *climax*, and *falling action* (or *resolution*).
See also **Climax; Conflict; Drama; Falling action; Fiction; Rising action; Story**

Poetry A form of literary expression that uses line breaks for emphasis. Poems often use connotation, imagery, metaphor, symbol, allusion, repetition, and rhythm. Word patterns in poetry include rhythm or meter, and often rhyme and alliteration.
See also **Alliteration; Connotation; Figurative language; Meter; Repetition; Rhyme; Rhythm**

Point of view The position from which the events of a story seem to be observed and told. A first-person point of view tells the story through what the narrator knows, experiences, concludes, or can find out by talking to other characters. A third-person point of view may be *omniscient*, giving the narrator unlimited knowledge of things, events, and characters, including characters' hidden thoughts and feelings. Or it may be *limited* to what one or a few characters know and experience.
Example of First-Person Point of View: I'm really hungry right now, and I can't wait to eat my lunch. **Example** of Third-Person Limited Point of View: Olivia is really hungry right now and she wants to eat her lunch. **Example** of Third-Person Omniscient Point of View: Olivia is really hungry right now and she wants to eat her lunch. The other students are thinking about their weekend plans. The teacher is wondering how she will finish the lesson before the bell rings.
See also **Character; Fiction; Narrator**

Propaganda A type of persuasion that twists or doesn't tell the whole truth. Types of propaganda include *glittering generalities* (using impressive words to skip past the truth), *transfers* (using appealing ideas or symbols that aren't directly related to the topic), *testimonials* (using the words of famous people), *plain folks* (showing that a product or idea has the same values as the audience), *bandwagon* (claiming that everyone else is doing it), and *name calling*.
See also **Persuasive writing**

Prose A form of writing in which the rhythm is less regular than that of verse and more like that of ordinary speech.
See also **Poetry; Rhythm**

Proverb A short saying that expresses a general truth. Proverbs are found in many different languages and cultures. **Example:** An apple a day keeps the doctor away.

Purpose An author's reason for writing. Most authors write to entertain, inform, or persuade. **Example:** An author's purpose in an editorial is to persuade the reader to think or do something.
See also **Expository nonfiction; Narrative writing; Persuasive writing**

R

Realistic fiction Fiction in which detailed handling of imaginary settings, characters, and events produces a lifelike illusion of a "real" world. **Example:** Although Upton Sinclair's *The Jungle* is a work of fiction, the author's graphic, detailed descriptions of the slaughterhouse workers' daily lives led to real changes in the meatpacking industry.
See also **Fiction**

Repetition The repeating of individual vowels and consonants, syllables, words, phrases, lines, or groups of lines. Repetition can be used because it sounds pleasant, to emphasize the words in which it occurs, or to help tie the parts of a text into one structure. It is especially important in creating the musical quality of poetry, where it can take such forms as alliteration and rhyme.
See also **Alliteration; Poetry; Rhyme**

Report A usually short piece of nonfiction writing on a particular topic. It differs from an essay in that it normally states only facts and does not directly express the writer's opinions.
See also **Essay; Nonfiction; Topic**

Resolution See **Falling action**

Rhyme The repetition of ending sounds in different words. Rhymes usually come at the end of lines of verse, but they may also occur within a line. **Examples:** *look, brook, shook*
See also **Poetry; Repetition; Rhyme scheme**

Rhyme scheme The pattern of rhymed line endings in a work of poetry or a stanza. It can be represented by giving a certain letter of the alphabet to each line ending on the same rhyme. **Example:** Because the end word of every other line rhymes in the following poem, the rhyme scheme is *abab*:

Winter night falls quick (a)
The pink sky gone, blackness overhead (b)
Looks like the snow will stick (a)
Down the street and up the hill I tread (b)

    See also **Poetry; Rhyme; Stanza**

Rhythm The natural rise and fall, or "beat," of language. Rhythm is present in all language, including speech and prose, but it is most obvious in poetry.

    See also **Meter; Poetry; Prose**

Rising action The part of a plot that presents actions or events that lead to the climax.

    See also **Climax; Conflict; Exposition; Falling action; Plot**

S

Setting The time and place in which the events of a story occur.

Short story A brief, fictional narrative. Like the novel, it organizes the action, thought, and dialogue of its characters into a plot. But it tends to focus on fewer characters and to center on a single event.

    See also **Character; Fiction; Novel; Plot; Story**

Simile A type of figurative language that compares two unlike things by using a word or phrase such as *like, as, than, similar to, resembles,* or *seems.* **Examples:** The tall, slim man had arms as willowy as a tree's branches. The woman's temper is like an unpredictable volcano.

    See also **Figurative language; Metaphor**

Song lyrics Words meant to be sung. Lyrics have been created for many types of songs, including love songs, religious songs, work songs, sea chanties, and children's game songs. Lyrics for many songs were shared orally for generations before being written down. Not all song lyrics are lyrical like poems; some are the words to songs that tell a story. Not all poems called songs were written to be sung.

    See also **Folk literature; Poetry**

Speech A message on a specific topic, spoken before an audience; also, spoken (not written) language.

Stanza A group of lines that forms a section of a poem and has the same pattern (including line lengths, meter, and usually rhyme scheme) as other sections of the same poem. In printed poems, stanzas are separated from each other by a space.

    See also **Meter; Poetry; Rhyme scheme**

Story A series of events (actual or imaginary) that can be selected and arranged in a certain order to form a narrative or dramatic plot. It is the raw material from which the finished plot is built. Although there are technical differences, the word *story* is sometimes used in place of *narrative.*

    See also **Drama; Plot**

Style The way a writer uses language to express the feelings or thoughts he or she wants to convey. Just as no two people are alike, no two styles are exactly alike. A writer's style results from his or her choices of vocabulary, sentence structure and variety, imagery, figurative language, rhythm, repetition, and other resources.

    See also **Figurative language; Genre; Imagery; Repetition; Rhythm**

Symbol A word or phrase that serves as an image of some person, place, thing, or action but that also calls to mind some other, usually broader, idea or range of ideas. **Example:** An author might describe doves flying high in the sky to symbolize peace.

    See also **Figurative language; Imagery**

T

Textbook A book prepared for use in schools for the study of a subject.

Theme The underlying message or main idea of a piece of writing. It expresses a broader meaning than the topic of the piece.

    See also **Topic**

Tone A writer's or speaker's attitude toward his or her topic or audience or toward him- or herself. A writer's tone may be positive, negative, or neutral. The words the writer chooses, the sentence structure, and the overall pattern of words convey the intended tone.

    See also **Connotation; Figurative language; Literature; Mood; Rhythm; Topic**

Topic What or who is being discussed in a piece of writing; the subject of the piece.

    See also **Theme**

Index of Skills

personal reading journal 531
plot diagram 81
prediction chart 11
problem-and-solution chart 236
question-answer chart 177
sequence chain 159
story map 26
story plan 621
T chart 216, 383, 442
theme chart 72, 492
time line 196
tree diagram 461
Venn diagram 164, 366
visualization chart 333, 345

I

Independent reading
content library 1, 79, 167,
243, 321, 391, 469, 549
digital library 6, 30, 54, 86, 110,
134, 172, 200, 220, 248, 270, 294,
328, 350, 370, 396, 420, 446,
474, 496, 526, 554, 574, 594
leveled library 1, 79, 167,
243, 321, 391, 469, 549
Inferences, make 41, 64, 194,
209, 289, 415, 441, 451, 461, 569
make with textual evidence 197,
226, 257, 571
Informal English (see Formal/
informal English)
Internet 1, 27, 28, 74, 79, 107,
108, 161, 196, 236, 237, 292,
331, 367, 384, 386, 442

J

Judgments, make 71, 129, 365, 541

L

Language Functions
ask and answer questions 7, 9, 29
ask for and give
information 173, 175, 199
clarify and verify 295, 297, 317
define and explain 87, 89,
109, 271, 273, 293
describe an event 201, 203, 219
describe animals and
things 329, 331, 349
elaborate 371, 373, 387

engage in conversation 135, 137, 163
engage in discussion 421, 423, 445
express ideas and opinions 55, 57, 75
express opinions 397, 399, 419
give and follow
directions 527, 529, 545
give information 31, 33, 53
justify 447, 449, 465
make comparisons 249,
251, 269, 351, 353, 369
negotiate 575, 577, 593
persuade 555, 557, 573
retell a story 111, 113, 133
summarize 221, 223,
239, 497, 499, 525
tell an original story 51, 475, 477, 495
use appropriate
language 595, 597, 625
Language learning strategies
acquire vocabulary
basic 10, 25, 34, 49, 58, 71, 90, 105,
114, 129, 138, 159, 176, 195, 204,
215, 224, 235, 252, 265, 274, 289,
298, 313, 332, 345, 354, 365, 374,
383, 400, 415, 424, 441, 450, 461,
478, 491, 500, 521, 530, 541, 558,
569, 578, 589, 598, 621, 658–668
grade-level 10, 25, 34, 49, 58, 71,
90, 105, 114, 129, 138, 159, 176,
195, 204, 215, 224, 235, 252,
265, 274, 289, 298, 313, 332,
345, 354, 365, 374, 383, 400,
415, 424, 441, 450, 461, 478, 491,
500, 521, 530, 541, 558, 569,
578, 589, 598, 621, 658–668
learning techniques
reviewing 25, 49, 71, 105, 129,
159, 195, 215, 235, 265, 289, 313,
345, 365, 383, 415, 441, 461,
491, 521, 541, 569, 589, 621
language
academic using/reusing
speaking activities 28, 108,
162, 132, 218, 316, 348,
367, 386, 494, 543, 592
writing activities 27, 73, 292, 443
basic using/reusing
speaking activities 28, 30, 52, 73,
74, 107, 131, 165, 172, 218, 220,
237, 241, 319, 389, 467, 547, 627
writing activities 25, 49,
71, 105, 129, 159, 195, 215,
235, 265, 289, 313, 345,

365, 383, 415, 441, 461, 491,
521, 541, 569, 589, 621
monitor production
oral language 33, 89, 137
written language 29, 163, 239
Listening
distinguish between facts and
opinions 237, 279, 571
evaluate spoken messages
for bias 52
follow oral instructions 527,
529, 538, 545
for a purpose 28, 30, 52, 73, 74,
107, 131, 165, 172, 218, 220, 237,
241, 319, 389, 467, 547, 627
give oral instructions 527,
529, 538, 545
identify main idea and details
in spoken messages 368
paraphrase spoken messages 368
summarize presentations 52,
223, 316, 368, 385
**Listening (second language
acquisition)**
academic vocabulary 493,
494, 522, 523, 622, 623, 624
basic vocabulary 84, 85, 170,
171, 181, 185, 186, 326, 327
comprehension
collaborating with peers 251,
273, 306, 373, 387
following directions 527, 529, 545
responding to questions
and requests 7, 9, 175
retelling 111, 113, 122, 221, 223
summarizing 111, 113, 122, 221, 223
taking notes 78, 166, 223,
237, 242, 320, 385
contextual support to
enhance/confirm spoken
language 475, 497, 575
distinguish English
intonation 15, 279, 634, 638, 655
sounds 58, 90, 176
English sound system 114, 204, 252
language structures 7, 8, 56,
249, 271, 272, 273, 296
linguistic support to enhance/
confirm spoken language 9, 87, 577
meaning from media for
concept attainment 31,
55, 186, 214, 249

language attainment 31, 55, 186, 201, 214, 249

monitor understanding of spoken language 51, 109, 132, 297, 317

new expressions 54, 55, 173, 394, 395, 575

seek clarification 173, 297, 306, 317, 329, 371

understand complex spoken language
Implicit ideas 315, 417, 443, 588
Information 175, 353, 529

understand spoken language (situations familiar to unfamiliar)
general meaning
contexts 449, 557, 591
language 223, 251, 297, 519, 520
topics 52, 107, 574
important details
contexts 266, 292, 346
language 387, 495, 525
topics 386, 443, 522
main points
contexts 291, 543, 593
language 137, 423, 577
topics 160, 368, 386

visual support to enhance/confirm spoken language 87, 111, 135, 295, 397, 421, 447

Literary elements & devices
allusion 669
descriptive language 669
hero or heroine 670
mood 671
narrator 671
style 240, 673
tone 198, 673
topic 388, 673
word choice 392, 393, 402, 462, 463, 467, 590
see also Character, Figurative language, Plot, Poetic elements, Point of view, Setting, Sound devices, Theme

M

Main idea (as comprehension strategy) 470, 522

Manage text
notetaking 78, 390
outlining 265
previewing 11, 59

Mechanics (see Capitalization and Punctuation)

Media Literacy
analyze media 92, 93, 96, 237, 591
distinguish fact and opinion 237
food commercials 591
create media 131, 292
comic book 131
technical manual 292
digital library 6, 30, 54, 86, 110, 134, 172, 200, 220, 248, 270, 294, 328, 350, 370, 396, 420, 446, 474, 496, 526, 554, 574, 594
evaluate media 267
evaluate techniques used 237
use media for research 386
use the Internet for research 1, 27, 28, 74, 79, 107, 108, 161, 196, 236, 237, 292, 331, 367, 384, 386, 442

Monitor comprehension, see self-monitor

P

Paraphrase 147, 211, 213, 311, 359, 368, 381, 413, 431, 438, 455, 509, 520, 540, 541

Persuasive text 550, 551, 627, 672
appeals 550, 570
propaganda 550, 572, 672
techniques 590, 626

Plan reading 11, 12, 25, 35, 36, 49, 59, 60, 71, 77
preview and predict 11, 59
preview and set a purpose 35

Plot 26, 80, 81, 116, 130, 140, 160, 165, 314, 442, 672
climax 26, 80, 160, 669
complications 26, 160, 669
conflict 26, 80, 160, 669
exposition 670
falling action 26, 80, 160, 670
resolution 26, 80, 160, 672
rising action 26, 80, 160, 673

Poetic elements
meter 671
repetition 464, 672
rhyme 464, 672
rhyme scheme 673
rhythm 464, 673
stanza 464, 673
verse 464

see also Figurative language, Sound devices

Point of view 2, 12, 36, 50, 672
first-person 2, 12, 36, 50
third-person 50

Predictions 11, 59

Prior knowledge (see activate prior knowledge)

Prior experiences 6, 30, 54, 86, 110, 134, 172, 200, 220, 248, 270, 294, 328, 350, 370, 396, 420, 446, 474, 496, 526, 554, 574, 594

Purposes for reading 36, 37, 46, 62, 66, 70, 94, 96, 98, 100, 102, 118, 142, 180, 182, 184, 186, 188, 190, 192, 208, 210, 214, 228, 230, 232, 234, 256, 258, 260, 262, 278, 280, 282, 284, 286, 288, 302, 304, 336, 338, 340, 342, 358, 360, 362, 368, 378, 380, 382, 428, 432, 434, 454, 456, 458, 482, 504, 506, 508, 510, 512, 514, 516, 518, 534, 536, 538, 540, 562, 564, 566, 582, 584, 586, 602, 609, 618

Q

Questioning 177, 178, 195, 205, 206, 215, 225, 226, 231, 232, 235, 241
question the author 205, 208, 211
self-question 177, 180, 182, 184, 191
types
evaluative 50, 197, 416
interpretive 177, 191, 205, 208, 212, 225, 226
literal 177, 180, 182, 184, 191, 195, 225, 226, 340, 381, 512, 537, 612
universal 25, 265, 345

R

Reading (second language acquisition)
decode using skills 13, 37, 61
demonstrate comprehension by
analytical skills 25, 106, 123, 157, 158, 225, 313, 385, 470, 471, 483, 588, 599, 619, 620
employing basic skills 41, 233, 281, 341
expanding reading skills 108, 333, 334, 381, 383, 522, 571

inferential skills 41, 299, 308,
  401, 402, 404, 406, 408, 425, 426,
  428, 430, 432, 436, 451, 452, 454
retelling 147, 431, 479, 480, 525, 565
shared reading 198, 256,
  278, 520, 534, 568, 586
summarizing 147, 431,
  479, 480, 525, 565
taking notes 27, 196
prereading supports 90, 93,
  94, 177, 179, 354, 357, 358,
  360, 362, 377, 380, 403
use peers/teachers' support to
  develop background
    knowledge 30, 86, 446, 474, 526
  develop grasp of language
    structure 32, 33, 174, 175, 476
  develop vocabulary 114,
    314, 327, 558, 598
  enhance/confirm
    understanding 67, 409, 431, 608
  read content area text 177,
    245, 325, 333, 501
use visual/contextual support to
  develop background
    knowledge 6, 30, 86, 172, 294
  develop grasp of language
    structure 32, 33, 174,
    175, 202, 476, 477
  develop vocabulary 246, 247,
    311, 326, 327, 459, 473
  enhance/confirm
    understanding 130, 418, 522, 533
  read content area text 48,
    189, 261, 276, 287, 305
written classroom materials
  English vocabulary 80,
    168, 322, 323
  environmental print 515
  language structure 222,
    223, 352, 353, 476, 477
  sight vocabulary 204, 354, 374
Research 27, 28, 89, 107, 108,
  161, 218, 292, 367, 386
Research/Research Plan
  collect/gather 28
  electronic resources 1, 27, 28, 74,
    79, 107, 108, 161, 196, 236, 237,
    292, 331, 367, 384, 386, 442
  online sources 1, 27, 28, 74, 79,
    107, 108, 161, 196, 236, 237,
    292, 331, 367, 384, 386, 442

follow plan to gather
  information from
    advanced search
      strategies 107, 161, 367
    relevant print 107
organizing
  draws conclusions 386
  graphic to organize 218, 292
  gives reasons for conclusions 386
  marshals evidence to explain 28
  paraphrases findings 107, 108
  summarizes findings 108
projects
  collect data 28
  explore animal adaptations 108
  explore dragons across
    cultures 161
  find area 73
  give an informative report 367
  make a technical manual 292
  report about names and places 27
  report on Lithuania 443
  research animal vision 107
record data 78, 386, 390
synthesizing 386
topic 27, 28, 108, 386, 443
  brainstorm 27, 89, 107
  consult with others 27,
    107, 108, 218, 219
  decide on topic 27, 28, 108, 386, 443
  formulate major research
    question 28, 443
Resources
  Diaries 452, 669
  electronic texts 376
  journals 276, 671
  literature 2, 80–83, 290, 318, 670,
    671
  maps 322
  newspapers 226, 671
  speeches 673
  textbooks 502, 673
Respond to texts 25, 49, 71, 105,
  129, 159, 195, 215, 235, 265, 289,
  313, 345, 365, 383, 415, 441, 461,
  491, 521, 541, 569, 589, 621
  analyze literature 25, 159,
    313, 415, 521, 589
    arguments in persuasive text 570
    character and plot 130
    drama 622
    imagery in poetry 347

myths 268
    persuasive language 590
    plot 26
    plot and setting 160
    point of view 50
    realistic fiction 314
    song lyrics 464
    support in persuasive text 571
    symbols in poetry 524
    text structure 26, 50, 106,
      196, 236, 266, 522, 542
    theme 492
    tone 198
  evaluate literature
    biography 216
    characters 417
    historical fiction 442
    imagery 416
    informational text 197
    word choice 462
  reflect on reading 77, 165,
    241, 319, 389, 467, 547, 627
  support responses
    citing textual evidence 197, 216, 571
    paraphrase 147, 211, 213, 231,
      311, 359, 368, 381, 413, 431,
      438, 455, 509, 520, 540
    using experience 6, 30, 54, 86,
      110, 134, 172, 200, 220, 248, 270,
      294, 328, 350, 370, 396, 420, 446,
      474, 496, 526, 554, 574, 594
    using prior knowledge 2, 4, 6,
      7, 30, 31, 54, 55, 80, 84, 86, 87,
      110, 134, 168, 170, 172, 200, 201,
      220, 221, 246, 248, 249, 270, 271,
      294, 295, 322, 326, 328, 350,
      370, 371, 392, 394, 396, 397,
      420, 421, 446, 447, 470, 472, 474,
      475, 496, 497, 526, 527, 550, 552,
      554, 555, 574, 575, 594, 595

S

Self-monitor 91, 92, 105, 115,
  116, 129, 139, 140, 159, 165
  clarify ideas 91, 105
  clarify vocabulary 115, 129, 139, 159
  reflect on understanding 77, 165,
    241, 319, 389, 467, 547, 627
    make connections 253, 254, 265,
      275, 276, 289, 299, 300, 313, 319
    personal 299

American Express Publishing Corporation: "Soup for the Soul" by Kristin Donnelly is comprised of excerpts from "Soul-Soothing Soups" from the November 2006 issue of FOOD & WINE magazine. Text copyright © by Kristin Donnelly. Reprinted by permission of FOOD & WINE magazine, a publication of American Express Publishing Corporation.

Carmen T. Bernier-Grand: "Indian Summer Sun" by Carmen T. Grand. This work was first published in ONCE UPON A CUENTO edited by Lyn Miller-Lachmann published by Curbstone Press. Used by permission of the author.

Diana Chang: "Saying Yes" by Diana Chang. Copyright © Diana Chang. Used by permission of the author.

Charlesbridge Publishing: "The Flag We Love" by Pam Muñoz Ryan. Text copyright © 1996 by Pam Muñoz Ryan. Illustrations copyright © 1996 by Ralph Masiello. Used with permission of Charlesbridge Publishing, Inc. All rights reserved.

Curtis Brown, LTD.: Copyright © 1983 by Sue Alexander. First appeared in NADIA THE WILLFUL. Published by Alfred A. Knopf, Inc. Reprinted by permission of Curtis Brown, LTD.

Estate of Dr. Martin Luther King, Jr.: "I Have a Dream" by Dr. Martin Luther King, Jr. Reprinted by arrangement with The Heirs of the Estate of Martin Luther King Jr., c/o Writers House as agent for the proprietor New York, NY. Copyright 1963; copyright renewed 1991 Coretta Scott King.

Farrar, Straus and Giroux, LLC: "The Clever Magistrate" from THE CH'I-LIN PURSE by Linda Fang, illustrations by Jeanne Lee. Text copyright © 1995 by Linda Fang. Illustrations copyright © 1995 by Jeanne Lee. Reprinted by permissions of Farrar, Straus and Giroux, LLC. "The Three Chicharrones" from RED RIDIN' IN THE HOOD AND OTHER CUENTOS by Patricia Marcantonio. Copyright © 2005 by Patricia Marcantonio. Reprinted by permissions of Farrar, Straus and Giroux, LLC.

Georges Borchardt, Inc.: DRAGON, DRAGON AND OTHER TALES by John Gardner. Copyright © 1975 by Boskydell Artists, Ltd. Reprinted by permission of Georges Borchardt, Inc., for the Estate of John Gardner.

Groundwood Books: "Chief Koruinka's Song" from MESSENGERS OF RAIN AND OTHER POEMS FROM LATIN AMERICA. Compilation edited by Claudia M. Lee Copyright © 2002 by Groundwood Books. First published in Canada by Groundwood Books Ltd. Reprinted by permission of the publisher.

Hyperion Books for Children: From MARTIN'S BIG WORDS. Text copyright © 2001 by Doreen Rappaport. Illustrations copyright © 2001 by Bryan Collier. Reprinted by permission of Hyperion Books for Children. All rights reserved.

Lee and Low Books, Inc.: "In My Dreams" by Francisco X. Alarcón is from POEMS TO DREAM TOGETHER: POEMS PARA SOÑAR JUNTOS. Text © 2005 by Francisco X. Alarcón, illustrations copyright © 2005 by Paula Barrgán. Permission arranged with Lee & Low Books, Inc., New York, NY 10016. PASSAGE TO FREEDOM: THE SUGIHARA STORY. Text copyright © 1997 by Ken Mochizuki; illustrations copyright © 1997 by Dom Lee. Permission arranged with Lee & Low Books, Inc., New York, NY 10016.

Naomi Long Madgett: "Midway" by Naomi Long Madgett. From STAR BY STAR © 1965, 70. Reprinted in CONNECTED ISLANDS: NEW AND SELECTED POEMS by Naomi Long Madgett. By permission of the author.

Daisy Myrie: "Market Women" by Daisy Myrie from NEW SHIPS: AN ANTHOLOGY OF WEST INDIAN POEMS, edited by Donald G. Wilson, Savacou Publications Ltd.

NASA: "Between Earth and Space" astronaut journal excerpts are from the journal entries of the Johnson Space Center astronauts, which can be found online at www.nasa.gov/centers/johnson/astronauts/journals_astronauts.html.

National Geographic Society: "A Lion Hunt" by Joseph Lemasolai Lekuton. Reprinted with permission of the National Geographic Society from the book FACING THE LION by Joseph Lemasolai Lekuton with Herman Viola. Copyright © 2003 Joseph Lemasolai Lekuton with Herman Viola. "Mireya Mayor: Ultimate Explorer" is adapted from "Mireya Mayor: Primatologist/Conservationist" at www.nationalgeographic.com. Used by permission of National Geographic Society.

Penguin Books Ltd: From ZLATA'S DIARY: A CHILD'S LIFE IN SARAJEVO by Zlata Filipovic, translated by Christina Pribichevich-Zoric (Viking 1994, first published in France as 'Le Journal de Zlata' by Fixot et editions Robert Laffont 1993). Copyright © Fixot et editions Robert Laffont, 1993. Reproduced by permission of Penguin Books Ltd.

Penguin Group (USA) Inc.: "Diary Entries", from ZLATA'S DIARY by Zlata Filipovic, translated by Christina Pribichevich-Zoric, copyright © 1994 Editions Robert Laffont/Fixot. Used by permission of Viking Penguin, a division of Penguin Group (USA) Inc.

Marian Reiner: "Argument" from OUT LOUD by Eve Merriam. Copyright © 1973 by Eve Merriam. Used by permission of Marian Reiner.

Scholastic, Inc.: "Getting Involved" by Jonathan Blum. From "School Spirit" by Jonathan Blum. Published in SCHOLASTIC ACTION, May 8, 2003. Copyright © 2003 by Scholastic Inc. Reprinted by permission. "Taking Action" by Genet Berhane. From "Matt Cavedon Says Enough is Enough!" by Genet Berhane. Published in SCHOLASTIC NEWS: Online Edition. Copyright © 2007 by Scholastic, Inc. Reprinted by permission. From ANY SMALL GOODNESS: A NOVEL OF THE BARRIO by Tony Johnston. Scholastic Inc./The Blue Sky Press. Copyright © 2001 by Roger D. Johnston and Susan T. Johnston as Trustees of the Johnston Family Trust. Reprinted by permission.

Simon & Schuster, Inc.: "Quilt" by Janet S. Wong. Reprinted with the permission of Margaret K. McElderry Books, an imprint of Simon & Schuster Children's Publishing Division, from A SUITCASE OF SEAWEED AND OTHER POEMS by Janet S. Wong. Copyright © 1996 by Janet S. Wong. All rights reserved.

Emma Suárez-Báez: "Almost Evenly Divided" by Emma Suárez-Báez. Copyright © 1999 by Emma Suárez-Báez. Used by permission of the author.

Susan Bergholz Literary Services: From THE HOUSE ON MANGO STREET. Copyright © 1984 by Sandra Cisneros. Published by Vintage Books, a division of Random House, Inc., and in hardcover by Alfred A. Knopf in 1994. Reprinted by permission of Susan Bergholz Literary Services, New York, NY and Lamy, NM. All rights reserved.

Dr. Florence Wambugu: "Is genetically modified food a good way to feed the world?" is from "Taking the Food Out of Our Mouths" by Florence Wambugu, published in THE WASHINGTON POST, August 26, 2001. Dr. Florence Wambugu is now the CEO of Africa Harvest, whose vision is "An Africa free of hunger, poverty and malnutrition". The Foundation's vision is to use science and technology - especially biotechnology - to help the poor in Africa achieve food security, economic well-being and sustainable rural development. For more details, visit www.ahbfi.org.

Photography

3 (b) Time & Life Pictures/Getty Images. **5** (tl) Imagezoo/Images.com/Corbis. (tr) Visuals Unlimited/Corbis. **6** (b) Rick Gayle Studio/Corbis. **7** (t) Sylvain Grandadam/The Image Bank/Getty Images. (b) Jonathan Kirn/The Image Bank/Getty Images. **8** (b) Milk Photographie/Corbis. **10** (bc) Urs Kuester/National Geographic/Getty Images. (bl) PM Images/Getty Images. (mc) Burazin/Getty Images. (ml) Brian Drouin/National Geographic Image Collection. (mr) Stockbyte/Getty Images. (tc) Image Source/Corbis. (tl) Jodi Cobb/National Geographic Image Collection. (tr) Stockbyte/Getty Images. **24** (r) Richard Nowitz/National Geographic Image Collection. **29** (b) Photodisc/Getty Images. **30** (b) Lind Holthaus Crumpecker. (bg) Carl & Ann Purcell/Corbis. **31** (r) WorldFoto/Alamy Images. (bg) Paul Souders/WorldFoto/Alamy Images. **32** (b) Julie Harris/Alamy Images. **33** (b) Rob C. Nunnington/Gallo Images/Corbis. **34** (bc) Randy Olson/National Geographic Image Collection. (bl) John Eastcott and Yva Momatiuk/National Geographic Image Collection. (mc) Tom Grill/Corbis. (ml) Jeff Foott/National Geographic/Getty Images. (mr) Gerry Broome/AP Images. (tc) Yellow Dog Productions/Photographer's Choice/Getty Images. (tl) Brian Drouin/National Geographic Image Collection. (tl) Medford Taylor/National Geographic Image Collection. **36-37** (LesOp) Richard Du Toit/Minden Pictures/Getty Images. **38-39** (t) Roy Toft/National Geographic Image Collection. **39** (b) Lind Holthaus Crumpecker. **40** (c) DLILLC/Corbis. **42** (c) Wendy Stone/Corbis. **43** (c) Paul Souders/The Image Bank/Getty Images. **45** (c) Corbis. **46** (c) Randy Wells/Stone/Getty Images. **48** (t) Lind Holthaus Crumpecker. **52** (c) Jeff Greenberg/PhotoEdit. **53** (b) Peter McBride/Aurora Photos. **54** (b) Craig Tuttle/Corbis. **55** (c) Archivo Iconografico, S.A./Corbis. (bg) Comstock Images/Jupiter Images. **56** (b) Peter Titmuss/Alamy Images. **57** (t) Holger Winkler/A.B./zefa/Corbis. **58** (bc) Somos/Veer/Getty Images. (bl) Otis Imboden/National Geographic Image Collection. (mc) Cleve Bryant/PhotoEdit. (ml) Altrendo Images/Getty Images. (mr) Brian Drouin/National Geographic Image Collection. (tc) Richard Olsenius/National Geographic Image Collection. (tl) Michael Blann/Digital Vision/Getty Images. (tr) Randy Faris/Corbis. **70** (c) Eric Gay/AP Images. **81** (b) Photodisc/Getty Images. **83** (c) Photodisc/Getty Images. **85** (t) graficart.net/Alamy Images. **86** (b) Dennis Johnson/Papilio/Corbis. (bg) Doug Perrine/Seapics. **87** (c) Stuart Westmorland/Corbis. **88** (b) Stuart Westmorland/Corbis. **89** (t) H. Schmid/zefa/Corbis. **90** (bc) Jim Reed/Corbis. (bl) John Burcham/National Geographic Image Collection. (mc) Beverly Joubert/National Geographic Image Collection. (ml) James Ingram/Alamy Images. (mr) Jason Edwards/National Geographic Image Collection. (tc) John Cumming/Digital Vision/Getty Images. (tl) Juniors Bildarchiv/age fotostock. (tr) Roy Toft/National Geographic Image Collection. **92-93** (LesOp) Stephen Frink Collection/Alamy. **94** (l) Stephen Frink Collection/Alamy. (r) 2005 Norbert Wu/www.norbertwu.com. **95** (b) August Sycholt/AGE Fotostock. **96** (l-r) Mark Payne-Gill/Naturepl.com. **97** (l-r) Mark Payne-Gill/Naturepl.com. **98** (l) David A. Northcott/Corbis. **99 (b)** Klaus Uhlenhut/Animals Animals. **100-101** (b) Doug Perrine/Seapics.com. **102** (b) Michael Nichols/National Geographic Image Collection. **103** (t) Michael & Patricia Fogden/Corbis. **104** (tr, bc, br) Robert Sisson/National Geographic Image Collection. (bl) Chris Johns/National Geographic Image Collection. (tc) Paul Zahl/National Geographic Image Collection. (tl) Bruce Dale/National Geographic Image Collection. **110** (b) Images.com/Corbis. **112** (b) David Diaz. **114** (bc) Terry Vine/Digital Vision/Getty Images. (bl) Somos/Veer/Getty Images. (mc) David Young-Wolff/PhotoEdit. (ml) Don Hammond/Design Pics/Corbis. (mr) Peter Krogh/National Geographic Image Collection. (tc) Alistair Berg/Digital Vision/Getty Images. (tl) Photodisc/Alamy Images. (tr) Andy Sacks/Photographer's Choice/Getty Images. **138** (bc) Mary Kate Denny/PhotoEdit. (bl) The Gallery Collection/Corbis. (mc) Kenneth Garrett/National Geographic Image Collection. (ml) Nikolaevich/Taxi/Getty Images. (mr) Stock4B/Getty Images. (tc) Photodisc/Getty Images. (tl) Barry Austin Photography/Photodisc/Getty Images. (tr) Town Hall, Malaga, Spain/Bridgeman Art Library. **133** (t) Rabbit running from Wolf's House, illustration from 'Brer Rabbit' (gouache on paper) by Virginio Livraghi (20th Century). **134** (b)

Blue Lantern Studio/Corbis. **136** (b) Images.com/ Corbis. **157** (c) Photo courtesy of Joel Gardner/ Flat Out Films. **158** (c) PhotoObjects.net/ Jupiterimages. **161** (b) The Bridgeman Art Library/ Getty Images. **169** (r) Superstudio/Getty Images. **171** (t) Peter Turnley/Corbis. **172** (b) Bettmann/ Corbis. (bg) Rob Bartee/Alamy Images. **173** (c) Bettmann/Corbis. **174** (b) Rogelio V. Solis/AP Photo. **175** (t) Wally McNamee/Corbis. **176** (bc) Ace Stock Limited/Alamy Images. (bl) Danny Lyon/ Magnum Photos. (ml) David Young-Wolff/ PhotoEdit. (tc) James L. Amos/National Geographic Image Collection. (tl) James P. Blair/ National Geographic Image Collection. (tr) Reuters/Corbis. **178** (l) Carl Iwasaki/Time Life Pictures/Getty Images. **178-179** (LesOp) Spider Martin. **180** (c) Library of Congress, Prints & Photographs Division, FSA/OWI Collection, [LC-DIG-fsa-8a03228]. **181** (c) Hulton Archive/Getty Images. **182** (b) Bettmann/Corbis. **183** (r) Carl Iwasaki/Time Life Pictures/Getty Images. **184** (r) Carl Iwasaki/Time & Life Pictures/Getty Images. **185** (b) Copyright 2003. The University of Michigan Photo Services. All Rights Reserved. (t) Carl Iwasaki/Time Life Pictures/Getty Images. **186** (t) Corbis. **187** (r) Bettmann/Corbis. **188** (c) Flip Schulke/Corbis. **189** (r) Gene Herrick/AP Images. **190** (tl) Time Life Pictures/Time Magazine, Copyright Time Inc./Getty Images. **190-191** (tr) Grey Villet/Time Life Pictures/Getty Images. **192-193** (t) Francis Miller/Time Life Pictures/Getty Images. **194** (bg) Paul Edmondson/Jupiterimages. **195** (t) AP Photo/Gene Herrick. **200** (b) Bettmann/ Corbis. **201** (r) Bettmann/Corbis. **202** (b) Time & Life Pictures/Getty Images. **204** (bc) Alison Wright/National Geographic Image Collection. (bl) Stephen St. John/National Geographic Image Collection. (mc) William Lovelace/Express/Getty Images. (ml) Dalmas/SIPA Press. (mr) Mario Tama/ Getty Images. (tc) The Granger Collection, New York. (tl) Rebecca Cook/Reuters/Landov. (tr) allOver photography/Alamy Images. **209** (b) Fox Photos/Getty Images. **212** (t) Donald Uhrbrock/ Time Life Pictures/Getty Images. **214** (b) Ernst Haas/Getty Images. (t) Candlewick Press. **217** (b) Julian Wasser/Time Life Pictures/Getty Images. **220** (b) Dana White/PhotoEdit. (bg) Nicemonkey/ Alamy Images. **221** (c) Tony Freeman/PhotoEdit. **222** (b) David Young-Wolff/PhotoEdit. **224** (bc) Jim Wright/Star Ledger/Corbis. (bl) Chuck Savage/ Corbis. (mc) Joel Sartore/National Geographic Image Collection. (ml) Jeff Greenberg/Alamy. (mr) Annie Griffiths Belt/National Geographic Image Collection. (tc) Robert Sciarrino/Star Ledger/ Corbis. (tl) Bobby Model/National Geographic Image Collection. (tr) Lee Celano/AP Images. **228** (t) Bruce Kluckhohn. 229 (c) Bruce Kluckhohn. **230** (t) David L. Moore/Alamy Images. **232** (l) Steve Miller/AP Images. **233** (r) Corbis/Jupiterimages. **234** (c) Boundless Playgrounds. **244** (l) NASA/JPL/ PIRL/UofArizone/Michael/Peter Arnold, Inc. (r) NASA/National Geographic Image Collection. **245** (l) Myron Jay Dorf/Corbis. (r) Stocktrek Images/ Getty Images. **247** (t) Daniel L. Geiger/SNAP/ Alamy Images. **248** (b) Tim Kiusalaas/Corbis. (bq) The Stocktrek Corp/Brand X/Corbis. **249** (l) Kayte M. Deioma/PhotoEdit. (r) Paul Thompson/Eye Ubiquitous/Corbis. **250** (b) James L. Stanfield/ National Geographic Image Collection. **252** (bc) Chris Cheadle/Alamy Images. (bl) JTB Photo Communications, Inc./Alamy Images. (mc) Dustin Steller/Design Pics/Corbis. (ml) Quilla Ulmer/Jim Reed/Photo Researchers, Inc.. (mr) Tim Kiusalaas/ Corbis. (tc) Riser/Glen Allison/Getty Images. (tl) Corbis. (tr) Eddie Hironaka/Image Bank/Getty Images. **254-255** (LesOp) NASA/JPL/Image Envision. **256** (c) NASA-JPL - Mars Pathfinder/ digital version by Science Faction/Getty Images. (t) ESA/K. Horgan/Stone/Getty Images. **257** (ml, mc, bl, bc) Scott Tysick/Masterfile. (tr) NASA/Roger Ressmeyer/Corbis. **258** (ml, mc, bl, bc) Scott Tysick/Masterfile. **259** (bl) A-JPL-Caltech - Cassini/digital version by Science Faction/Getty Images. (br) Photos.com/Jupiterimages. (tl) LASP/ NASA/Handout/Reuters/Corbis. (tr) NASA/Time Life Pictures/Getty Images. **260** (b) StockTrek/ Photodisc/Getty Images. (t) Photodisc/SuperStock. **261** (r) NASA/Getty Images. **262** (b) Reuters/ Corbis. (t) World Perspectives/Stone/Getty Images. 263 (r) Images.com/Corbis. **268** (b) Stock Illustration Source/Getty Images. **270** (bl) Michael Lewis/Corbis. (br) Anthony West/Corbis. **270** (bg) NASA, ESA and the Hubble Heritage Team (STScI/ AURA). 271 (r) NASA/Roger Ressmeyer/Corbis. **272** (b) Rex Stucky/National Geographic Image Collection. **274** (bc) NASA/ESA/The Hubble Heritage Team (STScI/AURA)/P. Knezek (WIYN)/ Space Telescope Science. Institute. (bl) Transtock. (mc) Vince Streano/Corbis. (ml) Joe McBride/ Stone/Getty Images. (mr) Creatas Images/ PunchStock. (tc) Lester V. Bergman/Corbis. (tl) NASA Human Space Flight Gallery. (tr) Visuals Unlimited/Corbis. **276** (tl) image100/Corbis. (bl) NASA Human Space Flight Gallery. **276-277** (LesOp) NASA/Roger Ressmeyer/Corbis. 278 (l) Hubble Image: NASA and ESA; Acknowledgment: K.D. Kuntz (GSFC), F. Bresolin (University of Hawaii), J. Trauger (JPL), J. Mould (NOAO), and Y.-H. Chu (University of Illinois, Urbana); CFHT Image: Canada-France-Hawaii Telescope/J.C. Cuillandre/Coelum; NOAO Image: G. Jacoby, B. Bohannan, M. Hanna/NOAO/AURA/NSF. **279** (r) NASA Human Space Flight Gallery. **280** (r) NASA Human Space Flight Gallery. **281** (r) NASA Human Space Flight Gallery. **282** (r) NASA Human Space Flight Gallery. **283** (bg) John Marshall Mantel/Sipa Press/NewsCom. **284** (t) NAS/Roger Ressmeyer/ Corbis. **285** (l) Larry Dale Gordon/The Image Bank/Getty Images. (r) NASA Human Space Flight Gallery. **286** (r) NASA Human Space Flight Gallery. **287** (b) NASA Human Space Flight Gallery. (t) image100/Corbis. **288** (r) NASA Human Space Flight Gallery. **292** (b) image100/Corbis. **294** (bl) Atlantide Phototravel/Corbis. (br) Gabe Palmer/ Alamy Images. **296** (b) Corbis. **298** (bc) Somos Images LLC/Alamy Images. (bl) Image Source/ Corbis. (mc) ColorBlind Images/Iconica/Getty Images. (ml) Darren Robb/The Image Bank/Getty Images. (mr) BrandX/Jupiterimages/Alamy Images. (tc) Will & Deni McIntyre/Corbis. (tl) bilderlounge/ Corbis. (tr) Kevin Dodge/Corbis. **301** (c) Lou Wall/ Corbis. **302** (r) Images.com/Corbis. **307** (r) Archivo Iconografico, S.A./Corbis. **311** (c) Carmen T. Bernier-Grand. **314** (b) Comstock/Corbis. **322** (l) Paul A. Souders/Corbis. (r) Craig Tuttle/Corbis. **323** (c) National Geographic Digital Media. (r) Huetter, C./Arco Images/Peter Arnold, Inc. (b) George Grall/National Geographic Image Collection. **324** (t) Klaus Nigge/National Geographic Image Collection. **325** (t) Michael Melford/National Geographic Image Collection. (br) National Geographic Digital Media. **327** (t) Peter Arnold, Inc./Alamy Images. (b) Jupiterimages/Botanica/Jupiter Images. **328** (b) DLILLC/Corbis. (bg) Robert Llewellyn/zefa/Corbis. **329** (t) Tom Brakefield/Photodisc/Getty Images. (b) Nick Greaves/Alamy Images. (bg) Penny Tweedie/Corbis. **330** (b) Joel Sartore/National Geographic Image Collection. **332** (bc) Thomas Mangelsen/Minden Pictures. (bl) Karen Kasmauski/National Geographic Image Collection. (mc) Dennis MacDonald/Alamy Images. (ml) Charles O'Rear/Corbis. (ml) F Hart/The Bridgeman Art Library/Getty Images. (tc) Joel Sartore/ National Geographic Image Collection. (tl) Comstock Images/PunchStock. (tl) Riser/ Ableimages/Getty Images. **334-335** (LesOp) Michele Westmorland/Corbis. **336-337** (l) Jeff Greenberg/PhotoEdit. 337 (r) Skip Brown/National Geographic/Getty Images. **338** (l) Philip Schermeister/National Geographic/Getty Images. **341** (bg) Stuart Westmorland/Getty Images. (br) C. & D. Frith/Frithfoto/Bruce Coleman Inc.. (mr) Robert P. Carr/Bruce Coleman Inc.. (tr) Nicholas Parfitt/Getty Images. **342** (b) Tom Brakefield/ Stockbyte/Getty Images. **343** (bg) Liu Jin/AFP/ Getty Images. (bl) Christopher Talbot Frank/ Photex/zefa/Corbis. (ml) Joel Sartore/National Geographic/Getty Images. (tl) Chris Johns/ National Geographic Image Collection. **349** (b) Brian J. Skerry/National Geographic Image Collection. **350** (b) Joe McDonald/Corbis. (bg) Ralph A. Clevenger/Corbis. **351** (tr) Tom Brakefield/Corbis. (br) DK Limited/Corbis. **352** (b) Chris Johns/National Geographic Image Collection. **354** (bc) Michael S. Quinton/National Geographic Image Collection. (bl) Dorling Kindersley/Mike Downing/Getty Images. (mc) Raymond Gehman/ National Geographic Image Collection. (ml) Blend/ PunchStock. (mr) Tim Laman/National Geographic Image Collection. (tc) David R. Frazier Photolibrary, Inc./Alamy Images. (tl) image100/ Corbis. (tr) Paul Nicklen/National Geographic Image Collection. **356-357** (LesOp) Steve Bloom Images/Alamy. **358** (c) Layne Kennedy/Corbis. **359** (t) Dr. Dale Miquelle/Wildlife Conservation Society. **360-361** (b) Ilya Naymushin/Reuters/Landov. **361** (t) Dr. Maurice G. Hornocker/National Geographic Image Collection. **362** (t) Pavel Filatov/Alamy. **364** (bc) China Photos/Getty Images. (bl) Purestock/ Getty Images. (br) Michael Nichols/National Geographic Image Collection. (mc) Michael K. Nichols/National Geographic/Getty Images. (mr) Jimin Lai/AFP/Getty Images. (t) Martin Harvey/ Alamy. **366** (t) Layne Kennedy/Corbis **370** (b) Mark Thiessen/National Geographic Society. (bg) Boyd & Evans/Corbis. **371** (t) Steve Kaufman/Corbis. (m) George H. H. Huey/Corbis. (b) Gary W. Carter/ Corbis. (bg) Macduff Everton/Corbis. **372** (b) Alissa Everett/Alamy Images. **373** (b) Taylor S. Kennedy/National Geographic Image Collection. **374** (bl) National Aeronautics and Space Administration. (mc) Citizens' Voice, Dave Scherbenco/AP Images. (ml) Klaus Nigge/National Geographic Image Collection. (mr) Paul Chesley/ National Geographic Image Collection. (tc) Jeff Greenberg/The Image Works, Inc.. (tr) Michael Nichols/National Geographic Image Collection. **376** (t) Roger Antrobus/Taxi/Getty Images. (tl) Mark Thiessen/National Geographic Image Collection. (tml) Ben Graville/eyevine/Zuma Press. (bml) Mark Thiessen/National Geographic Society. (bl) Mark Thiessen/National Geographic Image Collection. **376-377** (LesOp) Mark Thiessen/ National Geographic Image Collection. **378** (bcl) Mark Thiessen/National Geographic Image Collection. (mbl) Mark Thiessen/National Geographic Image Collection. (mcl) Ben Graville/ eyevine/Zuma Press. (tcl) Mark Thiessen/National Geographic Image Collection. (tl) Roger Antrobus/ Taxi/Getty Images. (tr) Mark Thiessen/National Geographic Image Collection. **379** (mc) Mark Thiessen/National Geographic Image Collection. (tl) Roger Antrobus/Taxi/Getty Images. **380** (br) Mark Thiessen/National Geographic Image Collection. (tc, ml) Mark Thiessen/National Geographic Image Collection. (tl) Roger Antrobus/ Taxi/Getty Images. **381** (bc) Jason Edwards/ National Geographic Image Collection. (br) Andreas M. Gross/Westend 61/Alamy. (tc) Mark Thiessen/National Geographic Image Collection. (tl) Roger Antrobus/Taxi/Getty Images. **382** (bl) Pete Oxford/Minden Pictures/Getty Images. (tc) Mark Thiessen/National Geographic Image Collection. (tl) Roger Antrobus/Taxi/Getty Images. **384** (c) Mark Thiessen/National Geographic Image Collection. **386** (b) Roy Toft/National Geographic Image Collection. **393** (b) Photo by Eliot Elisofon/ Time & Life Pictures/Getty Images. **395** (tl) Bettmann/Corbis Sygma/Corbis. (tr) Corbis. 395 (b) Michael A. Keller/Corbis. **396** (b) Annie Griffiths Belt/Corbis. **398** (b) SW Productions/ Photodisc/Getty Images. **400** (bc) Corbis. (bl) Larry Williams/Corbis. (mc) Rob Walls/Alamy Images. (ml) Stockbyte/Getty Images. (mr) Blend/ PunchStock. (tc) Todd Gipstein/National Geographic Image Collection. (tl) Jodi Cobb/ National Geographic Image Collection. (tr) Bubbles Photolibrary/Alamy Images. **412** (b) Jamel Akib. (t) Nancy Yamin. **413** (r) Robert Harding Picture Library Ltd/Alamy Images. **414** (c) Images.com/ Corbis. **418** (c) Hans Neleman/The Image Bank/ Getty Images. **420** (b) KRT Photograph via Miami Herald/Newscom. **421** (r) Al Messerschmidt/Getty Images. **422** (b) Getty Images/Jose Luis Pelaez. **423** (t) AP Photo/HO, Randy Rodriguez, AIN. **424** (bc) Thomas J. Abercrombie/National Geographic Image Collection. (bl) Howard Davies/Corbis. (mc) Thinkstock/Corbis. (ml) Loungepark/Taxi/Getty Images. (mr) Myrleen Ferguson Cate/PhotoEdit. (tc) Stuart Westmorland/Science Faction/Getty Images. (tl) Inmagine/Alamy Images. (tr) Jodi Cobb/National Geographic Image Collection. **439** (t) Petras Malukas/AFP/Getty Images. **440** (b)

David Bergman/Miami Herald/NewsCom. (t) Lee & Low Books. **446** (b) Alexandra Boulat/SIPA Press. **447** (t) Tramp Cascade/Workbook Stock/Jupiter Images. (b) Randy Faris/Corbis. **448** (b) AP Photo/The Roanoke Times, Eric Brady. **450** (bc) Michael Newman/PhotoEdit. (bl) Frances Roberts/Alamy. (mc) Jon Feingersh/zefa/Corbis. (ml) Pat LaCroix/Photographer's Choice/Getty Images. (mr) Bill Curtsinger/National Geographic Image Collection. (tc) Purestock/Getty Images. (tl) Radius Images/Jupiterimages. (tr) Mark Dyball/Alamy Images. **452-453** (LesOp) Alexandra Boulat/SIPA Press. **454** (b) Chris Rainier/Corbis. **456** (b) Michael S. Yamashita/Corbis. **457** (r) EPA/AFP/Getty Images. **459** (t) Aidan Crawley. **460** (c) Images.com/Corbis. **462** (c) AP Photo/Saleh Rifai. **465** (b) Getty Images/PhotoAlto. **471** (t) Roaring Lion Image Research LLC. (b) Simon Marcus/Corbis. **473** (t) Corbis. (b) Beathan/Corbis. **474** (b) Jeff Cadge/The Image Bank/Getty Images. **476** (b) Getty Images/Illustration Works. **478** (bc) Robert Sciarrino/Star Ledger/Corbis. (bl) Jupiterimages/Thinkstock/Alamy Images. (mc) Michelle Pedone/Zefa/Corbis. (ml) Ryan McVay/Photodisc/Getty Images. (mr) David Young-Wolff/PhotoEdit. (tc) Raymond Ortiz Godfrey. (tl) Bonnie Kamin/PhotoEdit. (tr) Vincent Mo/zefa/Corbis. **487** (c) Linda Fang. 490 (l) Joel Sartore/National Geographic/Getty Images. (r) Suk-Heui Park/Photographer's Choice/Getty Images. **496** (b) Stapleton Collection/Corbis. (bg) iStockPhoto. **497** (t) Bettmann/Corbis. (b) Digital Stock/Corbis. **498** (b) Kenneth Garrett/National Geographic Image Collection. **500** (bc) Seth Wenig/AP Images. (bl) Bob Daemmrich/PhotoEdit. (mc) Marty Honig/Photodisc/Getty Images. (ml) Joseph H. Bailey/National Geographic Image Collection. (mr) PNC/Photodisc/Getty Images. (tc) Spencer Platt/Getty Images/Getty Images. (tl) Raymond Ortiz Godfrey. (tr) Paul B. Southerland/AP Images. **502-503** (bg) Martin Ruegner/Getty Images. **503** (LesOp) Peggy & Ronald Barnett/Corbis. **504-505** (b) Wally McNamee/Corbis. **506** (b) Michael Ventura/PhotoEdit. **507** (c) Joseph Sohm/Visions of America/Corbis. **509** (b) The Signing of the Constitution of the United States in 1787, 1940 (oil on canvas), Howard Chandler Christy, (1873-1952) Hall of Representatives, Washington D.C./The Bridgeman Art Library International. **510** (b) Bettmann/Corbis. **511** (b) Dennis O'Clair/Stone/Getty Images. **512** (b) Brooks Kraft/Corbis. (ml) Photograph by Steve Petteway, Collection of the Supreme Court of the United States. **513** (r) Bettmann/Corbis. **514** (b) Bettmann/Corbis. **515** (b) Frank Siteman/PhotoEdit. **516** (b) Bettmann/Corbis. **517** (c) Bettmann/Corbis. **519** (bg) Terry Eggers/Corbis. (c) Smithsonian Institution/Corbis. **520** (b) Digital Vision/Alamy. (t) Heather Shimmin/iStockphoto. **524** (t) Stephen St. John/National Geographic Image Collection. **526** (b) Leland Bobbé/Corbis. **527** (c) Bob Daemmrich/Corbis. **528** (b) Vince Bucci/AFP/Getty Images. **529** (t) AP Photo/Mark Humphrey. **530** (bc) Jim West/Alamy Images. (bl) Corbis. (mc) Bob Daemmrich/Stock Boston/IPNstock. (ml) David Young-Wolff/PhotoEdit. (mr) Joel Sartore/National Geographic Image Collection. (tc) David McNew/Getty Images. (tl) Paul Schutzer/Time Life Pictures/Getty Images. (tr) Frances Roberts/Alamy Images. **532-533** (LesOp) Bob Daemmrich/The Image Works, Inc. **534** (t) Dean Mulso. 535 (b) Dean Mulso. (c) Dean Mulso. **536** (c) Randy Belice/NBAE via Getty Images. **537** (bg) burke/triolo productions/Brand X Pictures/Jupiterimages. **538** (c) Mary Kate Denny/PhotoEdit. **540** (c) Jeff Greenberg/PhotoEdit. **550–551** (t) Graham Dean/Corbis. **552** (bc) image 100/Corbis **551** (l) 100281.000000/Getty Images. (r) Todd Gipstein/National Geographic Image Collection. **553** (t) David R. Frazier/Photolibrary, Inc./Alamy Images. (bl) Paul Cooklin/Brand X/Corbis. (br) Hugh Threlfall/Alamy Images. **554** (bl) Chris Knapton/Alamy Images. (br) Stocksearch/Alamy Images. (bg) Corbis. **555** (c) Myrleen Ferguson Cate/PhotoEdit. **557** (b) AP Photo/The Conway Daily Sun, Jamie Gemmiti. **558** (bc) Roy Gumpel/National Geographic Image Collection. (bl) blue jean images/Getty Images. (mc) David De Lossy/Photodisc/Getty Images. (ml) Raymond Ortiz Godfrey. (mr) Mike Greenlar/Syracuse Newspapers/The Image Works. (tc) ThinkStock/Jupiterimages. (tl) Melissa Farlow/National Geographic Image Collection. (tr) Mark Thiessen/National Geographic Image Collection. **560-561** (bg) imagewerks/Getty Images. 561 (LesOp) Dr. Florence Wambugu/Cornell University. **562** (b) USDA/Photo Researchers. 563 (r) Issouf Sanogo/AFP/Getty Images. **564** (l) Lynn Johnson/Aurora/Getty Images. **565** (t) Robb Kendrick/Aurora Photos. **566** (l) G. Dimitras/AFP/Getty Images. **567** (c) Chris Rogers/Rainbow. **572** (bc) Dennis MacDonald/Alamy. (bl) Frank Lukasseck/Corbis. (mc) Stockbyte/PunchStock. (ml) Joseph Van Os/The Image Bank/Getty Images. (mr) Carolyn Kaster/AP Images. (tc) Bob Bird/AP Images. (tl) Tom Sistak/AP Images. (tr) Richard Olivier/Corbis. **574** (b) Emilio Ereza/Alamy Images. (bg) Justin Lightley/Photographer's Choice/Getty Images. **575** (c) David Young-Wolff/PhotoEdit. **575** (c) Lawrence Dutton/Getty Images. **576** (b) IMAGE13/Getty Images. **577** (b) dbphots/Alamy. (t) Frans Lanting/Corbis. **578** (bc) Stephen St. John/National Geographic Image Collection. (bl) Richard Nowitz/National Geographic Image Collection. (mc) Stockbyte/Getty Images. (ml) Jim West/PhotoEdit. (mr) Chad Ehlers/Alamy Images. (tc) David P. Hall/Corbis. (tl) Patrik Giardino/Iconica/Getty Images. (tr) Peter Dazeley/Photographer's Choice/Getty Images. **579** (mc, mr, bc) O. Louis Mazzatenta/National Geographic Image Collection. **580** (bl) Steve Hamblin/Corbis. (br) Michael Newman/PhotoEdit. (b) Edmund Neil/Eye Ubiquitous/Corbis. **580-581** (LesOp) Rebecca Wittmuss. **582** (l) Rebecca Wittmuss. **583** (r) Rebecca Wittmuss. **585** (r) Rebecca Wittmuss. **586 (r)** iMaggio/Kalish/Corbis. **587** (r) Atlantide Phototravel/Corbis. **588** (bg) W. Cody/Corbis. **598** (bc) Dennis MacDonald/Alamy Images. (bl) Kris Timken/Digital Vision/Getty Images. (mc) Digital Vision/Alamy Images. (ml) Michael Newman/PhotoEdit. (mr) Tom Grill/Corbis. (tc) Gareth Brown/Corbis. (tl) Joel Sartore/National Geographic Image Collection. (tr) David Young-Wolff/PhotoEdit. **583** (c) Justin Guariglia/National Geographic Image Collection. **584** (t) Frank Robichon/epa/Corbis. **585** (b) Phil Schermeister/Corbis. (t) Phil Schermeister/Corbis. **586** (r) Photodisc/Alamy. **590** (b) Getty Images/MIXA. **594** (b) Hemis/Alamy Images. (bg) Rich Reid/National Geographic/Getty Images. **595** (t) Stewart Cohen/Blend Images/Getty Images. (b) Michel Newman/PhotoEdit. **596** (b) Haensel/zefa/Corbis. **596** (bc) David R. Frazier Photolibrary, Inc./Alamy. (bl) Image Source/Corbis. (mc) Alaska Stock LLC/Alamy. (ml) Harvey Lloyd/Taxi/Getty Images. (mr) Jeff Hunter/Image Bank/Getty Images. (tc) Richard Cooke/Alamy. (tl) Peter Macdiarmid/Reuters/Corbis. (tr) Bertrand Gardel/Hemis/Corbis. **598–599** (bg) Tim Davis/Corbis. **600** (b) David Muench/Corbis. **601** (bl) Dan Fagre, courtesy of Glacier National Park Archives. (br) Karen Holzer, courtesy of Glacier National Park Archives/U.S. Geological Survey, Northern Rocky. Mountain Science Center. (tl) T.J. Hileman, courtesy of Glacier National Park Archives. (tr) Carl Key, courtesy of Glacier National Park Archives. **602** (b) Michael Quinton/Minden Pictures. **603** (bl) DLILLC/Corbis. (br) Courtesy of NASA. (tr) Courtesy of NASA. **604** (l) Peter Pinnock/Getty Images. (r) Tim Laman/National Geographic Image Collection. **605** (r) David Woodfall/Stone/Getty Images. **606** (b) AP Images. (c) Kevin Schafer Photography. (t) Morales/AGE fotostock. **607** (b) Kevin Schafer/Corbis. (c) Gary Bell/Oceanwideimages. (t) Roger Eritja/Alamy. **618** (bl) Lawrence Manning/Corbis. (ml) Petra Wegner/Alamy. (mr) Toho/Kobal Collection. (tc) Dana White/PhotoEdit. (tl) Carolyn Kaster/AP Images. (tr) Gunter Ziesler/Peter Arnold/Alamy. **624** (c) Michael Greenlar/The Image Works. Geographic Image Collection. (tl) moodboard/Corbis. **629** (b) Michael Noonan. (t) Charles R. Knight/National Geographic Image Collection. **630–631** (bg) Owaki/Kulla/Corbis. **631** (b) Mike Simons/Getty Images. **633** (bg) Thinkstock Images. **634** (b) Frank Lukasseck/IFA Bilderteam. (bg) Thinkstock Images.

Fine Art

xv *Puzzled*, 2006, Elizabeth Rosen. Acrylic on canvas, courtesy of Morgan Gaynin Inc., NY. **13** *Divercity*, 2005. Acrylic on chipboard, courtesy of Morgan Gaynin Inc., New York. **14** *Los Angeles*, 2002, Jose Ramirez. Mixed media on canvas, private collection. **16** *El Lonche*, 1993, Simon Silva. Oils, used with permission of the illustrator and Bookstop Literary Agency, Orinda, California. **19** *Trois Pepiers*, 2007, Frank Romero. Oil on linen, collection of the artist. **21** *Untitled*, 2001, Sandro Chia. Oil on canvas © VAGA, New York. **22** *Santa Fe Roadside Prickly Pear*, year, Claudette Moe. Acrylic on canvas, collection of the artist. **55** *Young Girl at the Window*, 1925, Salvador Dali, Oil on board © Salvador Dali, Gala-Salvador Dali Foundation/ARS, NY/Archivo Iconographico, S.A./Corbis. **166** *Marching*, 2005, Gil Mayers. Collage © Gil Mayers/Superstock. **242** *Tar Beach 2, 1990*, Faith Ringgold. Silkscreen on silk, Philadelphia Museum of Art, Philadelphia. **301** *Juanita IV*, 2004, Lou Wall. Oil on canvas © Corbis. **305** *Muchacha en la Ventana (Girl in the Window)*, 2000, Graciela Genoves. Zurbaran Galeria, Buenos Aires, Argentina © Zurbaran Galeria/Superstock. **307** *Girl in a Shawl*, 1910, Isidro Nonell. Oil on canvas © Corbis. **308** *State of my Heart*, 2005, Elizabeth Rosen. Mixed media collage, collection of the artist, courtesy of Morgan Gaynin Inc., New York. **310** *Spring Thaw*, 2005, Elizabeth Rosen. Acrylic on canvas, private collection, courtesy of Morgan Gaynin Inc., New York. **312** *Small Echo*, 2004, Graham Dean. Watercolor on paper, private collection/Bridgeman Art Library. **320** *Tiger's Garden*, 2006, Alfredo Arreguin. Oil on canvas, private collection. **390** *Tree*, 1994, Ron Waddams. Acrylic on board, private collection. **518** *Preamble*, 1987, Mike Wilkins. Painted metal on vinyl and wood. Smithsonian American Art Museum, Washington DC/Art Resource, NY. **548** *Bowl of Life*, 2004, Jose Ramirez. Mixed media on wood, private collection, Los Angeles. **568** *The Marketplace*, 1988, Carlton Murrell. Oil on canvas, private collection/Bridgeman Art Library. **601** *Wounded Sleep*, 2006, Durga Bernhard. Gouache and ink, collection of the artist. **605** *Aurochs and Deer*, 2004, Cecilia Henle. Oil on canvas, collection of the artist, www.henlestudio.com. **610** *Indian Camp*, Eanger Irving Couse (1866-1936), Oil on canvas © Christie's Images/Superstock. **613** *Mountain Buck*, 2000, Durga Bernhard. Gouache on paper collage, Michael Densmore collection. **617** *Teepees in the Moonlight*, Ralph Albert Blakelock (1847-1919), Oil on canvas, Christie's Images, New York © Christie's Images/Superstock. **619** *In Depth*, 2006, Carmen Hathaway. Acrylic on canvas, collection of the artist.

Illustrations

17 (molcajete) © 2004, Lorraine J. Karcz/FoodShapes/Fotosearch, **48** (World map locating Kenya and United States) Mapping Specialists, **60-69** ("The House on Mango Street") Rafael Lopez, **78** (frog) © Bill Mayer, **111** ("The Rooster and the Jewel") Meilo So, **116-127** ("The Three Chicharrones") Bill Mayer, **135** (king and queen) Vitali Konstantinov, **140-156** ("Dragon, Dragon") Brandon Dorman, **158** (Komodo dragon map) Mapping Specialists, **231** (Thailand map and globe) Mapping Specialists, **295** (students) Ben Shannon, **360** (Siberian Tiger map and globe) Mapping Specialists, **382** (Madagascar map) Mapping Specialists, **397** (parents and son) Steve Bjorkman, **402-411** ("Nadia the Willful") Jamel Akib, **460** (person holding earth) © Joel Nakamura, 2001, **468** (blindfolded lady with scales of justice) Teofilo Olivieri/Images.com., **475** (brothers and chores) Ben Shannon, **480-489** ("The Clever Magistrate" and "The Clever Old Woman") Marilee Heyer